1993

The Building of Renaissance Florence

School of Verrocchio, Madonna with Child and saints (detail)

THE BUILDING OF RENAISSANCE FLORENCE

An Economic and Social History

Richard A. Goldthwaite

THE JOHNS HOPKINS UNIVERSITY PRESS
BALTIMORE AND LONDON

This book has been brought to publication
with the generous assistance of the National Endowment
for the Humanities.

Originally published, 1980
Second printing, 1982
Johns Hopkins Paperbacks edition, 1982
Second printing, 1985
Softshell Books edition, 1990
Second printing, 1991

The Johns Hopkins University Press
701 West 40th Street
Baltimore, Maryland 21211-2190
The Johns Hopkins Press Ltd., London

The paper used in this book meets the minimum requirements
of the American National Standard for Information Sciences—
Permanence of Paper for Printed Library Materials,
ANSI Z39.48–1984.

PHOTO CREDITS (by page number) Alinari/Editorial Photocolor Archives: frontispiece, 125, 127, 151, 153, 232, 236, 253, 255, 271, 290, 303, 323, 354; Archivio di Stato, Florence: 180, 182, 310, 312; Fogg Art Museum, Harvard University, Cambridge, Mass.: 149; John and Mable Ringling Museum of Art, Sarasota, Fla.: 315; Niedersächsische Landesgalerie, Hannover: 299; Soprintendenza ai beni artistici e storici, Florence: 134, 137, 222, 226, 308, 326, 330, 336, 341, 374, 380; Toledo Museum of Art, Toledo, Ohio: 395; Vatican Library, Rome: 128, 129; Author (Pineider, Florence): 131, 133, 140, 141, 205, 235, 294

Library of Congress Cataloging in Publication Data

Goldthwaite, Richard A.
The building of Renaissance Florence.

Includes index.
1. Construction industry—Italy—Florence—History. 2. Architecture—Italy—Florence—History. 3. Florence—Economic conditions. 4. Florence—Social conditions. 5. Florence—History. I. Title.
History. I. Title.

HD9715.I83F563 338.4′7624′094551 80–7995
ISBN 0–8018–2342–0
ISBN 0–8018–2977–1 (pbk)

To

FREDERICK B. ARTZ

a builder of houses

of intellect

Contents

ILLUSTRATIONS

ORDERS OF PAYMENT

THE ARCHITECT

TABLES, CHARTS, GRAPH, AND MAPS

TABLES

GENEALOGICAL CHARTS OF GUILD CONSULAR FAMILIES

Preface

The monographs in this book have as their subject the building activity that resulted in the Renaissance city of Florence. The Introduction presents a survey of that activity. In the chapters following this, the subject is approached as a market phenomenon to be looked at from both the side of demand and the side of supply. On the demand side (Part I), the discussion takes up first the economic conditions in the city that permitted the considerable expenditure represented by building (Chapter 1), and then the political, social, and cultural forces that produced, through the needs and taste of the upper class, a demand for building (Chapter 2). On the supply side (Part II), where the major research effort has gone, the various forces of production that went into building are surveyed: organization of work (Chapter 3), the building-material industries (Chapter 4), the labor force (Chapters 5 and 6), and the aesthetic component, the architect (Chapter 7). Because construction by its very nature requires many different kinds of workers, ranging from unskilled manual laborers to highly talented artists, some working as day laborers and others as small entrepreneurs, this description of the industry offers, in effect, a cross section of working-class society in Renaissance Florence. The entire discussion of Part II, therefore, complements the focus on the upper classes found in Part I by filling out a picture of the society and economy of Renaissance Florence. The Conclusion attempts to assess the social and economic consequences of this building activity, finding that the conspicuous consumption we associate with the Renaissance was not altogether wasteful but, on the contrary, resulted in considerable internal development and, ultimately, a more mature economy.

In planning the book in this way the objective has been to show how one major economic activity—building—generated by demand from the upper classes, and employing a cross section of the lower classes, can be the point of departure for a social and economic history of the city. Moreover, since the products of this activity were major architectural monuments, much of the discussion bears directly on an evaluation of the material conditions of artistic activity. Architecture is thus related to its social function on the one hand and to the productive forces that brought it into existence on the other. In fact, the conclusion contains a hypothesis to explain the remarkable flourishing of the arts for which Renaissance Florence is most famous. Finally, since much of this discussion of the construction industry in Florence has no counterpart in the historiography of medieval and early modern Europe, an effort has been made to place Florentine materials in the widest possible geographical and chronological context. It is hoped that this occasional shift of perspective beyond the city walls of Florence will throw some light on the history of the construction industry in pre-industrial Europe, for it is one of the industries most neglected by scholarship, despite its fundamental importance in any economy.

Notwithstanding the breadth of this scheme, two subjects of central importance to a fully comprehensive study of building activity—architectural style and construction technology—are not dealt with. Both lie beyond the competence of the author. Moreover, it can be fully anticipated that the picture presented here will have to undergo some major redrawing once the current work of a number of art historians comes to fruition. This work includes Diane Finiello Zervas's on Orsanmichele, Brenda Preyer's on fifteenth-century palaces, Beverly Brown's on the Santissima Annunziata, Margaret Haines's on intarsia artists, Harriet Caplow's on Maso di Bartolomeo, Caroline Elam's on urban development, and Suzy Butters's on the building projects of the first grand dukes, as well as a number of dissertations on other relevant topics. All these scholars will have so much new archival material to bring to bear on the building of Renaissance Florence that in the meantime it is probably foolhardy for anyone to venture into the subject at all; I would never have dared to do so without the generous encouragement of them all. I can only hope that this approach of an economic historian will open some new horizons on the Renaissance urban scene, however much the paths traveled herein will have to be recharted as we learn more about the buildings and builders encountered along the way.

The reader needs to be prepared for one problem of terminology. The word *mason,* which is so central to our understanding of the history of building craftsmen in northern Europe, has no exact Italian translation, a fact that points to a very different division of skills in the two areas. In Italian a distinction is made between freemasons, on the one hand—hewers, scapplers, sculptors, and others who work with cut stone—and layers, setters, or simply wallers, on the other. The former are generally known as *scarpellini* or *scarpellatori* in Florence (or, less commonly, as *maestri di scarpello, lastraiuoli, scultori*), and sometimes as *tagliapietre, spaccapietre,* or *piccapietre* elsewhere in Italy. The masons who used stone to build walls were everywhere known as *muratori* (or *maestri di cazzuola, maestri di murare*). *Muratori,* however, also laid bricks and were engaged otherwise in construction activity. These were two distinct groups of craftsmen, in many places having separate guilds. In the following discussion, therefore, *scarpellino* has been translated as *stonecutter* and *muratore* as *waller.* The use of the latter term is perhaps not the most felicitous solution, but it avoids the problem of using the standard English nomenclature. *Mason* obviously would not do because of all the implications that term has as a result of the considerable scholarship on the northern mason in the Middle Ages. *Builder* would be an exact translation if understood literally, but the term is even looser in English since it can be used to refer to the patron who builds as well as to the construction worker. *Muratore* literally means *wall-builder;* and although the term *waller* in English suggests an artisan of modest status, it is precisely because it has a narrower meaning in English that it is less likely to lead to confusion with other crafts. The reader will simply have to accept the waller as a craftsman who could do everything from laying bricks and stones to major contracting. The reader can, at any rate, be assured that the terms *stonecutter* and *waller* as used in this discussion reveal the exact distinction in the documents between these two kinds of craftsmen. The word *mason*—apart from its application to craftsmen in northern Europe—is used for Italy only in its general meaning of the artisan-builder when in the context of the discussion both stonecutters and wallers might be referred to. For example, the guild of Maestri di Pietra e di Legname, which commonly included workers who built in stone, brick, and wood, and which was found in so many Italian towns, will sometimes be referred to simply as the masons' guild. The word *maestro,* when standing alone, has also been translated as *mason.* Further discussion of the differences between stonecutters and wallers in Florence will be found in Chapter 6 on pages 320–21.

The Florentine monetary system is explained in the text of Chapter 6. The discussion in that chapter gives the reader a better sense of the real value of money. Appendix 1 can be consulted for a conversion table of the florin and the soldo *di piccioli* (and therefore the lira). The standard abbreviations for monetary units are f. for florin, lb. for lira, s. for soldo (one-twentieth part of either the florin or lira), and d. for denaro (one-twelfth part of a soldo). In the Florentine system of dry measures the staio was equal to 24.7 liters (or about 0.7 bushel) and the moggio was 24 staia. The braccio was about 2 feet (58.36 centimeters).

References (mostly to unpublished sources) for the numerous unnoted observations about building-craft guilds in other Italian towns are found in Appendix 2.

The research for this book could never have been undertaken without the generous support of American institutions dedicated to the patronage of scholarship. The Harvard University Center for Italian Renaissance Studies at Villa I Tatti in Florence and The National Endowment for the Humanities provided support for two years of research in Florence; an invitation from The Institute for Advanced Study at Princeton, with further support from the National Endowment for the Humanities, made it possible to spend yet another year thinking it all over and writing it up. Most generous of all has been The Johns Hopkins University, which supplemented these grants and allowed me freedom from my normal duties there.

For one pursuing such a vast subject and working in a field where the materials are so abundant and the scholarship so specialized, even the most casual conversation with a colleague, the slightest comment about particular matters, can sometimes lead to important discoveries or insights. To single out all the people I am indebted to for help over the years of putting together this book would therefore be impossible, and, in any case, I would not consider it a gesture of my appreciation to relegate any one of them to the crowd that would result from a listing of all their names here. Thanks to an invitation from Staale Sinding-Larsen to give a series of lectures on the subject of this book at his institute of architectural history in the architectural faculty of the university at Trondheim, I was compelled to take an overview of the subject and get my thoughts in order early on in this project, so I was immeasurably aided in directing subsequent research. Those who made the special effort to give me a critical reading of parts of the manuscript at some point in its evolution include Marvin Becker, Judith Brown, Shannon Brown, Sue Greene, Kent Lydecker, Reinhold Mueller, Giuliano Pinto, Marco Spallanzani, Phoebe Stanton, and, above all, my colleagues—faculty and students—in The Seminar of the Department of History at The Johns Hopkins University.

The Building of Renaissance Florence

ABBREVIATIONS

ASF	Archivio di Stato, Florence
ASI	*Archivio storico italiano*
Badia di Fiesole	Innocenti, ser. CXLI
Badia di Firenze	ASF, Conv. sopp. LXXVIII
BNF	Biblioteca Nazionale, Florence
Carte strozz.	ASF, Carte strozziane
Catasto	ASF, Catasto
Fabbricanti	ASF, Università dei Fabbricanti
Flor. Mitt.	*Mitteilungen des kunsthistorischen Institutes in Florenz*
Innocenti	Archive of the Ospedale degli Innocenti, Florence
JEEcH	*Journal of European Economic History*
JSArH	*Journal of the Society of Architectural Historians*
Leg. tosc.	Lorenzo Cantini, ed., *Legislazione toscana* (Florence, 1800–1808)
Maestri	ASF, Arte dei Maestri di Pietra e di Legname
S. Miniato	ASF, Conv. sopp. CLXVIII
S. Spirito	ASF, Conv. sopp. CXXII
Ss. Annunziata	ASF, Conv. sopp. CXIX
Statuta (1415)	*Statuta Populi et Communis Florentiae (1415)* (Freiburg, 1778–83)
Statuti (1325)	Romolo Caggese, ed., *Statuti della repubblica fiorentina*, vol. 2: *Statuti del Podestà* (Florence, 1921)

INTRODUCTION

The Buildings of Renaissance Florence

The Thirteenth Century

FEW cities in pre-industrial Europe expanded as rapidly as Florence in the thirteenth century. It was at this time that Florence joined the upper ranks of Europe's great cities. Before the last quarter of the twelfth century, when a new set of walls went up, Florence was smaller than Pisa and probably not much larger than several other towns in Tuscany and central Italy. A century later, however, Dante and Giotto grew up in a city that had a population conservatively estimated at nearly 90,000, a four- to sixfold increase; and during their lifetime they saw yet another set of walls go up that, in anticipation of even further growth, incorporated five times the area of the earlier walls, coming close to being the largest ever built by any European city.

Under the most favorable circumstances, building to accommodate such remarkable growth would have been hurried and haphazard. It was all the more so in a medieval commune still in the throes of growing pains, often hardly able to assure much more than the semblance of public authority as it struggled to work out institutions of government sufficiently comprehensive to embrace the diverse groups within its corporate structure. As the population grew, people packed themselves on top of one another in great tenement houses built in the tradition of the old Roman insulae, with shops below and crowded, dark, living quarters stacked five or six floors above. Tightly compressed against one another in narrow, crooked streets, most buildings were put up in brick, rubble, and wood too hurriedly to be safe against the ravages of frequent fires and the occasional flooding of the Arno. Few buildings of any kind stood out to break the architectural monotony of this congested urban scene. The families of old magnates and rising merchants, still untamed by a civic mentality, kept their urban profile confined to the great towers around which were clustered their homes and wherein they took refuge from the violence of private vendetta and factional strife. The cityscape fairly bristled with these towers, so characteristic of all Italian towns; but for all their expression of private status they did little to relieve the anonymity of communal architecture.

What stood out were the churches, above all those of the new orders of mendicant friars spawned by the rapid growth of towns all over Italy and dedicated to serving the needs of an urban society. By the second half of the thirteenth century these new communities had won their way into the hearts of the urban masses and boldly asserted their presence in conspicuous building programs. They located their monastic complexes all around the periphery of the densely populated center, in the open spaces where there was enough room for the great churches and vast squares they needed to accommodate the public they sought to attract, often in competition with one another. The Humiliati at Ognissanti, the Servites at the Santissima Annunziata, the Augustinians at Santo Spirito, the Carmelites at the church of the Carmine, and, the largest of all, the Franciscans at Santa Croce and the Dominicans at Santa Maria Novella—all these establishments were rebuilt or built anew in the second half of the century.

A mass of tenements, towers protruding everywhere, a few monumental complexes scattered here and there around the outer rim—this was the Florence of the thirteenth century. The urban sprawl had little overall organization (beyond the grid pattern at the core that was predetermined by the city's Roman foundation) and few points of focus to pull parts of it together visually. The cathedral complex, consisting of the baptistry and the church of Santa Reparata, was the monumental ecclesiastical center of the city, but as these structures, built in the eleventh century, became engulfed by the subsequent expansion of the city, the scale of their monumentality was considerably reduced. Santa Reparata could not compare to the new cathedrals of Siena and Pisa, towns that Florence was rapidly leaving behind in size and wealth. Political authority was given presence by the erection of the Palazzo del Popolo (the Bargello) in 1255 to house the city's chief police and judicial official; but this severe, castlelike structure was located off at the side, away from the center of the city, and tucked into the urban texture without enough surrounding space to put it into much relief. The political and ecclesiastical centers were thus separated in Florence. The market squares, the heart of the city's bustling economic life, were in yet another area. The chief local market was the Mercato Vecchio, located at the geographical center of the city and corresponding to the forum of ancient Roman times (and to the Piazza della Repubblica of today); the grain market was a few steps away,

Map of Florence showing: walls of 1173–75 and 1284–1333; the central squares of (1) the Mercato Vecchio, (2) the grain market (Orsanmichele), and (3) the Mercato Nuovo; and major churches and public buildings.

in the square of Orsanmichele; and the banking center, the heart of a growing financial empire abroad, was a few steps beyond, in what today is the Mercato Nuovo. The physical separation of cathedral, town hall, and marketplace distinguished the urban organization of Florence from that of many central and north Italian cities where the political and economic centers overlapped, sometimes in close proximity to the ecclesiastical center, in large, multifunctional squares with major public buildings, loggias, and fountains (Padua, Cremona, Modena, Perugia, Pistoia). The map of medieval Florence reveals no such centrality.

About the time Dante was born the spirit of a new political order inspired Florentines to insist on greater assertion of civic values against the centrifugal forces of a corporate society and to give more coherent shape to communal government. The constitutional process by which the new political morality worked itself out was slow and painful—Dante himself was not altogether freed from the viciousness as well as the despair of the older factionalism; but with the promulgation of the Ordinances of Justice in 1293, a firm constitutional foundation was laid for the development of a sound republican government. In the spirit of this nascent political order, a deliberate program was undertaken to cut the factious families down to size by truncating their towers, legislation was devised to give some order to future urban expansion, and major decisions were made to build public monuments worthy of a city that was one of the largest and richest in Europe. The new cathedral, begun in 1296, eventually became one of the two or three largest churches in Christendom; and the town hall of the new government, underway by 1299, was no less impressive for its size alone. Both, moreover, were distinctively new kinds of buildings and were destined to be milestones in the history of European architecture. By 1299 new walls (planned since 1285) were going up that pushed the boundaries of the city outward to take in five times the area ringed by the older walls. Planned in optimistic expectation of further growth, they embraced vast amounts of open space, reaching much beyond the built-up populated center. That expectation was never realized, of course, and the walls were not entirely filled up until the nineteenth century. Nevertheless, the people of Florence had taken the first step toward endowing the city with a monumentality worthy of its size and wealth, and the optimism, grandeur, and imagination that characterized these first stirrings of urban renewal continued to inform the spirit with which the city was built and rebuilt throughout the Renaissance.[1]

Civic Monuments

As in most medieval Italian towns, the cathedral project in Florence was undertaken as a public building program. In 1296 the cornerstone was laid to

[1] No attempt has been made to annotate the following discussion with full bibliographical references to the vast and well-known literature on the buildings of Florence. An approach to that literature can be made from the recent bibliographies in the periodically updated *Firenze e dintorni* of the Touring Club Italiano and in Giovanni Fanelli, *Firenze: architettura e città* (Florence, 1973). Only recent and specialized studies and those with particular interpretations are cited in the following.

initiate construction for replacement of the older church of Santa Reparata, located opposite the baptistry, with a much larger structure. An imposing sculptural program for the facade got underway almost immediately, under the direction of the first foreman of the works, Arnolfo di Cambio. Large parts of the building must have been up by 1331, when the discovery of the relics of Saint Zenobius (thought to have been the first bishop of Florence) under the crypt of the old church prompted the decision to change the original plans in favor of an even larger building. For the next quarter-century, however, work concentrated instead on the campanile, originally designed by Giotto but modified during construction by subsequent architects. It is not clear how much of the church had been built when the Campanile was nearing its completion in the 1350s, but only then were the crucial decisions made that were to determine the final size of the nave. The walls were erected by 1366, and then another, even more momentous decision was made to close the nave at the east end with a crossing whose centrality was as revolutionary in the history of church design as the solution eventually found for covering it over was in the history of architectural engineering.

Florentines had thus, little by little, committed themselves to a project that was to result in one of the largest churches in Christendom at the time, and they came to this decision notwithstanding a considerable falling off of their numbers during these very years (see table 1). Under similar circumstances of population decline, planners in nearby Siena put a sudden halt to construction on their bold new project to incorporate the existing church as a mere transept of a vastly enlarged structure. Florentines, on the other hand, went ahead: by 1379 the nave was vaulted, and for the next forty years work progressed on the crossing even though no one was sure how such an enormous space was to be covered. With the appointment of Brunelleschi in 1418 the cupola, the largest groin vault ever built in the west, got underway. Crowning a building already notable for its size and resplendent with its marble facing, the cupola so dominated the entire city that it brought the urban sprawl into sharp architectural focus—which, in fact, has determined the way Florence has been seen ever since by virtually every artist who has tried to take in the totality of the new cityscape.

Unlike most medieval Italian towns, Florence did not limit public prestige architecture to its cathedral complex. Contemporaneous with construction of the cathedral, a political center of no less architectural significance was taking shape on the other side of town. With the constitutional changes of the 1280s and 1290s establishing the guild republic headed by the priorate, there was need for a new public hall, one that could accommodate the growing number of citizen committees in charge of the increasingly complex governmental operations and also serve as the personal residence for the priors during their term of office. The result was the Palazzo dei Priori, since the sixteenth century (after the Medici duke abandoned it as his official residence for the

Pitti palace) known as the Palazzo Vecchio. This great hall, with its tower and baldacchino, its complex rustication, its distinctive north facade, and its open centralized courtyard with portico, surpasses most other Italian city halls of the period for the originality of its architecture. As the prototype of the later patrician palace, it has been labeled one of the most original buildings in the history of Italian architecture. The vicinity around it quickly became the political center of the city, especially with the opening up of the great square to the north and west, completed in the late 1380s. As Florence continued to expand its dominion over much of northern Tuscany and increase its involvement in peninsular politics, other governmental buildings went up around the square and the palace. The loggia for the priors (which, like the palace itself, took on a new name as the Loggia dei Lanzi with the advent of the Medici dukes) was the most monumental of these structures; but scattered throughout the vicinity were new palaces for the office of the Condotta (administrators of military expenditures) and the tribunal of the guilds (the Mercanzia), both facing the square, and a variety of lesser buildings for other offices behind the palace as well as a new mint, largely rebuilt in the 1420s, behind the loggia. Much of this building was not of monumental scale, but the opening up of such a vast square around two sides of the palace set off the inherent grandeur of that building and brought the entire space under the imposing dominance of its soaring tower.[2] Monumentality was much more a spatial creation here than in the relatively cramped quarters of the massive structural complex of the cathedral. The Piazza della Signoria, moreover, was a purely political center, in no way confused by market activity as were the places of government in most other Italian towns.[3]

The urban scene was now polarized by the cathedral and the Palazzo dei Priori. Halfway along this axis, in the square of Orsanmichele, the commune undertook another building project during these same years that was probably part of a scheme to link the cathedral and government centers. Since at least the end of the thirteenth century the city grain market had been located here, and as in all medieval towns the communal government interfered in that market to control prices and assure supply for the well-being of the population. The square was therefore a central place in the life of the city. In 1336, following the destruction by fire of a small wooden loggia used by officials for the city's market activity, construction began on the present building of Orsanmichele. Over forty meters high, built entirely of stone, and vaulted on two floors, it is perhaps the most imposing grain market that any medieval

[2] The growth of this square has been traced by Nicolai Rubinstein, "The Piazza della Signoria in Florence," in *Festschrift Herbert Siebenhüner*, ed. Erich Hubala and Gunter Schweikhart (Wurzburg, 1978), pp. 19–30.

[3] Jürgen Paul, "Commercial Use of Medieval Town Halls in Italy," *JSArH*, 28 (1969), 222.

city ever built. It was planned as a large loggia spreading over much of the square and open on all sides as a protected marketplace. On the pillars inside can still be seen the opening of the chutes through which the grain was to be released from the storage bins located in the two floors above. After the completion of the ground floor of the new structure in the 1350s, however, and while construction of the upper floors proceeded, the arcades were walled up to create a sanctuary. Obviously, this enclosure caused the loss of open space necessary to a marketplace, and in fact the grain market was soon relocated behind the Palazzo dei Priori, where the present loggia (now enclosed as a cinema) was built at the beginning of the seventeenth century. The relocation of such an important market must have changed the traffic patterns of the city, clearing the area of the kind of popular and perhaps occasionally unruly meeting-place so vividly described and even illustrated in the chronicle (the famous Biadaiuolo Manuscript in the Laurenziana) of the early fourteenth-century grain dealer, Domenico Lenzi.

Despite this change in function, the new building of Orsanmichele was completed as designed. It was transformed into a communal oratory, functioning inside as the hall of one of the city's largest confraternities dedicated to alms-giving and outside as a religious center for the guilds, who were assigned tabernacles on the facades for celebration of their annual feast days. This great free-standing monument, in other words, became symbolic of communal charity and of the guild structure of Florentine society. It is still today almost as prominent on the Florentine cityscape as the cathedral complex to the north and as the political complex to the south. That there was a grand scheme to unite all three places to give the city a monumental axial center is implied by the plan of 1388 and 1389 to widen the street that connects all three, Via Calzaiuoli, and to require owners of private buildings along it to rebuild the facades of their property according to uniform standards.

The sheer monumentality of these structures—the cathedral, the Campanile, Orsanmichele, the Palazzo and Loggia dei Priori—deserves more emphasis than most modern observers of the fourteenth-century architectural scene have given it. Moreover, it is remarkable that the city's enthusiasm for building was not daunted by the very considerable loss of population it underwent during the fourteenth century, even *before* most of these projects were completed or even conceived.

All this building culminated in one of the grandest programs of public sculpture undertaken since antiquity. As the cathedral reached its conclusion at the beginning of the fifteenth century, the sculptural decoration of the facade, which had been suspended after Arnolfo's death in 1302, was resumed on a much larger scale. From 1399 to 1427 eight life-size figures in marble were commissioned representing church fathers, martyred saints, evangelists, and prophets, and after 1415 work began on six additional statues for niches on the east and north facades of the Campanile. An additional project was under consideration from 1410 to 1415 to mount colossal statues, over three times the height of man, on the tribune around the base of what was to be the cupola. A terracotta figure of Joshua by Donatello actually was put into place and survived until the seventeenth century; but another, also given to Donatello, in marble, got only as far as the order for the block of stone; and a third figure, to be covered with metal plates, never left the drawing board. The project ended here, a fanciful symbol of the soaring ambition the Florentines had for the cathedral complex.

Meanwhile, work progressed on the doors to the baptistry opposite the cathedral. For half a century, from the 1401 competition for its second doors almost to the time of his death in 1455, Lorenzo Ghiberti was employed virtually full time on the two sets of doors that established him as one of the great virtuoso craftsmen in the bronzesmith's art. At Orsanmichele another ambitious sculptural program got underway with the legislation of 1406 instructing the guilds to contribute statues of their patron saints for their respective places around the outer facades; by 1427 fourteen more life-size figures in stone were completed. The richest guilds—the Calimala (importers and exporters of cloth), the Cambio (bankers), and the Lana (wool manufacturers)—decided, in competition with one another, to pay ten times the cost of a marble figure to have theirs in bronze; so Ghiberti had yet another occasion to demonstrate his virtuosity, making the largest figures cast in bronze since late antiquity. The flurry of sculptural activity generated by these commissions at both the cathedral and Orsanmichele, all in the span of a generation, as well as the monumental scale and civic function of the programs, go a long way to explain both the artistic atmosphere and the material conditions that nurtured the first generation of Renaissance artists.

In the Florence we see today the monumentality of these building projects is more apparent than any broader ideals of urban planning that may have inspired communal policy. Yet there was some degree of rationality in the way the commune organized public space. During the urban explosion of the later thirteenth century, open spaces were preserved and even enlarged at Santa Croce and Santa Maria Novella, the churches of the most popular of the preaching friars, and at the Carmine. Efforts were made to assure order by establishing regularized street patterns in new areas being built up, for example in the Santo Spirito and the Ognissanti areas. Building legislation, in addition to being directed toward the usual objective of maintaining the safety and health of the citizenry, reveals a preoccupation with appearances and convenience in fixing minimum heights to house fronts, in widening, straightening, and paving streets, in clearing streets of overhanging upper stories (*sporti*), and in calling for beauty and dignity in all this work. Uniformity of facades was projected, if not altogether realized, in central thoroughfares around the apse of the cathedral and along Via Calzaiuoli to the extent that windows were to have a uniform height and facades were to follow a single model. But, obviously, in the already densely built-up center any attempt to extend urban ideas of spatial organization beyond the central ecclesiastical, political, and market squares was hardly imaginable. Out in the countryside, however, communal urban ideas could be more fully realized in the new towns occasionally built as centers of military and administrative authority in recently conquered territories. These places—San Giovanni, Terranuova, Castelfranco, in the upper Valdarno, and Firenzuola and Scarperia north of the Mugello—were laid out with a large central square and streets following a grid pattern. All in all, the evidence adds up to a fairly comprehensive urban ideal. It is often assumed that appreciation of regularity and the geometrical organization of space in urban planning originated in the Renaissance; but a spirit of order, equilibrium, and central focus had long characterized the attitude of communal Florence toward public space.[4]

Institutions and Churches

Florentines' interest in public building was not exhausted in the central monumentality of the cathedral, the Piazza della Signoria, and Orsanmichele alone. These buildings arose as the expression of the collective concern of the citizenry, but they were just one manifestation of that concern. Building—and rebuilding—was a widespread phenomenon throughout the city from the second half of the fourteenth century onward. It is not always easy to delineate public and private roles; much building was sponsored by institutions like guilds, parishes, and welfare foundations that were, in effect, public, or quasi-public, organizations with close ties to the government.

In the second half of the thirteenth century the government made direct subsidies for construction to the popular mendicant orders that catered to the needs of the urban population. Subsequently the commune continued a policy

[4] For a recent description of Florence at the time of Dante with full bibliography see Ugo Procacci, "L'aspetto urbano di Firenze dai tempi di Cacciaguida a quelli di Dante," s.v. "Firenze" in *Enciclopedia dantesca*, II (Rome, 1970), 913–20. The subsequent literature includes: Guido Pampaloni, *Firenze al tempo di Dante: documenti sull'urbanistica fiorentina* (Rome, 1973); Franek Sznura, *L'espansione urbana di Firenze nel Dugento* (Florence, 1975); Renzo Manetti and Mariachiara Pozzana, *Firenze: le porte dell'ultime cerchie di mura* (Florence, 1979). The point about the spirit of order in pre-Renaissance urban planning was made by Nicola Ottokar, "Criteri d'ordine, di regolarità e d'organizzazione nell'urbanistica ed in genere nella vita fiorentina dei secoli XIII–XIV," in his *Studi comunali e fiorentini* (Florence, 1948), pp. 143–49; and this is the theme of Wolfgang Braunfels, *Mittelalterliche Stadtbaukunst in der Toscana* (Berlin, 1959). The urban planning of new towns has been studied by David Friedman, "Le terre nuove fiorentine," *Archeologia medievale*, 1 (1974), 231–47.

of modest support for building programs at a large number of churches by assigning percentages of specific incomes, such as gate gabelles. On occasion much larger sums were appropriated outright. For example, in the fifteenth century the monastery at San Pancrazio received a grant through its Gonfalone (one of the sixteen political subdivisions of the city); and the church of Santo Spirito, representing an entire Quarter of the city, got much support for its new building from the Monte officials (who administered the public debt and therefore virtually all the city's fiscal affairs).

The guilds were also major patrons of building. Besides their tabernacles at Orsanmichele, almost all of them, including the smallest, built new halls sometime after the mid-fourteenth century; and although not one of these buildings can claim much mention in the history of architectural style, some were imposing buildings and were conspicuously located on public squares. More important, however, were the activities of the guilds as patrons of welfare foundations. Beginning in the latter part of the fourteenth century several of the major guilds opened hospitals with building programs that resulted in the distinct development of that genre in Florentine architecture. The Calimala built the hospital of Bonifazio, founded in 1376, and the Cambio took over the building of the hospital of San Matteo following the death of its benefactor, Lemmo Balducci, in 1389. As if not to be outdone, the guild of Por Santa Maria, elevated by the success of the silk industry in the later fourteenth century to the ranks of those guilds dominated by the city's wealthiest men, founded the orphanage of the Ospedale degli Innocenti in 1419 and undertook one of the most important building programs in the entire history of the city. At about the same time the state put the hospital of San Paolo under the patronage of the Giudici e Notai (lawyers and notaries) in hopes of a reform that also may have included a building program, although the extensive building that eventually got underway there after 1451 seems to owe little to guild support. In 1335 another major guild, the Medici e Speziali (doctors and apothecaries), was given the patronage of the church of San Barnaba, which was slowly rebuilt under its auspices. Of the seven major guilds, only the Vaiai e Pellicciai (furriers) and the Giudici e Notai seem never to have undertaken a building program as sponsor of a public or religious institution.

It was no coincidence that hospitals figured so prominently in guild patronage. As a consequence of recurrent plague in the fourteenth century, establishments for the sick proliferated outside the older hospices (*ospedali*), where they had been taken care of along with pilgrims, orphans, and the poor. According to Cristoforo Landini there were thirty-five hospitals at the end of the fifteenth century. These new hospitals did not specialize in the treatment of particular illnesses, although some specialization occurred later—with the foundation of San Bastiano as a lazzaretto for plague victims after

1464, the establishment of the Incurabili as a home for syphilitics in 1520, and the transformation of San Paolo into a short-term convalescent home in 1592. Santa Maria Nuova, which had long been a hospital for the sick, was considerably enlarged into a vast complex that made it by far the largest such institution in the city, but many of these hospitals were so small that it is unlikely they were founded simply to satisfy a pressing need for more hospital beds. Most were founded either by rich patricians who left large bequests for that purpose, especially in the generation after the Black Death, or by religious communities organized to perform some kind of social welfare function. However small some of these operations were, they all required not only wards for the sick and a chapel but also cloistered quarters for the religious group that constituted the resident staff. This last feature had much the greater architectural significance, for the staff could easily outnumber the patients and often was made up of both men and women, who had to be accommodated in separate quarters.[5] The public statement made by the larger foundations was heightened by the monumental loggias that stretched across the facades of their buildings.

Monasteries were also the sites of much building activity. Some of this building resulted from altogether new foundations, like the large number of communities for women that sprang up beginning in the second half of the fourteenth century. By 1540 they numbered over forty.[6] Although many were lodged in small houses, each community, like a hospital, had its minimum requirement for a chapel area and some kind of cloistered residence. In addition to these local foundations, many new monastic communities moved into the city around 1400, and even though they generally took up residence in older establishments, they nevertheless asserted their presence in new building programs—for example, the Olivetians at San Miniato (1373), the Cistercians at Cestello (1442), and, at Fiesole, the Third Order Franciscans at the new house of the Hieronymites (1415) and the Lateran canons at the Badia (1442). Likewise, reform movements within older orders marked their success with building programs—for example, the Benedictine Observants at the Badia (1418), the Franciscan Observants at San Salvatore al Monte (1419), and the Dominican Observants at both San Domenico at Fiesole (1406) and San Marco (1436). At both new and old foundations, moreover, the new life-style of friars, who were for the first time allowed to have private cells, was accommodated by the replacement of the traditional second-story dormitories with rows of cells opening on loggias around the

[5] The literature is cited in Richard A. Goldthwaite and W. R. Rearick, "Michelozzo and the Ospedale di San Paolo in Florence," *Flor. Mitt.*, 21 (1977), 224, 280.

[6] Richard C. Trexler, "Le Célibat à la fin du Moyen Age: les religieuses de Florence," *Annales, E.S.C.*, 27 (1972), 1329–50.

courtyard. This often necessitated major remodeling of cloisters into the double-decked arcades characteristic of Renaissance monasteries, the first examples of which are, in fact, found in Florence.[7]

Whatever the internal dynamic for change that provided religious communities with the excuse for undertaking so much building activity, few buildings would actually have been built had there not been considerable financial support for them. In the final analysis that activity was another manifestation of private patronage. The wealthy had always supported the church in its various institutional forms by financing building programs; but after the mid-fourteenth century the pace of private patronage was much increased—at least patronage expressed itself more conspicuously in the coats of arms that began to appear everywhere on architectural projects undertaken privately on behalf of religious institutions. Many of the institutions that came into existence after the Black Death were creations of single donors; that so many of them were so small indicates a widespread desire to have a personal memorial. But less expensive outlets for patronage existed in every parish church as well as in the mendicant orders' half dozen or so monasteries, whose cloistered internal spaces were accessible to the laity. The possibilities were seemingly infinite as men competed to build a new sacristy or high altar in their parish church, an entire cloister in their preferred monastery, or, more commonly, a family chapel in the church where they had traditional family associations—all "signed" with the donor's arms. If civic buildings were an outlet for the collective conscience, religious architecture flourished because it represented the happy convergence of a different kind of public duty and purely private interests.

The desire for private chapels was the major catalyst that brought about the boom in church construction. Private chapels were nothing new, but earlier only the very rich had them, and they were mostly confined to the transepts of major churches. By the fifteenth century, however, there was hardly a church in the city that did not feel the impact of remodeling, or rebuilding, to accommodate a surge in demand for chapel space arising now not only from the rich but also from men somewhat further down in the social hierarchy. At Santa Trinita chapels were added to the nave (a major one by a teacher of commercial arithmetic), and after 1362 these were worked into the more coherent design of a chapel-lined church that became a standard plan. All of Brunelleschi's churches met this functional requirement, most notably Santo Spirito, where the nave and presbytery were enclosed in an outer ring of thirty-eight chapels belonging to families in that quarter of the city. The Santissima Annunziata was transformed in a similar fashion, with five chapels along each side of the nave and nine around the crossing. Virtually all new

[7] Wolfgang Braunfels, *Monasteries of Western Europe: The Architecture of the Orders* (Princeton, 1972), p. 136.

churches constructed during the Renaissance, for example those at Cestello and San Salvatore, follow the same plan. Much new church construction was, in fact, financed by the selling of private chapel space. In the patrician republic of Venice no such demand arose for rebuilding the city's churches in the fifteenth century; by the same token, when the Brunelleschian model for church design was transplanted abroad, as for example at Ferrara in the churches of Biagio Rossetti, the result was likely to be a building whose many starkly vacant chapels point up the social validity of the original idea in Florence.

Private Palaces

With the exception of the loggias of a few hospitals, privately sponsored institutional construction was often not apparent to the public from the street. Architectural embellishments were concentrated inside the residential quarters of religious communities and behind church doors. Few of these buildings made much of an impression in their external appearances, and it is one of the curious facts in the history of Florentine architecture that virtually no church in the city has a complete Renaissance facade. For that matter, not even the elaborate sculptural program for the cathedral was completed, and, for all the building's monumentality, its facade remained largely unfinished throughout the Renaissance. If the streets of Florence changed in their appearance during this period, it was mostly the result of entirely private building in the realm of domestic architecture.[8]

Before the second half of the fourteenth century the urban residence of the rich did not constitute a distinctive architectural form. Giovanni Villani, in the 1330s, had more to say about their rural seats. Some buildings in the city were quite impressive for their size, but facades received little aesthetic treatment. Rustication of stone surfaces was crude, and there was little articulation of stories and not much applied decoration, except perhaps a family coat of arms. The ground floor had arched openings leading into shops or the interior of the building, and there was no particular focus on a principal entrance. If anything, these buildings must have given the city something of a visual unity in the general uniformity, if not indeed monotony, of their facades, but this was owing less to policy or notions of style than to artisan traditions in handling materials, their rule-of-thumb techniques for arching openings, and their conservative inclination to use existing buildings

[8] For the literature on domestic building and further details see Richard A. Goldthwaite, "The Florentine Palace as Domestic Architecture," *American Historical Review,* 77 (1972), 977–1012. A general discussion of family buildings on the medieval urban scene (but with considerable emphasis on Genoa) is Jacques Heers, *Le Clan familial au moyen âge* (Paris, 1974), chs. 4 and 5.

as models for new ones. Members of a great family tended to reside in clusters of these anonymous buildings. The architectural symbols of their presence in an area were an open loggia, where they assembled on ceremonial occasions, and a great tower, where they took refuge in more violent times. Both became obsolescent in the Renaissance. The towers, once symbols of the strength and independence of great family groups, were torn down in the course of the late thirteenth and early fourteenth centuries by the commune in pursuit of its policy of asserting public authority over private interests. Loggias, whose declining social utility is not clearly understood, were something that most families felt no need to build after the fourteenth century.

The Peruzzi were one family that attempted to give the conglomeration of its residences some public architectural identity. The buildings along Via de' Benci at the west end of the square of Santa Croce have an apparent uniformity, above all in the four arches linking the buildings across the side streets opening off Via de' Benci, each arch conspicuously marked with the Peruzzi coat of arms. These buildings, which may incorporate the earlier city walls along this line, mark the confines of the residential area of the family clustered around its square behind. No other family at the time, however, seems to have architecturally asserted its presence so boldly—and few were in a position to.

Sometime after 1400 domestic architecture began to come into its own with the development of the private patrician palace. A conscious effort was made to set off the facade of the individual residence from the anonymity of the medieval buildings around it. Greater focus was achieved by giving emphasis to the principal entrance; eventually a standard palace-type emerged and all other openings were eliminated, so that, with shops removed, the building became more exclusively a residential property. Strip lines separated the standard three-story elevation, and more decorative elements were added in the form of window moldings, cornices, and ironwork. The prototype for this new architectural genre seems to be the articulated three-story facade on the north side of the Palazzo dei Priori, which is symmetrical and centers on a single entrance leading into an open arcaded courtyard within. It may not be irrelevant to its role as a model for domestic architecture a century after its construction that the Palazzo dei Priori was not only the symbol of republican government but also the residence of the priors during their tenure in office. That model became the standard format of the private palace. Modifications took place mostly in the decorative elements—the treatment of the facade surface, the elaboration of classical details, and the addition of other features from the bench below to the crowning cornice above.

Palace facades fell roughly into two categories, rusticated stone or intonaco (a kind of painted plaster), but combinations of the two and differences in the degree of rustication permitted considerable variation. Facades with stone revetment varied according to how the material was handled, the possibilities ranging from roughly hewn blocks of highly irregular sizes (the Neroni palace) to blocks that were completely finished, flat, and carefully patterned (the Bartolini palace). These options were not infrequently used in combination, with a different treatment of each story, as most notably (and probably originally) in the Medici palace; or the ground story alone might be rusticated, with the upper ones in intonaco. The flat, even quality of a facade in intonaco allowed greater elaboration of contrasting stone elements used for windows and doors. The surface itself could be treated in a more purely decorative way by being either worked in sgraffito, a technique by which a design was incised through plaster to a painted surface underneath, or (much more rarely) frescoed. A third facade type is represented by Alberti's Rucellai palace with the applied classical order of its entablature-pilaster system and the bricklike pattern of the canalization in the flat stone surface that disguises the identity of the stone blocks out of which it is made; but this palace had no imitators in Florence, despite its absolute originality in the history of architecture. Another curious stylistic limitation of Florentine architecture was the failure to elaborate the decorative possibilities of brick, although it (along with rubble) was the basic structural element used in virtually all of these buildings. The basic palace-type was not much influenced by subsequent stylistic developments elsewhere in Italy, although it was subject to some curious elaborations by builders in provincial towns like Colle Val d'Elsa, Cortona, Castiglion Fiorentino, Barga, and Volterra, where in the ducal period local elites looked to the capital city for inspiration but at the same time tried to do something original.

Within, the courtyard became a standard feature of the plan of the building. Earlier palaces did not have internal courtyards, or if they did, the space was likely to be cramped, irregular, and without much ornamentation. The palace-type that developed in the fifteenth century, however, invariably centered on the regularized space of an arcaded courtyard embellished by columns, capitals, moldings, cornices, oculi, and sometimes an open loggia above. Vaulted double-ramp internal staircases were also an innovation; but apart from the occasional appearance, toward the end of the fifteenth century, of a detached column at the landing, they remained severely simple. Vaulting of the ground floor permitted the addition of carved stone corbels, but otherwise the internal architectural decoration was generally limited to fireplaces and water basins in stone and to the woodwork of paneling and ceilings.

Benedetto Dei wrote (about 1470) that thirty of these palaces were built in his own time. Somewhat over half a century later Benedetto Varchi republished Dei's list, adding thirty-five palaces that he considered worthy of mention, plus about twenty that were built after Dei wrote, and he concluded that anyone who wanted to list them all "would have too much to do." All of of this building amounted to what today we would call urban renewal. These palaces considerably enlarged the domestic space for the family; and because from one-third to one-half of their ground plans were taken up by open courtyards, their construction meant clearing a large area of built-up urban property. The Strozzi palace, one of the largest of all, occupied a block that had been gutted of a house with a tower belonging to the counts of Poppi, a "large house" with three shops on the ground floor, four other houses, and nine separate shops, some with living accommodations. Over twenty houses were swept away by the Medici palace. Even the much smaller Bartolini palace replaced half a dozen houses as well as an inn, and many a normal-sized palace incorporated several older structures into a single dwelling behind a new facade. The settings of many palaces were further enlarged by extensive gardens—so many that both Dei and Varchi listed them in their description of the city.

The palace was primarily an expansion of interior private space. Only a few projects for a square to set off the palace as a private monument can be documented, and not many of them were realized at the time. The Pitti palace had a square to enhance its location on high ground at the edge of a built-up area, and there were vague plans to link the Medici palace with the church of San Lorenzo around a square. Giovanni Rucellai went the furthest by opening up a square in front of his strikingly original palace and erecting a loggia opposite, but he apparently had little interest in either the spatial or stylistic integration of the whole.

These vast blocks of private property were inserted in the congested center of the city, not in the open areas of the periphery, and public display was confined to facades whose beautiful proportions often blind us to their extraordinary height. Their formidable massiveness marks the limits of the civic world. Most palaces were located in the narrow streets of the medieval city, where they cannot be easily seen (as anyone who tries to photograph them knows only too well), and hardly any were placed on already existing squares. By the sixteenth century the concentrations of them in certain streets, like Via Tornabuoni, Borgo Pinti, Via de' Ginori, and Via Maggio (where they displaced sixty wool shops), were significant enough to change the general character of the neighborhood, but in general they were widely scattered throughout the old city. Nevertheless, more than anything else it was the collective effect of their monumentality that transformed the anonymous medieval city into the Renaissance city we admire today.

The Renaissance City

Much of the housing left empty by the population losses of the fourteenth century must have been insubstantial and inadequate for the more prosperous city of the Renaissance, but it is difficult to assess the extent to which building (or rebuilding) went beyond the conspicuous monuments of private and institutional patrons to effect an overall physical transformation of the city. According to Alamanno Rinuccini, writing in 1462, the construction of so many and such large private palaces by the rich in itself caused serious problems of dislocation for the masses, and he refers (although not too clearly) to efforts by the commune to encourage investment in better housing for them.[9] Subsequently, legislation was designed to promote building in the vast outlying area between the populated center of the city and the third circle of walls, which had never been built up and was turned over instead to gardens and farms. In 1474 a twenty-year tax relief was offered for every house put up on previously unbuilt land. This inducement must not have been sufficient, for the legislation was repeated in 1489, with the promise that anyone who built within five years would have tax relief for forty years; by the time the deadline was reached in 1494 no one had taken advantage of the exemption, and the legislation was renewed once again.[10] The commune announced its willingness to sell the land it owned in these areas to developers and made efforts through the Roman Curia to get ecclesiastical institutions to put their large holdings on the market.[11] The legislation expresses explicit concern for the beauty of the city as well as for what is referred to as a housing shortage. The tax advantage held out by the commune, however, would have been attractive only to real estate developers, men who wanted to build rental properties, for houses used as residences by their owners had long been exempt from taxation. Vast undeveloped areas beyond the built-up core of the city but still within the walls remained conspicuous on maps and aerial views of the city until the nineteenth century.

Within the built-up core of the city, on the other hand, a certain amount of speculative building went on. In 1512 the masons' guild itself began work on an apartment over its hall as an investment, and the place was rented on a three-year lease long before it was finished. Several large institutions invested

[9] *Ricordi storici di Filippo di Cino Rinuccini dal 1282 al 1460 colla continuazione di Alamanno e Neri suoi figli fino al 1506*, ed. G. Aiazzi (Florence, 1840), p. xc.

[10] ASF, Provv. 165, fols. 26r–27r (26 April 1474); Provv. 180, fols. 16v–17v (27 May 1489; published by Giuseppina Carla Romby, *Per costruire ai tempi di Brunelleschi: modi, norme e consuetudini del Quattrocento fiorentino* [Florence, 1979], pp. 41–42); Provv. 184, fols. 120r–21r (11 March 1493/94). The spirit of this legislation is still found several years later in the proposals of Domenico di Roberto Cecchi, *Riforma sancta et pretiosa . . . per conservatione della città di Firenze et pel ben comune* . . . (Florence, 1496/97), p. 23 (now reprinted in Umberto Mazzone, *"El buon governo." Un progetto di riforma generale nella Firenze savonaroliana* [Florence, 1978], p. 191).

[11] A letter from the Signoria to its ambassador in Rome is quoted in Piero Sanpaolesi, "La casa fiorentina di Bartolommeo Scala," in *Studien zur toskanischen Kunst: Festschrift für Ludwig Heinrich Heydenreich zum 23. März 1963*, ed. Wolfgang Lotz and Lise Lotte Möller (Munich, 1964), pp. 278–79 note; related documents are published by Romby, *Per costruire*, p. 46.

more substantially in the building of what today might be called row houses, which were to be rented or sold. Between 1489 and 1503 the hospital of Santi Filippo e Jacopo del Ceppo in Via dei Tintori put up a row of six houses. In 1510 the wool guild dismantled one of its stretching plants in Via de' Servi to clear a site for a dozen three-story houses, which were to be sold, and about 1575 it erected an apartment house designed by Ammannati in Via degli Alfani at the corner of Via della Pergola. Other houses were put up by the Cambio and the Mercanzia. The loggia begun in 1516 by the Servites of the Santissima Annunziata to match that of the Innocenti opposite served as a facade for a row of houses behind (although they were not finished until over half a century after the loggia itself). In the second half of the sixteenth century surveys made by ecclesiastical institutions of their property holdings commonly include illustrations of urban buildings, and on many of these appear modest row houses that seem to have been built according to uniform standards, probably during the fifteenth and sixteenth centuries. Bonsignori's aerial view of Florence at the end of the sixteenth century, in fact, shows a substantially built city that is still recognizable today, not just in its great monuments but in its ordinary buildings as well.[12]

With all of this building there is little evidence of systematic planning. Palace-square combinations were few, and almost all remained incomplete. Single monuments, private or otherwise, when located in large squares do not seem to have set any criteria for the organization of the larger space, except perhaps for the straightening of street frontages. The loggia of the hospital of San Paolo, for example, was placed prominently on a large square opposite Santa Maria Novella, but in no relation to it that might have imposed more geometric coherence on subsequent development of the square. Only in the square of the Santissima Annunziata did Brunelleschi's loggia of

[12] The additional floor to the masons' guild hall is discussed on p. 257 herein. For the Lana properties see "Le case dell'Arte della Lana in Via de' Servi," in *L'illustratore fiorentino: calendario storico per l'anno 1908*, ed. Guido Carocci (Florence, 1907), pp. 165–66; and Mazzino Fossi, *Bartolomeo Ammannati, architetto* (Naples, [1966]), pp. 101–3. The Ceppo's project is recorded in the building accounts for the fourth and fifth houses, 1490–1505 (ASF, Incurabili 12), and in summary accounts in ledgers of general administration (Incurabili 79, fol. 80; and 100, fol. 65). The surviving building accounts for the Servite loggia project are Ss. Annunziata 846 (ledger, 1516–25), 847 (income-outgo journal, 1516–26), 849 bis (1577–80); the houses are referred to by Iodoco Del Badia, "La loggia a destra nella piazza della Ss. Annunziata di Firenze," *Arte e storia*, 1 (1882), 82–83. The houses of the Cambio and the Mercanzia, as well as many more in Via del Campuccio, are noted in a memorandum by Francesco Baldovinetti published by C. von Fabriczy, "Aus dem Gedenkbuch Francesco Baldovinettis," in *Repertorium für Kunstwissenschaft*, 28 (1905), 543–44. Illustrations of row houses in the property records of San Pancrazio have been published by Leonardo Ginori Lisci, *Cabrei in Toscana: raccolte di mappe, prospetti e vedute, sec. XVI–sec. XIX* (Florence, 1978), pp. 41 illus. 24, and 207 illus. 231.

the Innocenti project the ordering of the space that materialized a century later with the addition of an identical loggia opposite, and, a few years afterwards, the portico of the church on the third side of the square. Moreover, despite the demand for chapels that occasioned the rebuilding of most of the city's churches, church facades got little attention and stood prominently incomplete on their squares even when (as at San Lorenzo) the open space had been extended at great cost to set off the new building. As for private palaces, they did not so much organize space as make an appearance in it, and with all the elaboration of facade types, more expressive of the private whims of their owners than of the ideals of urban order, palaces, if they did anything, jolted the tradition of uniformity and order of earlier town planning. More than one writer has commented on the apparent contradiction between, on the one hand, civic ideals and an aesthetic sense of geometric order and, on the other, lack of urban planning and the individuality of private architecture. In the history of urban planning with respect to what actually got built in Florence (as opposed to what the theorists talked about), the Renaissance lies dormant between the age of the earlier commune and the age of the Medici princes. Tourists from Montaigne to the present cannot be taken to task too severely for not finding the much-vaunted beauty of Florence immediately apparent on their first walk through the city's streets.

If not a better planned city for all this building, Florence was at least a better built city and a safer place to live. Manetti (in his life of Brunelleschi) commented on the crude method of building evidenced in the older structures and still seen in his day, and their fragility is noted in the annals that record the ravages wrought on them by disasters of all kinds. Devastating fires broke out in 1293, in 1301, and again in 1304, when (according to Villani) over 1700 buildings—palaces, towers, and houses—were destroyed. The danger of fire was so great that Paolo da Certaldo advised keeping rope and sacks around the house so that when the alarm came a person could get his goods and himself out as quickly as possible. The great flood of 1333 swept away many of the buildings all along the Arno, too many (says Domenico Lenzi) to be enumerated. And then there was the mob, ever ready to turn itself loose, in the faction-ridden society of this earlier period, to wreak its vengeance on the enemy of the moment. Salutati's despair about the situation was not all rhetoric: "How many and magnificent houses of citizens and how many palaces have been destroyed by the internal discord of our citizens! How many have been annihilated by fires sometimes set deliberately, sometimes caused by chance."[13]

By the fifteenth century there was little talk of this kind of destruction. Buildings were more substantial, since construction materials were almost

[13] Quoted in Hans Baron, *The Crisis of the Early Italian Renaissance* (Princeton, 1966), p. 109.

entirely brick, stone, rubble, and tile. Walls were massive enough that fireplaces were normally set in interior walls and kitchens moved from the top to the ground floor. Timber was reduced by the widespread vaulting of ground floors and the substitution of stone for the outside supports (*sporti*) of overhanging floors. Looking at these structures, seemingly built for an eternity and having already endured half a millennium, it is difficult to see how fire, flood, or even the willful action of the most violent mob could do much damage to them. In fact, hardly any evidence of such destruction can be turned up anywhere in the annals of the Renaissance city.

Florence was also a remarkably clean city by European standards of the time. At the beginning of the fifteenth century Goro Dati commented on how well the streets were paved "with flat stones of equal size so that they were always clean and neat, more so than in any other place," a feature that for the next two centuries or so invariably impressed visitors from across the Alps.[14] Although apparently the pavement of streets was largely a private expense, they were kept reasonably clean by an extensive drainage system of sewers dumping into the Arno that was maintained by the city. Moreover, palaces commonly had their own private source of water. Dati and Varchi both make the point that most had their own wells, making it possible (as Dati says) to get fresh water, even to the top floors. When in 1476 the sons of Messer Giannozzo Pandolfini undertook remodeling of their father's house to divide it between them, they saw to it that another well was dug to assure each residence an independent water supply.[15] Buildings were also fitted out with internal latrines, probably very like the closets that emptied into cesspools below that can still be seen in the Davanzati palace (and that were illustrated by Francesco di Giorgio). These were the responsibility of the building's owner, and the records of the Parte Guelfa for the sixteenth century are full of litigation over problems relating to cesspools shared by several households. One clothmender made a note in his book of memoranda of the cost for the annual emptying of a cesspool (from 1520 to 1524), and a scene in the *Decameron* (VIII, 9) is set at the ditches near Santa Maria Novella, which was one of the city's dumping-grounds for this refuse.[16]

Plumbing of all kinds was a major feature of palaces put up in the Renaissance. Building accounts are full of expenses for wells, cesspools, cisterns, sinks, latrines (*necessari, luoghi comuni, agiamenti*), and the tile

[14] Creighton Gilbert, "The Earliest Guide to Florentine Architecture, 1423," *Flor. Mitt.*, 14 (1969), 46.

[15] Goldthwaite, "Florentine Palace," p. 1001.

[16] The administration of the city's sewage system in the sixteenth century is described in Giorgio Spini, ed., *Architettura e politica da Cosimo I a Ferdinando I* (Florence, 1976), pp. 212–13, 231–34, 317–18. The book of the cloth-mender (*rimendatore*) Marco di Zanobi is ASF, S. Paolo 106: every year he paid a *votapozzi* from lb.1 to lb.1 s.15 for emptying the pool of so-many buckets of *roba* (fol. 12r).

piping that constituted the plumbing system; and contracts for foundations commonly included stipulations for leaving holes and openings to accommodate the system. Occasionally events about the plumbing were considered important enough to be recorded among the memoranda Florentines were ever compiling about the notable events in their lives—like the bursting of two latrines and the flooding of a room in the house of Agnolo di Niccolò Benintendi in 1473, and the discovery by Bartolomeo di Lorenzo Banderaio in 1539 that the cesspool for his latrine was actually under the house of his neighbor.[17] When the doctor Antonio di Ser Paolo Benivieni made improvements in the plumbing of his house in 1487, he described the complete system. On investigating the drainage from a downstairs latrine, he found that it emptied into a cesspool along the street, and he rerouted the drainage from a sink so that it connected up with another latrine and thereby helped flush it. Two years later he had three new cesspools dug for the emptying of latrines and sinks above and for the drainage of rainwater from the courtyard and roof. Benivieni tells us he recorded these plumbing improvements so the system would be understood by whoever might take up residence there in the future. It may also have been his natural instinct as a medical man to take a particular interest in the sanitary system of his house. The system Benivieni installed is exactly that described in the architectural treatises of two near-contemporaries, Alberti and Filarete.[18]

[17] ASF, S. Paolo 74 (memoranda of Benintendi, 1469–78), fol. 85r; S. Paolo 129 (memoranda of Banderaio [who later changed his name to Berti], 1514–39), fol. 87r.

[18] Benivieni describes his improvements in his book of memoranda (1484–1500): ASF, Notarile antecosimiano, B 1324 (bound in with his father's protocol), fols. 196r and 207r. "Ricordo chome a dì 15 di settembre 1487 ricerchai nella volta di casa mia per la fognia dell'agiamento di chamera terrena e tròvala a piè del pilastro in verso Francesco del Cittadino, nel chanto del pilastro, e era ripiena perchè è una fognia. Va in un pozo che è lungho la via. E nel chanto più là, lungho el muro, trovai quella dell'aquaio di sala, che era rovinata, e riprèsila. E òlla messa nella fognia dello agamento, acciò lavi quella che non si riempie. E sopra detta fognia ò fatto uno ismaltitoio nel mezzo della volta. A memoria di chi succedrà." "E ò fatto fare nella volta sotto la chamera uno pozzo insino all'aqua: è a piè del truogolo maggiore, e à il chiusino di sopra in che entra l'aqua del truogolo e gli agiamenti di camera terrena e di camera e di su insino al tetto e l'aqua etrandro dell'aquaio. Ancora ò fatto uno pozzo insino a l'aqua nella volta della chameretta in sulla chorte, nel quale entra tutti gli agiamenti da in llì in su e chosì anchora l'aqua [che] piove nella chorte, [n]el pozzo, et nel chanto a piè dello agamento e al lato in verso la schala va in detta volta, cioè tra le schala e 'l muro dell'agiamento. Item ò fatto fare uno pozzo da smaltare nella volta sotto la chamera terrena [che] è in sulla via, cioè la chameretta, da smaltare l'agiamento di detta chamera a direttura sotto detto agiamento, e à il chiusino medesimamente chome gli altri. A memoria di chi succedrà." The theorists' descriptions are Leon Battista Alberti, *L'architettura*, ed. Giovanni Orlandi (Milan, 1966), p. 90; and Antonio Averlino detto il Filarete, *Trattato di architettura*, ed. Anna Maria Finoli and Lilliana Grassi (Milan, 1972), p. 124. Cf. the relatively

A survey of building in Florence during the Renaissance would not be complete without a description of the villas that dotted the countryside. Although outside the city walls, these buildings were nevertheless put up by the urban upper classes as second homes, and they therefore fall fully within the economic and social context of architectural patronage during the Renaissance. Many of the city's older families had long had country seats, usually associated with the place of their origins. Florentines, says Giovanni Villani (*Cronica*, XI, 94), were considered mad for the wild expenditures they lavished on these places, and the sight of so many such residences invariably left an impression on visiting foreigners. In the fifteenth century another generation of country houses grew up, either as a result of rebuilding or building anew. As an architectural phenomenon, however, the Tuscan villa represented an extension of the town palace into the countryside and did not much advance the history of villa style in Renaissance Italy. This interest in the villa cannot be linked to any change in estate management by townsmen making "a return to the land," and in any event the villa did not function as an estate headquarters in any way other than as the residence of its owners. The villa was primarily a social phenomenon, an expression of the desire for an escape into the tranquillity of the countryside that was in part inspired by the model of the ancient Roman landed patriciate then becoming familiar through the literary taste of the humanists. Two centuries after Villani expressed his amazement at the craze of his countrymen for building outside the city, Florentines were still building with such a passion that, according to the Venetian ambassador, a man could easily be induced to spend a hundred times his income for (what the Venetian called) a palace in the countryside.[19] The sight of all these "palaces" scattered in the hills around Florence inspired Ariosto to speculate (with full poetic license) that if they were all gathered together within one set of walls the result would be a city not even two Romes could equal:

> Se dentro un mur, sotto un medesmo nome,
> fusser raccolti i tuoi palazzi sparsi,
> non ti sarian da pareggiar due Rome.
> (*Le Rime*, Capitolo XI)

---

primitive system of Francesco di Giorgio Martini, "Architettura civile e militare," in the edition of his *Trattati di architettura ingegneria e arte militare*, ed. Corrado Maltese, II (Milan, 1967), 335–37.

[19] Arnaldo Segarizzi, ed., *Relazioni degli ambasciatori veneti al senato*, 3 vols. (Bari, 1912–16), III, pt. 1, 19. The Renaissance villa is still a major problem in the history of architecture; the literature is surveyed in the discussion of Kurt W. Forster, "Back to the Farm: Vernacular Architecture and the Development of the Renaissance Villa," *Architectura*, No. 1 (1974), 1–12.

The Ducal Presence

Florence got her prince with the establishment of the Medici duchy of Cosimo I in 1537, and almost immediately the city was endowed with a new kind of architectural splendor. The earlier Medici had an avid interest in architecture, but their patronage was not so explicitly designed to impress the physical mark of their authority on the urban scene. Cosimo il Vecchio, inspired by the notion of the humanists that a great man expresses the magnificence of his status and quality through architecture, sponsored building projects to enhance the newly gained position of his family in Florence. Although his patronage of architecture was more generous than that of any other of his class, it hardly went beyond the limits of patrician propriety in a state that was, to all appearances, still a republic. Besides financing the construction of buildings outside the city walls—family villas, the monastery at Bosco ai Frati, the Badia at Fiesole, the church of San Bartolomeo—he invested heavily in the monastery at San Marco, and his interest in rebuilding the family parish church of San Lorenzo was so keen that fellow parishioners were somewhat discouraged from joining him in the enterprise, leaving the place all the more conspicuous as a Medici monument. Yet, Cosimo never went as far as Giovanni Rucellai did by putting his name prominently across the entablature of the facade at Santa Maria Novella; indeed, none of the Medici put a facade on San Lorenzo at all. Cosimo's palace was the grandest ever built in the city and certainly made its mark on the urban scene, but he had rejected an even grander scheme presented to him by Brunelleschi. Moreover, at the end of the century the building was overshadowed by the Strozzi palace and rivaled by several others.

Cosimo's grandson, Lorenzo, was not a builder on the same scale, although he had a deeper personal interest in architecture. It has been claimed that he made his own designs for buildings, and his aggressive interest in other men's building projects suggests that his approval of them was a quasi-official requirement. Lorenzo wished to project abroad an image of Florence as an art center, and presumably he was anxious to see the city itself enhanced with architectural monuments appropriate to his ambitions. His project for a villa in the northeast part of the city, which would have significantly reworked a large piece of the urban fabric in the area of Via Laura and Borgo Pinti, anticipated the grandiose schemes of later princes; but although it gave a stimulus to private building in the area, it was still on the drawing board at the time of his death in 1492.[20]

[20] Caroline Elam, "Lorenzo the Magnificent and the Florentine Building Boom," *Art History*, 1 (1978), 43–66. For Medici patronage of building and interest in architecture, see p. 95 herein.

These fifteenth-century Medici made themselves much more conspicuous to their fellow citizens by putting up prominent buildings than by appearing in any official capacity on the innumerable committees that ran the city's government, but their architectural presence was hardly commensurate with the reality of their political power. The shattering of the last vestiges of republican pretensions in 1530, however, left the family free to take off its disguise and assert its princely power, now embellished by ducal status. Indeed, architecture became a means of communicating the new arrangements to the city.[21] The first duke, Alessandro, asserted the military presence of the new government in the massive Fortezza da Basso (built in the years 1533 to 1535), and a later grand duke reasserted it in the fortress of the Belvedere, as high above the city as anything could be and in plain view from any number of points in the center below. Cosimo I (who reigned from 1537 to 1574) took up residence in the Palazzo dei Priori itself but eventually moved to the Pitti palace, which he enlarged and further set off by opening up a great square in front. He collected the guilds and other administrative offices together in one large center of bureaucratic power, the first modern office building, the Uffizi, which was erected adjacent to the Palazzo Vecchio (as the Palazzo dei Priori was called after the move of the ducal family to its new residence), and which was to be adorned with statues of illustrious Florentines, whose presence around the square was to recapitulate a history of greatness culminating in the building itself.[22] And, as if to leave no doubt about the new political arrangements, the bureaucratic and personal centers of government were later linked by the Corridoio Vasariano, which extended from the Uffizi to the Pitti palace high above the street on an arcade, crossing the river and boldly cutting through the urban maze on its way.

There was not much occasion for rebuilding outside the ducal sphere since so many of the city's churches, monasteries, and palaces had been built so recently. Public squares, however, now got some attention, especially with the erection of great loggias. The Mercato Vecchio was embellished with Vasari's Loggia del Pesce, the entire square of the Mercato Nuovo was enclosed by an open arcade, and the grain market eventually (in 1619) got its loggia, while the hospital of Santa Maria Nuova was covered (from 1611 to 1618) with a loggia that extended around the better part of the square in front. The ducal presence was also accented by the conspicuous new palaces erected by some of the men, mostly foreigners, who rose to power under ducal auspices in the bureaucracy and at court—Grifoni, a ducal secretary; Almeni, the

[21] The building projects of the first grand dukes are surveyed in Spini, *Architettura*.

[22] Georg Kauffmann, "Das Forum von Florenz," in *Studies in Renaissance and Baroque Art Presented to Anthony Blunt* (Edinburgh, 1967), pp. 37–43; Johanna Lessmann, "Gli Uffizi: aspetti di funzione, tipologia e significato urbanistico," in *Il Vasari storiografo e artista: Atti del Convegno internazionale nel IV centenario della morte* (Florence, 1974), pp. 233–47.

chief of the ducal wardrobe; Ramirez di Montalvo, tutor of Cosimo's son and heir, Francesco; and Mondragone, a confidant of Francesco's. In addition, the government encouraged large-scale private building by enacting legislation favoring builders who needed more space but were blocked by owners of contiguous property who refused to sell.

The addition of these buildings on a princely scale was one way in which the city reflected its new status; its display of the emblems of Medici rule was another. The Medici arms were attached to buildings all around town, and so where a goodly number of ducal busts. In the Piazza della Signoria the older sculptural assertions of republican freedom got their responses from the new duke: counterbalancing Michelangelo's David was Bandinelli's Hercules (the symbol of Cosimo I), and over Donatello's Judith loomed Cellini's Perseus, holding on high the head of Medusa, symbolic of (Medicean) victory over (republican) confusion and rabble. The square was much more significantly modified, however, by the fountain of Neptune, another reference to Cosimo, this time to his maritime ambitions. The granite column from the baths of Caracalla presented to Cosimo by the pope was erected in the square of Santa Trinita as a monument to justice, celebrating the final military victory at Montemurlo that had brought him to power. In polarity with this column, opposite an axis marked by the elegant new bridge of Santa Trinita and Via Maggio (the most patrician of all streets), was another, bearing a statue of peace, erected in the square of San Felice to commemorate the victory at Marciano that led to the conquest of Siena and the final rounding out of the Tuscan state. Cosimo and his son Ferdinando I were each commemorated with a large equestrian monument in a prominent square, and, finally, the Medici got their pantheon with the immense and richly worked Cappella dei Principi attached to San Lorenzo, begun in 1604. These stamps of Medici power scattered throughout the city did not entail any spatial reorganization comparable to the baroque plans of other princes; but as ubiquitous reminders to the public of the family's presence, they gave the urban scene a kind of unity that it had never had before.

It would be an exaggeration to describe the transformation of Florence in the Renaissance as a "building boom" because of the overtones that phrase has in a modern industrial economy. Nevertheless, the prestige building undertaken throughout the city was considerable by any standard, be it the size of buildings, the number of projects, the quality of architecture, or the total effect on the appearance of the city. It is difficult to think of any other city in all of Europe, from the days of ancient Rome down to the end of the Middle Ages, that was so transformed, and unlike most cities that underwent notable rebuilding in subsequent periods, Florence was not at the time undergoing much of an expansion. The improvement in the conditions of employment was important for the evolution of the medieval master mason into the architect, and the multiple responsibilities open to him by so much new building are surely part of the explanation for the innovation of ideas that makes this period such an important chapter in the history of architecture. In fact, the history of art is in a real sense tied to the history of these buildings, since they were the occasion for all those forms of decoration, from liturgical objects to pictures and frescoes, that constitute a good part of the artistic heritage of the Renaissance.

The importance of all this building, however, goes well beyond the realm of art history. Besides style, buildings have functions, and for the social historian new buildings represent a change of the setting in which life plays itself out. To the extent that they fulfilled new spatial needs, the new buildings put up in Florence during these years are documents of social change; by the same token, they gave a new style to the lives lived within. For the economic historian these buildings represent a massive reappropriation of wealth. The Renaissance in art is itself a phenomenon of conspicuous consumption, and buildings were by far the most expensive form of that consumption, both in their direct costs and in the indirect cost of their furnishings and the new life-style they brought into existence. This wealth came from somewhere, and the movement of so much wealth—its *recycling*, we might say today—was bound to have reverberations throughout the economy, even if they did not reach "boom" intensity.

In short, to study the buildings of Florence is to learn much about the city's economic, social, and cultural foundations. Where wealth came from, who had it, why it was spent the way it was, how the forces of production across the entire spectrum of labor—from unskilled workers to artisan-entrepreneurs—were organized, how the city was affected by all the activity throughout the marketplace centering on the demand for buildings and the supply of buildings—buildings that spatially redefined the life-style of the men who lived in them and buildings that opened up new outlets for the skill and creative imagination of the men who built and decorated them—this is the program for the ensuing discussion. The totality of that building in all of its component forces and in all of its wider repercussions constitutes much of what we still admire in the culture of Renaissance Florence.

PART I

Demand: The Patrons

CHAPTER ONE

The Wherewithal to Spend: The Economic Background

THE study of precapitalist economic systems has not yet clarified how demand fits into its scheme of things. Economic historians seldom talk about it, and it has hardly any identity in their analysis. Demand arises from taste and needs that give direction to motivation, and such subjects generally fall outside the realm of traditional economic history. Whatever its roots, however, demand was conditioned by what the economic system would permit. The decision to spend large amounts of money for something like the building activity that is the subject of this book presupposes the availability of money to spend. The basic economic questions about the building of Renaissance Florence, therefore, are: What was the level of wealth in the city? How did the city's social structure determine the way the wealth was spent? Was there some change in the level, structure, or nature of wealth that may help explain the relatively sudden release of money at the beginning of the fifteenth century that enabled the conspicuous consumption we associate with the Renaissance to take place?

The fundamental proposition advanced here is that by the fifteenth century extraordinary amounts of wealth were accumulating in the hands of a relatively large number of Florentines. The fall in population by as much as one-half to two-thirds that Florence, like other European cities, suffered in the second half of the fourteenth century in itself accounts for higher per capita wealth of the survivors. In fact, the city was smaller in population than it had been for almost two centuries, and those who remained were enjoying the fruits of the considerable economic development that had taken place in the meantime. Moreover, the considerable expansion of the Florentine territorial state precisely in these years, over the century following the Black Death, brought greater wealth into the capital city, which clearly dominated the regional economy. More importantly—and this is the central theme in the ensuing discussion—during these same years the economy successfully adjusted its performance to a changing situation in international markets in a way that stimulated growth in the textile industry and strengthened the operations abroad of the commercial and financial sectors. The result was a highly favorable balance of payments. During the late fourteenth and early fifteenth centuries much of this wealth was absorbed by the military costs of the city's territorial expansion and its emergence as a major Italian power; but after the first third of the fifteenth century, with the stabilization of the political order abroad and the consequent lightening of the tax burden at home, the profits that were flowing into the city from international commercial and financial operations became available for consumption spending.

In short, more money was spent on luxury goods in the Renaissance because more money was available, and the spirit with which Florentines began to consume in the fifteenth century and the culture that spending generated reveal the Florentines' optimism about the economic situation. Moreover, that spending, by calling into existence new forms of production, in itself brought about some major improvements in the performance of the economy during this period. No sector better illustrates that proposition than construction, where so much money was spent.[1]

[1] The current state of Florentine studies does not permit easy generalization about the economic situation during the Renaissance. Although many monographic studies have been dedicated to various aspects of that economy, most scholarly attention has concentrated on individual operators and enterprises rather than on general problems; and it is hardly possible to get a synthetic view of any one sector of the economy, let alone the economy as a whole. Nevertheless, the scholarly literature is rife with opinions about the performance of the economy, running the entire gamut of possibilities from depression to boom (this literature is cited in Richard A. Goldthwaite, *Private Wealth in Renaissance Florence: A Study of Four Families* [Princeton, 1968], p. 235 note 2). Moreover, many careless observations have been made about economic conditions at specific moments in the life of the city by political historians who feel obliged to invent economic explanations for political events (thus, for example, hard times are assumed to be behind any political crisis), a kind of upside-down Marxism. In view of this state of affairs the interpretation that follows can only be highly tentative, but it is, hopefully, sustained by a more systematic argument and informed by a more comprehensive overview than most others so that perhaps the grounds for future discussion will be better defined.

The bibliography on the economic history of Florence can be approached through Armando Sapori, *Le Marchand italien au moyen âge* (Paris, 1952) and the same author's collected studies, *Studi di storia economica*, 3 vols. (Florence, 1955–67).

Florence and the European Economy

The economic system in which Florence developed as one of the great centers of early European capitalism had its origins in the so-called commercial revolution of the eleventh century, when merchants from all over northern Italy ventured forth to take advantage of the opportunities for trade in the expanding European economy. The basis of that trade was the relation between an undeveloped area and a developed one, between northern Europe, where markets for luxury goods opened up once the political situation began to stabilize, and the older markets in the Levant, where many of those goods were to be found. Italy was located halfway between these market areas and lay in the midst of the sea that facilitated transport, so the Italians were destined to be the middlemen—the traders and shippers. Everywhere in northern Italy, in small towns and large ones, entrepreneurs collected what capital they could and went forth to exploit market opportunities; and in the course of the next two centuries they built up a network of commercial relations that spanned all of Europe, from England to Egypt, and that was the lifeline of the developing European economy.

What set Florence on its own course in making a way in the larger economic system was the local development of a major industrial sector whose production was geared to markets abroad. Unlike the other Italian cities it is often compared to—the maritime ports of Genoa and Venice—Florence, by the time of Dante, was a large industrial city; and yet, unlike the great wool-producing cities in the Low Countries with which it is also compared, it fully participated in the international commercial system of the Italians. In other words, Florence developed both an industrial and a commercial sector, giving it one of the strongest economies in medieval Europe.

Geography favored the development of the cloth industry. Located on one of Italy's largest rivers just at the point where, after taking in the watershed of an exceptionally long tract of the Apennines, it comes out of the hills into a flood plain, Florence had, on the one hand, an abundance of rapidly flowing water for the cleaning of wool and, on the other, easy access to the sea at the port of Pisa, whence the entire Italian commercial network abroad, from northern Europe to the Levant, could be exploited for both the supply of raw materials and market outlets for production. The steady rise of population in Europe from the eleventh century onwards generated demand for clothing that led to the development of local industries everywhere, but few cities anywhere in Italy—and none of the neighboring hill-towns of Tuscany—had the same potential for raising the level of local production to the point that the industry became oriented primarily toward export markets.

Originally the industry took its wool from the hills of the hinterland and sold its products in the rapidly growing urban markets nearby; but as production increased, merchants went farther afield for raw materials, and as quality improved, they expanded into new markets. By the end of the thirteenth century they were bringing wool from England and also cloths from the Low Countries and elsewhere in northern Europe for finishing, dyeing, and then reexporting. The success of this industry in expanding its markets lay in the improvement of the quality of its product to a point that it could compete with northern European cloths, especially those from the Flemish cities. These northern cities had been the leaders in manufacturing luxury cloths that were sold all over Europe, including Italy; but since the marketing of much of this cloth was in the hands of Italian merchants, it was not difficult for aggressive Florentines to push their own products once these were competitive. Moreover, the heavy urban concentration of the Italian population assured Florence a large market potential close at hand. By 1300 the city had far outstripped all of its neighbors—and indeed most other European towns—in size and wealth as an industrial center.

The presence of a strong industry importing raw materials from one part of Europe and exporting its products to another part strengthened the economy's commercial sector by making available that much more capital for investment in international trade. Florentines were to be found virtually everywhere throughout the vast international commercial network of the Italians, and in some of the major markets they were the single most important group of merchants. Their gold florin, first issued in 1252, became a standard international currency for all of Europe, and the use of their commercial network for the execution of foreign exchange and international transfer of credits led to their preeminence in international banking and finance. Since Florentines established colonies in virtually every major center of trade in Europe, the financial network built up by them was as vast as the commercial system itself. The service they could perform in moving funds and extending credit had by the fourteenth century brought them into the highest sphere of papal and princely finance. They were the ubiquitous agents of transfer and exchange in the international ebb and flow of payments. In the traditional historiography the names of their leading merchantile and banking companies—Frescobaldi, Bardi, Peruzzi—symbolize the high point of all Italian banking in the Middle Ages.

Of the vigor of the leading sectors of the Florentine economy during the period of the so-called commercial revolution there can be little doubt. The full weight of the historiographical tradition is behind the proposition that Florence rapidly moved into the vanguard of this expansion, becoming one of the wealthiest cities in Europe, and the well-known details need not be rehearsed here. Yet in the most fundamental respect the economy was not successful; it could not handle the population growth that in the fourteenth century reached the upward limits of what could be supported. The situation must have been desperate by the time the city was hit by the Black Death

TABLE 1
Population of Florence, 1172–1632
Estimates of Population

Year	Russell	Fiumi	de La Roncière	Herlihy/ Klapisch	Beloch
1172	10,000				
1200	15–20,000	50,000			
1260		75,000			
1280		85,000	100,000		
1300	96,000	95,000	110,000		
1338		90,000	100,000	120,000	
1347		76,000	90,000		
1349			32,000		
1352			41,000	42,000	
1362			70,000		
1364			54,000		
1373			60,000		
1375			53,000	60,000	
1379			56,000		
1380		54,747		54,747	
1400				60,000	
1427				37,144	
1441				37,036	
1458				37,369	
1469				40,332	
1480				41,590	
1520					70,000
1551					59,557
1562					59,216
1632					66,056

SOURCES: Josiah Cox Russell, *Medieval Regions and Their Cities* (Newton Abbot, 1972), p. 42; Enrico Fiumi, "Fioritura e decadenza dell'economia fiorentina," *ASI*, 116 (1958), 465–66; Charles M. de La Roncière, *Florence, centre économique régional au XIVe siècle* (Aix-en-Provence, 1976), pp. 693–96; David Herlihy and Christiane Klapisch-Zuber, *Les Toscans et leurs familles: une étude du catasto florentin de 1427* (Paris, 1978), pp. 173–88; Karl Julius Beloch, *Bevölkerungsgeschichte Italiens*, II (Berlin, 1939), 148.

(this is discussed in chapter 6). Florence was as devastated by that event as any place in Europe, losing perhaps one-half of its population (depending on what estimates one accepts) at the middle of the century and perhaps one-third again by the beginning of the fifteenth century (table 1). A number of historiographical problems have arisen over events of the fourteenth century and the effect of the general crisis that the entire European economic system is thought to have suffered in the late Middle Ages primarily as a result of the sequence of plagues drastically reducing the population. Demographic disaster, however, did not altogether cloud the local economic scene.

Over the course of the fourteenth century the Florentine economy was reasonably successful in making adjustments to the changing situation, and in many ways those adjustments add up to a strengthening of its economic system with respect to both the performance of the leading sectors abroad and the well-being of the population at home.

The major development in later fourteenth-century Europe that assured the continuing success of the Florentine economy was a rise in demand for banking services and for luxury goods of all kinds—above all, cloth. In part luxury consumption was a consequence of the more concentrated wealth in the hands of those who had survived the demographic disasters—and much has been made of their greater propensity for spending as a result of the psychological shock they suffered during those events. In part, too, this demand was generated by new needs and taste arising out of the consolidation of power by a number of princes all across Europe that resulted in the elaboration of bureaucratic government, the building-up of the military complement of power, and the growth of the sedentary court with its highly ceremonial life-syle. These events were particularly notable in Italy, where the heretofore fluid political situation coagulated into a more stable multistate system, for the most part in the hands of princes of one kind or another. Taking up permanent residence in cities, these men sought to consolidate their position and establish their legitimacy by engaging in the kind of consumption we associate with the spendor of the Italian Renaissance. These urban courts in Italy and their counterparts elsewhere in Europe were the markets that stimulated the production of, and commerce in, luxury goods; the resulting intensification of activity throughout the commercial system challenged the Florentines to retool their home industry for the production of the kind of cloths required by the new demand and to improve their banking services for investment in government finance. The zeal with which they went about this is evidenced by their appearance wherever business opportunities opened up—and by their success in dominating whatever market they operated in.

No level of international finance was any higher than the papacy, whose needs for credit transfers throughout its far-flung organization accounted for the rise of Tuscan banking in the first place. And no one profited more than the Florentines from the soaring fortunes of the papacy as a secular power at the the end of the Middle Ages—from the bureaucracy it built up at Avignon to tighten its hold on the international network of ecclesiastical finances, from the sumptuous court it set up once back in Rome, and from the large territorial state it carved out for itself in central Italy.

Avignon was an important base for Florentine commercial operations as a central place for the collection of wool throughout southern France for export to Italy and the Levant, an independent activity in the area that gave Florentines an advantage over the Genoese and Venetians in the competition for papal business. By plugging into the papal financial network at its center, major firms were able to build up an extensive system of branch operations all over Europe. The strongest of these firms at the end of the fourteenth century, the Alberti, with extensive control over papal finances throughout Europe, established its position in the papal network so securely that it was able to survive the break in diplomatic relations between the papacy and Florence occasioned by the War of the Eight Saints (1375 to 1378); nor was the firm's business much hurt by reverses suffered by the family in the city's internal factional strife that resulted eventually in the family's exile for over a quarter of a century, from 1401 to 1428.[2]

After the Great Schism divided the church in 1378, Florentine firms—Alberti, Spini, Ricci, Medici—took their chances with the Roman claimants, eventually planting their roots in Rome; and Florentine commerce and banking reaped the harvest once the Council of Constance (meeting from 1414 to 1417) unified the church and the papacy was reestablished in its historic capital. The close ties both Martin V and Eugene IV had with Florence are to be seen as partly a result of Florentine banking interests, above all those of the Medici, who made their fortune in papal business. With the growth of the papal capital as a market for Florentine cloths, Florentines became more conspicuous, dominating virtually every aspect of the rapidly expanding luxury trade. Moreover, the capital accumulated from these commercial profits was available for investment in the papacy itself, now more than ever in need of funds to pursue its policy of state-building in central Italy. It was thus that Florentines were able to dig deeper and deeper into papal finances as treasurers and tax collectors, at times virtually taking over the fiscal administration of the papal state and claiming possession of the papal tiara itself as security. Rome remained one of the most important centers for Florentine banking down through the two Medici pontificates in the sixteenth century. For all their involvement with papal finances, however, Florentines held a position in the papal state that was built on the solid economic basis of the international commercial system they operated; and their business as merchants did not seriously suffer during those moments when any one of them lost papal favor in financial affairs.[3]

[2] Yves Renouard, *Les Relations des papes d'Avignon et des compagnies commerciales et bancaires de 1316 à 1378* (Paris, 1941), pp. 106–17; idem, *Recherches sur les compagnies commerciales et bancaires utilisées par les papes d'Avignon avant le Grand Schisme* (Paris, 1942). The papal interdict imposed on the Florentines from 1376 to 1378, as much as it hurt business for Florentine bankers at the Curia, hardly disrupted the Florentine economy; cf. Richard C. Trexler, *The Spiritual Power: Republican Florence under Interdict* (Leiden, 1974), ch. 3.

[3] The prominence of Florentines in fifteenth-century Rome has been emphasized in the work of Arnold Esch; see, most recently, his "Importe in das Rom der Frührenaissance. Ihr Volumen nach den römischen Zollregistern der Jahre 1452–62," in *Studi in*

A second Italian capital whose growth at the end of the Middle Ages opened important new opportunities to merchants and bankers was Naples. Under the Angevins, Florentines had had a commanding position in foreign trade, and the new regime established in 1435 with the conquest of the kingdom by the Aragonese fully appreciated their presence for the well-being of the realm. In fact, the banking services of the Florentines were essential to the fiscal health of the kingdom; and when Alfonso the Magnanimous was compelled to outlaw them in 1447 in line with his opposition to the Medici, he found that he could not so easily dispense with them. Florentines remained active despite the ban, and the king granted safe conduct to certain of them, in violation of his own policy. Florentines continued to receive special privileges from Alfonso's successor, Ferrante, who was anxious to develop commerce and banking in his capital, and for the rest of the century they dominated the markets in Naples and other cities in the kingdom, especially in Puglia. Although this aspect of the economic history of the kingdom in the fifteenth century is poorly documented, many Florentine fortunes were known to have been made there, including those of two of the most prominent palace-builders in the Renaissance—Filippo di Matteo Strozzi and Giuliano di Leonardo Gondi, both of whom had close personal ties with the king himself.[4]

Both Rome and Naples were capitals of states with wealth out of proportion to their territorial extent in Italy—Rome was the financial capital of the official organization of European Christendom, now finally strengthened by territorial independence and a solid bureaucratic structure; and Naples, after its conquest by Alfonso I, was the capital of a state spreading across the Tyrrhenian Sea to Aragon, Valencia, and Catalonia, with its flourishing port of Barcelona. Both cities experienced rapid growth, especially Naples, whose population reached 200,000 by the mid-sixteenth century, making it one of the largest cities in Europe. Great quantities of wealth flowed into both places, much of it brought by aristocrats who were induced by the

---

memoria di Federigo Melis (Naples, 1978), III, 381–467. For the Medici in Rome, see Raymond de Roover, *The Rise and Decline of the Medici Bank, 1397–1494* (Cambridge, Mass., 1963), and George Holmes, "How the Medici Became the Pope's Bankers," in *Florentine Studies: Politics and Society in Renaissance Florence*, ed. Nicolai Rubinstein (London, 1968), pp. 357–80. The references to Florentine activity in the early sixteenth century are cited by Melissa M. Bullard, "*Mercatores Florentini Romanam Curiam Sequentes* in the Early Sixteenth Century," *Journal of Medieval and Renaissance Studies*, 6 (1976), 51–71.

[4] Nunzio Federigo Faraglia, "Studi intorno al regno di Giovanna II d'Angiò: mercanti e banchieri forestieri nel regno; povertà della Regina," *Atti della Accademia pontaniana*, 26, No. 9 (1896), 11–14; Goldthwaite, *Private Wealth*, pp. 238–39; Alberto Grohmann, *Le fiere del Regno di Napoli in età aragonese* (Naples, 1969), pp. 273–80; Mario Del Treppo, "The 'Crown of Aragon' and the Mediterranean," *JEEcH*, 2 (1973), 161–85; H. Lapeyre, "Alphonse V et ses banquiers," *Moyen Age*, 4th ser., 16 (1961), 124–27.

attraction of the new courts to take up urban residence. These courts, among the most sumptuous in Europe, were major new outlets for the quality products being manufactured in Florence. It has been estimated that in the fifteenth century one-half of the luxury cloth supplied to Rome came from Florence and that Roman consumption alone accounted for as much as one-tenth of the output of the Florentine industry.[5]

A third major market for Florentine cloths that opened up later in the fifteenth century was the Turkish Empire. With the Mongol and Turkoman invasions and the disintegration of the Mamluk Empire in Syria and Egypt in the late fourteenth century, demand for local luxury crafts collapsed, and the region went into a general economic decline. In this situation Italian luxury cloths (like Chinese ceramics) enjoyed a competitive advantage over local products. These markets grew with the expansion of the Ottoman Empire, which culminated in the restoration of Constantinople, after 1453, as one of the great entrepôts of the Western world. The city's long decline under the last Byzantine rulers to a size of no more than 100,000 was now reversed, and by the third quarter of the next century it had a population of almost three-quarters of a million. The sumptuous court of the sultans and their elaborate bureaucracy endowed the place with much of its former splendor and assured its importance as an emporium for the luxury trade. Cloths were among the leading items in this, as in all, luxury markets; and because the native cloth industry was incapable of meeting the demand, Italian producers profited most of all from the new situation. Florentine merchants, formerly active in Constantinople, quickly came to terms with the new rulers, entering into trade agreements with the Sultan within a year of the conquest. Almost fifteen years later Benedetto Dei listed fifty-one Florentines active in the area, and by the end of the fifteenth century they had organized themselves into a formal trading community in Pera. Even the Venetians felt threatened by the strong presence of Florentines in what had traditionally been their territory. In addition, many merchants from the Balkan region of the Ottoman Empire showed up in Florence to purchase cloths. Most of this trade was in woolens, but Florentines were also able to push some silk cloth in this area that supplied raw silk for their home industry—a fact that marks the clear industrial advantage Italy had over the Near East.[6]

[5] The flow of wealth into Alfonso's new capital from the rest of his kingdom is emphasized by Del Treppo, "Crown of Aragon," pp. 166–67. For the importance of Rome as a market for Florentine cloths see the study of Arnold Esch cited in note 3 to this chapter.

[6] The bibliography on Florentine trade in the Ottoman Empire is noted in Bruno Dini, "Aspetti del commercio di esportazione dei panni di lana e dei drappi di seta fiorentini in Costantinopoli, negli anni 1522–31," in *Studi in memoria di Federigo Melis* (Naples, 1978), IV, 1–54; for the Ottoman side of this trade see Eliyahu

Scattered all across the Western world, and yet linked through the technical facilities for dealing with one another, the Florentines had what was in effect Europe's only international banking system, and more than any other money their gold florin was the international standard of value.[7] Well before the end of the fourteenth century Florentine capital and business know-how had asserted its strength to the point that even the most vigorous competitors could not resist the penetration by Florentines into their home areas. The need for their capital and banking services thus led the Venetians in 1382 to reverse a longstanding policy of protectionism and come to terms with Florentines by letting them finally set up shop in Venice and invest in Venetian maritime trade, and Florentine capital contributed significantly to the growth of the textile industry in Ragusa in the fifteenth century.[8] In Barcelona, the great center of maritime commerce in the western Mediterranean, local merchants persisted more vigorously in their hostility to the growing presence of these foreign competitors at the end of the fourteenth century, but the Florentines eventually moved in under the protection of the king, who recognized the superiority of their financial services despite the continuing protests from his own subjects.[9]

It was almost entirely under Florentine auspices that a major center for international clearance and speculation in exchange opened first in Geneva and then in Lyons. When the prince-bishop of Geneva announced a liberalization of his usury policy to encourage business at the fairs there, Florentine companies were quick in setting up branches to take advantage of conditions favorable to their traffic in bills of exchange (1387). With the Hundred

---

Ashtor, "L'exportation de textiles occidentaux dans le Proche Orient musulman au bas Moyen Age (1370–1517)," in *Studi in memoria di Federigo Melis* (Naples, 1978), II, 303–77. The success of one fifteenth-century silk producer in selling his products in the east is documented by Florence Edler de Roover, "Andrea Banchi, Florentine Silk Manufacturer and Merchant in the Fifteenth Century," *Studies in Medieval and Renaissance History*, 3 (1966), 271–75.

[7] The Florentine florin is the common denominator in the comparative study of Peter Spufford and Wendy Wilkinson, *Interim Listing of the Exchange Rates of Medieval Europe* (Keele, 1977).

[8] The forthcoming study of Frederic C. Lane and Reinhold Mueller on banking in Venice will trace the presence of Florentines in Venice. Florentine activity in Ragusa is assessed by Bariša Krekić, "Italian Creditors in Dubrovnik (Ragusa) and the Balkan Trade, Thirteenth through Fifteenth Centuries," *The Dawn of Modern Banking* (New Haven and London, 1979), pp. 247–49.

[9] On Florentines in the Aragonese Kingdom around 1400 see Alberto Boscolo, "Mercanti e traffici in Sicilia e in Sardegna all'epoca di Ferdinando I d'Aragona," in *Studi in memoria di Federigo Melis* (Naples, 1978), III, 271–77; Maria-Teresa Ferrer i Mallol, "Intorno all'assicurazione sulla persona di Filippozzo Soldani, nel 1399, e alle attività dei Soldani, mercanti fiorentini, a Barcellona," in *Studi in memoria di Federigo Melis* (Naples, 1978), II, 441–78.

Years War raging in France, Geneva replaced Paris as the trading-place for the entire area—but only until the situation in France finally settled down, when Louis XI, anxious to promote Lyons as a rival place of business, scheduled fairs there to compete with those in Geneva. In 1463 he granted all kinds of concessions to merchants to induce them to bring their business into his kingdom, and before the year was out the first Florentine bank opened its doors. By 1470 the Florentine colony had organized itself into an official corporation (*nazione*). Almost five-sixths of the 169 firms that can be identified as operating in Lyons down to the end of the century were Florentine. The emigration of Florentines spelled decline for Geneva and assured the preeminence of Lyons as the principal trading and banking center north of the Alps. In the sixteenth century many Florentines in Lyons took the traditional path of their trade into the highest realm of royal finance and ended up as French noblemen at the court in Paris.[10]

Florentine firms were found all across the continent beyond the Alps. Only in northern Germany was their penetration somewhat blunted by the organized resistence of the Hanseatic cities. In Poland Florentines were the leading Italian merchants, especially active in the commerce of luxury cloths.[11] In Hungary they put their commercial wealth and financial skills at the disposal of the monarchy, receiving, in return for political loans, control over mines, customs, and other tax revenues; and in the early sixteenth century they had a monopoly in the purchase of all precious metals mined in Transylvania.[12] In England, although no longer involved so much in royal finances as were their predecessors in the early fourteenth century, Florentines were still the most prominent bankers in effecting international payments, especially to the papacy and the Low Countries. The leading house there during the first third of the fifteenth century was the Alberti, the members now conducting their business in exile from their native city.[13] From their banking place in Bruges, Florentines were essential to the flow of international payments on which the cloth industry of northwestern Europe had long been so dependent, this commercial business being more important than govern-

[10] Jean-François Bergier, *Genève et l'économie européenne de la Renaissance* (Paris, 1963); Goldthwaite, *Private Wealth*, p. 239 (on Lyons, with further bibliography).

[11] Henryk Samsonowicz, "Relations commerciales Polono-Italiennes dans le bas Moyen Age," in *Studi in memoria di Federigo Melis* (Naples, 1978), II, 287–301; Sapori, "Gli italiani in Polonia fino a tutto il Quattrocento," in his *Studi di storia economica*, III, 149–76.

[12] S. Goldenberg, "Notizie del commercio italiano in Transilvania nel secolo XVI," *ASI*, 121 (1963), 255–88.

[13] G. A. Holmes, "Florentine Merchants in England, 1346–1436," *Economic History Review*, 13 (1960–61), 193–208; M. E. Bratchel, "Italian Merchant Organization and Business Relationships in Early Tudor London," *JEEcH*, 7 (1978), 10–11 (on the Frescobaldi).

ment finance for most of them.[14] In the luxury trade that began to pick up in this area so quickly in the fifteenth century, however, Florentines, though active, were probably less important than their competitors from the maritime republics of Genoa and Venice.

Florentines did not fail to take advantage of the opportunities that opened up in the Atlantic trade with the expansion of Portugal and Spain. From the time that they began to buy wool in Spain, first in the eastern kingdoms of Aragon and then in Castile, they roamed all over the Iberian peninsula looking for business opportunities. Although there is as yet no study that takes an overall view of their activity in the area, scattered evidence about particular merchants indicates something about the networks they built to the Atlantic islands, to Africa, and eventually to the New World. They dealt in a great variety of items, including, besides the traditional luxury products, African slaves, sugar from Madeira, and more common goods like grain, fish, and leather from Portugal. Among the Italians doing business in the peninsula the Florentines seem to have had a notable presence in Portugal. One of the chief companies there, the Cambini, had its own ships sailing the Atlantic coast and covered the voyages of others with insurance. It provided Henry the Navigator with his copy of the Florentine edition of Ptolemy, and when his brother the cardinal died in Florence the home office became the executor of his estate, in charge of building his tomb in San Miniato. The Marchionni, another merchant family that over several generations played a major role in Portuguese colonial expansion, had companies dealing in coral and in the slave trade between Africa and Brazil. Girolamo Sernigi, of another long-established family of merchant-bankers in Lisbon, wrote letters back to Florence reporting on Vasco da Gama's arrival in India and assessing the commercial possibilities arising out of that event, and one of the first factors in Goa was yet another Florentine, Francesco Corbinelli, who for a dozen years handled much of the business of the royal treasury there.[15]

Although there is no way to assess it quantitatively, all this activity, encircling virtually the whole of Europe, from Constantinople to the Atlantic

[14] Raymond de Roover, *Money, Banking, and Credit in Mediaeval Bruges: Italian Merchant-Bankers, Lombards, and Money-Changers* (Cambridge, Mass., 1948).

[15] Charles Verlinden, "La colonie italienne de Lisbonne et le developpement de l'économie metropolitaine et coloniale portugaise," in *Studi in onore di Armando Sapori*, I (Milan, 1957), 617–28; Virgínia Rau, "Un florentin au service de l'expansion portugaise en outre-mer: Francesco Corbinelli," in *Fatti e idee di storia economica nei secoli XII–XX: studi dedicati a Franco Borlandi* (Bologna, 1977), 277–86. Much of the literature on Italians in the Iberian peninsula is noted in Charles Verlinden, "From the Mediterranean to the Atlantic: Aspects of an Economic Shift (12th–18th Century)," *JEEcH*, 1 (1972), 625–46; and Federigo Melis, *Mercaderes italianos en España, siglos XIV–XVI* (Seville, 1976); idem, "Di alcune figure di operatori economici fiorentini attivi nel Portogallo nel XV secolo," *Fremde Kaufleute auf der iberischen Halbinsel*, ed. Hermann Kellenbenz (Cologne, 1970), pp. 56–73.

islands, from England to Poland, adds up to a much more dynamic commercial and banking sector than Florence had had before the Black Death. Whatever the general economic situation was in Europe at the end of the Middle Ages, trade intensified, the range of commodities traded enlarged, and luxury markets everywhere boomed—and Florentines cashed in on these opportunities. Moreover, Florence's trade was rooted in a thriving home industry supplying a product that was a staple in virtually every luxury market. The need for raw materials—wool from England, Spain, and Italy; silk from the Near East and Italy—and the demand for their finished cloths sent Florentine merchants everywhere throughout the Mediterranean and northern Europe, building up a network through which they could channel any other commodity for which there was a market, be it a rare spice or ordinary salt, and improving their banking services for the extension of credit, execution of international payments, and administration of government finance. For all its geographic breadth, however, the system was oriented to the Mediterranean, where major new centers of financial activity opened up in the revitalized papal state, first in Avignon then in Rome, and in the kingdom of Aragon once it had expanded into Italy. Moreover, its success at pushing its own products in the eastern Mediterranean helped Florence's balance of payments with that part of the world—a problem that perennially plagued the European economy as a whole well into modern times. The core area of banking and commerce was thus largely conterminus with the area to which its home industry was oriented for both its raw materials and its markets. This system, more concentrated in a confined geographical area and more interrelated in its infrastructure, gave the city a much sounder economic foundation than it had ever had before.

Performance of the Economy

If at the end of the Middle Ages the times were favorable for the development of the leading sectors of the Florentine economy, those activities could achieve a high level of performance only by making adjustments to meet the changing conditions abroad. Over the fourteenth century these adjustments added up to a major transformation of the cloth industry and considerable improvement in some of the ways merchants and bankers conducted their business.

At the center of the economy was, as always, the wool industry.[16] It

[16] The fundamental work on the wool industry is being done by Hidetoshi Hoshino. References to his numerous articles and the other literature can be found in his brief overall view of the history of the industry, *L'industria laniera fiorentina dal basso medioevo all'età moderna: abbozzo storico dei secoli XIII–XVII* (Rome, 1978).

improved the quality of its products, expanded its markets abroad, and eventually diversified its production with the addition of silks. The initial phase of this expansion owed much of its success to the ability of Florentines to capture the Mediterranean markets for northern cloths, taking advantage of a favorable market situation at a time, the early fourteenth century, when the Flemish cities were beset by serious political and economic problems. It is striking, in fact, how, in upgrading the quality of their woolens to meet the competition, Florentines adopted a nomenclature for their products that derives from conscious imitation of the products against which they were competing. Eventually their production was so exclusively aimed at luxury markets abroad that cheaper cloths for local consumption were being imported, and complaints were heard about the difficulty of finding Florentine products in the local market.

Wool cloth fell roughly into two categories. The most luxurious (*panni di San Martino*), made from wool imported from England, came to enjoy a virtual monopoly in the traditional luxury markets of Italy and long remained a staple of the industry. The reorientation of the industry, however, resulted from the development of a strong second-line product (*panni di Garbo*), made from wool found closer at home, in the Mediterranean. This wool originally came from north Africa, then from Provence and Catalonia, and when political and economic problems in these areas interrupted supply at the beginning of the fifteenth century, a new source was found in Italy itself, in the Abruzzi and Lazio. Toward 1500 yet another supply channel was opened with the importation of Castilian wool, and in the sixteenth century Spain became a major source of raw material for the industry. Production had its ups and downs as it adjusted to these geographical shifts in supply, and political instability and other problems in these various areas often resulted in moments of depression in Florence; but in the long run the industry prospered. Markets for these cloths, as we have seen, lay almost entirely within the Mediterranean area.

This industrial sector was further strengthened by expansion into the production of silk, the most luxurious of cloths.[17] Although silk had long been the leading industry in nearby Lucca, there is little evidence for an industry in Florence much before the end of the fourteenth century. The

[17] The only historical survey of the silk industry is the brief review of guild statutes by Piero Pieri, *Intorno alla storia dell'arte della seta in Firenze* (Bologna, 1927), reprinted in his *Scritti vari* (Turin, 1966), pp. 3–29. The fundamental study of the organization of the industry is Florence de Roover, "Andrea Banchi," where there is a bibliography of the older literature. See also Gino Corti and J.-Gentile da Silva, "Note sur la production de la soie à Florence au XVe siècle," *Annales, E.S.C.*, 20 (1965), 309–11; Roberta Morelli, *La seta fiorentina nel Cinquecento* (Milan, 1976); and, on the guild, *L'oreficeria nella Firenze del Quattrocento* (exhibition catalogue; Florence, 1977), sec. III.

1335 statutes of the guild of Por Santa Maria, made up mostly of retail sellers of clothing including silk, do not suggest that much manufacturing was going on. Silk workers exiled from Lucca began showing up in Florence about that time, however; and it is generally thought that the industry got underway as a result of their enterprise. In any case, guild records in the second half of the century identify silk workers as a distinct category (*membrum*) of the membership and reveal a growing concern with production.

By 1429, when the statutes were revised, silk manufacturers clearly dominated the guild, which afterward was commonly identified as the silk guild. By this time, too, the commune was making efforts to promote the industry, holding out the advantage of tax relief for reelers and spinners who took up residence in the city and encouraging the planting of mulberry trees in the countryside. Most of the raw silk for the industry, however, was imported from the Caspian Sea area, from Spain, and from elsewhere in Italy (the Romagna, the Marches, the Abruzzi, and Calabria). It was not until later, when the grand-ducal government more energetically pursued a policy of getting mulberry trees planted, that the local source of supply became significant.

As with the wool industry, growth in the production of silks cannot be quantitatively assessed with precision. Benedetto Dei counted 83 shops around 1470, a figure that may be seriously questioned but yet may have some significance for the relative importance of the industry if compared to the 280 wool shops counted in the same survey. In 1527 the Venetian ambassador reported the value of the output of the industry as two-thirds that of wool production.[18] The quality was renowned throughout Europe, even in the north, where Florentine wool did not sell, although the best markets were largely in Italy itself and the Mediterranean, including the Turkish Empire.

In summary, the performance of the textile sector over the period of the Renaissance was very strong. Even in view of the sharp decline of the working force in the half-century following the Black Death, the few production figures we have for wool indicate that there was no decline in per capita output in the industry. Furthermore, the quality of that output increased, and the sector was further strengthened in the fifteenth century by an increasingly vigorous silk industry. With virtually all of this production directed to foreign luxury markets, the city was assured a secure source of wealth from abroad.

The upgrading of the quality of wool in the course of the fourteenth century and the expansion into silk in the fifteenth century raised the requirements for skilled labor and so brought on a transformation within the work-

[18] Arnaldo Segarizzi, ed., *Relazioni degli ambasciatori veneti al senato*, 3 vols. (Bari, 1912–16), II, 28–29.

ing class employed in the sector. In the wool industry, where more skilled labor was needed as the quality of cloths improved, this gradual transformation within the work force probably lies behind some of the problems that erupted in the Ciompi revolt (although that event has never been placed in the context of a structural disjunction in the industry). The introduction of silk in the fifteenth century raised the quality of labor found in the textile sector as a whole, since silk requires a more skilled labor force than that employed in wool. Much less manual labor of the kind necessary for the washing, combing, and carding of wool was needed, because even the physical handling of silk requires less manpower. Weaving of silk was much more demanding than weaving of wool: looms were more elaborate, and the highest skills were required to weave the patterns for the damask, brocades, and figured satins that the industry was noted for. Moreover, most silk weavers, unlike wool weavers, lived in the city. The local production of silk, finally, generated more jobs for craftsmen in related trades: goldbeaters, who made the gold and silver threads for the most luxurious figured cloths; tailors, embroiderers, and related craftsmen, who made the cloth into clothes, belts, hats, purses, liturgical vestments, altar hangings, and all those other luxury items of "high fashion" for which Florence was famous; and designers, who planned patterns for figured cloths and styled the finished pieces (a clear, but unstudied, link of the industry to the fine arts that explains some of the extraordinary demand in the city for the work of artists[19]). In other words, as more and more of the cloth sector was taken over by the production of silk, the work force in the cloth industry as a whole was reconstituted with an ever-larger component of skilled labor. Whereas the labor in this sector at the time of Dante was largely composed of unskilled, and lowly skilled, wool workers, with many of the more skilled weavers living outside the city, by the fifteenth century skilled labor had become a much more significant component of the city's population. They were highly diversified in their skills, many of them working as independent entrepreneurs. Collectively, as well-paid artisans, they constituted a new "middling" class whose earning power effected a socially downward redistribution of wealth and whose spending stimulated the consumer-goods crafts, including the decorative arts.

The traditional view of the performance of the commercial and banking sector of the economy has been somewhat distorted by its focus on the spectacular success of a few international banking firms, above all, the Bardi and the Peruzzi. On the surface the record of these great firms is impressive.

[19] Some recent studies point to the extraordinary knowledge painters had of clothing: Annarosa Garzelli, *Il ricamo nella attività artistica di Pollaiuolo, Botticelli, Bartolomeo di Giovanni* (Florence, 1973); Elizabeth Birbari, *Dress in Italian Painting, 1460–1500* (London, 1975).

With (at one time or another) over twenty-five partners, as many as twenty-five branches throughout Europe, and a staff of over a hundred; with assets of two to three times the fixed income of the Florentine state; and with their hands deep in the treasury of one of the great feudal monarchies, these enterprises have played the role of corporate giants in the mythology of medieval economic history. To observe that after their dramatic collapse in the 1340s no firm operating on such a grand scale ever again turned up on the business scene, however, is no argument for decline. The simple fact is that even at the time no more than three or four companies ever reached their size, the others being enterprises of only several partners.[20] The great companies of the fifteenth century—Strozzi, Medici, Cambini—also had few partners, but many a fifteenth-century investor had more capital tied up in his company than any individual Bardi or Peruzzi. What happened after the failure of the 1340s was not a decline in banking but a general shift in the foreign orientation of the economy that eliminated the function these few large firms performed (and the problems their abnormal size created).

Well into the fourteenth century a central problem in the Florentine system was the geographical gap between payments for raw materials in England and receipts from sales of finished cloths in southern markets, a gap that could not be bridged by sale of luxury items in a place as relatively underdeveloped as England. Fortunately, payment problems in England, resulting from, first, remittances by the English church to Rome and, secondly, the cost of the king's overriding political interests on the Continent, where he was continually at odds with the French suzerain from whom he held vast areas in vassalage, created a conjuncture of interests in the flow of credit that brought the Italians and the English king together—the king had to make payments to the Continent, where the Italians had large receipts from sales, and they in turn needed money in England to pay for wool. The Italians found the solution by advancing credit to the king abroad in return for liens on his tax receipts at home, which were then used to buy wool—a solution that depended on the precarious and inextricable involvement of a few leading banking houses in the English fiscal system. With one hand raking in vast amounts of credit from their Italian contacts and with the other dipping deeply into the English royal till, these banks became abnormally large operations by standards of business organization of the time. The result was that, first, too much credit became tied up in their operations and, secondly, they became subject to the whims of a feudal monarch who could at any moment withdraw his support and renege on his debts—hence the sequence of bankruptcies the Italians suffered at the end of the thirteenth and early fourteenth centuries, culminating in the greatest of all crashes, those of the Bardi and Peruzzi in the mid-1340s. But the fact that down to that time the banks and

[20] See the rosters of the guild, ASF, Cambio 6, 8, and 10.

the king, after each falling-out, nevertheless turned around only to fall right back into one another's arms is proof of how much each needed the other.[21]

The failure of the Bardi and the Peruzzi marked the end of this long flirtation between the king and the Tuscan bankers. No banking house ever again got so inextricably involved in English royal finance. It was not that Italian bankers had, finally, learned a lesson in royal perfidy, nor was it that their credit operations had been constricted by any deep crisis in their economy at home. The disengagement occurred because, quite simply, in the course of the fourteenth century England became less of a nodal point in the Florentine commercial system. Earlier in the fourteenth century dependence on English wool meant a disjunction between the source of raw materials for the home industry and the markets where Florentines sold their wares, with the result that there was too much of a demand for money in a backward area on the edge of the international luxury market; but later, as Florentines began to take more wool from places closer at hand, from Spain and from Italy itself, the cloth industry, the mainstay of the city's economy, became oriented toward the core of the European commercial system around the Mediterranean for the supply of its raw materials, just as it had always been for its markets. This reorientation was strengthened by the contemporaneous diversification of the industry into silk, which was found only in the Mediterranean area. There was, in other words, considerably more of an overlap of the markets where Florentines bought and sold. Moreover, this recession of England from the Florentine industrial-commercial system occurred at a time when both the English payments to the papacy and military expenditures on the Continent began to fall off, so that England had less need of Italian bankers to handle international payments. By the fifteenth century supply channels and sales outlets were tied closely together in the old and well-developed trade network at the Mediterranean core of the European commercial system, and credit and goods flowed throughout the area without the likelihood of the kind of glut that dependence on a single remote and peripheral area had created earlier.

It was an altogether healthier economic situation as a result. Nothing like the banking failures of the 1340s, with their disastrous consequences throughout the city, ever occurred again. Still at a stage of development where foreign trade involved a high degree of speculation, the Florentine economy of the Renaissance saw its share of bankruptcies; an entire archive of impounded company accounts survives as testimony to the business that came

[21] I have suggested this interpretation in "Italian Bankers in Medieval England," *JEEcH*, 2 (1973), 763–71. Data confirming this thesis are presented by Hidetoshi Hoshino, "La questione della lana inglese nell'evoluzione dell'arte della lana fiorentina del Trecento," *Annuario dell'Istituto giapponese di cultura in Roma*, 15 (1978–79), 67–97.

before the special section of the merchants' court (the Mercanzia) set up to handle the resulting legal problems. The biggest crisis of the fifteenth century, in 1464 and 1465, however, produced only ripples that left most companies in the banking community untouched. It was presumably caused by an entirely local situation in the Levant, at the edge of the European banking system, and had little to do with the kind of problem inherent in the very structure of the system that lay behind the earlier banking failures.[22]

No small part of the continuing success of banking and commerce was due to the business technology that made the mechanism of the system work. The roots of business practice were in the earlier period; and the entire subject of this history of business techniques is riddled with controversy about when and where the first instance of this or that device occurred. The isolated example in the earlier period, however, becomes common practice later on. Business practice improved steadily over the fourteenth century with the refinement of bookkeeping (and recordkeeping generally), credit instruments, insurance, business organization, and other techniques; and the development of elementary schools of commercial arithmetic taught men the fundamentals of how to deal with these practices. Virtually everyone in Florence who was in business, whether artisan or international merchant, used these techniques. The following discussions include descriptions of how they were exemplified in the way the kilnmen Da Terrarossa organized the business side of their enterprise; in the way the stonemason-foundryman Maso di Bartolomeo kept his accounts; in the way ordinary construction workers handled written orders of payment, used giro operations, "thought" in terms of a money of account, and, in general, trusted to a system of private recordkeeping for so many of their transactions.

This technology made the mechanisms of the business system function more efficiently at home and abroad; the merchants' court developed in the fourteenth century to handle business affairs with increasing effectiveness engendered confidence in that system; and a personal rapport among operators of all classes—*fiducia* is the term used by business historians—which was hardly disturbed even by political exile from their native city, held everything together. The vast international operations of the well-know merchant of Prato, Francesco di Marco Datini (who died in 1410), marks the singular success, not of a lone merchant-adventurer or an exalted royal favorite, but of a sedentary and diversified investor who—as an "establishment man"—worked efficiently through the highly sophisticated system of international

[22] De Roover, *Medici Bank*, pp. 359–60. A new reference to these failures has come to light, thanks to the discovery by Mark Phillips of the "Diverse notizie istoriche . . ." of Marco Parenti: BNF, Magl. XXV, 272, pp. 15–17. Parenti attributes the problem to debasement of the *grosso*, but only a few bankers felt the effects.

commerce and banking Florentines had built up among themselves by the end of the fourteenth century.[23]

The Florentine economy was additionally strengthened in the fifteenth century by greater control over the transportation facilities on which trade depended. The importance of shipping in an economy like Florence's hardly needs comment: the records of just one merchant, Francesco di Marco Datini, mention the names of 3,000 different ships in a fourteen-year period, from 1391 to 1405. Unlike its great rivals, Genoa and Venice, Florence built up its commercial system in the thirteenth and fourteenth centuries as an inland city without its own port and without a fleet. With the decline of Pisa after the battle of Meloria in 1284, Florence was in a better position to obtain port privileges; but since the relations between the two cities were not always friendly, Florentines by no means depended entirely on this one port as a commercial outlet. Much of its shipping was in the hands of the Genoese, who often used several other Tuscan ports as points of entry and exit; and much of the eastern trade was directed overland to Ancona and put in the hands of Venetians. Increasingly toward the end of the fourteenth century, however, we hear of Florentine merchants owning their own ships—the Alberti, for example, had ships serving England and Catalonia, and in the fifteenth century the Cambini had ships sailing the Atlantic coast in the expanding Portuguese Empire. The conquest of Pisa in 1406 and the purchases (from Genoa) of Porto Pisano and Livorno in 1421 gave Florence its own outlet, and many firms immediately established offices there. The next step, the setting up of a state-controlled galley system in imitation of that of the Venetians, was taken immediately, and although this system never established Florence as a maritime power (and in fact was abandoned in 1480), it contributed substantially, at least for a time, to the improvement of its control over an essential facility in its commercial system.[24]

The investment habits of Florentines in the fifteenth cenutry, if not further proof of the vitality of the economy, at least indicated that their confidence in that economy was not flagging. The vast expenditure for private building that is one of the themes of this book is not to be seen as a withdrawal of capital from more productive enterprise by a propertied class undergoing a change of heart about their business traditions for either cultural or economic reasons. Some of the men who spent most lavishly on building projects were successful merchants whose investment portfolios reveal no intention of closing shop. For example, Filippo Strozzi, who had enough cash on hand to pay the entire cost of his new palace with plenty left over, kept up his

[23] The literature on business technology is cited in the compilation of Federigo Melis, *Documenti per la storia economica dei secoli XIII–XVI* (Florence, 1972).

[24] Michael E. Mallett, *The Florentine Galleys in the Fifteenth Century* (Oxford, 1967).

businesses to the day of his death; Giuliano Gondi, who stipulated in his will that his sons were to finish building the palace he had started, also exhorts them to keep up the family business, since it had been going for such a long time; and we have Giovanni Rucellai's own words about the satisfaction he derived from his successful career as a banker.

Rich Florentines took the cloth industry for granted as an investment, most of them, even merchant bankers for whom such a business was a small operation in relation to their international trading and banking companies, participating as partners in either a wool or silk shop. Giannozzo Alberti (in *Della famiglia*) strongly recommends investment in a cloth shop on the grounds that it provided the income necessary for the maintenance of a family with suitable dignity but did not require much work and bother (and, he adds, since this kind of investment had a social utility in the employment it provided, it also endowed the investor with a certain moral virtue).[25] Giannozzo reveals here the mentality of a veritable rentier, such was his confidence as an investor in the stability of the industry. Other Florentines, moreover, worked hard as active partners in their cloth shops, and not the slightest stigma of ignobleness was associated with such employment—something that always impressed the Venetian ambassadors. The merchant-aristocrats from the lagoons marvelled that these upper-class Florentines, with their cloaks draped over their shoulders so they would have greater freedom of movement, were seen in their shops doing manual labor without any concern about what the public thought. At the beginning of the seventeenth century the Venetian ambassador noted the withdrawal of the upper classes from involvement in business affairs as younger men found court life more attractive; and such a late date for his observation on this change in life-style is evidence of how long the cloth industry maintained its central importance in Florentine life.[26]

In the Renaissance the upper classes made no marked move to "return to the land," a theme that occurs repeatedly in the history of European urban elites at that point where they lose their nerve and seek the security and prestige of investment in landed estates. In 1427 the upper 2 to 3 percent of the city's wealthiest men had no more invested in real estate than in business.[27] Like Giovanni Rucellai they recognized the pros and cons of land as an investment and concluded that land helped round out and balance—but should not dominate—an investment portfolio.[28] Many of the biggest

[25] *I primi tre libri della famiglia*, ed. F. C. Pellegrini (Florence, 1946), p. 319.

[26] Segarizzi, *Relazioni*, III, pt. 2, 42 and 176; Eugenio Alberi, ed., *Relazioni degli ambasciatori veneti al senato*, II (Florence, 1859), 21 and 327.

[27] David Herlihy and Christiane Klapisch-Zuber, *Les Toscans et leurs familles: une étude du catasto florentin de 1427* (Paris, 1978), p. 254.

[28] *Il zibaldone quaresimale*, ed. Alessandro Perosa (London, 1960), pp. 8–9.

portfolios show no higher share of total investment in land than the 7 percent in Filippo Strozzi's and the 12 percent in Francesco Sassetti's, the manager of the Medici bank; and like these two successful merchant-bankers, many probably had more tied up in their town house than in income-yielding real estate, be it in the city or in the countryside. Most all Florentines of any substance, including even artisans, had property outside the city—many still do—and we can always turn up a few men who had extensive landholdings and nothing else. The Medici had vast estates already in Cosimo il Vecchio's generation, so vast that in some areas the family enjoyed what was virtually a feudal presence; and Lorenzo's interest in his cheese factory and stock farming (especially on his estate at Poggio a Caiano) anticipated the relatively enlightened agricultural policy of Cosimo I.[29] Before the sixteenth century, however, there was no marked tendency for the upper classes to build up large compact estates and virtually no interest in introducing new methods of estate management or farming technology. Purchasing land, which yielded a much lower return for one's investment than business, was no way to build up a fortune. Moreover, no particular prestige was attached to owning land. For all the interest in building villas, temporary retirement to them did not induce anything like a rentier mentality or (what has been called) a villa psychology.[30]

The history of just about any family whose economic fortunes can be traced over the four or five generations spanning the Renaissance will turn up more entrepreneurs of one kind or another than rentiers, and not one of these families could be classified a rentier family over the entire period. Since the practice of partible inheritance could reduce even a rich man's sons to a modest status, most men were compelled to invest both time and capital in the advanced sectors of the economy if they wanted to make their own fortunes. Indeed, the lack of legal devices to protect the integrity of estates beyond one generation, especially in view of the nascent dynastic sense that explains much of their interest in building, can be seen as a mark of the confidence Florentines continued to have in the business traditions of their economy.

The story of the performance of the Florentine economy in the Renaissance can be recapitulated in the language of one of the economist's models—the linkage theory of economic development. From the thirteenth century onward, Florence experienced an impressive export-led growth in her economy, the staple being cloth—first wool, then both wool and silk. The quality of the

[29] The scattered references to Lorenzo's interest in agriculture have been assembled by Philip Foster, *A Study of Lorenzo de' Medici's Villa at Poggio a Caiano* (published Ph.D. diss; New York, 1978).

[30] For general remarks and reference to the literature on this argument, see Goldthwaite, *Private Wealth*, pp. 246–51.

product was continually improved, and by the fifteenth century virtually all the production linkages around the staple were fully developed. The "non-industrial forwarding operations" of selling abroad and finance went beyond the business of the staple to become independently one of Europe's leading commercial and banking systems; only the link to transportation remained undeveloped. Development of backward linkages was blocked only by the geographical requirements of the raw materials, although even here the situation much improved in the fourteenth century as supply channels were open to sources closer at hand in the Mediterranean; and by the sixteenth century, one of the final links in the chain of supply was being forged with the establishment of the silkworm culture in the area of Pescia.

At this point further growth of the Florentine economy could have come only by using profits to invest in capital equipment with the hope of breaking the technological barrier to increased industrial production. Instead, the Florentine economy took a different turn. As the men who made their fortunes in the forward sectors of the economy spent more and more of their wealth, a consumption linkage was opened to other productive forces in the economy. Because building was the most expensive of their new tastes, the construction industry received a major stimulus, and it, in turn, activated its own set of linkages, both backward to the bulding-material industries and forward, by complementarity of use, to the craft industries producing all those goods men needed to fill up their new and enlarged built-environment. This forward linkage from construction generated new demand, therefore further strengthening the consumption linkage originally derived from the staple. In other words, by that marvelous process of "one thing leading to another," an upward shift in overall demand was induced within the local economy that resulted in the growth of the luxury-arts sector, which included the kind of building that is the subject of this book. This sector grew because much of the enormous wealth that had accumulated in Florence was invested in it. In the discussion that follows, it becomes apparent how the particular character of this sector was determined by the way the social structure of that wealth shaped demand; how the success of the sector in meeting virtually the entirety of that demand precluded recourse to foreign luxury markets and therefore loss of wealth from the economy; and, finally, how investment in this sector brought about a real transformation in the economy, one that was more important than mere growth or greater wealth because that investment, calling for more skilled workers, for a greater variety of skills, and for more highly developed skills, was in the most basic factor of production—human capital itself. This was the notable achievement of the economy of Renaissance Florence—and, in the final analysis, this is what the Renaissance was about.

The Florentine economy began to run down with the decline of its staple, and this happened with the collapse of the wool industry and the slow retrenchment of the silk industry as it concentrated more and more on the production of simpler cloths. The wool industry remained strong down to about 1600. In the second half of the sixteenth century it was producing a cloth that for the first time in the history of the industry found markets in northern Europe, and the value of its production was much more than that of silk—50 percent more in 1588, according to the Venetian ambassador. By that time, however, competition was appearing everywhere: the Low Countries made inroads in the Spanish markets, local industries in Italian towns took their toll in Italy itself, and the Venetian and German industries became highly competitive in the Turkish market, once called the "stomach" of the Florentine industry. When the Dutch and the English moved into the Mediterranean at the end of the century with their "new draperies," Florence was virtually out of the picture. After 1600 production fell off sharply.[31]

Silk also confronted growing competition from other Italian cities and, north of the Alps, from Lyons, but the industry maintained some strength by cutting back on production of highly luxurious brocades and other items subject to the vicissitudes of taste and concentrated instead on plain cloths that could be sold as a kind of standard product in most markets. In turning to the production of simpler goods, the industry was probably able to reduce costs by employing more women and children (whose numbers reached an astounding proportion of the labor force employed in the industry by the seventeenth century); and economies were also achieved by the grand duke's policy of promoting the planting of mulberry trees virtually everywhere, so vigorously pursued that in the 1590s one observer anticipated that within twenty-five years Tuscany would no longer need import silk at all.[32] Silk was to remain the only major manufactured item Tuscany exported down to the early nineteenth century.

In the sphere of international banking and commerce, decline came fast in the sixteenth century. With German bankers moving into that sphere backed by the Hapsburgs and with Genoese bankers cashing in on their ties with Spain to handle the immense business growing up around the influx of gold and silver from the New World, the Florentines, without the backing of a major political power to support them in the increasingly enlarged stage of international power politics, were left behind, and they were not a significant force in the rapid expansion of the European commercial system over the entire globe. Many Florentines set up shop in Antwerp when it became a major international entrepôt for northwestern Europe, but their presence there, even among the Italians, was never as overwhelming as it had been in so many places in the preceding century. Nevertheless, Florentines remained

[31] For decline of the wool industry see R. Romano, "A Florence au XVIIe siècle: industries textiles et conjoncture," *Annales, E.S.C.*, 7 (1952), 508–12; F. Ruiz Martín, *Lettres marchandes échangées entre Florence et Medina del Campo* (Paris, 1965).

[32] Paolo Malanima, *I Riccardi di Firenze: una famiglia e un patrimonio nella Toscana dei Medici* (Florence, 1977), pp. 58–59.

active in banking and commerce, where great fortunes could still be made throughout the sixteenth century. The Florentine upper classes did not, economically or socially, ever pull up their business roots—or, worse yet, deny they had ever had them. By the early seventeenth century, however, when the Venetian ambassador found the younger generation less interested in business and more attracted to the pleasures of a different kind of life, Florentines had lost out to Dutch and English enterprise and were no longer even marketing their own silks in the Mediterranean. Although an old ambition was finally realized with the growth of Livorno as one of the great entrepôts of Mediterranean trade, that success was induced by ducal policy directed to assuring its status as a free port and owed little to the initiative of local enterprise needing an outlet for business abroad. Livorno's bustling international commercial life had little to do with anything happening within the Tuscan economy—and there was less and less going on in Tuscany that had anything to do with economic life beyond the region's frontiers.[33]

Decline of gross national product and per capita income is not the foredrawn conclusion to these events in the economic world of late Renaissance Florence. The government of the early Medici dukes certainly did its share in trying to stimulate the economy to keep it going, in many ways anticipating mercantilist policy of a later period. Beyond encouraging the planting of mulberry trees and boosting the port of Livorno, it investigated the possibilities of direct trade with India; it reclaimed large tracts of land for agricultural purposes in the lower Arno valley; it set up a monopoly for the marketing of iron from the island of Elba and undertook searches for other metals on the mainland; it opened new quarries in the area of Carrara, but now on its own, Tuscan, side of the border; it experimented with the manufacturing of porcelain; it spied on the Venetians to learn how to set up commercial glass works; it promoted the entire range of luxury crafts at court by gathering jewelers, wood carvers, goldsmiths, miniaturists, distillers, clockmakers, ceramicists, cosmographers, and a host of others together in the new building of the Uffizi. If all this did not induce growth, it was not for lack of trying; and if ultimately the relative decline of the Florentine economy was not arrested, it remains an open question how much of an absolute decline there

[33] On the relative decline of Florence in the international economy, see José-Gentile da Silva, "Aux XVIIe siècle: la stratégie du capital florentin," *Annales, E.S.C.*, 19 (1964), 480–91; Amintore Fanfani, "Effimera la ripresa economica di Firenze sul finire del secolo XVI?" *Economia e storia*, 12 (1965), 344–51; R. B. Litchfield, "Les investissements commerciaux des patriciens florentins au XVIIIe siècle," *Annales, E.S.C.*, 24 (1969), 685–721; Dante Zanetti, "Commercio estero e industria nazionale: setaioli fiorentini e mercanti inglesi nel XVII secolo," in *Studi in memoria di Federigo Melis* (Naples, 1978), IV, 445–58; Jean-Pierre Filippini, "Il porto di Livorno ed il Regno di Francia dall'editto del porto franco alla fine della dominazione medicea," *Atti del convegno "Livorno e il Mediterraneo nell'età medicea" (1977)* (Livorno, 1978), pp. 3–25.

was once Florence severed its satellitic ties to the wider world economy and turned in upon itself.[34]

Level of Wealth

The success abroad of its forward sectors assured Florence a favorable balance of trade. Except for the supply of raw material for its cloth industries, the economy depended little on imports from abroad. The domestic economy was virtually self-sufficient. Tuscany was well provided with wood for fuel, with clays and stone for construction, and with iron, copper, and other minerals for local industry; and after the population decline of the fourteenth century the agricultural sector was capable of meeting basic food needs. Finally, local crafts were able to satisfy the growing demand for luxury goods, so that Florentines were less and less interested in foreign products in this category. The favorable balance abroad, therefore, was largely made up with payments.

Although the paths bullion traveled to make up the trade balances have never been charted, merchants' accounts document the extraordinary quantities of it coming into the city. From Geneva the Medici company sent at least 35,000 florins in gold over a period of less than three years (from March 1443 to December 1445), and almost all the cash shipments sent out by the much smaller company of Della Casa and Guadagni in one year (from September 1453 to September 1454) went to Florence: 5,414 scudi in florins, cameral florins, Venetian ducats, and marks. From Naples and other places in Italy the company of Filippo Strozzi sent home about one shipment of cash a month during the period 1473 to 1477, averaging around 4,000 florins a year. In 1466 one of the city's galleys returned with 40,000 ducats in gold taken on somewhere during the course of its voyage from Flanders and Spain. It was not always possible to convert profits to cash, however, and the difficulties of handling credits in northern Europe suggested to Raymond de Roover, the only historian to comment on this trade advantage, that one of the reasons for the eventual decline of Florentine banking was the strangulation of trade resulting from the accumulation of credits abroad that could not be transferred home in any form.[35]

[34] A positive assessment of the local economy is made in the article by Jordan Goodman and Judith Brown, "Women and Industry in Florence," *Journal of Economic History*, 40 (1980), 73–80.

[35] De Roover, *Medici Bank*, pp. 150, 195–96, 271, 317, 326–27, 373–74; idem, "La balance commerciale entre les Pays-Bas et l'Italie au quinzième siècle," *Revue Belge de philologie et d'histoire*, 37 (1959), 374–86. The shipments by Della Casa and Guadagni come from their ledger edited by Michele Cassandro, *Il libro giallo di Ginevra della compagnia fiorentina di Antonio Della Casa e Simone Guadagni, 1453–*

The flow of bullion from the Ottoman Empire was likewise built into the structure of trade with the eastern Mediterranean, where Florentines increased their sales of wool and found little to buy except raw silk, pepper, dyes, a few luxury items, and an occasional slave. Because this was one area where they never set up banking operations, there was no other way to handle profits but bring them home. An accomanda contract made by Battista di Taccino in 1462 for the sale of wool cloths in Constantinople strictly limited the goods his agent was to buy with the proceeds, specifying a preference for cash. Another venture undertaken by Bernardo Banchi and Piero Segni in 1463, based on an accomanda contract that similarly restricted their agent, ended with the importation of 1,456 florins, about 90 percent of gross sales. From one trip made in 1523 and 1524 to Constantinople to sell wool, Daniele di Carlo Strozzi brought back 2,273 ducats and 1,927 gold sarafi; the next year the administrators of the estate of his brother Girolamo, who died there, sent about 4,000 ducats to Florence. Insurance contracts taken out by Florentine merchants on shipments from the Ottoman Empire from 1524 to 1526 also document this flow of gold and silver to Italy. By this time raw silk in the Turkish markets cost so much that Florentines, now with other sources closer at hand in Italy itself, no longer wanted to buy one product that had heretofore been a staple in the eastern markets. By this time, too, the luxury trade from the east was in clear decline. In this situation, with gold being taken out of his empire in ever-larger quantities, Sulieman tried to prevent its exportation, momentarily frightening the Florentines with the prospect that all trade would end between the two places, but, fortunately for them, the export restriction never took effect.[36]

The movement of all this bullion into the city could hardly have gone unnoticed. The evidence for its abundance is striking: it shows up in the hands of the rich as plate and jewelry on their household inventories, and in the hands of the most humble worker as the wages handed out to him on payday. Moreover, by the fifteenth century the working of gold and silver became one of the city's major luxury crafts. In 1322 the goldsmiths in Florence, theretofore organized outside the official guild system, were sufficiently numerous to be accepted into the system as a separate "member" of the guild of Por Santa Maria. During the rest of the century (from 1320 to 1399) 258 goldsmiths were matriculated. Only 7 of these claimed the right

---

1454 (Prato, 1976), fols. 266, 282, 380, 660; the Strozzi shipments come from two of his books of business memoranda: Carte strozz., ser. V, 26 and 30. The thesis that the balance of payments in northern Europe generally favored Italy has been outlined by Harry Miskimin, *The Economy of Early Renaissance Europe, 1300–1460* (Englewood Cliffs, N. J., 1969), pp. 138–58.

[36] Dini, "Commercio di esportazione," pp. 13 (table), 16, 49–50. Battista di Taccino's contract is in Innocenti, ser. CXLIV, 199, fols. 141v–42; Segni's profits are recorded on his accounts, Libri di commercio 13, fols. 14 and 19.

to a reduction of the matriculation fee on the grounds of having a relative already in the guild, the others presumably being outsiders attracted to this new profession. In the following century a much higher percentage of the 308 matriculated goldsmiths claimed this benefit. By this time goldsmiths were the third largest group to matriculate in the guild (after silk merchants and clothcutters). In the first Catasto of 1427, 43 men identified themselves as goldsmiths (not counting beaters of gold), and half a century later Benedetto Dei listed 44 goldsmith shops (in addition to 30 goldbeating establishments). A shop inventory dating from the 1360s indicates how much business Florentine goldsmiths were doing at the papal court in Avignon by that date.[37] Subsequently, the travel abroad of many goldsmiths themselves to serve the luxury-loving courts of Renaissance Italy can be documented; Florentines replaced the Sienese as Italy's most noted workers in the craft. The importance of the goldsmith's shop as the training-ground for men who then went on to become major artists in other media has often been noted as an explanation for the remarkable versatility that is virtually the hallmark of the Florentine artist. In this sense the city's artistic achievement is partly a consequence of the enormous accumulation of wealth in its most concrete form—gold and silver.[38]

Where did all this wealth end up? During the period from the late fourteenth century to the early 1430s the state must have raked off much of the city's wealth to meet the expenses of one war after another, which was the cost Florence had to pay as it came of age as a major Italian power. In the recent historiography, dominated as it is by political historians who see the matter from the point of view of a government desperately looking for ways to pay the military bills that were coming in too fast, much has been made of the considerable fiscal burden and the way it must have borne down on the economy and private wealth. The complaint of Goro Dati that, with all the problems war brought to the businessman in the 1420s, "the greatest damage to me was the terrible tax burden imposed by the commune," has been loudly echoed in the modern scholarly literature, since there is no problem in documenting the sentiment with other complaints—taxes were no less odious then than they are now.[39] Fiscal burden, however, is not an

[37] R. Piattoli, "Un inventario di oreficeria del Trecento," *Rivista d'arte*, 13 (1931), 246–47.

[38] Much of the evidence for the craft has been collected by Alessandro Guidotti, "Gli orafi e l'oreficeria a Firenze dalle origini al XV secolo attraverso i documenti d'archivio: posizione sociale ed economica, organizzazione del mestiere," sec. III of the exhibition catalogue *L'oreficeria*. Further comments on the goldsmith's craft are made herein, pp. 414–15.

[39] Gene Brucker, ed., *Two Memoirs of Renaissance Florence: The Diaries of Buonaccorso Pitti and Gregorio Dati* (New York, 1967), p. 141.

economic indicator, nor is war altogether negative in its effect on an economy. Taxation is a form of redistribution of wealth, and since the enormous sums poured into the wars Florentines waged in the early fifteenth century were for the most part spent locally within the city's own territory (whose economy the capital clearly dominated), it is not an unreasonable hypothesis that wartime taxation was in fact an economic stimulus, at least for certain sectors of the economy.[40] The alarm expressed by one speaker before the innermost circle of the city's power elite in 1431 that the tax system was not touching the substantial wealth accumulated by workers and artisans during wartime is not to be dismissed out of hand as upper-class grumbling over its own tax bills.[41] Chapter 6 discusses the fact that, for the "little man," wages remained high and prices remarkably low during the decade of the 1420s, and even prosperous artisans were able to avoid direct taxation (or forced loans) because of a generous system of deductions. Giovanni Rucellai, looking back at mid-century over the recent history of the city, regarded the years around 1420 as the period of its greatest wealth (*colmo della riccheza*).[42] This was precisely the moment when the city announced its intention to invest in an expensive galley system. Perhaps no better evidence testifies to the ability of citizens somehow to pay their tax bills—for all their complaints about them—than their willingness to keep up the extravagant public building program at the cathedral during these very years of "crisis."

Nevertheless, any taxation cuts into disposable income, and taxes were undeniably high during these years of war. The rich merchant of Prato, Francesco di Marco Datini, paid about 1,300 florins a year in taxes (in one form or another) from 1400 to 1406; and although this may not seem very much for a man with an estate easily worth up to 100,000 florins, these were years of relative peace. The burden was substantially heavier in the later 1420s, especially after the outbreak of war with Lucca in 1429. Matteo Palmieri, with an estate worth about 5,000 florins, paid about 430 florins a year from 1428 to 1433; and Matteo di Simone Strozzi, worth about the same, paid about 300 florins from 1425 to 1432—not insignificant sums for

[40] The numerous account books (in Arezzo) of the condottiere Micheletto Attendolo provide the material for a study of war expenditures; a cursory glance through them suggests that much of his enormous appropriation from the Florentine state was spent in the Tuscan countryside for provisioning. The economic domination of Florence over its territory is a thesis developed by Herlihy and Klapisch, *Toscans*, pp. 259–60, but their emphasis on the exploitative nature of this domination will have to be modified in view of the forthcoming study of Pescia by Judith Brown.

[41] Anthony Molho, *Florentine Public Finances in the Early Renaissance, 1400–1433* (Cambridge, Mass., 1971), p. 156. A similar sentiment expressed before the city fathers at this time is recorded by Giovanni Cavalcanti, *Istorie fiorentine*, I (Florence, 1838), 79.

[42] Rucellai, *Zibaldone*, p. 62.

these men of middling status within the upper class.[43] Any tax burden in Florence, however, must be understood not as taxation in a strict sense but as forced loans, so that in fact what was paid to the state was not altogether lost. A man could not cash in the credits he got in return for forced loans, but he could sell them; despite the decline in their market value during the 1420s (a sure indication of the loss of confidence that the state could ever get out from under its debt burden), shares were still worth from 25 to 30 percent of par value in the early 1430s—the extent, in other words, to which payments to the state did not represent a loss. Moreover, these "loans" paid interest, varying from 3 to 8 percent, and although these figures cannot be taken at their face value outside the context of a complex debt operation that has not yet been thoroughly studied, they nevertheless represent a return that further reduced the loss represented by actual payments to the tax officials (the figures cited earlier for Datini and Palmieri have been adjusted to reflect this return). These "tax" payments, in fact, were really a (forced) shift of investment or consumption funds. It is also worth noting that the rich men who carried the floating debt by extending substantial short-term, high-yield loans to tide the state over moments of great need when income from normal sources was inadequate to keep up the cash flow made handsome profits during these years, much more than the 8 to 10 percent they could reasonably expect from their business investments.[44]

What is most impressive about the bills rich citizens received from treasury officials for loans to the state is that they were paid out of income or savings. Neither Datini nor Palmieri nor Strozzi dug into his capital, so far as we can tell. Most assessment reports (the famous Catasto documents) made by the city's richest men show no reduction in landholdings over these years, and there is little evidence that these men withdrew capital from business. In short, the wealth was there, and once the state got out from under the burden of wars, its citizens found themselves with an immense amount of disposable income to spend. The beginning of relief came in 1434 when Cosimo de' Medici returned from his short exile to assert his leadership of the dominant political faction. Military expenditures declined considerably, and long periods of peace during the ascendancy of the Medici probably account for much of their success with the upper classes. The system of

[43] The amount of forced loans paid by Datini and Palmieri have been calculated by Molho, *Finances*, pp. 94–99; The record of Strozzi's payments is in his ledger, Carte strozz., ser. V, 11, fols. 24, 35, 63, 74, 87, 110, 134; his wealth is estimated in Goldthwaite, *Private Wealth*, p. 45.

[44] Molho, *Finances*, pp. 171–75; cf. Frederic C. Lane's observations on Molho's material in his review of this book in *Journal of Economic Literature*, 11 (1973), 545–46; and the criticism by Paolo Cammarosano, "L'analisi del Molho sulla finanza pubblica fiorentina," *Studi medievali*, 16 (1975), 887–906.

forced loans was under less pressure and the burden on private wealth lightened.

Fiscal policy has not been studied from the public side, but the great number of private accounts for the period after 1434 show that taxes were often a relatively insignificant item of expenditure. For example, Matteo Palmieri, who in seven years, from 1428 to the end of 1434, had paid f.3,187 lb.148 to the state, paid, over the next twenty-five years, to the beginning of 1460, only slightly more—f.3,649 lb.906. Moreover, Palmieri, who kept a record of these matters over his entire adult life, eventually got back almost two-thirds of his payments in the form of interest: until 1460 the interest account on his books was debited f.4,239 lb.570 as against his total payments of f.6,836 lb.1054.[45] If in the late twenties and early thirties he was able to take losses on large loans to the state without cutting into his patrimony, how much more money he must have had to spend during the last twenty-five years of his life! A generation later, in the 1480s, the son of Matteo Strozzi, Filippo, the builder of the great palace, paid much lower tax bills than his father, although he was twenty times wealthier, and (over the seven and a half years for which we have a record of his payments) only one-fifth as much as Datini had paid at the beginning of the century, although Filippo was every bit as wealthy as Datini. Even during the difficult—and costly—Savonarola regime Strozzi's widow paid an average annual tax bill of only about 450 florins—and she continued to keep up her share of construction expenses on the family palace.[46] Disposable income, in other words, rose considerably in the fifteenth century—and this was the period when business was booming as a result of the stabilization of the Italian political scene; when new markets for Florentine goods opened in Naples, Rome, Constantinople, Lyons, and elsewhere; when, in short, all the evidence points to an extraordinarily favorable balance of payments. And this was the period, beginning with the advent of the Medici, when private spending for building and the arts soared.

Social Structure of Wealth

There can hardly be any doubt that by the fifteenth century a considerable amount of wealth had accumulated in Florence, whether the analysis of the

[45] ASF, Acquisti e doni 7, fol. 121v.

[46] Filippo's accounts show that he paid 458 florins from April 1481 to September 1483 (Carte strozz., ser. V, 36, fols. 93 and 193), 786 florins from February 1487 to November 1488 (Carte strozz., ser. V, 44, fols. 58 and 240), and 787 florins from January 1490 to December 1491 (Carte strozz., ser. V, 51, fol. 47). His wealth is assessed in Goldthwaite, *Private Wealth*, p. 60. His widow's tax bills from 1495 to 1500, a period of war and civil disturbance, added up to only 2,673 florins; Carte strozzi., ser. V, 54, fols. 131, 141, 157, 185.

state of the economy at that time is as optimistic as presented in these pages or not, for it is this extraordinary wealth that permitted the heavy expenditure for new buildings and their decoration. The nature of that spending, however, was conditioned no less by the structure of wealth than by the level of wealth. Wealth was distributed among a relatively large number of men, and once they started spending for the "extras" that today we consider art, something different happened in the history of patronage. Demand was no longer confined to just a few public or ecclesiastical institutions, as it had been earlier in medieval towns, including Florence itself, or concentrated in princely authority, as it was elsewhere in Renaissance Italy. It was now the composite force of a multiplicity of actions by private persons all converging on a single urban market.

The distribution of wealth is accurately documented in written reports Florentines made for the Catasto of 1427. One-quarter of the total wealth of the city was in the hands of 100 men (heads of households), and one-half of the liquid wealth—commercial and industrial capital and credits—was in the hands of 250 to 300 men (2½ to 3 percent of all those filing declarations). By standards of the time these figures probably represent a fairly wide distribution of wealth. This point can be illustrated by a comparison of a list of the top 600 assessments for the 1427 Catasto with an assessment, made in 1500, of the 100 wealthiest merchants in Nuremberg, a city then about half the size of Florence in 1427. In the German city 37 merchants were assessed from 10,000 to 100,000 Rheingulden (worth at the time about one-quarter less than the same number of florins), and the 63 others fall into a bracket ranging from 10,000 down to 1,000 Rheingulden; on the Florentine list of the highest 600 assessments, 86 men fall in the top bracket extending upward from 10,000 florins to 116,000 florins (not a very different distribution from that in Nuremberg, considering the population difference), and the second bracket containing all the rest has a cut-off point of about 1,500 florins. In other words, at the top level of wealth the Nuremberg merchants could almost hold their own with the Florentines, but at the next level the Florentines outnumbered them well over nine times. It is remarkable that Nuremberg's richest merchants could compare so well with the richest Florentines; but the considerably higher number of Florentines in the middling bracket reveals the extraordinary difference between the two cities with respect to the amount and distribution of wealth—and Nuremberg was one of the wealthiest cities north of the Alps, certainly wealthier than the other southern German towns. According to the assessments reported in the 1427 Catasto, after allowing for all deductions except that for household dependents, 1,649 Florentines were worth at least 1,000 florins, equal to about fifteen times what a well-paid craftsman earned in a year. This class of the city's wealthiest men was not dominated (as in Nuremberg) by a few inordinately wealthy men. Moreover, wealth in Florence was highly fluid, not frozen by social or business structures.[47]

The fundamental fact about the structure of wealth within the upper classes is the diversification of investment capital into strong industrial, commercial, and financial sectors and its further fragmentation within those sectors among a large number of relatively small capitalist enterprises. Cloth shops, between those that produced wool and silk, numbered in the hundreds and were of various sizes. Even the largest of these partnerships, with a capital of approximately 5,000 florins and an annual output of about 300 cloths, at the most no more than 2 or 3 percent of the total production of the industry, had no significant share of the market.[48] In the commercial-banking sector, companies were many fewer and much larger in capital formation, but no one company or combination of companies dominated the others, nor did the power of their capital concentrations extend oppressively into the industrial sector, which was dependent on them. For instance, the company of Filippo Strozzi sold raw materials to, and bought finished cloths from, dozens of shops; and not one of them was any more dependent on him than he was on any one of them. In the operations of commercial firms abroad, with their diverse interests and the whole of Europe as their stage, there was room for all. The Medici company, perhaps the largest on record, with a capital of 72,000 florins (in 1451), did not dominate any of the great international banking places where it operated. In no way a central bank to which the others were inextricably tied, the Medici firm, even with the political standing of its owners, had nothing like the position in the business world the Bardi and Peruzzi had a century earlier. The history of Florentine banking and commerce in the Renaissance could be written with no more than passing reference to the Medici as the largest, perhaps (from a noneconomic point of view) the most interesting, but certainly not the dominant, firm. The transformation in the

[47] The figures for Florence come from Herlihy and Klapisch, *Toscans*, pp. 251–54 (but their interpretation suffers from failure to make any comparisons with other places). I have not used their computer materials to collect more exact data, but see the tables of the highest 150 declarations in each quarter of the city published by Lauro Martines, *The Social World of the Florentine Humanists, 1390–1460* (Princeton, 1963), App. II. The Nuremberg evidence is published by Helmut Haller von Hallerstein, "Grösse und Quellen des Vermögens von hundert Nürnberger Bürgern um 1500," *Beiträge zur Wirtschaftsgeschichte Nürnbergs*, I (Nuremberg, 1967), 117–76. Further comparison of the Nuremberg and Florentine figures would require extensive discussion of a number of complicated problems.

[48] The lowest annual production figures cited in the literature are 10,000 to 12,000 cloths for the years 1425 to 1430; Hidetoshi Hoshino, "Per la storia dell'arte della lana in Firenze nel Trecento e nel Quattrocento: un riesame," *Annuario dell'Istituto giapponese di cultura*, 10 (1972–73), 65–68. Production was closer to 20,000 later in the century.

international structure of the economic system that occurred in the later Middle Ages, described earlier, precluded the domination of the system by any one firm.[49]

This fragmented business structure reflects the limited power of capital in the hands of any one investor. Since the basis of all business organization was the partnership contract creating a pool of investment capital, there was, behind the array of cloth shops, banks, and trading companies, an even greater number of investors. Most of these partnerships were in fact dominated by a single investor, or by a family block of investors, but few of these men spread their investment capital beyond two or three businesses. The Medici—always a special case—were probably as extended as any, with, however, no more than three cloth shops (one silk and two wool, none any larger than a host of other such shops) and a single banking office in Florence, which, at its most extended (in 1470) had eight branches abroad (four in Italy and four north of the Alps). Piero di Gino Capponi, in 1485, had a bank, a wool and dye shop, a shop for goldbeating, and two companies abroad (in Pisa and Lyons). Filippo Strozzi had only one trading company in Florence and two abroad (in Rome and Naples).[50] This fragmentation of investment capital and the restricted nature of the typical investment portfolio are clearly discernible in the only survey we have of the city's investors, a list drawn up in 1451 for purposes of a special tax on business investments. By no means complete nor altogether accurate in the figures reported, the list nevertheless has the names of hundreds of investors, few of whom are down for a share in more than one partnership.[51]

This picture of the fragmentation of investment capital is not essentially changed by looking behind the facade of its business structure to the private sphere from which investment funds came. On the one hand, there no longer was that corporate sense relatives had earlier shared about maintaining a certain cohesion among themselves in handling their financial affairs; on the other, patrimonies were not yet burdened by inalienability and durable legal ties as they came to be later. No longer did brothers—like the sons of Villano di Stoldo (Villani), in 1322—think about drawing up a pact (*fraterna*) tying the hands of each to their common financial interests.[52] And no longer did a man think that such a community of family interests extended

[49] This interpretation of the banking system is further elaborated in my "Il Banco Medici," to appear in *I Medici e la banca nel Quattrocento fiorentino* (Milan, 1980).

[50] For the Medici see de Roover, *Medici Bank*; for Capponi and Strozzi, see Goldthwaite, *Private Wealth*. In the era of the Peruzzi, partners were restricted in investing outside their own companies; Armando Sapori, *Una compagnia di Calimala* (Florence, 1932), p. 39.

[51] This document is published by Anthony Molho, "The Florentine 'Tassa dei Traffichi' of 1451," *Studies in the Renaissance*, 17 (1970), 73–118; but see the comment herein, chapter 4, n. 48.

[52] Michele Luzzati, *Giovanni Villani e la compagnia dei Buonaccorsi* (Rome, 1971),

into the future so that he could burden the patrimony of his heirs by the debts of his own failures—in the way the Peruzzi, who failed in 1345, committed their descendants for the next century to pay off their debts in full.[53] Ownership of property was individual, not familial; according to the practice of partible inheritance, once a father was dead his property was divided, usually without prejudice, among his sons. A town palace, built as the symbol of the dynastic aspirations of its builder, was most likely protected by his last will and testament from ever leaving the possession of his descendants, but this did not mean common ownership and shared residency by individual parties, not even if they were brothers. Other real estate, with the possible exception of an ancestral property in the countryside where the family had its origins, was not subject to such claims.

Not until the sixteenth century did the notion that wealth somehow had its own integrity as something inviolable and permanent, to belong forever to a family, gain currency, and only then did inalienability and fideicommissa begin to complicate the inheritance of property by mandating that an entire patrimony be kept intact. No fifteenth-century Florentine had that dynastic sense of property that compelled Riccardo Riccardi, in 1616, first, to tie up the better part of his estate with a fideicommissum preserving it "not only to the third, fourth, fifth, sixth, and seventh generations, but to the thousandth and beyond, in perpetuity and into infinity," and then, worrying about perpetuity, to oblige oldest sons to marry by the age of thirty, on penalty of paying 500 scudi annually to their poorest relative (to be increased to 1,000 scudi if they reached the age of thirty-two without having married) and of losing their privileges as first-born should they reach thirty-six still celibate.[54]

The division of an estate was not only a legal fact; it was a social fact, as well. However strong the ties of affection among members of a family, their investment interests often diverged. It was not unusual for sons of an entrepreneur to remain partners in their father's business; but it was no more unusual for them, once having come into their shares of the patrimony, to follow separate investment interests. In the industrial sector, with its numerous but relatively small partnerships in wool and silk shops, companies had no family continuity, although sons might independently follow in their father's footsteps. In the commercial-banking sector, with many fewer but

p. 16. The Villani pact lasted almost twenty years but eventually was the cause of litigation among the brothers (p. 45).

[53] Armando Sapori, *La crisi delle compagnie mercantili dei Bardi e dei Peruzzi* (Florence, 1926), p. 170.

[54] Malanima, *Riccardi*, pp. 114–15. The loose and informal nature of legal ties on property in the fifteenth century is illustrated in the discussion of Francis William Kent, *Household and Lineage in Renaissance Florence: The Family Life of the Capponi, Ginori, and Rucellai* (Princeton, 1977), pp. 135–44. See also Goldthwaite, *Private Wealth*, pp. 271–72; and Giulio Vismara, "L'unità della famiglia nella storia del diritto in Italia," *Studia et documenta historiae et iuris*, 22 (1956), 255–59.

considerably larger companies, partnerships among brothers were more common, although a surprising number of these great international firms were not family partnerships at all (and therefore had no continuity as such). A partnership of brothers, in any case, rarely continued beyond their lives to take in the next generation of cousins in the way that the great fourteenth-century companies of the Bardi, Peruzzi, Alberti, Strozzi, and others gradually absorbed the sons of several brothers and sometimes even their sons. For the fifteenth century it is hardly accurate to talk of "family" companies with a life beyond two generations except in the sense of a father-son continuity, with perhaps a stray relative here and there holding a share. The renewal of partnership contracts among the Medici heirs has created the illusion of a family company that endured for four to five generations, but the history of the capital investment originally amassed by Giovanni di Bicci de' Medici is somewhat eccentric as a result of limited proliferation of the lines descending from him and the political pressures on Cosimo, his son, and grandson to prevent the break-up of the company's capital formation despite serious rifts with the collateral line of Pierfrancesco. The investment history of other fifteenth-century families—Gondi, Capponi, Strozzi, Guicciardini—reveals little interest in the pooling of resources beyond the second generation. The business history of Renaissance Florence is written about individual, not family, firms (which is not to say, incidentally, that a businessman did not offer jobs in his company to any number of miscellaneous relatives).[55]

Wealth widely distributed in many hands unbound by ties of wider family interests got shifted about with great frequency, and since what a man did with it depended on his own performance, those who handled the better part of the city's wealth saw much mobility within their ranks. The practice of partible inheritance was enough to keep up the pace of this mobility. Once a patrimony was divided among men who felt no obligation, and often little disposition, to pool resources, each heir took his share and went off on his own, his fortune more or less in his hands. The history of a fifteenth-century "family" fortune beyond one generation thus disintegrates into many different lines, each following its own variable course in a process of repeated and

[55] For the last four families mentioned here see Goldthwaite, *Private Wealth*; for the Bardi, Peruzzi, and Alberti see the articles in Sapori, *Studi di storia economica*; for the fourteenth-century firm of Carlo Strozzi, see Marco Spallanzani, "Una grande azienda fiorentina del Trecento: Carlo Strozzi e compagni," *Ricerche storiche*, 8 (1978), 417–36; for the Medici, see Goldthwaite, "Il Banco Medici." The process of family fragmentation of business interests can be seen in the history of the Alberti firms through the later fourteenth century: Sapori, "La famiglia e le compagnie degli Alberti del Giudice," in his *Studi di storia economica*, II, 983 (and n. 6, with further references to Renouard's studies); Arnold Esch, "Bankiers der Kirche im Grossen Schisma," in *Quellen und Forschungen aus italienischen Archiven und Bibliotheken*, 46 (1966), 277–398 (indexed for names); Holmes, "Florentine Merchants," pp. 193–98; idem, "Medici," pp. 360–61.

inevitable furcation. In a later period this course was altered by a countervailing force that, gaining its strength from a growing sense of dynasty and concern about status, inspired men (like Riccardo Riccardi) to take steps to keep their patrimonies intact at whatever cost.

Private wealth was all the more fluid for being so exposed to the instability that was in the very nature of a business economy of the premodern variety. If (as discussed earlier) the stability of the cloth sector engendered a rentier mentality among investors, the commercial-banking sector had ups and downs that could dramatically make and break fortunes. This sector was oriented to speculation in markets abroad and was not at all protected by a state banking system at home holding in the reins of money and credit, and men with investments in it were exposed to the unlimited liability of the partnership contract underlying business organization. The diary of Gregorio Dati (who lived from 1362 to 1435) is eloquent testimony of the vicissitudes of a businessman's fortune. Dati's father, though not wealthy, was well established in the business world, but he died when Dati was only twelve without leaving much of a patrimony for his sons. Dati started out as a minor partner in the silk business and then ventured into foreign trade, with a particular interest in Spain, and in 1395 he was able to set up his own company. We learn from his own testimony that he often suffered heavy losses, leaving him with debts and involving him in extensive litigation. Repeatedly he came to the brink of complete ruin—only to be saved by the dowries of his several wives and advances from his well-placed brother, the general of the Dominican Order. In the end he came out on top; the last assessment we have of his wealth is his 1427 Catasto declaration of 3,000 florins in assets.

One of the implications of the fluidity of wealth in a society where the moneyed class did not protect itself by exclusive guild barriers or by legal and political privilege is social mobility. *Mobility* is a relative term, and the phenomenon has yet to be studied in Florence, but it is apparent that the upper classes were always having to make room for men with new wealth. The rise of Francesco di Marco Datini (who lived from 1335 to 1410) to the ranks of the very rich is the best documented. Born the son of a local merchant in Prato but (like Dati) left an orphan (by the Black Death) without much of a patrimony, Datini made his own way as an apprentice in Florence and then ventured abroad to find his fortune in the great international markets, especially in Provence. He built up a vast network of international banking and commercial operations and a substantial wool establishment in Prato that brought him a fortune worth over 100,000 florins, as large as any in the city. Although not quite a story of rags to riches, Datini's may have been the business success of the century—he has certainly left his mark on the economic history of the entire period, much of which is written from the vast archives of his business records.

Many a Florentine palace tells the story of this mobility. Lorenzo Ilarioni's and Bono Boni's had to be sold off in the wake of bankruptcy; Bartolomeo Barbadori's, designed by Brunelleschi, never got built because mounting debts forced a halt to construction; and how many others—undertaken in the euphora of rising fortunes—were sold off by heirs or—like those of Filippo Strozzi, Giuliano Gondi, and Giovanni Rucellai—were left incomplete because heirs shared no collective interest in continuing the work and no one of them was financially up to doing it on his own? Who knows what change of fortune lies behind the transfer of so many of these palaces out of their builder's (or buyer's) family into another within a generation or two of their construction? And, finally, to put private wealth into a different perspective regarding the palaces: How many palaces, if they could have called forth the dead and opened their doors to the immediate forebears of their builders, would have found themselves crowded with artisans like Canacci, Pucci, Gaddi—just to mention some of the names of the upwardly mobile men in the crafts that are touched on in this book?

Much of the history of the construction of these palaces and of their ownership was determined by the nature of wealth—its wide distribution and its fluidity brought on by business fortune and partible inheritance. Although the group through whose hands wealth circulated remained fairly contained in the long run, individuals within those ranks had diverse fortunes, and new fortunes were not uncommon. This structure of wealth shaped demand not only for architecture but for all the arts and crafts in the luxury category. The market was crowded with consumers, and new faces were continually showing up to renew their ranks. Moreover, the redistribution of wealth in the city brought on by the increase in the number of highly skilled craftsmen and by a rise in wages to an all-time high in the fifteenth century meant that men of more modest stature also found themselves with something left over to spend for those "extras" beyond life's necessities, including even art. The high level of total spending for the arts, in other words, was the result of an aggregate of individuals each spending at a relatively low level, whereas in the courts of northern Italy, with larger individual concentrations of wealth in the hands of a single prince and his small circle of courtiers, spending was more spectacular, although perhaps less in its total value than in Florence. In Florence, precisely because there were many agents of demand, a veritable marketplace for the decorative arts came into existence, a place increasingly crowded with buyers and sellers, where the demand-and-supply mechanism developed well beyond the personal relations of princely patron and dependent artisan. It is characteristic of the Renaissance in Florence that the decorative arts, flourishing not in a court but in the marketplace, came to constitute a distinctive sector of the economy, one whose growth marked a new stage in the economic history of the city.

CHAPTER TWO

The Reasons for Building: Needs and Taste

THE economy determines the context in which spending is possible. It sets the limits of demand. The economic variables that impinge on demand, however, can only shape demand, not create it. Demand itself arises from other sources. Men build because they have need for specific kinds of enclosed space, and the appearance of the buildings they put up is very much a matter of taste. Needs and taste can obviously be measured by their economic results on the supply side, but the forces determining needs and taste are generally considered under the independent categories of psychology, social conditions, and, more broadly, culture. Traditional economic history has little place for them in its scheme of things. Buildings have functions and style, and the motives for building them cannot be understood in the usual terms of economic analysis.

Function is the easiest tool of analysis to explain major building activity. People use buildings for specific purposes, and as their needs change so do the demands they make on the places where they do what they have to do, whether it is work, sleep, pray, or play. Apart from demographic growth and the consequent need for more buildings, extensive urban building, or rebuilding, can often be explained by social transformations giving rise to demand for altogether new kinds of buildings. In the nineteenth century the range of building types that came off the drawing boards of architects expanded considerably to accommodate the increasing complexity of life brought on by the industrial revolution.

In the Middle Ages significant building—that is, building of architectural importance—was very much confined to religious life. For this reason medieval architecture reflects the history of the church, although this wider cultural context in which building took place has been little remarked. For example, the continuing infrastructural transformation of the church, with the frequent proliferation of new organizations within its vast structure, was forever creating occasions for building and rebuilding. Church-building has therefore been a particularly notable activity in periods of internal upheaval when new religious communities were founded and splinter groups in the guise of reform movements broke away from older ones. Much religious building at the end of the Middle Ages can be seen in this light, and so can the building boom of the counter-reformation church. In Florence the Observant movements within the orders of friars, the proliferation of convents, and the formation of communities for the operation of welfare institutions like hospitals and orphanages all created occasions for new buildings, and to this extent the rebuilding of Florence can be explained as part of the larger picture of religion in late medieval Europe.

Building inspired by these general religious movements, however, does not account for much of the transformation of the local architectural scene. What was new on that scene was the rise of demand for significant building within the secular world from both the public and private sectors. Even much of the remodeling and rebuilding of churches resulted from the need to accommodate more private chapels. Yet, this public and private demand cannot be altogether explained by new needs arising from profound social changes in the structure of either politics or society at large, since there was nothing really new about the functions these buildings performed. The various civic buildings did not differ in any significant way with respect to function from the kinds of buildings to be found in just about any Italian town. The chapel-lined church evolved to accommodate the growing demand for chapels, but the private chapel itself was nothing new, nor for that matter (in the context of European architecture) was the chapel-lined church itself. And, finally, private residences had of course always existed—some of them, despite their architectural anonymity, probably every bit as large as many a Renaissance palace. In the fifteenth century, however, more men wanted larger and more impressive homes, more men wanted their own chapels, and collectively they wanted more impressive civic buildings. Something had changed in their lives to generate this demand.

In the final analysis what is most distinctive about building activity in Florence as seen in the tradition of urban building in medieval Europe is not just the rise in demand for new buildings. It was above all a taste for architecture, a desire to give these buildings a certain physical presence, and an interest in new ideas about how to do this. In other words, building was undertaken in a spirit informed by a consciousness of public space and inspired by the desire to make a distinctive mark in it. Architecture, as Alberti recognized, is essentially a civic activity, and the new spirit with which Florentines built was generated in the atmosphere of the civic world that took shape in Florence during the fourteenth century and that in fact found its highest expression in the public building programs that radically reorganized the city's central public spaces. The monumentality of all these projects—not only their size but also their elaborate sculptural programs and the plan to put them all in some kind of spatial relation to one another—is a basic fact about the city's view of itself. That collective vision came into focus over a century and a half of public building, and by the fifteenth century it was inspiring private builders to see their own projects in a new perspective. This sense of a civic context for building, both private and public, opened a new chapter in the history of architectural patronage, and, it is important to add, the results would have been most impressive for the amount of building alone —even without the stylistic innovations that also opened a new chapter in the history of architectural style.

Civic Spirit and Public Building

The welling up of civic pride that overflowed in public building was brought on by that remarkable course of events from the end of the thirteenth to the beginning of the fifteenth century that transformed the Florentine state and along with it the Florentines' very perception of the political world. During the century and a half beginning at the building of the town hall and ending at the crowning of the cathedral with Brunelleschi's cupola, Florence put its internal affairs into an impressive new order, carved out a large territorial state extending over much of Tuscany, and asserted itself as a major Italian power.[1]

In the thirteenth century the city was just one of several in the area, each vying with the others to extend its influence beyond the immediate countryside to which it was confined. By the fourteenth century Florence's rivals were clearly on the wane as competitors. After the disastrous battle of Meloria in 1284 Pisa was pushed out of the maritime world where it had won wealth and power and slowly declined to a provincial port. With the increasing orientation of the region's economy toward cloth production, the older bank-

[1] The major general works surveying this background—all recent and with full bibliographies—are: Marvin Becker, *Florence in Transition*, 2 vols. (Baltimore, 1967–68); Gene Brucker, *Florentine Politics and Society, 1343–1378* (Princeton, 1962) and its sequel *The Civic World of Early Renaissance Florence* (Princeton, 1977); Hans Baron, *The Crisis of the Early Italian Renaissance* (Princeton, 1966).

ing capital of Siena, high in the hills and without the resources to expand its local cloth industry, was outstripped by the economic growth of Lucca and Florence. As to Lucca, its concentration on the production of silk cloths assured a more durable prosperity but excluded it from the rapidly expanding markets for wool. In short, of all these Tuscan towns Florence had the most dynamic economy, and as it pushed ahead in the international markets abroad, one of the rewards was the steady growth of its territorial state at home.

At the beginning of the fourteenth century that territory barely extended beyond the narrow valley of the Arno on either side of the city upstream just into the Valdichiana along its western part as far as Montepulciano and downstream as far as Empoli, where the valley opens up into the wide plain extending to the sea. This territory was bounded on the west by the Elsa, and on the east it did not yet reach as far as the Apennines. In the second quarter of the fourteenth century an aggressive policy got underway to extend those boundaries. The valley of the Ombrone northwest of Florence was secured by the final pacification of Pistoia (1329); with the crossing into the Valdinievole and the occupation of Pescia (1329), Fucecchio (1330), and Barga (1341), Florence rounded out its western possessions in the wide Arno valley toward Lucca, Pisa, and the sea. In the hills to the south of this area Florence pushed westward across the Elsa to San Gimignano (1354), Volterra (1361), and San Miniato al Tedesco (1374). The conquest of Pisa itself came in 1406, and that city's stout resistance and the continuing rebelliousness of its population only sharpened the Florentines' sense of the significance of this expansion to the sea, culminating in the purchase of Livorno in 1421. Meanwhile, Florence consolidated its power in the upper Arno valley and in the Mugello, affixing the stamp of its authority in new fortifications (for example, at Borgo San Lorenzo in 1351) and carefully planned new towns established as military outposts at Firenzuola (1332) and Terranuova (1337). Arezzo came into the widening Florentine orbit in 1384, Cortona in 1411; and then began the move into the Casentino against the last holdouts of local feudal lords in this mountainous region. With its conquest in 1440 the last gap was closed in the stretch of Apennines that formed a natural barrier to Florence's further expansion. As the map of Tuscany shows, in the early fifteenth century the Florentine state had essentially the shape of the modern region less the extensive Sienese territory to the southwest and, to the extreme northwest, Lucca and the narrow strip of Tyrrhenian coast above Pisa.

The formation of this territorial state was not merely a matter of provincial politics. For the Florentines it meant the emergence of their city as one of the major powers of Italy. What was happening in Tuscany occurred all over northern Italy: as a few towns enlarged their territory at the expense of others the fluid political situation left by the failure of German imperial schemes gradually coagulated around a few dominant states. Their relations, in turn,

Tuscany

eventually reached a point of stasis in the precarious "balance of power" established at Lodi in 1454 that was to assure the peace of Italy until it was jarred by foreign invasions. Florence was one of the states involved in this balance. Its policy of expansion in Tuscany did not occur in regional isolation; the more it came to dominate the region, the more it came up against the greater Italian powers abroad. Tuscany's central position in the peninsula put it in the path of the ambitions of others—of the papacy, at a time when

Cardinal Albornoz was trying to secure a state in preparation for the return of the popes from Avignon; of the Visconti lords of Milan, who had by the end of the fourteenth century conquered much of the Po valley and were setting their sights southward; of the kings of Naples, for whom Tuscany was one approach to getting a stranglehold on the intervening lands of the pope. These princes often supported the local enemies of Florence in pursuit of their own schemes, and the struggle against them from the last quarter of the fourteenth century through the first quarter of the next had its moments of high drama. Much has been made of the psychological and cultural implications of the political crisis facing Florence in 1401 and 1402, when for a brief but tense moment before his sudden death it looked as if the Visconti duke, who had surrounded Florence, was about to deliver the final blow to Florentine independence. The drama of this one event may have been overstated by modern scholarship, but there is little doubt that the general threatening situation abroad for this fifty-year period made a deep impression on Florentines, especially in view of their eventual success at survival against what at times seemed insurmountable odds.

Florence at the time of Dante for all of its economic vitality was little more than just another regional city-state; a century later it was a major Italian power sharing the peninsular political scene with popes and princes. This was a fundamental experience in the Florentines' political education. The widening of their horizons beyond the confines of Tuscany to the entire peninsula was an important process in the formation of that distinctive view Florentines had of their city and the political world of which it was a part.

The very nature of the Florentine state within underwent a profound transformation during this same period, and much of that change was related to territorial expansion and the broadening of political horizons abroad. At the time of Dante the political order can be defined as a loose corporate structure typical of medieval towns, in the instance of Florence one held together somewhat precariously by a government with roots in a complex guild structure. Even a man the stature of Dante was scarcely capable of rising above the emotions generated by the instability and violence that racked the city. By the fifteenth century, however, corporate loyalties had lost much ground to a higher sense of political order. It is not that there was an institutional development toward bureaucratic centralization along the lines we associate with the "rise of the modern state," but nevertheless Florentines had clearly begun to recognize a higher public authority in their political affairs. Despite an unwieldly republican system of overlapping legislative bodies and innumerable citizen committees performing executive functions, they were able to develop a more coherent view of their political world. Control over their territory was effected through a hierarchy of military vicariates and captaincies, and relations with the great powers abroad were conducted by an increasingly rational system of ambassadors. At home the nucleus of a stable, professional bureaucracy appeared in the form of the chancery, whose eminent humanist secretaries became eloquent spokesmen for the city. Furthermore, heavy military expenses put pressures on the state to formulate a more coherent fiscal policy. The older, ad hoc system of borrowing money was put into some order with the funding of the public debt in 1345 into the Monte, an institution that as a result of the continuing rise of military expenses soon became the central treasury of the state. In 1427, a little less than a century after the setting up of the Monte, the institution of the Catasto, with its impersonal and objective procedures for assessment of private wealth for tax purposes, was the mark of how fiscal policy, in affecting the pocketbook of every Florentine, was successful in engendering the kind of confidence in state institutions that brought them all more securely into the orbit of public authority.

The rise of Florence from provincial commune to Italian power was something less than spectacular considering the amount of time in which it was accomplished, but Florentine chroniclers—for the most part practical men of affairs and not professional intellectuals—document the general optimism with which Florentines regarded progress along the way. From the anonymous writers of the thirteenth century to Villani, these men told a success story. The earlier ones exalted the glorious origins of the city shrouded in the mystery of myth and legend and recounted with pride the more recent events in the commune's struggle for survival. Villani in the mid-fourteenth century put everything on a grander scale. In his rambling chronicle packed with immense detail he broadly surveys the wealth and power of the city in a way that clearly indicates a sense of accomplishment beyond the political arena. A little more than half a century later this generally positive view of Florentine history was brought into sharper focus by Goro Dati. He sees the city more baldly as a power entity locked in a struggle with other powers in a way that anticipates Machiavelli a century later. His exclusive focus on foreign affairs and his strong sense of power politics can be seen as the mark of the precocity of Florentines in coming to an understanding of the wider political world that they had entered in the course of territorial expansion.

This sense of the state as power was enhanced by a growing conviction that Florence also had a certain ideological stance. That ground was not very firm, or at least not very clearly staked out; but what gradually emerged was a positive attitude about the state that helped mollify the despair earlier Florentines had felt about the nature of political life within their city. For all their pride in the successes of the struggle for survival abroad, the earlier chroniclers were not so confident about the way politics were conducted at home. Even Dante, when faced with the necessity of finding a political solution to the local situation, settled for the fantasy of a revived empire rather than any hope of strengthening political morality within the city. The most any of his contemporaries could propose was the stock Christian appeal to virtue and justice, which did little to inform a citizen's behavior with a particular civic consciousness. The wars of the fourteenth century, however, seem to have made Florentines feel that their city, after all, stood for something. In their justification for these wars, in appeals for support, in tirades against their enemies, they tried to stake out their ideological ground. There was much talk of liberty, but the concept long remained vague, little more than a cry against bad government, tyranny, and foreign domination. Salutati, appointed chancellor in 1375, only occasionally gives a republican twist to the term by suggesting that *liberty* implies the freedom to participate in government. The breakthrough came with Salutati's successor, Leonardo Bruni, who went farther than anyone else in defining *liberty* as a specific quality of a republic. Despite his vigorous defense, however, no one went beyond to elaborate a political theory of liberty and republicanism; yet, for all their vagueness, the terms became charged with a fervor that strengthened the emotional ties binding citizens to their state. If this did not inspire more acute analysis of the theoretical structure of their constitution, it gave Florentines a new way of looking at their historical foundations, for they now rejected the traditional thesis of the Roman origins of their city in the empire for a new one rooting their traditions in the republic. This revisionism was of no little importance in arousing that historical interest so fundamentally a part of the Renaissance outlook. The seriousness with which men took history—for instance, when they tried to remake Brutus into a republican hero and rescue him from the lowest pit of hell, where he had been relegated by Dante for his betrayal of the empire—bespoke a new civic consciousness.

By the beginning of the fifteenth century Florentines had a more coherent and a better-defined view of themselves. They ruled a large territorial state that was a major Italian power; their government had a degree of institutional cohesion and the force of public authority; and their sense of politics had at least a tinge of ideology. Moreover, the economic life of the city expanded the context in which they saw themselves well beyond the political sphere. Their cloth industry produced for the markets across Europe from England to Egypt, and their merchants had all these places tied up in a great international banking and commercial network. They hoped, too, to become a maritime power when they took to the sea with the inauguration of a galley system in 1421, shortly after the conquest of Pisa. Their gold florins circulated everywhere as the most universal of international currencies. Their familiarity with the world can be documented by the travel abroad of any number of merchants and by the vast correspondence of the more sedentary ones—like Francesco di Marco Datini, who received in an eight-year period (from 1392 to 1400) 16,000 letters (an average of 6 a day) from 200 cities. As Goro Dati proudly asserted (and he had the authority of his own experience to appeal to), business gave Florentines a sense of the wider world, a larger context for their view of policy: they "know all the doors of entrance and exit to the world," they "spread their wings over the world and have news and information from all its corners." With their cosmopolitan outlook on the world it was only natural that storytellers like Boccaccio set their tales in places all over Europe. A worldwide breadth of vision, the central importance of Florence itself—these made up the self-image that was taking clearer shape in the Florentine mind at the end of the fourteenth century.

Florentines' pride inspired them to write about their city as no other Italians did. A rich tradition of historical writing exalted their accomplishments, and collections of biographies sang the praises of their more prominent citizens. With the continuing re-etching of their self-image, Florentines came to know themselves with unprecedented insight. At the level of popular poetry, Antonio Pucci, if not distinctive for his literary quality, nevertheless articulated this *fiorentinismo* in the way he captured the spirit of the city, its history, its vitality, and its people. Recited in the streets and squares, Pucci's poetry must have helped give consciousness to deep feelings among the less articulate. In fact, language itself became the mark of Florentine pride. By the end of the fourteenth century Florentines could look back on a long literary tradition that had transformed their dialect into a refined and sophisticated language. Giovanni da Prato celebrated Dante, Petrarch, and Boccaccio as the three crowns of Florence for their contributions to the historical evolution of Tuscan to the point that it had become a medium for the subtlest feelings and the most profound thought. Elsewhere in Italy hardly a vernacular writer of importance can be turned up, other dialects remaining undeveloped for lack of a stronger literary tradition. Not surprisingly, therefore, once the new humanism began to resuscitate classical Latin, it was in Florence where men took up the cause of the vernacular; such a debate made no sense anywhere else in Italy.

The notion that there was something unique and superior about their culture was thus deeply anchored in the historical consciousness of Florentines, and in their very language. It was almost as if Providence had singled them out for a special destiny, a feeling evoked by chroniclers and poets, who hailed the city as the daughter of Rome, and by apocalyptic visionaries, who sought to arouse it to the destiny of renewing Christianity. Savonarola's millenarian message could only have made sense to a people who were ready to see themselves as the chosen ones, men with pent-up historical urges awaiting some kind of legitimization. Boniface VIII called the Florentines, with their rarefied self-esteem, the fifth element, and some would say that something of this essence survives in the city even in our own times.

The civic pride Florentines took in their city extended also to the urban fabric, more so than for any other people in Europe. Their aesthetic sensibilities were aroused and conditioned by the lively school of painting established by Cimabue and Giotto, else these artists and their successors would never have made it into the growing list of great Florentines as enumerated by contemporaries; it should be noted that the fame Giotto enjoyed in his own time and long after extended much beyond the elite circle of intellectuals like Dante, Petrarch, and Boccaccio. In other words, Florentines were learning how to look; and as the built environment came within their purview they enthusiastically set about to enhance its beauty in accord with their pride in the state. We see this in building regulations and urban planning and in the way chroniclers describe their city. Dino Compagni, about 1300, and Giovanni Villani, in the 1330s, noted the beauty of the place, albeit only generically and in passing. Coluccio Salutati, at the end of the century, was struck by the splendor of the sight of it all as taken in from the hilltops around—before he descended to comment gloomily on the deterioration that was beginning to set in on some of the most notable structures.[2] With the characteristic grandeur of the humanist vision of things, Leonardo Bruni, at the beginning of the fifteenth century, saw the setting of the city in its outlying territory as a neat arrangement of concentric circles centering on the tower of the Palazzo dei Priori.

In Goro Dati's description, however, we get a more original approach and perhaps the first statement anywhere in Europe of a genuine aesthetic pleasure felt upon looking out on an urban scene.[3] Whereas the famous description of Villani, like its medieval models, consists of city walls and churches evaluated quantitatively rather than qualitatively and generically rather than specifically, Dati sets his focus on secular monuments and reveals a real sensitivity to their architectural quality. He wrote his description in the mid-1420s, by which time there was much to be seen that was new and exciting; and his account rings with enthusiasm. He has something to say about the Palazzo dei Priori, the adjacent loggia, Orsanmichele, and the cathedral complex; and he goes on to mention hospitals, orphanages, private palaces, as well as churches. Not surprisingly, he gives measurements for the cathedral, which, after all (as he boasts), was to be the biggest in Christendom; but his eye is also sensitive to coloristic effects of marble surfaces, to the working of stone, to the great sculptures at Orsanmichele, and, finally, to the space in which a building is located. All the pride that was welling up in Florentines as a result of their political, economic, and cultural achievements is here brought to bear on the physical transformation of the city that was then taking place. This convergence of civic pride and aesthetic pleasure goes a

[2] The passage from Salutati's *De seculo et religione* is quoted in Michael Baxandall, *Giotto and the Orators: Humanist Observers of Painting in Italy and the Discovery of Pictorial Composition 1350–1450* (Oxford, 1971), p. 67.

[3] Creighton Gilbert, "The Earliest Guide to Florentine Architecture, 1423," *Flor. Mitt.*, 14 (1969); Christian Bec, *Les Marchands écrivains à Florence, 1375–1434* (Paris, 1967), pp. 172–73.

long way to explain the public building program that inaugurated the Renaissance in architecture.[4]

Attitudes about Private Spending

Although examples of private prestige building can be found before the fifteenth century, wealthy Florentines were generally under strong restraints against spending their wealth too conspicuously. As men engaged in business they were constantly under fire from popular preachers for the evils that seemed to be inherent in the business world. With their passion for making money merchants exposed themselves to the vice of materialism, and too many of their practices smacked of usury, a subject the preachers of Florence were especially articulate on. No serious churchman failed to recognize the essential role of the merchant in society, but it was incumbent on the upholders of Christian morality to point out the only too obvious moral pitfalls awaiting men who were primarily interested in making money. Moreover, matters were not made any easier for the merchant by the social criticism of Franciscan extremists preaching their doctrine of poverty. Merchants were under constant suspicion from all quarters, and under the circumstances it was better not to invite trouble by spending money too conspicuously. The tension over these matters was somewhat more evident in Florence than in many other places in Europe precisely because it was one of the most advanced centers of capitalist growth.

If this morality was not enough to restrain them, there were also social pressures to contend with, for in the faction-ridden political world of the Trecento it was simply good business sense not to let others know just how wealthy one was. As one anonymous fourteenth-century merchant put it: "Spending a lot and making a big impression are in themselves too dangerous."[5] "Never show off your wealth," advises Giovanni Morelli, "but keep it hidden, and always by words and acts make people believe that you possess one half as much as you have; by following this advice you cannot be too badly cheated."[6]

[4] André Chastel has suggested that much public building in Florence was undertaken in conscious rivalry with other cities, including Rome: *Art et humanisme à Florence au temps de Laurent le Magnifique* (Paris, 1961), pp. 181–82. Interpretations of major works of art in public places that emphasize a special relation between Rome and Florence include Eve Borsook and Johannes Offerhaus, "Storia e leggende nella Cappella Sassetti in Santa Trinita," *Scritti di storia dell'arte in onore di Ugo Procacci* (Milan, 1977), I, 289–310; and the theme looms large in George Holmes, *The Florentine Enlightenment, 1400–50* (London, 1969).

[5] Gino Corti, ed., "Consigli sulla mercatura di un anonimo trecentista," *ASI*, 111 (1952), 118.

[6] As quoted in Robert S. Lopez and Irving W. Raymond, eds., *Medieval Trade in the Mediterranean World* (New York, 1955), p. 423.

Winds of change, however, slowly cleared the air of these doubts about wealth. Erosion of the usury doctrine relieved the businessman of the burden that weighed most heavily on him. The refinement of business practices involving the extension of credit, including the mechanism by which the society collectively committed itself to a permanent, funded public debt, raised serious questions about the validity of the traditional restrictions on lending money. Earlier notions about usury began to look too simplistic, and church intellectuals concerned with the problem were compelled to recognize the realities of an increasingly complex economic world and hence to be more systematic and careful in their examination of theory and practice. Two of the most sophisticated and even daring of all fifteenth-century thinkers who took on the thorny problem of usury were in fact the local saints Bernardino and Antonino, the latter the bishop of the city. The ideas of these two popular preachers were hardly confined to the usual audience of scholarly discourse. They recognized the reality of a veritable money market with alternatives for investment and admitted that a man with money to spare and many options for its use should not be penalized for lending it by having to sacrifice a return on it—a dangerous notion that opened up a host of problems for the traditional argument against usury. They also made much of the notion of risk, which from the beginning had been a loophole in the medieval discussions of usury through which it was possible to escape the tight confines of narrow and simplistic condemnations. Having allowed themselves to be led down these precarious paths, thinkers like Bernardino and Antonino found themselves caught up in a convoluted casuistry the contradictions and inconsistencies of which eventually brought on the kind of belittling criticisms that much late scholasticism was to suffer in the early modern period.[7]

As merchants found that more and more of their practices were being cleared of moral contamination it would not be surprising if they began to feel something of the uncertainties in the arguments against the others. Fifteenth-century business records show them less careful in trying to disguise the charging of interest, and sometimes even explicit about it. Although some extraordinary instances of how seriously men could still feel guilt for usurious practices have been documented for the fifteenth and early sixteenth centuries, they generally showed less concern for it in last wills and testaments, where traditionally the usuror cleared his slate by doing restitution. When restitution is explicitly mentioned in fifteenth-century wills, it is likely to take the form of a generalized gift to charity rather then rectification of particular offenses against specified victims. Bishop Antonino inveighed against this easy and ultimately irresponsible way out of the problem, but he was fighting

[7] Raymond de Roover, *San Bernardino of Siena and Sant'Antonino of Florence: Two Great Economic Thinkers of the Middle Ages* (Cambridge, Mass., 1967); Bec, *Marchands*, pp. 253–77.

a losing battle against a new confidence that was no longer likely to be dented by such moral onslaughts. By the beginning of the sixteenth century the bishop's court had resigned itself to defining usury as little more than the charging of excessive interest, and the few practices that remained suspect (like pawnbroking) had nothing to do with the normal conduct of business by merchants and bankers.[8]

Meanwhile, the Florentine merchant toed a thin line between guilt and common sense, between religious imperatives and self-interest. Francesco Datini's friends advised him not to set up a local bank in Florence in 1398 because of the moral dangers inherent in that line of business, but he went ahead anyway—and at the end of his life left his huge estate in a charitable bequest. According to Vespasiano da Bisticci, guilt gnawed deeply into Cosimo de' Medici's conscience, but if he built San Marco partly to make up for his ill-gotten gains, he did not do it altogether in a spirit of anonymous, self-effacing piety. These merchants confidently called on God to help them in their business, evoking Him and a host of favorite saints in the first lines with which they invariably open their account books, and scratching in the sign of the cross at the top of each page thereafter; and they kept their bargain with Him in bequests, endowments, and buildings to His glory—and to theirs. Much of the religious art of the Renaissance, as has often been said, is a result of the ambivalence men felt in the matter of God and profit.

Some intellectuals came to the help of these merchants by supporting their case with a rationale for wealth that undermined the traditional Christian ideal of poverty. Whereas humanists in the fourteenth century, like Petrarch and Salutati, shunned wealth primarily out of their commitment to the stoic notion of the contemplative life, their followers at the turn of the century tended to regard the problem of wealth in the context of civic life. These so-called civic humanists attempted to promote a sense of public morality by exalting the active life, and to buttress their argument they appropriated certain notions found in Aristotle about the importance of wealth in achieving virtue. Leonardo Bruni, who translated the Pseudo-Aristotelian *Economics*, emphasized riches as the foundation of the state not only because wealth provided the material well-being for the security of the state but also because it presented a moral challenge to the active citizen. Liberality presupposes possession of wealth, and (as these men saw it) the test of virtue is not to be passed by fleeing the world with its material encumbrances but, on the contrary, by mastering wealth in ways that demonstrated one's moral stature. Such ideas were picked up by moral thinkers like Alberti and Palmieri, and they got wide circulation in public orations and vernacular

[8] Richard C. Trexler, *Synodal Law in Florence and Fiesole, 1306–1518* (Vatican City, 1971), pp. 110–12.

writings. They were not ideas unknown in the Middle Ages—Saint Thomas, after all, had read Aristotle, too—but there is a new secular tone in the emphasis these humanists put on the active life and its civic content and in the particular accent they gave to the private achievement of the individual. The proper use of wealth was no longer confined to charity. For Alberti possessions are necessary to the happiness of the family; it is through wealth that one builds friendships, gains authority among his fellows, and finds fame. The private and civic satisfactions that the wealthy man can thereby gain for himself in the social and public world go beyond what most earlier moralists chose to consider, let alone concede as proper, and these were exactly the pleasures that men in the fifteenth century were beginning to enjoy more openly.

These humanists were not economic thinkers any more than were any other intellectuals of their times. They were not interested in economic analysis or any justification of the economic system with respect to psychological, social, and moral values. A defense of capitalism was not what they were about. What they were doing was, in a sense, merely finding a place for the merchant in a traditional scheme of things where it was thought proper for man to seek a certain honor and glory in this life. They were inspired, of course, by classical notions (for example, of Aristotle) of the appropriateness of lavish expenditures for the achievement of greatness and prestige, but their orientation toward glory-seeking was not discordant with the medieval chivalric spirit, which was in any case much more familiar to the unlettered businessman since it was so much a part of the world abroad he dealt with. In short, the lust for money, roundly condemned throughout the Middle Ages from Saint Augustine on, was justified not on its own terms but as a means to satisfy the desire for glory, an ambition also condemned frequently enough in the Middle Ages but nevertheless sustained by the countervailing force of the aristocratic ethos. That ethos was now transmuted into classical terms by the humanists with their emphasis on the civic life. The humanists, in other words, were more traditional than innovative; all they did was to give a twist to an old tradition in order that the merchant also be able to fit into it, more or less on his own terms. It must be added that only a few humanists took up this subject at all, and the ideas of those who did are merely asides to the main thrust of their thought. Their influence on later economic thought was negligible, and we cannot be certain how much weight their ideas carried in their own day with merchants themselves. But that they took up the subject at all shows their sensitivity to a psychological problem of no little concern to the society they were trying to address.[9]

[9] The larger context in which these ideas are to be seen has been sketched out by Albert O. Hirschman, *The Passions and the Interests: Political Arguments for Capitalism Before Its Triumph* (Princeton, 1977).

Without a full-scale theory of a capitalist economy the entrepreneur could not buttress his case for the defense of private wealth by claiming to have a vital role in a higher scheme of things. He could take some solace, however, in the explicit recognition of his importance to the well-being of the state and of society in general. By the beginning of the fifteenth century it was a commonplace that trade was the lifeblood of the state. Official spokesmen defending the city's cause abroad considered trade as one of its great achievements, bringing as much honor to the state as military power; and thinkers like Alberti were only too ready to admit the obvious—that trade and industry brought the city wealth and created employment. In the amplified context of the early fifteenth-century civic world, therefore, the merchant could claim a certain dignity, and many upper-class Florentines who looked down their noses at the humble crafts and vulgar retail trade were quick to put the international merchant in a different category.[10] It was also a commonplace—though never a theorem worked out in any of its implications or an argument developed for extravagant living—that the spending of money had considerable social benefits. We have already observed that the city fathers in the 1420s recognized how so much of the money they appropriated for military expenditures ended up in the pockets of artisans and tradesmen. One of the arguments made for the legislation devised at the end of the fifteenth century to encourage building by granting tax breaks was that "a great treasure would thereby be released, with the money changing hands six times a day throughout the whole city, so that the country would be restored and the poor would find gainful employment, a good thing for everyone and for the state, and an honor to the city."[11]

In the fifteenth century the rich man felt a little less doubtful about his moral position, somewhat enheartened by a new notion of wealth, and considerably more confident in his social and civic status, and he began to relax the social and moral restraints about spending too conspicuously. Instead of "don't spend," the advice tended to be "don't spend more than you can afford"—an economic, not a moral, imperative. The very word for *savings*, with all the force of the middle-class's system of values behind it, became redefined, losing its passive connotation of hoarding and coming to mean active investment in possessions, including even household furnishings (*masserizia*).[12] Alberti (echoed by Rucellai) can only prescribe moderation

[10] A subject discussed by Lauro Martines, *The Social World of the Florentine Humanists, 1390–1460* (Princeton, 1963), pp. 30–34.

[11] Domenico di Roberto Cecchi, *Riforma sancta et pretiosa . . . per conservatione della città di Firenze et pel ben comune . . .* (Florence, 1496/97), p. 23. (now reprinted in Umberto Mazzone, *"El buon governo." Un progetto di riforma generale nella Firenze savonaroliana* [Florence, 1978], p. 191).

[12] For example, the advice of Gino Capponi: "regolatevi nelle spese, perché dallo spendere più che non si può ne nasce cose molte nocive"; Gianfranco Folena, ed.,

in this kind of spending—but after a good deal of thrashing about he is none too clear about where the line is to be drawn. Meanwhile, more and more men opened accounts in their books for *masserizia* alone. Cosimo de' Medici (according to Vespasiano da Bisticci) thought that no good could come from any attempt to disguise one's wealth—except at the tax office. Florentines did indeed become less inhibited in their spending, more conspicuous in their consumption; today we celebrate their enthusiastic accumulation of luxury objects in our devotion to the Renaissance of the arts. When Guicciardini, in the early sixteenth century, looked around and saw all this spending, he recognized that although "the people of Florence are generally poor, our style of living is such that everyone wants very much to be rich."[13] Savonarola railed against the acquisitive spirit that had come over the Florentines, whereas Machiavelli, with cynical resignation, chalked it up to the inherent nature of man, which could perhaps be contained but not essentially changed. Doubts and fears about wealth lingered on, of course, the Savonarolan episode being a recall of older notions. In general, however, the Renaissance was more confident about wealth: greater pride was taken in it, and certainly there was a new dimension to the enjoyment of it.

Nothing is more telling about Florentines' attitudes toward wealth than the famous Catasto reports of private wealth required for purposes of levying forced loans (or what in effect were taxes) on citizens. That Florentines were prevailed upon to file complete financial statements, including accounts of both real estate and liquid wealth, is surely one of the milestones in the history of public accountability of private wealth for tax purposes, and virtually every historian who has studied Florence uses these documents in grateful appreciation of that fact. The innovation of 1427 marked an improvement over a system of assessments by neighborhood committees based only on personal impressions, an imprecise and disquieting system, to say the least. Now, instead, as one citizen declared with considerable relief to the officials in his assessment report, "It seems to me that today we are finally on the right road, since I see that you want to find out the truth."[14] The Catasto meant that taxes were now determined in the light, as Giovanni Rucellai

---

"*Ricordi* politici e familiari di Gino di Neri Capponi," in *Miscellanea di studi offerta a Armando Balduino e Bianca Bianchi* (Padua, 1962), p. 37. Alberti's use of the word *masserizia* is subjected to an acute linguistic analysis by Daniele Bonamore, *Prolegomeni all'economia politica nella lingua italiana del Quattrocento* (Bologna, 1974), pp. 37–46.

[13] *Ricordi,* ed. Raffaele Spongano (Florence, 1951), no. B19. Guicciardini's polemic against luxury in the "Discorso di Logrogno" is discussed in J.G.A. Pocock, *The Machiavellian Moment* (Princeton, 1975), pp. 135–38.

[14] Quoted in Elio Conti, *I Catasti agrari della repubblica fiorentina e il catasto particellare toscano (secoli XIV–XIX)* (Rome, 1966), p. 64.

said, not in the dark and by opinion.[15] In a real sense Florentines had decided to go public with their private wealth. If they did this because they were more confident about their civic world, they could do it more easily because they were also less worried about the social view of wealth.

No less remarkable as documentation for this new attitude toward wealth are their account books of private administration, the most characteristically Florentine of documents (as distinct from business accounts), setting the city off from all others at the time. Increased possessiveness called for a closer scrutiny of spending, and their account books swell with the details of expenditures, neatly categorized, on the principle that it was somehow useful to have not just a balance sheet of one's net worth but also the total picture of a lifetime's accumulation of expenditures. Any number of private account books will show at a glance just how much its writer spent throughout his entire life for food, clothing, household goods, and other personal items without yielding the slightest clue where the money came from. For purposes of their permanent records what they did with their money was clearly more important than how they made it—more honorable and more satisfying, as Giovanni Rucellai put it. The getting of money was nothing new in Florence, but something was new with respect to the spending of it.

The Taste for Building

At the center of the humanist justification of the social value of wealth was the concept of magnificence, the visual expression of a man's inherent worth that gained him respect, friendship, and authority. Magnificence was a public concept expressed in display—in elaborate ceremony and in possessions, above all, buildings. As enduring private monuments that adorned public space, buildings assured the fame that great men seek. "Since all agree that we should endeavor to leave a reputation behind us, not only for our wisdom but our power too," asserts Alberti, "for this reason we erect great structures, that our posterity may suppose us to have been great persons." Once the building became the measure of the man, its construction became a moral act. For Alberti "the magnificence of a building should be adapted to the dignity of the owner"; Palmieri warned that "he who would want . . . to build a house resembling the magnificent ones of noble citizens would deserve blame if first he has not reached or excelled their virtue." This theme could be played in a Christian mode as well, as it was when the Augustinian canon Timoteo Maffei came to the defense of what seemed to many to be the

[15] Giovanni Rucellai, *Il zibaldone quaresimale*, ed. Alessandro Perosa (London, 1960), p. 9.

extravagant building activities of Cosimo de' Medici. Taking up Saint Thomas's notion of magnificence as virtue Maffei made the point that a building—he had in mind the Badia at Fiesole, subsidized by Cosimo—was the material evidence for the quality of its builder and a worthy example for others to follow. As the Duke of Milan was told in a report from his Florentine correspondent on the newly built Medici palace, "Because of the magnanimity and greatness that you have, you too would want to do something worthy—and not only equal this but surpass it if that were possible."[16]

This rationale for building was not just so much rhetoric. Building was widely regarded as the mark of the man, worthy of mention in any biographical assessment. Hardly anyone writing about Cosimo de' Medici failed to mention his building. Giovanni Rucellai, himself no mean builder, considered all of Cosimo's building "worthy of a crowned king," and it was the only thing a much simpler man, the money-changer and scribe Bese Ardinghelli, commented on when he briefly noted Cosimo's death in his book of memoranda.[17] Fame came to Filippo Strozzi almost as soon as work began on his great palace. No one less than the duke of Ferrara sought plans and details of the building, and at home and abroad the project loomed as a monument to a man and his family. Even a modest shopkeeper like Luca Landucci, viewing construction from his shop across the street, could see that the Strozzi palace was something obviously destined to last almost an eternity.[18]

The argument that fame could be achieved through building made a great deal of sense to Florentines and to upper-class Italians everywhere. Unlike the feudal elites of northern Europe, they lived in cities, where there was a public to whom they could display their status with appropriate monuments; and with ruins all around to remind them of the grandeur that had been Rome's, they had a model to follow in their desire to make their mark on the future. Inasmuch as the new architecture of the Renaissance consciously imitated that of Rome, style itself became an important element of the immortality these men sought in their buildings.

To assure that immortality, construction could be timed in harmony with the cosmic order. Alberti insists on the importance of astrology in determining the day when building was to get underway (II, xiii). Marsilio

[16] Rab Hatfield, "Some Unknown Descriptions of the Medici Palace in 1459," *Art Bulletin*, 52 (1970), 233. The Alberti and Palmieri remarks are cited in Richard A. Goldthwaite, "The Florentine Palace as Domestic Architecture," *American Historical Review*, 77 (1972), 990. For the idea of magnificence in architecture see A. D. Fraser Jenkins, "Cosimo de' Medici's Patronage of Architecture and the Theory of Magnificence," *Journal of the Warburg and Courtauld Institutes*, 33 (1970), 162–70.

[17] BNF, Tordi 2, fols. 147v–48r.

[18] F. W. Kent, "*Più superba de quella de Lorenzo*: Courtly and Family Interest in the Building of Filippo Strozzi's Palace," *Renaissance Quarterly*, 30 (1977), 311–23.

Ficino and the bishop were among the astrologers who advised Filippo Strozzi to begin filling in the newly dug foundations of his palace on 6 August 1489 and to start actual construction two weeks later. The astrologers consulted by Duke Alessandro de' Medici in 1534 to determine the day when the foundation stone for the Fortezza da Basso was to be laid agreed on the month of July but had some differences over the actual day, and so one of the Duke's advisors, the bishop of Assisi, sent the astrological diagram (made by the provincial of the Carmelites) to Francesco Guicciardini in Bologna to get the opinion of astrologers there. Then, on the day that was finally decided upon, the astrologers kept the assembled crowd waiting until they determined that the right moment had finally arrived for the first foundation stones to be put into place.

Under the circumstances the foundation ceremony was an appropriately solemn event. Filippo Strozzi himself was the first to pick up the shovel to fill the foundations of his palace, and he tossed in a commemorative medal made for the occasion with a portrait of himself on one side and his personal device on the other. A chance passer-by (who made a memorandum of the event) was invited to take a turn at the shovel and throw in a coin. He was so excited that he rushed home to get his small children, and he had his son throw in a coin along with some flowers to impress on the boy the importance of the occasion. Meanwhile, masses were being said in several places around town. The entire community of Santo Spirito and the construction staff were on hand when they began filling in the foundations of the new sacristy on 3 December 1489, and amidst burning incense the site was blessed with holy water. At the Fortezza a mass was said at the site, and then two marble stones commemorating the bishop of Assisi and the duke were set into place and three medals commemorating the bishop, the duke, and the pope tossed in. A medal was also cast to be thrown into the new foundations of the Uffizi at the beginning of construction there in 1560.[19]

"I think," wrote Giovanni Rucellai, "I have given myself more honor, and my soul more satisfaction, by having spent money than by having earned it above all with regard to the building I have done." He—like Filippo Strozzi, Giovanni Bartolini, Giuliano Da Gagliano, and others whose accounts have been used for this study—probably kept careful track of what he spent for construction so that he could see, quite literally at a glance, exactly what the record of spending was. Da Gagliano even isolated those expenditures that

[19] Richard A. Goldthwaite, "The Building of the Strozzi Palace: The Construction Industry in Renaissance Florence," *Studies in Medieval and Renaissance History*, 10 (1973), 113–14; J. R. Hale, "The End of Florentine Liberty: The Fortezza da Basso," in *Florentine Studies: Politics and Society in Renaissance Florence*, ed. Nicolai Rubinstein (London, 1968), pp. 518–20 (with an illustration of the astrological diagram); Umberto Dorini, "Come sorse la fabbrica degli Uffizi," *Rivista storica degli archivi toscani*, 5 (1933), 21; S. Spirito 128, fol. 105r.

went for the facade of his palace and so had a separate accounting of just what the public presence alone of his project had cost. Benino de' Benini, the hospital manager at San Paolo, kept a cumulative account of all the money he spent over almost half a century in rebuilding the property of that complex. Furthermore, in all the vast paperwork of accounts and memoranda he generated during his long tenure the only note Benini made about the eight-year period when he was concurrently manager of the much larger and more prestigious hospital of Santa Maria Nuova, perhaps the biggest administrative job in town, was a list of all the building undertaken there under his supervision.[20]

Just to make sure that a building brought the builder the fame he sought he might put his signature into the very fabric for all to see. One trick was to adapt a motif from the family arms to the decoration of capitals, a practice that has no known precedent anywhere in the history of architectural decoration.[21] Capitals abound with such conceits as the balls of the Medici (in the church at Bosco ai Frati, perhaps the earliest example) and the crossed chains of the Alberti (in their loggia in Via de' Benci), the dolphins of the Pandolfini and the Pazzi, the poppy of the Bartolini, the rose of the Ricasoli, and the griffin of the Rustici, all in courtyards of town houses.[22] Bartolini also worked his family's poppy into the frieze along the string line of his palace at Santa Trinita and inscribed his motto over the Via Porta Rossa entrance. The personal device of Giovanni Rucellai, the sails of fortune, run all along the front of his palace, and they appear also on the facade he financed at Santa Maria Novella. Giuliano Gondi had his personal device put into the step ends of the staircase of his palace. None of the builders, however, was quite as exuberant as Filippo Strozzi in stamping personal marks all over his building. He did it discreetly and in good taste, and they do not overwhelm one, but the Strozzi crescents are nevertheless there, carved into every appropriate space on Filippo's palace: the spandrels of the windows, the metal lanterns and standards on the facade, the bases of the corbels inside—and these interior corbels, among the most richly carved in the city, are also replete with his personal insignias of the sheep and the falcon. Strozzi did not go so far as to inscribe his palace, but he had less modesty when he rebuilt the rural oratory at Lecceto, where the visitor is immediately overwhelmed by Filippo's name incised in greatly oversized letters on the entablature above the main altar. Matteo Palmieri went so far as to mount a bust of himself on the

[20] Richard A. Goldthwaite and W. R. Rearick, "Michelozzo and the Ospedale di San Paolo in Florence," *Flor. Mitt.*, 21 (1977), 269–71.

[21] Howard Saalman, "The Authorship of the Pazzi Palace," *Art Bulletin*, 46 (1964), 391–92.

[22] Some of these are illustrated in Leonardo Ginori Lisci, *I palazzi di Firenze nella storia e nell'arte* (Florence, 1972), I, 50–51.

facade of his house—which calls to mind his comment about the moral quality of a building as the expression of its builder.[23] The builder of the hospital of San Paolo was also commemorated by portraits in two terracotta medallions on the great loggia overlooking the square of Santa Maria Novella. And across that square, and high above it, written across the facade of the church, is the name of Giovanni Rucellai, so prominent that it is almost legible from the hillsides on the other side of the river overlooking the city.

Innumerable other builders contented themselves more modestly by simply attaching a shield bearing their family arms to whatever they built, whether for themselves or for the church. Their demand must have assured a brisk business for the sculptors who produced the great number of these items in stone and terracotta that still adorn every nook and cranny of the city. Saint Antonino took it for granted that private patronage for the building of new churches was a kind of publicity-seeking and pleaded instead for the anonymity of donations for repairs of existing structures; and Savonarola scolded these builders because he could not get them to give 10 florins to the poor, whereas if he asked them to pay 100 florins for a chapel in San Marco they would do it just to display their family arms—"for your honor, not for the honor of God."[24] The clergy's outrage, however, no longer counted for much in dampening all this egotistical enthusiasm for building. When Castello Quaratesi was told he could not have his arms displayed on the proposed new facade for Santa Croce he simply withdrew his support for the project and founded his own church. There is no other city in Europe where buildings identify their builders so conspicuously and in such a variety of ways.

Florentines were no less modest abroad. When in 1462 a Florentine broker in Geneva, obviously trying to get a little work for himself, approached Piero de' Medici about sponsoring some kind of building project in one of the city's churches, he pointed out that, whereas the arms of all the other Florentine merchants in the city were to be seen in the churches, there was no mark of the Medici presence, although they had been established longer than anyone else and had made the greatest profits there.[25] Nor were Florentines outdone by any other urban elite in Europe in putting their arms on other objects, such as furniture, silverware, and ceramics. In Venice—to make once again that inevitable comparison—one has to look long and hard

[23] Irving Lavin, "On the Sources and Meaning of the Renaissance Portrait Bust," *Art Quarterly*, 33 (1970), 209, where it is suggested (without, however, any evidence) that this may have been done by other builders as well.

[24] Cited by Marino Ciardini, *I banchieri ebrei in Firenze nel secolo XV e il Monte di Pietà fondato da Girolamo Savonarola* (Borgo San Lorenzo, 1907), pp. 95–96. For Saint Antonino see Fraser Jenkins, "Magnificence," p. 163.

[25] Jean-François Bergier, *Genève et l'économie européenne de la Renaissance* (Paris, 1963), p. 284.

to find anything, be it a building or a plate, with any patrician's coat of arms. Indeed, the Florentines were hardly outdone by the later excesses of the baroque—or by the gaucherie of the nouveau riche in our own time.

With all the signs of ownership embedded in its fabric, a palace was marked for all time, and the testaments of many builders show that in fact this is what they had in mind. Despite the nearly universal practice of partible inheritance these men were nevertheless concerned that their palaces remain forever in the hands of their descendants. Giovanni Bartolini (who died in 1544) left his palace, stamped with his family's coat of arms and boldly inscribed with his personal motto, to one of his brothers, or, should his line become extinct, to the line of a second brother, or, on the extinction of that line, to the oldest male of the next nearest line. Filippo Strozzi, who died in 1491, when his great palace was barely begun, made careful provision for its completion and then, desperately trying to anticipate all genealogical eventualities, elaborated in tedious detail the procedures for the inheritance of the building so that it would never pass out of Strozzi hands. Giovanni Rucellai made the same point with more economy but greater force when he stipulated that his palace never even be rented to anyone else and that, whatever happened to his family, it was under no circumstances to become the residence of any other Florentine family. On the extinction of the Rucellai it was to pass to the commune for the residence of a foreign ambassador or perhaps (more appropriately?) even a foreign prince—provided, of course, that he was not Florentine or of Florentine origin. Even without these testamentary bonds a family residence, it seems, could not be sold by its owner without granting relatives the first option to buy—as Lorenzo Verrazzano found out, in 1533, when he put up for sale his half of the Gianni palace, which he had inherited from his sister (who had married a Gianni).[26]

The monumental family palace decked out with all the evidence of its ownership and legally projected to be forever a family possession became the preeminent symbol of status for the patrician. In contrast, to judge from testamentary preoccupations, the villa, often associated with the family's indistinct origin in its rural past, did not weigh so heavily on the family conscience. Francesco Sassetti was explicit in giving his sons permission to sell his great villa at Montughi in the event it became too costly. It was, in short, the urban residence alone that really mattered.[27]

[26] For Strozzi and Rucellai the references are cited in Goldthwaite, "Florentine Palace," pp. 991–92; the Bartolini will, dated 3 July 1538, is in the Archivio Bartolini Salimbeni, Villa di Collina (Vicchio di Mugello). Verrazzano's one-month notice to the three sons of Francesco di Giovanni Gianni, who occupied the other half of his palace, is in ASF, Carte Gianni, filza 60/246.

[27] Sassetti's last will and testament is discussed in A. Warburg, "Francesco Sassettis letzwillige Verfügung," in his *Gesammelte Schriften*, I (Leipzig, 1932), 143.

In an earlier epoch, town houses of the rich were in themselves not very conspicuous. A family's presence in the city was more apparent from the concentration of its various households in a particular section of the city, perhaps clustered around the remains of a great tower or in the vicinity of a family loggia. The house itself counted for little. However large, it was lost in the anonymity of its architecture and the multiplicity of its functions—like the home of Alessandro di Ser Filippo Borromei, one of the half dozen or so wealthiest men in the city at the beginning of the fifteenth century, which he described as a palace but much of which was rented out, including five shops.[28] Moreover, mobility of a household from one home to another was certainly not unknown. In 1394 Giovanni Morelli, for example, changed his residence from one section of the city to another in order to get a better break in his tax assessments, at the time made by one's neighbors (this was before the institution of the impersonal procedures associated with the Catasto of 1427). In Alberti's dialogue on the family, one of the participants, Giannozzo, considered this moving around from one house to another serious enough to hold forth on the subject, insisting that for practical as well as spiritual reasons it was better that the family be permanently established in one house. And establishing their families in one house was precisely what many wealthy men at the time were trying to do.[29]

"A noble house in the city," commented Michelangelo after over a century of palace-building by his countrymen, "brings considerable honor, being more visible than all one's possessions." He saw no surer way of establishing the status of his family, perhaps the greatest ambition of his spectacular career, than by building a palace—"because (he mistakenly, if not deceitfully, boasted) we are citizens descended from the noblest of lines." Sending money to Florence in order to get his family back on its feet, he instructed his brother first to buy an appropriate house and then to think about investing in other property.[30] Looking over the palace scene in the seventeenth century, Ferdinando Del Migliore, in his *Firenze città nobilissima illustrata* (1684), concluded that in Florence, like in ancient Rome, it must have been because ownership of a building in the city was the requisite for citizenship that her noble citizens competed with one another in building veritable palaces, not mere houses.

The quantity of all this building is not unrelated to the emergence of a new architectural style. Quantity never in itself assures quality, but zeal for building sometimes inspires new ideas about architecture, especially when new buildings

[28] Catasto 81, fol. 523.

[29] Giovanni di Pagolo Morelli, *Ricordi*, ed. Vittore Branca (Florence, 1956), pp. 338–40; Leon Battista Alberti, *I primi tre libri della famiglia*, ed. F. C. Pellegrini (Florence, 1946), p. 288.

[30] Cited in Ugo Procacci, ed., *La casa Buonarroti a Firenze* (Florence, 1965), p. 6.

are being put up to establish the public presence of important men and institutions, whether merchants and monastic orders in Florence or banks and corporations in New York City, rather than to satisfy mere functional needs. Florence was already the scene of lively competition among men in business and politics and among rival institutions within the church that were vying for support, and building became another way of asserting presence in the public arena. In rejecting Brunelleschi's plan for his palace, Cosimo de' Medici (unlike his architect) presumably recognized that there was, however, an upper limit to what society would allow a private person to have, although the house he finally got certainly exalted his family above all the others. And Filippo Strozzi at the end of the century did not upstage the Medici without worrying about it (if we are to believe his son). Churchmen-builders also had a sense of what their colleagues were doing, like the Dominican Observants, who no sooner had papal approval for their reform movement within the Dominican Order (in 1421) than they organized a building committee at Santa Maria Novella to keep up with what was going on at other churches. When this is the spirit in which building is initiated, any innovation in style is likely to generate its own demand. Modernization for its own sake thus becomes a factor in the complex formula explaining the forces that converge in the marketplace to get new buildings built.

The Knowledge of Architecture

While intellectuals worked out a rationale for building, many more ordinary citizens learned about architecture by participating directly in the management of construction projects, not only in the private sphere but in the public one, as well. The characteristic institution that involved them in this activity was the *opera*—the works, or building, committee. Corporate bodies of medieval urban society—guilds, confraternities, the commune itself—normally set up such committees from their membership to supervise new construction; if the committee was also charged with the financing of construction, it could evolve into an autonomous body with its own financial resources that remained in existence after completion of work to maintain the building and administer its property. The permanent, autonomous building committee was a common institution in Florence. The commune traditionally went about putting up its buildings by setting up committees and assigning control over them to one of the major guilds. The parish normally had its own committee, and—what seems to be a more marked custom in Florence than elsewhere—even monastic establishments had recourse to lay building committees to broaden the basis of support for their construction projects. Members of these committees gained considerable experience in building practice, and with the great amount of building undertaken in Florence in the hands of such committees, opportunities for service were open to a large number of men.

The city's oldest and most prestigious monument, the baptistry, had long been in the care of a committee chosen by the Calimala, the oldest of the upper-class guilds; at the end of the thirteenth century this guild took over the additional responsibility for new construction at Santa Croce, partly subsidized by the commune. Although during the early stages of construction of the new cathedral the commune shared representation on the building committee with the bishop and the chapter, eventually, in the 1320s, it shifted all responsibility for the works committee to the major guilds collectively; and then in 1331, after the decision was made to enlarge the original plans, it put the committee in the hands of the wool guild alone. With its ongoing operations this workshop had a more or less permanent professional staff, and much other communal construction was assigned to it—for example, the Campanile, the Loggia dei Priori, and the Piazza della Signoria. The cathedral building committee, therefore, became something like a public works board with control over what was in effect a large construction company. The grain market at Orsanmichele, however, was assigned originally to the guild of Por Santa Maria, the fourth of the great upper-class guilds, and later to the Parte Guelfa.

Almost all the building undertaken by the church in the Renaissance was put in the hands of building committees consisting of laymen. The institution facilitated the raising of funds from private sources, and if contributions came also from public revenues, the committee was likely to be set up under formal communal auspices. In 1383 the monks of Santa Trinita requested the commune to name a committee from its parishioners and to authorize it to raise money for their new church. In 1415 the major councils of the commune elected citizens to the committee set up for the rebuilding of San Lorenzo. In 1422 a lay committee was organized to direct new work at Santa Maria Novella. In 1428 a provision set up a works committee for Santo Spirito. In 1445 another provision named four laymen to sit along with two friars from the Santissima Annunziata to oversee construction of the new church and monastic buildings there. In short, the works committee of laymen was a well-developed institution in Florence, one that was normally used to direct the construction of public and ecclesiastical projects. There seem to have been few church projects that were not under the direction of such an authority.

The lay building committee was by no means unique to Florence. It was a characteristic institution of city-states as far back as ancient Greece, where the construction of temples was often put under the supervision of prominent citizens who were not professional builders or artisans in the construction industry. In medieval Europe, however, the lay building committee was less common outside of Italy. Much church property in northern Europe was inextricably tied into the feudal system of proprietory rights, whereas in the towns, the great cathedrals went up under the auspices of the bishop or the chapter, not local lay patriciates (who in many places were explicitly excluded from participation in the enterprise).[31] In Nuremberg, a city in so many respects comparable to Florence, a single official supervised public building. He was, in effect, a bureaucrat with a long tenure—like the patrician Endres Tucher, author of a well-known description of the post in the fifteenth century. The major parish churches of Nuremberg were similarly the responsibility of a single official, who was accountable to the city council. Closer to home, in Venice, public building was supervised by the Salt Office, and the building of the church of San Marco, by a division of the Procuratia. Both of these communal boards had broad administrative responsibilities of which building was just a small part, and neither saw the rapid turnover in personnel so characteristic of Florentine committees. Is it not also indicative of this basic difference between patronage in Florence and Venice that apparently in none of the half-dozen-or-so parish and monastic churches in Venice where the architect Sansovino worked did he have to deal with a lay building committee specifically set up for that purpose?[32]

The building committee opened up patronage to a large number of men. Service on it brought them into active participation in the building process, giving them responsibility for the finished project and practical experience with organizational and technical problems of construction. Those who served conscientiously and had some imagination were likely to be aroused to think more seriously about architecture and to refine their knowledge of it. Furthermore, by the very nature of their task, whether the project was a guild hall, a hospital, or a parish church, these men were compelled to think about architecture in a public context.

The size of a works committee and the tenure of its members (the *operai*) were not fixed and could vary from time to time for any one committee. There were usually three to six seats on a committee, and the term of office was normally at least a year, sometimes longer. Rather than a cash salary, operai customarily enjoyed a remuneration in the form of gifts from the sponsoring organization. The operai of the Innocenti received spices (such as saffron and pepper) and dining utensils (such as bowls, platters, and serving

[31] This is a recurrent theme in the survey of the building history of several cathedrals by Henry Kraus, *Gold Was the Mortar: The Economics of Cathedral Building* (London, 1979).

[32] For Nuremberg see Lon R. Shelby, *Gothic Design Techniques: The Fifteenth-Century Design Booklets of Mathes Roriczer and Hanns Schmuttermayer* (Carbondale, Ill., 1977), pp. 12–13 (and further references indicated there); and for Venice, Deborah Howard, *Jacopo Sansovino: Architecture and Patronage in Renaissance Venice* (New Haven and London, 1975), ch. 4.

baskets). In the years from 1437 to 1444 such presents for one operaio cost about ten lire a year. At Santo Spirito they were each given a goose every year. Committees met only occasionally, perhaps once a week. They generally left the day-by-day direction of building in the hands of a salaried purveyor. The size of any additional staff depended on the nature of the project.

A works committee was the financial agent for the handling of income and disbursements relative to the construction enterprise. Committeemen personally authorized contracts, checked the accounts, and in general watched over the interest of the institution they served. Morever, these men were inevitably drawn into problems of an artistic nature. They frequently had to consult with experts from outside the committee's own workshop about technical and design problems, and not infrequently they found themselves sitting down for discussions with leading artisans in the building trades as well as painters, goldsmiths, and others who had design expertise. Sometimes they could resolve their uncertainties only by sampling a wider range of opinion from their own associates. In 1427 the works committee of the Innocenti called in the consuls of the sponsoring silk guild together with some masons and "many merchants" to get final approval for "a certain design" for their project, and afterwards they celebrated the occasion with a meal for the entire assemblage.[33] In 1478 the Santo Spirito committee called in three foremen from the communal office of the Tower Officials to get cost estimates, and in 1479 they consulted with some of the city's "most knowledgeable and reputable architects" to get advice about the tribune.

Making a decision on whether the principal entrance at Santo Spirito was to have three or four doors was a major problem for that committee. It was thought that Brunelleschi originally planned four doors, although no one was clear about what he had in mind. In 1482, after consulting with four masons, the committee voted for three doors, although two of the five members felt so strongly against this solution that they refused to attend, sending their sons instead so the vote could be unanimous. Although the decision was reconfirmed the next year and a model ordered, doubts lingered; in 1485 the committee sought the outside opinion of five or six citizens on the matter. The problem was not finally resolved, however, until a year later, when the whole question was thrown open to a general assembly of forty-two interested citizens. After listening to arguments on the matter by several leading masons and architects, each guest spoke his own opinion, and then they voted along with the committee, thirty to seventeen, in favor of three doors, although

[33] Innocenti, ser. CXX, 1 (general accounts), fol. 146 (published by Manuel Cardoso Mendes and Giovanni Dallai, "Nuove indagini sullo Spedale degli Innocenti a Firenze," *Commentari*, 17 [1966], doc. 11).

twenty would have preferred to delay a decision until they could see models of each solution.[34]

Through citizen works committees, and the constituency they on occasion appealed to for help, architectural problems were opened up to a large number of men in the upper classes. On the one hand, a committee provided plenty of opportunity for anyone with his own ideas about building to come forward with them, and on the other hand, service on a committee broadened the building experience of many men and brought them into the ambience of architectural ideas. Even men named to a committee without any particular interest in architecture likely gained a certain expertise during their tenures. At Santo Spirito there is a remarkable continuity of men in the two-year tenures, and some members were replaced only on death. The works committee of the Innocenti saw greater turnover, but several members continually reappear.

The works committee of the Innocenti was in fact a group of strong-willed men, if we are to believe Manetti. In his life of Brunelleschi Manetti blames the committee for its interference in construction during Brunelleschi's absence, with the result that wrong decisions were made that the architect was forever having to rectify. Manetti singles out one committeeman (whom out of respect he does not name) as being especially arrogant for not wanting to recognize the exclusive authority of Brunelleschi in settling architectural questions, although this man later repented of his errors when they were pointed out to him by the architect. Vasari picked up this story and, writing a century later, did not hesitate to identify the culprit as Francesco di Francesco Della Luna, a silk merchant and one of the richest men in the city. Della Luna, in fact, as a guild consul when the original decision was made to build, must have been involved in selecting Brunelleschi as architect and going ahead with one of the most innovative designs in the history of architecture. He sat on the building committee from 1427 to 1430 and again from 1435 to 1442, longer than anyone else. His association with the project spans an even longer period of time. His name appears (for unclear reasons) in the building accounts at the beginning of construction in 1419, and from the mid-1430s to 1450 an account was kept open in his name, although most of the activity on it other than purchases of some wood from him are not explained. In addition, Della Luna was occasionally called in for his advice along with other prominent citizens and artisans by the works committee of the cathedral—for decisions about the choir (1435) the latern (1436), and the sacristy (1442)—and in 1438 he served a term on the committee. He must have had some reputation as a man with opinions about architecture to have been remembered by Vasari over a century after his death, although the historiographical tradition that made him into an

[34] S. Spirito 128 (journal and memoranda), fols. 29r, 59r, 80r. On the models see herein, p. 376.

architect was inspired by sheer fantasy. Della Luna's fame, at any rate, has its roots in a situation where members of building committees had their own ideas about architecture and were capable of an aggressive interest in the project they were responsible for.[35]

Another man whose keen eye for architecture has already been noted is Goro Dati. He (along with Della Luna) was consul of the silk guild at the time the decision was made to build the new orphanage of the Innocenti, and he was on the building committee two years later. Moreover, he was singled out by Manetti (in his life of Brunelleschi) as one of the men "of intellect, reputation, and standing" who were in the audience when the first appeal was made for the rebuilding of the church and monastery of Santo Spirito. The nature of Dati's involvement with these two projects is uncertain, but his description of Florence (probably written during these years, in the mid-1420s) reveals something of the architectural sensibilities he could bring to bear on a decision to be made by a works committee.[36]

There were probably other men like Dati and Della Luna who had more than a passing interest in architecture. Cosimo de' Medici is the only one we know much about, not only because his patronage was more extensive, but also because his prominence in the political life of the city assured the kind of documentation lacking for most other men. As the city's biggest private builder Cosimo undoubtedly had a considerable interest in what he was paying for, although it would be going too far to call him an amateur architect. His biographer, Vespasiano, tells us that Cosimo followed closely the building of all his projects and that many men came to get his advice about what they were building. In the laudatory poem by Giovanni Avogrado we are shown a scene in which Cosimo is walking around the site of the Badia talking about what he wanted here and there while his mason trailed along, taking everything down in detailed notes. When Cosimo inspected Manetti's model for the crossing of San Lorenzo he made many critical observations, including some of a technical nature.[37]

The preeminent patrician-architect of the fifteenth century was Cosimo's grandson, Lorenzo the Magnificent. A man of considerable literary talent, Lorenzo's artistic sensibilities were also attuned to architecture. He was, for example, interested enough in Federigo da Montefeltro's new palace in Urbino that he asked the Florentine architect Baccio Pontelli to send him detailed plans of the building, including measurements and decoration. Lorenzo also had thoughts of his own about architecture, and although he was not the builder that his grandfather had been, he nevertheless got his ideas across

[35] The tradition on Della Luna is assessed by Gilbert, "Guide," p. 37, n. 12.

[36] Ibid.

[37] The evidence is collected by E. H. Gombrich, "The Early Medici as Patrons of Art: A Survey of Primary Sources," in *Italian Renaissance Studies*, ed. E. F. Jacob (New York, 1960), pp. 282–97.

to other builders about what they should be doing by asserting his prerogative as the city's prince-in-disguise. His success at this is particularly well documented toward the end of his life, from about 1485, when we know that he was studying Alberti's treatise on architecture. In that year—no doubt at his own behest—he was delegated by the Parte Guelfa and the office of The Ten to take responsibility for the design of the new church of Santa Maria delle Carceri, which was to be built in Prato in commemoration of a miracle that had occurred the preceding year. He made at least two trips to Prato to look over the site, and he instructed the local works committee to send proposals to him in Florence, from which he selected the model of Giuliano da Sangallo. Shortly thereafter Lorenzo began to involve himself actively in the building of the new sacristy at Santo Spirito. He joined the works committee, and thereafter they deferred to his judgment in matters of design. Again, Sangallo was his choice, and the committee was attentive in seeing that the architect follow his wishes. It was presumably on the basis of an idea by Lorenzo that Sangallo worked out the design for the villa at Poggio a Caiano; his hand has also been seen in the Palazzo Strozzi, where, according to the builder's son, construction got underway (in 1489) only after much subtle maneuvering to bring Lorenzo around to supporting a gigantic private project that savored of the spirit of challenge to his own patronage. He actually submitted an entry in the 1491 competition for a new facade for the cathedral. Lorenzo's interest in architecture was recognized abroad by the duke of Calabria and Ferdinand II of Naples, each of whom requested his help in selecting an architect for a new residence; the two architects he recommended —Giuliano da Maiano and Sangallo, respectively—submitted innovative designs that were perhaps inspired by Lorenzo himself. There were obviously political objectives to Lorenzo's architectural policy—to enhance the beauty of the city at home and its prestige as an art center abroad—but he shaped that policy to open an outlet for his own architectural imagination.[38]

The passion for building and the interest in architecture were by no means confined to Florence. It is one of the notable features of Italian Renaissance culture that architecture began to arouse the interest of the wealthy and the powerful—popes, princes, and, eventually (following the Florentines), local patriciates everywhere. Once the political situation stabilized and the rulers of Italy's many states felt reasonably secure in the precarious but effective balance of power that had been reached in the mid-fifteenth century, they sought legitimization and fulfillment of their authority in the magnificence of

[38] Mario Martelli, "I pensieri architettonici del Magnifico," *Commentari*, 17 (1966), 107–11; Gombrich, "Early Medici," pp. 304–11. Other nonprofessional designers who have been turned up in the scholarly literature include Antonio di Migliorino Guidotti (Brenda Preyer, "The Rucellai Loggia," *Flor. Mitt.*, 21 [1977], 194) and Giovanni di Ser Paolo (Hannelore Glasser, "The Litigation Concerning Luca Della Robbia's Federighi Tomb," *Flor. Mitt.*, 14 [1969], 15–16.

buildings, in line with the thinking of the humanists, who by this time were beginning to influence the style of government. The projects that were undertaken throughout Italy in the second half of the century are too numerous and too familiar to need enumeration here. Something of the satisfaction they gave their sponsors can be felt in the lengthy and careful description by Pius II of the rebuilding of his native town of Pienza. Pius, however, never makes the slightest suggestion that he himself had had anything to do with the planning of it all, except in his insistence that the cathedral be laid out like a hall church of the type he had admired during his stay in Germany. He simply turned things over to his architect, who, after everything was finished, was called into the papal presence, thanked, and rewarded. Other princes are thought to have entered more actively and creatively into the planning of their building programs. Federigo da Montefeltro had strong views about what he wanted in putting up his great palace in Urbino, and he was probably as much responsible for its design as the architect. In letters Lodovico Gonzaga wrote to his architect, Luca Fancelli, he shows himself well versed in technical matters of construction, absorbed in the progress of building, and ready to criticize what he did not like. Ercole d'Este was interested enough in architecture to direct enquiries into the new palace he had heard was being built in Florence by Filippo Strozzi, and he followed all the construction he sponsored at Ferrara with knowledgeable and lively interest. Ercole read Alberti's treatise before building his own palace in Ferrara, and he himself may have made architectural drawings.[39]

It was, after all, for men like these, the enlightened patrons, and not the mason-architects, that Alberti wrote his treatise. His close friendship with some of the leading artists in Florence as well as his own contacts in upper-class society gave him a sense of the audience available for the kind of highly theoretical work on the subject he set out to write about. The more practical-minded Filarete also understood the implications of the widespread enthusiasm for architecture in his day: a great building in his eyes was not just the creation of an artist but (to use his metaphor) the child born of the true marriage between architect and patron. Perhaps more buildings in Florence than we suspect could claim such a lineage.

The amateur architect was one of the characteristic personages in Renaissance society. Given the humanist notion of magnificence, the public nature of architecture for urban elites, and the fascination of the times with the classical models they found all around them, it is no wonder that architecture

[39] Ludwig H. Heydenreich, "Federigo da Montefeltro as a Building Patron," in *Studies in Renaissance and Baroque Art Presented to Anthony Blunt on His 60th Birthday* (London and New York, 1967), pp. 1–6; Clifford M. Brown, "Luca Fancelli in Mantua: A Checklist of His 185 Letters to the Gonzaga," *Flor. Mitt.*, 16 (1972), 155; Charles M. Rosenberg. "The Erculean Addition to Ferrara: Contemporary Reactions and Pragmatic Considerations," *The Early Renaissance, Acta*, 5 (1978), 51–53.

had a special meaning to upper-class patrons in a way that painting and sculpture did not. It was more accessible to the amateur, both from the point of view of his knowledge about it, derived from classical prototypes, and from the point of view of his ability to express his ideas about it, either in drawings and sketches, however rough, or in instructions to his builders during actual execution. If architecture could therefore be "practiced" by the amateur without any contaminating involvement in the lowly crafts, it was also the first of the fine arts to gain full intellectual respectability by the standards of the time: it presupposed knowledge of the classical past and it early gained a mature theoretical formulation. We know that patrons like Lorenzo the Magnificent and Ercole d'Este read Alberti, whereas it is not at all certain that architects did. Moreover, the patron obviously had a practical interest in architecture, whether he was a prince overseeing the construction of military installations that needed to meet highly technical requirements or a patrician planning the house in which he was to reside. And, finally, because buildings were expensive, took time to construct, and could not be contracted out, the patron, having a vital interest in watching the use of his resources in any major construction he undertook, was in a real sense actively involved in the building process if in no other way than watching the accounts—and that involvement could easily mean creative interference in the artistic execution from the moment he looked over the first designs submitted to him by his architect. This amateur interest in architecture on the part of the upper classes was one of the reasons the architect was able to put his social status on a securer ground earlier than other kinds of artists, but it also led to artistic problems in his working relation with his patron that hardly bothered the painter and sculptor and that still continue to plague the architect.

The Need for Space

Most private construction in Florence was undertaken to remodel or build anew chapel areas in churches and residences. A prominent element of display characterized both of these undertakings. Chapels, rather than being tucked away within one's house for private use, as they were to be in a later epoch, were carved out of public space inside churches; and the upper-class home got a noble and formidably massive facade that decisively cut off the family from the public world but at the same time made it clear to everyone just who was inside. Since buildings of both kinds, moreover, had a utilitarian function in the lives of their owners, the enlargement of ecclesiastical and domestic spaces inevitably affected their owners' life-style—if the enlargement of space was itself not the result of a desire to change that style. Private construction, in other words, is an important fact in the social history of the city; any attempt to explain the motives for building must eventually deal with the large social question of how men organized their lives in space or, rather, how they organized space to live the kind of lives they wanted.

Chapels did not first appear in Florence during the Renaissance. They began to proliferate within churches throughout Europe during the thirteenth century to make space for more altars, especially in the churches of the preaching orders, and for private burial. In Florence extra chapels were for the most part confined to the transept of the older churches, until such a surge in demand for them arose in the fifteenth century that, as already observed, most of the city's churches virtually had to be rebuilt to accommodate them. The chapel-lined church became a distinctive local type. Brunelleschi had a decided penchant for this kind of church plan, which he at one point hoped to impose on the cathedral itself. These chapels were places belonging to private persons, not to guilds, confraternities, or other corporate institutions (as in so many other cities). Clearly, in the fifteenth century more men wanted chapels, including many of modest estate, far below the ranks of those generally considered patricians.[40]

A private chapel represented a major contribution by its donor to the fabric of the church and so brought him the benefits of a good work; since most carry the signature of their donors in the form of a family coat of arms and perhaps some other more personal symbols, they also gave their patrons the satisfaction of having a permanent and public record of their generosity. The chapel may also have served as the final resting-place for the builder and his family, and if an endowment had been set up to pay for periodic votive masses, the place, in their view, would continue to bring them real benefits, even after death. There were, therefore, many advantages to be had from a chapel for both the soul and the ego (not to mention the body), and in both this world and the next. Whether the rise in demand for chapels in the Renaissance was the result of a greater importance men attached to any one of these various benefits or whether it was simply a matter of the general affluence that gave greater means for more men to satisfy these traditional feelings is not easy to say.

It is usually assumed that chapels were family places and that the proliferation of them has something to do with what was happening at the moment in the upper-class family. There can hardly be any doubt that men built chapels with their families in mind, but what did they have in mind as the family? How far did they reach outwards through the various degrees of

[40] For some notable examples see Creighton Gilbert, "The Patron of Starnina's Frescoes," in *Studies in Late Medieval and Renaissance Painting in Honor of Millard Meiss*, ed. Irving Lavin and John Plummer (New York, 1977), I, 185–91; Rab Hatfield, *Botticelli's Uffizi "Adoration": A Study in Pictorial Content* (Princeton, 1976).

consanguinity to gather relatives in one way or another into these sacred places? The larger family, or cognate group, usually had traditional associations with a monastic church in the neighborhood where a common ancestor had established his residence and where his descendants continued to reside. The family in this larger sense, therefore, generally had its burial places in the same church, and it was not unusual that the family members also shared the patronage of a chapel there.

The rebuilding of Santo Spirito after the fire of 1471 was largely financed by the sale of its many chapels, and so provides the material for a case study of the family nature of chapel building.[41] Some of these chapels were clearly purchased by large groups of relatives. Zanobi Biliotti made arrangements for the purchase of a chapel "in the name of the house of all the Biliotti" (after a relative, Giannozzo, who had purchased it for himself alone, was not able to pay for it), and an agreement signed by eleven of them specified the different assessments on each, which varied probably because of the signers' differing relationship to the founder of the patrimony they all shared. In a meeting of all the heads-of-households of the Ridolfi consorteria, also eleven in number and not closely related, the cost of the chapel was simply divided equally among all present. Family agreements to share expenses, however, were not always kept, for the continuing harmony among even close relatives could not be taken for granted. Francesco Petrini, who shared with his brother Andrea half the cost for one of these chapels at Santo Spirito, at one point protested to the building committee that he did not want any trouble with his relatives, Zanobi and the sons of Giovanni Petrini, who were responsible for the other half but who apparently were not keeping their commitments; he went so far as to tell the committee that if his relatives did not want to pay their share the family arms could be taken down and the chapel given to whomever the committee pleased. When the committee looked into the matter the other Petrini registered surprise at this action and asked for time to think about it. Whatever the outcome, it was clear that for this group of relatives purchasing a chapel put a strain on family harmony.

Most chapels at Santo Spirito were financed not by large groups of diverse relatives but by brothers or fathers who considered them investments for their own offspring alone. Although a chapel-builder undoubtedly took pride in confirming his family's prestige by building a chapel in its traditional church or attaching the family coat of arms (rather than a personal insignia) to one in another church, new chapel space probably did not serve any social function for his various relatives outside the immediate household. Many chapels were in effect private burial plots erected in line more with dynastic ambitions to establish a lineage descending from one's self rather than with a wider social

[41] Memoranda of the meetings of the building committee are included in S. Spirito 128.

concern to accommodate other relatives. They were typically designated—for instance, in the will of Filippo Strozzi—for the builder's descendants alone. Even one who had no surviving sons, Francesco Pepi, explicitly left his burial chapel at Cestello for his widow and daughter (if she so desired) without mention of other lines through which the family was to survive. Many of these chapels appear primarily as monuments to their builders, some with conspicuous sarcophagi and highly personal iconographic commemoration in the pictorial or sculptural decoration. The small semicircular chapels at Santo Spirito, however, were designed in such a way that it would have been difficult to set up tomb monuments in them, as the Capponi found out in 1488 when they installed one for their great ancestor Neri. Many chapels, finally, were simply memorial chapels where the builder was not even buried and where the only indication of his personal benefaction was a periodic votive mass (probably financed by an endowment, not by voluntary gifts from remembering relatives). For some men, like Piero di Donato Velluti, who died in 1411 leaving money for the building and maintenance of a chapel in Santo Spirito if he were not to be survived by sons or if they had no male descendants, the chapel was a substitute monument for the dynasty they lacked.

The existence of a traditional family chapel certainly did not preclude the building of another by men who had reasons for wanting one of their own. At San Lorenzo there were several Ginori chapels, although the family was at the time a new one on the scene: the son of the first chapel-builder built one for himself, and his grandson built another. Lodovico Capponi, whose family had bought one of the chapels at Santo Spirito, nevertheless bought (in 1525) and decorated one for himself in another church, Santa Felicita. Likewise, Giovanni de' Bardi, despite the conspicuous and ancient association of his family with Santa Croce, bought a chapel for himself at Santo Spirito, and he left money in his will for the building of another in the church of Cestello—and his nephew and heir founded yet another at the Santissima Annunziata. In fact, almost all of the chapels at Cestello, a new chapel-lined church built at the end of the fifteenth century, were purchased by men whose families were traditionally associated with other places and who regarded their new chapels as a purely private, not a familial, matter.[42]

It therefore cannot be said that in general men built chapels to enhance the corporate sense of the family as a laterally extensive social group. To what extent, in fact, the chapel served any social function at all as a place where relatives assembled for votive masses or other religious ceremonies involving

[42] Alison Luchs, *Cestello, A Cistercian Church of the Florentine Renaissance* (New York, 1977); Francis William Kent, *Household and Lineage in Renaissance Florence: The Family Life of the Capponi, Ginori, and Rucellai* (Princeton, 1977), pp. 103 (Ginori chapel) and 105 (Capponi chapel).

the family remains obscure. Such important social events in the life of the family as baptisms, marriages, and funerals, during which relatives beyond the household are likely to assemble, did not take place in chapels.

Palaces, being residences, had a more precise social function than chapels.[43] The fundamental fact that has to be recognized if we are to understand why men wanted them is their monumentality. The casual tourist roaming the streets of Florence is likely to overlook the immense size of these buildings. They are so beautifully proportioned that their scale is utterly disguised, and they are so numerous that too much about them is simply taken for granted. Monumentality, however, is not just a matter of size. It also consists of architectural design. Decorative facades enhanced the public presence of a building, and the lively interest of builders in them helped refine that consciousness of style we associate with the visual sensibilities Florentines developed in the Renaissance. The monumentality of a palace was also an economic fact. Palaces were obviously built to make a big impression, and the zeal with which men set about doing this is evidenced in what they were prepared to spend on construction. Easily one-third to one-half of the owner's estate could be tied up in his palace. Some builders so strained their resources that they could not complete the job, or so burdened their estate that their heirs sold the building. A few went bankrupt, and although the connection between building and bankruptcy is tenuous, who can say that the capital tied up in construction could not have helped ease the crushing pressures from creditors? Despite all the prohibitions, legal and moral, against alienating a family palace, a surprising number of these buildings, primarily for financial reasons of one kind or another, changed hands within a generation or two of their construction (or purchase).

Despite the great cost of these palaces, the value of the investment was limited to the domestic economy of their owners. If they were not regarded as part of a scheme for the development of urban property to provide rents from shops and apartments, neither did they count for much within the business operations of their owners. Unlike the Venetian palace, which often doubled as a warehouse for its owner's commercial interests, the Florentine palace was not a place of business. Palace-owners with cloth and banking interests preferred to keep their businesses in the few areas where such establishments were traditionally located rather than incorporate them into their homes, even if it meant, as it did for many, paying high rents. When in the later fifteenth century palaces began to go up in Via Maggio, one of the traditional centers for the wool industry, the shops were closed down; by the mid-sixteenth century few remained in the entire Oltrarno quarter of the city. In

[43] For much of what follows on the palace, with more detail on some matters, see Goldthwaite, "Florentine Palace."

his account of the building of his father's palace, Lorenzo Strozzi says that he considered shops a blight on the beauty of a palace, and we can infer that most men shared this view. A man's home served as a place of business only to the limited extent that he worked out of his private study supervising his investments and, if he directed international operations as a merchant and financier, keeping up his correspondence and exerting central accounting control over his far-flung affairs. The structure of the vast Medici enterprise, like many others, thus centered on the study (*scrittoio*) in the Medici palace, but the cloth shops and the bank in Florence where the company dealt more directly with the public were located elsewhere. A palace, therefore, did not figure prominently in the investment portfolio of its owner. Even its rental value as a residence, should its owner ever have to think of that prospect, did not represent much of a return on the capital it took to put up such a structure.

In short, practically all a man got when he built a palace was a house. As a one-family dwelling a palace not only asserted the family's magnificent presence to the public without but also secured for it a greatly enlarged private world within, and its formidable facade marked the clear delineation between the two. It must have been as great a relief for men of the times as it is for us today to escape from the crowded, narrow, crooked streets into the immense open and ordered spaces within one of these palaces. Even the windows, high above the noise and dirt of the street life below, served little more than to permit the penetration of light: within they are too high to permit easily peering out, and in any case they were usually covered not with transparent glass but with translucent, oiled cloth, a feature that evoked comment from northern visitors like Fynes Moryson as late as the end of the sixteenth century.

The fullest implication of the size of the new home a builder moved his family into is to be found inside. What kind of family life was it that was played out in such a large space? The first point to be made in answer to this question is that these palaces are much larger than at first glance they seem to be with respect to the domestic space they actually provide. The inflation of space within represented by the overall size of the building went much beyond merely practical requirements. Under inspection by the modern homebuilder's eye for floor space of actual living area, the typical palace shrinks into something somewhat smaller, albeit still quite large by modern standards —and, for that matter, by standards down to the time they were built. For all the vertical extension of these palaces, there are never more than three main floors, whereas modern standards would allow at least six. Much of the space, moreover, is not fully enclosed. A central area was left open as a courtyard, which penetrated into arcades on the ground and (usually) top floors. What remains are three floors of a single file of connecting rooms around three or four sides of an open core. The palace, in short, was a house that was inflated by pushing it out from the center around a completely private outdoor space. The actual number of rooms for living purposes might number no more than a dozen in even a large palace.

This immense open space within these houses was not crowded with people. The history of the ownership of a palace as it can be traced through tax records, wills, inventories, and accounts reveals that the residents of most numbered no more than a married couple and their children. The household might temporarily expand as sons married and began their own families under the paternal roof, but it contracted when, after the death of the father and the inevitable division of the estate, brothers sooner or later moved out to establish their own homes until the palace remained in the hands of just one of them, once again the residence of one man and his immediate family. Equal division of estates among all sons was normal in fifteenth-century Florence, and the inalienability of a palace did not exempt it from that division. "And in dividing the estate, you, Neri," says Gino Capponi to his son, "take the house in Florence—and don't worry about its value."[44] Most fathers did not leave specific arrangements for assignment of the family residence, but there is no reason to think that eventual division was not anticipated. For practical reasons it might come under the joint ownership of brothers for awhile, and then, invariably, within a few years one brother bought out the others. Men without sons were likely to be more precise about the immediate disposition of their houses. Giovanni Bartolini, who left his estate to one brother and the five sons of another, specifically designated his palace for the brother alone and his equally prestigious urban villa at Gualfonda (no longer standing) for just one of the nephews. The donation of the Pandolfini palace by Giannozzo to his nephew Pandolfo d'Agnolo in 1520 required that it go to Pandolfo alone and then pass to his descendants by primogeniture. In the early fourteenth century, when there were stronger and more enduring economic ties binding relatives together, ownership of the family home was subject to the most complex fractionization; but in the fifteenth century it was normal that the title to a palace be clearly in the name of one man. The Pitti palace, however, was an exception: when it was sold in 1550 to the Medici there were seven parties to the sale, representing no fewer than thirteen Pitti heirs.[45]

Instances of subsequent physical remodeling of palaces into separate quarters to accommodate a division of a household are not unknown, but the standard palace plan of a single series of rooms around an open courtyard

[44] "Ricordi," p. 36.

[45] Francesca Morandini, "Palazzo Pitti, la sua costruzione e i successivi ingrandimenti," *Commentari*, 16 (1965), nos. 1–2, 44, n. 28. The Bartolini will is cited in note 26 to this chapter; the Pandolfini will is in the Carte strozz., ser. II, 116, doc. 2. For specific examples of what happened to the ownership of palaces, see Goldthwaite, "Florentine Palace."

with loggia on the top and bottom floors presented difficulties for a division of rooms. In contrast, the Venetian palace is neatly divisible floor by floor (with mezzanines often inserted between), since it is without the complications brought about by the presence of an open courtyard; on each floor the long central hall down the middle from one end of the house to the other (and sometimes separate internal staircases) provided the further convenience of isolating separate quarters. The Venetian palace was seemingly designed from the outset in anticipation of the household needs of a proliferating family.[46] There are some notable examples of Florentine palaces designed to accommodate more than one household—the Busini, the Strozzi, the Rucellai, the Gondi, the Rustici, the Strozzino—but they depart from the standard plan in having separate apartments within, each with its own entrance from without.

It must have been a memorable day for a palace-builder when he finally moved his family into its new quarters, not least of all because the opening up of so much space for so few people must in itself have been an exhilarating experience. These new homes—even those of such rich men as Filippo Strozzi, who had purchased over a dozen properties to get his building lot, and Giovanni Rucellai, who acquired half a dozen adjacent houses to be incorporated into his own—were much larger than the residences these men had had before. Under the circumstances these palace-builders could not have had much furniture to take with them on moving day, and it probably took some time before they knew what to do with themselves in their newly inflated private world. One thing they could do was to start filling it up with objects of all kinds (more is said about that in the conclusion), but even fifty years after moving into the great Strozzi palace, the family of the builder's son was rattling around in quarters with some of the largest and grandest rooms still completely empty.[47] The owner of a new palace was probably slow in changing his way of life to realize the full potential of the greatly increased space for holding more furnishings, for the more specialized use of its rooms, and for the elaboration of social ceremonies on a larger scale. In the Quattrocento the functional demands on domestic space were still limited.

It is difficult to get much sense of the kind of life the small family group led in its relatively small number of large rooms set into such an immense space. From what one can tell from the slight evidence about the organization of palace interiors, rooms seem not to have been laid out to accommodate

[46] Although James Davis, *A Venetian Family and Its Fortune, 1500–1900: The Donà* (*Memoires of the American Philosophical Society*, 106 [1975]), pp. 2–8, makes the argument that the extended family lived under one roof, the evidence he presents in fact points to a custom no different from that in Florence, i.e., the growth of the household family lasted only as long as a father lived.

[47] Carte strozz., ser. V, 110, fols. 139ff (1542).

complex use of space. Not even the architectural theorists were much concerned with this kind of problem. Although Alberti went beyond Vitruvius by talking about interior arrangements of houses, he says little that reflects the social realities of Florentine upper-class life. For all their interest in practical service arrangements, these Florentine theorists down to Vasari il Giovane show little interest in the function of rooms. On their plans the terms (*sala*, *saletta*, *camera*, and so on) used to designate rooms seem to have more to do with size (or, as in Serlio, with shape) than function. The same terms are used in household inventories, and an analysis of the use of domestic space according to the furnishings recorded in these documents suggests that, with the exception of a dining area and of a bedroom-study combination that constituted the private apartment of the head of the household, most rooms were intended for generalized use. As in an earlier era, beds were still found distributed throughout.

More than one critic has commented on the lack of comfort of these Renaissance interiors, but such an anachronistic sensibility is an outgrowth of the subsequent history of interior decoration. Florentine furniture is notable for its massiveness and the architectural quality of its forms, and both features derive from the function of furniture in the immense spaces it was designed to fill. Characteristic pieces like the credenza, the high-back chair, and the cassapanca were in a sense decorative extensions of a severe architectural context. They were conceived as structures, with no upholstering to compromise their mass, and decoration was taken almost entirely from the architect's vocabulary. Only slowly was the architectonic quality of space decorated away by the evermore ornateness and delicacy of furniture forms and materials and by the accumulation of bibelots—until all sense whatsoever of structure dissolved into the excesses of the rococo and the overstuffed comfort of the nineteenth century.

The palace interior, moreover, was not a theater for an elaborate ritual of domestic life that required a large retinue of servants. The number of servants that show up in the private papers of a rich family in the fifteenth century is much smaller than might be expected in such large houses. A great household like that of Giovanni Rucellai might have half a dozen or so—his staff of four men and four to five women servants (including slaves) comprised stable hands, domestics, and a tutor for his children—but the normal upper-class home had only two or three, although the number increased rapidly in the sixteenth century as rich men settled down in their larger homes.[48] A large portion of the population consisted of servants of one kind of another,

[48] The servant population of Florence at the middle of the sixteenth century is tabulated in Pietro Battara, *La popolazione di Firenze alla metà del '500* (Florence, 1935), pp. 68–70. One hundred fifty households had six or more, 260 households had five or more.

but it was not easy for an employer to keep them at a time when wage rates were generally high and employment opportunities relatively good. Some writers of books of memoranda, at any rate, record a striking turnover of household servants, who often did not stay as long as a year.[49] "Experience shows," says Guicciardini, "and I have seen this to be the case with my own servants—that as soon as they get their fill, or as soon as the master is unable to treat them as generously as he has in the past, they leave him flat."[50] For many heads of households it was more convenient to spend fifty to a hundred florins to buy a female slave. Hardly anyone had more than one slave, however, and she was invariably freed sometime before her death and provided with a degree of financial help. Other than wet nurses, who were lavished with gifts (and who usually lived out), ordinary household servants do not show up in private accounts as much of an expense (for instance, for food and clothing) or in wills as objects of esteem for faithful service. In his treatise on the family, Alberti dismisses servants as inferior persons (else they

[49] For example, Antonio di Leonardo di Rinieri Rustici, a local banker, recorded the following tenures of a female servant in his house (all on a salary of 9 to 11 florins): 15 to 27 Feb. 1415; Mar. to Jul. 1415; Jul. 1415 to Jan. 1416; Jan. 1416 to Jul. 1417 (at this point he bought a slave for f.50 but sold her in 1417 for f.65); Sep. 1417 to Aug. 1418; Aug. to Sep. 1418; Sep. to Oct. 1418; Oct. to Dec. 1418; Dec. 1418 to Mar. 1419; May to Jul. 1419; Jul. 1419 to Jan. 1420; etc. Carte strozz., ser. II, 11 (memoranda of Rustici, 1412–36).

The notary Andrea di Cristofano Nacchianti recorded less of a turnover than Rustici but occasionally added some explanations: one woman came to work in Mar. 1478 but left in Nov. because she did not like the work; one who came in Nov. 1481 stayed on the job until 1487; one came in May 1487 and left in Jun. 1491 to work for someone else; her replacement came in Jun. but left in Dec. when caught robbing; in Feb. 1492 he made a contract with a mother to have her daughter as a servant for eight years (to be paid at the end of the period); subsequently other women served from May to Oct. 1495; Dec. 1495 to May 1498; Sep. to Dec. 1498 (at which point a previous employee returned for a few months); May 1500 to Jan. 1501. The salaries ranged between 7 and 8 florins. Innocenti, ser. CXLIV, 633 (accounts of Nacchianti, 1471–1508).

Things were no better with the rich banker Bartolomeo di Tommaso Sassetti, who recorded the following tenures: in Mar. 1473 a woman came to work but left the same day; her successor stayed only a few days; others were employed from Apr. to Jul. 1473; May to Oct. 1473; Oct. to Dec. 1473; Nov. 1473 to Aug. 1474; Apr. to May 1474; May to Jun. 1474; Jul. to Dec. 1474; Aug. to Sep. 1474; Dec. 1474 to Jan. 1475; Jan. to May 1475 (this one was fired "because she was a thief"); Aug. to Nov. 1475; 2 days in Dec. 1475; a few more days in Dec. for her successor; Dec. 1475 to Jun. 1476; Jan. to Mar. 1477 (and this one returned in Jun. to stay until Feb. 1478). Sassetti paid salaries ranging from 7 to 9 florins. Carte strozz., ser. V, 1750 (ledger of Sassetti, 1471–77).

The examples could be multiplied from many other household accounts. Note that all the salaries of these servants were quoted as florins per year.

[50] *Maxims and Reflections of a Renaissance Statesman*, trans. Mario Domandi (New York, 1965), p. 42.

would be more gainfully employed), and when, at the beginning of the fourth book, one appears on the scene, he enters as an object of comic relief. Nor were servants so prominent in the lives of the upper classes as to make much of an appearance in the imaginative literature of the period. Servants had little presence in Florentine life as faithful and beloved family retainers or as players in an elaborate household ritual of service and ceremony.

It has been said that the sympathetic adjustment of the psyche to the precisely ordered spatiality within these houses resulted in a more rational and more modern mentality in accord with the so-called humanistic spirit of the Renaissance. However that may be, the new spatial world of domestic life in its very vastness and emptiness challenged the inhabitants to fill it up and thus to define its uses. In this sense simply the availability of so much space induced a new life-style. In his adjustment to palace life, therefore, the Florentine went beyond physically setting himself apart from his society. The more space he had to fill up, the more he consumed, and the more conspicuous his consumption became, the greater was the social distance he put between himself and the ranks of ordinary men—a distance that his ancestors probably did not know even though they may have been every bit as wealthy. In other words, these palaces, in opening up a world of private space as an appropriate theater for the exuberance of wealth, set off a kind of social fission, physically and socially isolating their owners and vertically stratifying society.

The palace was not peculiar to Florence. Its development as an architectural form was a notable feature of urban life throughout Italy during the Renaissance, whereas outside of Italy the history of domestic architecture in the early modern period is not written about town houses but about the country seats of landed aristocrats. The great town houses that were built in seventeenth-century Paris were largely hidden from public view, opening on courts walled off from the streets, and many a great French aristocrat who spent lavishly on his country place was satisfied with renting a home in the capital. In England the rich spent extravagantly for remote and secluded country houses and were content to establish their London residences in planned terraces and squares. Only in Italy do individual town houses constitute a good part of the material for the history of architecture. Within that history the Renaissance palace in Florence has a prominent place for its priority in time; it also differed from palaces elsewhere because of the peculiar functional demands made on it as a residence. The way in which Florentine domestic architecture was shaped by the distinctive quality of upper-class life can therefore be put into relief through a comparison of these palaces with the kinds of homes built by elites in other Italian cities.

Venice was the only other city in Italy that had much of a tradition of domestic architecture before the sixteenth century. It was, in fact, the one city in all of Europe where there was an older tradition of palace-building, although the merchant's house was distinctly different from the Florentine palace in both style and function. Venetian palaces were built in a conservative Gothic-Byzantine style that endured to the end of the fifteenth century without showing the individual elaborations in particular buildings that are so characteristic of Florentine palaces. Moreover, the Venetian merchant did not regard his home exclusively as his residence. Warehouses were located on the bottom floor of the grandest of them, and, as has been said, domestic space above, divided vertically by a central corridor and uncomplicated by interior courtyards, could be neatly organized into separate apartments to accommodate more than one household of the family.[51]

In fifteenth-century Genoa, a city of comparable wealth, the patrician residence had no particular architectural identity. Although family groups had a distinct presence in the city because of their concentration in one locality, the only notable architectural features of residential complexes were anonymous towers and porticos of the kind that had long become both stylistically and functionally obsolete in Florence. When Genoese nobles began building sumptuous palaces in the sixteenth century, they did so in the continuing spirit of the collective family. The palaces along the Strada Nuova, one of the most impressive stretches of urban residential architecture in the Renaissance, were put up by only four families still clustering together in the medieval tradition of corporate solidarity; Via Balbi, somewhat later, represented yet another family concentration. Furthermore, many of the most sumptuous of the new palaces erected in the sixteenth century have shops on the street floor, a feature usually rejected by Rubens in his publication of these palaces as not suitable to the nobility of their primary function.[52]

When the urban elites of other Italian cities began to build town houses in the sixteenth century, the houses were on the whole grander than the earlier Florentine Renaissance palace because they had somewhat more complex functions. Palace-building was a particularly notable activity in those places where the regime, whether princely or oligarchic, was heavily weighted in favor of closed aristocracies for whom the family palace was more than a mere residence and a symbol of status. The vast palaces that appeared on the Roman scene were designed to provide a quasi-public space to accommodate the elaborate ceremonial life-style of the papal aristocracy, especially cardinals.

[51] Howard, *Sansovino*, p. 131.

[52] Ennio Poleggi, *Strada nuova: una lottizzazione del Cinquecento a Genova* (Genoa, 1968). General observations on medieval Genoese domestic architecture are made by Jacques Heers, *Gênes au XVe siècle* (Paris, 1961), pp. 197 and 569–70; and by Diane Owen Hughes, "Kinsmen and Neighbors in Medieval Genoa," in *The Medieval City*, ed. Harry A. Miskimin et al. (New Haven, 1977), pp. 95–111. The propensity of the Genoese to include shops on the ground floor of new sixteenth-century palaces is remarked on by Emmina De Negri, "Dei palazzi 'mercantili' genovesi: a proposito del Palazzo di Ambrogio de Nigro a Banchi," *Bollettino ligustico, 1966* (1968), especially pp. 57–59.

Similarly, in provincial Bologna, another place notable for its palaces, the senatorial families who dominated the political scene after the establishment of the papal regime in 1506 needed those grand staircases and sumptuous rooms that make their palaces so distinctive as settings for the official ceremonies with which they brought their public life into their homes.[53] Tommaso Marino, the Genoese merchant who made a fortune in Milan and ended up buying a dukedom and marrying off his children into the local nobility, was a little perplexed by the immense new home designed by Galeazzo Alessi to accord with his new station in life: "There are only a few rooms that can be enjoyed," he wrote in 1578, "since loggias, porticos, hallways, stairways, and other public places [*pompe*] take up most of the space and leave little for habitation."[54]

The public presence of the aristocratic family in these and other cities was of such importance that several branches might go together to establish their separate residences together behind a common facade with a central entrance to integrate them as a single architectural entity. Eventually the desire for an imposing public facade reached the point where the palace far outstripped residential quarters and incorporated an entire urban business block, including both residential and commercial rental space besides the family apartments, all packed into a single architectural entity. In eighteenth-century Turin the palace of a great family was thus considered an investment like any other, with a calculated fixed income from shops and apartments to supplement the prestige such a structure returned to its owner.[55]

In this wider context of Italian domestic architecture the fifteenth-century Florentine palace appears as a particular kind of building. Public life did not penetrate into it either by way of formal political functions its owner may have performed for the state or by way of a highly formalized ritual of upper-class social life. Its economic value scarcely went beyond its domestic function, and, moreover, that function in a social sense was limited to the immediate family of the owner. His palace isolated him from more distant

[53] G. Cuppini, *I palazzi senatorii a Bologna: architettura come immagine del potere* (Bologna, 1974).

[54] Cited by C. L. Frommel, "Galeazzo Alessi e la tipologia del palazzo rinascimentale," in *Galeazzo Alessi e l'architettura del Cinquecento*, Acts of the International Congress in Genoa, 1974 (Genoa, 1975), p. 168. Frommel goes on to observe that this preponderance of public places was a characteristic of Roman palaces in the first half of the century.

[55] Francesco Cognasso, *Storia di Torino* (Turin, 1959), p. 337; Augusto Cavallari-Murat, "Gian Giacomo Plantery, architetto barocco," *Atti e rassegna tecnica della Società degli Ingegneri e degli Architetti in Torino*, new ser., 11 (1957), 322–23; S. J. Woolf, "Some Notes on the Cost of Palace Building in Turin in the 18th Century," *Atti e rassegna tecnica della Società degli Ingegneri e degli Architetti in Torino*, Sept. 1961, pp. 1–8. Cf. Gérard Labrot, "Le Comportement collectif de l'aristocratie napolitaine du seizième au dix-huitième siècle," *Revue historique*, 258 (1977), 50–51.

relatives, whatever pride they may have taken in its splendor, as much as it did from the public. Even as a monument to its builder's dynastic ambitions it was not designed in anticipation of having to accommodate in any way a growing lineage. The palace facade established its owner's status, but within, it was very much one man's private residence.

Eventually, however, demands that they were not originally designed to accommodate were made on these palaces. The later remodeling of the Renaissance palace and the more precise planning of new ones point to the more careful articulation of spatial functions as upper-class life within became more stylized. Rooms came to have more specific functions. There had to be a chapel, a gallery, a great hall for festive ceremonies, a staircase more suitable for the grandeur with which the owner moved through his home, more service rooms to accommodate his staff of servants, and perhaps more apartments to house the straggling relatives he was more reluctant to send away as his sense of family became more socially extensive. The whole place became crammed with the accumulated furnishings of generations—furniture, pictures, sculptures, and stuffs of all kinds—until the very structure of the building is lost in the surfeit of decoration. The Florentine palace thus came into line with the kind of palace that had meanwhile sprung up in Rome, Bologna, Genoa, and the rest of Italy, marking a new age in the history of the upper classes.

The spirit of individualism that Burckhardt made so central to our appreciation of the Renaissance nowhere expressed itself with greater emphasis than in buildings, and this was no less true in bourgeois Florence than in the courts of the princes and condottieri of northern Italy. Florentines built to make a statement, for their contemporaries and for all time, about their magnificence. Chapels and palaces were family monuments only in the sense that they were bequeathed to a builder's descendants. They had little to do with his collateral relatives. In an earlier time the socially extensive family, the cognate group, probably participated in one way or another in the construction of those buildings that served them all—the loggia and tower. So it was, at any rate, that Giovanni Rucellai was able to get the cooperation of at least a few cousins (but not all) in building the family loggia opposite his palace, a building that theoretically, at least, could serve them all—if indeed in that day and age it still had any function.[56] When, however, Rucellai started buying up neighborhood houses from these same cousins in order to enlarge his own house, he did not find them so cooperative. "It was almost an impossible thing to do," he tells us, and by his own account they made him pay enormous prices to get what he wanted.[57] And no wonder, for what was

[56] F. W. Kent, "The Rucellai Family and Its Loggia," *Journal of the Warburg and Courtauld Institutes*, 35 (1972), 397–401.

[57] Rucellai, *Zibaldone*, p. 121.

in it for them? Carlo di Leonardo Ginori had the same problem when he tried to put together a site for his new palace at the beginning of the sixteenth century and had to change his plans when a first cousin simply refused to yield his own house for the project, even though he was offered another in exchange.[58] Once a man got his palace built, of course, his relatives may have come fawning in admiration (as Filippo Strozzi found out) in the hope that they could now cash in on their relationship—and this, in fact, may not have been beyond the calculations of a builder in a political society where such influence could count for much. Chapels and palaces, however, were not social space for use by the wider family beyond one's own household, and there is little evidence that relatives cooperated—or even were interested—in what one another was doing. Buildings passed to descendants, but only in a selective way that could eliminate many more than remained to enjoy the bequest. It was not the family in any laterally extensive social sense that mattered, it was the dynasty. And what was a dynasty if not, also, a monument to the magnificence of its founder?

[58] Kent, *Household*, pp. 129–30.

PART II

Supply: The Construction Industry

CHAPTER THREE

Organization of Work

Construction as a Problem in Industrial History

DESPITE the long tradition of scholarship directed to the history of European architecture in the medieval and the early modern periods, surprisingly little is known about the economics of building—about the cost of putting buildings up and about the impact such expenditures had on the economy as a whole. There are histories of style, of building types, of construction techniques and building materials, but for the most part we are without studies of construction as a problem in industrial organization. Only the English, with their characteristic affection for old buildings and their antiquarian zeal, have lavished scholarly attention on the history of the building trades. Although the industry satisfied one of man's most basic needs and was, even into the industrial age, one of his largest employers, it hardly finds a place in most surveys of the economic history of Europe, and a comprehensive view of its historical development is not easy to come by.

It is not difficult to explain why construction has been studied less than the other industries that provide man's basic needs—clothing and agriculture. One of the obvious reasons is that before the industrial revolution few technological innovations were introduced that essentially changed the ways buildings were put up. It is not that premodern architecture is without its great engineering feats. The entire tradition of Gothic architecture following the invention of the quadripartite vault represents extraordinary engineering talent and imagination, as do also a few single enterprises, such as the vaulted cupola of the Florentine cathedral. Nevertheless, Florentine builders in the

Renaissance and Roman builders in the baroque period were probably using a basic technology of lifting and moving devices and of building methods that were in a tradition going back to ancient Rome. Improvements in the subordinate industries, such as brickmaking and quarrying, did not have much effect on their organization as industrial enterprises, nor were building materials introduced that led to the foundation of new industries and new building methods. Not until the nineteenth century did both new technology and new materials begin to make much of an impact on the industry as a whole, and that change has taken place slowly throughout most of Europe.

Because of the peculiar nature of demand for construction, the industry underwent little structural change before the modern period, and in this sense, too, the subject leaves the historian with less to write about than do other industries. Construction has been shaped by a market that is distinctively different from the markets that have determined the course of the other basic industries. In the clothing and food industries the producer was oriented toward a commodity market that was highly generalized and remote, and he was likely to have no direct relation with the consumer. To write the history of these industries is to tell a story of continually advancing technology to accommodate ever-expanding and shifting markets, a story that reaches its climax in a stage of "revolutionary" reorganization. It is therefore not surprising that that history is written almost exclusively from the supply side of the marketplace. A peculiarity of the construction industry, on the other hand, was its dependence on a restricted demand. It was an industry that was almost exclusively local, not only with respect to its market but also with respect to its linkages to the subordinate industries that supplied building materials. Men occasionally had to go far afield to find building materials, especially stone or marble for monuments of architectural importance, but construction utilizing such materials was sporadic and was seldom organized with anything in mind beyond a specific project or, at the most, a local market. Moreover, the construction industry had a highly amorphous structure embracing a great variety of skills and manufacturing processes that were activated as forces of production only by direct commission for one project at a time. Because each construction enterprise involved a separate effort to coordinate supply through numerous independent channels and to mobilize labor for actual construction, manufacturing and labor organization in the industry depended on the specific nature of the demand. In the construction industry, in short, the producer had a direct relation with the consumer, and the market was circumscribed by a number of particular conditions.

When the industry began to change its traditional ways, it was the result of a quantitative leap in demand and not of a retooling with new technology. The urban expansion of the industrial era brought such a soaring demand for more and better housing and for a greater variety of nonresidential buildings and public works projects that in the early nineteenth century the construction industry, or at least divisions of it, finally began to introduce structural changes and organize operations on a larger scale. Nevertheless, despite the industrial revolution with its impact on both demand and technology, today the construction industry remains the least revolutionized of the heavy industries.

The central problem of the construction industry is the organization of supply and labor for a building project. Scholarly interest in a construction enterprise has been almost directly proportional to the building's scale, and the history of the industry, as it has been written to date, tends to focus on those large buildings that are often monuments in the history of architecture, as well. In any case, it is mostly for these buildings that we have documentation.

Description of mere size, however, is not the point of industrial history, nor is admiration of aesthetic quality. It goes without saying that almost from the moment of the birth of civilization men have succeeded in organizing themselves for the construction of buildings that, from the pyramids of Egypt and Mexico to the ancient cities of the Indus River valley, never cease to amaze us for their monumentality. For the sheer organization of manpower no project in Europe is comparable to those of the ancient world, for the obvious reason that no builder in Europe commanded the immense human resources that were available in the ancient and nonwestern despotisms. In short, the problem of industrial production in construction in pre-industrial Europe is not concerned with the mere size of an operation but with how management that did not have despotic power dealt with labor in the marketplace and how changes in demand for construction made an impact on industrial and labor organization in the private sector of the economy.

The Graeco-Roman world saw the beginning of the development of a market economy, and in its large urban centers much construction was contracted for in the marketplace. Temple-building in Greece is a case where even public authority had recourse to the market in contracting with independent artisans for work. Projects were usually supervised by building committees composed of prominent citizens who approved the design, contracted for labor, and organized the works project. Some labor was employed directly and some work was let out by bidding (although the lowest price might not be the only consideration) on contracts that could be comprehensive, precise, and detailed in their specifications. Temple-building, however, did not represent an exorbitant investment; because it was only an occasional activity, it hardly sustained a large industry. Domestic buildings were mostly of the wattle and daub type or were made of unbaked bricks; only the rich could afford wood and stone.

Without any other kind of prestige building to stimulate demand, therefore, the kind of skilled labor needed for temples was scarce. Skilled artisans, in fact, were like their medieval descendants—highly itinerate, traveling throughout Greece from one project to another; it has been argued that the problem of finding skilled labor to build a temple was more serious than finding the money to pay for it. Even in Athens, the largest city in the Greek world, where a boom in public building in the fifth century temporarily enlarged the ranks of artisans, there was no demand from any other sector of the economy to take up the slack once the boom was over, so eventually many artisans either went abroad or found a different way of making a living.

Under these market conditions, craftsmen could only be considered modest entrepreneurs. Contracts were usually small, involving no more than a few weeks of work; the larger ones often required that the patron make advances to the artisan. At Epidauros the largest contract let out for the temple amounted to only 1 percent of the total cost of construction, while the more normal contract came to less than half that. Little is known of the bargaining process for contracts, but it is a significant comment on the limited operation of the market in the ancient economy that for the pious artisan the honor of working on a temple could well be greater than his desire for profit.[1]

The situation in Rome was different. The Roman passion for public monuments—evidenced in all classes of society, from top to bottom—generated a lively demand for building, even if it was nothing more than the funerary monument ordered by a slave. The extent and wealth of the Roman world meant that all this building added up to a major industrial activity. With their extravagant wealth, the senatorial families number among the greatest builders of all times. The scale of quarry operations to meet their demand for carved stone outdid in some respects anything that has taken place in quarrying since then; it is likely that brickworks were equally impressive, if not for their organization as industrial enterprises, then at least for their levels of production.

These industrial operations, however, were not organized by using the normal procedures of the marketplace as that institution is generally understood. The immense labor forces that were required, including all kinds and degrees of skills, consisted largely of dependent and involuntary workers who did not work for wages contracted freely in the market. They were pressed into service by the force of arms or compelled by customary and legal authority working through social institutions, like slavery and clientage, that are peculiar to the ancient world. The same system was probably used also by the publicans who invested heavily in contracts for the construction of large public and private buildings. These men commanded enormous capital resources, and although little is known about how they organized their industrial

[1] Alison Burford, "The Economics of Greek Temple Building," *Proceedings of the Cambridge Philosophical Society*, new ser., 11 (1965), 21–34; idem, *The Greek Temple Builders at Epidauros* (Liverpool, 1969); Philip H. Davis, "The Delian Building Contracts," *Bulletin de Correspondance hellénique*, 61 (1937), 109–35.

enterprises, it can be assumed that they, too, circumvented the market in assembling their labor forces. Crassus, for example, used slaves for his infamous building activities in Rome; Frontinus tells us that some entrepreneurs who had public contracts for maintenance of aqueducts often misappropriated their labor force, which could number several hundred, for private ventures.[2]

Medieval Europe did not see construction on a scale anywhere near that of the greatest of these Roman building operations. In the first place, no political authority was in a position to sponsor the kind of public works project that explains the grandeur of much Roman architecture. In the second place, the feudal elite was a rural class, widely distributed throughout all of Europe, so that its effective demand was not concentrated in a few centers. The members of the feudal elite were, furthermore, not nearly as wealthy as the wealthiest Roman senators. In any case, as members of a warrior class their conspicuous consumption did not take such a prominently architectural form, and as members of a rural class they lacked the Roman inspiration for public building. A third reason for the lesser scale of building in the Middle Ages was the lack of an urban market of a large metropolitan center like ancient Rome. By the twelfth and thirteenth centuries European society began to assume a distinctive urban quality as towns sprung up everywhere, but no European city offered opportunities for speculative building and public works projects on a grand scale. By and large medieval cities were not the residences of feudal elites, and the demand for building in them was too low in quality and too diffused among their many constituent agents to have occasioned the concentration of investment that might have inspired large-scale building operations. What made Florence unique and accounts for its importance in the history of European architecture is that there, for the first time, the urban upper classes began to build conspicuously.

Feudal lords built fortifications in the countryside, and towns occasionally put up a communal monument, but the church was the great builder of the Middle Ages. It is around its structures—the great monasteries and, from the twelfth century on, the urban cathedrals—that the history of the construction industry in the Middle Ages, as well as the history of architecture, is usually written. Church-building, however, like temple-building in ancient Greece, was only an occasional activity, and investment in it was scattered throughout all of Europe.

The nature and structure of demand for building in medieval Europe was

[2] Helen J. Loane, *Industry and Commerce in the City of Rome (50 B.C.–200 A.D.)* (Baltimore, 1938), pp. 79–86; E. Badian, *Publicans and Sinners: Private Enterprise in the Service of the Roman Republic* (Ithaca, 1972), ch. 4; Richard Duncan-Jones, *The Economy of the Roman Empire: Quantitative Studies* (Cambridge, 1974), pp. 2–3 (with further reference to Plutarch on Crassus and to Frontinus). For the nature of labor in the ancient world see the analysis of M. I. Finley, *The Ancient Economy* (Berkeley, 1973), ch. 3.

thus distinctly different from what it had been in the Roman world. Even more significantly, the political, social, and economic system that emerged in medieval Europe limited direct control over the one major resource absolutely necessary for any building enterprise—manpower. Construction is a labor-intensive activity in both the preparation of materials and the actual construction. Although a building patron, be he bishop or knight, could find basic building materials in the quarries and woods of his estate and could turn over the considerable organizational problems of a building to his estate administration, his biggest problem was assembling the labor force to quarry the stone, fire the bricks, cut the wood, deliver materials, and put the building up. In the Oriental despotisms and in ancient Rome, nothing was easier than tapping the resource of labor, but the expansion of the market economy that is so central to the development of the West changed all that by redefining the basic terms of social organization. Slavery was kept very much at the periphery of the European social system, and the institution of serfdom, which was undoubtedly important in much feudal and monastic building in the early Middle Ages, was slowly eroded away in many parts of western Europe. By the thirteenth and fourteenth centuries neither slaves nor serfs—or even prisoners—were prominent in construction work; the European builder could hardly avoid the marketplace for labor.

For instance, when the prince of Acaia built his fortress at Fossano in the period from 1324 to 1332, he was able to cut some costs by using the labor service due him by residents on his lands, but he was still left with considerable bills to pay for wages of other workers as well as purchase of materials.[3] As to slaves, although generally not used for industrial work of any kind in Europe, they occasionally show up on construction gangs in the western Mediterranean, on the frontier between the Christian and Moslem world, in the form of enslaved Moorish prisoners. The royal works in the kingdom of Maiorca employed some in the early fourteenth century. Fifteen is the highest number recorded at any one time, however, and the fact that they were paid a daily wage suggests that their service was not altogether free from market conditions.[4] Eleven Moorish slaves (plus five other prisoners) worked on the towers and palisade built for the port of Cagliari in the years 1376 and 1377, but the authorities had to engage as many free laborers; here, too, the slaves were paid a daily wage (at about half the rate

[3] G. Falco, "Sulla costruzione del castello di Fossano (1324–1332)," *Biblioteca della società storica subalpina*, 163 (1936), 65–116. Few instances of villein service in construction were found by L. F. Salzman, *Building in England Down to 1540* (Oxford, 1967), p. 37 n.

[4] Marcel Durliat, *L'Art dans le royaume de Majorque: les débuts de l'art gothique en Roussillon, en Cerdagne et aux Baléares* (Toulouse, 1962), pp. 179–80.

paid to free workers).[5] The forced labor of slaves, serfs, and prisoners was, in short, a marginal phenomenon in the history of medieval construction.

For most of his labor, therefore, the medieval builder had to turn to the market, and none of these builders had the financial resources to buy labor in the market at the levels that despotic authority could command it by other means in nonwestern societies. There were, of course, noneconomic forces a builder could bring to bear on employment. It would not be surprising to learn that in the so-called Age of Faith a worker's religious zeal could soften his purely economic demands in dealing with a builder of a cathedral, just as working on a temple had its spiritual rewards in the Greek world. The image of the pious people of Chartres, joined by volunteers from Normandy, Brittany, and other far-away places, swarming around the construction site of their new cathedral after the fire of 1194, eager to work for the glory of God, is not to be taken lightly. It has been suggested that use of the institution of penitence as an instrument for getting the poor sinner to contribute his labor to the construction of churches may explain the rapidity of their construction along the pilgrimage routes of southern France.[6] We can doubt, however, that these spiritual powers of the church did much to improve its bargaining position for the normal kind of skilled labor it needed for most of its building.

Legal authority counted for somewhat more, and the traditional right of governments to require military service was one way labor could be impressed for public works, above all for construction of military installations. In this way a government could force its terms on the market to the extent that it commanded service, but it did not thereby circumvent the market, for it was still confronted with the necessity of paying the labor bills. The most notable examples of impressment of labor in medieval Europe are surely to be found in England in the later thirteenth century, during the Welsh wars, and in the mid-fourteenth century, for the building of Windsor Castle. For the campaign of 1282 and 1283 Edward I pressed 7,630 workers from all over England into service for clearing forests and building fortifications and castles. In these situations workers were required to bring tools and provisions and to stay on

[5] C. Manca, *Il libro di conti di Miquel Ça-Rovira* (Padua, 1969), pp. 97–105.

[6] Etienne Delaruelle, "L'Autel roman de Saint-Sernin (1096): confrères, pèlerins et pénitents," in *Mélanges offerts à René Crozet*, I, ed. P. Gallais and Y.-J. Riou (Poitiers, 1966), 388–89; Marcel Aubert, "La Construction au moyen âge," *Bulletin monumental*, 118 (1960), 249–51 and 254. Other examples of labor contribution are cited in Gwilym Peredur Jones, "Building in Stone in Medieval Western Europe," *Trade and Industry in the Middle Ages*, Vol. II of *Cambridge Economic History of Europe* (Cambridge, 1952), p. 502. Cf. Marcel David, "La Fabrique et les manoeuvres sur les chantiers des cathédrales en France jusqu'au XIVe siècle," in *Etudes d'histoire du droit canonique dédiées à Gabriel Le Bras* (Paris, 1965), II, 1115–16.

the job for the forty days traditionally due the sovereign for military service. During the building of Windsor Castle they had to be policed to prevent desertion, and proclamations were issued against employment of deserters and (in 1362) against employment of any mason in the private sector without permission. One chronicler observed that at the time "almost all the masons and carpenters throughout the whole of England were brought to that building, so that hardly anyone could have any good mason or carpenter except in secret."[7] Nothing on the Continent compares to the magnitude of these English examples, and in England itself the practice hardly survived the fourteenth century, at least on such a grand scale.

Governments, however, could always make demands on their subjects for military purposes, and this included work on fortifications. One of the popular images conjured up about life in the medieval world is that of the entire population of a town pitching in for the building of fortifications. In the fifteenth century a city as small as Nantes was able to order over 500 men to work on its walls, and in 1486 all the stonemasons of Genoa were required to contribute one day's labor at the Molo.[8] In Florence itself the new government of the Medici dukes was able to put as many as 3,000 to work at one time on the rush job to put up the Fortezza da Basso, all drafted into limited service from the countryside and provided with food and lodging but no wages.[9] Nevertheless, these ventures were of limited duration and for specific military purposes, and the authority often had to be prepared to pay something like the going market rates to workers so pressed into service. In other words, the possibilities of gathering a labor force for construction through this kind of recruitment were clearly limited, however impressive some instances of it were. Certainly by the early modern period no government could act as imperiously in the market as Peter the Great did in his kingdom on the fringes of western institutions. Needing all the masons he could find to get construction underway at St. Petersburg, he issued an ukase forbidding any masonry building throughout all of Russia so that masons would not be prevented from coming to work for him; but not even Peter, who allegedly commandeered 40,000 men to clear the ground and begin

[7] R. A. Brown and H. M. Colvin, "The King's Works 1272–1485," in *The History of the King's Works*, I, ed. H. M. Colvin (London, 1963), 180–84; cf. Salzman, *Building*, pp. 37–38.

[8] Michel Le Mené, "La Construction à Nantes au XVe siècle," *Annales de Bretagne*, 68 (1961), 390–91; Ennio Poleggi, "Il rinnovamento edilizio genovese e i magistri Antelami nel secolo XV," *Arte lombarda*, 11 (1966), 66–67.

[9] J. R. Hale, "The End of Florentine Liberty: The Fortezza da Basso," in *Florentine Studies: Politics and Society in Renaissance Florence*, ed. Nicolai Rubinstein (London, 1968), p.516. Examples of legislation in ducal Florence for impressment of labor and materials for public works are found in *Leg. tosc.*, VII, 384 and VIII, 187.

construction on his new capital, could keep them on long enough to get much of a city built.[10]

Limitations in the size of available labor forces goes a long way to explain the absence in the West of many buildings that compare in monumentality to those of the ancient despotisms. The most a medieval prince could muster for a rush job on the construction of fortifications was seldom more than several thousand. The daily work force of between two and three thousand employed on the great mosque in Istanbul in the mid-sixteenth century (of which almost half consisted of slaves and soldiers) was probably larger than could be found on any contemporary construction gang in the West working on a nonmilitary project.[11] It was a rare cathedral workshop that employed more than a hundred men for any length of time, the grandeur of these structures being more a monument to persistence and to the duration of an effort that could go on for centuries than it is to the scale of building operations. A labor force of a hundred men was about the most to be found even on a private project as well financed and so determinedly pushed forward as the Strozzi palace in Florence.[12] By the sixteenth century, as a result of changes in the technology of war that led to the organization of large standing armies of infantrymen, some European princes could appropriate troops to raise larger work forces than their medieval predecessors could have considered employing, and this helped them to build on a larger scale. For skilled labor, however, the market could not be avoided.

The nature of the demand for buildings in the Middle Ages meant that industrial organization remained on a small scale. Especially significant was the geographical diffusion of that demand, for as a result there was little stimulus for changing the highly localized structure of the industry, which has survived even to the present. It is not surprising, therefore, that in the Middle Ages and well into the early modern era the industry saw little technological and structural change. The task of the historian of this industry is less to trace growth in a linear sense than to use his materials to fill out a variegated picture of economic organization in pre-industrial Europe.

If construction is a major industry because it provides man with one of his essential needs, it is also an industry that is remarkably comprehensive in embracing a wide range of man's economic activities. It is a labor-intensive

[10] Iurii Alekseevich Egorov, *The Architectural Planning of St. Petersburg*, trans. Eric Dluhosch (Athens, Ohio, 1969), p. xxii ("Translator's Note on the Founding and Development of St. Petersburg").

[11] Omer Lutfi Barkan, "L'organisation du travail dans le chantier d'une grande mosquée à Istanbul au XVIe siècle," *Annales, E.S.C.*, 17 (1962), 1093–1106.

[12] Richard A. Goldthwaite, "The Building of the Strozzi Palace: The Construction Industry in Renaissance Florence," *Studies in Medieval and Renaissance History*, 10 (1973), 172.

industry, as noted, with only a small part of its productive capacity dependent on either machines or nature's vital powers. Even the value of basic building materials has only one major component—the cost of labor. That labor force comprises a vast number of skills and manufacturing processes, ranging from unskilled laborers to artists, from burning lime and firing bricks to carving highly decorative stonework. The scale of operations could also be impressive, with construction gangs that in some cases were probably the highest concentrations of labor found in any industry before the industrial revolution, however small they may have been by ancient standards. What industry in the private sector in early modern Europe had to have a staff organization as vast as, for example, that of the building crew of Saint Peter's in the early sixteenth century, with an architect, a co-architect, a general manager, a paymaster, three measurers and assessors, two treasurers, a secretary, five to ten supervisors and their assistants, and finally, the foremen of the various work crews?[13] Building accounts, in fact, have been the major, if not the exclusive, source for our knowledge of wages in pre-industrial Europe because the industry was one of the few that was organized for direct labor employment on a large scale. They have much to tell us about the nature of industrial organization in the various subordinate building-material industries, about the managerial and administrative problems in organizing all those component forces that have to be brought together to get a building erected, and about the economic conditions of life for a representative cross section of the laboring classes.

There is a direct relation between consumer and supplier that separates construction from industries that are oriented to more impersonal commodity markets. The central problem of construction is the form that relation takes. What were the possibilities for contracting for supply and labor? What were the contractual terms? To what extent could a patron relieve himself of involvement in the construction project by recourse to the market? How much of an entrepreneur could a mason-contractor be, and how developed were the building-material industries? In short, how was the industry organized to meet the demands made of it? How did the market in which it operated function?

Contracting for Construction

TYPES OF CONTRACTS. Wherever the economy centered on an active market it was common for men in most crafts to contract for work. Contracts made by craftsmen in the building trades survive from as early as classical Greece,

[13] James Ackerman, "Architectural Practice in the Italian Renaissance," *JSArH*, 13, No. 3 (1954), 5.

Andrea Pisano, wallers, ca. 1340

and contracts made during the Middle Ages can be found for virtually every part of Europe—those surviving in England have, in fact, been published.[14] Although this material has never been brought together in a comprehensive study, it appears at first glance to be remarkably homogeneous. The market situation in which craftsmen in the building trades proceeded in their work probably varied, depending on local conditions, from place to place across Europe, but certain features in the contracting procedures were commonly found in many places. Almost every feature of practice as described in the ensuing discussion of Florentine contracts has its counterpart elsewhere in Europe. The advantage of the Florentine materials derives from their greater abundance and diversity for this one place, allowing us, on the one hand, to

[14] By Salzman, *Building* (the 1967 edition of this book has additional contracts brought to the author's attention since the 1952 edition). English contracts have been discussed also by Brown and Colvin in *The History of the King's Works*, pp. 186–87; and by Douglas Knoop and G. P. Jones, "The Rise of the Mason Contractor," *Journal of the Royal Institute of British Architects*, 43 (1936), 1061–71. For contracts in ancient Greece, see the references in note 1 to this chapter.

study problems with considerable detail, and, on the other, to arrive at a more comprehensive view of the industry than we have for any other place.

The typical Florentine master waller was an independent worker who found employment as head of a miniscule crew consisting of no more than an assistant or an apprentice along with one or two manual laborers. His competence in handling the materials of Mediterranean construction was comprehensive: he could prepare foundations; erect walls of rubble, brick, and stone, and plaster and whitewash them; vault the area overhead; and cover the whole with a tile roof. In the fifteenth century there were men who specialized in some of these tasks—*fondatori, muratori, stuccatori, imbiancatori, copritetti*—but some wallers in fact did all of these things and often the terms used to identify them refer only to their work in a specific capacity at a given moment. In contrast, the more specialized terminology in medieval English usage for craftsmen in the building trades perhaps reflects the greater diversity of skills in an area of different building materials. This comprehensive range of skills that enabled the Florentine waller to satisfy most building requirements should have made it easier for him to organize the forces of production in the industry.

The degree to which the waller was prepared to take it upon himself to organize a construction project determined the kind of arrangements he was willing to make with his employers. There is much documentation for these arrangements in the copies of formal written contracts, the memoranda made about such contracts by employers in their account books, and the building accounts themselves. (Where both survive, the actual financial arrangements found in the building accounts are often more revealing about the terms of employment than the formal contractual agreement itself.) For purposes of a description of these arrangements, contracts can be categorized according to what the mason agrees to supply—either labor alone or both labor and building materials—and according to the financial terms of payment—either a flat fee or a rate on the basis of measure and value of work completed. The most ambitious contract is the contract in gross, one by which the waller agrees to supply all labor and materials for a construction project in return for an agreed price. The simplest arrangement, and the alternative to committing himself to any responsibility other than his own performance on the job, was for the waller to go to work for wages calculated according to a rate based on time, usually (in Florence) a day, a month, or a year; the waller thereby resigned himself to be a worker in a direct labor system. His ability to negotiate the terms of his employment on grounds other than going to work for a simple wage was limited by the difficulty in making estimates and anticipating costs, by problems of labor management and discipline (which became acute with an increase in the size of the labor force and in the duration of employment), and by his modest financial resources.

Small-scale contracting for labor alone on the basis of a task rate was

Nanni di Banco, Tabernacle of the Arte dei Maestri di Pietra e di Legname (detail from relief), ca. 1408.

widely practiced. Where building requirements were of the simplest kind it was no problem to calculate the amount of labor needed for particular work in order to come up with a task rate, especially since labor costs were assured by the stability of wages during most of this period. Many task-rate contracts for a variety of projects can be found scattered throughout the private accounts books of the period, some made by a waller working alone, some by wallers in association with one another, and some by one waller who was prepared to employ others and their crews. An example is the contract made in 1390 by an unnamed waller and Riccardo di Francesco Del Bene for the building of a laborer's cottage on Del Bene's property at San Casciano. Del Bene supplied stone, lime, sand, wood, and tiles; the waller was to be paid 2 soldi per braccio of wall and 1 soldo per square braccio of roof, "a ttutta sua spesa di maestero."[15] In 1464 Virgilio d'Andrea Adriani made a similar contract for work on the loggia in the courtyard of his house at Balatro (near Antella, now a suburb southeast of Florence). He was willing to provide materials, and two wallers, Benedetto di Papi from Balatro and Papi d'Antonio del Valligiana from Antella, joined forces in contracting to do walls for 2 soldi per braccio. After this was finished Papi d'Antonio contracted separately to vault the loggia and an adjacent room for s.4 d.6 per braccio "a ogni sua spesa" except for bricks, lime, and sand (and since he could not write, the

[15] ASF, Carte Del Bene 85 (cash book of Riccardo di Francesco Del Bene), fol. 19r.

contract had to be signed for him by a priest).[16] In another contract, of 1496, the waller Cristofano di Parente undertook the construction of an entire house in the city for Bernardo Masi, agreeing to do all the brickwork, plaster the exterior, and finish the roof for 2 soldi per braccio (a rate that would indicate that all materials were supplied by the employer).[17]

Many other labor contracts of this kind can be cited. Most of the construction involved, however, was not what could be called major projects, and few wallers contracted to do large-scale work on these terms. One of the larger

[16] Carte strozz., ser. II, 21 (accounts and memoranda of Virgilio d'Andrea Adriani, 1463–92), fols. 4r and 22r.

[17] ASF, Mss. 88 (memoranda of Piero di Bernardo Masi, 1452–1513 [but written about a decade later]), fol. 143v.

Shop of Pacino, illustrations from the *Cronaca* of Giovanni Villani, mid-fourteenth century. At left, Tower of Babel (top) and Temple of Mars (Baptistry of Florence). Above, Charlemagne rebuilds Florence.

contracts of this kind was let out by the commune for rebuilding part of the Bargello after the fire of 1332. The contract itself does not survive, but the accounts for the years 1345 and 1346 make reference to it. The prominent mason Neri di Fioravante and seven others joined forces (but clearly under his direction) in contracting to work for a task fee (rather than for a schedule of rates), and all materials were furnished to them by the building committee of the commune. Their price was 850 florins, and the accounts show that they received payments about once a month. Although this was a substantial contract (especially considering that it was made before the inflation of wages in the mid-Trecento), it was undertaken by an association of eight masons, not by a single entrepreneur, and when the fee is divided among the eight, each with his own work crew, the figures turn out to be approximately their collective earning expectations according to the current wage scale. Furthermore, the fee included only basic construction; work in other specialties within the building trades—carpentry, stonecutting, plastering, and whitewashing—was paid for separately by the commune.[18]

In 1387 the commune let out another moderately large contract for rebuilding the church of Santa Cecilia after the older structure had been destroyed in order to open up space for the Piazza della Signoria. In this contract Losti and Giusto, sons of Piero dell'Asserello from Campi, agreed to erect the entire structure from the foundations to the roof, including finishing the walls, according to instructions from the foreman at the cathedral. All materials were supplied to them, and a rate schedule was included. Without the accounts for this project, however, it is impossible to assess the full extent of the responsibilities assumed by the wallers.[19]

A final, and notable, example of a sizeable building project undertaken by wallers who were willing to take comprehensive responsibility for their work was the hospital of San Matteo, founded by a merchant from Montecatini, Lemmo Balducci. In a series of contracts let out from 1385 to 1400, two wallers, Romolo di Bandino and Sandro del Vinta, undertook to build a complex of buildings comprising separate wards for men and women, courtyards and service buildings, a portico on the street (which is still standing in the Piazza di San Marco), and a church; in addition, one contract calls for the construction of a completely new convent for the nuns of San Niccolò, who formerly had occupied the site and now had to be relocated and given new quarters. The work included foundations with underground vaults, walls to be plastered on the exterior and finished on the interior, the roofs, installation of stone door and window frames, and erection of columns for the loggia and the vaults over them. All the materials, including finished stone, were to be supplied. Bricks are not mentioned in the contracts, but since the building accounts do not survive there is no way of checking on which party paid for them. Complex and detailed schedules of rates were drawn up, and payments were to be made from time to time (one contract stipulates at the end of each month, following the measuring of that month's work). Once again, however, it is not possible without the accounts to ascertain how much financial responsibility the wallers assumed. The work force was larger than the usual team associated with a waller, for Romolo and Sandro were required not only to be in steady attendance themselves but to keep at least two other wallers on the job, along with as many laborers as needed. Both these men appear in the surviving records of the hospital for the next fifteen years, and

[18] ASF, Balìe 3 (provisions, appropriations, income, and expenditures relative to construction, 1345–46); for a summary of this phase of the construction see Luigi Passerini, *Del Pretorio di Firenze* (Florence, 1858), pp. 18–25.

[19] The contract is published by Carl Frey, *Die Loggia dei Lanzi* (Berlin, 1885), pp. 227–29.

Anonymous, illustration from a thirteenth-century Bible

it is likely that their employment on these terms was more or less continual during this entire period of the construction of the new hospital complex.[20]

One area of construction where it became normal procedure to contract for task rates was the preparation of foundations. Any waller could probably do this work, and sometimes, as in the San Matteo contract, the foundations were included in the contract along with the construction. In the fifteenth century, however, foundation work was more likely to be turned over to men who specialized in the operation. Zanobi di Sandro is one of the better documented of these: in 1485 he did the foundations at Santa Maria delle Carceri in Prato; in July 1489 he turned down a contract with Filippo Strozzi; over the next several months he was paid for work on the sacristy chapel of Santa Maria Maddalena di Cestello; and at the end of the year he attended a ceremony at Santo Spirito for filling the foundations for the new sacristy. *Fondatori*, or *maestri di fondamenti*—called here *founders*—appear on most projects in addition to the wallers who were responsible for construction. In charge of small crews of several laborers and supplied with their basic tools, these men were prepared to do the hard work of digging foundations as well as building supporting walls and filling in with gravel if required. They sometimes also dug wells. This work was usually let out on contract, even when for other phases of construction a direct labor system was organized, and the terms were invariably a task rate on the basis of square braccia of foundations prepared.

A number of contracts with founders survive. They are similar to each other in most respects, the major difference being in the obligation to supply gravel for fill. In the contracts let out by the Innocenti in 1419 with Ambruogio di Leonardo and in 1427 with Piero di Cenni and Nanni di Michele del Fogna, the founders were not required to supply fill, which was purchased by the building committee from sand and gravel dealers; but in another, of 1426, with Bartolo di Piero Maringhi, the rate paid to the founders included fill (but not lime). The rates were s.2 d.6 and s.1 d.6, respectively, for the first two, and 4 soldi for the last.[21] Even for the great Strozzi palace, where a direct labor system was set up for all other operations, foundation work was

[20] Five contracts, along with a number of periodic settlements of accounts with the wallers, are bound in with other miscellaneous papers of the hospital: ASF, Ospedali, S. Matteo 1, fols. 9–37; 123, fols. 5–7 and 21. One of these contracts is with three different wallers, Michele di Marco da Terrarossa, Leonardo di Paolo, and Giorgio di Tuccio; but they were specifically required to follow work already done by the other two contracting wallers. Some of these documents from the first volume cited above, including two of the contracts, are published by Piero Sanpaolesi, "Alcuni documenti sull'ospedale di S. Matteo in Firenze," *Belle Arti*, 1 (1946), 76–87; but his analysis is incorrect at many places.

[21] Innocenti, ser. VII (building accounts), 1 (ledger A), fol. 9r; 2 (ledger B), fols. 179–80 and 183.

Anonymous, illustration
from a fifteenth-century Roman
Breviary (detail).

let out on contract. The chief founder, Andrea di Luca Frilli, signed a three-year contract (it was later extended a year) to prepare foundations at the rate of 2 soldi per square braccio, not including fill. Over the four years he worked on this project, Frilli earned an average of 550 lire a year, a figure that at current wage rates indicates that he must have had a crew of no more than two or three laborers.[22] Contracts with founders do not include specifications about work involved, although it can be assumed that this was generally known beforehand. The Innocenti contracts specify that work was to be done according to measurements forthcoming from the building committee, while the Strozzi contract with Frilli was made for the stipulated duration of three years of full-time employment. Because founders worked for a task rate, accounts of payments to them usually include detailed measurements of work completed in the credit entries (documents of obvious importance for archaeological research). Actual payments, however, were made regularly, usually weekly (on what basis cannot be determined) during the period of construction.

Enough projects like all of these surveyed so far for which a waller contracted to do the work on a rate basis can be turned up in the archives to

[22] Goldthwaite, "Strozzi Palace," pp. 142–44.

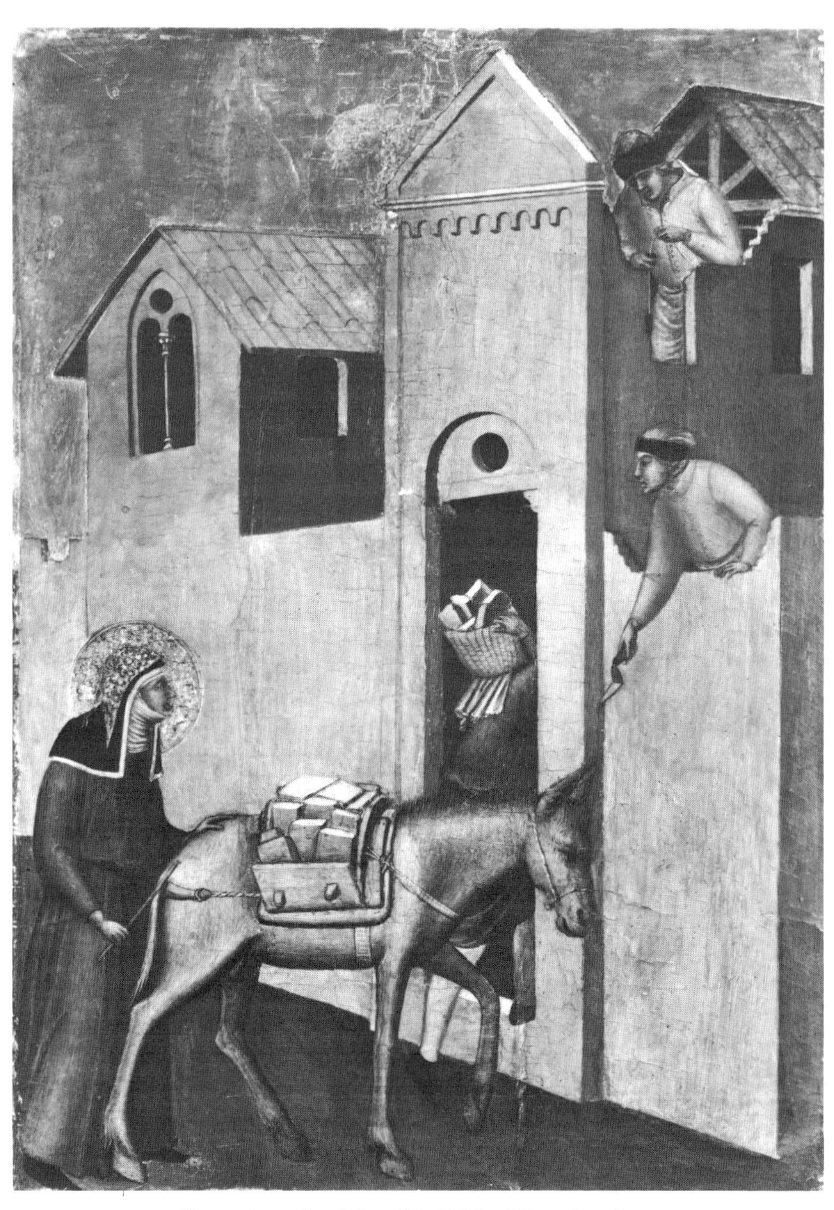

Florentine school, Sant'Umiltà builds a church
in honor of St. John the Divine (panel from the Life
of Sant'Umiltà), 1341 (?).

assure us that labor contracts for task rates (and, rarely, for task fees) were not unusual among the wallers of Florence. It was much less usual, however, for them to go the next step and contract for supply of materials as well. When they did, it was generally for modest projects. Many contracts can be found of the kind made in 1395 by Nanni di Cecco, a waller from Settimo, by which he agreed to rebuild a doorway and steps of a rural building belonging to Nofri di Palla Strozzi at Roncigliano: Strozzi provided a stone lintel and the lock, but otherwise Nanni was responsible for the work "tutto a ssue spese," for which he received a fee of 5 lire.[23] In 1341 a waller named Antonio contracted with the confraternity of Orsanmichele to build a complete house, including digging foundations, hauling away dirt, building brick vaults, and erecting stone walls. Antonio provided all the materials except iron, lead, and wood, and a rate schedule for the various parts of the building was included in the contract.[24]

Another labor-and-supply contract for less complex work but probably work of greater value was that made in 1432 between the wallers Berardo di Giovanni and Stefano di Jacopo, on the one hand, and Cosimo and Lorenzo de' Medici, on the other, for the building of about one thousand braccia of garden wall. This work included digging the foundations according to specifications, filling them with gravel and mortar, hauling away dirt, and building the wall according to specified thickness, height, and materials. The wallers provided all the materials themselves (gravel, sand, lime, unfinished stone, and their equipment) and organized the work force; they were to be paid according to a task rate on the basis of measure and value (8 to 9 soldi per braccio of measured wall, a rate that clearly included materials). According to the terms of the contract the total cost would have amounted to over 125 florins, roughly the equivalent of a waller's optimum earnings over two years, no small enterprise for one of artisan status.

The accompanying building accounts, however, reveal some of the realities of the financial arrangement not reflected in the contract itself. Despite the terms of the contract the Medici were not able to turn everything over to the wallers and await the completion of the project for a final settling of accounts. The wallers did not have enough capital to see them through even part of the work, and the Medici had to make advances to them almost on a weekly basis. Furthermore, the Medici made numerous payments for purchase of lime and its transport; on the books these financial operations have nothing to do with the wallers' accounts. There is no way of knowing to what extent these additional expenditures by the Medici represented a compromise of the terms of the contract, but it is certain that the wallers were not prepared to finance

[23] Carte strozz., ser. III, 279 (accounts of Nofri di Palla Strozzi, 1394–99), fol. 32.

[24] G. Milanesi, "Documenti inediti dell'arte toscana dal XII al XVI secolo," *Il Buonarroti*, 2d ser., 14 (1880), 224–25.

such an extensive project even though they had signed a comprehensive labor-and-supply contract for a job where the materials were of the simplest kind.[25]

A similar financial limitation on the part of the waller is found in the accounts that accompany another labor-and-supply contract, this one based on a task fee rather than a task rate. In 1489 the prominent waller Jacopo di Stefano Rosselli contracted to do some work for the notary Andrea di Cristofano Nacchianti. The job involved some structural adjustments between two adjacent properties, a "new" house and an "old" one that were apparently hereby to be joined into one; it also included building a new staircase and a fireplace, raising part of a roof, and building a loggia. Rosselli was to do the work "a tutte le sue spese" for 57 florins (and he was also to have the wood from the old roof), a sum roughly equivalent to a year's wages for one of his status. The contract is silent on whether the waller was responsible for financing the project, but Nacchianti's accounts show that in fact he himself paid the ongoing expenses for labor (to Rosselli himself, to his son, to other wallers and workers, as well as to a stonecarver) and for materials, especially bricks. Since the accounts are incomplete, it is not possible to determine whether these payments were eventually balanced against the contracted fee or what the financial settlement consisted of, but, once again, the accounts complement the contract in revealing the arrangements for financing the enterprise.[26]

There are labor-and-supply contracts for more significant construction than any of the examples cited so far, but they are not accompanied by accounts to complete the picture of the financial arrangements. Most come from an earlier period. In April 1348 one of the city's most prominent wallers, Benci di Cione, who worked at the Bargello, Orsanmichele, the cathedral, and the Loggia dei Priori, contracted to build an entire chapel, from the foundations to the roof (completely described with measurements in the document) for the nuns of Santa Maria del Fiore of Fiesole. He agreed to supply stone, wood, iron, mortar, and labor, to pay most all other expenses, and to finish the work within six months for the flat fee of 440 florins, no small figure before the inflation of wages that began to take place later that year.[27] In 1350 Neri di Fioravante recognized in a notarial act receipt of payment of 200 florins for the construction of the Falconieri chapel in the Servite church of Santa Maria (the Santissima Annunziata), including his labor and expenses of stone, wood, and mortar; it can be inferred that this was work he had contracted to do for a task fee.[28] Two contracts for the building of the Mercanzia,

25 ASF, Mediceo avanti il Principato, 131/D (accounts for building the wall), fol. IV.

26 Innocenti, ser. CXLIV, 633 (accounts and memoranda of Ser Andrea di Cristofano Nacchianti, 1471–1508), fol. 94 left.

27 Milanesi, "Documenti," pp. 231–33.

28 Ibid., p. 234.

Spinello Aretino, Foundation of Alessandria della Paglia
by Pope Alexander III, 1407.

apparently for successive stages of the construction, are known to have been let out to masons who were willing to do the work and who were apparently also prepared to supply the basic building materials of stone, rubble, and brick. The deliberations of the Mercanzia officials record an authorization of payment of 350 florins to Giovanni di Lapo Ghini in December 1359 according to "certain agreements" (*certi patti*) for the building of their new palace that are not explained; other items in the same appropriation of funds include expenses for iron, lead, and mortar, but not for stone or bricks. In a contract for further building made a year later, in December 1360, with Berto di Martignone, a copy of which is inserted into the deliberations, complete building specifications are spelled out, including the officials' obligation to supply iron, lead, wood, and mortar. All other expenses were Berto's responsibility, and the rate of 12 soldi per square braccio of wall to be paid to him indicates that he provided more than just labor. Apparently both Giovanni di

Lapo Ghini and Berto di Martignone were prepared to organize the work force and provide some of the construction materials—one for a task fee, the other for a task rate.[29]

Some of these last contracts are veritable contracts in gross—that is, the contractor provided materials and labor for a single task fee. The lack of building accounts, however, precludes any assessment of the actual financial commitment the contractor made. In any case, none of these examples can be considered a large-scale project by standards of the time. Contracts in gross are in fact rare for major construction in the fifteenth century. The largest turned up in this study is one made in 1459 for a refectory with a dormitory above at Sant'Ambrogio with the waller Michele di Mariano, who supplied labor, bricks, and lime (but not stone and iron) for lb.1,600 s.10 (about 300 florins).[30]

No research to date has brought to light evidence that any construction entrepreneur operated at the level suggested by Vespasiano da Bisticci in his comments on the men to whom Cosimo de' Medici let out contracts for his building programs. One of these contractors ("uno suo fattore di tutte le muraglie che faceva") cheated Cosimo and made more than his fair share of profits. The other, named Lorenzo ("uno maestro intendentissimo"), faced ruin because, out of deference, he was reluctant to bring to Cosimo's attention his mounting operating costs. Vespasiano gives us no names or specific details except to mention such exaggerated figures for the amounts of money involved in both instances—100,000 florins—that we can wonder whether he was not fabricating the incidents to illustrate certain aspects of Cosimo's personality by registering his reaction to a cheat on the one hand and to an overly deferent employee on the other. Cosimo did indeed spend large sums for building projects, but the two about whose financing some judgments can be made on the basis of surviving accounts—San Lorenzo and the Badia at Fiesole, both among his largest projects—were certainly not undertaken by single entrepreneurs working on a contract in gross.[31]

[29] G. Milanesi, *Nuovi documenti per la storia dell'arte toscana dal XII al XVI secolo* (Rome, 1893), pp. 56–58. The building history of this palace is summarized by Iodoco Del Badia, *La nuova sede nei palazzi della Condotta e della Mercanzia* (Florence, 1907), pp. 15–19.

[30] ASF, Conv. sopp. LXXIX (S. Ambrogio), 121 (accounts), fols. 16v–17r.

[31] Fragmentary building accounts for San Lorenzo survive in the Biblioteca Laurenziana; those for the Badia are in the Innocenti, ser. CXLI, 1–6. On the possible identity of *maestro* Lorenzo as Lorenzo d'Antonio di Geri, see Ugo Procacci, "Cosimo de' Medici e la costruzione della Badia fiesolana," *Commentari*, 19 (1968), 80–97.

One final contract in gross calls for comment apart because it is known only secondhand as described by an observer of doubtful accuracy. This is the contract for the building of an Alessandri palace reported in Georges Rohault de Fleury, *La Toscane au moyen âge: lettres sur l'architecture civile et militaire en 1400* (Paris, 1874), II, 141–219. The contract was made after competitive secret bidding with a mason named

THE NATURE OF THE CONTRACT. The selection of anyone for a position as important as a construction supervisor was usually a personal matter involving informal procedures. The institution that was continually involved in building or extensive maintenance and the individual owner who went from one building project to another customarily had recourse to the same waller, who thereby tended to become permanently associated with his patron, although he was not necessarily a full-time employee and certainly not a client in the political and social sense of that term. The several projects undertaken by Filippo Strozzi before the great palace was begun—a smaller palace in the city, a villa, and two oratories in the countryside—were all under the direction of Stefano Rosselli and his son Jacopo; it was therefore to be expected that Jacopo Rosselli was Strozzi's first choice as foreman also on the palace (and Cronaca may have gotten his job as head stonecutter because he was Jacopo's son-in-law).[32] Some builders must have left the selection of the construction staff to the architect, even when the architect did not work at the construction site. The team of wallers and stonecutters that went to work on the new building at the hospital of San Paolo designed by Michelozzo was the same that had long been associated with the architect in its previous employment at the Santissima Annunziata; likewise, the appearance of the same team of craftsmen at the Da Gagliano and Bartolini palaces is probably to be explained as the choice of the consulting architect of both, Baccio d'Agnolo.[33]

Although the more formal and objective procedure of selecting wallers on the basis of competitive bidding for work contracts was probably not used extensively in Florence, one notable instance of recourse to this method is known. The building committee of the Innocenti made at least two public announcements soliciting bids for construction work at the new orphanage. The announcement of 17 April 1428 stated the terms: walls were to be erected on the already prepared foundations according to stipulated height and thickness, with materials (to be provided by the works committee) specified; bids were to consist of a proposed schedule of task rates and to be written, sealed, and presented to the building committee and its purveyor; all bids were to be kept secret, and the contract would be let out to the lowest bidder. The committee

---

Gerardo and was accompanied by a plan that he was to follow. Gerardo was to demolish older walls and to provide the labor and materials for extensive new building, and for this he was to receive 5,100 florins a month for a year, with additional work to be paid for according to a schedule of rates. He made a security deposit of 50 florins and named two guarantors. Rohault de Fleury then proceeds to describe at great length (and with considerable verisimilitude) the building history of the palace, presumably drawing his material from an account book in the Alessandri archives. The monthly amount to be paid to Gerardo is certainly not accurate, and without the document itself it is not possible to check on the rest of this account.

32 Goldthwaite, "Strozzi Palace," pp. 149–50.

33 On teams of craftsmen associated with architects see pp. 383–84 herein.

also announced bids for vaulting of the hospital's portico after the columns were in place, for plastering and painting the walls, and for installing the tie rods; and, again, the bidder was to present task rates for work alone (and the method of measurement was stipulated in the announcement). To judge from a contract drawn up on 11 June 1428, winning bids for both these jobs came from Antonio and Francesco di Geri, who in fact had been the lowest bidders for an earlier contract, in 1422. Unfortunately the written bids do not survive, and it is not known how the building committee proceeded to make its selections. This instance of opening up work at the Innocenti to competitive bidding is especially interesting because it suggests, on the one hand, that the architect, Brunelleschi, had no close ties with wallers, and, on the other, that the wallers had repeatedly to submit new bids for additional work to keep their employment.[34]

Agreements on the terms of employment were usually incorporated into a written contract if work was undertaken under any arrangement other than a direct labor system. These documents were made in two copies, one for each party (although what survive today are mostly copies entered as memoranda in

[34] The announcements are items no. 8 and 14 among loose papers in ledger A of the building accounts: Innocenti, ser. VII, 1. The second of these is published by Manuel Cardoso Mendes and Giovanni Dallai, "Nuove indagini sullo Spedale degli Innocenti a Firenze," *Commentari*, 17 (1966), doc. 16.

Apollonio di Giovanni, illustrations from the *Aeneid* (details), mid-fifteenth century.

the owner's books of accounts), and they were signed and witnessed by one or more outside parties. Generally, however, they are not highly standardized, and they do not take on the form of well-formulated legal documents. As a rule labor contracts were not notarized (they were more likely to be notarized if drawn up in Florentine territory beyond the city walls). Florentines had abandoned the notary for most agreements that did not involve the transfer of property and money (hence in the absence of private documents other than notarial acts before the mid-fourteenth century, little can be known about the construction industry in the earlier period[35]). Contracts were nevertheless legal documents, and in the event that one of the parties went to court (at either the Mercanzia or a guild) to settle claims relative to a breach of contract, the contract constituted the major evidence, along with the parties' account books and the judgment of any outside consultant who might be called in for an opinion.

Characteristic of the legal informality of labor contracts in the construction industry is the absence of penalty clauses, bonds, and sureties. Although examples of all these features can be found, they are rare, and they become rarer in the fifteenth century. In the 1427 Innocenti contract for the roof of the children's residence hall, the waller Piero d'Antonio Cioffi produced a guarantor who also signed the contract, agreeing to be responsible for damages

[35] Franek Sznura, *L'espansione urbana di Firenze nel Dugento* (Florence, 1975), p. 21.

and shortcomings up to a value of 100 florins.[36] This exceptional arrangement (unique among the many Innocenti contracts) may be explained by the special precaution the orphanage's building committee wanted to take in contracting for the roof of the central building in the complex where the children themselves were to reside. In the San Matteo contract of 1388 with three masons for additional buildings to that new hospital, a clause was added stipulating a penalty of 100 florins to be paid by either of the parties (the owner or the contractors collectively) in the event of failure to observe the contract (50 florins were to go to the other party and 50 florins were to be paid to the commune).[37] On the Strozzi palace project the founder Andrea Frilli accepted a contract (after it had been turned down by another founder) with a penalty clause holding him responsible for half the damage should any of the foundations collapse. In view of the enormous load his foundations were to carry, it is perhaps not surprising that Filippo Strozzi added this stipulation, although one might wonder how he thought he could have collected any damages from a man of Frilli's modest financial status as an artisan.[38] Sometimes penalty clauses were directed to enforce the full-time commitment of the waller to the job. In 1318 Lapo di Ricco, who contracted (apparently for a task fee) to keep three other wallers and laborers on the job full time building a shop for a Calimala merchant, agreed to pay the owner 40 soldi for every day they did not work;[39] in a 1399 labor contract for chapel construction at San Pancrazio, Vanni di Filippo from Rovezzano agreed not to take other work under penalty of 15 florins.[40] The additional device of clamping down some kind of control on the waller by requiring an outside judgment of work completed, a common feature of artists' contracts at the time, is rare in construction contracts. One example appears in the 1341 contract already cited between the confraternity of Orsanmichele and the waller Antonio for construction of a house, where a final clause names the waller Gherarduccio as judge of the quality of Antonio's work.[41]

In general, however, when Florentine owners made labor contracts, they did not seek to protect themselves by stipulating controls over the waller's work such as penalties, sureties, bonds, and outside judges—all of which were characteristic, for instance, of English building practice in this period.[42] It was nevertheless possible to have recourse to the courts whenever problems

[36] Innocenti, ser. VII (building accounts), 2 (ledger B), fols. 180r–81r.

[37] The contract is published by Sanpaolesi, "S. Matteo," pp. 77–79; see pp. 367–68 herein.

[38] Goldthwaite, "Strozzi Palace," pp. 142–43.

[39] Milanesi, *Nuovi documenti*, pp. 21–22.

[40] Published by Marco Dezzi Bardeschi, "Il complesso monumentale di San Pancrazio a Firenze ed il suo restauro (nuovi documenti)," *Quaderni dell'Istituto di Storia dell'Architettura*, 13th ser., fasc. 73–78 (1966).

[41] Milanesi, "Documenti," pp. 224–25.

[42] Salzman, *Building*, p. 52.

arose. In Modena legislation held the waller responsible for guaranteeing his product by requiring him to pay damages if the structure did not hold up for ten years, and the liability could be shifted to his workers if their negligence in the matter could be established.[43] In Florence the silk guild took such action in 1361 against the foreman Benci di Cione at their sponsored project of Orsanmichele: they petitioned the commune to appropriate and sell all of his property in compensation for his incompetence and defective workmanship on the job.[44] Most cases involving disputes over contractual agreements, however, probably went before the masons' guild. For instance, in 1543, after looking over a written agreement and calling in other evidence, the consuls made a judgment against a waller for work on the roof of a house; in another appeal in 1548 they ordered a waller to live up to the terms of his contract and complete his work satisfactorily within a set time on penalty of reimbursing his client all the money already received in payment.[45] Unfortunately, the guild deliberations contain only the final action by the consuls and nothing of the background hearings and materials leading up to that action. To judge from the surviving deliberations of the sixteenth century, however, the consuls dealt with few such cases.

The labor contract was a document that existed primarily to commit the contractor to a project and to establish the financial terms of his agreement with the employer. It included other conditions, of course, but the document did not follow a highly standardized formula, and it is difficult to generalize about other kinds of clauses. A contract could be quite detailed in specifying what was to be built. In the San Matteo contract of 1385 with Romolo di Bandino and Sandro del Vinta, a complete set of measurements was included —for the depth of foundations and thickness of foundation walls, for the lengths and thickness of the buildings' walls, for the vaults—and instructions were given about what materials were to be used and how walls were to be finished. It was not unusual that contracts for more ambitious buildings also included references to plans the wallers were to follow, a subject that is discussed herein with regard to architectural practice. If the owner provided building materials, it is usually specified that any material not left in the building (as the formula put it),[46] such as wood for scaffolding, was to be furnished by the wallers. Sometimes the length of time in which work was to

[43] Melchiorre Roberti, "Il contratto di lavoro negli statuti medioevali," *Rivista internazionale di scienze sociali*, 40 (1932), 44.

[44] Saverio La Sorsa, *La compagnia d'Or San Michele* (Trani, 1902), p. 104.

[45] Fabbricanti 4, fol. 233v; 5, fols. 67v–68r.

[46] For example: "e debba dare la detta badessa calcina, mattoni, pietre, ferrame, e concio e ongni cosa abbi a rimanere nel detto lavoro; e el detto Lorenzo debba mettere ponti, armadure di volte, taglie, canapi, e tutto quello bisongnia per detto magisterio"; ASF, Conv. sopp. LXXXII (S. Apollonia), 10 (building accounts), fols. 3v–4v (1429).

be completed was stated, and some contracts required the masons to work full time on the project and to keep a certain minimum work force fully employed on the site. In short, a wide range of possibilities existed for establishing contractual terms between employee and waller. Almost any conceivable arrangement can be found; some, obviously, appear more frequently than others, while some appear to be completely eccentric within general practice (to judge from surviving examples). It is therefore difficult to make many generalizations about conditions of employment on the basis of contracts alone.

To settle accounts for a contract that defined work in terms of measure and value, an outsider had to be called in to take all the appropriate measurements. This job was generally left to professionals, the teachers of commercial arithmetic (*maestri d'abbaco*), of which Florence had a plentiful supply.[47] They did their measuring in the presence of a witness for each of the two contracting parties, who then shared the cost of the measuring. The building-crafts guild—the Arte dei Maestri di Pietra e di Legname—also approved assessors (*stimatori*) for judgment of work in connection with settlement of accounts, and with the reorganization of the guild in the sixteenth century, an official post of assessor was created for this function. More is said about this office in the discussion of guild activities. In the early fourteenth century, receipt of the employer's final payment to the mason was sometimes notarized; but in the fifteenth century, by which time the legal status of account books had gained universal confidence, masons simply signed a statement in the employer's account book acknowledging receipt of payment.

Whatever role contracts played in the professional practice of the Florentine waller, no written document tells the whole story of the relations between him and the owner. Fortunately, building accounts go a long way toward filling in the realities of the financial situation. These records indicate that wallers were limited in their ability to contract more extensively because they had little if any liquid capital at their disposal. Whether he committed himself to a comprehensive general contract or to a labor contract for a task or rate fee, the chances are that he did not have the financial resources to see his way through his payroll obligations up to the final settlement of accounts. In two of the examples of comprehensive labor and supply contracts described previously—the Medici contract for a garden wall and the Nacchianti contract for remodeling of a house—the wallers could to no significant degree finance their operations; if the same detailed information existed for other projects let out on contract, we would probably find that this was in fact the situation in which all the wallers of Florence found themselves.

Regardless of the terms of the contracts they made, therefore, wallers in-

[47] Richard A. Goldthwaite, "Schools and Teachers of Commercial Arithmetic in Renaissance Florence," *JEEcH*, 1 (1972), 428.

evitably had to be given frequent advances against the eventual charges to their employers. This condition was written into the San Matteo contracts—one stipulating that payments were to be made at least once a month, another that they were to be made from time to time. Accounting evidence suggests, however, that periodic payments to contractors while work was in progress was such a standard procedure that there was no reason for inserting provisions for payment into the contract. Sometimes payments were made in rounded figures (so many florins, for instance, whose value in lire might not correspond to the value of payments due), sometimes they were calculated on the basis of the going wage rate for all members of the work crew. The usual procedure seems to have been for the owner, regardless of the terms of the contract, to assume the ongoing payment obligation for the work crew, including even the wages of the contractor, at the standard wage rates; his payments were considered credit against the settlement of accounts at the end of construction. For example, on the accounts of the hospital of Santa Maria Nuova for the building of a patients' ward in the years 1414 and 1415 and a new chapter room and pharmacy in the years 1428 and 1429, the wallers who contracted to do the work (for the former project there were four) and their work crews were paid regularly according to the current wage rates; at the end of construction the value of their work was calculated according to a schedule of task rates established in prior agreements, and the difference between this value and the accumulated totals of wages already received was given to the wallers to settle the account.[48]

From the owner's point of view this financial limitation on the part of the waller meant that he could not contract away the obligation to meet the (usually weekly) payroll of the work force employed on a construction project. It is not surprising, therefore, that many projects, certainly most of the larger ones, were organized not by contracts but by a direct labor system in which the owner became an employer of wage labor and the wallers worked as salaried employees. If the work force was small, consisting of no more than the crews of one or two wallers, the waller might be the intermediate paymaster between employer and laborers, but all payments were based on a wage rate. For unskilled laborers the time rate was always a day's wages, and it was frequently so also for wallers, stonecutters, carpenters, and other skilled laborers. Given his inevitable responsibility for meeting the payroll, the owner found the daily wage contract the most convenient, for it gave him the flexibility he needed to deal with labor in an enterprise where for many reasons employment was subject to frequent fluctuations. The direct labor system was preferable when the owner wanted building to go forward rapidly (one thinks of Filippo Strozzi) and therefore needed an organization on a larger scale than any artisan could handle on his own. It

[48] S. M. Nuova 5046, fols. 27v, 36, 46, 93v, 101, 108, 119; 5047, fols. 9, 25.

was also a more satisfactory procedure for those projects that, because of inadequate or sluggish financing, went forward too slowly to make a formal contract of any advantage to either party (and many institutional projects were of this kind).

A labor contract based on a time rate rarely took a written form, not even when it was made with a foreman who was to work for a monthly or annual salary. A written contract was drawn up, however, for the building of Santa Maria delle Carceri in nearby Prato. In 1485 the building committee employed Giuliano di Francesco da Sangallo as foreman for the new church, and the terms were written down, and even notarized.[49] Sangallo was to receive a daily wage of 30 soldi for every day he actually worked on the site, and he agreed to see the work through to its completion, following all instructions from the building committee. Although he was assured that he could keep a waller and a stonecutter in continual employment, their wages as well as all arrangements with laborers were to be determined by the committee. The agreement was written out probably because Sangallo's residence in Florence raised some question in the committee's mind about the regularity of his attendance at the building site (and in fact, because of other commitments, he did not stay on the job long).

Although it was not the custom for a mason who took on employment on the basis of a time rate to have the terms of his employment incorporated into written contracts, something of the nature of his informal agreement with his employer can often be found in the entries of payments to him on the employer's accounts. When Cronaca went to work on the Strozzi palace as head stonecutter with an annual salary, Filippo Strozzi made a memorandum of their agreement that Cronaca was to hire stonecutters, supervise their preparation of the stone for the wallers, keep records of their work, and make designs and models for stonework; these terms were frequently repeated in the entries for his wages over the duration of his employment for the following fifteen years.[50] Cronaca worked as a salaried employee in a direct labor system, however, without a contract formally defining the mutual obligations of employee and employer. Most Florentine masons probably worked under similar informal arrangements.

Thus the contract was an instrument that only to a limited extent served to relieve the owner of the organizational problem in a construction project. Contracts for supply helped to assure a schedule of delivery, and labor contracts clarified financial terms and committed masons to the projects, but neither contract freed the patron from financial administration. For this reason labor contracts rarely offered advantages over a direct labor system. In

[49] The document is published in G. Marchini, "Della costruzione di Santa Maria delle Carceri in Prato," *Archivio storico pratese*, 14 (1936), 62.

[50] Goldthwaite, "Strozzi Palace," p. 124.

any case, whether an owner used a direct labor system or whether he let out construction work by contract, he could not avoid a close financial involvement in the operation—and, in the final analysis, he simply may not have wanted to relinquish complete financial control. He invariably had to keep detailed accounts, and it is thanks to the survival of those records that we know so much about how the industry operated.

THE LIMITS OF ENTREPRENEURSHIP. Enough examples of various kinds of contracts can be found for us to conclude that the entire range of contract possibilities was open to Florentine wallers. To the extent that they contracted at all, however, they contracted only on a small scale; the most realistic option was to contract to do work for a task rate on the basis of measure and value. For anything but the simplest construction project wallers were reluctant to concern themselves with supply of building materials. Moreover, their financial involvement was limited; they made virtually no investment in the enterprise, they assumed little financial control over the operation, and more often than not they ended up working on salary, sometimes despite the formal terms of a contract. Their work gangs were composed of only an apprentice or two and perhaps as many laborers, and they seldom made contracts where they were responsible for a much larger labor force. At San Matteo, for instance, where two masons promised to keep a minimum number of other masons and laborers employed full time on a project that included everything from foundations to roofs for a sizeable hospital complex, probably no more than a dozen workers ever showed up for work at any one time.

Few wallers, furthermore, could count on steady, long-term work on one job. Instability of employment was endemic to the construction industry, and the more enterprising waller-contractors were subject to the industry's erratic rhythms only slightly less than day laborers. With the seasonableness of the industry, the problems of financing, and the play of various forces, political and otherwise, in the labor market, it was rare that employment on a building project could be maintained at a constant level for more than several months. If the waller worked on a task contract, it was probably for a small job that did not for long relieve him of worry about where the next contract was to be found.

Wallers had little capital tied up in their work. They had their own tools, and when work was taken on contract they were generally prepared to supply the equipment they needed, such as scaffolding, rope, and smaller lifting devices. They did not work out of shops; no mention of shops is made in their tax returns, and none appear in the shop census of 1561. Although they often went into association with one another (as *compagni*) for purposes of specific projects, wallers are not known to have organized formal partnerships in the business sense of that term. Moreover, there is no evidence that they profited from their supply channels by investing in the building-material industries. Those who had property to report to the tax officials declared land and houses rather than kilns, quarries, or woods. Not many, however, made enough from their craft to invest in anything at all. Of the wallers who so identified themselves on their declarations for the 1427 Catasto, only six had an estate worth more than 300 florins. After taking a generous deduction of 200 florins for each dependent, few of these men had much to worry about from the tax office. The waller who was best off was Francesco di Geri, who with his brother Antonio did much of the masonry work at the Innocenti. With a house rented out, Monte credits worth 340 florins, and other miscellaneous credits, Francesco declared an estate of 598 florins; his brother was worth only half that. Neither added significant real estate holdings to his estate over the next twenty-five years.[51]

Despite their modest profile as entrepreneurs, wallers often displayed quite considerable supervisory talent. Whether he worked as his own boss on a small project or as a foreman on a large one, he likely had responsibilities that went beyond the formal terms of his employment. Although he made no financial commitment to supply materials, he could assume the responsibility for selecting suppliers and controlling the quality of their products, thus serving as a consultant, if not indeed the agent, of the employer on these matters. When it came to supervising labor, the waller who was the general foreman of the works had supervisory powers not only over laborers and any other waller who might be employed on the project but also over other craftsmen, such as carpenters, painters, stonecutters, and founders, even though they were employed on independent terms by the employer.

It was the task of the foreman of the works to coordinate the efforts of all these men into a reasonably efficient operation. Most foremen were wallers but it certainly was not unusual for a stonecutter to be selected for the job, especially, of course, if stone was a major material in the building. On the typical job the crew under a foreman was small, not much more than a dozen men and usually fewer, but there were those foremen, for instance at the new sacristy at San Lorenzo and the Strozzi palace, who were in charge of a work force whose ranks on occasion swelled to over a hundred men. It is hard to think of any other industrial enterprise in Florence organized as a direct labor system that required the coordination of a work force so large, so diverse, and so concentrated at one site as that necessary for a large construc-

[51] Information about wealth comes from the survey of those taxpayers who declared their occupation represented on the printout by David Herlihy, "Census and Property Survey (Catasto) of the City of Florence, Italy, 1427 with Additions of 1428." The references to the Catasto reports of Francesco and Antonio are 65, fol. 308; 76, fol. 246. Cf. their sons' reports: Catasto 707 (1451), fols. 401 (Francesco's sons) and 536 (Antonio's sons). Antonio's son Lorenzo was foreman at the Badia of Fiesole (see note 31 above); and another, Andrea worked at the chapel of the Portuguese cardinal in San Miniato and, along with his two sons, at San Bartolomeo.

Pesellino, Construction of the Temple of Jerusalem, mid-fifteenth century.

tion project. The foremen on these projects probably had the most developed supervisory talents in their society. The names of the successive foremen, culminating in Brunelleschi, at the cathedral come immediately to mind, but many other private projects underway throughout the city were only slightly less challenging to the supervisory and managerial talents of their foremen.

Only on the largest projects, however, could a waller (or a stonecutter) hope to find a full-time job as foreman. There were few posts of the kind Cronaca had as head stonecutter at the Strozzi palace, for which a part-time salary was paid on a steady basis, regardless of the pace of construction. The larger ecclesiastical institutions usually kept a foreman on salary as maintenance supervisor for their extensive building complexes, and he could find work elsewhere in his free time. In the second decade of the sixteenth century a property owner in the vicinity of Santa Croce frequently gave out small jobs to a waller named Battista, who is identified as the foreman at that monastery.[52] Virtually all the foremen at the cathedral after Brunelleschi

[52] ASF, Archivio Gherardi 169 (accounts of Lorenzo di Matteo Morelli, 1513–16), fols. 16 and 21; 170 (1516–20), fols. 25 and 33.

were in effect such part-time employees working on salary, and they show up concurrently on other projects. If the foreman worked for daily wages, however, he knew that if there was no work there would be no pay, and every foreman had to face the probability of a complete shutdown of the workshop every so often. We have seen how Giuliano da Sangallo, when he went to work as foreman at Santa Maria delle Carceri, was warned that he would be paid nothing for the days he did not show up. Few of these men were as fortunate as the foreman at Santo Spirito, Giovanni di Mariano: although he worked for a daily wage, he nevertheless had something like a guaranteed minimum income, for he was promised at least 12 lire a month (approximately equivalent to his pay for twelve days of work) if during periods of inactivity at Santo Spirito he was unable to find work elsewhere.[53]

The absence of large-scale contracting in Florence should not obscure the fact that the organization of the building trades was nevertheless sufficiently developed to have facilitated an effort to coordinate them all into a single entrepreneurial venture. Many of the conditions favorable to contracting were present in Florence. The waller's training in the tradition of Italian building practice gave him comprehensive mastery of almost all the skills needed for most construction, and producers of building materials were sufficiently numerous and independent that it was possible to contract for supply, with delivery to the building site included in the bargain. Furthermore, building costs could be estimated beforehand with reasonable accuracy. Rates for basic materials were standardized, and it did not require a high level of arithmetic skill to calculate the quantity of material needed to build walls of given dimensions. A standard problem in the numerous manuals of practical arithmetic of the period included calculations of number of bricks needed for a given wall. In Book IV of his treatise on architecture Filarete estimates the full cost of building walls at Sforzinda by using calculations for the number of bricks needed for the total volume, the amounts of sand and burnt lime (which he sets at a ratio of four to one) required for laying 1,000 bricks, and the number of wallers and laborers who can do a braccio of the wall per day. That labor costs could be estimated for normal kinds of construction is clear enough from the widespread practice of masons of contracting for task rates, and the refinement of their calculations is reflected in the detailed schedule of rates one finds in payment records for the various parts of a building, from foundations to the roof, including walls built to different specifications and standard pieces of *pietra serena*, such as moldings, columns, and capitals. Neither building materials nor building techniques changed throughout the period, and with a long tradition of building in brick and rubble and finishing walls with plaster and whitewash, most masons must have possessed a fairly accurate sense of unit costs. In any case,

[53] S. Spirito 128, fol. 82v.

Master of San Miniato, St. Barbara honors the Trinity by having a third window opened in the tower where she is imprisoned (detail).

the highly standardized accounting procedures used by owners to keep track of building expenses—neat categorization of expenditures, fully descriptive entries, and double entry—facilitated cost analysis. Finally, this was a time when such calculations were not threatened by price instability of either materials or labor.

The lack of capital has been suggested as one difficulty facing the waller who wanted to organize these forces of production. He had no access to credit from either his employees and suppliers, who required frequent cash settlement of accounts, or capitalists, who had not organized institutions through which investment (as opposed to consumption) credit could be channelled to artisans. Advances on contracts were, of course, a form of credit, and it is possible that some enterprising wallers were able to increase their profits from construction ventures by relying on this kind of financing from the employer himself. With factor inputs (labor and materials) relatively fixed in cost, however, a contractor had little prospect of cutting his expenses to increase profits.

Perhaps the most serious obstacle to increasing the scale of those operations was the unwillingness to organize labor for the purpose of making a profit. It was a fundamental fact in a labor-intensive industry like construction before the industrial revolution (when labor was not yet disciplined by the factory system) that hardly anyone was prepared to contract for the organization of a large labor force (this observation is clarified in chapter 6). When a waller contracted for extensive building and assumed the full responsibility for labor, he was more often than not committing himself to a long duration of work rather than to supervision of a large labor force.

However favorable some market conditions were for contracting, the marketplace lacked an atmosphere conducive to exploiting those conditions. This was not an age of speculative building for profits, and the patron no more than the waller felt any inclination to go about organizing large numbers of workers in an entrepreneurial enterprise. Most patrons caught up in the building zeal of the new era had too much of a personal interest in their projects even to think about turning everything over to anyone else.

Throughout early modern Europe the basic structure of the construction industry did not advance much beyond the artisan stage represented by the Florentine situation. The mason had little potential for expanding his enterprise. Equipment was not a major capital expense, and investment in the building-materials industry did not necessarily assure lower costs so that he could improve his competitive advantage in the market. In many parts of Europe (but not in Florence) local craft traditions stood as barriers to a higher level of integration of skilled workers, and there was little point—even had it been possible—in mobilizing ordinary laborers into a more effective labor force, since demand was sporadic, pick-up labor plentiful, labor costs relatively fixed, and the working man still undisciplined by the modern industrial system. In short, the mason had few opportunities for cutting expenses. In the absence of technical innovation, little efficiency was to be gained through reorganization, and in the absence of a booming market, the effort would hardly have been worthwhile.

This view of the industry should not be distorted by the grandeur of many construction projects or by the growing number of big contractors and speculators in the building markets of the expanding cities of early modern Europe. With the rapid growth of large capital cities, governments found themselves engaged in major construction projects, ranging from widening streets and opening squares in accord with new ideals in urban planning to putting up fortifications in response to the threat of a rapidly changing military technology; in the private sector some of the largest cities underwent what was virtually a boom in upper-class housing. In this situation both mason-architects and capitalists found increasing opportunities for turning a

Sodoma, St. Benedict appears to two monks and gives them the design for the building of a new monastery (detail), 1505–1508.

profit, but their entrepreneurial efforts did not bring about any significant change in the basic structure of the construction industry.

What a mason-architect had to contract out were his own talents—his technical expertise, his practical knowledge about subcontracting, his supervisory abilities. For example, the architect Vignola and a colleague made a contract in 1548 with the investors in a public project to build a canal in Bologna, including three locks, a gateway through the city walls, docks in the city, and two guardhouses; the work was to be done within one year for 6,000 scudi, plus or minus 500 scudi, depending on how the employers were satisfied with the results.[54] The contract does not specify the details of the financial arrangements, and the accounts are missing, but since Vignola had to put up security (which came from an outside guarantor), we can surmise that financing was entirely in the hands of the men who let out the contract. Vignola certainly did not have this kind of capital, and it is difficult to know where he would have gotten it. Moreover, it is unlikely that he went about the work as an industrial entrepreneur. In late sixteenth-century Milan a number of large contracts for canals and fortifications were let out to architect-engineers, who simply proceeded to organize work through the usual subcontracting mechanisms.[55] In other words, with financing out of their hands, these men really contracted to work as supervisors and technical experts, not as building entrepreneurs. Such men might, quite naturally, try to cut expenses—this is why so many architects throughout the early modern period advised their patrons not to rely on contractors—but they were not inspired to reorganize the forces of production into a business enterprise.

Nor did it make much difference in the organization of the industry when a large-scale contract was taken by a capitalist investor rather than a mason-entrepreneur. The most notable contractor of this kind in the sixteenth century—and perhaps the first of a new breed of building speculators—was surely Gilbert van Schoonbeke, the enterprising brewer of Antwerp.[56] In 1551 van Schoonbeke, with the support of a few fellow investors, undertook the building of a major section of the new fortifications of Antwerp. His investment went where he presumably thought the profits were to be made—to the supply of materials. He opened a complex of fifteen brickyards, complete with sixty houses for workers, and elsewhere he set up several limekilns; he organized work at an immense peat bog employing at least a hundred workers; and he arranged for supply of wood. At the building site he had large buildings erected to house workers. The construction work itself, however, he subcontracted to half a dozen or so masons, who themselves organized the work force in the traditional way, including the financing of it between the intervals when they were paid by van Schoonbeke for completed sections of the walls. Van Schoonbeke invested his capital in the production of building materials for a guaranteed customer and used his financial power to speculate in subcontracting away the responsibility for actual construction. What attracted

[54] Guido Zucchini, "Il Vignola a Bologna," in *Memorie e studi intorno a Jacopo Barozzi pubblicati nel IV centenario della nascita* (Bologna, 1908), pp. 229–34.

[55] Domenico Sella, *Salari e lavoro nell'edilizia lombarda durante il secolo XVII* (Pavia, 1968), pp. 42–43.

[56] Hugo Soly, *Urbanisme en kapitalism te Antwerpen in de 16de eeuw: de stedebouwkundige en industriële ondernemingen van Gilbert van Schoonbeke* (Brussels, 1977).

him (and other Antwerp investors) was the enormous size of the contracts—the total cost for the entire project has been estimated at 2,000,000 florins. Once the fortifications were completed, however, no other work on anything like this scale was available; and, in any case, Antwerp was by that time in clear decline. In other words, contracts like these were regarded as one-time ventures for a sure profit, not as part of the ongoing business of a construction entrepreneur.

Speculation in building became more important in the early modern period with the increased demand for substantial housing by the middle and upper classes crowding into some of the growing capital cities of Europe, above all, London and Paris.[57] Large amounts of capital were attracted by schemes undertaken to develop residential property, and with the easier availability of credit, even for craftsmen, some artisan-builders could make their fortunes in these enterprises. During the boom of sixteenth-century Antwerp, for example, masons could buy land for an annuity, build on it, and then sell it for an annuity—and so turn a good profit. The scale of this kind of speculation was much higher in London, where after the great fire of 1666 a procedure was developed for carrying through extensive building schemes that then remained the standard pattern during the boom in better residential property that London (and other English cities) enjoyed over the next century. Speculators bought or leased large pieces of urban property on which they developed an extensive housing project in the hope of assuring themselves income from ground rents through long-term leases. Actual construction was regarded as a stage in this development process to be contracted out in order to avoid further investment in the scheme. The building contractor—usually an artisan-builder—leased single lots for a token rent from the developer until the house was built, or contracted directly to undertake construction; but, whatever the terms, he in turn subcontracted to other trades rather than organize the entire building process himself. These men were themselves small speculators who managed to finance relatively large contracts (by their standards) with the credit they received from the developer (in token rents), from their suppliers and subcontractors, and from mortgages they took out on the houses that were to be built—arrangements that were possible only because of the extraordinary availability of credit in eighteenth century England. The profits to be made in these ventures came, for the developer, from speculation in getting the land and organizing the estate development, and, for the builder, from being able to contract for construction on credit;

[57] These building procedures have been well studied in England: John Summerson, *Georgian London* (London, 1948); C. W. Chalklin, *The Provincial Towns of Georgian England: A Study of the Building Process, 1740–1820* (London, 1974); Ron Neale, "Society, Belief, and the Building of Bath, 1700–1793," in *Rural Change and Urban Growth, 1500–1800: Essays in English Regional History in Honour of W. K. Hoskins*, ed. C. W. Chalklin and M. A. Havinden (London, 1974), pp. 253–80.

both enterprises involved speculation, not a more efficient organization of the building process itself.

General contracting, by which the contractor himself organized the forces of production into a single enterprise rather than subcontract for them, did not appear in England until the beginning of the nineteenth century. The original stimulus to set up this kind of operation came from the large and exacting public contracts the government let out for barracks during the years of the Napoleonic threat, and the impetus was sustained by demand for extensive building arising from various other quarters about the same time as a result of the urban transformations brought about by the industrial revolution. The first innovator in organizing a modern construction firm is generally thought to have been the master carpenter Thomas Cubitt. He had his own brickyard and workshops and directly employed bricklayers, masons, carpenters, smiths, plumbers, plasterers, roofers, glaziers, and other specialized craftsmen as well as carters and laborers, to whom he was able to offer full-time employment going from one project to another. By the mid-nineteenth century there were some half dozen such contractors in London, each employing about one hundred and fifty men.[58]

Despite notable examples of large-scale enterprises, construction has remained an industry of small firms. In England, France, and the United States—and no doubt elsewhere as well—the typical construction company is a small enterprise with operations confined to an immediate locale and organized around extensive subcontracting. In the United States many firms are short-lived, single-owner enterprises, whose capital is mostly in equipment. Even large firms achieve few economies of scale and have a relatively low capital investment. More efficient management control of the industrial process has been limited by the custom-built nature of the product, the separation of the design process from production, and the lack of durable relations between management and the forces of production resulting from the extensive use of subcontracting. Construction, in short, remains the least revolutionized of the heavy industries.[59]

[58] Hermione Hobhouse, *Thomas Cubitt, Master Builder* (London, 1971); E. W. Cooney, "The Origins of the Victorian Master Builders," *Economic History Review*, 8 (1955–56), 167–76; idem, "The Organization of Building in England in the 19th Century," *Architectural Research and Teaching*, 1, No. 2 (1970), 46–52; H. J. Dyos, "The Speculative Builders and Developers of Victorian London," *Victorian Studies*, 11 (1967–68), 641–90.

[59] For the present state of affairs in the industry see, for the U.S.A., Peter J. Cassimatis, *Economics of the Construction Industry*, Studies in Business Economics, No. 111 (New York, 1969); for France, T. J. Markovitch, "L'industrie française de 1789 à 1964. Titre IX: construction," *Cahiers de l'Institut de science économique appliquée*, No. 174 (1966), 143–94; for England, Marian Bowley, *The British Building Industry: Four Studies in Response and Resistance to Change* (Cambridge, 1966).

Managing the Enterprise

ADMINISTRATIVE ORGANIZATION. The organizational problem of erecting a building breaks down into three distinct tasks: supply of materials, construction operations, and financial administration. A modern contractor assumes all these responsibilities for his client, but we have seen that in Florence masons were prepared to make such comprehensive contracts only in exceptional instances. Rarely could an owner, after engaging a mason, sit back, watch construction go forward, and wait for the bills to come in. There is no reason to think that any wealthy Florentine even considered this a desirable way of doing things. His sense of property was personal, and a property-owner, be he a private person or an institution, had no reason to entrust any aspect of the administration of his property to an artisan. Given the mentality about wealth in precapitalist societies, it was quite natural that an owner wanted to keep a close personal watch over purchase and use of materials needed for construction and over expenditures of his money for labor. He was, therefore, inevitably involved in a web of special relations with suppliers and workers, and even though much of the supervision of actual construction could be left to his foreman, he himself ultimately carried the burden of responsibility for supply of materials and financial administration.

The employer's task of supplying his workers with materials was greatly facilitated by the independence of the forces of production supplying those materials. There were manufacturers and dealers prepared to supply virtually anything, and the owner had recourse to them in the marketplace. If he wanted to assure himself of a reasonably steady pace of supply during protracted building activity or purchase materials that had to be made to order, such as wood beams, ironwork, and, above all, decorative stonework, he most likely dealt with suppliers through contracts. These contracts (*allogazione* is the usual term found in the documents) were written, signed, and witnessed, but not usually notarized unless an advance payment was made by the buyer. The terms varied according to circumstances. The price is generally quoted as a rate charge, and almost always it is clearly stated that price included delivery to the building site. Contracts were generally made for materials bought in large quantity, such as bricks or sand and lime for mortar. For the construction of the Strozzi palace, for instance, these were the only items that were the subject of written contracts.[60] For the orphanage of the Innocenti, on the other hand, almost all materials were purchased through contractual agreements with suppliers—not only bricks, lime, and sand, but

[60] Goldthwaite, "Strozzi Palace," pp. 157–59.

also wood, gravel for fill of foundations, some of the stonework, and the iron tie rods for the portico. In all essential details supply contracts for most items resemble those for stone and brick, which are discussed in the following chapter.

The chief function of the contract in these instances was to assure supply and delivery when it was important to keep workers on a regular schedule. The concern is explicit in the Innocenti contracts: two required the supplier to meet all the orphanage's requests for his product within the duration of the contract; another, with a supplier of sand used for mortar, required that he not do work for anyone else within the stipulated time of the contract; and the contract for wood was accompanied by a complete list of what was required, an advance payment, and a schedule for three additional installments to guarantee delivery. Such contracts often included penalty clauses holding the supplier responsible for expenses resulting from any failure on his part in meeting obligations. It is not clear, however, what recourse a buyer might have in such an event, since a supplier could hardly have been in a financial position to pay much of a penalty. A memorandum was made in the Innocenti books about the protest (apparently to the guild) against a sand supplier who failed to meet his contractual obligation, but there is no evidence about the action taken against the supplier or any compensation the orphanage received for the inconvenience. A San Miniato contract for bricks defines the penalty to be imposed on the kilnmen for failure to meet the supply schedule as payment of any increase in costs suffered by the monastery should it have to buy bricks from another dealer.[61]

Agreement on costs was less of a concern in contracts than assurance of a steady supply. Two of the Innocenti contracts—one for the tie rods of the portico, another for the stone oculi of its facade—state that costs were to be determined at a later time. The cost of most materials, especially those not produced to special order, was so uniform as a result of normal forces of the marketplace (there were no controls) that it was probably not a major consideration in making a supply contract. There were generally accepted notions of what constituted a fair market price, and for this reason bidding was most likely not practiced as a procedure for selecting particular suppliers. In early nineteenth-century England it was still not the practice to let out contracts on the basis of competitive bidding since price was not a major variable.[62] Competitions with submission of written bids, however, were not altogether unknown in Florence (as discussed earlier).

[61] Many of the Innocenti contracts are recorded in ledger B of the building accounts: Innocenti, ser. VII, 2, fols. 176–89. The San Miniato contract is cited herein, p. 185 n. 26.
[62] Cooney, "Victorian Master Builders," p. 174.

To the extent that the owner was responsible for supply, he had to keep track of how his money was being spent, just as, regardless of the terms of his arrangements with his foreman for building operations, he had to assume financial responsibility down to the weekly payroll. It is a basic fact about building in Florence that the owner kept the financial record, and because of the high standards of accounting practice for which the city is famous, the result of this recordkeeping was the abundant documentation that is the foundation of this study. Building accounts appear everywhere, as separate accounts in ledgers of general administration—private, institutional, and public—and as entire books kept just for the administration of a building project—*libri della muraglia*, as they are universally called. No less impressive than the abundance of these records is their uniformity as accounting documents, even so far as the terminology and format of the entries. Expenses are carefully categorized into materials and labor, credits and debits are divided, items are registered in double entry, and total expenditures are often collected and summarized on comprehensive accounts. The remarkable detail and organization of these documents have already been cited as evidence for the deep personal involvement of Florentines in their building projects.[63]

Between supply and financial administration a builder was confronted with considerable managerial responsibility. On the normal project, where the work crew was small and construction proceeded slowly, arrangements for supply were probably worked out by the owner with the help of his foreman, who could advise about suppliers and check supplies as they came in. On larger projects, however, these tasks could not always be left to the foreman, and in any case, the authority to contract and make payments was rarely delegated to him. If the owner for one reason or another could not give his attention to these matters—if for instance, the project was large and he was a busy man, like Filippo Strozzi, or if the owner was an institution that had to work through an administrative staff—someone who could manage the operation had to be found. Such a person was called the purveyor of the works (*provveditore*). Most large institutions, like hospitals and monasteries, had purveyors for the general administration of their property who might also take on responsibilities for any building undertaken by the institution, but on a large project this job could be full time. Being entrusted with the owner's personal interest in the enterprise and responsible for his property, the purveyor was a man who enjoyed his employer's full confidence. Almost all who can be identified are men with clerical or low-level administrative

[63] The Strozzi accounts are described in Goldthwaite, "Strozzi Palace," pp. 136–42.

backgrounds; they did not come from the ranks of the building crafts. Although they did not form a distinct professional group, some may have gone from one job to another on the basis of their expertise in directing construction projects.[64]

The purveyor was something like a business manager whose responsibilities complemented the technical operations that were in the hands of the foreman. He was involved in actual construction to the extent that he made arrangements for supply, checked on deliveries, and looked out for the security of the workshop. In addition, he was in charge of the financial administration—making disbursements and keeping the accounts. At both the Innocenti and Santo Spirito his records were subject to inspection by members of the building committee and to periodic audits conducted by accountants called in for that purpose. The purveyor's accounts included the payroll, although it was the foreman's task to keep the daily employment record of workers, since he had supervisory control over them. At Filarete's Sforzinda the foreman sent chits to the paymaster vouching for the employment of workers, and in Florentine building accounts enough references to these (they are called *polizze*) turn up to assure us that this was a general practice. At Santo Spirito the head stonecutter, Salvi d'Andrea, not the foreman, kept the employment records (and sounded the work bell), and he was paid a small supplement to his wages for every six months or year that he did this.[65]

Although he kept accounts, the purveyor did not always handle cash and actually make payment. The purveyor selected by Cardinal Giulio de' Medici in 1519 for the building of the new sacristy at San Lorenzo, Giovan Battista Figiovanni, accepted the task only on condition that he not have to handle money. He kept the accounts but made payments by written orders directed originally to the cardinal's treasurer at the archbishop's palace and later, after Giulio was named pope, to the Medici's bankers in the city. After 1530, however, when he returned to the job following the shut-down of the workshop during the interlude of the last republic, Figiovanni had to assume the responsibility for the cash box himself because of difficulties of making payment through local bankers. The building committee at Santo Spirito kept its funds in deposit at the bank of Piero Mellini, and the purveyor wrote orders of payment on that account, which included the payroll. Nevertheless, some cash had to be kept on hand for occasional direct payments to workers and suppliers at the site, and the separate ledger kept for this activity survives

[64] Like the broker in Geneva, Antonio di Ser Pagolo, who tried to get a building commission from Piero de' Medici "perchè n'ò lla praticha . . . [and] perchè in tale lavori ne prendo grande chonsolazione"; cited herein, chapter 2, n. 25.

[65] Salvi was paid for "avere tenuto conto degli scioperii" (1482), "per avere tenuto il ruolo 4 anni al chonto degli scioperii" (1487), and "per avere tenuto l'oriuolo e tenere richordo d'opere e scioperi" (1492); S. Spirito 128, fols. 56v, 85v, and 217v.

in the Santo Spirito archives.[66] At the Innocenti, a new foundation that at the time of building was still raising money for its endowment, the building committee had a treasurer (*camerlingo*) who handled all payments for construction expenses on written order from the purveyor, but here, too, the purveyor often made cash payments out of his own pocket, for which he was reimbursed. For the Innocenti the surviving accounts include also those of the purveyor of the sponsoring guild, who was responsible for keeping records of all financial affairs of the new orphanage, including building.

The first items that invariably appear on any set of building accounts are expenditures to get the purveyor's operation going—purchase of the account books themselves, pen, ink, sometimes a desk, and other equipment. The vast paperwork produced by the administration of the workshop of the Strozzi palace included journals, employment rosters, record books, cash books, and the ledgers (which alone survive). The workshop was so large that the purveyor, Marco di Benedetto Strozzi, needed the assistance of a cashier just to handle the cash box, and from time to time he carried additional assistants on his staff to help keep an eye on the horde of workers at the construction site and the several contemporaneous quarry operations elsewhere. The ledgers Marco kept of all this activity are notable for the degree expenditures were categorized into separate accounts, for the detail of information in the entries, for the summary organization of expenditures in collective accounts, and for the periodicity and duality of entry. They are a monument to his administration of the workshop, in their own way almost as impressive as the palace itself.[67]

Giovan Battista Figiovanni, the purveyor at the new sacristy of San Lorenzo, had a task almost as great as that of Marco Strozzi, and we have some of his comments on what it meant to be in charge of such a large workshop.[68] A canon at San Lorenzo, he was called into service by the Medici in 1519 to supervise the building of the new sacristy, and later the library, at his monastery; he remained on the job for fifteen years, broken only by the three-year interlude of the last republic. The workshop was large, often with as many as ninety men on the employment rosters; Figiovanni's job was not made any easier by having to work with an architect as temperamental as Michelangelo. The paperwork alone must have been considerable. In his comments on his work nothing is clearer than the devotion and zeal he had for the task, which was obviously fired by his pride in being associated with such an illustrious patron. He boasts about his close supervision of every

[66] S. Spirito 127.

[67] Goldthwaite, "Strozzi Palace," pp. 136–42.

[68] Gino Corti, "Una ricordanza di Giovan Battista Figiovanni," *Paragone*, 15, No. 175 (1964), 24–31; reprinted in Alessandro Parronchi, *Opere giovanili di Michelangelo* (Florence, 1968), pp. 165–87.

detail. He arranged for purchase of bricks and rubble and contracted for stonework, and

> every morning at dawn I am there key in hand with everything open, awaiting the wallers and laborers to give them their orders. I never dress up except on holidays, and I am never out of arm's reach of the wallers and laborers. I want everything that goes on, however minute it be, to originate from me. Everything passes through my hands, and I do not trust even my hands because I want to see everything with my own eyes in order that the wallers do not use brick where they could use rubble. I have employed sixty, eighty, even ninety men; and I have never had a moment to myself and do not now. Everyone marvels that I can handle it and that I can give such an operation so much supervision, order, and admirable smoothness without there ever being any confusion. At the beginning Michelangelo wanted me to take on an assistant and pay him three or four ducats a month; but I wanted to do everything myself so that what turns out to be good is mine, and likewise what turns out badly. And I shall show that this management saves one ducat a day by not being allowed to flounder.

Figiovanni's zeal to serve the Medici was so great that, as he put it, even if they made him pope their account with him would not be balanced—and he wanted the proof to be the success of this construction project.

SOME EXAMPLES OF PRACTICE. Like many institutional building projects, the orphanage of the Innocenti was organized under the direction of a building committee set up by its sponsor, the guild of Por Santa Maria, commonly known as the silk guild.[69] The committee proceeded to organize the building operation through contracts both for supply and for labor, some (as previously noted) opened to competitive bidding. The orphanage complex went up building by building, with new contracts for each rather than a single contract for the whole. The first contracts were let out in 1419, and measurements to settle builders' accounts were taken in 1422 for the children's residence, in 1423 for the church, in 1424 for other rooms on the courtyard, and in 1426 for the children's dormitory. At this time the portico was ready for roofing, and work on the courtyard itself was contracted out, and in 1427 and 1428 building was also proceeding on the garden side. Most of the complex was finished by the end of 1432, by which time the books showed total accumulative expenditures of f.2,809 lb.19,460 s.15 (all together about 7,700 florins), although these figures did not include various services and materials contributed to the project by everyone from carriers and sand dealers to gold-

[69] Innocenti, ser. VII (building accounts), 1–4 (ledgers A, B, D, and E, 1419–51); ser. CXX (general administration), 1–2 (ledgers A and B). Published extracts of these accounts appear in: Cornel von Fabriczy, *Filippo Brunelleschi, sein Leben und seine Werke* (Stuttgart, 1892); Mendes and Dallai, "Innocenti"; G. Morozzi and A. Piccini, *Il restauro dello spedale di Santa Maria degli Innocenti, 1966–1970* (Florence, 1971).

smiths, which the accountant did not evaluate in monetary form since "they were given for God." Thereafter work proceeded at a much slower pace on the loggia of the courtyard, the second floor over the portico, and elsewhere; the hospital was not ready to open its door for operation until 1445. During this second phase of construction, in contrast to their earlier practice, the orphanage authorities used a direct labor system, employing both wallers and stonecutters as needed on a daily basis.

Virtually the complete set of contracts for the first phase of construction, up to 1432, survives—supply contracts for wood, bricks, lime, sand, gravel, and decorative stone elements, and labor contracts for foundations, masonry, and roofing. The principal waller from 1419 to 1422 was Ambruogio di Leonardo, and after 1422 his place was taken by the brothers Antonio and Francesco di Geri. These wallers, however, did not have commanding positions as the chief foremen. They contracted to do work for task rates, and they went from contract to contract, at least three of which were assigned after competitive bidding. Furthermore, other wallers worked independently on foundations and roofs, and the principal stonecutters, Albizzo di Piero and Betto d'Antonio, did much of the installation of their own work for the portico.

The works staff at the Innocenti was therefore somewhat amorphous, but it was directed through the central administration of a purveyor appointed by the building committee. His salary of 36 florins a year indicates the importance of his task as at least a half-time employee. Two successive appointments were made to this post in the first two years of construction (one of whom complained that the salary was too low), but with the appointment in November 1421 of Buto di Niccolò the building committee found a purveyor who was to stay on the job throughout the rest of the first phase of the building program, until November 1432. When the pace of construction fell off after that year, the salary was reduced to 12 florins. The purveyor kept the building accounts and cleared all payments to be made on his written order by the treasurer, and for lack of any other permanent personnel on the works staff, above all a foreman, he must have functioned as a general manager of the works, checking on contractual obligations, coordinating various activities, and tending to a myriad of details from organizing occasional festivities for the workers on completion of certain tasks to going off to Pistoia to consult with the architect. Brunelleschi, who was retained as a consultant and was frequently on the building site, was of course an important part-time member of the staff. He is at least once called a "chondottore," and in the early years he was paid something like a consultant's fee. Compensation for his labor was included along with the purveyor's salary in the 60-florin deduction for staff expenses on the project the guild claimed in its 1429 tax report.[70]

[70] For details, see ch. 7 herein.

The building committee at Santo Spirito went about its work in a different way. This church, also designed by Brunelleschi, was begun in 1436, but work proceeded slowly until destruction of much of the older structure by a fire in 1471 gave greater urgency to the new project. Major construction got underway shortly thereafter and continued for twenty years, until the mid-1490s, and many of the records for this phase of construction survive.[71] Rather than contract extensively for labor, the building committee set up a direct labor system and engaged a foreman, the waller Giovanni d'Antonio di Mariano, called Scorbacchia. Scorbacchia went to work for daily wages ranging from 20 to 22 soldi, but since (at least at one point, when apparently there was a lag in construction) he was guaranteed a minimum monthly income of 12 lire, he enjoyed some security during periods when there was not enough work to give him regular employment (on the condition that he did not take employment elsewhere). Serving alongside Scorbacchia was a foreman of the stonecutters, a position of obvious importance in a largely stone building like Santo Spirito. This man was Salvi d'Andrea. Since he made models and served as a consultant to the committee, along with outside architects, on matters of design, Salvi can also be considered the supervising architect. He too worked for daily wages, but he earned supplements for keeping the daily employment record of workers and for his work on architectural models. Scorbacchia and Salvi d'Andrea directed a labor force that at times numbered as many as two or three dozen wallers, stonecutters, and laborers.

Since the entire labor force was salaried, all expenses connected with the building operation were paid by the building committee. It bought wood for scaffolding, rope, pulleys, lifting devices, and the other materials and equipment needed in construction that wallers who worked on contract were usually prepared to supply. To keep the stonecutters' tools in shape a smith was added to the staff on a monthly salary of 16 lire plus expenses. Most of the building materials were purchased from suppliers who provided delivery to the site, but for much of the decorative stonework in *pietra serena* the committee set up its own transportation system, employing carriers and buying oxen for them in exchange for credit against eventual carriage charges (this is the way Strozzi also handled the transportation problem). The complexity of the organization of the fabric workshop at Santo Spirito emerges in the rich detail of the surviving account for miscellaneous expenses, which included payments for everything from the clock to mark workers' time on the job and the lock and keys to secure their workshop to the soap needed to oil down finished stone.

The administration of the fabric workshop at Santo Spirito was in the

[71] S. Spirito 67 (notes of meetings of the congregation of friars, 1440–1557), 127 (building accounts, 1471–81), and 128 (the purveyor's journal of appropriations and miscellaneous memoranda, 1476–97).

hands of a purveyor. He attended meetings of the building committee and executed its instructions, and he also acted for it as a legal representative (*procuratore*) and as a general administrator (*sindaco*) for the property that had been assigned to the committee in financial support of the project. His main task, however, was the general administration of the work itself. He kept the building accounts and ordered payments from the treasurer (which up to 1486 was the bank of Piero di Francesco Mellini, one of the most important in the city and a firm closely connected with the Monte, through which much of the financing of the project was handled). There were only two purveyors throughout the two decades of building—Piero di Bartolomeo de' Rossi, and, after his death in 1483 (and with a couple of interruptions occasioned by absence on government service), Zanobi di Ser Jacopo Landi. The long experience these men had in their jobs must have counted for much in organizing the staff of such a large and prolonged works project.

The works staff at Santo Spirito, headed by the purveyor-accountant, the foreman, and the chief stonecutter, embraced a full range of responsibilities in directing construction activity. But the patron, too, had a role to play, and a picture of the extent of that involvement emerges from the purveyor's financial records, where he made notes on his periodic meetings with the church building committee. At Santo Spirito the committeemen had in effect lifetime appointments: they were continually reconfirmed in their office, and in the case of death the vacancy was invariably filled by a close relative of the deceased. These men had a knowledgeable and personal interest in the building. Their major concern was of course financial, and they were much involved in dealing with both the buyers of the church's many chapels and the state, which partially subsidized the project. At least once the committeemen paid out of their own pockets to keep construction going forward in a moment when funds were short. They were just as concerned with the administration of their funds as they were in collecting them. They made all decisions about what was to be built, authorizing the purveyor to proceed with construction section by section as the church went up and fixing the levels of employment that were to be maintained. Their appropriations for expenditures by the purveyor were carefully earmarked, including such fundamental decisions as the wage rates to be paid to workers. They looked over the purveyor's accounts and signed their approval in his books, and outside accountants were paid to make a more complete audit. Only occasionally did they leave it to the purveyor to determine amounts to be paid—for example, for models. The purveyor was clearly their agent, and their numerous detailed instructions, often written down by the staff notary, reveal how closely they followed the work and how much they kept the purveyor in tow. Moreover, the committee continually made decisions regarding costs, technical matters, and design; in such matters they called in outside masons, architects, and even fellow patricians for their opinions and advice (as noted earlier). The works staff, in short, was far from being autonomous or freed from the continual interference of the patron.[72]

Not all ecclesiastical and institutional building in Florence was undertaken under the supervision of a works committee, and in fact many projects were not financed well enough to maintain much of a works organization at all. An example is the building program of the hospital of San Paolo.[73] This ancient institution of Franciscan tertiaries, having fallen into some disorder in the first half of the fifteenth century, was reformed in 1451. Under the administration of the new manager, the priest Benino de' Benini, a building program got underway that was to include the imposing portico in the Piazza Santa Maria Novella and, behind it, extensive building around two new cloisters on either side of an older hospital ward. Benini commissioned no less skilled an architect than Michelozzo to draw up the plans, and the monumental portico is itself evidence of his ambitions for the enlarged complex of the hospital whose reform he was charged with. Benini, however, did not enjoy the beneficence of a generous donor for his project; not even the official patron of the hospital, the guild of notaries and judges, did much to help subsidize the project. Money therefore came in slowly, and building was drawn out over the next forty-five years. The portico, clearly planned from the beginning, was finally completed in 1496, just a year before Benini's death.

With this pace of building activity, contracting for labor was not feasible, and nothing like a real works staff ever evolved. Benini, who as administrator of the hospital kept his own accounts and watched over the cash box, simply absorbed the building operation into his normal administrative work. He bought materials, including finished stonework, as needed, and employed a waller with a miniscule gang of workers for daily wages whenever (presumably) finances permitted. To be sure, he had a master plan by Michelozzo, and he was careful always to engage the same craftsmen—the wallers Nencio di Lapo and his son Nanni, and a supplier of stonework, Zanobi di Luca Succhielli—all of whom had been closely associated with Michelozzo earlier at the Santissima Annunziata and who were presumably familiar with the architect's ideas. When Succhielli died Benini simply continued giving out work to his son Giovanni, as he did with Nanni after Nencio's death. A master plan and the availability of the same artisans, however sporadically employed, simplified Benini's task as organizer of work. For one with his professional talents as an administrator (he was for a time concurrently manager of Santa Maria Nuova, the city's largest hospital) it probably was not difficult to get even a large project like San Paolo built with little organizational effort, as long as the pace of work was slow. Of course, Benini's personal interest in building

[72] See ch. 2 herein.

[73] Richard A. Goldthwaite and W. R. Rearick, "Michelozzo and the Ospedale di San Paolo in Florence," *Flor. Mitt.*, 21 (1977).

(which was commented on in chapter 2) counted for much in keeping things on track, but much building in Florence for which financing was sluggish probably went forward with an organizational effort that was hardly beyond the capacity of the patron's own administrative talents.

In some respects construction projects for private persons, especially palaces constructed *ex novo*, presented more of an organizational problem to their builders. Not only were many of these palaces exceptionally large buildings requiring a fairly complex labor force, but the pace of their construction was probably much greater than that for institutional and ecclesiastical projects. The financing of a private residence was likely to be more secure from the outset and less dependent on long-range projections, and we can well imagine that the owner felt some urgency to see his project through to its conclusion.

The largest of all private palaces built in the fifteenth century, that of the wealthy merchant-banker Filippo Strozzi, is also the best documented.[74] It was begun in 1489 on a design by Giuliano da Sangallo but executed under the supervision of Cronaca, who is probably responsible for the decorative details, including the cornice and the courtyard, as well as for a further elevation of its imposing height as a result of a decision to vault two (rather than just one) of the three floors. The job of putting up this enormous structure was additionally complicated by the full-scale quarry operations that were necessary to supply the massive blocks of *pietra forte* that face the building on three of its facades. Since Strozzi had more than enough cash on hand at the outset of construction to pay for it all, no problems of financing arose to obstruct the building's progress. The palace was almost finished in about fifteen years of continual building activity at a cost of over 30,000 florins (not including the site), representing a rate of input probably unequaled by any other construction project in the city (or, for that matter, by few other industrial enterprises of any kind).

Confronted with the size of the projected building, the additional operations at the quarries, and the desired pace of construction, the owner was under pressure to organize a works staff to handle an exceptionally large-scale task. He was able to assure supply of materials (except stone) by letting out long-term contracts, but for construction he could not have done other than undertake the direct employment of wage labor. Only the founders, as usual, worked on contract (one of these worked full time for four years). The foreman in charge of the fabric workshop was Mariotto di Papi, whose exceptionally high salary (by the standards of his profession) of 60 florins corresponded to the extent of his responsibility. Directly under him were always several other wallers. Cronaca, a part-time member of the staff (with a salary of 36 florins), acted not only as executing architect but also as the chief stonecutter, who was responsible for the quarry operations, the prepara-

[74] Goldthwaite, "Strozzi Palace."

tion of the stone for the facades, and negotiations with the independent suppliers of finished work in *pietra serena.* A carpenter and a smith were at times employed on salary. Under this staff of some six to eight men worked a labor force numbering from fifty to one hundred construction workers and stonecutters, both at the site and in as many as four quarries. In addition, six carriers were usually employed in hauling stone, and although they worked for a rate per load, Strozzi had to finance their operation by extending credit for the purchases of oxen and carts. The administration of the works was in the hands of a distant relative of the owner, Marco di Benedetto Strozzi, who was the purveyor and accountant, with a salary of 30 florins; he had his own staff of a cashier and, occasionally, an assistant or two to help keep employment records and pay wages. It is difficult to imagine that any building other than a few public works projects employed such a large labor force. However active Filippo Strozzi himself may have been in setting up the operation, by the time of his death in 1491, just two years after the ground-breaking ceremony, the staff had evolved as an autonomous body able to keep construction going steadily forward for over a dozen more years, despite considerable political turbulence during that time.

Two other private projects for which complete building accounts survive are the palaces of Giovanni di Bartolomeo Bartolini in Piazza Santa Trinita[75] and Giuliano di Piero Da Gagliano in Via Ricasoli (later incorporated into the Gerini palace).[76] The architect for both was Baccio d'Agnolo, and both went up at the same time. Construction at the Bartolini palace got underway in February 1520, and the body of the building was up by May 1523 (although interior finishing went on for another decade). Work on the Da Gagliano palace began in February 1522 and by May 1528 the owner and his family were able to move in. The Bartolini palace was a completely new structure; its owner had purchased over half a dozen shops and houses (including a hotel and the workshop of the painter Bernardo Rosselli), all of which had to be cleared from the site so that new foundations could be prepared. It has two facades fully faced with stone. For thirty-three months of construction the project employed usually from twelve to eighteen wallers and laborers, and ten more years of finishing and decorating (up to 1533) brought the price of the building to more than 11,000 florins (not including 1,930 florins paid for the site). Its imposing presence on the

[75] Archivio Bartolini Salimbeni, Villa di Collina (Vicchio di Mugello): 211 (ledger of building accounts, 1520–27), and 284 (ledger of Giovanni di Bartolomeo di Leonardo Bartolini, 1515–29), in which there is an account of building expenses beginning on fol. 281. See Lorenzo Bartolini Salimbeni, "Una 'fabbrica' fiorentina di Baccio d'Agnolo: le vicende costruttive del palazzo Bartolini Salimbeni attraverso i documenti d'archivio," *Palladio*, 3d ser., 27, fasc. 2 (1978), 7–28.

[76] Archivio Salviati, Pisa: ser. IV, 13 (ledger of building accounts, 1522–28) and 14 (accompanying journal and memoranda, 1522–28).

square, with its niches, semidetached columns, pediments over the windows, and incised inscriptions on its facade, represents the particular taste of its owner, who broke with a long tradition of Florentine palace style.

The Da Gagliano palace—now lost in rebuilding—was a more modest project, and in fact it was probably a remodeling of an older building. The building accounts include no expenditures for the site and little for foundation work. Moreover, it had a stuccoed, not a stone, facade. Not many more than a dozen men were ever employed on it, and when the owner took up residence after six years of construction, he had not spent much more than 1,500 florins, less than Strozzi spent each year. Nevertheless, the architect of the palace was the most prominent architect on the scene at the time. Its stucco facade with window and door frames in stone, three stories high and three windows wide, was imposing enough in the mind of the owner that he opened a separate page in the building accounts for its cost. Neither the Bartolini nor the Da Gagliano palace approached the scale of the Strozzi palace, but taken together, one as a new palace and the other as an extensive rebuilding project, they are more typical of the kind of construction enterprise represented by most of the domestic architecture of the period.

In organizing the work for their projects both Bartolini and Da Gagliano followed the same procedures used by Filippo Strozzi. They contracted for supply (including carriage) of construction materials and set up a direct labor system. Bartolini contracted for all the stone, both *pietra forte* and *macigno*, that was needed for the facing of his palace, and the rates he paid included finishing and delivery to the site. This option was not open to Filippo Strozzi, probably because of the quantity of stone he needed and because the special nature of the rustication he wanted required closer supervision, whereas the component parts of the facade of the Bartolini palace were standard shop products. At any rate, the building organization of the Bartolini project did not have to carry the burden of working quarries and employing gangs of stonecutters, and the difference this convenience made in the fabric workshop is reflected in the account for miscellaneous expenses, where there are no payments for tools, smiths, and those other items connected with preparation of stone. For the organization of the labor force for construction, both Bartolini and Da Gagliano did exactly what Strozzi did: wallers and laborers were employed for direct wages (even the foreman at both sites worked for daily wages rather than on salary), stonecutters for task rates, carriers for rates per load of rubble hauled away, founders for rates according to contracts, artisans with special skills, like smiths and carpenters, for task rates for finished work. Da Gagliano kept his own books and for the most part paid out wages himself, whereas Bartolini, who was one of the most prominent bankers in the city, turned both his cash box and his accounts over to an employee. The accounts for both projects are set up in double entry and are categorized in exactly the same way, and since terms of payment for virtually all materials and labor were essentially the same, the similarity in the format of their accounts extends even to individual entries.

The difference in these palace projects was principally in the degree of refinement in the organization of the works staff, and this depended on the extent of the building operations. The Strozzi project, involving not only construction of one of the largest private buildings in the city but also extensive quarry operations, employed at times more than one hundred men. In order to enable it to delineate responsibilities, the supervisory staff was large, highly specialized, and employed on a long-term basis (mostly on salary). At the Bartolini palace the staff was composed of only three men at the top: the accountant-cashier may have doubled as a purveyor (although he is never so identified in the documents), the architect was retained as a consultant on a part-time basis, and the foreman worked regularly, although for a daily wage rather than a salary. There was hardly any staff to speak of at the Da Gagliano project: the architect was not retained on a salary beyond the first year (and to judge from his total earnings of 8 florins, his responsibilities were never extensive), and Da Gagliano himself kept the accounts, probably in fact functioning as his own purveyor in close contact with the foreman. The differences in scale in these three projects obviously made a difference in the size of the staff and the refinement of responsibilities, but with respect to the general principles of building operations, the three were organized in the same way. They represent the normal way of going about getting a palace built.[77]

[77] The same procedures were followed at the other palace projects for which separate building accounts have survived, for example the palace of Alamanno d'Averardo di Jacopo Salviati in Via del Palagio, 1499–1500 (Archivio Salviati, Pisa: ser. II, 32), and the palace of Francesco di Piero Baccelli in Via dell'Anguillara, 1581–82 (ASF, Archivio Galli Tassi 1480/34). The foreman at the Baccelli palace was Jacopo dell'Ancisa; the design has been attributed to Ammannati; see the comment of Mazzino Fossi, *Bartolomeo Ammannati, architetto* (Naples, [1966]), p. 197.

In this account of construction procedures I have not dealt with the cathedral workshop because so many of the documents have been published and its activity has been well studied. Moreover, given the size and the duration of the project, and the fact that financing was in the hands of the state, the organization of the workshop was by no means typical.

CHAPTER FOUR

Production of Materials

Bricks and Lime

FLORENCE by the fourteenth century was a city largely built of bricks, although the appearance of what has survived of the late medieval and Renaissance city belies that fact about its construction. Florentine masons and architects seem not to have cared about using brick other than as a basic building material. There are earlier medieval examples of window moldings, columns, capitals, and other decorative elements made in brick, but these soon were made of stone. Brickwork never entered the canon of Renaissance architecture, despite its recognition by Alberti, echoing the authority of Vitruvius, and despite the architectural development of decorative brickwork elsewhere in Italy and even close at hand, in Tuscany. Florentines, instead, preferred to cover up their brick-and-rubble walls with either stone or stucco. Not until the Palazzo Grifoni, begun in 1557, is there an example of dressing brick used (probably by Ammannati) on a principal facade for aesthetic effects—and the building remains an isolated venture that did not inspire any further consideration of the material. By that time, however, as a result of a new aesthetic that owes much of its origins to Florence itself, brick was losing out to stone and stucco surfacing everywhere in Italy, even in places, like Bologna, with strong traditions in brick architecture. It surely is a matter of taste that Florentines never wanted to leave bricks exposed in their more notable buildings, although not much is made of this stylistic point in the literature of architectural history.[1] Strolling through the streets today, one is hardly aware of how basic a building material brick is.

THE HISTORY OF BRICKS. In ancient Rome brickmaking was the only industry in which the upper class invested. It was, in a sense, a rural industry founded on the human and material resources of the estates of the rich, and investment in it did not compromise their nobility as members of a landed aristocracy. The vast pools of labor at the disposal of estate-owners enabled some kiln operations to produce at an impressive level. Archaeological evidence attests the extraordinary size of kilns, and the study of brickstamps has revealed the wide distribution of their production. The large market for bricks that made this development possible was created by the urban concentration of Roman society, especially after the foundation of the empire. Rome itself was largely rebuilt at that time, and built once again after the fire in Nero's reign, and there was an increasing use of baked rather than sun-dried bricks, to permit the vertical growth of many of the city's buildings. One Roman lady is on record as owning forty-six separate kiln sites. With their characteristic instincts the emperors, too, were not unaware of the profits to be made in this expanding market for building materials, and by the third century, as owners of some of the largest brickyards in the city, they had a virtual monopoly of production.[2]

Rome survived in many forms after the fall of the empire in the West, and one of the legacies it left to early medieval Europe was the bricks it had made, which, like the stone it had quarried, continued to be used and reused by a younger (and poorer) society that regarded the vast outmoded building of the past as little more than convenient warehouses of ready-made building materials. As late as the eleventh century the Normans were still drawing on these supplies to build churches in their newly conquered kingdom of England.

[1] Observations on the use of brick in Florence have been made by geologists and geographers rather than by architectural historians. See Francesco Rodolico, *Le pietre delle città d'Italia* (Florence, 1965), pp. 252–53; and Renate Müller, *Die Entwicklung der Naturwerksteinindustrie im toskanischen Apennin als Funktion städtebaulicher Gestaltung* (Frankfort, 1975), pp. 44–45. Even in discussions of the Palazzo Grifoni the use of brick goes virtually unremarked except for casual comment about coloristic effects; for example, see Mazzino Fossi, *Bartolomeo Ammannati, architetto* (Naples, [1966]), pp. 61–67.

[2] A general discussion of the Roman brick industry is to be found in Helen J. Loane, *Industry and Commerce in the City of Rome (50* B.C.–200A.D.) (Baltimore, 1938), pp. 101–5; and Herbert Bloch, "The Roman Brick Industry and Its Relationship to Roman Architecture," *JSArH*, 1 (1941), 3–8. Tapio Helen, *Organization of Roman Brick Production in the First and Second Centuries* A.D.: *An Interpretation of Roman Brick Stamps* (Helsinki, 1975), investigates what stamps have to tell us about the industry.

Although there is evidence for bricks in Carolingian Europe and later Anglo-Saxon England, the industry did not make much headway in the early Middle Ages, in part because natural materials so plentiful in many areas of Europe supplied simpler building needs, and in part because the Roman technique for making bricks, which probably survived in Italy, was not suitable for the poorer clays of northwestern Europe. The invention of a way to make bricks from these materials has been attributed to the Cistercians in Denmark around 1200, and the technology was diffused through their monastic network. From then on, splendid examples of brick architecture appear in buildings scattered across Europe from southwestern France to eastern Prussia. In a few places bricks are found as common building materials, namely in Italy and the area in northern Europe extending from Flanders and the Netherlands across Lower Saxony, Holstein, and Denmark to Brandenburg and the lands of the Teutonic Knights. There has been much debate on the origins and diffusion of brick architecture in the North, but little comment on the industry that produced the bricks.[3]

In Italy, where building in brick has a tradition that goes back as far as the eleventh century (if indeed it was ever interrupted after the demise of Rome), the brick industry has a notable if also largely unremarked history.[4] Major brick structures from the eleventh and twelfth centuries are to be found in the churches of Bologna, Modena, Parma, Pavia, and other towns of the Po Valley; in the following centuries much civic and military as well as ecclesiastic construction was executed in brick. It was amidst this flourishing of brick construction in Italy that masons refined their handling of the

[3] E. M. Jope, "The Saxon Building-Stone Industry in Southern and Midland England," *Medieval Archaeology*, 8 (1964), 113; Gwilym Peredur Jones, "Building in Stone in Medieval Western Europe," *Trade and Industry in the Middle Ages*, Vol. II of *Cambridge Economic History of Europe* (Cambridge, 1952), p. 501. The old debate on north German brick architecture is summarized and sensibly appraised by Alfred Kamphausen, *Die Baudenkmäler der deutschen Kolonisation in Ostholstein und die Anfänge der nordeuropäischen Backsteinarchitektur* (Neumünster, 1938). For further bibliography see Konrad Maier, "Mittelalterliche Steinbearbeitung und Mauertechnik als Datierungmittel. Bibliographische Hinweise," *Zeitschrift für Archäologie des Mittelalters*, 3 (1975), 209–16. The subject of the invention of brickmaking in the north is taken up in articles by W.J.A. Arntz: "Tijdstip en plaats van ontstaan van onze middeleeuwse baksteen," *Bulletin van de Koninklijke Nederlandse Oudheidkundige Bond*, 6th ser., 7 (1954), 23–38; idem, "De middeleeuwse baksteen," *Bulletin van de Koninklijke Nederlandse Oudheidkundige Bond*, 6th ser., 70 (1971), 98–103.

[4] Brick architecture in Italy is surveyed by C. Roccatelli and Enrico Verdozzi, *Brickwork in Italy: A Brief Review from Ancient to Modern Times* (Chicago, 1925), and there are some useful observations in Francesco Malaguzzi Valeri, *L'architettura a Bologna nel Rinascimento* (Rocca San Casciano, 1899), pp. 32–36. Comment on the industry in Lombard times is made by Ugo Monneret de Villard, "L'organizzazione industriale nell'Italia Langobarda durante l'Alto Medioevo," *Archivio storico lombardo*, 46 (1919), 21–27.

material and created a distinct brick architecture. They made much of the polychromatic effects of different shades of bricks; they cut and molded them into different shapes and devised special molds to prefabricate decorative details in terracotta; they built them into a variety of architectural details like moldings, arches, pilasters, columns, and capitals; they varied courses and applied decorative bands against fields of plain brick. Of more economic importance than this imaginative use of brick in the occasional architectural monument is its widespread diffusion as a building material in more ordinary construction as the awareness of the fire hazards of high-density living in the booming Italian towns of the twelfth and thirteenth centuries led to an investment in more substantial buildings.

The architectural evidence for the rise of the brick industry in northern Italian towns is complemented by the increased mention of kilnmen and kiln products in early guild and communal documents. The first guild of kilnmen on record dates from the early thirteenth century in Venice, and there was one in Verona by 1319. A list of guilds at Orvieto in 1300 includes both limeburners and tile-makers. Where kilnmen belonged instead to the masons' guild, statutes commonly have specific rubrics regarding their work. In some of these guilds kilnmen emerged as a distinct group (*membrum*) with its own corporate identity. In the guild at Padua kilnmen are mentioned from 1294 onwards as members of the guild committee approving statutory changes, and in 1310 the guild had a regulation forbidding masons to accept employment on any project where bricks did not come from a fellow guildsman. The 1325 roster of the wallers' guild of Ferrara includes many kilnmen, and the statutes required that offices be divided (though not equally) between masons and brickcutters (*tagliapietracotta*). At Bologna by 1335 the kilnmen had their own meeting times and special regulations within the guild of wallers. During the next two centuries kilnmen formed their own guilds in Ferrara, Rome, Parma, and Modena.[5]

Paralleling the emergence of a corporate consciousness among brickmakers was the growing concern of communal governments with the regulation of an industry so vital to the public interest. The documentary material here, too, attests the growth of the industry in Italy. In the thirteenth century towns everywhere began to pursue a vigorous policy to control prices and set measurement standards for kiln products of all kinds. Legislation was also directed to assure the public's supply of bricks; Venice (and perhaps Padua) had communal kilns to supply public works. Parma required each town in its territory with a baptismal church to build a kiln at the expense of the local inhabitants and to fire it twice a year; at Parma itself five firings were required of kilns. At Venice attempts were made to stimulate production by setting the number of firings at each kiln, extending loans to kilnmen, and

[5] Extant guild records are listed in App. 2 herein.

forbidding export of bricks and lime. In Florence a 1325 statute shows the government's concern that there be a sufficient number of kilns to supply that city's needs.[6]

The evidence of guild and communal documents, not to mention the archaeological record, points to considerable activity in the brick industry in the medieval Italian towns, probably more so than for any other place in Europe. We are, however, little informed about the progress of the industry (as distinct from the development of style) elsewhere, including those places where brick was a common building material and where notable examples of brick architecture can be found. Only for England, where more is known about the construction industry in general, and for Holland has a basic outline emerged for the history of brickmaking.

Evidence for the earliest production in England has been pushed back to the twelfth century with the documentation for building at Little Coggeshall Abbey (Essex). Hull, founded by Edward I in 1293, had a municipal brickyard within a few years of its foundation, and it became England's first town built of brick. Nevertheless, for the building of the Tower of London great quantities of bricks were brought from Yprès in 1278 and again in 1283, and bricks continued to be imported from Flanders for the royal works over the next two centuries. By the fifteenth century, however, the level of production reached in some places occasioned legislation standardizing brick size and shape. The climax of the growing demand for bricks came with the great houses built by Wolsey and by King Henry VIII himself. Although the advantage of brick for them was the speed with which construction could go forward and the lower costs of a less skilled labor force, these men obviously did not consider the material incompatible with their dignity, and their taste contributed to the development of an impressive brick architecture in sixteenth-century England. Nevertheless, outside a few areas in the east of the country, bricks were used even in the sixteenth century only for important buildings in England and hardly ever for the home of anyone below high gentry status.[7]

[6] G. Micheli, "Le corporazioni parmensi d'arti e mestieri," *Archivio storico per le provincie parmensi*, 5 (1896), 68–70; Giovanni Monticolo, *I capitolari delle arti veneziane*, 3 vols. (Rome, 1896–1914), I, 79–93 and 213–33; *Statuti* (1325), pp. 252–55; Duccio Balestracci and Gabriella Piccinni, *Siena nel Trecento: assetto urbano e strutture edilizie* (Florence, 1977), pp. 65–72.

[7] Nathanial Lloyd, *A History of English Brickwork* (London, 1928); L. F. Salzman, *Building in England Down to 1540* (Oxford, 1967), ch. 8; Jane A. Wight, *Brick Building in England from the Middle Ages to 1550* (London, 1972), ch. 1; Malcolm Airs, *The Making of the English Country House, 1500–1640* (London, 1975), ch. 11. Some observations on the industry in the nineteenth century are made by Raphael Samuel, "Mineral Workers," in the book edited by him, *Miners, Quarrymen and Saltworkers* (London, 1977), pp. 25–26 and 43–46. The modern industry in Britain has been surveyed by A. Zaiman and W. A. MacIntyre, *Economic and Manufacturing*

Everywhere in Europe the history of the industry closely follows developments in vernacular architecture related to improvements in the general standard of housing. The evidence for brickmaking so early in the Italian towns, in other words, is probably a comment on the better living conditions that generally prevailed there. In any case, the veritable revolution in housing that took place in early modern Europe finally brought bricks to the fore in many places as the essential material for all kinds of buildings, from the simplest structures to great monuments of architectural quality. The economic expansion of those centuries meant urbanization, greater wealth, and the disposition of more men to invest in substantially better housing, with the result that brick production began to pick up over much of the Continent. Whereas in medieval France, for instance, there was little vernacular building in brick, by the eighteenth century the production of bricks was important enough to merit major publications on kilns.[8] In England brick was a vital ingredient of the so-called Great Rebuilding, and cheaper transport resulting from the canal system built up in the eighteenth century further stimulated the industry. When the industrial revolution got underway, brickmaking may have been the building-material industry with the largest market in Europe. Measurement of the commerce in bricks from that time on, in fact, has been one way of getting at a general index of construction.

In this early modern chapter of the story of bricks Holland has a unique place.[9] Good clay and peat were among the few natural resources of the country, and they were the raw material and fuel essential to the development of a brick industry. The area was one of the few with a tradition of brickmaking going back into the Middle Ages. As just noted, Flemish bricks were being exported to England as early as the thirteenth century. Dutch cities had municipal brickyards and were regulating the industry by the fourteenth century. The prosperity that commercial expansion brought to Holland in the sixteenth century had a significant impact on demand in the construction market, and since brick was the only building material that could be produced in plentiful supply, kilns became a major industry. Industrial growth was facilitated by the expansion of an inland waterway system that made pos-

---

Aspects of the Brick-Making Industries, Building Research Special Report No. 20 of the Department of Scientific and Industrial Research (London, 1933). A recent and general history of bricks in England, well supplied with illustrations, is John Woodforde, *Bricks to Build a House* (London, 1976).

[8] The conference report, *La Construction au moyen âge: histoire et archéologie*, Actes du congrès de la Société des Historiens Médiévistes de l'Enseignement Supérieur Public, Besançon, 2–4 juin 1972 (Besançon, 1973), has nothing on bricks or kilns. On the eighteenth-century interest in kilns see note 28 to this chapter.

[9] The best general history of brickmaking in any country is Johanna Hollestelle, *De steenbakkerij in de Nederlanden tot omstreeks 1560* (Assen, 1961), which has a full bibliography and an English summary.

sible the economic transport of clays, fuel, and the finished product—all bulky, cheap materials. It has been claimed that already in the seventeenth century the per capita production of the Dutch industry was twice that of England at the end of the eighteenth century, when the industrial revolution was well underway. Moreover, since bricks came to be used as ballast for outgoing vessels in the country's international shipping empire, the industry supplied bricks literally to the world—to England, the Baltic, and further afield to Asia, Africa, and the Americas. Dutch bricks turned up everywhere, and in some places their importation left its mark in the history of local architecture—for instance in the Baltic towns and in colonial America.[10] Holland in these early modern centuries was the first place where an industry grew up that produced a basic building material that was bulky, heavy, and relatively cheap for more than a local market. Indeed, it is likely that no building-material industry has ever had a more widespread distribution of its products. In any case, the highly developed Dutch industry provides a useful comparison (to the extent that the current scholarly literature will permit) for a study of the industry in Florence, another center of early capitalism.

KILNS. Whereas the building-material industries of woodworking and quarrying merely prepare raw materials for use, a kiln operation is a full-scale industrial process that transforms raw material into manufactured products—stone into quicklime, clay into bricks and tiles. Moreover, it is an industry whose development is subject to many variables—types of fuel, qualities of clay, the level of kiln technology, climate and seasonal changes, facilities for transport, the availability of alternative building materials, and, of course, taste. Each of these is a factor in the formula that determines the nature of brickmaking, and since each combination of them depends on physical environment and historical development, the industry varies in different parts of Europe at different times. It is not surprising, therefore, that the history of brick and lime production has yet to be written, for it requires a synoptic vision of many local operations, few of which, in fact, have ever been studied.

Roman kilns were of the pit-type, with fire chambers dug into the ground and the ovens above; they were partly embedded and partly walled, but were fully exposed to the elements at the top.[11] In medieval Europe bricks were commonly burnt in a clamp (or heap), a largely temporary structure that was built of the bricks to be fired and dismantled after each firing. With ashes mixed into the clay so that the bricks created their own heat and with fuel

[10] W.J.A. Arntz, "Export van Nederlandsche baksteen in vroegere eeuwen," *Economisch-Historisch Jaarboek*, 23 (1947), 57–133.

[11] On Roman kilns see Norman Davey, *A History of Building Materials* (London, 1961), ch. 8; and the references in Marion Elizabeth Blake, *Ancient Roman Construction in Italy from the Prehistoric Period to Augustus* (Washington, 1947), p. 302.

packed between the stacks of bricks, a clamp simply burned itself out. Although kilns were not unknown, clamps were used extensively throughout the early modern period, the technique being the normal procedure for making bricks even in England and Germany well into the nineteenth century. Clamps were especially suitable where coal was in plentiful supply. They were elastic in their size, which could be changed to meet the specific demand of the moment, and capacity could be increased up to half a million bricks. Moreover, clamps could be made on the spot at a building site, hence reducing carriage costs. As long as the demand for bricks was sporadic it made no sense to invest in permanent industrial structures.

In those few medieval towns, such as Bruges, the Hanseatic cities on the Baltic, and Hull in England, where brick was a common building material and demand therefore was somewhat more sustained, bricks were made in more or less fixed places, often under communal auspices. In these brickyards there was likely to be something approximating a kiln properly speaking—that is, a permanent structure. A commonly found type consisted of a platform over vaulted fire chambers, often dug into the ground, with a walled area above forming the oven, which was open at the top. They resembled the Roman pit-type kiln. Such a kiln, a small stone-walled one with a capacity of only 5,000 bricks and dating from the late thirteenth century, has been excavated at Narwym near Neidenburg in the lands of the Teutonic Knights.[12] Subsequent development saw refinement in the firing chambers and flues and an increase in the mass of the oven walls. A notable kiln of this type in late eighteenth-century Le Havre was singled out by the *Encyclopédie*; a great massive structure with an oven capacity of 5,415 cubic feet, it could hold 100,000 bricks.

In Holland, where the industry reached its highest productive capacity, the installations used for firing bricks were in effect permanently walled clamps. These scove (or Scotch) kilns, as they are called, can be found elsewhere, but they are notable in Holland for their enormous size. They were open at the top, and the fire chambers were made by stacking the bricks in such a way that small arched channels were left open below into which fuel was fed from openings in the outer walls. This system was made possible by the use of easily packed peat rather than wood or coal as fuel. A seventeenth-century Dutch kiln could produce 600,000 to 650,000 bricks in one firing, and a century later the *Encyclopédie* reported even larger kilns in Holland with a capacity of up to 1,200,000 bricks. With such giant kilns, Dutch kilnmen

[12] Franz Krüger, "Der Ziegelstein," *Jahrbuch für historische Volkskunde*, 3–4 (1934), 144–45; see also Eberhard G. Neumann, "Die Backsteintechnik in Niedersachsen während des Mittelalters," *Lüneburger Blätter*, 10 (1959), 24–25. Both of these articles are good introductions to technical, as opposed to stylistic, aspects of brick architecture in Germany.

were obviously confident about the new markets that had by that time opened up for bricks. Nevertheless, overproduction was always a threat, and it was as a hedge against this that some three dozen kiln operators in Rijnland in the mid-seventeenth century protected themselves by making cartellike arrangements to limit the annual number of firings at all brickyards. Such practices reflected the growing importance of this industry and anticipated the organization of Dutch kilnmen into guilds (a much later development there than in Italy).[13]

The development of kilns with completely enclosed ovens is obscure. By the eighteenth century substantial structures of this kind were being built in England;[14] the *Encyclopédie* documents (and illustrates) the massive vaulted kilns that were then in use in France. The normal kiln of this type in the pre-industrial era seems to have had a capacity of only up to 20,000 bricks. Being fixed in their productive capacity, they were probably kept small to assure more efficient use for small loads. Kilns as permanent and fully enclosed industrial structures of any kind, however, were relatively rare in Europe before the nineteenth century.

Florentine kilns were permanent installations, and they appear to have been fully developed as industrial structures, perhaps among the first in Europe. That they were substantial establishments is indicated by assessments of them

[13] On the Dutch industry the best I have been able to come up with, besides the general overview in Hollestelle, *Steenbakkerij*, and the articles by Arntz cited in note 3 to this chapter, are two articles by B. W. van der Kloot Meyburg: "Een productiekartel in de Hollandsche steenindustrie in de zeventiende eeuw," *Economisch-Historisch Jaarboek*, 2 (1916), 208–38; and "Eenige gegevens over de Hollandsche steenindustrie in de zeventiende eeuw," *Economisch-Historisch Jaarboek*, 11 (1925), 79–160 (with a late sixteenth-century plan of a kiln on p. 83). An excellent discussion of Dutch kilns is found in Gabriel Jars, *Art de fabriquer la brique et la tuile en Hollande*, published in 1767 as part of *Descriptions des arts et métiers, faites ou approuvées par messieurs de l'Académie royale des sciences* (Paris, 1761–88); this was the source for the discussion in the *Supplément à l'encyclopédie ou dictionnaire raisonné des sciences, des arts et des métiers*, II (Amsterdam, 1776), 69–70 (with illustrations in vol. V, the first volume of plates). See also Jacobus Alida van der Kloes, *Onze bouwmaterialen* (Maassluis, 1908–), II, 72–76 (with illustrations). Hollestelle, *Steenbakkerij*, includes reproductions of scenes of brickmaking in Dutch miniatures, paintings, and engravings from the fifteenth to seventeenth centuries (to which should be added another fifteenth-century illustration reproduced in Sandra Hindman, *Text and Image in Fifteenth Century Dutch Bibles* [Leiden, 1977], illus. 46).

[14] Joseph Arnold Foster, *Contributions to a Study of Brickmaking in America*, 6 vols. (published privately, Claremont, Cal., 1962–71), IV, 9; Richard Foster and Charles Steel, "Restoring an Oxfordshire Brick Kiln," *Country Life*, 158 (1975), 924 (a tall conical structure); P. J. Drury, "Post-Medieval Brick and Tile Kilns at Runsell Green, Danbury, Essex," *Post-Medieval Archaeology*, 9 (1975), 203–11 (one of these a bottle kiln seventy-five feet high).

Kilns in the environs of Florence, ca. 1600

for tax purposes of 100 to 200 florins and sometimes as high as 300 florins.[15] These values represented the capitalization of rents, and the higher rents were as much as had to be paid for the most expensive premises in the city—for instance, a prosperous cloth shop. A kiln property, however, most likely included not only the industrial establishment itself (the kiln) but also the raw material in the form of claypits; furthermore, the kilnman might live on the premises and may have been able to farm some of the land. Not all kilns were large structures. Kilns where only lime was burned were of much less value than brick kilns; in the tax records for Impruneta, an important center for the production of floor and roof tiles, the assessed value of most kilns was a modest 30 to 40 florins.[16]

The making of bricks was largely, though not completely, a rural industry. The firing of bricks took place outside the city walls not only because of practical considerations of accessibility to clays (or limestone) and firewood but also because, for obvious safety reasons, communal legislation restricted their location in the city.[17] Urban kilns were not altogether unknown, for unbaked bricks brought into the city (presumably to be baked) were explicitly exempted from gabelle charges.[18] Streets at one time or another known as Via delle Fornaci were located toward the walls and away from the populated center—a distant track of Via de' Serragli, the last bit of Via Agnolo—and the current Via della Fornace lies just beyond Porta San Niccolò. Some of the brick suppliers for the Bargello project of 1345 and 1346 are identified as residents of communal parishes.[19] Later building accounts, however, show that brick and lime almost always came from outside the city. Few kilns are recorded in the tax returns of 1427 as being in the city, and the only two listed in the 1561 census of the city's business establishments (*botteghe*) were both on the outskirts, in Via della Pergola and at the Porta San Pier Gattolini.[20] There were, of course, kilns just outside the city gates, especially on the Oltrarno side. A 1590 government survey of clay pits in the immediate vicinity of the city lists seven: three outside the Porta San Niccolò, one at the Porta San Pier Gattolini, one at the Porta San Frediano, and two on the other side of the river.[21] The greatest concentrations of kilns further away but still

[15] Based on descriptions of eighteen kilns found in the 1427 Catasto records of nine *gonfaloni.*

[16] Catasto 723, fols. 1–175 passim (Impruneta, 1451).

[17] *Statuti* (1325), p. 253; *Statuta (1415)*, II, 206–8.

[18] *Statuta (1415)*, II, 210.

[19] ASF, Balìe 3 (building accounts for the Bargello, 1345–46).

[20] Pietro Battara, "Botteghe e pigioni nella Firenze del '500: un censimento industriale e commerciale all'epoca del granducato mediceo," *ASI*, 95 (1937), II, 15.

[21] Gigi Salvagnini, "Famiglie e mestieri fiorentini: gli Zuti, fornaciai di Ricorboli," *Granducato (osservatorio fiorentino di storia, arte e cultura)*, 2 (1976), 40–42. See the illustration on p. 182 herein.

Kiln at Ricorboli, 1622

serving the city seem to have been to the south on either side of the Greve, between Impruneta and San Casciano, and to the west along both valley walls of the Arno downstream, from the Porta San Frediano to Lastra a Signa on the left bank and toward Sesto at the foot of Monte Morello on the right bank.

A few accounts have turned up for the construction of kilns that provide some details about the nature of them as structures. For one kiln built in 1465 there are payments for vaulting, an overhanging tiled roof, and a portico about 13 meters long and almost 4 meters high.[22] For another, a "fornello da quociare chalcina," 5,000 tiles were purchased for the roof of the kiln proper (*fornace*), and 3,150 more for the oven (*fornello*) and portico.[23] These sizeable structures were possibly not very different from some old kilns still to be found in the environs of Florence, which for the most part, however, date from after the sixteenth century. The main block of these buildings, themselves built of brick, houses the ovens and the fire chambers, and across the front is a vaulted area generally opened on the outside by high arched bays. Although the porticos described in the accounts for the construction of kilns might have been the drying sheds for bricks, the term may also refer to this partially opened work area where the fires were stoked and perhaps fuel stored. The remains of old kilns are usually located on hillsides with the fire chambers at the lower level in front, partly to help increase the draught, and with the ovens above therefore accessible for loading from the ground level higher up the slope in back. A communal statute of 1415 limits the height of kilns to 9½ braccia (about 5½ meters), but this restriction was probably

[22] ASF, Archivio Gherardi 326 (ledger of Andrea di Cresci di Lorenzo di Cresci, 1463–71), fol. 108 (with measurements of walls of the portico) and passim. The kiln was built as a donation to the convent of Santa Maria Maddalena at Caldine, a foundation of the Cresci family; G. Carocci, *I dintorni di Firenze*, 2 vols. (Florence, 1906–1907), I, 174–75.

[23] S. Miniato 57 (accounts of S. Bartolomeo), fol. 14r.

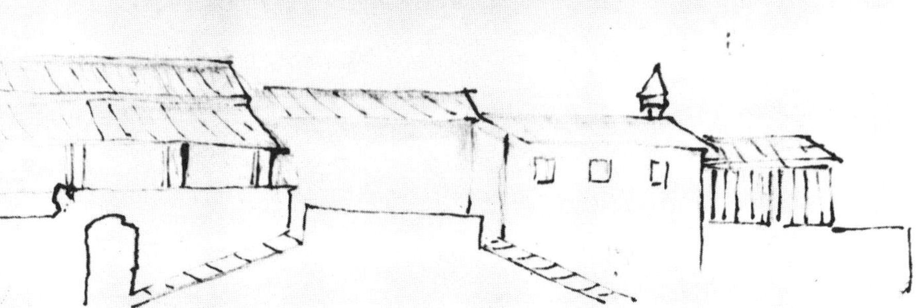

directed to structures only within the city walls, where fire was a constant danger.[24]

Kilns were the most prominent industrial structures drawn in on the maps made for an early seventeenth-century survey of the Florentine countryside (illustration p. 180). Some kilns survive that have great vaulted "porticos" reaching the full height of the building in front. A few at least three centuries old are still in operation, albeit with some modernization of the chambers, and others, now converted to different uses, abound. All together they constitute substantial material for archaeological study of this industry.

Some precise information about production levels of these kilns is to be found in an inquest conducted by the government in 1568 in response to a complaint from kilnmen about price controls imposed on their products.[25] One of the experts called in to look into the matter, Piero Pagni, came up with a cost analysis of kiln operations to show that the current prices were not in fact unreasonable. In his report Pagni submitted production figures for a single firing of each of two kilns he was familiar with (table 2). Assuming that a kiln working full time would have sixteen firings a year, or about one every three weeks, he estimated that one kiln could produce 1,280 moggia of lime and 272,000 bricks (with 320 moggia of charcoal as a by-product), and the other 1,440 moggia of lime and 160,000 bricks (plus 352 moggia of charcoal). He concluded that this level of production assured the smaller operator an income of 80 ducats a year, enough (according to Pagni) to be happy, and the larger operator an income of 150 ducats, "which would be comfortable for anyone." It is to be noted that the larger of these kilns had about the productive capacity of the kiln described in the *Encyclopédie*, but its maximum annual production of sixteen firings was less than half of a single firing of a Dutch installation in the seventeenth century.

[24] *Statuta (1415)*, II, 209.

[25] ASF, Capitani di Parte (numeri neri) 272, item 205.

TABLE 2

Balance Sheets for Single Firings at Two Kiln Sites, 1568

Kiln at San Niccolò, in Florence		lb. s. d.	Kiln at Ponte a Ema		lb. s. d.
Production					
Lime: 80 moggia @ lb.6		480. 0. 0	Lime: 90 moggia @ lb.6 s.10		585. 0. 0
Bricks: 17,000 @ lb.10 s.10 per 1,000		178.10. 0	Bricks: 10,000 @ lb.13 per 1,000		130. 0. 0
Charcoal: 20 moggia @ lb.4		80. 0. 0	Charcoal: 22 moggia @ lb.2 s.10		55. 0. 0
TOTAL		738.10. 0	TOTAL		770. 0. 0
Expenses					
Rent of kiln		10. 0. 0	Rent of kiln		8. 0. 0
Fuel		405. 0. 0	Fuel		333. 6. 8
Labor		153.10. 0	Labor		109. 0. 0
firing	70. 0. 0		firing	70. 0. 0	
molding	42.10. 0		molding	32. 0. 0	
stacking wood	7. 0. 0		stacking wood	7. 0. 0	
carriage at kiln	34. 0. 0				
Operations		103. 3. 4	Operations		83.16. 8
limestone	63. 0. 0		limestone	63. 0. 0	
rent of quarry	1. 3. 4		sand	11. 6. 8	
clay	8.10. 0		losses	2.10. 0	
depreciation	4.10. 0		miscellaneous	7. 0. 0	
losses	26. 0. 0				
			Delivery to Florence		200.13. 4
TOTAL		671.13. 4	lime @ lb.1 s.5 d.4		
			per moggio	114. 0. 0	
			bricks @ lb.8 s.13 d.4		
			per 1,000	86.13. 4	
			TOTAL		734.16. 8
Profit		66.16. 8			35. 3. 4

SOURCE: ASF, Capitani di Parte (numeri neri), no. 722, item 205.

NOTE: These balance sheets reproduce item for item those of the document (see text). Not all the items on one sheet correspond to those of the other, and there are some expenses that are missing.

These figures for kiln output in the later sixteenth century are substantially larger than the quantities of bricks contracted for, and delivered, that are recorded in earlier building accounts. The largest contract for the supply of kiln products turned up in this study, made between the monastery of San Miniato and the kilnman Cipriano di Durante from Galluzzo in 1446, called for delivery of 50,000 bricks and 100 moggia of lime within five months.[26] At the Strozzi palace, where the demand for bricks was probably as high as at any other site throughout the entire century, the purchase of bricks from any one producer never went higher than 7,000 a month. The supply contracts Strozzi let out to the kilnman Salvatore d'Antonio d'Andrea (who rented his kiln at Campi from Strozzi) required delivery of 12,000 bricks from June to September 1490, 20,000 bricks from April to August 1491, and 20,000 bricks from August to November 1491. During the same period Strozzi bought bricks from other producers, including one, Jacopo di Francesco at Monticelli, who supplied bricks (along with lime) at about the same rate as Salvatore. Neither, however, supplied more than 50,000 bricks in a year's time.[27]

That even the largest purchases of kiln products for construction projects before 1500 do not match the levels of production Pagni assumed were typical in 1568 may indicate that kilns increased their productive capacity in the sixteenth century, but given the current state of research on kiln technology it would be foolhardy to venture into that subject in these pages.[28] Our knowledge of kiln technology in pre-industrial Europe has enormous

[26] S. Miniato 160 (accounts), fol. 69v.

[27] Richard A. Goldthwaite, "The Building of the Strozzi Palace: The Construction Industry in Renaissance Florence," *Studies in Medieval and Renaissance History*, 10 (1973), 157–59 (with further references to kilnmen in the building accounts).

[28] The best discussions of limeburning and the making and firing of bricks before the industrial revolution are still those in the eighteenth-century *Descriptions des arts et métiers*: Henri Louis Duhamel du Monceau, *L'Art du tuilier et du briquetier* (1763); Charles René Fourcroy de Ramecourt, *Art du chaufournier* (1766); and Jars, *Art de fabriquer*. These were the sources for the enlarged article on bricks in the *Supplément à l'encyclopédie*, II, 54–70 (which, however, includes additional material, especially in the plates). The first volume of plates with illustrations accompanying the article in the first edition (Amsterdam, 1762) is also to be consulted. Much interesting material is collected in the various documents on brickmaking in England and America from the fifteenth to the nineteenth centuries published by Foster, *Brickmaking*. The subject of bricks and brick kilns is hardly mentioned in the standard histories of technology: Maurice Daumas, ed., *A History of Technology and Invention: Progress through the Ages*, trans. Eileen B. Hennessy (New York, 1969), especially I, 491–92 and II, 80; and C. Singer, E. S. Holmyard, A. R. Hall, and T. J. Williams, eds., *A History of Technology*, II (Oxford, 1956), 304–5 and 388. Brief discussions of techniques can be found in: Lloyd, *English Brickwork*, pp. 29–38; Davey, *Building Materials*, pp. 64–85; the May 1936 issue of the *Architectural Record*, which is dedicated to brick in all its aspects; and the standard national encyclopedias, each of which points out local peculiarities of the industry.

gaps. Not even the innovations that later modernized the industry—the mechanization of both the tempering of clays and the molding of bricks, the elaboration of the flue system to produce the down-draught kiln, and the development of various processes for continual firing—figure in the larger history of industrial technology. In the absence of a study of the clays in the environs of Florence with respect to the properties that make them suitable for brickmaking, and for lack of archaeological investigation of kiln structures in Tuscany, any discussion of the technology of brickmaking runs the risk of entanglement in the unknown.

The one obvious advantage of a permanent installation is its much more economic use of fuel. In Florence a high share of the total cost of operating a kiln went for wood. The three balances presented in tables 2 and 4, which are for kilns where firing of bricks was secondary to limeburning, all agree in putting fuel costs at the same level, just over 60 percent. Since comparative data for other places are not easy to come by, it is difficult to assess what such seemingly high costs meant for the industry in Florence. At the much larger dual-purpose kiln in Alsace (which is discussed later), fuel accounted for only 42 percent of total production cost. Kilns where bricks alone were fired consumed less fuel: only 31 percent of the selling price of bricks produced by the great kiln at Le Havre went for wood, and in a late seventeenth-century account of brickmaking in England the cost of fuel was estimated to be only 3 shillings per thousand bricks as compared to 7 shillings for the labor that went into the making and firing of them.[29] The continuing use of clamps in the north of Europe despite their greater inefficiency in the consumption of fuel and despite the unevenness in the firing of bricks was not unrelated to the lower cost of fuel. As late as the early nineteenth century one observer of the industry in England could still consider a clamp better than a kiln even though it took almost three weeks for the average clamp to burn itself out as compared to the one day in which the firing of a kiln could sometimes be completed.[30] In Italy the supply of wood of the kind suitable for kilns—not heavy timber but brushwood, faggots, and so on—was not abundant, and fuel could not be taken for granted. The Romans saved something in fuel by digging their pit-type kilns into the ground so that they were partially insulated. The building of permanent kiln installations in Florence was probably not unrelated to heavy fuel costs.

In the history of technology lime and brick kilns are treated as two different installations since each process required a different kind of oven. In Florence, however, the two processes could be brought together at one kiln site and even in one structure. Although on some building accounts suppliers of lime and suppliers of brick fall into two distinct groups, and on tax records and

[29] Lloyd, *English Brickwork*, p. 35.

[30] Foster, *Brickmaking*, IV, 14.

property documents the specific nature of a kiln is often indicated, it is nevertheless clear that many kilns produced both items. Legislation on kilns appearing as far back as 1325 required that no kiln be fired to make bricks without also burning lime,[31] and Pagni's report leaves no doubt that production of bricks and lime could be part of the same operation at a single kiln. Furthermore, guild records in Florence make no distinction among kilnmen with respect to their product (as they do, for instance, in Bologna). In both of Pagni's examples, incidentally, lime was much the more important product with respect to gross sales. In another well-documented kiln operation (analyzed in some detail herein), a kiln was leased by the works authority for the building of the bridge at Santa Trinita in order to provide the project with lime, but with each firing the kiln also produced thousands of bricks. Since for the most part the bricks were not needed for the bridge and the sale of them did not bring in a significant sum, it can be concluded that the structure of the kiln made it desirable from the point of view of efficiency to operate the kiln in this way. In the eighteenth century there were dual-purpose kilns in Provence and Languedoc in which bricks and tiles were simply stacked on top of the limestone. One such kiln in Alsace could produce 1,398 cubic feet of lime and 30,000 bricks in one firing. This kiln's productive capacity was much greater than that of any of these Florentine kilns; moreover, the relative market value of two products was the reverse of what it was in a Florentine operation.[32]

In addition to firing technology, the physical environment also influences the organization of the brickmaking industry. Climate, fuels, clays—all vary from place to place, and the process of production as well as kiln technology will depend to an extent on these changing conditions. The writers of the history of the industry, therefore, will have to deal with the geography of the industry. For instance, it is in striking contrast to the seasonal nature of the industry in many places, even where kilns rather than clamps were used, that Florentine kilns were in fact worked all year. Pagni took it to be normal that a kiln could be fired about every three weeks, with the actual firing lasting only several days; on this basis he went on to calculate sixteen firings a year for one kiln. In early fourteenth-century Venetian legislation regarding kilns, the workyear was assumed to be six months, and in 1327 the authorities, wanting to assure sufficient production of bricks, required a minimum of five firings a year at each kiln.[33] In eighteenth-century Mantua an inquest into the industry relative to the proper level of price controls (similar to the 1568

[31] *Statuti* (1325), pp. 252–55; *Statuta (1415)*, II, 209.

[32] An extensive report on this kiln by a royal engineer is quoted and analyzed, especially with respect to the relative cost of this kind of kiln operation, by Fourcroy, *Art du chaufournier*, pp. 26–29; and a brief reference to these dual-purpose kilns elsewhere in France is made by Duhamel, *L'art du tuilier*, p. 13.

[33] Monticolo, *Capitolari*, I, 79.

inquest in Florence) revealed that sometimes only three firings were possible by the kilns of that city. Here (as the inquest brought out) the problem was the length of time it took for the clay to dry sufficiently so that the bricks could be fired, since the clay of the region did not dry out quickly and wet weather could further prolong the drying process. The Mantuan kilnmen tried to compensate for these limitations by making their bricks smaller than regulation size, and this brought them up against public authority and occasioned the inquest.[34] In Holland the seventeenth-century cartel in Rijnland limited production to several firings a year, usually three; according to the *Encyclopédie* a firing could last as long as five or six weeks, with another three required for the kiln to cool off to the point where it could be unloaded. The Alsatian dual-purpose kiln was fired as frequently as every two and a half weeks; although a completely enclosed structure, it too was limited to an eight-month season. In all of these places, and likely elsewhere as well, the industry was seasonal—kilns were closed down in the damp winter months. Even during the normal firing season, moreover, clamps could be affected by the weather. There are several sixteenth-century instances in England of failure by kilnmen to meet contracted production levels because of bad weather.[35]

Although kilns were shut down, winter was not necessarily a dead season for the industry, for in some areas the drying time for clays required bricks to be made so long in advance of their firing that brickmakers might in fact work the year around. Alberti advised that clay dug in the autumn be weathered throughout the winter; then in the spring it could be molded into bricks (although he goes on to suggest ways that bricks can be made in both winter and summer). In modern Italy the season for working the clay and molding bricks normally extends from April to September, and unlike that in many areas, the climate there is favorable for a natural drying process. Clays, however, vary widely in the way they weather, work, dry, and fire; often the procedures used to organize work at a brickyard depended on the particular properties of the local clay as much as on anything else.[36]

INDUSTRIAL OPERATIONS. Kilns were usually located in the countryside for easy access to raw materials (clay and limestone), fuel, and temporary labor, not to mention the desirability of isolating a polluting and potentially dangerous industrial process. There is no evidence that the feudal nobility of

[34] Archivio di Stato, Mantua: Archivio Gonzaga, busta 3237, insert 20, doc. dated 21 January 1732 ("supplica dell'arte de' fornasari").

[35] Airs, *Country House*, pp. 104–5.

[36] Because there are so many variables affecting the production of bricks from one place to another, it is not useful to do a comparative study of brick prices; cf. F. Braudel and F. Spooner, "Prices in Europe from 1450 to 1750," *Cambridge Economic History*, IV (Cambridge, 1967), 417–18.

medieval Europe, like the landowners of ancient Rome, promoted the industry on their estates in response to the needs of urban markets growing up in their midst. With the increase in brick construction in the early modern period, however, some farmers in England on the periphery of urban markets turned to brick production during the off-season of the agricultural year. Larger estates in England often had more or less permanent brickyards to supply their own needs for new construction and maintenance, and production might also be directed to demand arising locally from other sources in the vicinity of the estate. Some of these estates continued to operate their brickyards until very recently, one at Ashburnham in Essex remaining in operation until 1968. These estate operations, however, were only marginally commercial enterprises. In general the production of bricks for urban markets fell outside the agricultural sector and beyond the pale of landowners' traditional interests in the extractive industries, such as mining. Lime, on the other hand, did arouse some interest in the eighteenth century in response to the rising demand for it not only as a building material but also as a product needed increasingly in farming. In Scotland some landowners, enlightened by the new ideas of their age about estate management, thoroughly industrialized the production of lime on their estates by building large stone kilns as permanent establishments and sometimes clustering these together in massive blocks for larger-scale operations.[37]

At a large construction site in late medieval England brickmaking was simply a part of the enterprise. Clamps were set up on the property of the builder, who might provide the equipment, including even the molds, and possibly much of the labor; they were operated only temporarily, for the duration of the demand arising from that specific construction project. Some of these ad hoc operations could nevertheless be quite large. Contracts are on record by which kilnmen committed themselves to make as many as 200,000 bricks, and for some projects the demand was such that the kilnman was assured work for several years. Yet, inasmuch as it was on commission, the employment of a kilnman was always temporary; to keep busy the kilnman had to take to the road and find another job between contracts and in off-seasons.[38] Many towns had communal brickyards, but the best-known of these, at Hull, throughout the fourteenth and fifteenth centuries was operated directly by the municipality rather than let out on contract.[39] The use of

[37] B. C. Skinner, "The Archaeology of the Lime Industry in Scotland," *Post-Medieval Archaeology*, 9 (1975), 225–30.

[38] Airs, *Country House*, pp. 104–7.

[39] The chamberlain's accounts for the operation of this kiln are the best documentation we have for such an enterprise outside of Italy before the early modern period. They have been studied by F. W. Brooks, "A Medieval Brick-yard at Hull," *Journal of the British Archaeological Association*, 3rd ser., 4 (1939), 151–74. Cf. Jean-Pierre Sosson, *Les Travaux publics de la ville de Bruges, XIVe–XVe siècles* (Brussels, 1977), pp.

temporary installations for the making of bricks on the construction site remained common in England, and in Germany as well, into the nineteenth century; in France the practice was not unusual at the beginning of this century.

Hardly any evidence exists about kiln operations as an ongoing artisan enterprise anywhere in medieval Europe. We can imagine that in those areas where there is a tradition of brick architecture, and around the larger cities that began to spring up all over late medieval and early modern Europe, the industry saw the development of independent artisan organization. In Italy, where a vigorous urban market for bricks developed early, temporary operations were nevertheless not unknown. One wealthy Pavese builder in the fifteenth century satisfied his need for bricks by doing exactly what a contemporary Englishman would have done: he engaged a kilnman to make bricks on his country estate.[40] In many places in Italy, however, the industry developed beyond the stage of being composed solely of itinerate kilnmen who traveled from one construction site to another as the occasion called for his services. Florence was not the only place where kilns were permanent industrial establishments with continuing operations. In Venice the market was sufficiently developed by the early fourteenth century that a kiln was considered a sound investment for income purposes, for when the government decided to appropriate funds for the building of new kilns in order to assure the public supply of bricks, it (characteristically bending public policy to the private interests of the ruling group) channeled those funds in the form of loans into the hands of poorer nobles so that they could build the kilns and enjoy the profits of the investment.[41] The nobles probably rented out their kilns and had little to do with their operation. That the expanding market for brick in late medieval Italy opened the way for some kilnmen to enter the market as small entrepreneurs running an ongoing business with considerable control over the industrial process is one inference that can be drawn from the appearance of separate guilds of kilnmen in some northern Italian cities and the formulation of communal laws to regulate their production. In Verona more concrete evidence for their success exists in their respectable showing on the tax rolls of the city.[42] Moreover, many building accounts attest the

---

75–77 (for the operation of the brickyard purchased by the city of Bruges in 1331).

[40] Carlo M. Cipolla, "Per una storia del lavoro in Italia (con documenti dagli archivi pavesi)," *Bollettino storico pavese*, 7 (1944), 78.

[41] Monticolo, *Capitolari*, I, 82 n. 1, 215–17, 225–26. According to Susan Connell, brickworks in Venice were normally owned by nobles, who rented them out to kilnmen on a type of production-sharing contract; "The Employment of Sculptors and Stone-Masons in Venice in the Fifteenth Century," Diss. Warburg Institute of the University of London 1976, p. 157.

[42] Amelio Tagliaferri, *L'economia veronese secondo gli estimi dal 1409 al 1635* (Milan, 1966), p. 147.

competitive bidding among producers to get large, long-term contracts to supply bricks—for instance, at the cathedral of Milan in the early seventeenth century.[43]

Few places in Italy or in Europe had the large regional markets with a steady demand for bricks that made the industry an attractive investment in seventeenth-century Holland. The enormous capacity of Dutch kilns made a brickyard, probably for the first time in the history of the industry, a relatively big business. It was so, for example, for one mid-seventeenth–century owner of two kilns, Theodosius Lempereur; furthermore, the record shows that he actively entered into their operation. For one kiln, in Leiderdorp, he made a contract with a foreman to organize the labor and direct operations in return for a rate charge on production, while Lempereur paid all expenses; for the other kiln, in Rijswijk, he went into partnership with the kilnman, whose one-quarter share was put up through a loan at an interest rate of 4 percent from Lempereur himself. In both instances Lempereur probably took care of fuel purchases and sales. The market value of one of his brickyards was 10,000 Dutch florins (or guilders). In an economy where a laborer made about one guilder a day, such a sum, as compared to the modest value of Florentine kilns, indicates how much larger these Dutch industrial establishments were. There was, at any rate, considerable capitalist penetration into the industry.[44]

The productive capacity of the brick industry in Florence did not approach anything like the levels reached by the industry in Holland, nor did the Florentine industry attract the interest of wealthy men. As permanent industrial establishments, however, Florentine kilns represented a capital investment in plant, as we have already seen, of up to several hundred florins, much beyond the reach of most artisans. That initial investment in most instances came from landowners who wanted to develop their property, but to judge from fifteenth-century tax records and private accounts, these men rarely went any further to invest also in the operation of their kilns. If anything, they paid for the upkeep simply out of an interest in seeing their property properly maintained. In a jointly filed tax return of members of the Alderotti family in 1427, for instance, a 20-florin deduction was claimed on a 45-florin rent from a kiln on the basis that this was what they had to pay out for maintenance expenses.[45] Owners preferred to rent their property to kilnmen rather than enter into partnerships with them. Rent was usually an annual fee, but contracts setting the rent as a percentage of production are not unknown.[46] Even

[43] Domenico Sella, *Salari e lavoro nell'edilizia lombarda durante il secolo XVII* (Pavia, 1968), p. 136.

[44] Kloot Meyburg, "Gegevens."

[45] Catasto 66 (S. Spirito, Ferza, 1427), items 739 and 775.

[46] For example, the contract, dated 6 October 1473, between Antonio di Francesco Baccelli and Antonio di Francesco Dini for rent of the former's kiln set the rent at

when the owner of a kiln needed bricks for his own building projects, he (like Filippo Strozzi) more likely than not entererd into a normal supply contract with his tenant kilnmen.[47] Not one set of building accounts has been turned up for a construction project where bricks (or lime) were supplied from a kiln set up and operated exclusively for that project. Regardless of the arrangement the owner of a kiln made for its operation, however, he was required (as of the Fabbricanti statutes of 1544) to pay a matriculation fee to the guild.

Brickmaking, therefore, was an independent artisan industry. By renting a kiln a kilnman could go into business without an initial capital investment in plant, and the additional cost of equipment was insignificant. He needed enough cash or credit, however, to get operations going to the point where income began to come in from sales.

Kilnmen worked largely on direct commission from owner-builders (not masons), although they probably had supplies of bricks on hand for smaller sales. Supply contracts are generally not notarized unless (as with some let out for the building of the Strozzi palace) an advance was made against future delivery to help pay for the cost of getting operations going. Otherwise, a brief memorandum entered in the client's account book sufficed. When Cipriano di Durante made the agreement with San Miniato cited earlier, his understanding of it was written down in one of the books of the monastery in his own hand (he says) just to make everything clear ("per chiareza"). His penalty for nondelivery was liability for any difference in the cost of bricks the monastery would have had to pay.

Production schedules were dependent on these commissions, for kilnmen could not rely on a steady demand for bricks from the general market, nor could more than a few have had enough capital to permit much of a build-up of inventory at the brickyard. Even a good customer, whose sustained demand a producer could count on, was hard to find. At the Strozzi palace, despite the intensity of building activity, no single kilnman supplied more than 50,000 bricks in a year's time. After Cipriano di Durante's final delivery at San Miniato the monks continued through the winter and early spring to buy bricks by the thousands from several other suppliers without, however, taking any more from Cipriano. There were, in other words, many suppliers in the marketplace, and ties with their customers were not tight. Firing of kilns must have been sporadic; indeed, underemployment (as following discussions point out) was the chief problem in the industry that the inquest of 1568 brought to light.

This artisan industry is not without its success stories. One can be told, on

---

20 soldi for every 1,000 bricks, or 15 soldi if Dini did not also burn lime; ASF, Notarile antecosimiano S501 (Bastiano Serforese), fol. 28r.

[47] Goldthwaite, "Strozzi Palace," p. 157.

TABLE 3
Balance Sheet of Benedetto da Terrarossa & Partners,
Kilnmen, 1427

	lb. s. d.
Assets	
Inventory and equipment	1,240.10. 0
Credits with 104 parties	2,218.12. 6
TOTAL	3,459. 2. 6
Liabilities	
11 creditors	581.10. 0
Capital (3 shares of lb.800 each)	2,400. 0. 0
Undivided profits	477.12. 0
TOTAL	3,459. 2. 0

SOURCE: ASF, Catasto, 81, fols. 313v–15r.

the basis of Catasto records, about the brothers Benedetto and Pagolo di Marco da Terrarossa. Their family probably came from a place called Terra Rossa near Trespiano on the road to Bologna, where in 1427 they and their father owned a farm. Although the name itself suggests their profession, their grandfather, Michele di Marco, had in fact been a waller. He was one of the contractors responsible for building a ward of the new hospital of San Matteo in 1388. In their 1427 tax declaration, however, Marco and his two sons report major investments in kiln operations. In addition to listing credits with two defunct partnerships for the operation of a kiln near Trespiano, they submitted a balance sheet of a current partnership for the operation of a kiln located in the city (table 3). Benedetto had a one-third share of the capital, worth 800 lire, and there were two other partners (Giovanni di Simone di Salomone and the previously mentioned Cipriano di Durante). The kiln was the Alderotti property mentioned earlier, one of the few inside the city, located near the church of Sant'Elisabetta delle Convertite in Via de' Serragli. The rent of 45 florins was as high as for any kind of industrial premises in the city, including cloth shops. At this point in the history of the family—Marco, aged sixty-five, was at the end of his career, and the brothers, thirty-six and thirty-two, were at the beginning of theirs—the members had, by artisan standards, a substantial but not exceptional estate consisting of their residence in the city, half of another urban house, and the large farm at Terra Rossa (worth 357 florins), besides their kiln business, although after deducting liabilities their net taxable wealth was a modest 339 florins. Moreover, both the father and grandfather were prominent in the affairs of the masons' guild, the Arte dei Maestri di Pietra e di Legname (for more on this see chapter 6).

The brothers, Benedetto and Pagolo, were presumably able to play off the advantages of operating a kiln in the city (no gabelle charges and reduced delivery costs) against the disadvantages (inaccessibility to clay and fuel). Their subsequent Catastro reports, filed jointly, tell the story of their growing enterprise. In 1438 they personally bought two-thirds of the kiln their partnership was operating, described in the sale document as a kiln for making bricks and lime. The share purchased by the Da Terrarossa had passed from the Alderotti family to Jacopo di Piero Bini and then was sold by the tax officials in settlement of his debts. The Da Terrarossa paid 160 florins for their share, and the kiln continued to be rented to their own partnership for 25 florins a year. In a partial list of the city's businesses drawn up in 1451 by the tax officials, the partnership, registered in Benedetto's name, was assessed at 500 florins, the top enterprise of its kind in the list and just over the line into the middle third of all 228 enterprises, a respectable showing for an artisan. Benedetto owned a three-eighths share, and his partners were the kilnmen Ugo d'Antonio Cioffi (three-eights share) and Antonio di Bartolomeo d'Agostino (one-quarter share).

In addition to operating the kiln rented from the brothers, the partnership invested some of its capital in another partnership, known under the name of Giovanni di Francesco & Partners, for the operation of a kiln outside the Porta San Niccolò, which they rented for 28 florins from Giovanni Capponi. This partnership also had a capital of 500 florins, and there were complicated ties of ownership between the two operations: not only was the partnership of Benedetto itself, as a single party, one of the partners in the San Niccolò kiln (for a 17½ percent share), but the two partners of Benedetto in addition invested privately in this second partnership—Ugo Cioffi, directly, for a 12½ percent share, and Antonio di Bartolomeo d'Agostino, indirectly, for a 25 percent share of Giovanni di Francesco's 33⅓ percent share. The fourth partner in the San Niccolò kiln operation, along with Giovanni di Francesco, Cioffi, and Da Terrarossa & Partners, was Bartolomeo di Piero Capponi. The complexities of these organizational arrangements for the operation of kilns demonstrate how formal business practices that were not unusual among the great banking and mercantile companies of the city had percolated down to the modest level of artisan enterprise.

It was presumably the profits made in the brick and lime industry that enabled Pagolo to make an investment in the wool partnership of one of the great merchants of the city, Lorenzo d'Ilarione Ilarioni. In the 1451 tax list of businesses Pagolo is down for a one-quarter share, assessed at 725 florins for tax purposes. The 1457 Catasto report filed jointly by Benedetto, then sixty-eight and unmarried, and Pagolo, who had seven children, further documents the success of their enterprise. At that time they owned five-eighths of the partnership (now with Cioffi alone) that rented their kiln, and they were themselves renting a second kiln. They had added to the property inherited from their father various parcels of land scattered in the vicinity of the southern slopes of Monte Morello from where they came—at Montughi, Novoli, Castello, and the environs of Prato. The residence on the property at Terra Rossa had been described in 1442 as a respectable house (*casa da signore*). Their total real estate holdings amounted to 1604 florins. Benedetto's last report, in 1469—he was then eighty and Pagolo was dead—listed the kiln (evaluated at 410 florins), a 35 percent share in a partnership for its operation with Antonio Cioffi and Matteo di Rinaldo Angeni, and real estate worth 1,857 florins.

Information on the economic history of his family ends after the death of Benedetto with the 1480 report of the three sons of Pagolo. The kiln at Sant'Elisabetta had been sold but another had been purchased; the partnership was still going, now with a declared capital of 1,000 lire, and was participated in by Marco di Pagolo (35 percent), Cioffi (40 percent), and Angeni (25 percent). It rented two sites, one for 26 florins and the other (from the Da Terrarossa themselves) for 130 lire. Contemporary building accounts attest the activity of this younger generation of the Da Terrarossa as suppliers of bricks. The fate of Pagolo's investment in the wool shop with Ilarioni, who had gone bankrupt in 1464, is not known, but his sons still had real estate (not counting their kiln property and residence) worth 1,525 florins. Another mark of Benedetto and Pagolo's success was their solid position in the elite that ran the masons' guild, which also included the families of their partners, Cioffi, Angeni, and Antonio di Bartolomeo d'Agostino.[48]

The kiln at San Niccolò, in whose operation the Da Terrarossa had a minor share in 1451, was the center of another large operation. In 1457 their partner there, Giovanni di Francesco, whose father had been a silk weaver, submitted to the tax officials a balance sheet of a completely reorganized business. The new company was still under his name, and he ran it for 20

[48] The Catasto declarations of the Da Terrarossa are as follows (all from San Giovanni, Vaio): 81 (1427), fols. 313v–15r; 628 (1442), fol. 183; 686 (1446), no. 179; 720 (1451), fols. 368–69; 832 (1457), fols. 149–54; 929 (1469), fols. 187–89; 1024 (1480), fols. 99–100. The 1451 tax assessments on businesses is found in ASF, Misc. rep. 21, insert 3 bis; this document is published only in part (and with errors) by Anthony Molho, "The Florentine 'Tassa dei Traffichi' of 1451," *Studies in the Renaissance*, 17 (1970) (for instance, the only kilnman of the five in the document to appear on the published list is Benedetto da Terrarossa, and he is identified as a baker). Cf. the 1451 Catasto report of the operator of the San Niccolò kiln, Giovanni di Francesco di Piero: 718 (San Giovanni, Chiave), no. 365. The 1438 sale document is among the papers of the notary Ser Pagolo Benivieni; ASF, Notarile antecosimiano B1323, fols. 103r–6v; and the transaction is reflected in the subsequent Catasto report of the Alderotti: 690 (1451), pt. 1, fol. 221. The guild activity of these men is mentioned herein in ch. 5; The prominence of Matteo and Marco di Pagolo as suppliers of bricks is remarked by Galeazzo Cora, *Storia della maiolica di Firenze e del contado, secoli XIV–XV* (Florence, 1973), I, 307.

The kiln outside Porta San Niccolò may have been on the site of the early seventeenth-century kiln documented by Salvagnini, "Gli Zuti."

percent of the profits, with the capital of 1,920 lire coming from two partners, Piero di Bartolomeo Capponi (or his sons) and the stonemason Giuliano di Nofri di Romolo. Besides the kiln at San Niccolò, which they rented for 30 florins from Giovanni Capponi, they also rented one from the monastery of San Miniato for 37 florins. The balance sheet Giovanni submitted listed credits with 130 persons totaling 4,142 lire (although many of these he wrote off as bad debts) and an inventory worth 305 lire. The list of debtors covers a cross section of Florentine society, ranging from artisans and shopkeepers through churches and ecclesiastical institutions to Cosimo de' Medici himself —whose debt, a mere 70 lire, was the largest.[49]

These enterprises are known only from tax records and clients' building accounts, and without the partnership accounts it is not possible to penetrate into their internal circumstances as business operations. These kilnmen undoubtedly kept accounts, however, for although the fame of Florentine economic history rides on the remarkable quality of extant records from the realm of industry, commerce, and finance dominated by the wealthy, enough accounts survive from all kinds of artisan enterprises to lead us to believe that accounting was widely practiced at all levels of the business world. Accounts for other kiln operations do survive. Two sets of these accounts are reasonably complete, and although both are late, dating from the same years in the second half of the sixteenth century, they fill out the record of this industry by documenting the manufacturing process itself.[50]

[49] Catasto 829 (S. Giovanni, Chiave), fols. 171–75. The reports of the other investors are: Catasto 832 (S. Giovanni, Vaio), fols. 814–15 (Giuliano di Nofri); 796 (S. Spirito, Drago), fols. 95 (Bartolomeo di Piero Capponi) and 108v (Nicola di Piero Capponi).

[50] Fifteenth-century accounts for the operation of kilns exist, but they are too fragmentary or sparse to merit extensive analysis, especially in view of the fact that where comparisons can be made with the complete records of the two later operations discussed in the text the operations appear to have been conducted in exactly the same fashion. See, for example, the accounts for the operation of a kiln at Colonica belonging to the hospital of Santa Maria Nuova: ASF, S. M. Nuova 40 (accounts, 1482–88), fols. 12, 112, 214, 326, 341. A small ledger survives for the operation of a kiln, from 1466 to 1469, located at the Badia of Santa Maria in Mamma, near San Giovanni Valdarno (at that time belonging to the Brigittine convent "Paradiso" at Pian di Ripoli just outside Florence): ASF, S. M. Nuova, Monache del Paradiso 205. The kiln was operated by two "maestri di murare e di fornace," and although they were employed on construction at the Badia, many of the transactions recorded in the ledger are sales to other parties. The accounts were kept by the Badia in correct double entry (with cash transactions cross-referenced to income-outgo books that no longer survive). There are, however, only thirty-five folios, and the title page is missing. An account (fols. 2 and 27) was opened for the expenses of operating the kiln, but the information is too sparse to merit analysis. The account book for four firings, from May to September 1533, of a *fornace di calcina* at Casignano near Bagno a Ripoli survives: Innocenti, ser. CXLIV, 346. This small book was kept by Bartolomeo di Simone de' Nobili for Raffaello Pucci. They were apparently partners in the operation,

The first set of these accounts comes not from a brick kiln but from a limeburning operation, and they survive because they were seized by the authorities in connection with settlement of the bankruptcy of the partnership formed to operate the kilns.[51] The kiln site was at Giogoli, south of Florence above Galluzzo, and it belonged to Francesco di Girolamo Tozzi. In January 1570 Tozzi went into partnership with Giuliano Mazzinghi, who was probably a kilnman (although he is not so identified in the documents). Tozzi invested 1,700 lire in cash (243 ducats) in addition to providing the use of his kilns and access to the limestone on his property. Mazzinghi put in no capital, and since the articles of association do not survive, nothing is known about the terms of his participation. The accounts do not show any payments to him or, indeed, withdrawals by him of any kind from operating funds. The typical Florentine arrangement would have been for the partnership to put a value on Mazzinghi's participation in the enterprise as the active partner, and this value together with Tozzi's cash would have formed the hypothetical capital (*corpo*) of the operation, with profits being divided between them according to the ratio of ownership.

The Tozzi accounts were kept in the best tradition of Florentine business practice, and they document the financial activity of the partnership for about five months of its operation, from January to May 1570. Among the first purchases of the new company, along with a small table and a stool, were four account books (of which the ledger and income-outgo book survive); other references are made to separate books recording sales of the company's two products, lime and the charcoal left over from firings. It is not clear who kept these accounts (they are all in the same hand); it may have been Mazzinghi. The staff included an administrator (*ministro*), Antonio di Piero Ambruogi, whose salary was 7 ducats a month. Ambruogi kept the cash box (but not the accounts), and he probably was responsible for paying workers and suppliers at the kiln site and collecting payments where deliveries were made, especially in the city.

---

although neither appears to have been a kilnman. There are only sixteen folios of accounts, and the information, once again, is too sparse to merit much of an analysis. Each firing produced 12 moggia of charcoal, 55 to 60 moggia of lime, and up to 8,000 bricks.

Another account book of a kiln, dated 1533–38, is inventoried as ASF, Carte del Sera 201, but it was lost in the flood of 1966 and as of the summer of 1979 had not yet been recovered. In a journal of landed possessions, 1546–62, of Messer Lorenzo di Piero di Niccolò Ridolfi (ASF, Libri di Commercio 67), a number of entries are for payments in connection with the operation of a kiln (e.g., fols. 2v, 6, 9, 34v, 92, 102v, 112v, 114v, 115, 117, 136, 136v); and perhaps among his numerous other books in this collection more information could be found on this enterprise.

[51] ASF, Libri di commercio 494 (income-outgo journal, 1570) and 497 (ledger, 1570); 495 and 496 are accounts of the kiln operation relative to bankruptcy proceedings against the owner beginning in 1572.

Tozzi made a trip to the kilns when they were first fired, and the occasion was celebrated by a meal of wine and blackbird for the workers. From January to April there were five firings, each one lasting six days and requiring two firemen and usually two laborers. During these periods the men had to work also at night, and they received a special wage for night work plus a bonus and some food for each firing. Among the first purchases in the accounts was a mattress for their use. During the downtime of two or three weeks, several unskilled laborers were employed emptying and cleaning the kilns, but the firemen worked only occasionally. Besides this work force at the kilns the partnership also paid men to quarry limestone and others to deliver the stone to the kilns. All together direct labor costs (including quarrying and delivery of limestone) constituted slightly less than 20 percent of total expenditures of the operation. The biggest expense by far—about 70 percent—was for timber and brushwood of various kinds (including its transport). There were miscellaneous expenses for kiln repairs, tools, measuring containers, mending of bags, and so forth; finally, the company paid independent carriers for delivery of the finished products—lime and charcoal—including gabelles on the former when it passed through the city gates.

The company sold 377 moggia of quicklime for lb.2,824 s.0 d.1 and almost 131 moggia of charcoal for a total of lb.525 s.4 d.8—a gross turnover of 478 florins in half a year of operation. There were dozens of customers, no one of them buying a significant share of the total production, although among them there were patrons of some of the city's most prominent current building projects—the Mint and the Pitti, Mondragone, and Montalvo palaces. A variety of small artisans bought the charcoal; barbers were particularly prominent among Tozzi's clients for this by-product of his industrial operation. The market for his products, in other words, was made up of many customers who bought on a small scale, and the demand was constant enough so that a business like Tozzi's was freed from dependency on large commissions.

The second set of kiln accounts document an operation undertaken by the building authority (*fabbrica*) of the Ponte di Santa Trinita.[52] This kiln, located at Ponte a Ema and belonging to Buonaccorso di Benedetto Pitti, was rented for twenty months, from 1 April 1568 to 30 November 1569, the period of the most intensive work on the bridge. The kiln was operated only for the purpose of supplying the bridge, but the accounts were set up to reflect a fully autonomous financial operation as if it were a private undertaking. For

[52] ASF, Depositeria generale 527 (the cover, title page, and the debit side of the first account are missing from this ledger). This kiln may have been the one at Ponte a Ema for which Pagni presented a balance in the same year (the production levels are almost the same), and in fact the accounts for the operation of this kiln may have been kept by the bridge building-authority for the purpose of analyzing costs in connection with the inquest of 1568.

example, cash received to cover ongoing expenses was credited to a capital (*corpo*) account in the name of the fabric as if it were the owner of the kiln, and all kiln products delivered to the bridge were charged to a separate account of the fabric as if it were a customer and were paid for in cash at the going market rates, including carriage and gate gabelles. The reason the accountant regarded all activity of the kiln as formally independent of the building operation, which, after all, was a government enterprise, may have been the government's effort to come to a better knowledge of operating costs in order to have a basis for setting price controls on kiln products, and in fact the exercise may have been a direct result of the inquest of 1568 discussed later. Although the kiln was obviously not a business enterprise, its finances were handled in such a way that the ledger probably reflects a financial picture not too different from that of a normal kiln operation. The balance sheet for its operation is presented in table 4.

The kiln had at least two furnaces (*fornelli*), one described as small. It produced both lime and bricks. The accounts and the cash box were in the hands of a general administrator (*ministro*), Giovanbattista Paganucci, whose salary of 72 florins annually indicates that he probably had a full-time job directing operations. The kilnman, Stefano di Bartolomeo Del Ruta, had an annual salary of 70 florins. The work force varied from week to week: on one occasion day laborers numbered eighteen, and over the year the mean number was eight. Their work is described as being at the kiln and at the quarry, which may refer to either the claypits or the lime quarry or both. Several molders (*spianatori*) were paid rate charges for unbaked bricks (lb.3 s.4 per thousand). There were separate carriage charges for unbaked bricks (one lira per thousand) and for delivery of limestone from the quarry. The largest expense, half of the total outgo, was for fuel—for timber and lighter brushwood, with a small amount going for olive husks, used to keep the fires up. Some of this wood was purchased from independent suppliers; the rest came from direct exploitation of woods where clearing rights had been purchased and woodsmen paid for cutting and delivery.

During the eighteen and a half months when the kiln was worked there were twenty-four firings, or one about every three weeks. A firing produced on the average 8,625 bricks (the mean was 9,000, and the highest number for a single firing was 11,000) and between 90 and 100 moggia of lime (the accounts are less precise for this product). The total production consisted of 207,000 bricks (*mezzane* and *quadrucci*), 2,700 small tiles (*tegolini*), and 2,199 moggia of lime. The lime was by far the most important of these products, constituting more than three-quarters of total gross sales, and almost all of it went to the fabric of the bridge. Only a small part of the brick and tile production, however, was needed for the bridge; the rest was sold. Sales of the by-product, charcoal, brought in almost as much as total brick production did.

The accounts of these two kiln operations point up one of the characteristic

TABLE 4

Balance Sheet for the Operation of a Kiln by the Fabric of the Ponte Santa Trinita, June 1568 to November 1569

		lb. s. d.
Production		
Sales		19,545. 4. 0
lime	15,085. 0. 2	
bricks	2,232.18.10	
charcoal	2,141.17. 4	
tiles	85. 7. 8	
Inventory at end of operation		351.10. 0
TOTAL		19,896.14. 0
Expenses		
Rent of kiln (f.16 lb.4 plus 4 moggia of charcoal, annually)		216. 6. 0 (1.2%)
Personnel		4,333.10.10 (24.0%)
administrator (f.72 annually)	867. 0. 0	
kilnman (f.70 annually)	897. 8. 4	
wage labor	1,608. 4. 4	
molders	960.18. 2	
Operating expenses		1,138.18. 8 (6.3%)
carriage of limestone to kiln	709.11. 8	
miscellaneous purchases	309. 1. 0	
petty expenses	67. 8. 0	
repairs to kiln	39. 9. 4	
sand for molders	13. 8. 8	
Fuel (delivered)		9,387.11. 4 (52.0%)
timber	1,374. 4.10	
brushwood	7,530. 4. 4	
oak branches	443.17. 0	
olive husks	39. 5. 2	
Delivery charges (transport and gabelles for lime, charcoal, bricks)		2,961.12.11 (16.4%)
TOTAL		18,037.19. 9 (99.9%)

SOURCE: ASF, Depositeria generale, no. 527.

NOTE: All the items on this table represent separate accounts in the ledger with the exception of the rent of the kiln, the salaries of both the kilnman and the administrator, which constitute a single account, and the delivery charges, which are treated as debits on the accounts of products sold.

features of the business of running a kiln, be it limeburning or brickbaking: the relative complexity, in comparison with most artisan activities, of managing this kind of industrial enterprise. Limestone had to be quarried, clay dug and molded into bricks, a steady fuel supply assured, a small work crew supervised, and transportation arranged for delivery of the finished product to the customer. Although much of this work—supply of limestone and fuel, and delivery of the finished products—was contracted out in the sense that it was paid for on a rate basis, the kilman was still left with the problem of coordinating supply with his work schedule, and the limited cash reserve of the normal kiln operation must have been a constricting pressure on his relations with both suppliers and carters. At the kiln he directed a work force consisting of the firing crew and various unskilled laborers who unloaded and stacked wood, carried bricks to and from the drying sheds and arranged them in hacks, loaded and unloaded the ovens, and assisted the carters.

The brickmolders would seem to have been independently in charge of their part of the operation, including working the claypits and tempering the clay as well as making bricks. This is the inference to be drawn from the relatively high rates they were paid at the Ponte di Santa Trinita kiln—4 lire, including carriage, for every thousand bricks—for (as we know from observers of the English industry) a good molder who worked in a carefully organized production line with assistants keeping him supplied with clay and continually carrying off the finished product could easily turn out several thousand bricks in a day's work. In England it was also customary for the molder (or brickmaster) to be paid a piece rate, with the count of his production being taken of the bricks that were successfully fired and therefore useable. A molder's work did not require much investment in equipment beyond the wood molds themselves and the shovels and wheelbarrows needed at the claypits (the animal-operated pugmill for mixing clays was a later development), but they had to pay for assistance according to how they set up their work and the rate at which they produced. If practice elsewhere is any indication, it is likely that Florentine molders used women and children, perhaps from their own families, to cut their expenses. In seventeenth-century Dutch kilns it was not unusual for women to work in brickyards as carriers, and English observers of the industry in the early nineteenth century took it for granted that the molder's helpers running to and from his work table to enable him to work at maximum efficiency were boys. In fact, legislation against child labor brought about major changes in the industry in England because it undermined the traditional system used to recruit labor.

The sporadic nature of employment at a kiln is seen in the fluctuation of the number of workers at the Ponte di Santa Trinita kiln. Given the capacity of the Florentine kiln, no more than two or three molders (along with however many assistants they may have had) would have been needed at any establishment; the two firemen at the Tozzi kiln, roughly corresponding to the costs of firing Pagni estimated for both the brick kilns he examined, probably represent the normal size of a firing crew. Add a varying number of manual laborers (the average was eight at the Ponte di Santa Trinita kiln), and the number of workers at a kiln site reaches upward to a dozen. Other than the molder and the fireman, it might be added, none of these laborers required special skills. The fact that the work force of such an operation—

for example, at the Ponte di Santa Trinita kiln—was as large as that employed by Theodosius Lempereur at one of his kilns, which had a much greater capacity, points up the greater efficiency of the Dutch industry. The difference also shows up, as one would expect, in a comparison of prices: whereas Lempereur paid a laborer 1 guilder for a day's work and sold his bricks for 3 to 5 guilders per thousand, in Florence the laborer's wage was more or less 1 lira a day (in the second half of the sixteenth century) but the price of bricks was 10 to 12 lire per thousand.

The operator of a kiln was continually, almost daily, paying a variety of ongoing expenses for fuel and raw materials as they arrived, for wages of his workers at least once a week, and for carriage and gabelle charges on deliveries to the city. Hence he had to be prepared to deal with a rapid turnover of capital. Expenses for Tozzi's operations amounted to just under 100 florins a month, those for the fabric's kiln somewhat more, and the surviving accounts of both attest the need to maintain a record of all this activity. Their ledgers display the sophisticated accounting practices that at least some operators were capable of using to keep that record straight. For the fabric's kiln the supply of ready cash was less of a problem since the operation was subsidized by the state. Some kilnmen who entered into contractual agreements to work virtually full time to supply a single building site stipulated a schedule of payments, including—for example, in the contracts let out by the Strozzi palace and the Innocenti projects—advances in the form of a loan to tide them over the time needed for starting up a new operation before production got underway. An operation like Tozzi's, however, which was not tied to any one construction project but depended on sales to numerous and various customers, required a fairly precise rhythm of expenses and income to assure an adequate cash flow. Therefore he had to make a substantial cash investment in the partnership to get things going. The low margin of profit in this industry, however, probably made it difficult for kilnmen without this kind of financial backing to maintain much of a cash reserve. This was presumably the problem that led to the bankruptcy of Tozzi himself, despite the cushion of his initial cash investment.

As to the practical problem of collecting charges from clients, who were more often than not several miles away, in the city, kilnmen generally used carriers as middlemen. The carrier worked independently, charging the kilnman a rate per load, out of which he paid the gate gabelles; if he was furnished with a written order of payment addressed by the kilnman to the customer, the carrier might also collect on delivery for the kilnman. Such written orders have been found tucked away in the pages of customers' account books, where they were placed after the appropriate entries had been made (see illustration p. 310). Some orders direct the client to pay only the transportation charges; others order full payment for goods received and delivery charges. These orders, incidentally, are documentation for the literacy of

Florentine kilnmen; the Dutch kilnman who signed the 1643 contract for operation of one of Lempereur's kilns could only put down a cross for his mark. The carters who made deliveries were an important independent link between producer and client, and although the Florentine guild statutes do not make much of them, they had special status in guilds elsewhere. In Venice carters formed a distinct group (*membrum*) within the guild of kilnmen, subject (in the early fourteenth century) to specific legislation regarding their part in the enforcement of communal regulation of kiln products. In Rome muleteers and carters come in for special mention in a rubric of the guild statutes that protected those who had contractual agreements with kilnmen from lay-offs due to bad weather.[53]

With as many small customers as the Tozzi kiln had on its books one wonders how the market functioned to bring together widely scattered consumers on the one hand and a remotely situated producer on the other. One outlet for sales may have been the middleman services of some retail food vendors (*pizzicagnoli*), who were subject to special guild fees because they dealt in kiln products.[54] The extent of the sales operation of some kilnmen can be inferred from a provision of the Fabbricanti statutes of 1544 permitting any kiln operator located outside the city to maintain a desk, records, and a sales representative (*fattore*) within the city walls (although not within a stipulated distance of any competitor).[55] Tozzi's administrator, for example, may have served as such a sales agent. The possibility that Tozzi himself was an active partner holding up his end of the business by drumming up sales in the city should not be excluded, however. Perhaps one advantage for a kilnman of going into partnership was that he could get not only the necessary operating cash to keep up production but also the services of an agent to promote sales.

It is widely held that in ancient Rome one of the devices used in the recordkeeping procedures either for production or for delivery of bricks was the brickstamp. The purpose of these brickstamps, however, is not at all clear, although they are the most discussed aspect of brickmaking in the ancient Roman world. A large percentage of Roman bricks are found stamped with signs or words (or both) that identify the slave who made the brick, the master of the kiln, the kiln itself, or the estate on which the kiln was located. This practice of stamping bricks continued into the Lombard period, but there is no evidence of the practice after that time. Examples turn up in northern Germany in the later Middle Ages, especially throughout lower Saxony, some of them going back as far as the twelfth century. Thousands have been found in Lüneburg dating from the last quarter of the fourteenth century to the

53 The statutes are cited in App. 2 herein.

54 See herein, p. 255.

55 Fabbricanti 1, fol. 64r.

sixteenth century, and examples from the fifteenth and sixteenth centuries come also from the Altmark and Schleswig-Holstein. The German marks were personal signs, like medieval stonemasons' marks; they are mostly confined to bricks used in places prominent in the design of the building. They can probably be seen in the medieval tradition of a master craftsman's signature.[56]

In Florence the only evidence for the use of stamps is a loose sheet inserted in one of the ledgers of the building accounts of the Innocenti that has a list of names of the kilnmen who supplied tiles (*embrici*) to the construction site; each name is accompanied by a drawing of his sign (illustration p. 205). Such a record suggests that brickstamps might also have been used in Florence for accounting purposes when there were several suppliers to the same project. No other documentation of the practice has come to light, however. The guild records are silent on the subject. The woodworkers' guild (Legnaiuoli) had much to say about the marks used by dealers in wood to identify the ownership of timber floated on waterways, but the only artisan guild to require the use of personal marks on manufactured products was the metalworkers' guild (Fabbri). Smiths registered their marks with the guild (the official guild register survives and has been published). Otherwise, such marks seem not to have been important among the artisans of Florence (including, incidentally, stonemasons).[57]

THE INQUEST OF 1568. Other aspects of the brick industry are brought out in the 1568 inquest for which Piero Pagni submitted the cost analysis

[56] The vast bibliography on Roman brickstamps can be approached through the references in Helen, *Brick Production*, which is the first of a large number of studies on the subject being undertaken by Finnish scholars. For Lombard practice see Monneret de Villard, "L'organizzazione industriale," pp. 23–24. The practice of stamping bricks in Germany is briefly noted by Rudolph Eberstadt, *Das französische Gewerberecht und die Schaffung staatlicher Gesetzgebung und Verwaltung in Frankreich vom dreizehnten Jahrhundert bis 1581* (Leipzig, 1899), pp. 417–19. A neat classification of these stamps in lower Saxony has been made by Neumann, "Backsteintechnik," pp. 36–42 (with many illustrations and further references to the few comments on the subject in the literature). Cf. Franz Krüger, "Mittelalterliche Ziegelstempel," *Forschungen und Fortschritte*, 10 (1934), 191–92; and idem, "Ziegelstein," pp. 154–55 (with illustrations). I have not seen Krüger's *Ziegelstempel in Lüneburg*, Festblätter des Museumvereins für das Fürstentum Lüneberg, 5 (Lüneburg, 1933).

[57] The Innocenti record of brickstamps is item no. 12 in an envelope of loose papers inserted into Ledger B of building accounts (1421–35): Innocenti, ser. VII, 2. On the use in general of marks and signs on industrial products in Florence, see Alfred Doren, *Le arti fiorentine* (Florence, 1940), II, 160–66. Stonemasons' marks, which have been much studied in northern Europe, are not commonly found in medieval Italian architecture. The peculiar markings found on some of the stones of the Rucellai, Medici, Pitti, and Pazzi palaces have not been studied.

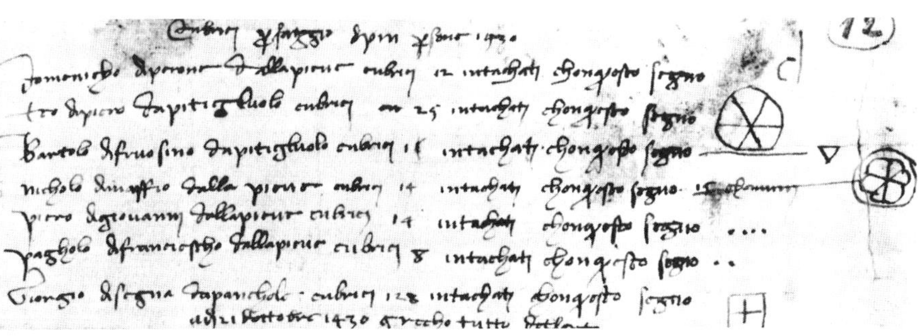

Enbrici per [?] di più persone 1430
Domenicho di Perone dalla Pieve enbrici 12 intachati chon questo segno
Teo di Piero da Piticghuolo enbrici 25 intachati chon questo segno
Bartolo di Fruosino da Piticghuolo enbrici 16 intachati chon questo segno
Nicholò di Maffio dalla Pieve enbrici 14 intachati chon questo segno
Piero di Giovanni dalla Pieve enbrici 14 intachati chon questo segno
Pagholo di Franciescho dalla Pieve enbrici 8 intachati chon questo segno
Giorgio di Segna da Panchole enbrici 128 intachati chon questo segno

Tilers' marks, 1430

of kiln operations already discussed.[58] This inquest followed an appeal by the consuls of the guild that the government revise its current price list for kiln products in view of the rising cost of everything from fuel to delivery charges. Obviously, behind this request was the mounting pressure of the inflation well underway by this time in the sixteenth century. Higher costs were beginning to take their toll in the variety of expenses a kilnman had to pay to operate his business, and he wanted to raise the prices of his products accordingly. The officials recognized that, indeed, conditions were not good among kilnmen and that their discontent was a threat to the city's supply of building materials; but with the characteristic myopia of bureaucrats the inquest evaded the deeper economic issue and cast about for a variety of other problems in the industry that were irrelevant to the policy of price controls. Although the officials thus failed to come to grips with the larger economic forces that were pushing prices upward everywhere in Europe at the time, they nevertheless sponsored an investigation that uncovered a number of specific problems in the industry.

The job of responding to the appeal from the guild landed in the office of the captains of the Parte Guelfa. The captains requested reports on the situation along with recommendations from two architects, Giorgio Vasari and Bartolomeo Ammannati, two purveyors of ducal works, Francesco di Ser Jacopo (or Seriacopi) and Bernardo Puccini, and, finally, Piero Pagni. All of the reports except that of Vasari survive. Ammannati's stands out as particularly notable in reflecting qualities of mind distinctly superior to the others.

[58] ASF, Capitani di Parte (numeri neri) 722, item 205.

Written in an extraordinarily careful and neat hand, it is a comprehensive survey of problems in the industry systematically and clearly laid out in fourteen points. It would do justice to a modern bureaucrat's notion of what a good report should be. The officials must have been struck by its cogency in comparison with the sketchy and limited nature of the other reports, for most of Ammannati's recommendations found their way into the final report.

Ammannati opened his report by declaring himself against a rise in prices because it might discourage building, and then, instead of turning to points directly relevant to the inquest, he brought up another matter of some importance to him as an architect. This was the deterioration in the quality of lime that apparently resulted from the bad situation among kilnmen, which led them to close the better quarries of limestone and take inferior stone from sources closer at hand, even from river beds. Ammannati recommended that the better older quarries (which he identified as those at Le Romituzze, Scandicci, and Pozzolatico) be reopened and that the duke go through with a current project of his to build a canal from the Porta al Prato to the Bisenzio, thereby encouraging the building of new kilns in the vicinity of Signa, where both fuel and limestone were available.

The fundamental problem in the industry identified by Ammannati and the others as being responsible for the economic hardships of kilnmen was underemployment: too many kilns were working below capacity. It was to prove this point that Pagni did his cost analysis, which showed that the official prices were not out of line with the profitable operation of a kiln and that if the kilnmen worked full time, they could do quite well. Although his figures are a little rough (compare the items on tables 2 and 4), Pagni at least did his homework by going out and looking at the accounts of two kilns. This was more than Bernardo Puccini and Francesco di Ser Jacopo did: they passed the buck, merely advising the officials that the purveyors of the ducal works open their own kiln and keep records to see whether the official prices were reasonable in relation to expenses. Francesco di Ser Jacopo thought it might be well to call together all kilnmen within three miles of the city to discuss the problem, adding that the occasion could also be used to exhort them to improve the quality of their products. It is not inconceivable, incidentally, that the accounts of the kiln operated in 1568 and 1569 by the works staff of the bridge at Santa Trinita were in fact kept for the purpose of doing such a cost analysis. The recommendations, in any case, took the form of requiring a minimum number of firings at each kiln: Pagni suggested that any kiln operating with less than one firing a month be closed down for ten years, while Ammannati came up with a minimum requirement of ten firings a year.

As most of these men saw it, a major problem had been created in the industry by the large building program of the duke. For one thing, his officials were commandeering molders, firemen, and other brickyard workers for these projects; Ammannati warned that the kilmen were complaining of this kind of interference with their molders in particular because it resulted in poor quality bricks. The practice was condemned in the final report. According to Pagni one mistake the government was making in organizing ducal projects was assigning agents (*ministri*) to deal with kilnmen. It would be much better, he claimed, to find someone to go into business as the partner of the kilnman, even if it meant advancing capital to him, for such a man would take much more interest in the operation than a salaried bureaucrat.

The 1568 inquest also points up the problem of fuel costs in the industry. At the time of the inquest a number of ducal construction projects were underway, and the demand for bricks was putting a heavy strain on fuel supplies. Ammannati proposed that in order to cut down on the demand for wood no kiln around Florence be allowed to produce charcoal alone; he also called for greater control over woodlands through clearer regulations and stronger enforcement. He found it especially deplorable that wooded areas were being ruined by poaching and that the culprits were encouraged in their ruinous practice by being permitted to take their loot into the city to sell it without paying the gate gabelle, since the wood was carried in on their backs. To put a stop to this it was decided that no wood was to be allowed into the city that did not enter in regulation form—that is, on the backs of animals. The mounting cost of fuel was the major concern behind a subsequent appeal made by the guild for changes in price controls, since the continuing inflation had rendered invalid the earlier cost analysis.[59] The guild suggested that wood for public projects might be brought from the Pisan plain by water so that the normal local supply channels of private operators not be interrupted. It was conceded that this would raise the cost of operating the public kilns, but the argument was made that a better wood supply would assure a better quality product for the duke and that this in turn would tend to make for higher standards in the private sector as well.

REGULATION OF THE INDUSTRY. Of all craftsmen in the various branches of the construction industry, kiln operators were most subject to regulation. Governments attempted to control the price of bricks in order to protect the public's interest in a basic building material; once this step was taken it was imperative to control the size of bricks, as well, for the kilnman, confronted with a fixed selling price, was tempted to cut his costs by reducing the size of his product. Even a slight diminution of a product that was manufactured by the thousands could mean considerable savings in drying time, in labor,

[59] This undated document is included in the file of papers on the 1568 inquest.

and in firing costs.[60] From the second half of the thirteenth century onward communal statutes in Venice, Padua, Pisa, Rome, Siena, and elsewhere fixed standards of measurement for bricks and for bags of lime and regulated prices of all kiln products.

Official models of regulation-size bricks were made to be used as checks. The Pisan statutes of 1286 refer to such a model; in Venice the model, stamped with the seal of the Giustizieri and enclosed in iron brackets to prevent tampering, was probably kept at the Rialto in the palace of the Ufficio di Giustizia, the magistracy in charge of supervising the guilds.[61] In other places the official model was made more available by being permanently displayed in a public place: in Padua it (along with a tile and a limebag) was sculpted in stone on the outside wall of the city hall; in Reggio Emilia a marble model was displayed under the arcade of the public grain market; in Piacenza the form was incised in a pilaster under the arcade of the Palazzo Gotico. Other towns where forms of bricks and tiles can still be seen in public places include Assisi, Bologna, Modena, Urbino, Verona, and Vicenza.[62]

Agents traveled about keeping a check on measurements and sizes, and in some of those places where kilnmen were organized into a guild this task was delegated to it. To the extent that the building-craft guilds regulated the industry, in fact, their statutes are mosly directed to these problems with kilnmen. The legislation, however, is generally not concerned with the quality of kiln products; little attempt was made to get control over the many variables determining the nature of the finished product by regulating raw materials or setting down standards for industrial procedures.

In Florence, too, there is a long record of communal legislation regarding measurement standards, price controls, and practices by kilnmen that tended to fix prices.[63] In the fifteenth century these regulations fell in the domain of the Grascia, the communal office that concerned itself generally with the

[60] Detailed analyses of what a change in the brick size could mean for costs at every point during the process of production were sometimes made in connection with protests by kilnmen of new regulations increasing the size of bricks. Such an analysis can be found in the report (cited in note 34 to this chapter) made in 1732 at Mantua following a protest of new brick regulations. Another exists for a similar situation in Baltimore in 1798: Lee H. Nelson, "Brickmaking in Baltimore, 1798," *JSArH*, 18 (1959), 33–34.

[61] Monticolo, *Capitolari*, I, 81.

[62] Emilio Nasalli Rocca, ed., *Statuti di corporazioni artigiane piacentine (s.XV–XVIII)* (Milan, 1955), p. 97 n.; Melchiorre Roberti, "Le corporazioni padovane d'arti e mestieri," *Memorie del reale istituto veneto di scienze, lettere ed arti*, 26 (1897–1902), fasc. 8, 94. The official models in Modena and Reggio Emilia are mentioned in early seventeenth-century guild documents; see App. 2 herein.

[63] *Statuti* (1325), pp. 252–55; *Statuta (1415)*, II, 206–8; *Leg. tosc.*, IV, 369–70; VI, 356–58; VII, 84–86; VIII, 182–86; X, 315–21; etc.

public's interest in the marketplace (above all, regulating sales of food),[64] but the enforcement agency that dealt directly with the industry was the Arte dei Maestri di Pietra e di Legname, the guild of the building crafts to which kilnmen belonged. The statutes of this guild do not survive, but the deliberations reveal the continuing concern of the guild with these matters.[65] In 1471, during deliberations about statutory reforms, the only specific statute referred to regarded the regulation of kiln products, and at that time a new statute was drawn up. In a subsequent deliberation in which the guild consuls are instructed to take an oath of office to uphold the guild statutes, the statute about kiln products is again the only one singled out for mention. In 1510, following the wisdom of experience (as the deliberation has it), a committee of eight was instructed to rewrite the statute for the greater clarification of certain procedures, especially the administrative mechanisms for enforcement and appeal. Again in 1533 another such committee was charged with the same task, this time on order of the new ducal government. Throughout the deliberations this is the only statute specifically mentioned that is relevant to practice in any of the building trades.

The guild statute of 1471, drawn up in response to public complaints about fraud in the industry, set up procedures for control; these were subsequently refined, especially by the ducal government, with respect to the machinery for enforcement and appeal.[66] Each limeburner was to keep on hand at the kiln regulation-size bags for measuring lime that were approved and marked by the guild (the official measure of a three-staio bag for the sale of grain was kept at Orsanmichele in 1325, and in the new market building erected there in the mid-fourteenth century it was incised in the inside wall above the door of the stairs leading to the storage area above). The basic brick was the *mattone*, which the 1325 statutes fixed at about twenty-nine centimeters in length, half that in width, and half the width in thickness. Later there were three official bricks—the *mattone*, the *mezzana*, the *quadruccio*—the sizes of which varied slightly from time to time. The *quadruccio* was slightly narrower than the *mattone*, and the *mezzana* was wider but considerably thinner. All these Florentine bricks corresponded roughly to the large medieval type found elsewhere, being thicker and a bit narrower than Roman bricks, and larger than the Flemish-type used in England, which was

[64] Kiln products, however, are not mentioned in the 1379 statute of the Grascia: M. Cristina Pecchioli Vigni, "Lo statuto in volgare della Magistratura della Grascia (a.1379)," *ASI*, 129 (1971), 3–70.

[65] For what follows see the guild deliberations: Maestri 3, fols. 17v–22r, 81v–84r, 92v–93r, 98, 102v–3r; and the discussion of guild administration in chapter 5 herein.

[66] Fabbricanti 1 (statutes of 1544), rubrics 8 and 12; Fabbricanti e Por San Piero 1 (statutes of the new guild conglomerate, 1583), rubrics 6 and 16.

closer to the size of modern bricks.[67] Regulations required that model brick-molds (*modani*) bound in iron and stamped with an official seal be on display at each brickyard; they were to be checked annually. The model mold was larger than the baked brick to allow for shrinkage during firing, but if shrinkage resulted in a brick smaller than the official size the kilnmen could request approval for a larger mold. In Bologna a 1566 addition to the guild statutes charged the officials with selecting the carpenters who made model molds for all kilns; in his diary the Bolognese mason Gaspare Nadi relates how he, as the responsible guild official in 1498, had old model molds (*modili*) used by kilnmen burned in a public square according to a rarely enforced statutory requirement.[68]

Enforcement of these regulations was in the hands of a guild agent, the *ricercatore* or searcher (he is so called in English documents), who was assigned an assistant (and, later, more than one). The searcher was to travel about on inspection tours, issue citations, keep a register of violators, and report violations to guild officials. His stipend was a percentage of the fines that resulted from his inspections. Informers were also encouraged by being offered a share of any fine resulting from their information. Inspections were to be made every eight days for kilns in the city, every fifteen days for those within three miles, and four times a year for those within ten miles. With the tightening of controls by the ducal government, kiln operators were required to notify the guild four days in advance of each firing; they were to keep complete records of their sales, including prices, quantity, and nature of all products sold; and they could not send their products off to the city without an approval slip from the guild stating quantity and destination. To check on measurements of delivered products, inspections were extended to

[67] The following table represents regulation sizes for bricks according to the 1544 statutes.

	Molds	Baked Bricks	
	s/d del braccio	*s/d del braccio*	millimeters
Mattone	10/8 X 4/6 X 2/10	10 X 4/4 X 2/6	290 X 126 X 73
Mezzana	10/9 X 5/6 X 2	10 X 5 X 1/9	290 X 145 X 51
Quadruccio	10/4 X 3/9 X 2/10	10 X 3/6 X 2/6	290 X 102 X 73
Roman brick	—	—	300 X 150 X 30
Medieval brick	—	—	250–380 X 125–190 X 45–80
Flemish brick	—	—	200–250 X 100–125 X 45–65

Further comparative information, especially for Roman and English bricks, can be found in L. S. Harley, "A Typology of Brick: With Numerical Coding of Brick Characteristics," *Journal of the British Archaeological Association*, ser. 3, 37 (1974), 63–87.

[68] Gaspare Nadi, *Diario bolognese*, ed. C. Ricci and B. Della Lega (Bologna, 1886), p. 236; for the Bolognese statutes, see App. 2 herein.

construction sites, where masons were required to keep a regulation three-staio measure on hand. Kilnmen were severely warned that inspections would be frequent and that whoever was found to be in violation of the regulations would be punished with no excuses heard, although precautions were taken to see that no one was victimized by enforcement abuse. The kilnman was primarily responsible for all violations, but if the abuse regarded the size of bricks, the molder was also subject to a percentage of the fine; and if the kiln was owned by a privileged party (such as a cleric) who was exempt from prosecution, then all the workers at the kiln—the kilnman, the stoker, the molder—were to share the fine. Any kilnman wanting to make bricks in non-regulation size had to have special permission. Such requests were occasionally presented by both kilnmen and builders.

Kiln operators were the only craftsmen in the building trades who came under controls of this kind. To judge from the surviving guild deliberations, appeal against fraud by kilnmen and condemnation of them for violations were by far the most recurring problems brought before the guild officials. The regulations regarded only measurements; except for an obscure stipulation about the kind of stone that could be burned to make lime, neither the commune nor the guild made efforts to assure quality control of kiln products.

There were, however, economic constrictions imposed on the industry. The sixteenth-century statutes limited kilnmen to the operation of no more than two kilns each within ten miles of the city, and an annual fee was to be paid to the guild for each molder's table in any brickyard. An early communal statute, incorporated in the dubious 1415 compilation, imposed a tax of 2 florins on each firing at a kiln, although no such payments turn up in the sixteenth-century accounts examined here. Control of market prices of kiln products was one of the primary objectives of the regulation of the industry. According to a rubric in the 1325 statutes (reiterated in the 1415 compilation), prices were to be determined by a committee of six representing the (at that time) six subdivisions of the city, but by the sixteenth century this authority was in the hands of the guild. In the later sixteenth century the newly formed guild of the Fabbricanti regularly issued a schedule of prices for the entire range of these products, and with the mounting inflation of that century provision was eventually made for annual review and adjustment. Finally, all kiln products that passed through the city gates were subject to gabelle charges.

Operating a kiln—with its labor crew, the constant need for materials and fuel, the sales campaign in the city, the organization of delivery of the finished product, and the constant turnover of cash—required more administrative, supervisory, and entrepreneurial talent than was required for the usual artisan enterprise. Some of the larger operators, like Benedetto da Terrarossa, must have developed some of these talents to a fair degree. To judge from the appearance of kilnmen in the consular elite of the guild and even in the more important bodies of communal government, their success won them more status in artisan society than one might think possible for men who did this kind of work. Kilnmen must have been a difficult and intractable lot, however. Besides being dependent on the vagaries of the market, kilnmen worked very much within the orbit of the public's interest, and they did not find it easy to manufacture their products under the constraints imposed on them by communal regulations. The authorities were continually on the alert to protect the public from their fraud, and they found themselves hounded by the searchers and more and more closed in by the guild and the state. Moreover, for all their talents only a few kilnmen could escape the hard conditions of their work, the evidence for which some carried in their very names, like Terrarossa, Rosso, and (perhaps) Rosselli. They were, joked the local wit Piovano Arlotto, the cleanest of all Florentines—because they alone washed their hands *before* going to the water closet.[69]

Stone

THE INDUSTRY IN THE MIDDLE AGES. The Romans did nothing that was not on a large scale, and if this is above all true of their building, the implication is that it was true of some of their quarrying operations as well. The organization of the production of marble objects, in fact, may never again have reached the degree of sophistication achieved in some Roman quarries.[70]

The commercial exploitation of quarries developed on a large scale in Rome because the structure and level of demand were favorable and investment in the industry was forthcoming. In the last years of the republic and especially after the foundation of the empire, Romans cultivated a taste for marble in conjunction with their distinctive penchant for building monuments. A brisk demand for the material arose from large spenders who were widely distributed over the Roman world; and since this demand was for products made from a relatively scarce raw material, the commercial viability of quarry exploitation was assured. In addition to the great marble quarries long worked in the eastern Mediterranean—in Egypt and the Aegean—Romans opened

[69] *Motti e facezie del Piovano Arlotto*, ed. Gianfranco Folena (Milan, 1953), p. 68.

[70] Roman quarrying has been discussed extensively by J. B. Ward-Perkins: "Marmo: uso e commercio in Roma," *Enciclopedia dell'arte antica*, IV (Rome, 1961), 866–70; "Quarrying in Antiquity: Technology, Tradition and Social Change," *Proceedings of the British Academy*, 57 (1971), 1–24; "Quarries and Stoneworking in the Early Middle Ages: The Heritage of the Ancient World," in *Artigianato e tecnica nella società dell'alto medioevo occidentale* (Spoleto, 1971), II, 525–44.

major quarries in north Africa, at Carrara, and in the Pyrenees. The imperial government provided the investment and organization needed to reach a high level of production. These quarries were in effect state industries worked by slave and other dependent labor. Such a system of production could only have existed in a society where it was possible to commandeer vast labor forces that included all levels of skills. In this respect Roman imperial quarry operations differed little from those of Oriental despots.

What made these Roman marble quarries so distinctive were the mass-production techniques with which operations were organized. Instead of producing exclusively for a ruler and a small court elite, Roman quarries directed production to meet a much more diffused demand; products were therefore more numerous, both in kind and quantity, and more variable in quality. Large and highly skilled labor forces were organized into something resembling an assembly line to turn out a variety of items, from decorative architectural details to major sculptural pieces, all highly standardized, with some quarries having their own distinctive designs. Many pieces left the quarries fully dressed, with only highlighting of details (such as fluting on columns) and polishing to be done at the site, where they were assembled like prefabricated parts. Some sculptured objects remained incomplete to the extent that the customer could add such individual details as an inscription on a sarcophagus or facial features on a statue. Distribution took place through a long-distance transport system that provided delivery throughout the Mediterranean and northern Europe. Archaeologists have salvaged ships laden with the products of these quarries and have uncovered well-supplied marbleyards at large port-towns where products were temporarily deposited before being moved on to local markets. The uniformity in marble work associated with the imperial style and found throughout the Roman world is a mark of how highly organized this industry, with its empirewide distribution system, was.

The cutting devices used by the Romans were the traditional ones that had been known in the Mediterranean since ancient Egyptian times. They were not of remarkable sophistication, and their use did not in any way depend on the imperial industrial system, which had instead been organized entirely around a plentiful labor supply. The Romans made no technological innovations in the working of quarries, and in fact there was no essential change in technology until the nineteenth century.

With the decline of the western empire the great Roman quarries closed down. Demand dried up as imperial authority collapsed, and the international commercial system that had sustained the industry fell a victim of the political disintegration of a changing world. The quarries in the foothills of the Pyrenees in the area of Toulouse survived the longest. Quarrying there went on with all the features of the earlier operations well into the Merovingian period, supplying sarcophagi and capitals to a market that extended over much of France, but they too were forced to close down following the Saracen invasions.[71]

In the immediate aftermath of the demise of the Carolingian Empire building in stone can hardly be found anywhere. Some Anglo-Saxon quarry operations were not insignificant in scope, to judge from the uniformity of objects made of the same stone and found in widely scattered buildings, but distribution rarely reached beyond seventy or so miles of the quarries, and the market was limited to the occasional church building.[72] Beginning in the eleventh century, however, construction in stone picked up all over Europe, especially for ecclesiastical buildings, but increasingly for fortification and for domestic use as well; in some areas the quarrying of stone became what might be called an important division of the local construction industry. Although the frontiers—geographical and chronological—of stone construction in Europe have not been clearly drawn, it is safe to say that because of the expense of carriage the demand for building stone for vernacular architecture was dependent on its availability in local quarries. Only for the most prestigious buildings, like cathedrals, did builders go farther afield for stone either because it was not present in the vicinity of the building site or because a particular quality of stone was required. The builders for the cathedral of Sens, for example, went one hundred miles to get the stone they wanted.

The few quarries worked to supply building stone for more than a local market were invariably located near rivers or the sea, which alone made such operations possible by facilitating long-distance carriage; production was sporadic, for the most part undertaken for the occasional construction of major ecclesiastical buildings scattered about in the market area of the quarry. In the western Mediterranean the availability of sea transport made it possible to expand momentarily quarry operations on Santanyí on the southeast coast of Maiorca when in the fifteenth century some notable orders for building stone came in from Barcelona and from Naples (for the Castel Nuovo).[73] The limestone quarries in Istria have a long history of supplying the ever-growing urban markets across the Adriatic in Italy, especially Venice, where from the eleventh century onward monumental building generated a steady demand for materials. In northern Europe one of the most active centers of quarrying throughout the Middle Ages was Caen in Normandy. Almost as

[71] Angiola Maria Romanini, "Problemi di scultura e plastica altomedievali," *Artigianato e tecnica nella società dell'alto medioevo occidentale* (Spoleto, 1971), II, 429.
[72] Jope, "The Saxon Building-Stone Industry," pp. 91–118.
[73] Marcel Durliat, *L'Art dans le royaume de Majorque: les débuts de l'art gothique en Roussillon, en Cerdagne et aux Baléares* (Toulouse, 1962), pp. 180–81; Juan Muntaner Bujosa, "Piedra de Mallorca en el Castelnovo de Nápoles: datos para la biografia de Guillermo Sagrera," *Boletin de la sociedad arqueologica luliana*, 76 (1960), 615–30.

soon as the Normans had conquered England they began to import white Caen limestone for the building of their new churches. For Canterbury Cathedral it was sent already cut to specifications. In 1278 seventy-five shiploads of this stone were sent for the Tower of London, and in 1287 the builders of Norwich Cathedral spent over twice the cost of the stone itself to get it delivered to their workshop. From the second half of the thirteenth century Caen stone appears as building stone all over the country and it was still prized four centuries later by the builders of Hatfield House.[74] In England itself quarries on the Isle of Portland began to produce for distant markets, including London, at the end of the Middle Ages; in the seventeenth century the use of Portland stone by Inigo Jones for several of his major projects increased its popularity. So much of the stone was needed for the building of the new Saint Paul's, however, that pressure for greater production strained relations with the quarriers on the island and overburdened both transport and unloading facilities.[75]

Another group of quarries that can be identified are those that, because of special properties of their stone, became centers for the manufacturing of small objects with wide market distribution. One of these centers was Tournai. Its gray limestone, which, when polished, appeared to be black, was used as a building material for many monuments in eastern Flanders, but already in the eleventh and twelfth centuries production included a wide range of ornamental pieces from baptismal fonts to funerary monuments, some probably fully finished before leaving the quarry zone. They show up throughout northwestern France and even beyond, including England. Their production, however, did not outlast the Middle Ages, probably because difficulties in adapting this stone for gothic vaulting sent its color out of fashion.[76] In England Purbeck "marble" from Dorset, also a limestone, enjoyed a similar demand from the twelfth to the fourteenth centuries; sculpture, church furniture, and architectural details made from it can be found all over the country. Its production also declined at the end of the Middle Ages, when

[74] On Caen stone see Salzman, *Building*, ch. 7; the references to its use at Hatfield House are in Lawrence Stone, "The Building of Hatfield House, 1607–1612," in his *Family and Fortune: Studies in Aristocratic Finance in the Sixteenth and Seventeenth Centuries* (Oxford, 1973), pp. 70–71.

[75] J. H. Bettey, "The Supply of Stone for Re-Building St. Paul's Cathedral," *Archaeological Journal*, 128 (1971), 176–85.

[76] The quarries at Tournai have been commented on by Paul Rolland in several places: "L'Expansion tournaisienne aux XIe et XIIe siècles: art et commerce de la pierre," *Annales de l'Académie Royale d'Archéologique de Belgique*, 72 (1924), 175–219; *Les Origines de la commune de Tournai: histoire interne de la seigneurie épiscopale tournaisienne* (Brussels, 1931), pp. 116–17 and 145–46; and, with Charles Camerman, *La Pierre de Tournai, Mémoirs de la Société belge de géologie de paléontologie et d'hydrologie*, n.s. 4 (1944), pt. 2 ("Son emploi dans le passé").

taste for new materials and designs from abroad began to outrun the conservative traditions of local craftsmen.[77] An altogether different kind of stone product that had even a wider distribution than most of these architectural and sculptural objects were the millstones made at the basalt quarries in the environs of Mayen in the Eifel. These quarries were worked in Roman times, and during the Middle Ages they supplied building stone to an extensive area in the middle Rhineland. The millstones that began to be produced here at the end of the Middle Ages, however, were shipped much farther afield; by the early modern period they turn up over a large part of central Europe from Danzig to the hinterland of England.[78]

No European stone has enjoyed more fame and a more extensive international market than the white marble of Carrara. So much of this stone was quarried in the period of the Roman Empire that long after the shutdown of imperial quarry operations Italians continued to live off that production simply by plundering Roman monuments. Around 1300 the minor building boom of Tuscan cathedrals at Pisa, Florence, Siena, and Orvieto resulted in occasional expeditions to Carrara to obtain marble, but transportation was such a major problem that these quarries did not replace more local sources. In this early phase of the revival of the quarries at Carrara production was sporadic and in the hands of contractors or agents of clients (for the most part cathedral building committees) who organized the entire enterprise, even sending stonecutters to the quarries for months, and sometimes for several years.

Toward the end of the fourteenth century rising demand, above all from Florence for the completion of the cathedral, with the cupola and the elaborate sculptural program then underway, gave rise to efforts by workers at the quarry zone itself to organize production. This development of the local economy was then sustained by the subsequent diffusion of Renaissance taste for marble throughout Italy and even northern Europe. Local quarriers at Carrara became more prominent in the operation of the quarries. Many were in fact Lombards attracted to the region by new opportunities. By the second

[77] Rosemary Leach, *An Investigation into the Use of Purbeck Marble in Medieval England* (Hartlepool, 1975).

[78] Much of the historical evidence for the trade in Mayen basalt is collected in a German dissertation by Josef Schmandt, *Die historische Entwicklung der rheinischen Basalt- und Basaltlava-Industrie* (Siegburg, 1930); and a recent archaeological study of the working of the quarries has been made by F. Hörter, F. X. Michels, and J. Röder, "Die Geschichte der Basaltlava-Industrie von Mayen und Niedermendig," *Jahrbuch für Geschichte und Kultur* [later: *Kunst*] *des Mittelrheins*, 2–3 (1950–51), 1–32; 6–7 (1954–55), 7–32. Evidence for these millstones in England is reported in Maurice Beresford and John G. Hurst, *Deserted Medieval Villages* (London, 1971), pp. 142–43.

half of the fifteenth century these local craftsmen were fully in charge of production. They were prepared to supply demand from abroad for stone blocks as well as decorative pieces, and they made all the local arrangements for transportation. There were eventually some twenty quarries open and forty to fifty master stonecutters working between the quarries and small workshops, and a guild was organized to protect their common interests.

This expanding market for Carrara marble reached the point in the sixteenth century that Genoese merchants began eyeing the profits to be made in this trade; supplied with capital and an international shipping service, the merchants slowly subordinated local artisans to their own marketing system. The government of the local Malaspina prince, in a brief effort to exploit the situation, tried to coordinate sales abroad by working through these merchants; when this failed the Genoese moved in on their own, buying quarries, employing shippers, and integrating local operations into their well-developed international commercial network. Business picked up considerably in the seventeenth century with the expansion of Dutch and English shipping into the Mediterranean and the development of the port of Livorno nearby. Dutch merchants found it worth their while to seek agreements with Genoa, the duke of Massa, and the grand duke of Tuscany for monopoly control over the export of marble from the entire region, and their well-stocked warehouses made Amsterdam the major distribution center for the expanding northern market—here was where much of the marble was purchased for the building of Versailles. Eventually, in the later seventeenth century, a few Carrarese merchants were able to wrest control of local operations from these outsiders. They bought quarries, organized the process of production, and saw to the distribution of stone throughout Italy and to Livorno for shipment abroad. With government protection of their interests secured through private arrangements, they were able to build up businesses that sustained the fortunes of their families for over a century—at least one of these, the Del Medico, gained access to the nobility as counts—until their grip was broken by the general economic policy of free trade adopted by the new Hapsburg regime in 1772.

With this widening of the market and intensification of commercial exploitation, production at Carrara increased, but it was now more dependent on the initiative of the merchant than on direct commissions from clients. To have more flexibility in the market, merchants limited production to standard decorative pieces of a simple kind and to blocks and slabs that (if they were to be finished at all) were worked in Genoa, in Amsterdam, or at the point of their ultimate destination according to the demand of the client. As a result the level of the skill of local craftsmen fell off considerably, and they eventually were reduced to little more than scapplers and hewers dependent on capitalists, whether outsiders or local men. What happened at the Carrara quarries, in other words, is the all too familiar story, so characteristic of the early modern development of capitalism, of the subordination of local forces of production to the growing power of international commercial capital.[79]

This panoramic survey of major quarry operations in medieval Europe fails to turn up one quarry zone that even by medieval standards, can rightfully be described as a center of significant industrial activity. The commercial exploitation of the quarries at Carrara once the Genoese merchants moved in on the scene probably went beyond anything known theretofore, but this was a far cry from the vast enterprises sponsored by the Romans at various quarry sites throughout the Mediterranean. Quarries where decorative objects were produced, like those at Tournai and in Dorset, could never have been very large operations, however impressed we may be by the wide diffusion of their products; in any case, they seem to have been on the decline at the end of the Middle Ages. Skilled stoneworkers were highly itinerate in the Middle Ages, going from construction site to construction site, and with the greater urbanization of European population in late medieval and early modern times, most tended to settle down in cities rather than at quarry sites, a general development that is not unrelated to what in fact can be documented as having happened in the working of Carrara marble. As to those quarries that have long histories of being worked for building stone, their production was undoubtedly sporadic, being completely dependent on the occasional demand arising from the construction of a prestige project within the delivery area. The production problems created at quarries as well developed as those on the Isle of Portland by the demand from just one large building—Saint Paul's—point up the low level at which many quarries, for all their fame, were probably accustomed to operate.

The fact is, however, that little is known about the history of quarrying as an industrial activity. Carrara is the only quarry zone in pre-industrial Europe whose economic development has been thoroughly studied. The evidence of quarrying in the Middle Ages consists mostly of art historical materials, the stone products themselves; the economic aspect of the industry remains largely undocumented. This absence of documentation is in itself evidence for the lack of much industrial development in most quarry zones. About the only written records that exist for medieval quarry operations are the accounts of client-builders, on whose sporadic initiative most quarrying

[79] Christiane Klapisch-Zuber, *Les Maîtres du marbre: Carrare 1300–1600* (Paris, 1969), is the definitive history of the subject down to the late sixteenth century. The next two centuries are covered in Marco Della Pina, "I Del Medico: l'ascesa di una famiglia nell'area economico-sociale della produzione marmifera carrarese," in *Aziende e patrimoni di grandi famiglie (sec. XV–XIX)*, Vol. II of *Ricerche di storia moderna*, University of Pisa (Pisa, 1979), pp. 141–224. The Dutch interest in this trade during the seventeenth century is remarked by Violet Barbour, *Capitalism in Amsterdam in the 17th Century* (Baltimore, 1950), p. 117.

depended and who usually were too removed from the quarries to be involved in keeping direct records of the production process.

As a natural resource the ordinary quarry, unlike a timber forest, had little economic value since so much labor was needed in the industrial process that transformed bedrock into a building material ready for use at a construction site. In rural areas landowners allowed peasants to exploit quarries on their property with a freedom they would never have permitted with their forests.[80] In general, the European landowning classes were little interested in industrial operations to exploit the natural resources on their property, least of all in an operation so labor intensive, so confined to local markets, and hence so limited in profit potential. Probably few took the initiative to organize the labor necessary to work quarries on their estates. They either leased them out or sold them, leaving the exploitation to others.

When a quarry was needed for a large building project it was sometimes possible to contract for both the working of the quarry and carriage, but usually the demand for stone generated by the building of a church was so exceptional that the patron could not rely on a well-developed commercial system to supply it. Hence he had to be prepared to take any initiative that was necessary to get his building materials. This meant that he rented or purchased a quarry outright and then set about organizing the working of it, so that in effect the quarry operation became a part of his overall building enterprise. For example, the building authorities of St. Victor at Xanten in north Germany in the fourteenth and fifteenth centuries, besides renting quarries and overseeing the working of them, had to arrange for the purchase and manning of ships for the river transport of the stone to the building site. The ships were bought at the place where they were loaded and sold at the end of the voyage; in the meantime the expenses of operation, including provisioning for the crew, were paid by the building authorities.[81]

Commercial operation of quarries, however, was certainly not unusual, although little is known about such enterprises. They existed to supply steady local demand, and down to more recent times they were modest ventures. Quarrymasters, whether renters or owners, generally had one or two partners but no more than several additional workers in their employ. As in ancient times, family traditions were strong. Because in most places the demand for stone was uncertain and quarriers were somewhat removed from urban markets, arrangements for operations of quarries were probably less dependent on monetary exchanges than on highly personal forms of cooperation and association among local stone workers. Nevertheless, entries in building

[80] Documentary evidence is presented by O. Chapelot, "La Construction rurale en Bourgogne," in *La Construction au moyen âge* (Besançon, 1973), pp. 249–50.

[81] Stephan Beissel, *Die Bauführung des Mittelalters: Studien über die Kirche des hl. Victor zu Xanten*, II (Freiburg im Breisgau, 1889; rpt. Osnabrück, 1966), II, 37–40.

accounts for the purchase of stone show that despite the small scale of a commercial quarry operation, the state of its products encompassed a great many possibilities. Stone, paid for either by weight or by measurement, might be completely dressed or only roughly cut for finishing later at the building site, and the price might include delivery or it might not.

In some places stonecutters who operated shops in the city served as middlemen between quarrier and client. Many of the quarries at Istria were owned by the men who worked them, and stonecutters in Venice bought the stone and had it shipped to their shops for finishing. Nevertheless, for some Venetian building projects the quarry operation was organized directly by the building patron exactly as it was in less developed urban areas. Local contractors who acted as middlemen in providing stone can be turned up all over Europe, although their exact relation to the working of quarries is often obscure. Such men were engaged by the authorities of St. Victor at Xanten, and we know that they brought stone from Cologne. To get the Caen stone for Hatfield House in the early seventeenth century, recourse was had to a merchant in London who bought a quarry at Caen and set up its operation. A fairly successful dealer in stone in the mid-fourteenth century has been turned up on Maiorca; here was a prominent entrepreneur in the local market who owned quarries and who left behind a large estate, including twenty-six slaves, some of whom may have been employed for quarrying and carriage for his business. In medieval Genoa, where stone was a major building material, the size of the city assured such a good market that some landowners in the surrounding hills where the quarries were located did not shun the profits that could be made by organizing production themselves and marketing the stone in the city.[82]

These scattered instances indicate the possibilities of making profits in the commerce of stone in local markets by entrepreneurs who were prepared to make arrangements for procuring stone at the quarry site and transporting it to the customer. Unfortunately, little evidence exists for the internal operation of these business ventures and for commercial quarrying generally. It is precisely the view of the industry from the marketplace that the Florentine

[82] The examples mentioned in this paragraph come from: Connell, "Employment," ch. 8; Beissel, *Bauführung*, pp. 37–39; Durliat, *Majorque*, pp. 181–82; Stone, *Family and Fortune*, pp. 70–71. See also P. Piétresson de Saint-Aubin, "La Fourniture de la pierre sur les grands chantiers troyens du moyen âge et de la Renaissance," *Bulletin archéologique* (1928–29), p. 578; A. Chauvel, "Etude sur la taille des pierres au moyen-âge," *Bulletin monumental*, 93 (1934), 435–50 (on tools); Douglas Knoop and G. P. Jones, "The English Medieval Quarry," *Economic History Review*, 9 (1938–39), 17–37; and Salzman, *Building*, pp. 124–25. Diane Hughes indicated to me the possibilities for profit in the Genoese market for stone, a subject that deserves study; evidence from notarial documents is indicated by Françoise Robin, *Sestri Levante, un bourg de la Ligurie génoise au XVe siècle, 1450–1500* (Genoa, 1976), pp. 214–17.

materials, notable above all for business records of all kinds, can most illuminate.

QUARRY OPERATIONS. Few cities in Europe have easier access to stone than Florence. Good building stone—an arenaceous limestone known locally as *pietra forte*—is located no farther away than the hills around the city immediately outside the city gates. Some of the earliest surviving notarial documents testify to quarry operations all along the left bank of the Arno from Santa Margherita a Montici to Monte Oliveto. A major quarry still being worked at the beginning of the sixteenth century was located within the city walls, now disguised by the Boboli Gardens but still recalled in the name of the little Via della Cava that opens from the Costa San Giorgio.[83]

Down to the end of the thirteenth century stone was used mostly in the form of rubble or roughly cut blocks, and it was a rare building, usually a church, that required something in the form of dressed stone. When a sculptural program was planned for the new cathedral at the beginning of the fourteenth century, men like Giovanni Pisano, Andrea Pisano, and Tino da Camaino had to be brought in from elsewhere to get things going. In the course of the fourteenth century, however, the working of stone became a more important local craft with respect to both quality and quantity of production. There were several reasons for this development. First, the building of the Palazzo dei Priori at the end of the thirteenth century introduced a highly refined taste for rustication that spread throughout the upper classes, eventually finding its finest expression in the richly elaborated facades of their fifteenth-century palaces. Secondly, the immense public projects undertaken in the fourteenth century—above all, the cathedral complex—created a sustained demand for more stone, including vast quantities of marble, and for elaborate sculptural decoration. Finally, at the beginning of the fifteenth century the introduction of the classical forms of moldings, columns, cornices, and a variety of other ornamental details used both inside and outside new buildings vastly enlarged the range and quality of stone production and generated new demand from the private sector for use of this kind of decoration in homes and chapels. The refinement of this taste for stonework through the fourteenth and fifteenth centuries implies a considerable development of the stone industry. More and higher-skilled stoneworkers were needed, and stylistic innovations opened up new possibilities for the development of their skills that obviously had consequences of inestimable value to the craft traditions of the city. There was probably not another city in all of Europe with such a large number of highly skilled stoneworkers as were

83 The most authoritative discussion of the stone of Florence is Rodolico, *Pietre*, pp. 239–54; and there are interesting remarks, especially on quarrying in recent times, in Müller, *Naturwerksteinindustrie*.

Mantegna, Madonna of the Quarries (detail), ca. 1485

found in Florence by the fifteenth century, and in fact the emigration of them throughout Italy was a phenomenon of considerable importance for the diffusion of Renaissance taste. In early seventeenth-century London, for example, a city several times the size of Florence, stonemasons were so scarce that to put up just one building, the New Exchange (in 1608), several recruiting trips had to be made into the countryside as far away as the west Midlands to find enough of them.[84]

One of the most important economic repercussions of the new taste in architecture was the quarrying of *pietra serena.* This famous soft gray stone came into its own in the Renaissance because of its suitability, both structural and aesthetic, for the ornamental details so characteristic of the new style.

[84] Stone, *Family and Fortune*, pp. 100–101.

Although not unknown before the Quattrocento, it was first used extensively by Brunelleschi; subsequently it became virtually the hallmark of Renaissance architecture. *Pietra serena* is a variety of *macigno*, the calcareous sandstone that is found extensively to the north of the city across the river valley on the southern slopes of the Apennines. The quarries used in the Renaissance were scattered on the hillsides between Fiesole and Settignano, especially on Monte Céceri above San Domenico and Maiano and around Vincigliata. When Vasari wrote his life of Michelangelo he described the area of Settignano as one abundant with quarries "which are continually worked by sculptors and stonecutters who are for the most part born there."

Quite apart from the rise in demand for more and better products, the stone industry flourished in Florence because of conditions that obtained for few other cities in Europe. In the first place, because stone was abundant and within easy reach of the market, it was economically feasible for an artisan to control the entire process of production from quarrying to delivery of finished products. Moreover, the structure of demand encouraged his enterprise. Not only was demand high, but it was widely distributed among a large number of purchasers whose individual level of demand was relatively low, however high there collective expenditures were. The stoneworker, therefore, was not dependent on a few large employers or patrons, and many commissions were sufficiently modest that he could handle them on his own. In other words, he operated as an entrepreneur in a busy and fairly crowded marketplace. In that marketplace, finally, he was not constrained by the regulatory activity of a guild or the monopolistic practices of an exclusive elite of guild masters. These conditions—the geography of the industry, the structure of demand, and the nature of the marketplace—meant that the industry was more malleable in the hands of enterprising artisans. This situation accounts for much of the vitality that sets off the stone industry in Florence from the industry in many other places.[85]

The upper classes who owned the land where quarries were located had little reason to invest in the industry. Because stone was so plentiful, a quarry was not a particularly valuable asset, and because quarrying was such a labor-intensive enterprise, it posed the kind of problems in the organization of industrial labor that merchant-investors of the period preferred to avoid. Landowners got what they could from quarries by renting them out and leaving the full exploitation of them to others. It was not always possible, however, to find a steady tenant, a quarrier who depended on that quarry for his living and who would take out a long-term lease. An owner might simply

[85] The rural isolation of the quarries of Purbeck stone and the conservatism of quarriers have been cited as the cause for their decline at the end of the Middle Ages. The effect of such conditions can be seen in the problems encountered in getting Portland stone for the building of St. Paul's in London; see note 75 to this chapter.

have to wait until a builder needing stone for a single project came along and rented the quarry on a temporary basis. Even then the usual agreement assured the owners not of a fixed rent but only of a charge for stone that was carted off. The rent, in other words, was tied to the depletion of the resource. Whatever agreement could be arranged, however, a quarry did not command a high rent.

This assessment of the economic value of quarries can be illustrated by examples of rental agreements made for the supply of stone for the Strozzi palace. When in the 1490s it was decided to undertake direct quarrying of *pietra forte* rather than rely on independent suppliers, the chief stonecutter on the project, Cronaca, was sent out on an exploratory mission to locate the best stone; eventually rental agreements were made with owners of four quarries—two in Boboli belonging to Lorenzo di Bernardo Ridolfi and Matteo di Giovanni Barducci, and two beyond the Porta Romana, one on the property of Lorenzo d'Alessandro Buondelmonti at San Donato a Scopeto and the other on the property of Messer Rinieri Guicciardini further out in Via di San Gaggio toward Marignolle. These quarries were rented out on terms that were essentially the same. The contracts, to run for two to three years, allowed Strozzi full access for workers and equipment and complete liberty in working the stone and removing it; the price was a fee per cartload: 13 soldi for stone from Boboli, but only 8 soldi from the others, since transportation costs were higher and the stone coming from outside the city gates was subject to a gabelle charge. The largest rent, paid to Ridolfi, added up to only lb.1,347 s.12 d.6 for seven years of intermittent quarrying on his property; the 3,122 lire paid in rent for all four quarters over a decade was a fraction of what it cost Strozzi to get all the stone he needed to the building site. When in 1500 the Strozzi rented a quarry of *pietra serena* on the property of Niccolò di Bartolomeo Valori in the valley of the Mensola under Monte Céceri, the lease had slightly different terms: besides a charge of 12 soldi per cartload of stone, there was also a nominal annual rent of 20 lire—still not much, but at least assurance to Valori of something during the long periods when the quarry was not being worked.[86]

The slight worth of quarries is also reflected in their low assessment for tax purposes. Apparently values were determined by capitalizing fixed rents without consideration of income earned from rate charges on stone actually quarried. In the declaration filed by Alessandro d'Ugo degli Alessandri and his brother in 1427 the numerous quarries on the family's extensive holdings on the hillside between Maiano and Settignano around the castle at Vinci-

[86] Another quarry in this area was rented by Girolamo Dei to a stonecutter for 8 lire every six months; Innocenti, ser. CXLIV, 353 (accounts and memoranda of Dei, (1503–27), fol. 106v.

gliata are evaluated only on the basis of their modest fixed rents.[87] There were six quarries, all contiguous, at a place called Trassinaia. Five were rented, and the sixth was taken by the cathedral workshop but no rent was registered since it was not being worked at the time (although its occasional use is documented by the published cathedral documents for the building of the cupola). A seventh quarry was listed in the woods of a farm "da' Tatti" and was rented as part of a larger property identified also as a farm. The five rented quarries brought in no more than a mere 3 to 8 lire a year, for a total of 29 lire; hence their capitalized value for tax purposes was only f.103 s.11 d.5. Nothing was reported about rate charges on stone carried away. That such charges were included in rental agreements, however, is implied in a subsequent declaration (1451) where the same rents are listed along with a protest that for some time several of the quarries had not earned anything at all. The receipt book of a quarrier who rented one of these quarries over a century later shows that in fact the rent he paid was 14 lire plus a charge on each load of stone carried off.[88] The Alessandri quarries were rented to quarriers on a long-term basis, for in the 1457 declaration they all had the same tenants (or their heirs) as they had had twenty-four years earlier, including the one rented by the cathedral (which was still closed). It was presumably this quarry, long leased by the cathedral but not paid for, that in 1560 was selected to supply stone to the Uffizi complex, because a dispute broke out between its owner, Maddalena Gaddi negli Alessandri, and Duke Cosimo over the latter's claim, which he could not document, that for the preceding eighty years the quarry had in fact belonged to the public.[89]

One property-owner who undertook the direct commercial exploitation of a quarry was the convent of Santa Felicita. The nuns there had a quarry on their property in what is now the Boboli Gardens, which had belonged to them as far back as the early thirteenth century. The quarry's location within the city walls meant that stone taken from it could be sold more cheaply since transportation costs were less and there were no gate gabelles to be paid, and it probably had a long history of being worked. How it was handled by its owner before 1489 is not known, but in that year, when the abbess and the

[87] This and subsequent Catasto declarations of the Alessandri are 80 (1427), fol. 77; 718 (1451), doc. 387; 1020 (1480), fol. 133. The earliest declaration is published by Howard Saalman, "I Tatti in 1427," *Essays Presented to Myron P. Gilmore*, ed. Sergio Bertelli and Gloria Ramakus (Florence, 1978), II, 353–56.

[88] ASF, Libri di commercio 352. This small *mezzana* was opened in 1557 by Simone di Antonio di Bernardo called il Coltrice and continued by his son Filippo and in turn by his heirs until 1619. Together with the Alessandri quarry Simone rented the Valori quarry, and he also had a workshop. On one of the Alessandri receipts it is stated that the quarry rented to Simone had always been held by his ancestors.

[89] Umberto Dorini, "Come sorse la fabbrica degli Uffizi," *Rivista storica degli archivi toscani*, 5 (1933), 15.

Ghirlandaio, St. Clement condemned to work in a quarry (detail), predella of Madonna Enthroned and Saints, ca. 1485.

prior appointed a new administrator for the convent's property, Guaspare di Simone di Niccolò Parigini, their instructions to him emphasized his direct supervision of quarry operations. They particularly stipulated that he was to keep accounts of the quarry, to make collections and payments, to sell and buy, and in general to do everything necessary for its operation. His compensation, in fact, was to be a healthy 20 percent cut of sales, although after a year on the job he was put on an annual salary instead.[90]

The surviving records of Santa Felicita do not permit an assessment of Parigini's administration of the quarry, but his dealings with one client can be observed through the building accounts of the Strozzi palace.[91] In the same year as Parigini's appointment Filippo Strozzi, then at the outset of the construction of his palace, drew up a contract with the prior of Santa Felicita for the supply of stone. The prior promised to supply hewed blocks of stone loaded on carts ready for delivery, and Strozzi agreed to take a minimum number of loads at a set price per load. Apparently, however, the prior had underestimated the cost of the operation, for Strozzi found himself continually advancing sums above and beyond the payments for the loads he received so

[90] "Ricordo come oggi . . . abbiamo tolto per nostro procuratore, rischotitore e sollecitatore d'ogni cosa apartinente al monisterio e in spetieltà della cava nostra di Firenze, cioè a tenere conto di detta cava dell'entrata e uscita e riscotere et paghare et fare tutto quello è bisogno a detta cava et vendere e conprare per detta cava"; ASF, Conv. sopp. LXXXIII (S. Felicita), 115 (Memoriale, 1458–1528), fol. 16 right.

[91] Goldthwaite, "Strozzi Palace," pp. 145–46.

that the prior could meet operating costs. Furthermore, Strozzi's need for stone was greater than the production capacity of the quarry operation, and he had to provide alternative sources of supply by renting the other quarries operated directly by his staff that have already been commented on. In fact, once he had taken the full amount of stone agreed on in the contract with the nuns he did not renew the arrangements, although he still had a large credit balance with the convent representing the difference between cash advances to the prior and the total charges for stone received. The prior had clearly misjudged the capacity of the quarry operation. Strozzi, however, was a most exceptional and demanding customer. His palace, perhaps the largest built in Quattrocento Florence, was faced on three sides with stone, and construction went forward at an unusually rapid pace. Presumably no independent quarrier in Florence was prepared to meet this demand or else Strozzi would not have resorted to setting up his own quarry operation. Most buildings required much less stone and went up much more slowly, and it is possible that a commercial operation like that of Santa Felicita could have satisfied the more modest demands of other builders.

Somewhat more is known about the quarry operations of another monastery, San Bartolomeo on Monte Oliveto, located just outside Porta San Frediano. These quarries of *pietra forte* are mentioned in the city's earliest notarial documents. Stone from them was used for construction of the Loggia dei Signori at the end of the fourteenth century, and the monastery's accounts include scattered references to two quarries being worked there throughout the fifteenth century. Normally they were rented out for sizeable sums, up to 50 florins, but these rental contracts may have involved a partnership operation that cannot be fully understood from the accounts alone. Sometimes only a fraction of a quarry was rented, and some contracts had a duration of only several months to accommodate a specific one-time need. The Baccelli, a large family of stonecutters, were regular tenants. In 1475 Francesco di Piero di Bartolomeo Baccelli made a contract to rent a quarry for three months at 25 florins a year, a rent that was close to the top level paid for industrial premises in the city. The only specifications of the rental contract regarded any eventual damage to a well and to the roadway as a result of quarrying. At the termination of at least one rental contract (in 1476) Baccelli was penalized 50 lire for leaving the quarry filled with dirt and rubble.

In 1481 Baccelli, together with another stonecutter, Giovanni di Filippo Calvani, organized a partnership with the monastery for the operation of the quarries. The articles of organization were written out, to be valid for two years (there were at least three renewals) with net profits going two-fifths to the stonecutters and three-fifths to the monastery. A separate set of books was kept for the business (of which one survives), and the formal nature of the organization is evidenced by the bookkeeping practice of crediting the monks on the partnership accounts for such things as the maintenance of a horse on their property and for the occasional use of one of their servants in business affairs. The partnership contracted for small orders of stone to be finished and delivered to building sites. Clients included Francesco Sassetti (for stone at Santa Trinita), Filippo Strozzi, Lorenzo de' Medici, and the building committee of Santo Spirito (for the front steps in 1477). The work crew, consisting of several manual laborers and two or three stonecutters, worked not only at the quarry but also occasionally in the city, putting finishing touches on pieces after delivery. Delivery was made by an independent carrier who charged per load (paying the gate gabelles himself), and occasionally the partnership had recourse to the services of a bill-collector (*riscotitore*), who was paid a percentage of his collections.[92]

As a consequence of the low value of quarries it was possible for stonecutters themselves to own the natural resource they depended on. The evidence for their ownership of quarries is scattered throughout the Catasto documents for Fiesole and Settignano. The 1429 declarations for the latter, for example, reveal one area where the quarries of several owner-operators were concentrated. Jacopo del Bora declared a quarry worth 15 florins, and adjacent to it was another, worth 25 florins, owned by Matteo di Domenico, which he claimed was used for his shop business. (Matteo was the father of the sculptors Bernardo and Antonio Rossellino, and Jacopo del Bora was probably his brother.) Next to these was a third quarry that was divided into two halves, one owned by Luca di Bartolo and the other by Nencio di Bartolo (who may have been brothers) and worth together f.11 s.9. This last quarry was identified as being "at the quarries" in Vincigliata; the same location was given for yet a fourth quarry, worth 15 florins and belonging to Antonio di Tomma'. All these men were stonecutters, and their quarries were contiguous in the immediate vicinity of the quarries of the Alessandri, who are in fact listed as the owners of adjoining property on two of these declarations. Other quarries, or parts of quarries, are listed on the tax declarations of stonecutters in Settignano but with insufficient evidence to be located precisely.[93]

[92] References to the monastery's quarry rentals are scattered in its account books: S. Miniato 23 and 55–59. The rental contract with Baccelli is in ASF, Notarile antecosimiano B1188 (Girolamo Beltramini da Colle), doc. dated 13 January 1474/75. Two account books of quarry operations survive: S. Miniato 174 (1482–88) and 170 (1532). On the Baccelli see Richard A. Goldthwaite and W. R. Rearick, "Michelozzo and the Ospedale di San Paolo in Florence," *Flor. Mitt.*, 21 (1977), p. 295 n. 124. Cf. Francesco Quinterio, "Note sul cantiere fiorentino del Quattrocento: l'orbita michelozziana," *Granducato*, 3 (1978), 21–30.

[93] The Catasto records for Settignano are 327 (1429), 981 (1469), 1072 (1480). In the fifteenth-century records most men who identified themselves as stoneworkers filed their declarations in the towns of Fiesole and Settignano and not in the rural parishes of Maiano and Vincigliata, where many of the quarries were. According to a census of 1841, 14 percent of the heads of households in the diocese of Fiesole (which did not include Settignano) were stoneworkers, and all were in the parish of

The value of these operator-owned quarries at Vincigliata ranged from 6 to 25 florins, more or less corresponding to the capitalized value of the rents paid for the Alessandri quarries. A piece of land or woods is sometimes declared as going along with the quarry, but improvements in the form of buildings are not mentioned. The tools and equipment needed by the quarrier were, however, an additional capital expense and could require an investment amounting to much more than the quarry itself. In his declaration Antonio di Tomma' added 8 florins to the 15-florin evaluation of the quarry as the worth of a mule that went along with the property, most likely standard equipment in this line of work. Some idea of the additional investment needed for the operation of a quarry can be had from the 1469 declaration from Fiesole of two brothers, Jacopo and Francesco, sons and heirs of Giovanni di Francesco di Sandro. This quarry came to the family in the dowry of their grandmother and apparently had been worked by their dead brother Antonio, but the brothers now reported to the Catasto official its recent sale to the stonecutters Benedetto di Benedetto and Vicenzio di Simone del Fora. The quarry, worked for block stone (*conci*), included a workshop (*fabbrica*) fully equipped with crow bars, pick axes, hammers, gouges, and chisels, as well as the bellows and anvil of a smithy. The property was sold for 67 florins, of which 40 florins was for the equipment alone.[94]

Marble was not found in the vicinity of Florence, and it was not a significant item of commerce in the local market. Virtually all demand for it came from the cathedral workshop. Whenever other builders had to purchase marble—for instance, for the chapel of the wonder-working image of the Annunziata, or for the private uses of a sculptor like Maso di Bartolomeo—they purchased it out of cathedral supplies. The cathedral authorities, therefore, organized the supply channel for the entire city. They did this through general contracts, the earliest of which dates from 1351. All the contractors seem to have been stonecutters. Their enterprise was no small matter, since they were committed to a long-term venture involving the operation of the quarries (even those as far away as Carrara), the transport over water and land and across international borders of heavy and bulky materials, and, finally, delivery at the workshop according to specifications, rates, and a set timetable. Although the value of such contracts could be as high as several thousand florins, it is likely that financing was entirely in the hands of the

San Romolo at Fiesole; Carlo A. Corsini, *Due comunità in Toscana nei secoli XVII–XIX: Fiesole e S. Godenzo. Studio di demografia storica*, pt. 1 (Florence, 1974), 70–71.

[94] Catasto 981 (Portate dei contadini, 1469–71), fols. 452–53, 583. Nothing can be said about working conditions at these fifteenth-century quarries; but those conditions were probably not very different from what they were in nineteenth-century England, described in Samuel, *Miners, Quarrymen and Saltworkers*.

cathedral authorities. Contractors, therefore, probably took little risks; but however high their margin of profit, they had only occasional opportunities to participate in these ventures since the progress of building at the cathedral was so slow and demand from other clients so limited. The commerce in marble, like the commerce in other building materials, was nothing that interested upper-class merchants.

WORKSHOPS. The production of *pietra serena* was an industrial process that extended to the finishing of all those ornamental details that are the indispensable components of Florentine Renaissance buildings. The industry required a high level of skill,[95] and the market offered much opportunity for specialization and entrepreneurial expansion. Some stonecutters confined themselves to quarry operations and sold only rough blocks cut to specified size for further dressing by others who in turn had small workshops where they produced highly carved decorative pieces like capitals and consoles. A number organized the entire process of production, from ownership of the quarry to the marketing of finished pieces cut to specifications, dressed, and ready for use by a builder. Benedetto di Benedetto, mentioned above as a party to the purchase of the quarry at Fiesole, was one such entrepreneur. It was in the workshop of his quarry that he probably turned out the great variety of pieces, from window moldings to capitals, that he is known to have sold to the Badia at Fiesole. He and his brother Bruogio appear on the monastic accounts for twenty years, from 1456 to 1477, as the chief suppliers for its rebuilding, in some years doing over 1,000 lire worth of business with this one client alone.[96]

The ease with which a customer could get what he wanted is illustrated in the building of the Strozzi palace, where finished pieces such as capitals, consoles, and moldings were bought from any number of independent artisans. Filippo Strozzi, in other words, did not have to make any effort to organize the forces of production by setting up a workshop for stonecutters at the building site—he simply went into the marketplace, where he found any number of artisans who were prepared to take his orders without coming to work on a payroll. A few had relatively large orders and were occasionally reengaged

[95] Technical procedures for carving stone are discussed by Louis Frank Mustari, "The Sculptor in the Fourteenth Century Florentine Opera del Duomo," Diss. Univ. of Iowa 1975, pp. 278–302. Cf. A. Chauvel, "Etude sur le taille," pp. 435–50; Pierre Noel, "Comment fut taillée la pierre en France depuis le début de l'ère chrétienne," *Congrès international des architects et techniciens des monuments historiques (Paris, 1957)* (Paris, 1960), pp. 118–26; A. Sené, "Quelques instruments des architectes et des tailleurs de pierre au moyen-âge: hypotheses sur leur utilisation," in *La construction au moyen âge*, pp. 39–58.

[96] Badia di Fiesole 1, fol. 17; 2, fol. 26; 3, fol. 22; 5, fol. 73; 6, fol. 29 (all building accounts).

over an extended period, while many others had only a single contract, sometimes only for a few pieces, but there were enough buyers and sellers in the market that Strozzi no more depended on any one supplier than any one of them depended on him as a customer.[97]

Stoneworkers undertook work on contract, and open competition through bidding was not unknown. It was apparently the procedure used at the Innocenti that resulted in the 1430 contract in which Lorenzo di Marocco, Nanni di Donato, and their associates agreed to do the work for the architrave, cornice, and pilaster of the corner section of the great loggia at a price lower than anyone else.[98] Over a century later, in building the Uffizi, the duke's concern about costs led him to announce a public competition for decorative stonework with bids to be submitted in writing; accusations circulated that Vasari profited from this situation by showing favoritism in letting out contracts without accepting the lowest bids.[99] Whether in fact bidding was or was not the usual procedure, the extraordinarily detailed rate schedules for decorative stonework (based on measurement) that are commonly found in both contracts and accounts for settlement of final claims leave little doubt that these stonecutters were sophisticated enough in their cost analysis to be able to submit bids on virtually any kind of stonework.

Agreements between the stonecutter and his customer once he had the job frequently show up as memoranda in the latter's accounts, and it can be assumed that these agreements were in fact often written contracts. For example, a memorandum in the accounts of the monastery of San Miniato regarding an agreement made in 1525 with Francesco di Jacopo from Settignano for the cornice and frieze of the new bell tower states that the agreement was written out and signed by both parties and inserted into the cover of the account book for reference.[100] Such agreements, however, were hardly ever notarized. Whether the contract was written out or not, stonecutters normally worked for either a flat fee covering the entire job or for task rates according to measure and value, the charge being for running braccia of completed stonework. Delivery to the site was invariably the responsibility of the stonecutter. A weekly payment on account was guaranteed in the contract for the supply of stone for the new bell tower at San Miniato

[97] Goldthwaite, "Strozzi Palace," p. 156. It is worth emphasizing the range of stonecutters' activities in the fifteenth century in view of some of the vague restrictions imposed by earlier legislation: *Statuti* (1325), p. 255; *Statuta (1415)*, II, 206.

[98] Innocenti, ser. VII (building accounts), 2 (ledger B), fol. 184.

[99] Dorini, "Uffizi," pp. 15–23 passim and 29–30 n. 2; Giancarlo Cataldi, "La fabbrica degli Uffizi ed il corridoio vasariano," *Studi e documenti di architettura*, No. 6 (1976), 130.

[100] The stonecutters were Bernardino di Piero di Bernardo, Francesco di Jacopo, and Domenico di Piero da Settignano; and their contract was worth 285 florins: S. Miniato 169, fol. 18 left.

Andrea Pisano, The sculptor, ca. 1340

in 1525,[101] and most building accounts show installment payments during the course of work to be normal procedure, whatever the contractual arrangements might have been. After delivery of all work friends of both parties, themselves usually stonecutters, might be called in to help take measurements and come to an agreement on rate and total prices (if this had not been agreed upon beforehand); final statements, where stonework is itemized, rates applied, and costs estimated, are appended to many building accounts.[102] Finally, the stonecutter might be asked to sign a quittance directly on the account book of his client.[103]

That there is not more evidence for competitive bidding and written con-

[101] Ibid., fol. 24.

[102] For example, at the Ospedale di San Paolo, to agree on price of work done by Francesco di Berto (ASF, S. Paolo 931, fols. 135 and 237), and at the Ss. Annunziata for the chapel of the Annunziata (Ss. Annunziata 844, fols. 42 and 51).

[103] Several examples of quittances signed by stonecutters occur in a book of accounts and memoranda of Bartolomeo di Michele Becchi, 1472–78: ASF, Libri di commercio 15, fols. 72 and 73 (Guiliano di Domenico Rondini), 79 (Sandro di Giuliano), and 81 (Filippo di Niccolò di Giovanozzo).

tracts including rates and that both parties were willing to submit charges to arbitration would seem to indicate a certain standardization of prices. Differences in final estimates for settling accounts, however, could vary considerably, especially when the decorative work was of high quality. When Maso di Bartolomeo finished work for Agnolo Vettori that included a fireplace mantel, a water basin, and a coat of arms, the four assessors who were called in came up with estimates ranging from 67 to 89 florins; unfortunately, we are not told how the differences were resolved.[104]

The amount of capital some stonecutters had tied up in their business—in materials, equipment, and credit—could represent a considerable investment for an artisan. As Benedetto di Benedetto and his colleagues found in the purchase of the quarry at Fiesole, the equipment for a major quarry operation could cost much more than the quarry itself. The 40 florins they spent for the quarry workshop was roughly equivalent to what one of them could expect to earn in a year. On their tax reports some stonecutters put down a comparable figure for the value of the inventory of stone kept on hand at their shops. Moreover, since these men usually worked on contract for task fees, they had to be prepared to forego payment for work until the end of the job, in effect extending credit to their clients. If work lasted for several months a client usually made periodic payment in the form of advances, but larger contractors invariably found themselves at the time of final settlement of accounts with a large credit balance outstanding. When in 1455 accounts were settled on a contract for stonework at the Santissima Annunziata with Salvi di Lorenzo Marocchi, recently deceased, the work was valued at 2,160 lire, of which 480 lire was still due to him.[105] In 1478, after the confiscation of the property of Jacopo d'Andrea Pazzi as a result of the conspiracy against the Medici, Giuliano da Maiano put in a claim of 1,800 lire for unpaid work on the Pazzi palace and villa—and he attached eight pages from his account book showing the residual balance due.[106] To the extent that artisans like Salvi and Giuliano working on task contracts were not fully paid until the end of work, which on a large job could mean several months, they must have had sufficient cash on hand, or good enough credit, to meet operating expenses in the meantime.

Few stoneworkers' shops, however, were large establishments. Many inde-

104 BNF, Baldovinetti 70, fol. 52. The price of carpentry work could also be determined by arbitration, and in one case, when estimates were sought for work done in 1475 in the Palazzo della Signoria, the consultants could not agree, and one of them, Domenico di Domenico, submitted his own report, "et però lò facta sicondo la mia conscienza, et sicondo il mio parere"; Giovanni Gaye, *Carteggio inedito d'artisti dei secoli XIV, XV, XVI*, I (Florence, 1839), 252–53.

105 Cornelius von Fabriczy, "Michelozzo di Bartolomeo," *Jahrbuch der königlich preuss. Kunstsammlungen*, 25 (1904), Beiheft, 84–86 (a memorandum of the settlement); payments toward the balance due are recorded in Ss. Annunziata 689, fols. 256r et seq.

106 Arnoldo Moscato, *Il Palazzo Pazzi a Firenze* (Rome, 1963), pp. 70–72.

pendent suppliers probably worked out of quarries or in their homes. They associated informally with one another for the duration of specific projects, but they seem not to have gone in for formal partnerships like kilnmen, for instance, or painters.[107] None appears in the 1451 tax list of the city's business establishments, although the list is no more than half complete, with many smaller shops clearly missing. Benedetto Dei, writing about 1470, numbers at fifty-four the shops in Florence where stone and marble were worked, but he may have reached beyond the city walls in taking his count. Only twenty-two shops are listed in the more reliable census of 1562, which was limited to the city.[108]

The business of one of the more enterprising stonecutters, Maso di Bartolomeo, can be penetrated by way of his own set of accounts, the only such document to survive for one of his trade. Maso worked independently out of a rented shop in the city. He purchased stone from quarriers (and marble from the cathedral workshop) and employed a variety of assistants as needed, occasionally subcontracting work to others. He took orders on stone objects ranging from coats of arms and capitals to church steps; on certain jobs he was associated with men of no less stature than Michelozzo and Donatello. His clients included such eminent people as Vettori, Mellini, Del Pugliese, and the Medici themselves. He was called abroad to work on the ducal palace at Urbino, and he took a gang of his own workers for the quarrying operations he supervised there in connection with this commission. He also did metal casting. His brisk business in church bells and artillery pieces, not to mention more purely decorative objects, brought him business from princes abroad as well as occasional calls from the Dieci di Balìa to serve as a consultant in matters of weaponry. As an economic operator Maso made his way in the marketplace independent of the continuing support of any one patron, and in the true spirit of the Florentine entrepreneur he kept a complete set of accounts tied together in a comprehensive system and fully cross-referenced, of which the surviving record book tells us about all this activity and attests to his sophisticated knowledge of accounting techniques.[109]

To judge from the Catasto records of 1427, the year when declarations of wealth can be considered reasonably reliable, at least a few of these stonecutters enjoyed some considerable success by artisan standards of the time.[110] The

[107] Harriet McNeal Caplow, "Sculptors' Partnerships in Michelozzo's Florence," *Studies in the Renaissance*, 21 (1974), 148.

[108] Battara, "Censimento."

[109] BNF, Baldovinetti 70; Maso's career is summarized by Caplow, "Partnerships," pp. 168–72; see herein, p. 307, for further comment on his accounts.

[110] The generalization is based on the survey of those taxpayers who declared their occupation represented on the printout from David Herlihy's "Census and Property Survey (Catasto) of the City of Florence, Italy, 1427 with additions of 1428."

Anonymous, Pygmalion (illustration from Italian translation of Ovid's *Metamorphosis*), fifteenth century.

wealthiest of those who identified themselves as stonecutters was Piero d'Andrea. He and his son Giovanni show up in the building accounts of the Innocenti as major suppliers of finished pieces of decorative stone. They rented a shop in Via Tornaquinci for 10½ florins, and in the tax report its contents were evaluated at 100 florins. Something of the extent of their operations is reflected in the list they appended to their report of thirty-two debtors owing a total of lb.846 s.6 and twenty-five creditors due, all together, lb. 1286. They rented their house in the city for 8 florins but owned parcels of land worth, all together, 709 florins. The wide distribution of these properties—at Settignano, the home of many stonecutters, where Piero himself lived; at the Porta a Faenza just outside the city walls; and at Signa, considerably farther away from the city in the opposite direction—further suggests the expansive economic interests of the more entrepreneurial of these artisans. With Monte credits the net worth of father and son before deductions for personal examptions was just over 1,000 florins.[111]

Although apparently not much more than highly skilled workers in decorative stone, Piero and Giovanni enjoyed a prosperity that was comparable to an artist of no less stature than Bernardo Rossellino, the most prominent sculptor in Florence at mid-century and one who also enjoyed a major reputation in other Italian capitals. In his 1457 Catasto report Rossellino lists sixty debtors plus others too small to itemize for a total of 1,470 lire in credits outstanding, not counting 170 florins on deposit at the bank of Giovanni Rucellai.

111 Piero and Giovanni filed a joint report in Settignano and Piero filed one in Florence on which his father is included; they are not altogether identical. Catasto 76 (S. M. Novella, Leon Rosso), fols. 417v–18v; 327 (Contado, 1429), fols. 251v–53v; Innocenti, ser. VII, 1, fol. 56v.

Nanni di Banco, Tabernacle of the Arte dei Maestri di Pietra e di Legname (detail from relief), ca. 1408.

Rossellino conducted his own business out of a shop shared with his brothers and rented by them for 18 florins a year, and at the time of his declaration he had marble and other stone on hand worth 60 florins. In 1465, four years after his death, Rossellino's heirs declared real estate worth 777 florins and an obligation to spend 100 florins for the construction and endowment of a chapel for him at the church in Settignano.[112]

Bernardo Rossellino came from a large family of stonecutters at Settignano, and his career illustrates the possibilities open to men of talent with this background. Although he must have received advanced training as a sculptor, since his first known commission (at Arezzo in 1433) included figural carving, Rossellino appears for the first decade or so of his known activity as merely a supplier of decorative work like doors, window frames, and even simple block stone at various places (the Badia, San Miniato, the cathedral). When later he turned to the tombs and tabernacles in marble that established his reputation, he always revealed a strong sense of their architectural setting. It was as a stonemason, furthermore, that he gained the expertise in construction, leading eventually to a papal appointment in Rome, from 1451 to 1455, as foreman of the works on the numerous building projects of Nicholas V. Even during his last years in Florence his work included the preparation

[112] The tax reports are published by Frederick Hartt, Gino Corti, and Clarence Kennedy, *The Chapel of the Cardinal of Portugal, 1434–1459, at San Miniato in Florence* (Philadelphia, 1964), pp. 177–84; and by Ann Markham Schulz, *The Sculpture of Bernardo Rossellino and His Workshop* (Princeton, 1977), pp. 136–40.

of building stone for the Innocenti and the Santissima Annunziata as well as supervision of construction projects in Pienza and at the Florence cathedral. The line between, on the one hand, stonecutters who supplied major architectural members in stone and, on the other, sculptors, contruction supervisors, and even architects, was not clearly drawn.

The Supply of Other Materials

In the second book of his treatise on architecture Alberti deals with the basic building materials—stone, brick, lime, sand, and wood—that the architect, the mason, and presumably also the prospective owner of a building should know well in order to assure sound construction and a dignity appropriate to the structure. Stone and kiln products required extensive preparation, and inasmuch as the production of them was directed almost entirely to satisfying demand for building materials, they have been considered here as properly belonging within the scope of the construction industry. The other materials can be treated more summarily. The supply of sand and wood was a problem primarily of commerce and transportation: sand was used in its natural state, and the kind of wood delivered to the construction site was not the product of what is normally considered an industrial process. The supply of neither material, measured economically, was an important activity within the construction industry. As to metal products, such a small part of their total production ended up in buildings that the industry can rightfully claim independence from a subcategory under construction.

Sand and gravel were the two most common natural materials needed in construction—sand for mixing with lime to make mortar, and gravel for fill in foundations. The Arno had plentiful supplies of both, and legislation established builders' rights of access to this natural resource regardless of the ownership of property along the banks.[113] Supply was in the hands of men (called *renaiuoli*) whose service was primarily transportation. They worked on contract, being paid according to the area of foundations to be filled or to the quantity of sand needed for mortar. Written contracts with some of these sand-and-gravel dealers survive among the Innocenti documents. With their carts freed after delivery they were sometimes able to make additional money by carrying off waste and rubble from the building site. They also delivered rubble to be used as fill. Sand dealers were members of the masons' guild, but in the sixteenth century they were categorically exempted from dues because of their poverty.

Tuscany had a notable supply of timber. As late as the survey made by the

[113] *Statuti* (1325), pp. 400–401 and 415; *Statuta (1415)*, II, 448–49 and 462.

French in 1832 one-third of the region was estimated to be in forest. The location of Florence at the edge of the Apennines gave it an advantage for the exploitation of these resources. There was relatively easy access from the valley floor of the Ombrone to the forests on the higher slopes of the mountainsides stretching from Florence to Pistoia. The availability of timber was important to the medieval economy of Pistoia in determining the location of small ironworks scattered over the mountainsides; it also accounts for the later development of a local paper industry. The tract of the Apennines extending on the other side of Florence, though more remote, was penetrated by the valleys of the Arno upstream in the Casentino and of its tributary the Sieve through the Mugello, and hence there was relatively easy river transport to the city from the vast forests of the region. The men who floated wood down these riverways were protected by guild and communal legislation that recognized the legality of their personal marks on logs and gave them rights against owners of property along the river where the timber might wash ashore. Commerce in wood could be a lucrative business in late medieval Europe: timber merchants were able to enter the elite of more than one town—for instance, Toulouse and Strassburg—and in Florence itself one of the leading families in the masons' guild who made it into the patriciate, the Canacci, probably made its fortune in this business.[114]

In a mid-fifteenth-century proposal for a general sales tax it was estimated that total gross sales of wood for all purposes in the territory of Florence amounted to only 30,000 florins a year, hardly the level of a major industry.[115] Not all this commerce in wood was directed to supply construction. Wood was a major fuel resource, and the extent of its use to make things that had nothing to do with putting up a building can be judged by the existence of a guild of nonconstruction woodworkers (Arte dei Legnaiuoli), one of the largest of the minor guilds. After textile workers, woodworkers formed one of the largest groups of craftsmen in the city, their numbers having increased from the fourteenth to the sixteenth century more than for any other single category of worker. Many of these men made furniture, which, with the enlargement of the patrician home, became a major object of household expenditure; and much of that production met the highest artistic standards of the time.

In general, wood was not an important building material, especially by the fifteenth century, when most urban building was in brick, rubble, and stone. At the Strozzi palace, where despite two vaulted floors there were some large

[114] Michel Devèze, *La Vie de la forêt française au XVIe siècle* (Paris, 1961), I, 150–52; Philippe Dollinger, "Patriciat noble et patriciat bourgeois à Strasbourg au XIVe siècle," *Revue d'Alsace*, 90 (1950–51), 67; Philippe Wolff, *Commerces et marchands de Toulouse (vers 1350–vers 1450)* (Paris, 1954), pp. 284–86.

[115] This proposal by Lodovico Ghetti is discussed herein, pp. 345–46.

spaces above to be spanned by wood beams, not to mention extensive scaffolding and some extraordinary wood machinery to lift stone, the cost of wood plus all carpentry executed on the site came to no more than 12 percent of the total cost of materials (and less than 6 percent of total building expenses). The working of wood for building purposes (unlike the finishing of stone) generally took place on the construction site as part of the workshop operation. Strozzi bought his wood from various suppliers, but for builders who had less need than he the cathedral workshop, which owned vast tracts of forest lands in the upper Arno valley, was a popular place to buy wood. For example, when in 1430 wood was needed at the Innocenti, a contract was made with a carpenter, Jacopo di Sandro, who was then currently employed by the building committee of the cathedral. Sandro agreed to deliver the wood according to specifications, and the building committee of the Innocenti got permission from the cathedral officials for him and an assistant to cut it on their property.[116]

Although the preparation of wood up to the point where it entered the workshops of construction sites was not a major economic activity, it was important that men responsible for construction know something about its qualities—and this is why Alberti introduced the subject in his treatise. It was otherwise with metal products. "In fact," writes Alberti, "in order to obtain iron, copper, lead, glass, and other such products it is not necessary to bother oneself with anything other than the purchase of them and keeping them on hand so that you are never without them during the course of construction"—and he promptly drops the subject. Metal products were a small item in the shopping list of any purveyor for a construction project. Workers provided their own tools; nails, tie rods, braces, machinery parts, hardware, decorative pieces, and all other metal products were purchased ready-made in the market from smiths or commissioned on order from them, as Alberti observed. The construction industry does not therefore include the manufacture of metal products, and the metal-products industry, supplying a market that was much larger than that created by demand from construction, cannot, properly speaking, be considered as part of the building-materials industry. The fact that Florentine metalworkers survived the radical consolidation of guilds at the end of the thirteenth century still divided into three separate guilds indicates the diversity of their interests. Furthermore, the production of base metals was not a local industry. Although there was some mining of

[116] Goldthwaite, "Strozzi Palace," p. 190; Innocenti, ser. VII, 2 (building accounts, book B), fols. 186–88. On the timber forests owned by the cathedral workshop, see Enzo Settesoldi and Antonio Gabbrielli, *La storia della foresta casentinese nelle carte dell'Archivio dell'Opera del Duomo di Firenze dal secolo XIV° al XIX°* (Rome, 1977), where there is much information on the management of the forests and on the shipping and marketing of the timber but very little on the financial aspect of the business.

lead (at Pietrasanta) and copper (at Montecatini, near Volterra), supplies of these metals also came from northern Europe. Much more significant amounts of iron were produced in Tuscany, but two stages of the industrial process—mining and smelting—were located far beyond the city walls, and only the manufacturing of finished products took place within the inner orbit of the urban economy.

Florence was fortunate in having access to the mines of iron ore on the island of Elba, the richest in the Mediterranean. The exploitation of these mines dates to the beginning of the Iron Age itself, when they were developed as the economic foundations of Etruscan civilization. In the Middle Ages Elba was dominated by Pisa, and with the decline of this city in the fourteenth century the island ended up in the hands of the Appiani lords of Piombino (in 1399). These rulers left the working of the mines to the inhabitants of Elba but took control of the sale of the ore by letting out contracts (*magone*) giving merchants exclusive distribution rights within certain markets. The ore was mined, delivered to the port of Rio Marina, and there turned over to merchants operating out of mainland ports. In northern Tuscany the ore was distributed to various places on the higher slopes of the Apennines where there were both the power of mountain streams to work mills and the fuel (mainly chestnut forests) for the making of charcoal, essential for smelting. The greatest concentrations of these ironworks were Buti on Monte Pisano, the Pistoiese, the Mugello, and the Casentino. Some of these mountainside places also became notable centers for the production of finished iron products with their own local traditions of artisan specialization, especially in arms (for instance, Villa Basilica near Lucca, famous for its swords). The area of Pistoia (which not by chance gave its name to the pistol) enjoyed a certain preeminence because it was close to urban markets, including Florence, and had easier, more direct access to the forests on the higher slopes where smelting occurred.

The links between these stages in the process of production in the iron industry were the merchants. They shipped the ore from Elba, sold it to iron workers (*fabbrichieri*) on the mainland mountainsides, and then bought iron and iron products for resale to smiths (*fabbri*) in nearby cities and to markets abroad. This commerce was lucrative enough to attract capitalist entrepreneurs of no less importance than the Medici themselves. Lorenzo il Magnifico apparently made efforts to get control of the distribution of all the ore produced on Elba, but he had to satisfy himself with a contract for Pietrasanta and Pisa (1489). Cosimo I, however, was in a stronger position; in 1543 he, personally and not in the name of the state, got effective monopoly privileges over the production for shipment to his warehouses in Pietrasanta and Pisa. It is thanks to the records of the Medici that the commercial network is well documented, but since the Medici were only middlemen who did not enter directly into the industrial process at any point, the documents reveal little about industrial organization.[117]

[117] Piero Ginori Conti, *Le magone della vena del ferro di Pisa e di Pietrasanta sotto la gestione di Piero dei Medici e comp. (1489–1492)* (Florence, 1939); Raymond de Roover, *The Rise and Decline of the Medici Bank, 1397–1494* (Cambridge, Mass., 1963), pp. 164–66. For Italy generally see Domenico Sella, "The Iron Industry in Italy, 1500–1650," in *Schwerpunkte der Eisengewinnung und Eisenverarbeitung in Europa, 1500–1650*, ed. H. Kellenbenz (Cologne-Vienna, 1974), pp. 91–105.

For other mining enterprises in Tuscany see Roberta Morelli, "The Medici Silver Mines (1542–1592)," *JEEcH*, 5 (1976), 121–39; and Guido Pampaloni, "La miniera del rame di Montecatini Val di Cecina: la legislazione mineraria di Firenze e i Marinai di Prato, secolo XV, seconda metà," *Archivio storico pratese*, 51 (1975), 3–169.

CHAPTER FIVE

The Guild

Building-Craft Guilds in Europe

THE craft guild was one of the most characteristic institutions to appear on the medieval urban scene. In ancient Roman cities craftsmen had close association with one another; but being subordinated to a political system so highly organized on well-developed principles of public authority, these Roman corporations (*collegia*) fulfilled only social and religious functions and knew nothing of the protective and regulatory spirit in matters of their respective trades that inspired the medieval guild. The medieval Italian town, however, was more amorphously constituted than its Roman predecessor. As they evolved, the various component groups of medieval urban society—merchants, craftsmen, great families, political factions—sought corporate identity, partly in self-defensive reaction to traditional feudal and ecclesiastical authority and partly in pursuit of common interests and mutual assistance in the religious spirit of the times. Hence the medieval town took on a complex corporate structure that only gradually became integrated by a higher sense of public authority. The guilds were a vital part of this urban scene. They arose from the common interests of masters and apprentices in the same craft and other artisans closely associated in their work. Their appearance dates almost as far back as the foundations of the communes, and in most places they soon achieved full legal status in the eyes of political authority.

A guild was defined primarily by the particular economic activity that brought its members together, and the essence of the system was its defense of their common interests. As an exclusive institution it had monopolistic tendencies. It usually controlled access to its ranks by prescribing the pre-conditions of apprenticeship leading to the status of master of the craft, and for the further mutual benefit of its members it sought to supervise and regulate their work to assure quality and reduce competition. With this kind of authority over the lives of its members the guild needed a precisely defined organization with statutes, officials, and the machinery for administrative, legislative, and judicial procedures. No such constituted group, especially in the uncertain urban society of the time, could have been without its strong social bonds as well, and much of the guild's attention was directed to providing welfare benefits for its members and to sponsoring group religious activities. In fact, in some Italian towns—certainly in Ferrara, and probably in Venice and Padua as well—guilds had their origins in confraternities; the terms (*arte, confraternita*) are sometimes used interchangeably, for instance in the fifteenth-century statutes of the wallers' guild of Modena. Italian guilds were also variously known as *fraglie*, *misterie*, *scuole*, *società*, and *università*.

The guild scene was essentially no different in many towns in northern Europe, and guild particularism was a fact of urban life throughout medieval and early modern Europe. In Italy even a small city could easily have over a score of guilds. In 1277 Padua had thirty-six, at the beginning of the fourteenth century Orvieto had twenty-five and Bologna at least thirty-two, and in the next century Perugia and Verona had over forty. Among the greater metropolises Genoa had about forty already in the thirteenth century; in Venice, perhaps the largest Italian city, the number eventually reached well over one hundred, more or less the number of guilds in Paris and London, the only cities of similar size outside of Italy in the late Middle Ages. If anything there was a tendency for guilds to proliferate in the fifteenth and sixteenth centuries. With the growth of great capital cities and the development of new trades (like printing) and the refinement of old ones catering to the growing luxury demand of the rich, craftsmen with new skills and some who had formerly been subordinated to others (especially some in the clothing industry) now came forward with their own guilds. Rome, which began to grow only after the Schism, is a good illustration: fourteen guilds there dated their foundations to the fifteenth century, twenty-three to the sixteenth century, and twenty-four to the seventeenth century. The number of guilds in the much smaller town of Ferrara went from twenty-five in the early fourteenth century to thirty-eight by the end of the sixteenth century; another small city, Verona, had seventy guilds by 1741.

This is not to say that guilds were in all respects flourishing at the end of the Middle Ages. In those towns (especially in Tuscany) where in the thirteenth century guilds had come to the fore as the principal instigators of constitutional reorganization of the commune, they had already by the fourteenth century begun to lose much of their role in the political affairs of communal life, and with the assertion of the Renaissance state, inroads were made against their traditional authority in other areas, as well. In many places their activities were reduced to the confines of a confraternity. Amidst the many signs of their internal confusion and weakness at the end of the Middle Ages it is difficult to determine from the available literature how tightly they were able to maintain their grip on the regulation of economic activity. Much of the cause for the economic decline of Italy after the Renaissance has been laid to their stranglehold on the economy, and yet only toward the end of the seventeenth century are the first economic arguments heard against the guilds and their monopolistic practices.[1]

Construction workers, one of the largest craft groups in any medieval town, usually had some kind of guild organization. Masons' guilds are found virtually everywhere.[2] Sometimes their membership was narrowly defined as layers, setters, or wallers; but often, especially in smaller towns, a single guild embraced virtually the entire range of building tradesmen, from preparers of foundations to stucco workers and roofers, including stonecutters (or hewers), wallers, carpenters, and kilnmen. In many places—Piacenza, Perugia, Viterbo, and some of the Tuscan towns—these comprehensive guilds were called Maestri di Pietra e di Legname, masters of stone- and woodwork, or, more simply, masons; where stone was less important as a building material—especially in the Po valley—they were called more generally Maestri di Muro e di Legname, master wallers and woodworkers. Nonconstruction woodworkers and carpenters usually had a separate guild; but since it was not always easy to draw the dividing line between some of these skills, conflict of guild interest could arise between carpenters and masons over issues like installation of windows and roofing. Some statutes attempt to draw boundaries between the spheres of these two guilds. In those places where carpenters and masons after a long tradition of corporate unity separated to form their own guilds—Parma in 1424, Siena in 1441, Pisa in 1477—agreements were incorporated into their respective statutes to accommodate carpenters who worked on buildings and masons who undertook wood construction of any kind, dual membership sometimes being required. At Rome, too, some carpenters broke away from the wallers' guild in 1539; the separation occurred at Brescia in 1566 and at Milan in 1568.

The formation of more homogenous guilds often depended on local conditions favoring the development of certain skills. Stonecutters, for instance, had

[1] The best brief surveys of the history of Italian guilds are P. S. Leicht, *Operai, artigiani, agricoltori in Italia dal secolo VI al XVI* (Milan, 1959), pp. 105–28; and Amintore Fanfani, *Storia del lavoro in Italia dalla fine del secolo XV agli inizi del XVIII* (Milan, 1959), ch. 5; but except for the communal period, that history has not been well served by particular studies. The notion that in the early modern period guilds became more restrictive in their economic policies to the detriment of the economy has been challenged, at least for Venice, by Richard Rapp, *Industry and Economic Decline in Seventeenth-Century Venice* (Cambridge, Mass., 1976).

[2] In the ensuing discussion references to guilds of the building trades outside of Florence come mostly from their statutes, largely unpublished, which are listed in App. 2 herein.

their own guild in Venice, Genoa, and Rome, but not in places like Mantua, Modena and Bologna, where stone was not an available material. Guilds of kilnmen were latecomers, perhaps because it was not until the town had extended its jurisdiction effectively into the countryside, where kilns were usually located, that kilnmen became more urban oriented. The earliest guild of kilnmen appeared in Venice in the thirteenth century; other places in the Po River valley, such as Modena, Ferrara, Parma, and (probably) Mantua, where brick architecture was also common, had guilds of kilnmen by the sixteenth century. Roofers were another group of craftsmen in the building trades that had a tendency to assert their own identity. They appear as a distinct group (*membrum*) in the wallers' guild at both Bologna and Mantua and in the confraternity of the building crafts at Lucca, but apparently only in Verona did they have their own guild (in the fifteenth century).

To a large extent, of course, the proliferation of specialized guilds depended on the size of artisan groups. It was in the largest of these cities, Venice, that specialization reached its highest point, in part because artisans in any number of crafts were sufficiently numerous to form their own guilds. Wallers, stonecutters, house carpenters, kilnmen, limeburners, sand vendors, windowmakers, and makers of floors in terrazzo, not to mention the many different artisans in the related decorative arts—each had a separate guild in Venice. Some much smaller places, however, had their own peculiarities in guild specialization, like Orvieto, where in 1300 tile-makers, limeburners, and makers of millstones had guilds apart from that of the masons.

The history of the building crafts in Italy did not see the development of some of the features that give the mason in northern Europe such a distinctive quality among medieval craftsmen. Outside of Italy masons (and freemasons) organized themselves in ways that set them apart from other workers in the industry. Because building in stone and brick was less common in the north than in Italy, masons were a rarer breed; and partly for this reason they were highly itinerate, often on the move from one construction site to another. In many towns they were not organized at all or were included in a guild with other craftsmen. In London, despite its being one of the largest cities north of the Alps, the masons had no official organization until the third quarter of the fourteenth century, and they were not incorporated as a City Company until 1481. The London guild, moreover, was not notable for its corporate solidarity. In the rest of England masons' guilds hardly appear before the end of the fifteenth century.[3]

In northern Europe the working life of many masons centered on the more or less permanent workshop, or lodge, of the large projects, usually a cathedral, where their employment was concentrated. The lodges were places where

[3] Douglas Knoop and G. P. Jones, *The Medieval Mason* (Manchester, 1933), pp. 135–43; L. F. Salzman, *Building in England Down to 1540* (Oxford, 1967), ch. 2.

itinerate workers found bed and board during their employment; this overlapping of social and professional life intensified their solidarity as a craft group. There were regulations to order their personal relations, often along the lines of a guild model, and to set down the procedures for their work. Because of the itinerate nature of a mason's life, especially during the years he was a journeyman traveling from lodge to lodge, extensive networks of common ties were established that made for a high degree of uniformity among the lodges and bound these widely scattered craftsmen together. A sense of brotherhood, a kind of fellowship, grew up among them, although these sentiments were never institutionalized into anything like a guild or confraternity. It has been inferred from a fifteenth-century poem, which however has never been altogether understood, that English masons made efforts to codify the customs of various lodges and even held something like a general assembly every year. The regional network of German masons was better developed and eventually resulted in the 1459 meeting at Regensburg of master masons from lodges throughout the empire to unify their statutes into a general ordinance that then became standard for all lodges. At that time the empire was divided into four major jurisdictional zones of lodges, with preeminence given to the Strassburg Lodge, which dated from the thirteenth century. No further meetings of this kind were held, however, and no central institution was ever created.[4]

There was nothing similar to these regional organizations of lodges in France, and as in England, most towns were too small to see much of a development of building-craft guilds before the fourteenth century. Etienne Boileau's compilation, made in 1260, of the "laws and customs" of 101 trades in Paris includes one set for wallers, stonecutters, and plasterers, and it has often been assumed that they formed a guild. The point of these regulations, however, was to impose strict standards on the quality of work, not to deal with the usual organizational problems associated with guild statutes. In any case, whatever guild organization existed, masons (along with carpenters) came in for considerable royal supervision at the end of the thirteenth century. When in the fourteenth and fifteenth centuries masons' guilds sprung up in the larger French towns, their charters were frequently confirmed by the king, but this led more toward guild monopoly and greater regulation at the local level than toward unifying royal control. At the end of the Middle Ages French guilds were strong corporate institutions built around the privileges of the masters who controlled them. It was in reaction to this guild elitism that in the sixteenth century a voluntary movement among journeymen arose

[4] The best summary of masons' organizations—guilds, lodges, and regional institutions—in Germany and France, with full and recent bibliography, is Lon R. Shelby, "The 'Secret' of the Medieval Mason," in *On Pre-Modern Technology and Science: Studies in Honor of Lynn White, Jr.*, ed. B. S. Hall and D. C. West (Malibu, 1976), pp. 201–19.

to organize confraternities separate from, but complementary to, the guilds. Although these *compagnonnages* were local, travel put their members in touch with one another, and the closed nature of their organization as a confraternity generated a certain zeal on a kingdomwide scale that often led them into conflict with the local guild establishment of masters. Features of these peculiar regional organizations of northern masons, both confraternities and lodges, partly inspired the movement of freemasonry in the seventeenth century, a movement that subsequently has been responsible for much confusion and misunderstanding about the nature of the earlier craft organizations, especially as a result of the emphasis the later Masonic organizations put on ritualistic secrecy and mystery.[5]

Italian masons do not seem to have had the migratory habits of their northern colleagues. The development of towns in Italy meant greater concentration of urban building and stronger local guilds of the building crafts, and masons were therefore more firmly anchored, both geographically and institutionally. Although some, of course, traveled to various places and were attached to the workshops of great cathedrals along with other outsiders, these associations never became institutionalized to the extent that is found in northern Europe.

The one identifiable group among the traveling masons (and freemasons) in Italy are the Lombards.[6] The early medieval revival of building in stone that

[5] René de Lespinasse, *Les Métiers et corporations de la ville de Paris*, II (Paris, 1892), 597–601; Jean Gimpel, "La Liberté du travail et l'organisation des professions du bâtiment à l'époque des grandes constructions gothiques," *Revue d'histoire économique et sociale*, 34 (1956), 303–14; Emile Coornaert, *Les Corporations en France avant 1789* (Paris, 1968), pp. 227–33; Bronislaw Geremek, *Le Salariat dans l'artisanat parisien aux XIIIe–XVe siècles* (Paris, 1968), chs. 2 and 3.

[6] The presence of notable Lombard stoneworkers throughout Italy is catalogued in the superficial work of Giuseppe Merzario, *I maestri comacini: storia artistica di mille duecento anni (600–1800)* (Milan, 1893). The problem of their name has been reviewed by Carlo Cordié, "I maestri commacini ('impresari costruttori' e non 'comensi')," *Annali della Scuola Normale Superiore di Pisa: lettere, storia e filosofia*, 31 (1962), 151–72; and Mario Salmi, "Maestri comacini o commàcini?" in *Artigianato e tecnica nella società dell'alto medioevo occidentale* (Spoleto, 1971), I, 409–24. For their activity in Genoa see G. P. Bognetti. "I magistri Antelami e la Valle d'Intelve (sec. XII)," *Periodico storico comense*, new ser., 2 (1938), 17–72; and Ennio Poleggi, "Il rinnovamento edilizio genovese e i magistri Antelami nel secolo XV," *Arte lombarda*, 11 (1966), 53–68; idem, "La condizione sociale dell'architetto e i grandi committenti dell'epoca alessiana," in *Galeazzo Alessi e l'architettura del Cinquecento*, Acts of the International Congress in Genoa, 1974 (Genoa, 1975), pp. 360–61. Also useful is Ugo Monneret de Villard, "L'organizzazione industriale nell'Italia Langobarda durante l'Alto Medioevo," *Archivio storico lombardo*, 46 (1919), 1–83. Some broad interpretations of this phenomenon of migrant workers have been proposed by Eugenio Battisti, "Problemi di metodo: indicazioni per organizzare un repertorio delle opere e degli artisti della Valle Intelve," *Arte lombarda*, 11 (1966), 17–22.

took place in the Po valley gave rise to a distinctive Lombard style associated with a group of stoneworkers known as Maestri Commàcini (or Comacini). Whether they took their name from their reputed place of origin near Como or whether the name somehow refers to the practice of their craft has been a disputed point. The region was not a center of notable building, but it is not surprising that the stoneworkers who were needed for building in the Po valley came from the general area of the foothills of the Alps. Many became itinerant craftsmen, and already in the seventh and eighth centuries special. Lombard legislation was directed to their particular extra-urban situation outside the sphere of local authorities. Having perfected the skills of their craft on the prestigious monuments of Lombard architecture, they came to be much in demand outside the region as building picked up throughout northern Italy and beyond the Alps with the revival of the European economy. Lombard architecture was a tradition that builders elsewhere looked to for inspiration, and the Lombard masters, as they were called, were sought for their expertise and experience. Lombardy, in other words, came to be a training ground for masons who then spread out over Italy. There are few regions in Italy where at sometime or another Lombards do not show up at work on a local construction project, whether there was a local guild or not. The emigration went on for centuries, well into early modern times, but these masons retained ties with their place of origin, sometimes returning to take wives and buy land. Although they did not have any formal organization and they reveal no stylistic uniformity in their work, they shared a sense of community arising from their common origins that marked them with a certain identity in some of the places where they settled.

The accommodation of the Lombards to the guilds depended on local conditions, and some guild statutes make specific reference to them. In Viterbo the masons' guild is repeatedly referred to as the guild of the Lombards (Arte dei Lombardi) in fifteenth-century guild documents, although this may have been simply a contemporary way of identifying the craft rather than an indication of the specific origin of its practitioners. In Siena, on the other hand, a 1473 addition to the statutes of the stonecutters' guild spelled out the financial terms of the Lombards' relation to the guild and permitted the selection by them of a separate treasurer, who was to work with the guild official. Half a century later, in 1525, a provision of the Sienese guild of wallers and kilnmen directed to enforcing regulations about foreigners complained that in fact guild affairs had been too long in the hands of these men, who every year sent considerable amounts of money back to Lombardy, and that they did not properly observe the guild statutes. At Genoa, in an area whose incomparable opportunities for stoneworkers attracted the steady immigration of Lombards from the twelfth through the end of the sixteenth century, they were a veritable ethnic minority with a definite corporate identity. They were able to retain the privileges and immunities that they originally had in accordance with imperial law, and many never pulled up their roots in their homeland. Their identity was reflected in the local usage of calling all stonecutters Maestri d'Antelamo, a name derived from the place in the lake region whence many came. The division of these Maestri d'Antelamo and local wallers under separate consolates in 1520 is evidence of the government's continuing support of their monopolistic position as stonecutters. The Lombards in Lucca also maintained a distinct identity in the confraternity of San Bartolomeo, which was for all practical purposes a guild of construction workers; when in 1520 they protested the prejudice against them, the commune granted them independent status. In Rome, where the quickened pace of construction in the sixteenth century attracted many Lombards, they had their own confraternity. The eighteenth-century statutes of the wallers' guild there call for one of the guild's two consuls to be a Lombard.

L'Arte dei Maestri di Pietra e di Legname

It might be expected that in Florence, one of Italy's largest cities, guilds proliferated as they did in the rest of Italy and in Europe in general.[7] The evidence is not abundant, but it clearly points to the existence of a large number (perhaps over seventy) of craft organizations before the end of the thirteenth century. With the evolution of a new constitution for the city government based on guild membership and culminating in the Ordinances of Justice in 1293, however, the guild history of Florence begins to diverge sharply from other places. Guild constitutions were common in Italian towns at the time, but in Florence more than elsewhere the guilds' accommodation to the new political arrangement resulted in their internal transformation. Probably to simplify the new constitution, and to facilitate patrician control over it, the many particularistic craft organizations were consolidated eventually into some twenty-one more comprehensive corporations, which might well be called guild conglomerates. The various branches of the wool industry, for instance, which in a comparable industrial center in Flanders were represented by numerous guilds, were now in Florence all brought together in a single guild in which the capitalist-investor dominated, at least for political purposes, the mass membership of craftsmen. Not all crafts were included in the new twenty-one guilds; some continued to have an autonomous guild organization outside the system, although eventually these either faded away or were absorbed by one of the official guilds. Before the Ordinances of Justice there is evidence for three separate corporations for

[7] The standard history of the Florentine guilds is Alfred Doren, *Le arti fiorentine* (Florence, 1940).

quarriers alone: one for the manufacturers of millstones in the quarries of Santa Margherita a Montici, another for stoneworkers at Fiesole, and a third for those in the city who worked the outlying quarries. With the new constitution, however, the Arte dei Maestri di Pietra e di Legname—literally, the guild of masters in stone and wood—was created, which eventually absorbed these and all the other building crafts.[8]

Although as a single comprehensive guild the Maestri had its counterparts in other Italian towns, it was a more unnatural development for such a large city with so much building activity, where numbers alone would tend to work against unity of diverse interests among craftsmen. A small group can find cohesion even if the members' skills are various, but the cohesion is likely to be threatened by growth. In Pisa, for instance, the masons' guild and the woodworkers' guild at a certain moment in the fifteenth century found their numbers so reduced that they decided to join forces in one guild, but by 1477 the ranks had grown sufficiently to justify the separation again into two.[9] The new statutes of 1477 are explicit about the reason for the merger and in stating that the later separation was directly related to the size of membership. The history of the Sienese guilds puts the eccentric nature of the Florentine development into even more relief. There, too, in 1355, a new political constitution was based on the reorganization of all artisans into twelve guild conglomerates, with the Arte di Maestri del Legname (later called the Arte del Legname e della Pietra) incorporating the building trades. This political solution lasted only a few years, however, and then the guild fragmented: in 1441 the woodworkers separated from the others and in 1489 the wallers and kilnmen formed a new guild separate from that of the stonecutters.[10] In contrast to the constitution of these much smaller Tuscan towns, the Florentine political system that created the guild conglomerates survived over two centuries, to the end of the republic, so that the guilds were

[8] Robert Davidsohn, *Storia di Firenze*, VI (Florence, 1965), 58–59.

[9] The Pisan guilds suffered a decline after the conquest by Florence, when they were subordinated to the corresponding Florentine guilds, but revived with the reestablishment of their autonomy in 1459; Michele Lupo Gentile, "Le corporazioni delle arti a Pisa nel sec. XV," *Annali della R. Scuola Normale Superiore di Pisa: lettere, storia e filosofia*, 2d ser., 9 (1940), 197–200. In the fourteenth century Pisa, like other Tuscan towns, formed a guild government, but the building trades were apparently not included in the new corporate structure.

[10] In another Tuscan town, Lucca, the Compagnia di San Bartolomeo comprised seven *arti*, all the usual building crafts found in the Maestri of Florence, Pisa, and Siena. It dates back to the late twelfth century. Its surviving statutes (1361), however, are those of a confraternity, not a guild; and its relation to guild organization is not known. Nevertheless, it is significant that each of the seven crafts retained enough of an identity to have its own official (*guardia*). See App. 2 herein and E. Lazzareschi, "Fonti d'archivio per lo studio delle corporazioni artigiane di Lucca," *Bollettino storico lucchese*, 9 (1937), 3–40.

frozen in a structure that was unnatural in the sense that it had been imposed from without as a result of political considerations and did not necessarily respond to the internal interest of the craft groups that constituted the membership.

The reduction in the number of guilds through consolidation had a profound effect on the subsequent arrangement of all Florentine guilds and on the guild structure of society. A guild conglomerate embracing a variety of skills could not count on the same compatibility of interests among its members as a more particularistic guild of the traditional kind. As a result, guild regulatory controls loosened considerably. Moreover, the very size of these new corporations inevitably meant a threat to their social cohesion. In short, in the course of the fourteenth and fifteenth centuries the craft guilds in Florence receded from the economic life of the city and from the social and religious life of their members. They survived less as corporate-interest groups than as agencies of communal authority—a transformation clearly illustrated by the history of the Maestri.

The Maestri is one of the few minor guilds for which statutes do not survive, and in the absence of the regulations that held the guild together as a corporate body we do not have a clear picture of its formal organizational structure. Statutes for building-craft guilds exist for many Italian towns, however, and although they vary considerably in emphasis—some, for example, resemble statutes of a confraternity, having provisions only for religious and social activities, and others lack any such provisions at all—these statutes are similar in all of the standard categories into which their rubrics fall: matriculation regulations, internal government, religious holidays, and so on. There is little reason to believe that the statutes of the Florentine Maestri were very different. Nevertheless, statutes are generally concerned with the organizational problems common to all guilds and are rarely specific about the particular activity of the craft. Most could serve one craft almost as well as another. Furthermore, the constitution laid down by a statute may not be a good indication of how things worked out in practice. Fortunately, with respect to the day-by-day business of the Maestri of Florence we have something better than the statutes in a volume of deliberations of the guild consuls from 1466 to 1534, while three registers of matriculation records from 1358 to 1534 are a mine for analysis of the membership.[11] With the organization of the Fabbricanti in 1534 the documented record of the guild enlarges to include the new statutes and their subsequent additions as well as many more, and better maintained, registers of deliberations and matriculation accounts.[12]

[11] Maestri 1–4.

[12] ASF, Fabbricanti; and, for the enlarged conglomerate of 1583, ASF, Università dei Fabbricanti e Por San Piero.

Of the twenty-one guilds, the Arte dei Maestri di Pietra e di Legname may have had the largest membership. On a 1391 list of matriculated members of fourteen guilds, the Maestri membership numbered 915 out of 2,548 names; even allowing another 2,000 for the seven guilds missing from this list, including the very large Lana, the Maestri would still account for about 20 percent of the total.[13] The membership must have gone still higher in the fifteenth century, when the annual average of new matriculations during the periods for which there are rosters was fifty.[14] These figures, however, are somewhat inflated by the practice of multiple guild membership, so that many "outsiders" appear on the rosters. In the second half of the following century, when inquests were being made relative to relocating the guilds in the projected palace of the Uffizi and to assessing charges on them accordingly, the membership of the new guild conglomerate of the Fabbricanti, which had wide territorial jurisdiction, was estimated to be about 3,000, with 1,700 between the city and its *contado*.[15] Many men in the building trades, however, did not live in the city. On the opening of the guild's oldest surviving matriculation roster in 1358, 434 members were listed as city residents;[16] the number was virtually the same (440) when a new book of members' accounts was opened in 1465;[17] yet another century later the officials apportioning construction costs of the Uffizi estimated that only 350 practicing members of the enlarged Fabbricanti lived in the city.[18] The bulk of the membership lived outside the city in an uncertain area identified in guild records as the *contado*. The records are not sufficiently complete to break down membership figures into the various categories of skills constituting the building crafts, but it is certain that two major groups, stonecutters and kiln operators, found their employment, and most likely their residence as well, outside the city walls. On the rosters where residence can be established, the greatest concentration was in the immediate vicinity of the city—around Fiesole and Settignano to the north, where quarries of *pietra serena* were found, and all along the left bank of the Arno from Antella to Signa, and especially toward Impruneta, where there was a concentration of both kilns and quarries. The *contado*, however, spread over a much vaster zone, including the Mugello, the upper Valdarno as far as Figline and Montevarchi, and the area bordered by the lower Arno and the Elsa, with such towns as Empoli, San Miniato al Tedesco, and Poggibonsi.

[13] ASF, Mercanzia 219, fols. 50–90. After the Maestri the largest was the Legnaiuoli with only 199 members.
[14] Maestri 2 (matriculation records, 1388–1515).
[15] ASF, Mediceo 659a, fol. 7r.
[16] Maestri 1 (matriculation records, 1358–88), fols. 1–34.
[17] Maestri 4 (accounts of matriculated members, 1465–1534).
[18] ASF, Mediceo 659a, fol. 134r.

Nanni di Banco, Tabernacle of the Arte dei Maestri di Pietra e di Legname, ca. 1408.

The Maestri incorporated virtually all the building crafts. The most skilled were the masons properly speaking—stonecutters, woodworkers, and wallers, some of whom, of course, we think of today as veritable artists rather than as mere craftsmen. Their patron saints were the Quattro Coronati, the traditional patrons of stonemasons in medieval Europe and the usual patrons of the guilds in Italy where other building crafts were associated with stonecutters. The base of the Maestri's tabernacle at Orsanmichele (illustration p. 253), shows a waller (laying rusticated stone blocks) and three stoneworkers (working on a column, a capital, and a statue.)[19] The chief device on the arms of the guild, however, is the waller's instrument for mixing mortar (illustration p. 255). Skill, however, was not the criterion for membership. The ranks of the Maestri extended well beyond the master craftsmen in the building trades to include almost all workers above the level of manual laborers who had a degree of specialization or a certain economic independence. Besides masons they included quarriers, kiln operators, roofers, stucco-workers, house painters, vendors of sand, gravel, and wood, founders, cesspool-diggers, and even carters of stone and dirt. When the Maestri became incorporated into the Fabbricanti their section of this larger conglomerate was also to incorporate operators of kilns who made pottery and things other than building materials. There is no evidence that formal distinctions were made between these different "members" (*membra*) or skills within the conglomerate. Only a few guilds elsewhere in Italy had statutory provisions appropriating offices to distinct groups or otherwise clarifying their identity within the whole.[20]

Some craftsmen who worked on the periphery of the building trades were members of other guilds. Carpenters and woodworkers who for the most part did not work directly in the construction industry (including furniture-makers) and dealers in wood belonged to the Arte dei Legnaiuoli; smiths who made construction tools and equipment and were therefore often found on construction projects were grouped with other workers of ferrous metals in the Arte dei Fabbri. Numerous carpenters (*legnaiuoli*), however, are found also on the rosters of the Maestri, presumably because their work led them into the area of overlap between the two guilds, just as some retail

[19] Where the other building crafts had separate guilds from stonecutters they had a variety of patrons: Saint Marino was the patron of the wallers of Parma, Saint Thomas of the wallers of Venice, Saint Gregory of the wallers of Rome, Saint Joseph of the wallers of Brescia, Saint Francesco da Paola of the wallers of Ferrara (in 1590), Saint Geminiano of the wallers and kilnmen of Modena, Saint Peter Martyr of the kilnmen of Parma. On the Quattro Coronati see Pierre du Colombier, *Les Chantiers des cathédrales* (Paris, 1973), pp. 137–43.

[20] The wallers' guilds of Modena and Siena divided offices between wallers and kilnmen, and at Lucca the Confraternity of San Bartolomeo had seven *guardie* representing each group of craftsmen in the building trades that constituted it.

Luca Della Robbia,
Coat of arms of the Maestri,
mid-fifteenth century.

food vendors (*pizzicagnoli*) were required to pay a special matriculation fee because they dealt in kiln products.[21] Finally, a small but conspicuous group in the Maestri consists of those identified on the rosters by professional or guild tags that put them completely outside the orbit of the building trades, some of them coming from the major guilds. Membership in virtually every guild can be found among these men. Dual guild membership was possible in Florence, and it was not unusual. Membership in more than one guild, if it was not obligatory because of overlapping guild claims on a man's skill, was probably taken out for the advantages to be gained in a political system built on guild foundations. Hence it is not surprising to find some of these unlikely members of the Maestri even serving as guild consuls.

[21] Maestri 3 (deliberations), fol. 35r.

TABLE 5
Annual Budget of the Arte dei Maestri di Pietra e di Legname, 1429

Income		Expenditures		
Fees (less 10 percent for collection)	lb.448	Staff salaries		lb.295
Rent of house	32	two servants	184	
Miscellaneous (not specified)	60	notary	75	
		treasurer	30	
		lawyer	6	
		General operating expenses		59
		Religious ceremonies		64
		annual feast day	50	
		other	14	
		Consular expenses		150
		Offering to Mercanzia		30
TOTAL	lb.540	TOTAL		lb.598

SOURCE: Catasto 291, fol. 60; 293, fol. 22r (summary copy).
NOTE: The guild arrived at these figures by taking an average of the income and expenditures over the preceding three years.

Guild Activities

Despite the impressive size of its membership the Maestri had a surprisingly modest organization, and to judge from the financial report it submitted in 1429 for the Catasto officials, a kind of budget listing all its income and expenditures, guild business was slight (table 5). The only salaries that could possibly have been for full-time service were the two at 92 lire paid for servants; the guild notary (at 75 lire) could hardly have been even half time, the treasurer (at 10 lire for four months) much less than that, and the lawyer (at 6 lire) only an occasional consultant. Other employees of the guild were paid out of fees charged for the services they performed (and they therefore are not mentioned on the 1429 budget). These were the searcher and his assistant, who were responsible for enforcing regulations on measurements of kiln products, and the assessors provided by the guild to settle accounts on construction projects. Apart from the salaries paid directly to the staff the guild's general operating expenses listed on the 1429 budget, including heat and office supplies (but not social and religious services), added up to a mere 59 lire.

Even with this modest budget and a large membership, the guild had a precarious financial position. The 1429 Catasto declaration listed only one property besides the guild hall, a small house at San Marco rented out for 32 lire a year. Almost all the rest of the guild's income came from dues and matriculation and consulate fees. The 1415 compilation of communal statutes forbade the guild to impose fees on work done by its members,[22] and there is no evidence that it collected the kind of charges paid, for instance, by the wallers of Mantua and the stonecutters of Rome as a flat percentage of their contracts or by the wallers of Modena for every well, oven, and tomb they built or by the wallers of Ferrara for every chimney as well as every well, oven, and tomb. The Maestri had continuing problems in getting the members merely to pay their dues. In the 1429 tax report it claimed a 10 percent deduction on income from dues that went for collectors' fees, and many of the accounts in the one surviving book of members' accounts are in arrears. As late as 1600, notwithstanding the tightening up of ducal control over the guilds, complaints were made about the many craftsmen in the Fabbricanti who were not paying their dues—with the result that their names did not appear on the rosters.[23]

With this poor performance in collection of dues, its main source of revenue, the guild declared an income of only 135 florins (540 lire) in 1429, which was about 15 florins short of meeting the ordinary expenses of its small operation. In 1482, because of inability to meet expenses, staff salaries as well as dining expenses for the consuls were reduced, and in 1491 a special committee appointed to find ways to save money called for further reduction of these items.[24] Things were so bad that at some point during these years one of the two servants had to be dismissed, although by 1507 the slot could again be filled.[25] In 1512 thought was given to investing in the construction of an apartment above the guild hall in order to increase income, but two years later construction still was not finished, although the space was already rented out on a three-year contract.[26] Half a century later the ducal assessors considered the Fabbricanti the poorest of all the guilds and the least capable of paying its share of costs for new quarters in the Uffizi.[27]

Although the statutes are missing we have something that relates details that are probably closer to the realities of guild activity in a volume of the consuls' deliberations from 1466 to the end of the guild's history as an autonomous organization in 1534. Most of the business incorporated in these deliberations is purely administrative. The officials dedicated the better part of their time to financial problems, especially the collection of dues and fines, to elections and appointments for the internal administration of guild affairs, and to dealings with the Mercanzia for preparation of scrutiny lists. Planning of religious ceremonies also constituted a good part of the routine business of

22 *Statuta (1415)*, II, 212.
23 ASF, Mediceo 659a, fols. 162r–63v (printed ban of 27 October 1600).
24 Maestri 3 (deliberations), fols. 34v, 53r, 53v.
25 Ibid., fol. 77r.
26 Ibid., fols. 87–89 passim.
27 ASF, Mediceo 659a, fol. 7r.

the guild. For a while a hospital was a continuing preoccupation. Few deliberations regard particular problems of individual members. For this reason the decision to allow Michelozzo to settle his account with the guild by paying only one-third of the unpaid dues that had accumulated during his absence in Ragusa and Venice surely indicates something of his stature among his fellow craftsmen. All in all, the guild had so little business that one relatively small volume with one hundred folios sufficed for two-thirds of a century of deliberations. Furthermore, the condition of the other surviving books—the matriculation rosters and accounts—hardly permits us to talk about an attentive administration. There were periods when the matriculation rosters were not kept up at all, and in 1471 auditors were called in to look into what was called the shameful state of the accounts[28]—a charge fully justified by the surviving books, where the evidence of sloppy handwriting and infrequent posting increases with the passing of time. In 1467 a committee of four was appointed to renew the statutes and make reforms. Four years later, however, there was still so much disregard of guild statutes that "one clearly sees the guild and the men thereof falling into disorder with respect both to their well-being and to their honor, to the shame and burden of the entire city," and another committee, this time of twelve, was named to put things in order.[29]

The financial weakness of a guild with such a large membership and the low level of its organization point up the slight role of the guild as a regulatory agent in that sector of the economy defined by the construction industry. In an amorphous guild like the Maestri different craft groups must have lost any sense of being members of an exclusive and closed organization of a traditional kind with a homogeneous and manageable membership that could be closely regulated for their common interests. In fact, Florentines could easily cross craft and even guild lines in finding work, something that was not so easy elsewhere in Italy. Stonecutters in Venice, for example, were enjoined by their statutes not to allow any waller or carpenter to do their work, and in Rome they were told to have virtually nothing to do with wallers and carpenters by way of professional activity, not even to sell finished stone to them. There is no evidence of such restrictions in Florence, and in practice many artisans engaged in more than one craft. Whereas statutes elsewhere are careful to define the boundary between the mason's and the carpenter's work, many Florentine carpenters (*legnaiuoli*) worked in stone, and some became architects and served as foremen on construction projects. Moreover, it is a commonplace of art history that a significant portion of the city's artists—sculptors and architects as well as painters—began in the goldsmith's

28 Maestri 3, fol. 16r.

29 "manifestamente si vede l'arte e gli huomini di quella andare in disordine e d'utile e d'onore e con graveza e infamia da tutta la città"; ibid., fol. 16v (see also fols. 4r and 16v–22r).

craft, completely outside the widest scope of the construction industry and included in a different guild. Nothing prevented a sculptor of stone from working also in bronze and from invading the realm of the Arte dei Fabbri to set up his own foundry for casting anything from sculpture to munitions. It would be interesting to know whether this horizontal mobility among artisans in Florence weakened other, shall we say, status, barriers of the kind that prevented wallers elsewhere from doing anything so degrading as mixing mortar and carrying mixing pans (Modena) or carrying stone (Bologna) or digging for wells (Ferrara) and that forbade the unskilled laborers of Venice even to touch a trowel.

Only to a limited extent was the guild able to require membership of craftsmen from other guilds whose work led them into the construction industry. A certain success may be inferred from the presence on the rosters of the Maestri of many men identified as *legnaiuoli.* Ghiberti, however, did not become a member until 1426, late in his career, and Mino da Fiesole was well established as a sculptor before he became a member. As to the practice of architecture, the question of guild membership may have been more nebulous since the planning of a building was not limited to craftsmen, but the only evidence at hand is the famous incident of Brunelleschi's encounter with the guild. In August 1434 the guild consuls had him thrown into jail because he had not paid annual dues, but within a few days his employer, the powerful works committee of the cathedral, not only got him freed but also took action against the guild consul who had been responsible for the matter in the first place. Too many details are lacking in the documents for this case for us to draw any conclusion other than that the guild could obviously get the law on its side, at least temporarily, in moving against a man who was in effect no less than a public official and the city's most important architect, then at the pinnacle of his success.[30] In fact, the very prominence of Brunelleschi may have elicited, on both sides, the spirit of defiance that produced the incident. The attitude of the guild consuls toward Michelozzo's delinquency suggests more deference and a great laxity of policy.

Not only did men from outside the building trades come into the guild, but non-Florentine craftsmen (*forestieri*), who were often the target of guild restrictions elsewhere in Italy because there were so many of them, especially the so-called Lombards, met little opposition in Florence. In 1344 legislation was enacted that specifically gave carpenters and masons from outside Florence the right to practice their crafts. From a list drawn up two years later of all guildsmen who were considered foreigners (although some, but not their fathers, may have been born in the city), it is clear that the Maestri had by far the greatest concentration of foreigners, with ninety-five names,

[30] The references to this case are cited in Cornel von Fabriczy, *Filippo Brunelleschi, sein Leben und seine Werke* (Stuttgart, 1892), p. 97.

or 20 percent; and twenty-three of these came from Lombardy.[31] In 1355, after the depopulation of the Black Death, legislation was directed against the restrictive policy of all the craft guilds toward foreigners, who thereby were given the right to practice their craft on payment of a guild fee, whether the guild wanted to accept it or not. In the fifteenth century a non-Florentine had only to pay a special fee to the guild, but this was not always easy to collect, and on occasion was farmed out.[32] No evidence suggests that foreigners seeking work in the city found the guild an obstacle. Their right to work was continually reasserted, the guild was enjoined from imposing restrictions on them, and Florentine craftsmen who refused to work with them were subject to fines. The Fabbricanti statutes required only that outsiders register with the guild.[33]

Apprenticeship was the normal path leading to the practice of a craft and to formal admission into the guild. The statutes of the Maestri, had they survived, would presumably have told us something about the procedures, although those for the Fabbricanti are strangely silent on this. Statutes of guilds of wallers and stonecutters elsewhere are specific about the terms of the contract between an apprentice (*discepolo* or, if he was older, *garzone*) and a master, especially with respect to the former's commitment to see his apprenticeship through to the end. Master's were expressly forbidden to take on an apprentice who had already committed himself to someone else. The period of apprenticeship in the construction trades varied from place to place: it lasted at least one year in Verona, four years in Piacenza, five years in Bologna, five to seven years in Venice, six years in Genoa and Savona, six years for the stonecutters and eight for the wallers in Padua, and as long as the master thought necessary in Modena. After his training the apprentice in some places became a worker (*lavorante*) in his craft for a year or more before he could enter the guild as a fully established master, although the category of journeyman was unknown in guilds in many Italian cities, including Florence and Venice. In Perugia, after a year of work he had to prove his skill before a committee of three masters, and his candidacy had to be approved by a two-thirds vote of an assembly of no fewer than fifty members. The wallers of Rome had a committee of four with lifetime tenures to examine the candidates for master's status. Early Italian statutes do not mention the "masterwork." In fifteenth-century Venice there was no mastership

[31] ASF, Provv. 211, fols. 123–34.

[32] Maestri 3, fols. 4v, 30v, 36r.

[33] The earlier and somewhat contradicting legislation was incorporated in the *Statuta (1415)*, II, rubrics LXVI and LXVIII–LXIX. In the statutes of the Fabbricanti (Fabbricanti 1) non-Florentines are treated in rubric IX, ch. 21. The older legislation is reviewed by Doren, *Arti*, I, 110–14; but see also Niccolò Rodolico, *Il popolo minuto: note di storia fiorentina (1343–1378)* (Florence, 1968), pp. 55–59; and Davidsohn, *Firenze*, VI, 54–55.

test, but in a later period a stonecutter proved himself by producing a base for a column and a waller by making a balustrade *a sguancio* (the meaning of which is not clear) and a fireplace with chimney (although if he was the son of a Venetian waller and had been in the trade for five years he did not have to produce a formal masterwork). A 1711 addition to the stonecutters' statutes in Padua specifies that the matriculating member, working in an isolated place so that he could not be aided by others, was to sculpt a short column of normal size.

It may be significant that of all the craftsmen that constituted the guild only wallers and stonecutters are referred to as masters in Florentine building accounts. Only their crafts required a high degree of specialized training and only they often required trained assistants. Generally in the Florentine guilds, apprenticeship, more than being a formal program of training to maintain the monopoly of the guild, was designed to supply the master with cheap labor while the apprentice gradually learned the craft. Undoubtedly some men—the son, relative, or servant of a master—did not serve formal apprenticeships at all but learned while working alongside the master. Others made a simple contractual agreement with him. Contracts for apprenticeship of stoneworkers are not unusual, especially before the mid-fourteenth century, but they rarely spell out the particulars about the training program.[34] They mostly regard financial arrangements, which (as everywhere in Italy) came closer to resembling a wage agreement than a definition of personal dependency. Contracts were typically for only three years, and the minimum age for full guild matriculation was eighteen, although there were exceptions. What kind of masterwork was required, if any, is not known. An apprentice obviously did not have the independence of an ordinary worker. On the acocunts his wages are invariably recorded in one comprehensive payment made to the master, not separately, as was payment for others in the master's labor gang, and he often did not earn as much as a manual laborer.[35] It was characteristic of all Florentine guilds, however, that the terms *master*, *apprentice*, and *worker* did not imply social and legal distinctions: they referred to chronological phases, not to juridical categories. The Florentine guilds were not props in a patriarchal organization of working-class society, and there was nothing of the corporate spirit of domination that provoked the kind of

[34] A contract dated 1310 is published by G. Milanesi, *Nuovi documenti per la storia dell'arte toscana dal XII al XVI secolo* (Rome, 1893), p. 18. Cf. Nicola Ottokar, "Pittori e contratti d'apprendimento presso pittori a Firenze alla fine del Dugento," *Rivista d'arte*, 19 (1937), 55–57. A contract with a stonemason is summarized by Robert Davidsohn, *Forschungen zur Geschichte von Florenz*, III (Berlin, 1901), 223. Apprenticeship contracts for quarriers have been studied by Christiane Klapisch-Zuber, *Les maîtres du marbre: Carrare 1300–1600* (Paris, 1969), pp. 119–26.

[35] Varying practice with respect to payment of apprentices is noted by Geremek, *Salariat*, p. 52 and n.

reaction represented by the journeymen's organization often encountered in the more hierarchical society of northern Europe.

Whatever restrictive policies Florentine guilds devised with respect to admission of new members, they did not impose high matriculation fees and membership dues. Matriculation in a minor guild cost no more than several florins, a one-time expense that was not unreasonable for any skilled worker. In the fifteenth century the fee for matriculation in the Maestri was only 24 lire, less than wages for three months' work for a man with a low-level skill, and payment could be made in installments as low as 2 lire a year. Sons, sons-in-law, and brothers of members got considerable reductions,[36] and residents in the *contado* paid only 6 lire (although they had to pay 12 lire more if they came to work in the city). No distinction was made between wage earners and shop operators. Annual dues were only 12 soldi (for some they were only 6 soldi), and older, nonworking, members were exempted.[37] When dues went up in the sixteenth century many of the poorer categories of members were also exempted.[38] With such low rates it is not surprising that the guild, despite its considerable size, was confined to a tight budget.

Once he was on his own the craftsman did not have to worry much about guild control over his activities beyond the normal kind of regulations found in the statutes of craft guilds in the building trades elsewhere. These were designed to discipline him in the practice of his skill, especially with respect to honoring contracts, and to reduce the competition between him and his fellows at least to the extent of prohibiting interference in one another's work and with another's apprentices. The statutes of the Maestri likely contained an exhortation to produce quality work followed up with specific regulations to assure it, such as, for instance, the requirements that no craftsman take on more than one job at a time, and that he finish one job before taking on another. To foster the proper corporate spirit guilds generally had regulations about locating shops too close to one another, about any interference from others once work was undertaken, about doing business with any debtor of a guild member or with another of the same craft who was not a guild member. In the 1544 statutes of the Fabbricanti there is an insistence on honoring contracts, and monopolistic practices for purposes of speculation are condemned. The sixteenth rubric has the usual provisions designed to protect private interests against interference: a craftsman's employees could not be lured away until their tenures were completed; when they did leave he was assured that they could not set up a shop within a certain distance of his; and

[36] In 1468 the benefit of having a paternal uncle in the guild was abolished, but a paternal grandfather still helped; Maestri 3, fol. 9r.

[37] The age was sixty in 1466 but later went up to sixty-five; ibid., fols. 1v, 15r, 27r, 28v, 36v.

[38] In the 1544 statutes these men were exempt from all fees; Fabbricanti 1, rubric IX, ch. 25.

if he dropped any work no one else could take it up without his permission and that of the guild.

Other than this kind of legislation about interference in one another's work the guild does not seem to have introduced constraints into the economic world of the craftsman. On the one hand, it did not purchase raw materials or invest in capital equipment in the spirit of the monopolistic tendencies of some of the major industrial guilds. On the other hand, the guild did little to reduce the terms of competition among its members. It did not attempt to set the prices that craftsmen charged for their work; and there is no evidence that it regulated the length of the workday or fixed wage rates, a traditional way of cutting price competition, although it is possible that in practice masons fixed wages of ordinary laborers through collusion in the labor market. The 1544 statutes of the Fabbricanti, like the statutes of most Italian building-craft guilds, do not reveal any concern for an active policy of quality controls to assure standards; presumably a Florentine stonecutter was not, as were his Venetian colleagues, subject to guild inspections to check the quality of his work. Nor was he, as were stonecutters in Venice as well as in Padua and Ferrara and in many northern places, limited to a certain number of apprentices or other kinds of employees in his shop. He could compete in the bidding for contracts with the knowledge that he controlled a number of variables that went into his price, including, for the most artistic craftsman, noneconomic criteria in the evaluation of his work. The craftsman was on his own, and although his maneuverability in the marketplace was obviously limited, the confines were not determined by the institutional framework of the guild. Corporate solidarity in no medieval guild, least of all in Florence, was carried to the point that equality of income was considered possible or even desirable as the objective of regulatory policy.

It is therefore not surprising that in the surviving deliberations of the Maestri the governing body hardly ever took up those kinds of problems generally associated with the regulatory function of guild policy. The only effective intrusion into the economic activity of member artisans was the recurrent action taken to regulate kiln products, both burnt lime and bricks, according to standards laid down by the commune. The new statutes of the Fabbricanti did not extend regulatory powers beyond the limited areas already defined by the Maestri. Kilns were the only industry the new guild, like the old, attempted to control, and the regulations were essentially the same as they had been, albeit with considerably more detail in accord with the bureaucratic spirit of the new regime. For instance, it was specified that the assistants of the searcher were to wear the uniform of a blue cape and two silver badges with the guild's arms, and penalties for violation and the mechanisms for appeal were spelled out in every particular. The specific nature of these regulations are discussed in chapter 4; suffice it in this context to note again the continuing concern of guild officials with the problem. A large part of their staff was involved in enforcement, and violations filled most of the agenda for the meetings of the tribunal of the Fabbricanti.

One of the few services the guild provided—and it is not known whether it was obligatory—was the assessment of construction work in order to settle accounts between the mason and his client on jobs where he worked on contract rather than for wages. In their deliberations the consuls of the Maestri had to deal with this service,[39] and procedures were set out in the sixth rubric of the 1544 statutes of the Fabbricanti. The assessors (*stimatori*), who were chosen by the parties involved, may have been the arithmetic teachers who frequently turn up in building accounts. They were called in to measure what construction had been done and to evaluate it. The Maestri consuls were interested in this activity because of the fee the guild received for its authorization of the service, and for this reason they occasionally had to take steps to tighten control over the assessors. No one was to do any assessing but men chosen by the consuls, their names were to be confirmed by the guild notary, a deposit of 1 florin was to be made against the eventual fee payable to the guild, and the final report was to be approved by the consuls. Before 1476 their approval extended only to assessments up to 200 lire, with cases involving higher values going before the Mercanzia, but in that year all assessments became subject to consular approval. The fee was determined in different ways, sometimes as a percentage of the assessment, sometimes as a fixed amount for different asessment brackets, but in both cases according to a schedule of descending rates. The two parties were to share equally the cost of the fee; half was to go to the assessor and the other half to the guild, which usually appropriated it to a specific purpose such as the hospital or the wallers' confraternity. In characteristic bureaucratic fashion the new statutes of the Fabbricanti brought this service into the hands of four official assessors, two of whom were to be concerned with construction (the others assessed the value of animals in connection with activities of the other guilds that had been brought into the conglomerate).

One of the important functions of all guilds from their inception was the resolution of disputes within the regulatory territory they had carved out for themselves, however confined this may have been. Soon after the establishment of the Florentine guild republic a merchants' court, the Mercanzia, was set up that eventually came to dominate the system of justice exercised through the guilds, but the guilds retained much of their authority in cases that involved members' practice of their craft. Although the deliberations of the consuls of the Maestri hardly ever record settlement of disputes, building accounts occasionally produce instances of recourse to guild justice for resolution of breach of contract by suppliers and masons. For example, on 10 November 1429 the works committee of the Innocenti appealed to the guild for action

[39] Maestri 3, fols. 11r, 28v–29r, 67v–68r, 74v–75v, 79r.

against two sand-and-gravel vendors who had failed to supply the project according to the terms of their contract; nothing, however, is recorded about the guild channels through which the settlements were worked out.[40] We are better informed about the judicial activity of the guild in the sixteenth century since the deliberations of the Fabbricanti are filled with judicial decisions. This activity, in fact, must have consumed most of the guild officers' time. Few of these cases, however, involved disputes between wallers and their clients over contracts for construction work. Most are settlements of debt claims among members and sentences for violation of guild regulations (the latter directed almost exclusively against kilnmen). Unfortunately, the deliberations record only the settlements, and the background materials (claims, hearings, depositions, and so on) leading up to the final judgement by the consuls do not survive.

The absence in the Fabbricanti statutes of regulations relevant to industries within the building trades other than kilns strengthens the impression from the earlier Maestri documents that wallers, stonecutters, and other workers in these trades had in fact never been seriously regulated by guild policy. The small scope of self-regulatory powers was not unusual among the building-craft guilds of Europe, for everywhere municipalities tried to prevent monopoly formations in the interests of keeping urban building and maintenance costs down, even to the point of suppressing guilds altogether.[41] In Florence, with the shift of political power away from the guilds and the emergence of a higher sense of public authority in the fourteenth century, guilds must be seen as acting less in the self-interest of particular groups of producers than as agents of public policy. Communal legislation banning monopoly practices, combinations, and price-fixing was as old as the Ordinances of Justice, and many of these restrictions originally directed against guild policy by the commune came to be incorporated in the guild statutes themselves. It was in this spirit of public interest with respect to the building crafts that foreign craftsmen were permitted to work in the city, that measurement standards for kiln products were established, and that an assessment service was provided for settlement of construction contracts. The Maestri was the administrative organ for executing public policy in the realm of the building trades and served as the tribunal to handle the ensuing disputes. Moreover, since searchers and assessors were paid out of the fees they collected, the operation paid its own way. As to the expense incurred by the consuls

[40] Innocenti, ser. VII (building accounts), 2, fol. 183r.

[41] Sylvia Thrupp, "The Gilds," *Economic Organization and Policies in the Middle Ages*, Vol. III of *Cambridge Economic History of Europe* (Cambridge, 1963), p. 262. Something of this spirit is reflected in the Florentine legislation incorporated in the *Statuta (1415)*, II, rubric LXVI. Cf. Doren, *Arti*, I, 108–9 and II, 88, where it is claimed that the concern was less with the public interest in general than with the government's particular interest as a sponsor of public works.

in dedicating their time to playing this supervisory role, they must have been satisfied to attribute that to the price of the political prestige they enjoyed as members of the ruling class of the city. In short, guild activity can best be understood as a function of government working through older, outmoded, institutions and not yet incorporated in a central bureaucracy. It is in this sense that its reorganization into the Fabbricanti brought the guild several steps closer to the logical conclusion of a long historical process.

The guild served an additional public function by providing the city with its firemen. According to the 1415 compilation of communal statutes, a committee of five guildsmen for each quarter had the responsibility for tending to fires. The guild statutes of Ferrara required all wallers to come whenever the fire bell was rung. In Padua the fire brigade was composed of wallers, carpenters, and wine carriers. In both Padua and Ferrara the guild was also to meet the city's need for its members' skills on any public works project (the selection was made by lot in Padua).

The social activity of the Maestri is more difficult to assess. One might reasonably expect that a loss of social cohesion would be another logical conclusion to the history of a guild that had experienced concurrently growth in membership reaching into the hundreds and loss of a specific professional identity, and that as a result had lost its role as a regulatory agent of the corporate economic interest of the group. In the 1429 budget the only items for social festivities involving the general membership were religious celebrations. The guild paid nominal sums for a service on the first Sunday of every month at its altar in the cathedral (6 lire a year)[42] and for the burning of candles at its tabernacle at Orsanmichele (8 lire a year). In addition, it had patronage of a chapel dedicated to San Mamiliano (or Massimiliano) at the convent of San Giorgio, but on occasion the consuls deliberated about selling or renting the place to raise money.[43] The great social event of the year was the celebration of the day of their patron saints, the Quattro Coronati. The officials, accompanied by as many guildsmen as possible, made an offering at the Orsanmichele tabernacle and heard mass (in 1429, 50 lire was the budget for the occasion, with most of the money going for trumpeters and feasting); the day after, the officials heard mass at the chapel in San Giorgio. In the deliberations (starting in 1466) there is continuing concern about the unbecoming behavior of the guildsmen during these celebrations, many of whom (it was lamented) "come more to drink and eat than to make offerings or do their duty toward the guild, and not only do they eat but they conduct themselves less than properly, as if they were

[42] On this chapel see Giovanni Poggi, ed., *Il Duomo di Firenze* (Berlin, 1909), p. cxii.

[43] Maestri 3, fols. 8v–9r, 27v, 45r. At one time the church was known as Ss. Giorgio e Mamiliano. The description in Walter and Elisabeth Paatz, *Die Kirchen von Florenz* (Frankfort, 1955), II, 162–71, has nothing on the chapel of the Maestri.

in a tavern or in some other unbecoming place, to the great shame and expense of the guild and its membership."[44] The officials repeatedly attempted to control matters by limiting the amount spent on this occasion.[45] The Maestri were obviously keeping up at least the formal observation of the religious practices that were typical of building-craft guilds elsewhere (and indeed of all guilds)—extensive celebration of a few specific religious holidays and honoring of others by burning of candles, hearing of masses, and cessation of work—yet it is difficult not to feel that the enthusiasm of the membership left something to be desired.

Nothing anywhere in the documents of either the Maestri or the Fabbricanti indicates that guildsmen felt any of those social obligations toward one another that are typical of guild society elsewhere—visits to the sick, attendance at funerals, help in providing dowries for daughters, and other benefits for poor members. In many places, for instance Rome, perhaps the most important difference in guild statutes as they were renewed in the sixteenth and seventeenth centuries was the increase in welfare and religious provisions, a development undoubtedly related to the eclipse of the guilds by political authority and their retrenchment as social institutions. The welfare function of Florentine guilds, however, had always been less pronounced than that of guilds elsewhere, especially those in northern Italy, although some of the upper-class guilds were generous in the welfare programs they sponsored for the entire community. Virtually the only social obligation found in the surviving statutes of the minor guilds in Florence is attendance at funerals of deceased members; most of the statutes made no other demands along this line. With the development of the guild conglomerate these activities along with the more strictly religious ones may have passed to smaller, more intimate, and separate confraternities. Painters asserted their identity in the amorphous guild conglomerate of the Medici e Speziali by establishing the Confraternity of San Luca, probably in 1349. Although goldsmiths, carpenters, smiths, stonecutters, glass-workers, and even tailors occasionally turn up in its incomplete rosters over the next century and a half, suggesting that the nature of the confraternity approached that of a circle for artists, painters clearly dominated. Ghiberti, Donatello, and Andrea Della Robbia belonged, but few of the other prominent members of the Maestri appear on the rosters. In 1520 carpenters (*legnaiuoli*) founded a confraternity, although they presumably had a more homogeneous guild organization than most craftsmen.[46] Among the building tradesmen only wallers are known to have

[44] "Molti vengono più per bere e mangiare che per offerere o fare el debito loro verso de l'arte, e nonchè faccino collatione ma tengono modi meno che honesti come se fussino alla taverna o in altro luogho disonesto con gran vergogna e carico di detta arte e degli huomini di quella"; Maestri 3, fols. 2r–3r.

[45] Ibid., fols. 14v, 23r, 29r.

[46] ASF, Comp. rel. sopp., Capitolo 348.

had such a confraternity. It is occasionally mentioned in the guild documents in connection with their chapel of San Mamiliano at San Giorgio. In 1508, when the confraternity found itself without enough funds to perform its pious works, the guild came to its help by appropriating a percentage of fees from matriculating apprentices and from assessors for settling building accounts; in return the confraternity was to provide for a high mass and a meal for the consuls on the occasion of their visit to San Giorgio after the annual celebration of the guild's patron saints. To keep this event within proper bounds no more than 4 lire were to be budgeted for it.[47]

The Maestri may not have had much enthusiasm for elaborate religious celebrations and it may not have enjoined its members to take a personal interest in one another's welfare, but it was perhaps the only craft guild to aspire to build its own hospital (*ospedale*). When the one surviving volume of deliberations was opened in 1466, building was in progress. The hospital was located in the square of San Marco, possibly on the site of the small house reported as the guild's only income property on its Catasto report of 1429. Building went forward with much irregularity, however, and the state of guild finances must have made the project a precarious one from the beginning. Financing was sought through an assessment of 10 lire on the consuls for each tenure, a percentage appropriation of assessors' and searchers' fees, the sale of the tax on non-Florentine craftsmen, and the sale of patronage rights over the chapel at San Giorgio; but money came in so slowly that supervision of the project floundered and at times even lapsed. Meanwhile, the funds were deposited at Santa Maria Nuova. A building committee of two and a purveyor were appointed in 1467 and charged with keeping a separate set of accounts for the construction, but only four years later there were complaints that the project had for some time been without the direction of such a committee, and a special committee was appointed to put the matter in order. At that time a manager (*spedalingo*) was actually appointed, although the building was clearly still not completed. The project was soon abandoned, for after 1482 the property was rented out to Clarice de' Medici. After the expulsion of the Medici the guild officials made an effort to repossess the property, and once they had it back their intentions were to restore it as a hospital. Once again moneys were appropriated for the project, but in 1496 the property was rented out on a lifetime lease to a merchant from Pistoia for 8 florins a year. Money was still being collected in 1511 for this purpose, however, and deposited for safekeeping, now with the Badia. There is, however, no evidence in the subsequent records of the Fabbricanti for the

[47] Maestri 3, fols. 78v–79v. The history of this confraternity is a mystery. Another confraternity of wallers, dedicated to San Matteo, was founded in 1604 (ASF, Comp. rel. sopp., Capitolo 797); it was closed to members of other guilds and accepted only a limited number of craftsmen from the building trades who were not wallers.

existence of a hospital, and it seems the place never opened its doors to offer any services to guild members.[48]

In general, Florentine guilds did not have the social quality so characteristic of guilds elsewhere, for instance in Germany; with few exceptions their regulations were not directed to the social behavior of members. In this respect it is perhaps not irrelevant to observe that apparently none of the wealthy men in the guild elite of the Maestri came to the rescue of the proposed guild hospital, and that the writers of the new statutes for the union of the five guilds into the Fabbricanti had to deal with only one endowment set up by testamentary bequest (a dowry fund established in 1455 for daughters of poor carpenters). Whether the guild hall itself was much of a social center for members is impossible to say. Florentine guild halls are not known to have had large social rooms; nor, since most were built (or rebuilt) in the late fourteenth century, after the electoral reforms that took much of guild government out of the hands of the membership, did guild halls have spacious accommodations for general meetings. This is perhaps one reason that Florentine guild statutes do not have the kind of provisions relative to the authority of the consuls during meetings that are found in the statutes of masons' guilds elsewhere in Italy.

The hall of the Maestri was in the Chiasso de' Baroncelli, behind the Loggia dei Signori, where a number of minor guilds clustered—the Legnaiuoli, the Fabbri, the Calzolai, the Vaiai, the Correggiai (the Vinattieri were also nearby, in the vicinity of Santo Stefano).[49] Inside, the hall had a meeting-room where there was a terracotta Madonna with a square, ax, mallet, and trowel worked into the decoration, a piece commissioned in 1475 for 10 florins from Andrea di Marco Della Robbia (illustration p. 271).[50] Sometime after 1512 an upper story was added to be rented out as an apartment.[51] The hall of the Maestri was presumably larger than the halls of the other guilds amalgamated into the Fabbricanti, because it was selected as the hall of the new organization.

If the guild survived partly because it had become a corner on the political stage where a small elite could play its role, it must have lost something of what little corporate spirit it could still inspire among its members at large. There were complaints in 1494, in 1505, and again in 1511 that attendance at meetings of the governing body was insufficient to conduct

[48] Maestri 3, fols. 1r, 2r, 4v, 6r, 8v–9r, 14r, 16v–17r, 23v, 29r, 30v, 46r–49r, 60r, 60v, 61v–64r, 84r. Cf. Doren, *Arti*, I, 406 n. 3.

[49] The guilds' Catasto reports of 1429, from which the halls can be located, are collected together in Catasto 291; cf. Guido Carocci, "Le arti fiorentine e le loro residenze," *Arte e storia*, new ser., 2 (1891), 153–55, 160–63, 169–70.

[50] Allan Marquand, *Andrea Della Robbia and His Atelier* (Princeton, 1922), I, 18–21.

[51] See p. 257 herein.

business properly[52]—and it may have been that the recent constitutional changes after the expulsion of the Medici in 1494 made guild political activity less relevant in those final years of the republic. The vast majority of guild members probably had little reason to feel strongly about it. To the extent that the guild conglomerates in Florence had replaced numerous smaller and more intimate associations, their very size precluded the kind of political outlet that was so important elsewhere—in Venice, above all—in compensating the lower classes for their exclusion from communal governemnt. It could not have made much difference to most of them when the new ducal government lumped the masons together with various other craftsmen into the Fabbricanti.

In 1532 Duke Alessandro de' Medici abolished the distinction between citizens based on guild membership, and in 1534 a plan was drawn up to consolidate the fourteen minor guilds into four even larger conglomerates and to bring them under the direct supervision of the Monte officials as part of the duke's program to tighten control over municipal institutions of all kinds.[53] In this consolidation all craftsmen in the construction, wood, and ferrous-metal industries, previously organized in five guilds (Maestri, Fabbri, Chiavaiuoli, Corazzai, Legnaiuoli), were united in the Arte dei Fabbricanti.

The statutes of this conglomerate of the Fabbricanti, drawn up in 1542 and approved in 1544, introduced no essential changes in the basic economic and regulatory function of the guild. As a matter of fact, the older statutes of the five former guilds were cited as further references for clarification of any point not adequately covered in the new consolidated edition. The changes were primarily bureaucratic and administrative, with careful attention to detail, especially with respect to the machinery of guild operation. Regulations and instructions are lengthy and detailed, although they regard mostly procedures common to any guild and not specific activities of separate crafts. There is an insistence on extensive recordkeeping, even to the point of specific instructions about format and organization. Procedures for bringing cases before guild officials are spelled out in all details, including formulas to be used in the related documentation and a complete schedule of fees for every document and transaction in the legal process. The systematic organization of the Fabbricanti deliberations, the more perfunctory recording of business transacted, and the sheer bulk of the surviving paperwork (there are ten volumes of deliberations for the same period covered by one of the Maestri) must have been the result of a more efficient operation once the guild came under ducal auspices.

[52] Maestri 3, fols. 58r, 74v, 83v.

[53] Arnaldo D'Addario, "Burocrazia, economia e finanze dello Stato fiorentino alla metà del Cinquecento," *ASI*, 121 (1963), 422 n. The legislation is published in *Leg. tosc.*, I, 102–4. Such a consolidation had been proposed in the fifteenth century but never executed.

Andrea Della Robbia, Madonna made for the Maestri, 1475

With the changes introduced by the Medici principate the guild became clearly an agent of public authority. A single governing body and staff, appointed by, and responsible to, the Monte officials, now served all five groups; and a court of claims was set up, with appellate authority assigned to the Mercanzia. The guild also extended its jurisdiction throughout the entire territorial state of Tuscany. Its regulation of craft activities was almost entirely directed to the public interest. The two groups of craftsmen the statutes are most preoccupied with are kilnmen, whose products had to be made to conform to official weights and measurements, and blacksmiths, who were used as the key to effective regulation for the protection of buyers and renters of animals.

The conclusion to the eccentric history of Florentine guilds is that they ended up as little more than administrative offices of the state; their history after the demise of the amorphous structure of the republic and its replacement by a princely regime is little more than a process of bureaucratic consolidation. The move of the Fabbricanti along with other guilds and magistracies into the Uffizi—originally called the Fabbrica dei Tredici Magistrati—was the final step in the transformation of guild into state office. The building, in line with Cosimo I's penchant for giving architectural expression to political policy, was designed by Vasari as the physical symbol of the administrative consolidation of the new princely regime.[54] It was, moreover, a purely administrative reform that in 1583 united all the "heavy" industries of the Fabbricanti with the guild of the food trades (the Arte di Por San Piero, itself the result of the merger in 1534 of the Fornai, Oliandoli, and Beccai) to form one conglomerate comprising men who, fifty years earlier, had been divided into eight of the fourteen minor guilds.[55]

Far from destroying the guild system by incorporating it into its administrative system the ducal government confirmed it by streamlining its judicial and organizational structure. The new regime simply made explicit what had been implicit from the inception of the guilds. In the earlier and looser communal structure, guilds, despite their particularistic organization, performed what were essentially public services, especially (with the Maestri) in the settlement of disputes and inspection procedures for maintaining measurement standards; they now survived in a more bureaucratic structure as state agencies performing these same functions. It was not until the legislation of 1770 abolishing the guild magistrates that the guilds lost their power as corporate entities, although they did not altogether disappear from the scene even then.[56]

The Consular Elite

Florentine guilds lost many of the essential qualities of guilds elsewhere partly as a result of their political reorganization into the guild government that was the foundation of the Florentine republic; that they survived at all was partly due to their political role, although, as the locus of power shifted away

[54] The location of the Fabbricanti offices in the new structure can be seen in the plan published by Alfredo Forti, "L'opera di Giorgio Vasari nella Fabbrica degli Uffizi, 1560–80: cronologia ragionata della costruzione della Fabbrica dei Tredici Magistrati, del Corridoio Vasariano e del secondo piano della Galleria Medicea," *Bollettino degli ingegneri*, 19 (1971), No. 11, 23–28, and No. 12, 33–39; 20 (1972), No. 5, 13–26.
[55] *Leg. tosc.*, X, 258–60.
[56] Luigi Dal Pane, *La storia del lavoro in Italia dagli inizi del secolo XVIII al 1815* (Milan, 1944), pp. 230–32.

from the guilds to upper-class power elites, the guilds lost much of their political identity, at least for most artisans. The guilds remained the formal foundation of the republican constitution, but they ceased to be instruments of political power in the hands of their members. The growth of the supra-guild court of the Mercanzia, founded in 1309, gave the upper classes, with their base in the important major guilds, an increasing dominance over all guilds. When in the 1320s the Mercanzia became the central institution for a new electoral system for public office, the upper classes extended their influence into the internal affairs of the guilds.

This electoral system consisted of complicated procedures by which men were qualified as candidates for political office, the actual selection being left to a drawing from bags in which names of all those thus qualified had been placed. The basic qualification remained guild membership, but because the first steps in the further process of elimination in drawing up electoral lists traditionally occurred inside the guilds, one aspect of the development of the new electoral system was increasing interference by the Mercanzia into the guild itself in order to control the selection of eligible candidates for public office. This meant a direct control over the selection of the consular elites within each guild, since the process by which political eligibility was determined within the ranks of guildsmen was tantamount to the selection of those men who were also qualified to hold guild office. The minor guilds were not freed from this interference inasmuch as one-quarter of all public offices were allotted to them. The effect of these electoral reforms, in other words, was that internal guild affairs became more and more subordinated to strictly political considerations. By the fifteenth century, and especially after 1434, the entire process of guild elections had become an instrument of political faction, and guilds came to be controlled by a small number of elites who were more responsive to the ruling faction in the government than to their own membership. Indeed, as a result of the procedures by which they were chosen, these guild elites can probably be seen simply as extensions of the larger political elite; the advantage of holding consular office, far from being service to the guild, came to be that it automatically opened the door to the political arena beyond.[57]

The government of the Maestri was almost entirely in the hands of a small

[57] The political decline of the guilds in the fourteenth century is traced in John M. Najemy, "Guild Republicanism in Trecento Florence: The Successes and Ultimate Failure of Corporate Politics," *American Historical Review*, 84 (1979), 53–71. The electoral procedures of the guilds are outlined in Doren, *Arti*, I, 259–307; and the political system of which they were a part—at least its operation under the Medici—is exhaustively described in Nicolai Rubinstein, *The Government of the Medici (1434 to 1494)* (Oxford, 1966). Interesting material on the loss of social and juridical distinctions between the *maggiori* and the *minori* with respect to public office is cited by D'Addario, "Burocrazia," p. 387 n.

elite group that controlled election to guild offices. Administration and policy were directed by four consuls chosen for four-month tenures and two consultative groups: a council of eight or nine that sat also four months but assembled only occasionally and, meeting more rarely, a body (*corpo*) varying between thirty and sixty men, including the consuls and the councillors. The constitution of this larger "body," which had the ultimate authority for policy, was probably determined by eligibility for the consular office—which in turn was determined by a complicated (but typically Florence) procedure of co-option by these same men involving a "scrutiny" of the membership and then drawing of lots under the close supervision of the Mercanzia.[58] The basic constitutional structure of the guild—though not necessarily the electoral system—was typical of the guild organization of the building crafts elsewhere in Italy.

The consulate was the central organ of the guild not only because its members had executive authority over guild affairs but also because eligibility for the office automatically led to service both as a member of the council and the larger governing "body" and as an administrative official. Andrea di Marco Della Robbia, for example, who was guild consul five times, had thirty terms on the council and was three times a syndic and once a treasurer.[59] The Maestri consulate was, in other words, the office through which the men who ran the guild passed at sometime in their careers; a survey of these office-holders over the 126 years for which rosters survive, from 1389 to 1515, reveals how small the elite was that ran the affairs of this, the largest of Florentine guilds.[60] Of the 1,524 places on the consulate during this period the occupants of 1,358 (89 percent) are known. Few of these men, however, used surnames, and since most are identified by the Florentine usage of designating both father and grandfather, the analysis of the rosters must proceed on the assumption that a three-generation coincidence of names identifies a single person. If the names of the 1,358 consuls are subjected to this process of identification and if all the men who held the post fewer than five times are arbitrarily eliminated, the list of consuls shrinks to a mere 104 men who, taken all together, account for 866 places—57 percent of the total number of places for the entire 126-year period, or 64 percent of those for which there are names. Inasmuch as hardly any of these held office more

[58] These procedures were retained by the Fabbricanti and are described in the third and fourth rubrics of the 1544 statutes.

[59] The documents for Andrea's activity in the guild council are published in Marquand, *Della Robbia*, I, xvi–xxii.

[60] The members of each consulate are listed in the matriculation register: Maestri 2. There were six consuls up to 1393, and thereafter four. Of the total of 1,524 places filled from 1390 to 1514 the occupants of 166 cannot be identified either because of illegibility or because their names were never entered in the document.

frequently than once every two years (this may have been the effect of a statutory regulation[61]), each of these 104 men who served no fewer than five terms was active in guild affairs for a period of at least ten years. Thirty held office ten or more times, and the record was twenty-one times.

In the absence of surnames family ties among this consular elite of 104 men can be traced only to the extent that their trinomial identification permits the determination of father-son and fraternal relationships. More distant relatives are elusive, and nothing is known about relationship through marriage, although a high degree of intermarriage is to be expected within any craft group, and especially among the families of its leading members. Under these circumstances those families that can be identified from the rosters represent a narrow definition, and it is precarious to generalize about the family structure of the elite. By this definition, nonetheless, 29 of the 104 appear to have no immediate relatives within the group, and the remaining 75 fall into 33 families. Since only 6 of these families extended their guild activity over more than three generations, the consular elite appears not to have been an oligarchy that perpetuated itself on a familial principle, and indeed this is not surprising, since artisan families lacked the kind of solidarity and stability one might expect to find in the upper classes of society. Many of these men, however, had relatives who served on the consulate fewer than five times and hence, as a result of our arbitrary definition, do not appear in the inner group. These men account for an additional 150 places, bringing the total number of places held by the elite and all their blood relatives (as we can identify them) to 66 percent of all consular places (74 percent of those whose occupants can be identified). These figures would most certainly be higher if we had a better way of tracing family relationships. That in over a century and a quarter only 104 men and their immediate relatives account for (at the least) two-thirds of all the consular posts in a guild with hundreds of members is remarkable evidence for the development of elitism in the craft guilds of Florence.

Who were these men? Many are not identified by livelihood or by surname, and it is therefore difficult to say much about them. Some, however, are identified as wallers, stonecutters, woodworkers, and even kilnmen, and confirmation that they in fact practiced these trades comes from the appearance of their names in building accounts. Almost every mason who, from 1386 to about 1410, held the post of foreman of the works for the city's largest building authorities after the works committee of the cathedral, the Tower officials (in charge of streets, bridges, and river control) and the Castle

[61] In the second rubric of the Fabbricanti statutes there are regulations about frequency of holding office in the guild, and these applied also to both an office-holder's relatives and his partners.

GENEALOGICAL CHART 1

Guild Consular Families: Angeni

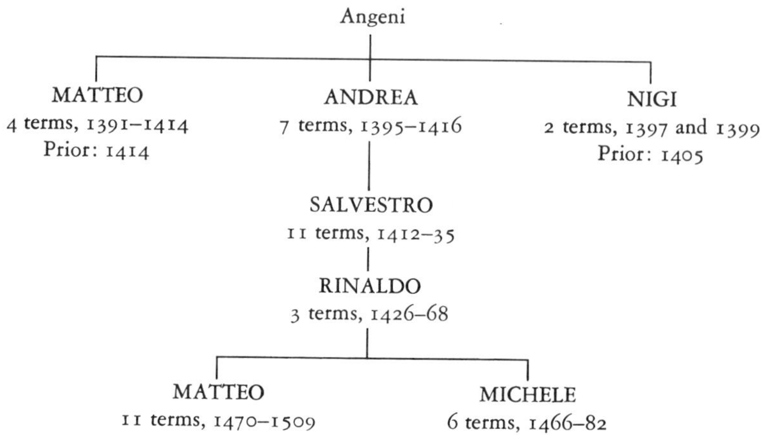

officials, served several terms on the consulate.[62] Leonardo di Giovanni Landi, who served eleven terms in the years 1406 to 1432, was one of the wallers who undertook the building of the main chapel at San Pancrazio in 1400;[63] Andrea di Berto di Martignone, who held the office five times in the years 1393 to 1417, was the son of the mason who contracted for work at the palace of the Mercanzia in 1360. Stefano di Jacopo Rosselli, who served five terms in the years 1459 to 1484, built the second story over the courtyard of the Innocenti in 1470, and his son Jacopo (seven terms, 1469–1515) did much building for Filippo Strozzi. Jacopo's brother Bernardo the painter held the office five times, and his son Michele and his son-in-law Cronaca held it once.[64]

Among those consuls who were stonecutters were Matteo, Andrea, and Nigi, all sons of Angeni (genealogical chart 1). Among them these brothers

[62] ASF, Mercanzia 78, fols. 75–76. The men were: Andrea (Antonio?) di Banco, Andrea Cioffi (see text following), Antonio Mazzini, Antonio Pucci (see text following), Basilio di Bartolo Brandini, Bartolomeo di Dino, Domenico Brunetti, Francesco del Cresta, Francesco di Dino Scambrella, Giovanni di Vanni Tresanti, Lapo di Martino, Leonardo di Giovanni (Landi?) "Buzzetti," Nigi di Angeni (see text following), Ristoro di Cione, and Stefano Gherardini.

[63] Marco Dezzi Bardeschi, "Il complesso monumentale di San Pancrazio a Firenze ed il suo restauro (nuovi documenti)," *Quaderni dell'Istituto di Storia dell'Architettura*, 13th ser., fasc. 73–78 (1966), pp. 50–51.

[64] On the Rosselli see Richard A. Goldthwaite, "The Building of the Strozzi Palace: The Construction Industry in Renaissance Florence," *Studies in Medieval and Renaissance History*, 10 (1973), 149–50. Stefano's work at the Innocenti is noted by G. Morozzi and A. Piccini, *Il restauro dello spedale di Santa Maria degli Innocenti, 1966–1970* (Florence, 1971), p. 38; and a job Jacopo undertook in 1489 has been noted herein, p. 136.

served thirteen terms (and perhaps more if Nigi could be equated with several others with a similar name) in the years 1391 to 1416, during which time all three turn up in the outgo journals of Santa Maria Nuova for small construction jobs of various kinds. Andrea's son Salvestro described himself as a mason in 1427. The fifteenth-century tax records reveal his family as one of only modest wealth. In 1480 his son Rinaldo, then 82, filed a declaration along with his two sons that included their residence in town, a farm worth 300 florins (with a *casa da signore*), and investments of 200 lire in a haberdasher's shop (for Michele) and 200 lire in the kiln partnership Matteo had with the Da Terrarossa. All these men show up in the list of guild consuls.[65]

Another consular family whose activity as stonecutters can be extensively documented was that of Nofri di Romolo (genealogical chart 2). Both Nofri (who served two terms) and his father worked at Santa Maria Nuova at the turn of the century, and Nofri (described as *lastraiuolo* from Settignano) was a major supplier of decorative stone for the new hospital of San Matteo in the first decade of the fifteenth century. His sons Giuliano (seven terms) and Andrea (thirteen terms) declared a jointly owned stoneworker's shop in their tax report of 1427.

Andrea was active from the second decade of the fifteenth century as a supplier of finished stone, including ornately carved decorative pieces, for such projects as the guild hall of the Linaiuoli, the Bigallo, San Miniato, San Lorenzo, the cathedral, and the hospital of San Paolo. In 1427 he and his brother declared net assets amounting to 724 florins. They owned a house in town and one in the country, along with two small vineyards, in addition to

GENEALOGICAL CHART 2
Guild Consular Families: Di Romolo

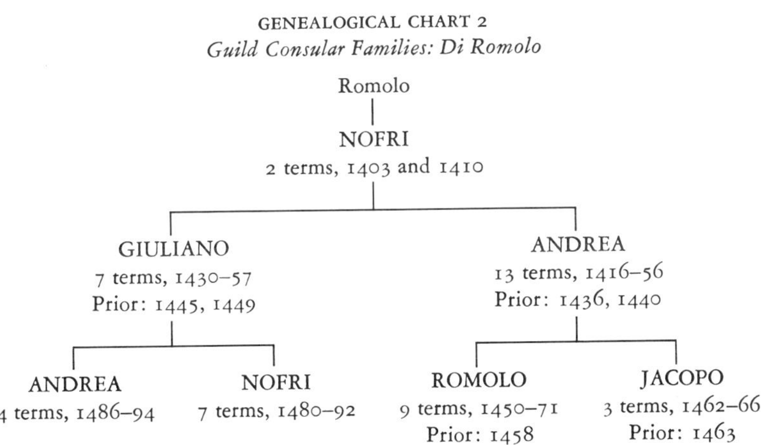

65 Catasto 78 (San Giovanni, Leon d'oro; 1427), fol. 461; 820 (1457), fols. 410–11; 1017 (1480), fol. 433.

GENEALOGICAL CHART 3
Guild Consular Families: Da Terrarossa

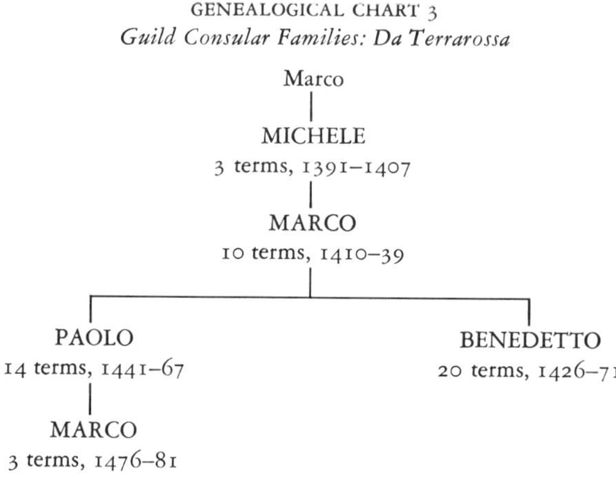

their shop and their residence. Their shop had an inventory worth 200 florins, and something of the scale of its business is indicated by the list attached to their report of 220 debtors for a total of 545 florins. In the 1430s Giuliano was active at Carrara, working on contract with the cathedral workshop. The brothers filed separate declarations in 1451, by which time each had his own shop and Giuliano owned a quarry; two years later Andrea also bought a quarry (from the sons of Lorenzo Marocchi for 30 florins). Andrea's sons, however, seem to have abandoned the family trade. In 1448 Andrea invested 100 florins to set up his eldest son, Romolo, in a haberdashery partnership (which had a capital of 300 florins); in the sons' first independent report in 1457 they describe their business as a thread-dealer's shop, and their recently deceased father's stoneworker's shop was in liquidation. Their real estate holdings alone (not counting their residence) were worth 763 florins—as much as their father had declared jointly with his brother as their total worth thirty years earlier. By 1480 the holdings of Romolo's sons amounted to 1,273 florins. Although he seems to have made his fortune outside the building trades, Romolo shows up along with his brother and cousins—whose trades cannot always be determined—on the consulate of the Maestri.[66]

[66] The Catasto records (San Giovanni, Drago) are the chief source for the financial history of these men: 52 (1427), fols. 127–30 (Andrea and Giuliano); 715 (1451), pt. 2, fols. 859–60 (Andrea) and 994 (Giuliano); 826 (1457), fols. 354–60 (Andrea's sons); 1018 (1480), fols. 555–56 (Romolo's sons); ASF, Misc. rep. 21, insert 3 bis (1451 business tax), fol. 23v (Romolo's haberdashery shop). Andrea's work has been documented by Charles Randall Mack, "The Building Programme of the Cloister of San Miniato," *Burlington Magazine*, 115 (1973), 448 n. 12; Isabelle Hyman, "Notes and Speculations on S. Lorenzo, Palazzo Medici, and an Urban Project

GENEALOGICAL CHART 4
Guild Consular Families: Cioffi

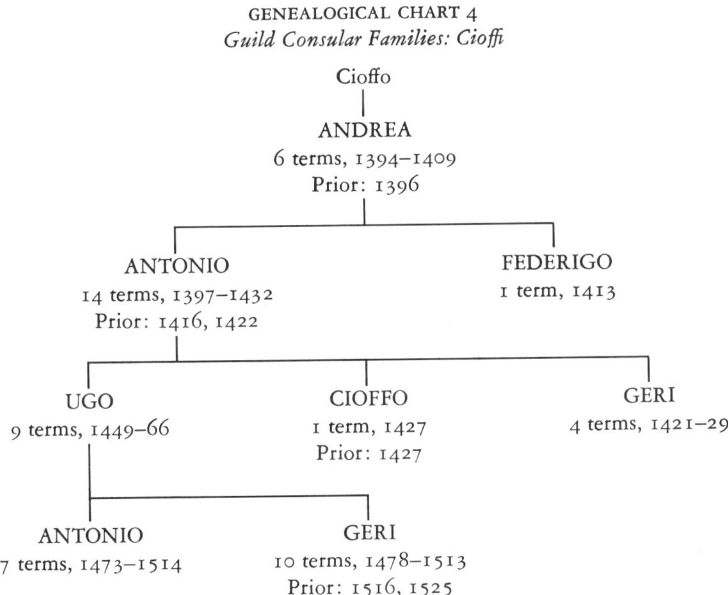

Among the guild consuls who were practicing kilnmen were the Da Terrarossa, whose enterprise in that craft has already been recounted on these pages. Marco di Michele served ten terms, and his two sons were among those with the longest record of service: between them Paolo, with fourteen terms, and Benedetto, with twenty, were on the consulate every year from 1441 to 1471 (genealogical chart 3). Moreover, three of their partners also came from families with an impressive record of consular service: Antonio di Bartolomeo d'Agostino and his brother and partner in the operation of a kiln, Rosso, each served seven terms, and their father served eleven; Antonio d'Ugo d'Antonio Cioffi, who held the post seven times, came from a family with four generations of service (genealogical chart 4); and Matteo di Rinaldo Angeni belonged to the consular family of stonecutters cited earlier.

Another consular family involved in the brick industry was the Del Rosso (genealogical chart 5). Rosso di Piero Del Rosso, who held the consular office nine times, was a major supplier of kiln products for the new hospital of San Matteo in the first decade of the fifteenth century. At least one of his seven sons appears on the consulate almost every year from 1433 to 1460. One of these, Guido, owned a kiln site, but in 1451 his orphaned sons re-

by Brunelleschi," *JSArH*, 34 (1975), 113; Richard A. Goldthwaite and W. R. Rearick, "Michelozzo and the Ospedale di San Paolo in Florence," *Flor. Mitt.*, 21 (1977), 287 n. 37.

GENEALOGICAL CHART 5

Guild Consular Families: Del Rosso

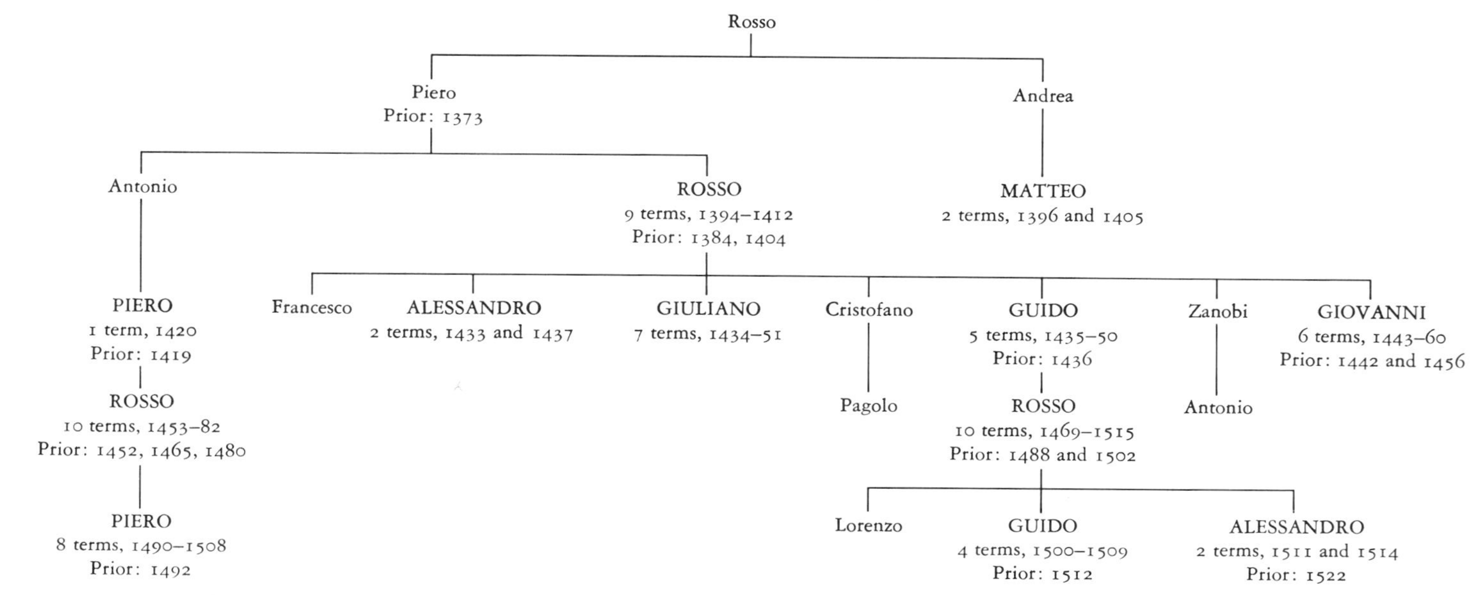

GENEALOGICAL CHART 6
Guild Consular Families: Canacci

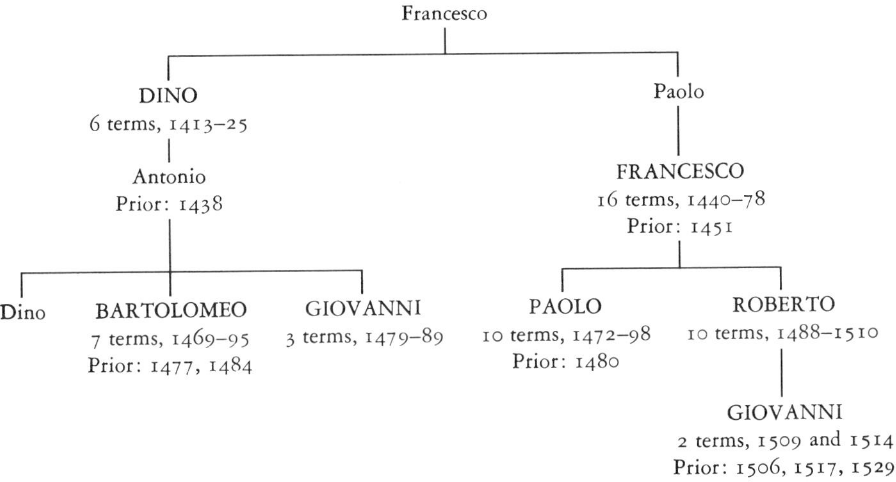

ported to the tax officials that it was not being used; Guido's brothers jointly declared a kiln site in 1451 and called themselves kilnmen in their report of 1457. None of their reports, however, reveals anything about their activity as kilnmen. Except for Guido the brothers always submitted a collective report, and none established a family in Florence. In 1442 Francesco was in Naples and Cristofano and Zanobi were in Hungary; in 1457 they declared among their liabilities expenses connected with a business failure in Venice and a debt owed to their "cashier," who had withdrawn to a Carthusian monastery. By 1469 a fourth brother, Giovanni, the last to survive in Florence, had joined the families of his two brothers living in Hungary. There is more than a suggestion in all of this wandering about that these brothers were undertaking something that went beyond the local operation of a kiln. None of the tax reports down to 1480, however, shows that any one of them ever built up property-holdings in Florence consisting of more than two or three items.[67]

One of the active consular families, the Canacci, made its fortune on the periphery of the construction industry, probably as wholesale dealers in wood, and ended up with considerable status by most criteria of their society (genealogical chart 6). Michele di Francesco is recorded as a carpenter

[67] The Catasto reports (S. Spirito, Ferza) of this family are: 66 (1427), fols. 203v and 238v–39r; 610 (1442), fols. 187 and 511; 690 (1451), fols. 76, 1105, and 1137; 790 (1457), fols. 130 and 747; 791 (1457), fols. 83–84; 908 (1469–70), fols. 369–70, 415, and 533.

working on the new guild hall of the Linaiuoli in 1419. In 1427 his two elderly brothers, Dino (then seventy-five) and Paolo (sixty-eight), reported sizeable estates, certainly much larger than the average artisan and approaching the level of the upper class. Dino's net worth (before the personal deduction allowed by the tax officials) was 1,452 florins, and Paolo's was 1,736 florins, and both were active in some aspect of the commerce of wood. Dino had three separate shops all together worth 709 florins, and Paolo reported proceeds of 665 florins from the recent sale of two shops (one to his brother) and debts involving dealings in wood in connection with his "new shop." Dino served six tenures as guild consul, and although Paolo never held that office his descendants for three generations served frequently. In 1451 Paolo's son Francesco declared two rented shops in the same location as his father's, but since their specific nature is not indicated his professional activity is not known. His estate, however, was substantial, with real estate worth 1,328 florins in 1469; the joint holdings of his sons eleven years later were worth 1,110 florins (not counting their residence). One of Dino's sons retained ownership of his father's three wood shops, but another, Antonio, left the trade before his father's death. In a report filed independently in 1427 Antonio declares ownership of a silk shop with its contents of cloths alone worth 2,230 florins, although after balancing his assets and liabilities his net worth was only 177 florins. Forty years later he had real estate worth 1,398 florins. He appears on the early Medici Balìe, and it was his son Dino who bought (in a different Gonfalone) the property where the great Canacci palace was eventually built. Dino d'Antonio, like his father, does not show up on the rosters of the Maestri consuls; his brothers, however, do. Most of the Canacci also took at least one turn on the priorate. The Canacci were a family of men who achieved wealth and status without altogether giving up their activity in the guild of the craft where they had their origins.[68]

The record of another of these consular families, the Pucci, documents the similar story of men who rose from an artisan craft to higher status yet nevertheless kept up their guild membership for political rather than professional reasons. Antonio di Puccio was a mason-carpenter whose record of activity includes some important contracts with the commune for construction in wood. In the years 1380 and 1381 he was one of three contractors who built the scaffolding for the vaults of the Loggia dei Priori, and the next year the same three undertook the completion of the roof over the vaults (in all these contracts the wood was to be supplied to the workers). In 1384 Antonio built

[68] The information on the Canacci comes from their Catasto reports (all from S. M. Novella, Leon Rosso, unless otherwise indicated): 74 (S. M. Novella, Vipera; 1427), fols. 118–19 (Antonio); 76 (1427), fols. 287v–88r (Dino); 405 (1430), fols. 222–23r (Giuliano di Dino); 707 (1451), fols. 613–14 (Francesco); 917 (S. M. Novella, Unicorno; 1470), fols. 325–28 (Dino d'Antonio); 919 (1469), pt. 2, fols. 359–60 (Francesco); 1012 (1480), fols. 208–9 (Paolo and Roberto di Francesco).

an elaborate wood model for the new church of the Santissima Annunziata. He was consul of the Maestri twelve times in the years 1390 (when the records start) to 1417. Moreover, he was prior twice. Once, in 1412, his involvement in politics ended in a temporary exile; it is likely that this political activity in itself indicates his rising ambitions. His sons, at any rate, were among the closest adherents of Cosimo de' Medici during the party strife of the 1420s and 1430s, and they must have gained an appropriate economic status, for they moved out of the building trades, though not out of the guild, where three of them also held the consular office a number of times (Puccio served 7 terms in the years 1416 to 1429; Giovanni: 5 terms, 1424 to 1444; Saracino: 3 terms, 1435 to 1439). In 1427 they jointly declared a modest investment of 362 florins in a partnership of haberdashers, and their total assets amounted to 1,612 florins. Shortly after the return of Cosimo de' Medici, Puccio d'Antonio matriculated in the Cambio and his brother Saracino in the silk guild. Puccio's son Antonio was a partner in the silk business of Luca Pitti in 1451, and by 1480 he had built up real estate holdings worth 6,547 florins. With a chapel in the Santissima Annunziata that cost him 500 florins, Antonio was well established in the upper ranks of Florentine society. In the fifteenth century these men and their descendants appear frequently on the rosters of political offices in the city, including the priorate and the Balìe.[69]

The few families surveyed here can be taken as fairly representative of the consular elite of the Maestri. Among them they account for more than one-quarter of the total number of posts on the consulate over 126 years (almost one-third of those whose occupants can be identified), and they include 42 of the 104 men who served five or more times. Many were active craftsmen in the building trades, others were descended from such artisans but had taken up a different trade. Some had substantial wealth and a few had upper-class status, while others appear to have had no more than several parcels of real estate beyond the earnings from the practice of their craft. One pattern that seems to emerge from this survey of consular families over several generations is mobility from the building crafts into commerce. The history of the Pucci and the Canacci are the notable examples, and ambition for a better way of

[69] A genealogy of the Pucci (1868) is included in Pompeo Litta, ed., *Le famiglie celebri italiane* (Milan, 1819–1902). The older Antonio's contracts with the commune are published by Carl Frey, *Die Loggia dei Lanzi* (Berlin, 1885), pp. 290–95; and his expense account for the model of the Ss. Annunziata is in Ss. Annunziata 841 (income-outgo journal, 1364–84), fol. 28. His descendants can be traced through Catasto documents (S. Giovanni, Vaio): 81 (1427), fols. 35 and 47v (sons of the older Antonio); 1023 (1480), fols. 11–16 (the younger Antonio); ASF, Misc. rep. 21, insert 3 bis (1451 business tax), fol. 2v. The political alliance of this family with Cosimo de' Medici is discussed by Dale Kent, *The Rise of the Medici: Factions in Florence, 1426–1434* (Oxford, 1978), pp. 122–23.

making a living may have been behind the decision of Andrea di Nofri di Romolo to set his son up as a haberdasher and of the Del Rosso to look for something better abroad. Given the peculiar role of the Florentine guilds in communal politics, participation in guild affairs was not irrelevant to men with higher ambitions.

Other upper-class names appear now and then on the rosters of consuls—Pandolfini, Martelli, Canigiani, Falconetti—but who they were, and how and why they got involved in the guild, cannot be ascertained. Some consuls were prominent craftsmen in other trades, like Guarante di Giovanni (consul four times in the years 1428 to 1443 and prominent in communal politics), a goldsmith associated with Ghiberti and documented for his work on reliquaries at the cathedral. Few of the consuls, however, were men who are known today for their artistic talent. Luca Della Robbia was consul nine times; his nephews, the brothers Andrea and Simone, held the post ten times between them. Toward the end of his life Lorenzo Ghiberti was a consul three times (in the years 1449 to 1453), and both his son Vittorio and his grandson Buonaccorso also appear as consul three times. Antonio Rossellino was in the office for two terms, and Michelozzo (in 1430) and Cronaca (in 1494) for one term each. Otherwise, despite their prominence as artists and despite the relative affluence of some of them (like Ghiberti), the more accomplished sculptors and architects left the politics of their guild to others.

Inside the guild hall the modest activity of running guild affairs—deliberating, hearing disputes, supervising administration, even officiating at ceremonies—was not without its own rewards. The consuls' meals and other benefits added up to an annual total of 150 lire, one-quarter of the budget reflected in the 1429 Catasto (already discussed at some length). The loss of the benefits of office suffered by Michelozzo while he was in Ragusa was one of the explicit considerations taken in reducing the debt on his membership account, which had fallen into arrears during his absence, although there is no evidence for his participation in guild affairs thereafter.[70]

In the final analysis, however, the men who ran the guild had more to do with the political elite that ruled the city than with the vast membership of the guild. Since their qualification for guild office meant approval by the politicians, the consular elite was in a sense an extension of the group of Florentine citizens who ran the city, and guild activity could therefore open the way to the wider arena of communal politics. Such opportunities could be

[70] "Item, si dice che 'sendo stato Michelozo di Bartolomeo, intagliatore, buon tempo absente da la cità, e non avendo esercitato l'arte nella cità nè nel contado nè etiam distretto di Firenze, e avendo perduto molti officii di detta arte, e' quali arebbe esercitati, e trovandosi in debito di buona somma di danari a' libri di detta arte, si dice che pagando detto Michelozo el terzo di quello à debito, s'intende libero e absoluto del resto, e pòssasi e debbi cancellare di tal debito dove fusse discripto debitore per chi apartiene"; Maestri 3, fol. 22v (22 December 1471).

measured by searching the many rosters of public office for the names of our Maestri consuls, but the kind of patience that would be necessary for the task did not go into this study. Most of these men, however, appear more conspicuously at the top of the political hierarchy as priors (these are indicated on the genealogical charts), and although this was largely a ceremonial office by the fifteenth century, election to it was not haphazard. More importantly, a number of Maestri consuls turn up on the Balìe, those ad hoc committees put together every so often during these Medici years in order to exercise what was in effect sovereign authority for one kind of constitutional reform or another. Balìe were composed of men who had been carefully selected by the power elite of the regime, and it can be assumed that behind the appearance of a name on the rosters of this body is a political career of some kind. Francesco di Paolo Canacci was a member of the Balìe of 1458, 1466, and 1471; Andrea di Nofri and his son Romolo between them sat on almost every Balìe from 1434 to the latter's death in 1472; and the Del Rosso turn up with only slightly less frequency. The door to wider political activity was not altogether closed on working guildsmen like Andrea di Nofri and the Del Rosso.[71]

Even men who moved up the social and economic ladder and no longer served actively in guild office did not always cut their ties with the guild. After the generation of the older Antonio Pucci's sons the Pucci no longer served terms on the consulate of the Maestri, but nevertheless they often designated the Maestri as their official guild association for purposes of their communal political activity. Since the minor guilds were allotted one-quarter of the communal offices, qualification through them gave men who belonged to the ruling class a better chance of gaining office. In a sixteenth-century document in which the author tries to show that the older distinction between public officeholders as major or minor guildsmen had lost all of its juridical and even its social meaning, the Pucci are singled out as an example of members of an obviously upper-class family whose social status was not tarnished by their association with a minor guild.[72]

Enough is known about the identity of the men who ran the guilds to make some conclusions about them. First, they were men who were acceptable to the power elite in communal politics, although they themselves were not necessarily in that elite. Secondly, despite the social mobility of some consular families many of the men who ran guild affairs were working artisans. Finally, the guild leaders were nevertheless more a political group than an economic one, and their control of guild affairs did not mean that they constituted an oligarchy in the business world of the construction industry. The Maestri was not a guild of the northern European kind where a small

[71] Rosters of the Balìe are published by Rubinstein, *Government.*

[72] D'Addario, "Burocrazia," p. 387 n.

inner group of master guildsmen closed itself off from the mass of apprentices and journeymen by erecting barriers in the form of examinations, masterwork requirements, and high matriculation fees and by reducing both apprentices and workers to formal legal categories of inferior status, nor within the ranks of the masters was there a distinction between those who worked for wages and the more entrepreneurial owners of shops. Although some consuls may have used their political influence to get some of the city's business (for example, through appointment to the post of foreman for a building authority), other prominent wallers and stonecutters achieved professional success or artistic prominence (and sometimes both) without ever making as much as a single appearance in the inner circle of the consular elite of the Maestri. It is not unreasonable to suppose that the artisans among the guild consuls were relatively well off by economic standards of their class, but they were not exclusively the leaders of their industry. It ought to be clear from the description of the construction industry presented in the preceding chapters that the industry in Florence was not organized in a way that put it largely in the hands of big contractors, like the men who controlled the guild in contemporary London and Bruges and in seventeenth-century Milan.[73]

[73] Domenico Sella, *Salari e lavoro nell'edilizia lombarda durante il secolo XVII* (Pavia, 1968), pp. 32–43; Thrupp, "Gilds," p. 262; Jean-Pierre Sosson, *Les Travaux publics de la ville de Bruges, XIVe–XVe siècles* (Brussels, 1977), pp. 189–201.

CHAPTER SIX

Labor

THE economic world of the working man in pre-industrial Europe cannot be easily recovered. If he kept any documents of his own, few have survived. Furthermore, the industrial system that provided him with work did not keep much of a record of his work. Most industries were organized on such a small scale that records were not necessary, and the few for which documentation survives did not maintain employment rosters, since much work was either organized on the putting-out system, which removed the workers from central accounting control, or paid for on a piece-rate basis, which makes it difficult for us to evaluate what he was paid for. Even Florentine businessmen, among the best record-keepers of all time, rarely had occasion to enter much information about industrial workers in their accounts. In the cloth industry, perhaps the best documented of all industries in Florence, capitalists kept records of their cloth when it entered and left the shops and while it passed through the various stages of the production process, but because little work was done in the shop itself, most cloth workers do not show up at all on the shop accounts. In fact, despite an abundance of documentation for the cloth industry, little is known about working conditions in Florence, a city that was one of Europe's leading industrial centers.

Construction, on the other hand, is well documented by employment records. By its very nature this industry more than any other brought many workers of varying skills together in one place and put them to work on a direct labor contract. Records were kept not because construction was a capitalist enterprise needing exact accounting to maximize profits, but because many builders were either institutions or men of property who simply wanted a record of the way their money was spent. Since most construction workers were paid a daily wage, not, as were so many of their contemporaries, a piece rate, a common denominator exists for comparing their wages through time. For this reason building accounts have long been mined for the data needed to establish an index for the history of the standard of living of the working man. Much more than wages, however, is involved in the contractual relations between employee and employer; building accounts have been little appreciated for what they have to tell us about the nonmonetary terms of employment. It is enough to skim off the wage data if one wants only to draw graphs of economic status, but a little more digging in these documents will yield other materials for rounding out our knowledge of the worker's economic existence.

Conditions of Work

A major component of the total labor force employed in the construction industry was the large pool of construction workers properly speaking—the unskilled laborers and masons who found employment going from one job to another and almost always working for a daily wage. On a modest structure built of brick and rubble the cost of labor at the construction site ranged between 25 and 40 percent of total costs. Where stone was used, more labor had to be employed simply to handle the material, and where it was finished at the building site, stonecutters had also to be taken on as day laborers. At the Strozzi palace, three sides of which are faced in stone, stonecutters constituted much of the labor force. Of the total construction cost there, 50 percent went for direct labor charges at the site, and of the 20 percent that went for the quarry operations, most was for labor charges.

Most of these construction workers earned daily wages. Only those skilled workers on the permanent staff of a large project might have their pay expressed as a monthly or yearly salary, although per diem adjustments were usually made if they worked anything less than full time. The smith Agostino di Simone Cioli earned 16 lire a month for the eighteen months he was on the job at the Strozzi palace, but once, when he was sick for only three days, they docked his wages 15 soldi a day.[1] The unusual arrangement the building committee of Santo Spirito made with its foreman guaranteeing him a minimum wage of 12 lire a month in periods of no work when he was unable to pick up work elsewhere has already been mentioned.[2] He did better than the much more eminent Giuliano da Sangallo, who, when he went to work for a daily wage as foreman at Santa Maria delle Carceri in Prato in 1485,

[1] Richard A. Goldthwaite, "The Building of the Strozzi Palace: The Construction Industry in Renaissance Florence," *Studies in Medieval and Renaissance History*, 10 (1973), 183.

[2] S. Spirito 128, fol. 82v.

was told he would not be paid for days he did not show up for work.[3] Unskilled laborers invariably worked for daily wages. At the beginning of construction at the Badia of Fiesole, the management took on several unskilled laborers at monthly salaries, but most of them did not work on those terms for even a month, and eventually all were being paid by the day.[4] A few other examples of salaried unskilled workers could be cited, but they all come from the countryside, where labor was probably less fluid than in the city.

No work meant no pay, a notion fully shared by the intellectuals—the scholastics and canon lawyers—who in general had little to say about wages except in their discussions of the just price. According to them only charity could be appealed to for any softening of the terms of the wage contract in case of sickness or any other cause of absence from work. Through the sixteenth century no writer on economic matters developed a doctrine of wages that attempted to put the traditional notion of the just wage as the market price for a day's work in a larger context of concern for the well-being of the working man. A day's work was the fundamental proposition in the wage contract.[5]

In Florence as throughout most of Europe the workweek lasted six days, from Monday through Saturday, with the possibility of an early quitting time on the eve of the Sabbath. Nevertheless, with about fifty religious holidays (apart from Sundays) scattered throughout the year when work was forbidden, a full-time laborer could hope to work at the most about 270 days in a year, or an average of about five or five and a half days a week. The interjection of these holidays into the workyear by the church had the effect of relieving the heavy burden imposed on the worker by an economic system that generally was not sensitive to his interests.

The critical view so readily taken by historians of pre-industrial Europe of the fact that the workday normally extended from dawn to dusk, or for as much as fourteen hours, is more informed by the prejudices of our own times than by much knowledge of the subject.[6] By the fourteenth century the

[3] Published by G. Marchini, "Della costruzione di Santa Maria delle Carceri in Prato," *Archivio storico pratese*, 14 (1936), 62.

[4] Badia di Fiesole 1 (building accounts, 1456–60), fols. 2–9.

[5] G. Barbieri, "Il giusto salario negli scrittori italiani del Cinque e Seicento," *Annali della Facoltà di Economia e Commercio dell'Università di Bari*, new ser., 9 (1949), 283–328.

[6] Micheline Baulant, "Le Salaire des ouvriers du bâtiment à Paris da 1400 à 1726," *Annales, E.S.C.*, 26 (1971), 465–66; Henryk Samsonowicz, "Salaires et services dans les finances citadines de la Prusse au XVe siècle et dans la première moitié du XVIe siècle," *Proceedings of the Third International Congress of Economic History (Munich, 1965)* (Paris, 1968), pt. 1, 541 (where it is stated that two hours of the workday

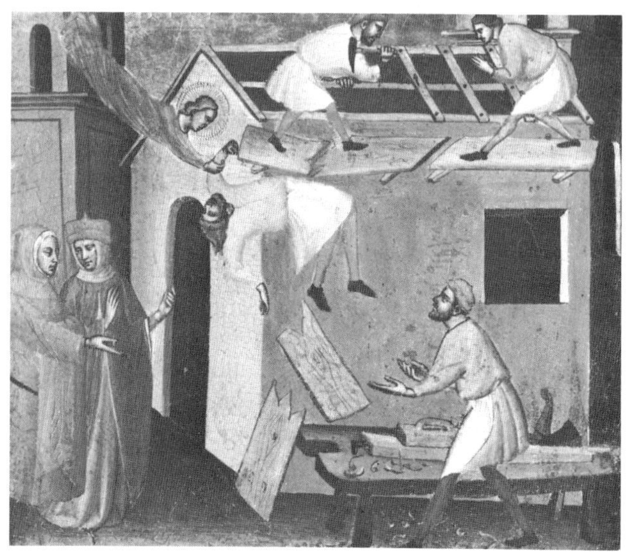

Lorenzo di Niccolò, Santa Fina appears and saves the life of a man who called on her as he was falling from the roof of a church where he was working (panel from Altarpiece of Santa Fina), 1402.

medieval notion that work-time was simply the duration of the day was being modified, at least in some of the larger centers of the cloth industry, by work-clocks. These were installed in public halls to mark a more precise division of time than had formerly been observed by the mere ringing of bells for the announcement of events in the public and ecclesiastical world. Early fourteenth-century legislation in Verona indicates that the town bell sounded the time to go to work, the beginning and end of the noon break, the mid-afternoon break, and the end of the workday. In fifteenth-century Florence some construction sites had their own clocks. At the Strozzi palace a bell was purchased for sounding the hours. At Santo Spirito there was a half-hour clock (*oriuolo di mezz'ora*), and the man who tended it and kept the employment record—sometimes the head stonecutter himself—got a bonus of 1 florin every six months for his trouble. If on the one hand these clocks served to impose a greater discipline on the worker, on the other they had the effect

were used for three meals); Bronislaw Geremek, *Le Salariat dans l'artisanat parisien aux XIIIe–XVe siècles* (Paris, 1968), pp. 81–82 (where the fourteen-hour day is said not to have included the break periods). In fifteenth-century Brussels the workday lasted from eight to thirteen hours (including breaks) depending on the season, and clocks struck the time according to a work and rest schedule; G. Des Marez, *L'Organisation du travail à Bruxelles au XVe siècle* (Brussels, 1904), pp. 243–47.

of making the worker more conscious of time. It has been said, in fact, that time—that is, the length of the workday—was more at issue than wages in labor disputes throughout Europe in this period.[7]

Nothing in the Florentine materials throws much light on the subject of the length of the workday. On the Strozzi accounts the occasional division of a day's wage into twelfths (or multiples thereof) is probably indicative not of a twelve-hour workday but of the duodecimal system Florentines used in all mensuration. Time off the job was, of course, taken for the noon meal. At the cathedral workshop (according to Manetti) Brunelleschi thought the lunch break was too much of an interruption, and to hurry up the pace of construction he opened a food concession at the building site for those workers who came to work without their lunches. The 1415 compilation of communal statues has a rubric (the sixty-sixth) on labor that restricts breaks and limits work on Saturdays, but the provision is stated with the lack of clarity characteristic of this document. In his treatise Filarete proposed an eight- to nine-hour workday at Sforzinda, exclusive of one hour off for lunch and half an hour for a mid-afternoon break—a schedule that he must have known as a construction foreman, for otherwise what sense did it make for him to propose such a liberal policy? Construction, after all, is hard work even for the most skilled, and the workday may have been shorter—or have had more break time—in this industry than in others.[8]

In view of what is usually said about workers in pre-industrial Europe, perhaps nothing is more notable about the conditions of employment for a Florentine worker than the extent to which wages were understood in purely monetary terms. The worker was invariably paid in cash, and little else was thrown into the bargain. Payment in kind was rare. Monasteries were the employers most likely to make occasional payments in produce to their workers. For instance, day workers at the quarries of San Bartolomeo at Monte Oliveto on the edge of the city sometimes received grain, wine, vinegar, and figs along with cash payments. While working at the Strozzi palace Cronaca was given wheat in lieu of cash, but this happened mostly in the later 1490s, when supply throughout the city was tight.

In most instances of significant payment in kind, the employee (like Cronaca) was working on contract, not for day wages or salary, and the quan-

[7] Jacques Le Goff, "Le Temps du travail dans la 'crise' du XIVe siècle: du temps médiéval au temps moderne." *Le Moyen Age*, 69 (1963), 597–613; cf. Armando Sapori, "Spazio e tempo: cambiamento di mentalità e di vita di una società," in his *Studi di storia economica*, III (Florence, 1967), 353–63. The subject of time and work as it is relevant to the immediate background of the industrial revolution is treated by E. P. Thompson, "Time, Work-Discipline, and Industrial Capitalism," *Past and Present*, No. 38 (1967), 56–97.

[8] This has been suggested by Luigi Dal Pane, *La storia del lavoro in Italia dagli inizi del secolo XVIII al 1815* (Milan, 1944), p. 251.

tities of produce he received as payment, usually the staples of grain and wine, not infrequently exceeded his needs for ordinary consumption purposes. When in 1465 Francesco di Filippo Guidetti contracted with the mason Domenico del Cresta to have work done on his house in Piazza Santa Felicita, part of the payment was stipulated as 70 staia of wheat delivered in Florence—enough wheat to supply five adults for a year (since delivery was made before work got underway, in what was in effect an advance payment, this labor contract was one of the few to be notarized).[9] A more striking instance of payment in kind occurs on the account kept by the Badia for Mino da Fiesole's work on the monument to Marchese Ugo (in the years 1469 to 1471). In two years the sculptor received more than 313 staia of wheat (plus some flour), 134½ barrels of wine (average consumption was about 7 barrels a year), small quantities of oil and wood, and cloth worth 294 lire. Of the 970 lire debited on Mino's account, 51 percent was in foodstuffs, 30 percent in cloth, and only 19 percent in cash. How Mino disposed of these supplies and why he agreed to be paid in this way can only be imagined. Given the enormous quantities involved, however, his situation is not what we usually have in mind when talking of payment in kind. His arrangement, in any case, is an exceptional one in the building accounts of the period.[10]

In recording payment in kind the accountant usually entered exact monetary values at current market prices as credits against the worker's wage claims. Rarely did an employer throw anything else into the bargain as an extra without debiting the worker's account for it. Occasionally, however, wine or a pair of shoes is mentioned in a wage entry but given no value, and contracts can be found with such informal arrangements specified. According to a contract the waller Pietro d'Arrigini from Bellinzona made in 1456 to build a wall for the nuns of Sant'Ambrogio, he was to be paid a rate on the basis of measure and value, but he also received a gown worth 10 lire and a pair of shoes for which no value was stipulated. In another contract, of 1429, the abbess of Sant'Apollonia agreed to give the waller Lorenzo di Giovanni da Ribuoia not only his meals along with his daily wages (to be adjusted accordingly), but also the use, by him and his crew, of one of the convent's houses (which had a single bed and no sheets).[11]

Throughout Europe payday for the worker who was paid by the day was Saturday. This is undoubtedly why in Rome Saturday was the day selected by the guild statutes for the collection of alms for the poor and the sick from the membership. In Nuremberg the city surveyor proposed paying workers

[9] ASF, Notarile antecosimiano S500 (Bastiano Serforese), fols. 30v–31r.

[10] Badia di Firenze 79, fol. 288.

[11] ASF, Conv. sopp. LXXXII (S. Apollonia), 10 (building accounts), fols. 3v–4v; LXXIX (S. Ambrogio), 121 (miscellaneous accounts), fol. 7r.

at noon so that their wives could shop in the afternoon before the market closed for the weekend.[12]

On large projects the employer or his agent made payment, not the foreman or supervisor (as at Filarete's Sforzinda). Sometimes the supervisor issued chits (*polizze, scritte*) to be redeemed by the employer's cashier on the building site. At Santo Spirito most of the operating expenses were paid out of an account with one of the city's leading banking houses (Mellini, later Capponi), and presumably workers dealt with an agent of the bank to collect their wages. That employers paid their workers directly and not through an intermediary who could rake-off something for himself is evidenced by the universal accounting practice of making separate entries, and even opening separate accounts, for all workers, whether skilled or unskilled; the full nature of these transactions can sometimes be confirmed by cross-references on the cash account. Apprentices, assistants, and even associates (*garzoni, fanciulli, compagni*) were usually paid through the mason to whom they were attached, but only rarely are masons given payments "to be given to the laborers" (as the accountant at Santa Maria Nuova once carefully specified). When it did happen that a mason's account was credited with the pay for the laborers in his work crew, the employer probably saw to it that each got his due. As one employer explained in a rare comprehensive entry for payment to both a mason and his laborer (or laborers), "each one of them got his share notwithstanding that (the payments) are recorded in [the mason] Francesco's name."[13]

A worker's cash earnings had to go a long way toward paying his expenses as a worker. Employers generally expected workers, even unskilled ones, to have their own tools. They make this explicit in contracts with founders and masons. In the Strozzi contracts with founders the employer agreed to pay for tools only if bedrock was struck and heavier equipment than normal was needed. On large projects, however, the employer often paid smithy expenses to keep metal tools in repair.

The worker was also on his own for his midday meal. This can be inferred from the anecdote about Brunelleschi's food concession at the cathedral. Building accounts are sometimes explicit about meal arrangements for the worker, stating the condition of his employment as being "at his expense" (*a sue*

[12] Friedrich von Weech, ed., *Endres Tuchers Baumeisterbuch der Stadt Nürnberg (1464–1475)* (Stuttgart, 1862), p. 62.

[13] "e ognino di loro ebe la partte sua nonestante che sieno ischritti in Franciescho"; Carte strozz., ser. II, 15 (accounts of Mano di Cambio Petrucci), fol. 17. Direct payment of laborers by the administration precluded the possibility that a foreman might take a percentage of their wages for himself; cf. B. Pullan, "Wage-earners and the Venetian Economy, 1550–1630," *Economic History Review*, 2d ser., 16 (1964), 407–26 (reprinted in Pullan, ed., *Crisis and Change in the Venetian Economy in the Sixteenth and Seventeenth Centuries* [London, 1968], pp. 146–74).

Apollonio di Giovanni, illustration from the *Aeneid* (detail), mid-fifteenth century.

spese). On the rare job where the employer offered work "at our expense" (*a nostre spese*), the worker's pay was docked, usually about 2 soldi. Moreover, whenever a wage payment is recorded at a lower than normal rate, invariably the explanation is added that the worker also got his expenses (*le spese*—that is, a meal). "Ebbe da noi le spese," explained the accountant at San Bartolomeo on the few occasions when he registered a wage payment of 2 soldi less than the normal wage for the manual laborers who worked for the monastery for about seventeen months in 1482 and 1483.

An incident at Santo Spirito—one of the few moments of drama recorded in any of these building accounts—verifies the idea that the worker was responsible for his food and tools. When, on 5 July 1496, the unskilled laborer Niccolò di Luca fell from a crane and died, the head stonecutter, taking it upon himself to return Niccolò's personal possessions to the widow, collected all those things that presumably an unskilled laborer carried to work—a purse, a pouch for his meat, a bottle, a small mallet, and a box. A considerable quantity of money was found in the purse—5 gold florins and lb.1 s.0 d.6 in small coin—which apparently they at first suspected could hardly have been Niccolò's, although it, too, was eventually returned to the widow. Niccolò di Luca had come to work that morning with his own tool and lunch box—not to mention what may well have been his life's savings.[14]

Some employers occasionally provided wine for their workers' refreshment and rewarded them with a meal on the completion of major phases of construction, although the examples strike one for the exceptionality of the custom. Institutions were likely to be more generous than private persons. At the Innocenti workers were dined with bread, cheese, and wine after the kitchen was vaulted; with a meal after the arms of the silk guild were mounted; with meat, bread, fruit, and four flasks of wine after the cloister was paved; with bread, meat, and half a barrel of wine after the wells in the garden were dug; and with another meal after the church was vaulted. At Santo Spirito refreshments were provided on the last day before Lent as well as on certain occasions marking the progress of construction. Wine was passed out when the first column of the church interior arrived, again when it was erected, and everytime thereafter when other columns were erected; when the last column was in place, the stonecarvers were treated to a large loaf of bread, three pounds of sausage, and four flasks of wine. In June 1481, in celebration of the completion of the tribune, the head stonecarver and the foreman were given the not inconsiderable sum of 25 lire, presumably to be spent for the workers.[15] In November 1487, on the completion and roofing of the front part of the church, they each got another 25 lire, and the sand dealer Fruosino di Berto got 20 lire as a "tip for good service."[16] Santa Trinita in 1361 was another site where the foreman, and sometimes other workers, were repeatedly (but not regularly) treated to something to eat.[17]

To judge from surviving accounts, private employers were less disposed to offer time out for such festivities. Strozzi offered food and drink, but only to selected workers, when the portals of his palace were arched and on several other occasions—not often in the fifteen years of construction. Other patrician employers were no more generous. Only once at the Da Gagliano palace, when the vaults of the loggia were completed, did the workers get something to eat (cheese, maccheroni, and fruit); there is no evidence in the accounts of the Bartolini palace that the workers there got anything at all. We can only assume that the tradition, still venerated in Florence, of offering a meal to

[14] "Richordo questo dì 5 di luglio [1496] Nicchолò di Lucha manovale chade d'in su l'antena e morì di fatto, e nella sua scharsella chavai, presente Antonio Sacchi, fi. cinque larghi d'oro e lb. una s. - d. 6, e' quali gli darò a cchi s'apartengho' quando saprò a chi gli ò a dare. Di poi per Salvi d'Andrea scharpelatore . . . manda' a ccha' sua e' sopradetti denari e la scharsella e uno charnaiuolo e una martellina e una sua chassa e uno fiascho, e disse detto Salvi gli consengniò alla donna sua"; S. Spirito 128, fol. 236v.

[15] "per bene andate e beveraggio pe' 'l compimento della tribuna"; ibid., fol. 159r.

[16] "per ben servito e mancia"; ibid., fol. 91v.

[17] ASF, Conv. sopp. LXXXIX (S. Trinita), 45 (journal, 1359–62), fols. 27v, 30r, 31v, 36v, 39r.

the workers on completion of major construction goes back as far as the Renaissance.

Although an account book, by its nature a document of cash and credit operations between employer and employee, can hardly be expected to reflect the extra-monetary nature of employer generosity, accounting practice assures us that the money an employer paid out for the sake of his workers did not go much beyond their contracted wages. Any payment for incidentals such as wine or food is almost always recorded within the autonomous accounting system set up for building expenses; such an expense is not usually charged to any of the other activities of the employer, thereby losing its identity as a building expense in his overall financial operations, be it a household or a monastery. With accounts as complete as some of these Florentine building records—for example, the Strozzi accounts—we can therefore be as confident about what the employer did not pay for as we are about what he did pay for. The market with its monetary nexus had thoroughly organized the ranks of labor, and employer largesse characteristic of a more informal and paternalistic regime was not to be expected. Incidents like the procession of construction workers at the Strozzi palace accompanying the body of their deceased employer to the church do not in themselves tell us much about the bonds between employer and employees—the commandeering of workers for participation in such ceremonies, after all, was not unknown even in early industrial America.

Construction work had its hazards, like the fatal fall of the laborer Niccolò di Luca at Santo Spirito, but few such incidents have been recorded. Several writers commented on the dramatic death of the waller Mariotto di Papi da Balatro, who was struck by lightning while clambering over the roof of the Strozzi palace to check on some leaks during a storm, but this accident did not occur during the normal course of a mason's work.[18] The perils of the craft, however, have been recorded by a waller himself, Gaspare Nadi (1418–1504) of Bologna, in a diary that spans a working life of half a century. In 1448 he fell while working on a mill at Prato and was laid up fifty-two days; in 1456 he (along with his apprentice) fell on the job, hurting his head, chest, arms, and legs; in 1472 he almost killed himself in a fall down a chimney and was able to return to work only after two months at home and 8 ducats in doctors' fees; in 1474 he fell once again—this time thirty-five feet—and although the fall itself did no harm, he got a bad kick from an ass he disturbed on hitting the ground; and, finally, in 1497 Nadi—now seventy-nine years old and still working—was struck on the leg by a piece of wood and was incapacitated for three weeks.[19]

[18] Goldthwaite, "Strozzi Palace," pp. 150–51.

[19] *Diario bolognese*, ed. C. Ricci and B. Della Lega (Bologna, 1886) pp. 26, 39, 73, 81, 221–22.

It was perhaps because of the hazards in this line of work that the Maestri alone of all the minor guilds tried so hard to open a hospital (the guild in Perugia also tried to get one built in the fifteenth century). The only concrete benefit of guild membership, however, was the lowering, or elimination, of guild fees for older nonworking members. Masons' guilds elsewhere in Italy provided help to the family of a deceased member and required his fellow members to attend the funeral. As already observed, this was one of the few standard guild provisions regarding fraternal relations among members that is found also in the statutes of Florentine guilds, and presumably the Maestri were no exception. In general, however, the construction worker could not count on many fringe benefits from any quarter. We have seen how Strozzi docked the wages of the smith Cioli for the few days he was sick. The cathedral opera—being naturally more charitable, or simply doing what was expected of it under the circumstances—paid some compensation to workers who were hurt in on-the-job accidents (in 1362 and 1365), but when it retired its foreman of eighteen years' standing, Giovanni d'Ambrogio, now too old and enfeebled to do his job, it paid him up to the end of the month—and that was all.[20]

Instability of employment was one of the basic conditions of life for construction workers in the pre-industrial period (and it is today). The seasonal nature of aggregate demand for labor dampened the worker's prospect of finding full-time employment the year around, and job opportunities depended entirely on the needs of individual projects. The guild did not organize the search for jobs, and there were no large labor contractors, not to mention construction companies, to offer reasonable stability of employment to the small gangs of assistants needed for their work, and not many unskilled laborers could have hoped to find this kind of durable association. The worker picked up jobs as he could find them, going from one site to another; most must have done a good deal of floating about, very much on their own in keeping themselves above the survival level.

In many cities in Europe workers of various kinds found jobs in central gathering places where every day employers came seeking labors. Such markets can be documented for cloth workers in the Flemish towns and for construction workers in Antwerp, Paris, and Milan. Workers who came to such a labor market were subject to discipline and regulation to avoid outbursts of violence, and employers were likely to work in collusion to minimize competition. The location of the labor market in a specific place, in other words, had the effect of subjecting wages to collective restraints. In seventeenth-century Milan the dozen or so masons who dominated the guild and controlled the largest construction projects had private understandings among themselves about the going wage in the labor market. In Florence, however, no such craft

[20] C. Guasti, *Santa Maria del Fiore* (Florence, 1887), pp. 149, 163–64, 318–19.

or guild elite can be identified, nor is anything known about a fixed location for the labor market.[21] The fourteenth-century statutes of the masons' guild in Bologna mention the guild hall as the clearing place where guildsmen found jobs, but unskilled laborers were explicitly forbidden to mill around outside the hall looking for work.

Employment was all the more fluid because most projects employed only a few men for a short duration, often no more than several weeks. A large institution like the hospital of Santa Maria Nuova that repeatedly, over decades, had recourse to the same workers for its building and maintenance needs did not offer any of them regular employment. Nor did the size of the project guarantee long-term employment. Inadequate financing often precluded the organization of work on a large scale; many major projects went forward by spurts of building activity followed by complete cessation of all operations, with the result that construction dragged on for many years. At the hospital of San Paolo the cloister complex designed by Michelozzo took almost half a century to build, and although one small team of wallers and stonecutters was used almost exclusively (and they were succeeded by their sons), the periods of employment were brief and far between.[22] At those sites where building activity proceeded steadily there were always moments when additional labor had to be taken on for brief periods of heavy work. It was a rare construction project, in short, whose employment rosters, for one reason or another, did not fluctuate considerably.

Workers came and went even at the largest sites where building activity was maintained at a steady pace and where, therefore, one might expect to find more stable employment conditions. An example is the Strozzi palace project. Here sluggish financing was no problem, since at the outset Filippo Strozzi had more than enough money to pay for the entire enterprise, all of it in cash stacked away at home; and there certainly can be no doubt about his determination to get his new palace erected as fast as possible. In fact, during the early years of construction the labor force of two or three dozen men was maintained at a constant level, and was not even subject to the usual seasonal fluctuation. The Strozzi project, in other words, must have offered the best employment opportunities available in the industry; that Strozzi himself considered the labor contracts a fairly permanent arrangement is strongly

[21] Geremek, *Salariat*, p. 128; idem, "Les Salariés et le salariat dans les villes au cours du bas moyen âge," *Proceedings of the Third International Congress of Economic History (Munich, 1965)* (Paris, 1968), pt. 1, 564 (see also the same author's "I salari e il salariato nelle città del Basso Medio Evo," *Rivista storica italiana*, 78 [1966], 376–78); Domenico Sella, *Salari e lavoro nell'edilizia lombarda durante il secolo XVII* (Pavia, 1968), pp. 33–37; H. van der Wee, *The Growth of the Antwerp Market and the European Economy (Fourteenth-Sixteenth Centuries)* (The Hague, 1963), II, 135–36.

[22] Herein, p. 384.

Apollonio di Giovanni, scenes from the *Aeneid* (detail), mid-fifteenth-century cassone panel.

suggested by the accounting procedures of maintaining individual worker's accounts, even those for unskilled laborers, in the ledgers. Further on in this chapter it is suggested that Strozzi's workers accepted wages that were at the lower level of the current scale because this project offered them more secure employment possibilities. Nevertheless, despite a relatively high level of employment, the labor force at the Strozzi palace underwent considerable turnover, with few workers staying on the job for more than several months. Of the eighty-nine stonecutters who show up on the rosters in the first 600 workdays—about two and a half years—one-quarter worked fewer than 50 days, one-half worked fewer than 100 days, and only two men worked more than 450 days. Throughout the first decade of work only about half a dozen stonecutters appear as regular employees. The fluidity of employment was even greater among unskilled laborers. Some of this fluidity is to be explained by short-term fluctuations in the demand for labor causing brief but periodic reductions of the work force when many workers were laid-off never to return—and, without any advantage of seniority in the determination of their wages, they had no reason to return if in the meantime they found work elsewhere. In the course of these fluctuations attrition of the original work force took its toll and the rosters gradually filled up with new men. Apparently work at the Strozzi palace was organized on the assumption that the availability of labor could be taken for granted. Management's employment policy depended entirely on the demands of the enterprise, and the enterprise was not planned to maintain a certain level of employment for a fixed labor force.[23]

With seasonal cycles of employment, the ad hoc mobilization of labor, the small scale and short duration of typical projects, and the sporadic nature of input at the larger ones, the construction industry could offer nothing like full-time employment for most workers. The workers must have regarded their employment prospects as being at the mercy of a somewhat capricious fortune. This is not to say that the worker who disappears from our view once he passes off the employment rolls of one project was not able to find work at another site, but high mobility in employment meant that the chances of his being periodically unemployed, at least for brief periods, were high.

Notwithstanding these odds against finding steady employment, there is no reason to believe that instability in employment was not partly a matter of the worker's volition. Accustomed to insecurity in employment, and without the prospect of wage increments for seniority, he lacked an incentive to tie himself to one job. For all the relative mobility in Florentine society a worker could hardly have had much hope for improving his economic and social status, especially if he was unskilled; nor was he driven by all those pressures that have converted modern man into a perpetual and insatiable consumer. The urban wage-laborer of the pre-industrial period must have expected little out of life beyond survival; in a period of relatively high wages, like that in Florence during most of the fifteenth century, what he could most afford was time off from hard work. As long as his workday might have been, he lived under a casual regime that gave him—perhaps despite himself—even more days off in a year than the one hundred or so official holidays. He probably thought himself fortunate if he could work as many as 200 days—or if he could get by without working any more than that.

Whether employed for a daily wage or for piece rates, most men worked very much on their own incentive. However oppressive the economic system

[23] Goldthwaite, "Strozzi Palace," pp. 173–77. For other specific examples of rapid turnover in employment rolls see: Corinne Beutler, "Bâtiment et salaires: un chantier à Saint-Germain-des-Prés de 1644 à 1646," *Annales, E.S.C.*, 26 (1971), 486 (where out of a total of 480 men employed, fewer than 5 percent worked more than a year); Baulant, "Salaire," p. 472; Maurice Meusnier, "Fondation et construction d'un collège universitaire au XIVe siècle: le Collège de Périgord à Toulouse," *Annales du Midi*, 63 (1951), 220; C. Manca, *Il libro di conti di Miquel Ça-Rovira* (Padua, 1969), pp. 97–105 (where in almost eleven months of construction on fortifications in late fourteenth-century Cagliari, 25 of the 34 unskilled laborers employed worked five days or less); Jean-Pierre Sosson, *Les Travaux publics de la ville de Bruges, XIVe–XVe siècles* (Brussels, 1977), pp. 238–55 (where of the 107 masons employed by the city of Bruges over twenty-nine weeks in 1480–81, more than one-third worked less than one week and over three-fourths worked no more than a month, and during thirty-five weeks of work in 1481–82, more than one-half worked fewer than five weeks).

may have been in its more brutal moments, it did not generate an attitude toward work like that conditioned by the rigors of the later industrial system. The revolutionary achievement of the industrial revolution was the attraction of workers into the wage-labor market and into factories; the conditioning of them to the discipline of steady, organized, and punctual work; and—not least important in their psychological transformation—the arousal of the expectation of security in employment.[24]

Money and Credit

The Florentine worker, both as a seller of his labor and as a buyer of life's necessities, was drawn into a market economy that was thoroughly monetized. Money itself, therefore, was a central fact of his life, and we would like to know more about how monetary problems affected him. Florence, like other Italian cities, had a bimetallic monetary system with the gold florin of international fame on the one hand and a variety of silver- and copper-based coins (*monete di piccioli*) serving the local market on the other. These petty coins had a variety of names, but for purposes of the written record of cash transactions their values were subsumed under the money of account known as the libra, or lira, with its vigesimal division and duodecimal subdivision into soldi and denari. The value of the lira was pegged to the gold florin. The problem of ascertaining values of payments in the local market made in silver- and copper-based coin but quoted in terms of the money of account is complicated, first, by the debasement of coin throughout the fourteenth, fifteenth, and early sixteenth centuries, and, secondly, by the steady depreciation of the lira with respect to the gold florin—two developments, obviously not unrelated, that resulted in an accumulation of a bewildering variety of coins in the local market and the appreciation of the gold florin. The lira-florin ratio rose more or less steadily from 3½:1 to 7:1 over the century and a half from 1350 to 1500 (see Appendix 1). It seems that there were two minimally different rates of exchange between the lira and the florin posted daily—an "official" rate at the mint and a commercial rate at the counter (*tavola*) of the bankers' guild; but nothing is yet known about the process by which these rates were determined.[25] Nor is it altogether clear why the

[24] J. R. Hicks, *The Theory of Wages* (London, 1963), p. 231; Christopher Hill, "Pottage for Freeborn Englishmen: Attitudes to Wage Labour in the Sixteenth and Seventeenth Centuries," in *Socialism, Capitalism and Economic Growth*, ed. C. H. Feinstein (Cambridge, 1967), pp. 338–50.

[25] Monetary policy with respect to debasement in the period of the republic is little understood; slightly differing explanations of it can be found in Carlo Cipolla, "Studi di storia della moneta. I: Movimenti dei cambi in Italia dal secolo XIII al XV," *Studi nelle scienze giuridiche e sociali* (University of Pavia), 29 (1948), 139; and

commune followed a policy of debasement and depreciation. In part it was a matter of the supply of silver: the international market for silver exerted pressures that were well beyond the power of the commune to resist, while the accelerating pace of economic activity in the fifteenth century demanded an ever-increasing supply of money.

Above the confusion of this monetary situation the gold florin reigned supreme. Because the gold florin was the international medium of exchange par excellence, the city and its merchants had a vested interest in maintaining its purity, and its appreciation in the local market could be taken for granted. These qualities of the florin have aroused the suspicion that there were strong social overtones to the bimetallic monetary system. The merchant pegged his finances securely to gold, while the little man confined to the local market presumably paid the cost of debasement. From the Black Death to the beginning of the sixteenth century the wages of the working man (which, as is noted later, remained nominally stable) lost their value in gold by about 50 percent. This appreciation of the florin offered obvious advantages to international merchants and bankers who wanted to cut expenses in the local market, but whether the fall in the cost of labor significantly improved the competitive nature of Florentine goods (above all, cloths) to the merchants' advantage abroad, and whether the merchants' profits made abroad kept pace with the increased buying power of the florin at home, cannot at present be known for lack of any comparative statistics on prices and wages as quoted in gold on the international market. An investor with a capital of 5,000 florins in 1500 was twice as wealthy as an ancestor 150 years earlier with the same amount, at least with respect to the labor such a sum could buy in the local market; but there is no way to compare these values in their respective international

---

Raymond de Roover, *The Rise and Decline of the Medici Bank, 1397–1494* (Cambridge, Mass., 1963), p. 32. A general discussion of money, legislation, debasements, silver content, and problems of the mint in sixteenth-century Florence is included in Giuseppe Parenti, *Prime ricerche sulla rivoluzione dei prezzi a Firenze* (Florence, 1939), pp. 38–71 (with a critical review of the older literature). See also M. Bernocchi, *La monetazione fiorentina dell'età dello splendore: indagine attorno al fiorino aureo* (*dispensa*, University of Florence, 1966–67), and the same author's paper to be published in the acts of the VII Settimana di Studio (1975) of the Istituto internazionale di storia economica "Francesco Datini" di Prato. Bernocchi has also written a history of the Florentine monetary system during the period of the republic: *Le monete della Repubblica fiorentina*, 4 vols. (Florence, 1974–78). The credit devices described in this chapter must have gone a long way toward making up for any lack of specie; cf. John Day, "The Great Bullion Famine of the Fifteenth Century," *Past and Present*, No. 79 (1978), pp. 3–54. The evidence for shortage of specie in Florence, however, is not impressive: David Herlihy and Christiane Klapisch-Zuber, *Les Toscans et leurs familles: une étude du catasto florentin de 1427* (Paris, 1978), p. 260, can cite only one reference to the problem in the city; see also herein, ch. 1.

Biagio d'Antonio (?), The Archangels Michael, Raphael, and Gabriel (detail), late fifteenth century.

markets so that something might be concluded about how the changing lira-florin ratio affected merchants and bankers who did business abroad and brought their profits home in gold.

How much debasement cost the working man is not easy to say. Although he saw the gold value of his wages erode, his real wages—that is, his ability to provide himself with life's essentials—were not necessarily affected. The discussion further on demonstrates, on the contrary, how high his standard of living was during much of this time. The gold florin moved irreversibly along its upward course without much apparent effect on the internal market of basic consumer goods needed by the laborer because his food and probably much of his clothing were produced within Florentine territory, where prices were determined more by local supply and demand than by the international market in gold and silver (at least until the later sixteenth century, when the city became increasingly dependent on grain imports from outside Tuscany).

The effects of debasement on the working man could hardly have been anything but negative, but the conclusion is not to be foredrawn that there was anything very dramatic about the situation. In the short run, during the lifetime of any one worker, this depreciation did not significantly reduce the buying power of his money, although it introduced another element of uncertainty in the market where he was trying to make a living. Moreover, because debasement was an occasional event, though it followed a steady trend, there was time for readjustment to new issues—and the common man may not have been so badly informed as we might at first suspect. Florence had long been an international commercial and banking center, and Florentines were familiar with many diverse foreign coins that circulated freely throughout the city. Moneychangers and speculators were numerous and ever-ready to effect exchanges of all kinds.[26] Furthermore, the strong business traditions of the city engendered considerable public confidence in private records of debits and credits, and (as the ensuing discussion of money and credit shows) the universal acceptance of the terminology and values of a money of account somewhat stabilized the monetary situation in the marketplace.

It would, at any rate be wrong to see the working man as always on the losing side of the changing lira-florin ratio. Long-term contracts were likely to be expressed in florins, and how he came out depended on his position in the contract. For example, rents contracted for periods longer than six months were generally (though not always) quoted in florins; therefore, as tenant, the worker found his rent slowly increased during a lease. On the other hand, the mason who contracted to do work for a flat fee had the advantage if the price was quoted in florins, as it usually was for large contracts. Likewise, if he worked for a salary stipulated in florins he in fact enjoyed a built-in raise to the extent that the florin appreciated in value with respect to the lira. Cronaca, who went to work at the Strozzi palace as head stonecutter for a salary of 36 florins, saw the value of that salary go up from 234 lire in 1492 to 252 lire in 1502, an increase of 8 percent in ten years.

For the working man the florin was more than just a value he knew in the abstract through contractual agreements. Gold, far from being confined by the social barriers scholars have erected around it,[27] commonly passed through the hands of ordinary men. Building accounts are replete with evidence that

[26] There is much useful information on this activity in Charles M. de La Roncière, *Un Changeur florentin du Trecento: Lippo di Fede del Sega (1285 env.–1363 env.)* (Paris, 1973), although this study is marred by the author's failure to recognize that his subject was merely a private speculator, not a money-changer in any official sense of that term.

[27] Carlo M. Cipolla, *Money, Prices, and Civilization in the Mediterranean World* (New York, 1967), ch. 3; idem, "Storia dei prezzi e storia della moneta: considerazioni critiche," *L'industria* (1950), pp. 604–6.

working men, even unskilled laborers, were frequently paid in gold. Many an entry is explicit that payment was in florins "in cash," and when an entry states only that the worker was paid a "gold florin," the exact nature of the payment can often be confirmed by a cross-reference to the cash account. Moreover, in many entries on cash accounts where payment in lire has a value corresponding only to the current exchange value of the florin (or multiples thereof) and not to any value corresponding to the time or work being paid for, we can guess that the worker had in fact been given a florin by his employer to be credited toward what was owed him. This happens with great regularity on workers' accounts in the Strozzi ledgers, and examples can be found in most other building accounts.

The accounts of the sculptor Maso di Bartolomeo provide many examples of an artisan himself paying his workers in gold. Maso's shop book records some payments of *fiorini larghi* to his employees in instances when the value did not correspond to any particular charge. The entry itself generally includes the current exchange value in lire (the money in which his accounts are kept) and sometimes specifies that the payment was in cash. On these occasions Maso, like Strozzi and a host of other employers, paid a gold florin toward what he owed a worker because he simply found it easier to hand out one small but valuable coin (which was sure to be accepted) than to be bothered with the weight and bulk of a lot of petty cash. Many workers at the Strozzi palace were paid in gold (in amounts that did not correspond to exact sums owed them, as calculated in lire), and some of the men paid in gold by Maso were as far down the social and economic scale as carters. Evidence for the working man's handling of gold also comes from the other side of the ledger, on accounts recording payment of their bills: for example, Giovanni di Mariano, the foreman at Santo Spirito, almost always used florins to pay his rent over a period of eight years, from 1477 to 1484 (and since his long-term contract stipulated the rent in lire and his landlord kept the record of his payments in lire, it cannot be inferred that Giovanni was required to pay in gold). In short, gold circulated well beyond the confines of the upper classes.[28]

Nor were the sophisticated banking practices that made this city one of the great financial capitals of Europe unfamiliar to the working man. Private banks were highly developed institutions in Florence and were so widely used

[28] The account book of Maso di Bartolomeo is cited herein, p. 234. Giovanni di Mariano's rental account is in a book of the Spedale del Porcellana: ASF, S. Paolo 433, fols. 7v–8r. In eight years he made only three payments through the Mellini bank, where he received his wages for work at Santo Spirito; and only four payments were made in kind—in cane, probably from his own land. Evidence for the handling of gold by masons in the mid-fourteenth century, of the same sort used here, is presented by Charles M. de La Roncière, *Florence, centre économique régional au XIV*[e] *siècle* (Aix-en-Provence, 1976), pp. 310–13.

for monetary transactions within the city that they touched the lives of many people. One banking instrument familiar to working men was the check, or at least an early form of it. Propertied men (and institutions) might well pay men who worked for them with drafts drawn on their current accounts with bankers. This is the way the workers who remodeled the main chapel at San Martino a Gangalandi in 1473 were paid. This project, carried out in accordance with the testament of Leon Battista Alberti, was financed by the executors in Rome, who assigned credits from the estate to an account at the bank of Guglielmo Rucellai and Matteo Baroncelli in Florence; their agent in Florence, Niccolò Corbizzi, who organized the construction project, paid the contracting waller, carpenter, and stonecutter out of the account by written orders (*polizze*) to the bank of Rucellai and Baroncelli.[29] Another instance of this practice of using a current account for payment of expenses for construction can be documented from the banker's side of the operation in a ledger of Bindaccio di Michele de' Cerchi, where an account kept in the name of Filippo di Giovanni Corbizzi (1476) for work on the house of Giovanni Zampini shows many payments to the entire range of craftsmen in the building trades.[30] And, just to round out the documentation for the payment of craftsmen through a bank, in yet another instance—this one involving not a craftsman in the building trades but nevertheless one of their class, a man who cleaned cesspools—one order of payment itself survives, a small slip of paper tucked away in the banker's ledger where it can still be checked against the entry on the principal's account.[31] This kind of instrument was frequently used for payment to men in the building trades. The carpenter Francesco di Nanni, for example, probably did not give it a second thought when he was paid, in 1462, for work on the chapel of the Annunziata with an order marked with the banker's sign of no one less than Piero de' Medici himself.[32]

For most working men involvement in the banking system probably went no further than the banker's office where they cashed in such drafts. Not many workers were likely to have deposit accounts with bankers. Unfortunately, despite the survival of an extraordinarily large number of account

[29] Marco Spallanzani, "L'abside dell'Alberti a San Martino a Gangalandi: nota di storia economica," *Flor. Mitt.*, 19 (1975), 245.

[30] During the six months the Cerchi ledger was open, April to September 1476, Corbizzi made three deposits and ordered forty-nine payments totaling f.87 s.4 d.9; ASF, Archivio Cerchi 316, fols. 27, 34, 35, 36.

[31] The order of payment is published by Marco Spallanzani, "A Note on Florentine Banking in the Renaissance: Orders of Payment and Cheques," *JEEcH*, 7 (1978), 156–57.

[32] Ss. Annunziata 844, fol. 49. For example: "Ane auti a dì 7 d'agosto lb. dieci s. sedici, cioè lb.10 s.16; portò e' detto da maestro Stephano di Servi per più opere à messo a fare l'armario degli arienti come la poliza mandata e segnata per mano di Piero [di Cosimo]; portò Guardino a detto maestro Stephano"; and other entries in this account indicate that Francesco carried the *polizze* to the bank.

books in Florence, only two ledgers have turned up for a local bank of deposit (Cerchi's, cited previously, and Francesco Datini's), and without such records there can be no comprehensive view of the social range of depositors in the Florentine banking system. Many private account books of third parties have entries registering transactions effected by artisans through banks, but the relation of these men to the banks is rarely spelled out. For example, on the property accounts of the hospital of San Paolo, which rented a house to Benozzo Gozzoli, the credits assigned to him for his rent came from the bank of Giovanni Rucellai, but the entries explain nothing about the specific arrangement the painter had with the bank.[33]

Although they may not have had the normal deposit accounts with bankers, artisans of substantial economic stature who were continually working for the rich could allow their credits to accumulate on their employers' books and then use their employers as agents for the payment of debts. A credit account thereby functioned as a current account from which credits could be assigned to third parties through the appropriate instruments. This practice of offsetting was facilitated in Florence by the widespread habit of keeping accounts and by the general confidence of the public at large in private written records of debits and credits. It was, therefore, relatively easy to make payments to third parties through the agency of one's debtors. Once again, the accounts of the sculptor Maso di Bartolomeo provide evidence that even an artisan could perform this function. The owner of the house rented by Maso used her credits with him to pay her bills: instead of collecting the rent in regular installments, she irregularly drew on her credit with Maso to make assignments through him to her creditors, in effect using that account as a current account and Maso as her banker.[34]

This system of offsetting could be extended even further by the transfer and retransfer of credits through the hands of several parties. In the incident cited previously where the Badia paid Mino da Fiesole by giving him wool, the wool was actually consigned to the sculptor by a dealer who rented his

[33] Benozzo rented the house from the hospital beginning on 1 November 1458 for 51 lire a year. The record of rental payments from him continues until May 1476; but given the nature of the hospital's surviving accounts, that record consists only of actual cash payments (twice made by his father, twice by the Medici bank, and from September 1473 on by the painter Piero di Lorenzo). Benozzo must have paid most of the rent (over 80 percent) in credit transfers. For his payments, see ASF, S. Paolo 744, fols. 26v, 44r, 45r; 745, fols. 16v, 21v, 56r; 746, fols. 2r, 3r, 8v, 18v, 33v, 37r, 38r, 39r, 40r, 42r, 45r, 46r. The house was identified as "delle case del Gherofano"; presumably it was one of several residences that constituted a complex of that name ("tutta l'abitatione chiamata Gherofano," "le case del Gherofano") adjacent to the hospital and bought by it in 1460 for its expanding building program; ibid., 741, fol. 17r; 978, fol. 34r. The first block of Via Palazzuolo going from Via de' Fossi was later called Via del Garofano.

[34] BNF, Baldovinetti 70, fol. 39v.

Sassetta, The patrician John having had a vision of Mary has a church built where he found a plan in the snow (from Altarpiece of the Madonna della Neve), 1430–32.

shop from the Badia and who got his rental account credited accordingly. In a sense such an operation is nothing more than barter, but its complexity required careful recordkeeping, presumably by the other parties as well as by the Badia. A more complicated instance of this kind of transfer, where the flow of credit was not circular within one set of books, as at the Badia, occurs in a payment made in 1452 by the administrators of the Santissima Annunziata to the heir of the stonecutter Meo di Bitocchio for work he had done for the monastery. Instead of cash payment Meo's heir wanted the credit transferred to a bishop (for what reason we do not know), but the bishop wanted his credit assigned to another party, who in turn ordered payment in his name to the Rucellai bank, who forthwith sent an agent to collect the money from the monastery.[35] Here, in other words, was a giro operation repeated four times before cash actually changed hands. Although the operation might appear less complex if the exact relation between these various parties were known, presumably each had to keep his own record at the point where the transaction affected his debit-credit relations. Whether these transfers were effected by written orders is not known, although we can be reasonably sure that if they were endorsement was not practiced. The giro operation, however, has yet to be studied in the context of Florentine credit instruments.[36]

Building accounts show that construction workers, too, used credits with their employers to pay their bills. Antonio di Marco, a laborer at San Bartolomeo, had his rent in 1489 paid by the mason for whom he worked;[37] another laborer, Luca di Pippo, had his wage account at Santo Spirito from 1477 to 1479 debited for a number of expenses—for his rent; for wood purchased for him; for payment of his daughter's dowry; for payment to a smith; and for the purchases of wheat, a bed, and a hat for his son Niccolò (who may have been the laborer who fell to his death in 1496).[38]

Luca di Pippo, incidentally, was one of many laborers whose accounts in this book of building expenses at Santo Spirito seem to record not their wages but only small credits withheld by the purveyor from their wages and drawn on later by them. Although the book is kept in lire, the amounts withheld are almost always equivalent to one or more florins, and the changes in the amounts withheld in lire correspond exactly to changes in the current rate of exchange between the lira and the florin—an indication of "thinking" in florins. When payments were finally made to the laborer, they were usually in cash (Luca di Pippo's account was an exception in this respect, and it was usually overdrawn). The account, in other words, seems to have functioned as a safekeeping account for the worker.

Occasionally the purveyor at Santo Spirito extended credit to some of his workers by paying their debts and then taking deductions from their wages until the monastery was paid back, but obviously only regular employees—like the head stonecutter himself, Salvi d'Andrea, who borrowed 80 lire to

[35] This document comes from the accounts of Ss. Annunziata 689, fol. 146r (account called "Questa è l'uscita del mese di luglio 1452. . . ."): "A opera e fabrica dell'acrescimenti della chiesa di sopra f. sei larghi, pagamo a l'erede di Meo di Bitochio, posto de' dare a libro nero segnato P c. 90; sono per parte di magior somma de' avere di manifattura delle priete di concio del detto lavorio à llavorate; e per lui pagamo a frate Mariano v[escov]o [Salvini of Cortona], e per lui a Paolo da Castangniuolo, e per lui a Giovanni Rucellai e compagni; portò Tomaso di Giovanni sta co' lloro di suo [sic] mano, al quaderno di chi porta c. 16, e a libre . . . lb.28 s.16.

[36] See the remarks of Federigo Melis, "Sulla non-astrattezza dei titoli di credito del basso medioevo," in *Studi in onore di Giuseppe Chiarelli* (Milan, 1974), IV, 3687–3701.

[37] S. Miniato 58, fol. 81v (rental account, S. Bartolomeo).

[38] S. Spirito 127, fol. 165.

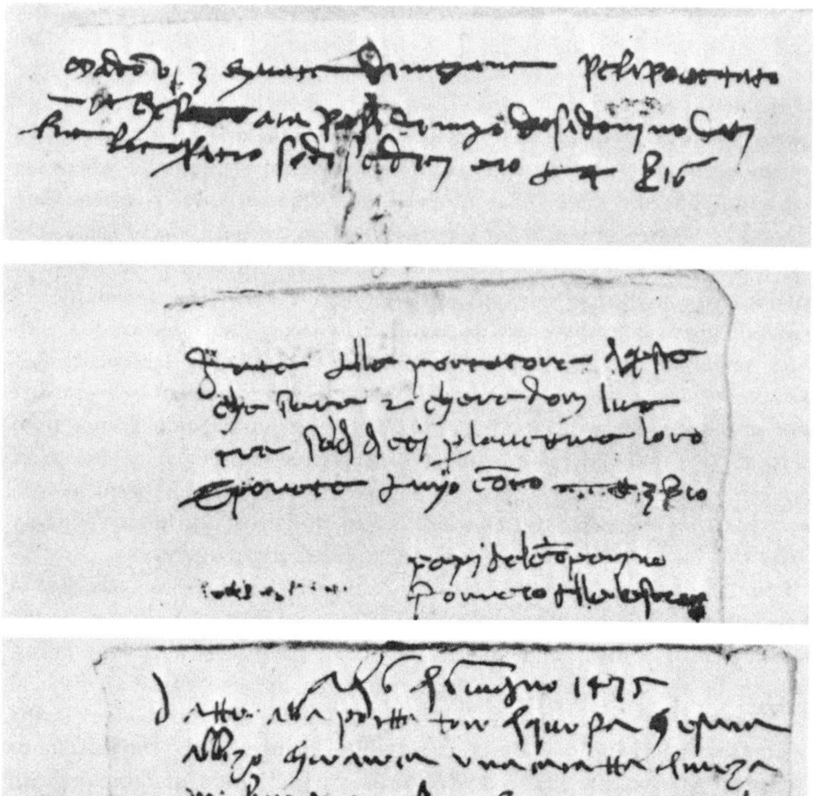

A kilnman's orders of payment, 1475. The handwriting pictured on p. 311 originally appeared on the reverse of the orders of payment shown above. The kilnman's account in his client's account book, showing the entries corresponding to these orders, is reproduced on p. 312.

Madonvi 3 charate di mezane pe' l'apporttatore, che sarà Papi Dovizo da San Donino, dati lire lire (?) quatro sodi sedici, cio' lb. 4 s.16.

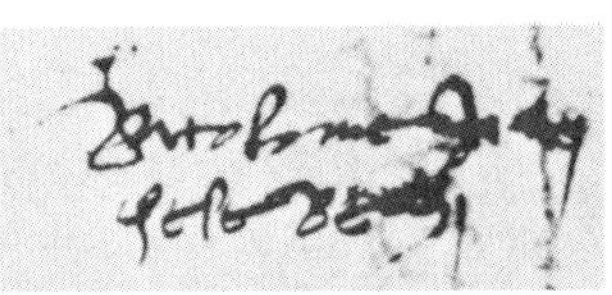

Batolome di Michele Bechi

Date all'aportatore di questo, che sarà 2 charadori, lire tre soldi dieci, per la vettura loro, e ponete a mio conto lb.3 s.10

Papi del Compagno
fornaio alla Lastra

Bartolomeo di Michele Bechi
in Firenze

A dì 6 di giugno 1475
Datte all'aporttatore di questa che sarà Albizo, che areca una caratta di mezane, lire una e s. quidici, e ponette a mio contto.

Piapi del Conpiagno
fornaciaio a lLastra

Bartolomeo tintore
in Firenze

A dì 7 di giugno 1475
Datte all'aportatore di questa che sarà Albizo, caradore, areca di mezane, lire una e s.15 e ponette a mio conto.

Piapi del Conpiagno
fornaciaio a lLastra

Bartolomeo tintiore
in Firenze

Papi di Nani del Chonpanno, fornaciaio, de' dare, a dì 5 di magio 1475, lb. quattro s. sedici, per lui a Papi da San Donino, charadore, portò contanti	lb. 4 s.16 d.-
E, a dì 6 di magio 1475, f. uno largo, portò e' detto contanti	lb. 5 s.12 d.-
E, a dì 11 di detto, lb.3 s.10, per lui a 'Ntonio di Michele da San Donino, charadore	lb. 3 s.10 d.-
E, a dì 13 di magio 1475, f. dua larghi, portò contanti	lb. 11 s. 4 d.-
E, a dì 7 di gugnio 1475, lb. tre s.10, per lui a Churado, charadore, portò contanti; rechò 2 charatte di mezane	lb. 3 s.10 d.-
[Total] lb.28.12	
E, a dì 10 di detto, f. uno largo, portò contanti	lb. 5 s.15 d.-
[Total] lb.34. 7	

Entries in account book of recipient of a kilnman's orders of payments. The first entry on the account corresponds to the first order of payment on pp. 310–11; the third entry, to the second order; and the fifth entry, to the third and fourth orders.

get his daughter married—were eligible for this kind of credit.[39] As a rule, however, construction workers did not get such extensions of credit (overdrafts) for future labor. Unlike piece-rate workers in the putting out system of the cloth industry, where capital goods exchanged hands, they were not bound to their employers in a way that reduced them to perpetual indebtedness.

In a society where so many transactions side-tracked the handling of money, the written record was all important. Orders of payments, promissory notes, tallies, and receipts—not to mention account books—were all part of the paperwork necessitated by an exchange system that had developed well beyond the cash nexus. The use of these instruments extended down to the lowest levels of artisan society, perhaps even into the ranks of the unskilled.

[39] S. Spirito 128, fols. 65r and 97v.

Some of the few examples of this paperwork that survive have been cited on these pages—for example, the books of receipts kept by the quarrier Antonio di Bernardo and the orders of payment written by the kilnman Papi del Compagno at Lastra directing his customer Bartolomeo Becchi in Florence to pay the carter who delivered bricks. Papi's orders (illustration, p. 310) have the essential characteristics of the instrument used in the banking system—the format of small slips of paper with the addressee's name on one side and the dated and signed order on the other, and the formal language of stock phrases like "pay to the bearer" and "post my account." Nothing could better illustrate how widely diffused these practices were even among artisans. It is noteworthy, incidentally, that Becchi made most of his payments to the carter in gold (see illustration on p. 312).

The declarations of wealth artisans made for the Catasto officials in 1427 are replete with long lists of their debtors and creditors. The stonecutter Andrea di Nofri di Romolo submitted a list of debtors with 130 names on it and added a single comprehensive value for 90 more whose debts, being under 4 lire each (1 florin), were too small to itemize; the total value was 2,178 lire. In the financial report on his kiln operation Benedetto da Terrarossa listed total credits of 2,219 lire with 104 men.[40] Evidence like this shows how extensively men were woven into a web of credit relations, how importantly credit figured in their lives, and how good they were at keeping the record straight.

These practices presuppose knowledge of reading, writing, and arithmetic, as well as a certain habit of mind about maintaining records, and it can be taken for granted that the practice of keeping accounts was widespread among craftsmen in the building trades. Carpenters and stonecutters, along with a host of other artisans, were forever hauling accounts before the court of the Mercanzia as primary evidence in cases involving debt settlement. When Giuliano da Maiano made his claims on the confiscated property of Jacopo Pazzi for unpaid work, he was able to show the authorities eight pages in his account book where the charges were itemized.[41] In 1474 the consuls of the Maestri brought a judgment against a mason for having falsified certain writings in his notebook (*quadernuccio*),[42] and it was to prevent the misuse of records that the sixteenth rubric of the Fabbricanti statutes forbade guildsmen to buy or accept as payment anyone else's documents of any kind, including accounts. Some examples of the accounts of kilnmen and stonecutters have already been cited on these pages, and dozens of others survive for many artisans of humble status from outside the building trades. These accounts are unique among working-class materials that survive in European

[40] These tax documents are cited herein, p. 195 n. 48 and p. 278 n. 66.

[41] Arnoldo Moscato, *Il Palazzo Pazzi a Firenze* (Rome, 1963), pp. 70–72.

[42] Maestri 3, fol. 25r.

archives, and that fact is not to be explained by their chance survival in this one city alone. Some of these accounts, like the book of Maso di Bartolomeo, reveal a systematic approach to accounting that in some respects is superior to the way many great London merchants kept their books as late as the seventeenth century.

Nothing in this discussion of money, instruments of payment, and record-keeping should be construed to suggest that the Florentine working man found himself in a marketplace where relations were highly impersonal and formal. On the contrary, the system of payment was loose and flexible, and its elasticity depended on the personal relation between employer and worker, between creditor and debtor. Take, for instance, the relation between the foreman at Santo Spirito, Giovanni di Mariano, a waller we have now encountered many times, and his employer on the one hand and his landlord on the other (both of whose accounts, fortunately, survive). Giovanni was paid regularly (usually every Saturday), but since he was often paid in florins for work evaluated in lire, his week's wage had to be rounded off on the accounts to the nearest florin, leaving either him or his employer with a credit balance. Likewise, when he used florins (as he almost always did) to pay his rent, which was stated in lire, a balance remained one way or the other. Moreover, despite any stipulation in his rental contract fixing the times when rent was due, he made his payments with no regularity. As noted, Giovanni was paid by the banker of the building committee of Santo Spirito; on the several occasions the bank paid his rent for him, or paid someone else for something he had purchased, this was done not through a current account in his name on the bank's books but by order to the bank from his paymaster at the monastery. This evidence could be much enlarged with examples from accounts of other workers. The picture emerges of a marketplace where, for all the ways its procedures anticipated later developments, personal relations were not yet left out of the cash nexus.[43]

The purely economic effects of the use of the written record for the extension of credit are not easy to assess. To what extent, for instance, did these practices contribute to an expansion of consumption credit? They surely expanded the money supply and thereby took up some of the slack caused by lack of coin, which has been cited as one of the reasons for debasement throughout this period. But did the practice of offsetting in fact arise out of shortages of coin? And was it a step back to barter and therefore economically retrogressive? Offsetting was common among merchants everywhere in

[43] The record of Giovanni's rental account is cited in note 28 to this chapter; the payments through the Mellini bank correspond to debit entries on his salary account, S. Spirito 127, fols. 164, 209, 231. An identical transaction for the purchase of a picture is noted herein, p. 404 note 12.

Piero di Cosimo, Building of a palace, ca. 1500

Europe, who often balanced their accounts with one another through exchange of goods rather than actual payment, and barter clearance of this kind was also used extensively both by peasants in rural areas only slightly penetrated by the market and by townsmen in growing commercial centers where money was often scarce.[44] The extent of the paperwork involved in these Florentine operations, however, suggests considerable sophistication in the use of substitutes for cash. But what in fact is to be said about the convenience, or inconvenience, of a practice that on the one hand might have saved men the trouble of handling money but on the other required them to take the time and care to keep their private records straight?

The Florentine habit of keeping written track of financial dealings meant that the monetary system was dominated by money of account. Moneys of account were common throughout Europe in the later Middle Ages, but perhaps nowhere more than in Florence was such a money widely accepted by the population for ordinary transactions, because nowhere else was there such a marked habit of keeping written accounts. Florentines used the lira for evaluating most of their transactions in the local market. Entries on accounts rarely indicate the actual coin used for payment (unless it was made in gold florins), and when money is mentioned in the popular vernacular literature of the period, even if the handling of specie is involved, it is usually expressed in values of the money of account. In other words, the Florentine's sense of

[44] The problem in rural France is alluded to by Jean Meuvret, "Circuits d'échanges et travail rural dans la France du XVIIe siècle," in his *Etudes d'histoire économique: recueil d'articles* (Paris, 1971) pp. 139–50 (now translated in Peter Earle, ed., *Essays in European Economic History, 1500–1800* [Oxford, 1974], pp. 89–99). Offsetting also figures in the discussion of consumption credit by van der Wee, *Antwerp*, II, 333–36.

value was conditioned by a system that in effect separated the measure of value from the medium of exchange.

To the extent that prices were tied to certain expressions of nominal value only, such as the lira with its soldo and denaro *di piccioli*, the existence of a ghost money (as Carlo Cipolla has labeled moneys of account) assured considerable stability in a monetary system racked by debasement as well as by fluctuation of the ratio between the two components of its bimetallic structure.[45] Prices for those goods most essential to working men and produced locally, such as food, clothing, and even housing, were likely to be less affected by debasement so long as the force of tradition backed up the acceptance of these nominal values (for instance, in the quotation of daily wage rates) and so long as the relation between the local economy and international markets was not changed by debasement. For men so dependent on the cash nexus the general acceptance of a money of account counteracted the uncertainties of evaluating coin subject to debasement as well as to clipping and the normal deterioration of wear. The monetary ghost, ironically, removed much of the uneasiness about an unstable reality.

By the fifteenth century in Florence it would have required only the slightest conjuration to bring off the materialization of this ghost in the form of paper money. In fact, this almost happened in a plan of about 1430 conceived by a modest silk merchant (significantly, not a banker), Andrea di Francesco Arnoldi, to reduce the extraordinary pressures of debt payment on the city's budget by monetizing the state debt. He proposed that the commune convert its debt into current accounts in the names of its creditors and then set up shop as an obligatory bank of deposit through which payment of all private debts above 10 florins was to be effected by mere transfer on its books. The monetary system, in other words, would have been one gigantic bookkeeping operation—offsetting writ large—centering on what in effect would have been a public bank. We know nothing about the reaction to Arnoldi's proposal—the paperwork alone probably boggled the mind of the city fathers, even as familiar as all Florentines were with complex accounting systems—but was he not merely being logical in tightening up and centralizing a system already in use, one so widely diffused throughout the society that it reached into the lives of even the working classes? Arnoldi explicitly recognized that his payment system would involve artisans, and indeed his 10-florin minimum was not above the level of the operations of many of them. After all, as he himself explained, "money and bank credit (*schritura di banco*) are both the same thing as cash." Otherwise, he asked, how could a city with no more than 150,000 florins in coin on hand at any

[45] The inertia of prices tied to certain nominal expressions has been remarked by Parenti, *Ricerche*, p. 43 (with reference to older discussions); and Marc Bloch, *Esquisse d'une histoire monétaire de l'Europe* (Paris, 1954), pp. 48–49.

one time ever have paid out the 4,000,000 florins that the war with Lucca alone had cost?[46]

Wage Rates

The graph on the following page lays out the history of wages in the Florentine construction industry from the early fourteenth to the late sixteenth centuries. The bottom cycle presents the annual averages of daily wages for unskilled and skilled workers; the second cycle presents the price of wheat, which, as the staple in the diet of the time, can be considered an index to the cost of living; the third cycle represents the real wages of unskilled workers by converting the wage rate into the wheat it could buy; and finally, the fourth cycle plots the eleven-year moving average of "wages-in-wheat" according to an index scale, with 100 as the highest level wages reached in the period from 1441 to 1451. Perhaps the most notable feature the graph reveals about the working man's situation is the lack of correspondence between the movements of wages and prices, or, in other words, the fluctuation of real wages. For the moment, however, the behavior of nominal wages alone is the matter at hand. One is struck by the fluctuation of annual averages and by certain features of the trend—the sharp rise after 1348, the long period of stability, and the absence of falls.

Data for the construction of a wage series are normally taken from one employer over a long period—usually an institution such as a hospital or monastery that was continually spending for ongoing property maintenance—because this kind of source assures a certain uniformity in employment conditions that facilitates the discovery of trends and the making of indexes. No less important than the long-term view that generalizes wages, however, is the reality of the specific moment in the working man's life when he had to face the fact of varying wage rates. To better reflect that situation the data sample used here was built from both the wages paid over a century by one institution, the hospital of Santa Maria Nuova, and the wages from dozens of other construction projects, some of long and some of short duration, some of major proportions employing dozens of workers and some consisting of barely more than the maintenance work done by a single mason and his helper. Moreover, the data that went into the annual averages on the graph represent different seasons during the year and all kinds of laborers within the two general categories of skilled and unskilled. The data sample for

[46] Carte strozz., ser. II, 86, insert 23. The document is discussed (but not published) by Raymond de Roover, "A Florence: un projet de monétisation de la dette publique au XVe siècle," in *Histoire économique du monde méditerranéen, 1450–1650. Mélanges en l'honneur de Fernand Braudel*, I (Toulouse, 1973), 511–19.

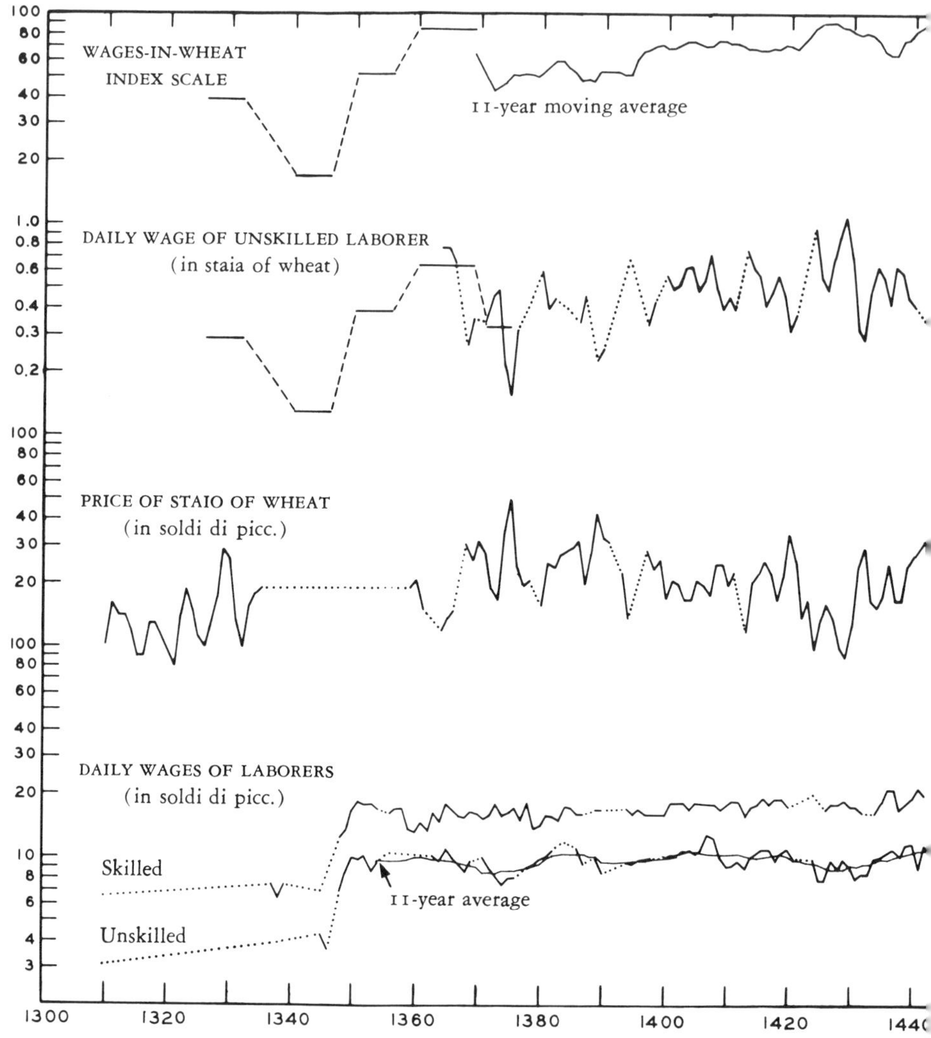

Workers' nominal and real wages, 1310–1599

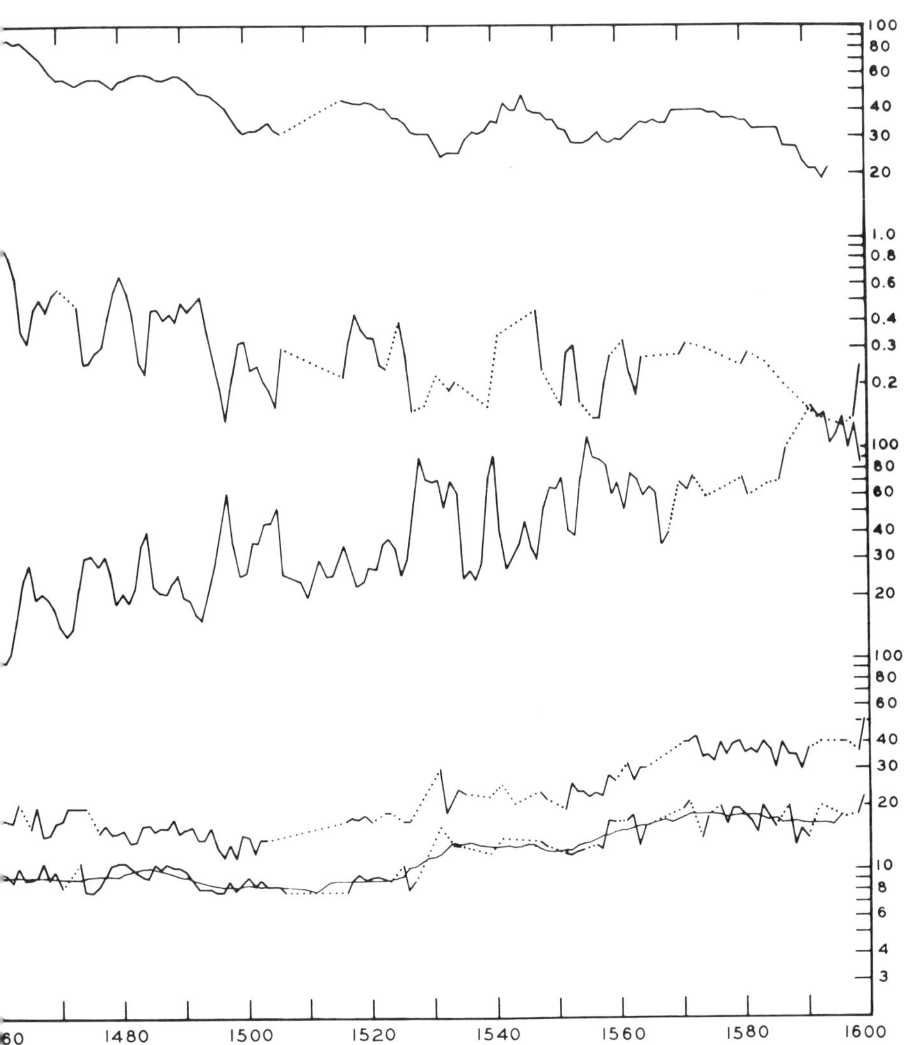

SOURCES: Wages: see Appendix 3. Grain prices: Richard A. Goldthwaite, "I prezzi del grano a Firenze dal XIV al XVI secolo," *Quaderni storici,* No. 28 (April 1975), 5–36. The data represented by the horizontal lines at the beginning of the graphs on the upper cycles come from Charles de La Roncière, "Pauvres et pauvreté à Florence au XIVe siècle," in *Etudes sur l'histoire de la pauvreté (Moyen Age–XVIe siècle),* ed. Michael Mollat (Paris, 1974), II, 680–81. The unfortunate grouping of de La Roncière's data in periods of irregular duration leads to some distortion; pre-1348 wages probably fell somewhere between the two levels indicated by his interpretation.

each year, therefore, reflects the widest possible range of wages, and the considerable fluctuation of annual averages is a result of this deliberate lack of uniformity of the variables in the data from one year to another. The annual fluctuation, in other words, can be regarded as defining the brackets within which wage rates varied according to the different qualifications of the worker, or the different conditions of employment, or both. These variables in the labor market are as important to the understanding of working-class life as is the trend of a highly generalized wage rate.[47]

The wide range of skills one expects to find among construction workers obviously accounts for much of the diversity in the schedule of their wages. Unfortunately, the Florentine terminology used to identify workers by skill is generic or vague, and records of wages do not often specify what is being paid for. Skilled laborers are identified only as stonecutters, wallers, and woodworkers, although within these groupings skills and the nature of work done could vary considerably. Nevertheless, the range of wages within each of these general categories is so nearly identical to the range in the others that in the preparation of the graph for an analysis of the history of wages all workers have been lumped together, with a distinction made only between skilled workers and unskilled laborers.

The category of stonecutters comprised a great variety of skills and a correspondingly wide range of rates. Occasionally the terms *lastricatori, lastraiuoli*, and *cavaiuoli* turn up in records of payments, but they refer more to the nature of the work being paid for at the time rather than to a distinct group of skilled workers, and the same men can sometimes be found at other projects (and sometimes at the same project) identified simply as *scalpellini.* This term was used for all men who worked in stone. For instance, on the Strozzi accounts the term embraces the entire range of workers involved in the process of the preparation of stone, from hewers and scapplers at the quarries to carvers of decoration, including the foreman in charge of them all, the architect himself. This lack of precision in the terminology of the documents precludes identification of the specific nature of work being paid for, and it is therefore impossible to draw up a schedule of rates for different tasks or skills. At the lower ranges stonecutters earned little more than manual laborers; at the upper range they earned more or less the average for all skilled workers as indicated in the graph. The most skilled, those who were self-employed artisans working on contract to carve decorative details in stone, were usually paid a task fee rather than a wage rate. However, at the Strozzi palace project, when several of the carvers who did the intricate details on the interior corbels (for which they were paid a flat fee) worked

[47] The particular problems of collecting this data and constructing the series are taken up in App. 3 herein, and all references in the following discussion to construction sites from which wage data come are also found there.

instead for daily wages in some other capacity, they earned no more than the standard rate being paid to stonecutters who were working on the rustication of the facade. In the fifteenth century wages of a stonecutter rarely went as high as 20 soldi. Only if he were a foreman would he be likely to earn more.

Wallers generally earned higher wages than stonecutters, probably because, unlike the latter, who worked alone, wallers were responsible for the small labor gangs who assisted them in laying bricks or stones. Although they did not often pay these gangs out of their own pockets, they had supervisory responsibilities over them. On large projects where several wallers worked under the direction of a foreman, each had his own gang. The wage rate for wallers varied less than that for stonecutters, usually falling between 16 and 20 soldi.

The daily wage rate for a mason—either stonecutter or waller—rarely went above 20 soldi in the fifteenth century. A few foremen, most of whom were wallers, were paid a somewhat higher rate. In the early stages of the construction of the Innocenti, where most work was contracted out, several wallers were occasionally employed for short periods at rates higher than 20 soldi. In 1422 Antonio di Domenico earned 25 soldi, and in 1424 the stoneworker Betto d'Antonio and the waller Antonio di Geri both got 24 soldi, while two of Antonio di Geri's assistants got 21 soldi. Twenty years later Betto d'Antonio earned 25 soldi at San Lorenzo. In a later stage of construction at the orphanage, when much of the work force was employed for wages, Antonio di Geri and his brother Francesco each earned 25 soldi, but their successors after 1444 were not paid as much. At the Santissima Annunziata, Zanobi d'Antonio was paid from 22 to 24 soldi for supervising the construction of the chapel of the Annunziata in the years 1461, 1462, and 1463; Nencio di Lapo was paid 22 soldi for building a dormitory during the same years. The foreman at the much bigger project of Santo Spirito, Giovanni di Mariano, was paid at a rate that fluctuated between 22 and 24 soldi, although he was also given some assurance of a minimum income to compensate for lack of work during slack periods. The 30 soldi paid to Giuliano da Sangallo at Santa Maria delle Carceri at Prato was an unusually high rate, earned perhaps because of the distance of the site from Florence.

On large projects, where the foreman had considerable responsibilities, he was likely to be put on an annual salary rather than a daily wage, and his earnings were generally somewhat higher than the maximum possible under the normal schedule of daily wage rates. At the Strozzi palace, one of the largest projects in the city, the foreman Mariotto di Papi da Balatro (a waller) earned a salary of 60 florins; the highest salary in the industry during the fifteenth century (as quoted in florins) was probably the 100 florins paid to Brunelleschi as foreman at the cathedral. In lire each of these salaries translates into a daily rate of 30 to 35 soldi.

Unskilled laborers were differentiated to the extent that rates could vary several soldi (or as much as 30 percent over the lowest rate) at the same project. For instance, on the employment rosters at Santo Spirito from 1477 to 1481 one manual laborer worker for 13 soldi, several worked for 12 soldi, and the rest were paid between 10 and 11 soldi. Any differences in their tasks, however, is disguised by the single term *manovale*, meaning *manual laborer*, with which all these workers are identified on the accounts.[48] The only workers whose wages fall below the minimum level of that of manual laborers were boys, sons, assistants, and apprentices directly dependent on a master mason. On his accounts the employer generally recorded the wages of these invariably anonymous dependents as part of a comprehensive figure paid the master, whereas he always carefully isolated, in separate entries or even in separate accounts, the wages of independent manual laborers who worked in the master's crew.

It is worth remarking on the absence of women and children (except those attached to masons) from the employment rosters of construction projects in Florence. Elsewhere in Europe women occasionally turn up in construction crews, some applying plaster and cement but most carrying small loads of materials and rubble and otherwise assisting men. Their wages were considerably lower than men's, sometimes by 50 percent. Women worked in many trades in the Middle Ages, probably doing more work than we suspect behind the doors of their husbands' shops, and only bad times were likely to drive them to the hard labor required on a construction site.[49]

The wage rates of construction workers throughout Europe at the time were subject to a seasonal fluctuation between summer highs and winter lows. The difference in fifteenth-century Florence amounted usually to a drop of about 10 to 20 percent in the winter. If we take the harsh view that the duration of a workday was fixed by the sun, the lower winter rate can be explained by a shorter workday. Relative demand, however, was probably the major variable, for construction activity then, as now, was subject to considerable seasonal variation. Winter was more likely to be a slack season

[48] Compare the more precise nomenclature and variations in rates of English and Lyonnais workers: Douglas Knoop and G. P. Jones, *The Medieval Mason* (Manchester, 1933), p. 71; and Richard Gascon, *Grand Commerce et vie urbaine au XVIe siècle: Lyon et ses marchands (environs de 1520–environs de 1580)* (Paris, 1971), II, 749–53.

[49] General comments on women in medieval construction are made by Jean Gimpel, *The Cathedral Builders* (New York-London, 1961), pp. 77–78; and specific instances of their employment in various periods are documented in L. F. Salzman, *Building in England Down to 1540* (Oxford, 1967), p. 71; Meusnier, "Collège de Périgord," p. 219; Pierre Goubert, *Beauvais et le Beauvaisis de 1600 à 1730* (Paris, 1960), I, 563; B. W. van der Kloot Meyburg, "Eenige gegevens over de Hollandsche steenindustrie in de zeventiende eeuw," *Economisch-Historisch Jaarboek*, 11 (1925), 87. Gino Corti has informed me of the presence of women among the laborers on the Siena cathedral before the Black Death: Opera Metropolitana, Siena: Uscita 328 and 330.

Sodoma, St. Benedict undertakes the building of twelve monasteries, 1505–1508.

because inclement weather conditions slowed down the pace of building and because work might be suspended to permit settling of new foundations. An overall view of a year's activity in the construction industry would show aggregate employment figures much lower in the winter, although on some large projects, like the Strozzi palace, employment rosters do not always conform to this pattern. The competing demand for labor from the agricultural sector is another explanation often advanced for higher wage rates in the summer, but seasonal migration was probably less important in a large urban center like Florence. So far as we know, no other major industry in the city had a regularly fluctuating pattern of demand for labor that could have affected the market for construction workers in such a way as to explain seasonal variations in their wages.

The seasonal fluctuation of wage rates did not occur precisely at the same

TABLE 6
Official Daily Wage Rates

Year	Laborers		Wallers		Foremen	
	summer	winter	summer	winter	summer	winter
1324	s. 3½	s.3	s. 7	s. 6		
1344	s. 4½	s.4	s.10	s. 8		
1415	s. 8½	s.6	s.18	s.12		
1534	s.11	s.9	s.18	s.15	s.24	s.20

SOURCES: Niccolò Rodolico, *Il popolo minuto: note di storia fiorentina (1343–1378)* (Florence, 1968), p. 106; *Statuta (1415)*, II, 211; ASF, Carte strozz., ser. I, no. 37, document no. 15 (copy of deliberations of the *riformatori*, 25 September 1534; another copy is located in ASF, Misc. rep. 2, no. 50).

time each year. Although legislation variably fixed dates between mid-September and early November for the beginning of the winter-rate period and between the end of January and the end of March for the beginning of the summer-rate period (see table 6), in practice, according to actual wage payments in the building accounts, the seasonal break came with no regularity and could vary from one year to another. Sometimes the seasonal adjustment was made in two or three stages, and there were years when wages were not subject to any seasonal adjustments at all.[50]

Although in a labor market without tight regulations wages fall within a range determined by the relation between demand and supply, slight variations can occur from job to job according to particular conditions of employment and the employer's disposition to spend. With as little precise indication as the Florentine documents provide about the nature of the work being paid for, it is next to impossible to compare wages of skilled workers on different construction sites in order to determine the extent to which employer attitude itself was a variable. Unskilled laborers formed a much more homogeneous group with respect to the nature of their work, and yet much of the fluctuation of their average wage rate is explained by the difference in rates from one job to another. Such differences can be attributed to the attitudes of employers trying to get what they want under the competitive conditions of the market, but we cannot extrapolate their attitudes from series of wage data alone. In 1477 most laborers at Santo Spirito were paid 11 soldi (10 soldi in the winter), whereas at the same time on a much smaller job at the hospital of San Paolo they were paid only 9 soldi (8 soldi in the winter). Perhaps, with a major project on their hands, the building committee of Santo Spirito was willing to pay a bit more to be assured of a steady and reliable

[50] Cf. Beutler, "Saint-Germain-des-Prés," p. 499; Meusnier, "Collège de Périgord," p. 220; Yves Durand, "Recherches sur les salaires des maçons à Paris au XVIIIe siècle," *Revue d'histoire économique et sociale*, 44 (1966), 473–76.

work force for what was a fairly complex building operation. In fact, in June 1481, with the laying-off of many workers accompanying the temporary slowdown of operations after the completion of the tribune, the committee called for a lowering of the wages of remaining laborers by 1 soldo (and of stonecutters' wages by 2 soldi).[51] Even though the committee's deliberations on the matter do not reveal any explanation, we can imagine that there is some significance to the timing of their decision about wages. Most of the highest wages in our sample come from construction sites of major projects like Santo Spirito and coincide with moments of considerable building activity.

A higher wage was not the only thing an employer could throw into the bargain: for the worker, security in his job could conceivably outweigh more money. Job security is certainly what Filippo Strozzi had to offer at his palace project, where from the beginning there were no problems of financing, no question about the patron's determination to see the job through, and no doubt that construction would last a good many years. Hardly any other site in the city could have offered the worker a better opportunity for full-time employment. Does this explain, then, why wages were at the bottom of the current wage scale? When Strozzi opened the palace workshop in 1489 he began hiring labor at 10 soldi, but within a year the rates dropped to 8 or 9 soldi, where they remained for the next five years. During these same years workers at some other sites were earning at least a soldo more—for instance, at the Spedale del Ceppo, which throughout the 1490s sporadically undertook construction on a series of houses planned as rental properties, and at Santo Spirito, where by 1489 rates had for several years been back at their earlier level of 10 and 11 soldi. Perhaps Strozzi offered lower wages because, unlike the Ceppo officials, he could promise more than just occasional work, or because he did not need the kind of work force required at Santo Spirito, where erection of columns and construction of complex vaulting in the church interior probably made it highly desirable to have a fairly constant force of reliable workers who were familiar with procedures. Construction at the palace was of a much simpler kind than that at Santo Spirito, and with its huge and efficiently organized workshop, Strozzi may have worried less about turnover in the workers' ranks than about mantenance of a high enough level of employment to keep up the pace of construction. And yet, the accounting system indicates that Strozzi considered at least his side of the bargain to be more than a temporary commitment: the ledgers include individual accounts even for manual laborers, whereas one would have expected these men to lose their identity in the accounting process by which the detailed information of their day-by-day employment recorded in journals and scrapbooks was summarized for transferral to collective accounts in the ledgers of permanent record.

[51] S. Spirito 128, fol. 52v.

Granacci, Joseph presents his family to the pharaoh
(detail), 1515–1518.

By following one man's working career as he passed from one site to another it might be possible to observe the extent to which his wages fluctuated as a result of what was required of him, whom he worked for, and what time of year it was; but to turn up this kind of information requires more patience and good fortune than the research that went into this study can claim. The best we can do is to reconstruct from some of the longer series of accounts the employment history of those workers who continually reappear on the rosters of a single project over a period of several years. The longest series used here comes from the expenditures of the hospital of Santa Maria Nuova for the upkeep of its buildings and, occasionally, for new construction of greater magnitude. The hospital did not have a permanent full-time maintenance staff, but it generally had recourse to the same men whenever work had to be done. The carpenter Boncienni, for example, worked regularly, but not full time, from 1363 to 1375 at a single rate, winter and summer, for various jobs ranging from working on walls to constructing beds for patients. Other workers, however, saw their wages subject to adjustments, although the reason—whether different work or different conditions imposed by the employer—is not often stated. One mason, Leonardo, worked for 20 soldi in September 1352; the next year he worked for 18 soldi, then 17 soldi; and in 1354 he earned only 16 soldi for work on the wall in the garden. The rates paid another mason, Pacino, from 1354 to 1356 varied from 16 to 18 soldi outside of any seasonal adjustments. Yet another mason, Duccio, was paid 16 and 18 soldi in 1357 and 1358, mostly for work on roofs, but over the next two years, until 1360, his pay sometimes fell as low as 10 soldi. Duccio's work, however, was not always related to his trade: one entry explains that the payment was made on the basis of two rates—16 soldi for making repairs on windows and a roof, and 14 soldi for helping in making wine (some of which he might also have received as part of his compensation). Another longtime employee of the hospital, the carpenter Maso di Corso, worked on an annual salary of 36 florins in 1412; later, from 1426 to 1441, he worked off and on at general maintenance, usually for a day rate of 18 soldi but twice for 20 soldi—once from mid-1429 to the end of 1431, when there was major construction on the chapter room and the spice shop (he was not foreman, however), and again briefly in 1438. The foreman for the building of the hospital's church of Sant'Egidio, Duccio di Feo, who was paid 20 soldi from the end of 1418 through 1420, during the last summer was given several extra lump-sum payments representing a retroactive raise (*rincrescimenti*) of 5 soldi a day.[52]

The hospital of Santa Maria Nuova, in short, did not follow a constant wage policy even for its regular workers. Wages at all levels throughout the century-long series from this institution fluctuate within the full range of the entire wage sample. The hospital administration presumably adjusted wages to the exigencies of the moment[53]—as did the builder of the new facade of San Lorenzo (in 1517), whose accountant recorded paying unskilled laborers at the rates of 8, 9, and 10 soldi "secondo li tempi."[54]

Dramatic events outside the labor market could have a temporary impact on wages. The Strozzi palace was one site where the employer can be observed readjusting wages as the result of political disturbances. The palace was not half completed when the city was thrown into the greatest turmoil it had experienced since the Ciompi revolt more than a century earlier. Late in 1494, while forces of the French king threatened to besiege the city, tensions within, already at the breaking point as a result of the general exasperation with the incompetent son and heir of Lorenzo il Magnifico, finally broke out in the revolution that brought Savonarola to power; his religious demogoguery and the ensuing political complications in foreign affairs kept the city unsettled for the next four years, until the self-styled prophet was burned at the stake in 1498. Life could not have been too easy for the working man during these years, when the price of bread rose higher and higher

[52] S. M. Nuova 5049, fols. 79v, 93r, 105r, 112r.

[53] The same observation can be made about the long series of wage data Parenti compiled from another institution in the sixteenth century, the convent of Santa Maria Regina Coeli. Other prosopographical studies of masons employed at Santa Maria Nuova in the mid-fourteenth century are presented by de La Roncière, *Florence*, pp. 310–32 (who fails to recognize, however, that the wage data are mostly for irregular maintenance work, not steady employment).

[54] C. Milanesi, "Due ricevute autografe di Michelangiolo Buonarroti ed un conto di spese concernenti alla facciata di San Lorenzo," *Giornale storico degli archivi toscani*, 1 (1857), 51–52.

and employment opportunities in construction were threatened by owners' second thoughts about the wisdom of such investments in times of trouble. In this situation employment at the Strozzi palace project, which proceeded as if to defy in its very massiveness the onslaught of ephemeral political events, must have looked even better. Strozzi, in any case, cut wages. The unskilled laborer, already working at a lower rate, lost the 1-soldo summer increment, and for the next few years worked at the single rate of 8 soldi the year around. Skilled workers were hit harder: stonecutters who had been earning 15 or 16 soldi (13 or 14 soldi, winter rate), including some who had seniority going back four years, had their wages slashed to 12 soldi (11 soldi, winter rate), and for a few the cut was even more drastic. Not until after the Savonarola episode did the rates for both categories climb back to the pre-1494 levels. Yet, during these same years rates at smaller projects elsewhere in the city seem not to have been affected. In 1497 the officials of the Spedale del Ceppo, resuming construction in a program to expand their rental properties, paid 10 soldi for laborers; and in 1499 Alamanno d'Averardo Salviati paid 9 and 10 soldi for work on his palace. In other words, the relation between supply and demand was not upset enough during these years of political instability to have much effect on the general level of wages, despite a temporary rise in the cost of living as a result of higher grain prices. The Strozzi were able to lower rates below their already low level presumably because in uncertain times favorable conditions of employment temporarily outweighed any demand for higher wages.

The range of rates paid unskilled workers, although not wide, remained nevertheless constant throughout the entire period from the mid-fourteenth until well into the sixteenth century. The diversity within that range is partly explained by different attitudes of employers about what they were prepared to offer. How much of a bargaining process went into the final decision can hardly be known. Workers were not so vociferous as to get their view of the matter registered in the documents. Vasari tells us what Brunelleschi did when at one point his workers insisted on higher wages: he simply dismissed them and began taking on Lombards; when the original workers found themselves without work and were ready to come back, he offered them even lower wages than before. Vasari is not a reliable authority as a historian, especially for facts of this kind in a time so long before his own; but, for all his fabrications, this anecdote assumes a situation in the labor market that he, in the mid-sixteenth century, took for granted.[55]

The relatively free play of these variables in the determination of wage rates suggests that the labor market operated without external controls. It was not unusual in medieval Europe for guilds and governments to formulate a wage-control policy, generally for the purpose of establishing a maximum,

[55] *Le opere di Giorgio Vasari*, ed. Gaetano Milanesi (Florence, 1973), II, 359–60.

although official rates do not usually correspond to wages actually paid.[56] In Florence little evidence has come to light that indicates much of an effort was ever made to fix wages. Indeed, in the mid-fifteenth century Saint Antonino, the bishop of the city and an economic thinker who wrote about the free operation of the market, roundly condemned price fixing along with monopoly practices.[57] The guild of building craftsmen had no policy on wages; when the commune did legislate to set the cost of labor (table 6), it was responding to specific problems of the moment rather than executing a policy of continuing market supervision. The legislation of 1344 revising the 1324 rates was designed (according to Niccolò Rodolico) for the benefit of the workers at a particularly difficult time for them, when price behavior was erratic; the price-fixing regulations of 1534 were set as a result of chaotic market conditions, probably connected to the political situation after the final demise of the republic. Legislation of this kind, however, is not frequent, and the official rate schedules correspond only in a general way to the reality of the labor market. Moreover, controls were limited to unskilled laborers and wallers, whose level of skill was fairly uniform. Apparently no attempt was ever made to bring order to the welter of skills among stonecutters by devising a detailed rate schedule for different kinds of work. In the extensive price-fixing regulations of 1534, which ranged over much of the retail market, the officials listed a variety of products of the stonecutter's craft but renounced any attempt to set prices on them because of their diversity in size and quality.

After everything is said about the variables that went into the determination of the wage rate, we are still left with the fundamental fact of the remarkable stability of nominal wages over a period of almost two centuries, a situation reflected in the eleven-year moving average on the graph. Controls are clearly not the explanation. To the extent that demand and supply determined the price of labor the stability of wages was a result of a general equilibrium of those forces. The loss of population in the fourteenth century and the slowness of its recovery kept supply tight, while the increased activity in construction in the fifteenth century stimulated demand. There is scattered evidence for at least temporary scarcity of labor, and on one occasion the shortage is de-

[56] Geremek, "Salariés," pp. 565–66; van der Wee, *Antwerp*, I, 46; Pullan, "Wage-earners," p. 172; Gascon, *Lyon*, II, 750–53. It has been said that beginning in the fourteenth century wage legislation in Italy generally became more protective of workers; Melchiorre Roberti, "Il contratto di lavoro negli statuti medioevali," *Rivista internazionale di scienze sociali*, 40 (1932), 44–47.

[57] Gino Barbieri, "Le forze del lavoro e della produzione nella 'Summa' di Sant'Antonino da Firenze," *Economia e storia*, 7 (1960), 17–18; Raymond de Roover, "Labour Conditions in Florence around 1400: Theory, Policy and Reality," in *Florentine Studies: Politics and Society in Renaissance Florence*, ed. Nicolai Rubinstein (London, 1968), p. 285.

Monument to a mule employed on the construction of the Pitti Palace, late sixteenth century.

scribed (by Landucci, in 1490) as specifically affecting masons and building materials.[58] Foreigners—Lombards above all, but also Germans and Poles—turn up on employment rosters of construction projects, and, as noted, the guild erected no barriers to keep them out or to restrict their activities.

Given the general equilibrium between supply and demand, wages must also have been kept within certain bounds by a strong sense of what a normal day's wages ought to be. On the demand side the need for labor in construction must have been elastic. Most men undertook building for prestige, not for profit, and at any time the supply of labor began to tighten in a way that put pressure on wages, the employer could reduce his operation or close it down altogether rather than offer higher wages to keep construction going. On the supply side, labor was fluid, since few men had anything like regular employment, and a reserve pool of labor that cushioned the market was built into the structure of work. On the one hand, employers took labor for granted in the planning and organization of work; on the other, the worker himself did not have the hope, if even the desire, for regular employment. In a situation where labor was neither highly organized by employers nor mobilized

[58] *Diario fiorentino dal 1450 al 1516*, ed. Iodoco Del Badia (Florence, 1883), p. 59; cf. Federigo Melis, *Documenti per la storia economica dei secoli XIII–XVI* (Florence, 1972), p. 108 (for labor shortages in Prato ca. 1400).

within its own ranks by an insistence on regular employment, demand and supply could fluctuate without upsetting the traditionally accepted notion of what a wage ought to be. Not even the temporary political disorders as serious as the Ciompi revolt in 1378 and the French invasion of 1494 and 1495 broke the inertia of custom.

That wages remained high despite the fall in prices at the end of the fourteenth century may be less a function of supply and demand than a natural resistance of nominal wages to downward movements. In the well-known study of seven centuries of English wages only once before the twentieth century do nominal wages drop. But if wages survive price falls, they are also slow to respond to price rises.[59] On the Florentine series, although prices began their rise at the end of the fifteenth century, nominal wages did not begin to make an upward adjustment to the rise in prices until toward the mid-sixteenth century, by which time price inflation had completed its slow but steady erosion of all that extra purchasing power gained after the disruption of the Black Death.

Real Wages

Most wage studies of the pre-industrial worker have been limited to construction workers because building accounts exist in far greater abundance than employment records of any other industry and because the daily wage rate that was the basis of the construction worker's contract provides a standard of value that can be used for comparisons through time and across space. These studies, however, are not explicit about the validity of using wages in construction as an index to economic conditions among industrial workers in general. It cannot be taken for granted that the skilled construction worker was typical. The very fact that he was a day laborer set him apart from most other skilled workers in an industrial system where measure and value were more important than time in the determination of wages. He may have worked a shorter workday, since construction required hard labor even from the most skilled, and he may have earned at a higher rate since he did not have steady employment. Irregularity of employment partly explains why construction workers rank among the best paid of industrial workers in the United States, and we might wonder whether this was not also true in the less urban areas of medieval Europe, where the mason was highly itinerant, often on the move from one place to another, seeking work. American construction workers have won high wages through their corporate strength,

[59] E. H. Phelps Brown and Shiela V. Hopkins, "Seven Centuries of Building Wages," *Economica*, 22 (1955), 195–206; "Seven Centuries of the Prices of Consumables, Compared with Builders' Wage Rates," ibid., 23 (1956), 296–314.

which is also rooted in the instability of their employment, and, likewise, of all artisans in medieval Europe, masons were most known for their corporate spirit, which was thought to smack even of secrecy. Because of their peculiar spirit, in fact, construction workers have held more tenaciously to the traditions of their craft than any other work group. The skilled construction worker, in short, was not a typical working man; a schedule of his wage rates may not have any relevance to wages of workers in other crafts and may not be an index even to his own earnings over an extended period of time.[60]

Unskilled workers, on the other hand, were less differentiated than skilled workers by the kind of work they did, so a study of their wages has implications that go beyond the construction industry. Regardless of where they worked, unskilled laborers were invariably paid a daily wage rather than a piece rate, and since presumably they lived close to a subsistence standard, their wages tended to be fairly uniform. Because some of these men specialized to a small degree, their wages oscillated slightly, as noted; but to the extent that they moved from one industry to another, going wherever sheer manpower was needed, their wages were less influenced by conditions peculiar to any one industry. Whether or not they did in fact move about to find work, there is no reason to believe that rates paid manual laborers in the construction industry were not typical for much of the unskilled labor in the city.[61] Because the unskilled worker's place was at the bottom of the economic scale, the history of his wages establishes a foundation from which it is possible to get some perspective on the higher ranks, not just of construction workers, but of working-class society in general.

To assess the purchasing power of what a worker earned for his labor it

[60] There are, surprisingly, no good comparative wage data to work with. Pierre Goubert, with little evidence and no systematic analysis, concluded that in seventeenth-century Beauvais, construction workers were, on the whole, better off than textile workers; Goubert, *Beauvais*, I, 569 and 571. Geographical mobility (and therefore relative scarcity) may explain why builders in late medieval England earned wages as high and even higher than builders in urban Italy; compare the data in Giovanni Vigo, "Real Wages of the Working Class in Italy: Building Workers' Wages (14th to 18th Century)," *JEEcH*, 3 (1974), 390 (table). On American construction workers, see Peter J. Cassimatis, *Economics of the Construction Industry*, Studies in Business Economics, No. 111 (New York, 1969), pp. 17–19.

[61] Because of the structure of the wool industry, accounts of manufacturers, who did not directly employ wage labor, have virtually no information on wage rates. There is some evidence, however, that the rates for unskilled labor in various branches of the cloth industry at the time of the Ciompi ranged from 8 to 10 soldi, the same as in the construction industry; see Federigo Melis, *Aspetti della vita economica medievale (studi nell'Archivio Datini di Prato)*, I (Siena, 1962), 491–92; Gene A. Brucker, "The Ciompi Revolution," in *Florentine Studies: Politics and Society in Renaissance Florence*, ed. Nicolai Rubinstein (London, 1968), pp. 320 n. 4 and 324 n. 2; Victor Rutenburg, *Popolo e movimenti popolari nell'Italia del '300 e '400* (Bologna, 1971), pp. 52–58.

is necessary to translate nominal wages into real wages. There is no lack of material in Florence for the construction of a comprehensive index to the cost of living for this purpose. Institutional accounts, like those customarily used in studies of this kind, exist in abundance for the fourteenth century onwards, and they have more data for a larger variety of items than the records that have been used for price studies in other places. Some of these materials have been used for two studies of the cost of living in the earlier period—Charles de La Ronciere's, for the mid-fourteenth century down to the Ciompi revolt,[62] and Giuliano Pinto's, for the decade beginning in 1395[63]—and for Giuseppe Parenti's classic construction of a price index for the later sixteenth and early seventeenth centuries.[64] Perhaps someone undaunted by the tedium of the task will eventually collect the immense amount of data that still lie buried in account books in order to extend our knowledge over the entire period of the Renaissance. Meanwhile, the only commodity for which there is a price series of long duration is wheat.[65] The reservations about interpreting the price of wheat as a cost-of-living index have long been recognized: wheat is by no means the only consumable man needs to maintain his existence, it can be substituted with cheaper cereals, and its price undergoes markedly more fluctuation than prices of other consumables and may be utterly unrelated to these other price movements. Still, wheat provided man with the main staple of his diet, and the long series for both wages and wheat provide a general backdrop against which the particular studies cited herein can be seen. With these materials the basis for analysis of the Florentine situation is at least as solid as it is for most studies that have been undertaken to ascertain the real value of wages in other places.

On the graph of workers' nominal and real wages for the years 1310 to 1599, wheat prices (the second cycle) have been used to translate the nominal wage of unskilled workers into values of the wheat they could purchase—in other words, into a rough index to real wages (the third cycle); and the fourth cycle translates the eleven-year moving average of this wage-in-wheat into an index scale, with 100 equal to the highest level wages reached in the

62 *Florence*, pp. 403–85.

63 Giuliano Pinto, "Personale, balie e salariati dell'Ospedale di S. Gallo," *Ricerche storiche*, 4 (1974), 143–61.

64 *Ricerche*. Cf. Aleksandra D. Rolova, "Alcune osservazioni sul problema del livello di vita dei lavoratori di Firenze (seconda metà del Cinquecento)," in *Studi in memoria di Federigo Melis* (Naples, 1978), IV, 129–46 (based on data in Parenti's study).

65 Richard A. Goldthwaite, "I prezzi del grano a Firenze dal XIV al XVI secolo," *Quaderni storici*, No. 28 (April 1975), 5–36. The first part of this series, for the years before the Black Death, is derived from the Biadaiuolo manuscript, and those data have been much more thoroughly studied in the edition of that document prepared by Giuliano Pinto, *Il libro del Biadaiolo; carestie e annona a Firenze dalla metà del '200 al 1348* (Florence, 1978).

period from 1441 to 1451. The history represented by the graph can be summarized as follows. The dramatic rise in nominal wages after 1348 brought an immediate gain in the worker's real wages. Wheat prices rose also, but they lagged behind wages; by 1360, when prices began to level off, the worker's earning power was improved by about 50 percent over what it had been before 1348. The level on the index scale (an eleven-year average) hovers around 50 from 1370 to 1390, around 70 from 1400 to 1420, and around 80 from 1420 to 1470. Then the decline begins. By the second quarter of the sixteenth century the index is in the 30s, lower than it had been since the Black Death. The subsequent rise in nominal wages is just barely able to keep up with the inflation of wheat prices, and the index remains more or less at the same level until the end of the century. In short, from the Black Death to the end of the fifteenth century wages were significantly higher than they had been previously, with a particularly high plateau stretching over the first two-thirds of the fifteenth century. Toward 1470, however, they began a slow decline that, toward 1530, reduced the wage earner almost to the level where he had been in the early fourteenth century; and at the end of the century, wages were as low as they had been on the eve of the Black Death.

Since the inertia of nominal wages lasted throughout much of this period, the movement of wheat prices accounts for most of the change in real wages. The curve of wheat prices more or less parallels the demographic history of the city as we know it in its general trends (table 1). The population declined by from one-half to two-thirds in 1348 (depending on one's estimates for the pre-1348 level), then began a recovery, but fell again after 1400 to a nadir of between 40,000 and 50,000 in the 1420s. This easing of demographic pressures kept wheat prices relatively low, so that, with fewer moments of tight supply, the temporary fluctuations so characteristic of the behavior of wheat prices, often spelling temporary misery even in the best of times, were less violent, especially after 1400. Down to the end of the fifteenth century no shortages occurred as disastrous as those of 1329 and 1346 and 1347, just before the population pressures eased. There is no evidence for anything worse than brief moments of scarcity, and despite the subsequent rise in wages, prices were not infrequently at a level as low as they had been in the 1320s.[66] Toward the end of the fifteenth century, when prices began to rise, population also increased, eventually reaching 70,000 in the first quarter of the sixteenth century; but by mid-century it had dropped back to about 60,000, where it remained for the next century or so.

[66] Further references to these moments of shortages are found in Goldthwaite, "Prezzi," pp. 18–22. It is to be noted that the data for the series of wheat prices before 1466 are random and uneven and their statistical validity is therefore much greater for the trend than for short-term movements.

The ability of the Tuscan countryside to support the city was obviously linked to this demographic history. Before the Black Death the city lived at a near-subsistence level and periodically had to face shortages of the most serious kind. It sought grain from outside the region, from places as far away as Sicily and Sardinia, but supply was sometimes not sufficient to relieve a desperate situation at home. The monumental size of the communal storage bin projected at Orsanmichele indicates the enormity of the problem faced by a government on constant alert against major crises in supply. The population decline of the fourteenth century, however, took the pressure off supply to the extent that eventually Tuscan agriculture itself could meet the demand and even diversify its production with other crops. In the fifteenth century the cost of food was relatively low, people ate better, and the countryside was capable of producing the basic food needs of the population. Wine, in fact, was even being exported. When in the sixteenth century the population began to approach former levels, provisioning in moments of tight supply was facilitated by the development of the Baltic grain trade and the efficient operations of the ducal government to obtain it.

However, just at that moment of stabilization of the population in the sixteenth century (in the whole of Tuscany as well as in the capital) new monetary pressures came into play that kept prices on their upward movement. With its commerce closely tied to Spain and a balance of payments very much in its favor, Florence was one of the first to feel the repercussions of the silver imports from the New World; one effect was an upward pressure on prices after the second quarter of the sixteenth century, despite stabilization of population. The wage index in Florence, in fact, rose much more rapidly than it did in many other places in Europe.[67]

The improvement of the Florentine worker's standard of living immediately after 1348 is a notable—and a dramatic—fact in the social history of the city. The nominal wage rate doubled within the year, and although wheat prices went up as well, their lag behind wages meant that the worker found the buying power of those wages very much increased. The severe labor shortage left behind by the plague had an especially sharp and immediate impact on the demand-supply mechanism of the labor market because the economy was geared to a cloth industry oriented to foreign luxury markets that were stronger than ever now that Europe's wealth was concentrated in the hands of fewer people. The demand for labor in Florence was therefore intense, and it had to meet a marked rise in prices. Even the communal trumpeters demanded a raise to keep up with the mounting cost of living—

[67] Parenti, *Ricerche*, pp. 149–66 and 231–40. The several series for Tuscan wheat prices in the sixteenth century have been put together and discussed by T. Damsholt, "Some Observations on Four Series of Tuscan Corn Prices, 1520–1630," *Scandinavian Economic History Review*, 12 (1964), 145–64.

Benozzo Gozzoli, Construction of the Tower of Babel (detail), ca. 1475.

BABIL

and got their wages doubled. Matteo Villani commented with considerable indignation on how, in a situation of relative abundance enjoyed by a reduced population, the little man refused to work in the usual jobs and demanded the most expensive and refined foods and the most showy clothes. It seemed to Villani that when food shortages occurred a few years later, in 1353, the lower classes did not much care, "because all were rich from their work, they earned greedily, they were ready to buy and enjoy the very best things notwithstanding the shortages, and they wanted them before the older and richer citizens got them—an unbecoming and astonishing thing to recount, but something seen continually, as we can give clear witness to."[68] Florentine chroniclers recorded this kind of upper-class indignation at the presumptuous demands of labor at the time, and in nearby Siena attempts were made to bring the situation under control through legislation. No contemporary comment, however, gives us any idea of the magnitude of what was happening.[69] It is curious, in fact, that the drama of these prices movements has not been remarked by later historians, for it cannot be often in the history of Europe, especially in the pre-industrial period, that such a radical change in prices occurred.

The rise of wages in the mid-fourteenth century meant a higher level of employment and the removal of the indigent and desperate poor to the periphery of society. One result was the relaxation of social pressures on two of the largest institutions of public assistance active before 1348, the confraternity of Orsanmichele and the Franciscan tertiary hospice of San Paolo, both of which had large endowments for the direct distribution of alms to the poor and highly systematized programs of poor relief. After 1348 the commune in effect appropriated the wealth of Orsanmichele to pay for one of the most imposing and expensive architecture monuments in the city, which served originally as the city grain market and later as a center for the public religious celebrations of guilds. By the end of the century the confraternity's treasury was depleted and its function was mostly limited to caring for its public tabernacle with a wonder-working image. During the same period the tertiaries of San Paolo shifted their activities from distribution of alms for the poor to the operation of a hospital for care of the sick, but by the end of the century their endowment had also fallen off and the moral fabric of the community began to come apart. In the second half of the fourteenth century charity increasingly found its public outlets in more specialized functions—hospitals for the sick, hospices for the old and the infirm, and homes for orphans—many of them small institutions with

[68] *Cronica*, I, iv; III, lvi.

[69] Aliberto Benigno Falsini, "Firenze dopo il 1348; le conseguenze della peste nera," *ASI*, 129 (1971), 466–75; Niccolò Rodolico, *Il popolo minuto: note di storia fiorentina (1343–1378)* (Florence, 1968), pp. 53–54; William M. Bowsky, "The Impact of the Black Death upon Sienese Government and Society," *Speculum*, 39 (1964), 30.

minimal operations. Confraternities sprung up that distributed relief to the "deserving poor"—like the Buonomini of San Martino—but this charity was organized on a small scale and represented now the extended sociability of a fraternal and civic kind rather than the more generalized religious consciousness that had inspired the large-scale welfare operations of the earlier, and poorer, era.[70]

The increase in the buying power of wages widened the margin between the worker's life-style and mere survival. If wages of unskilled laborers are to be taken as an index, the standard of subsistence changed remarkably at the middle of the fourteenth century, an improvement that has been obscured from the view of many historians by the Ciompi revolt of 1378. Discontent obviously fed that revolt, and the severity of conditions on the eve of the revolt can be well documented. And yet, however miserable the worker's standard of living was in 1378, it had significantly improved over what it had been in the first half of the century. The evidence for the economic discontent that has been considered the justification for protest in the later period only points up what must have been hopeless resignation to the even greater misery of the earlier period.

Moreover, in an economy with a strong industrial sector and little population growth, opportunities were good. The scramble by some to take advantage of the fluid situation created by plagues intensified the pace of economic efforts and heightened expectations. In the arena of much of this economic activity, the wool industry, workers such as carders, washers, menders, and shearers who were too far down in the hierarchy of skills to qualify for guild membership were capable of accumulating in one way or another enough capital to enter into partnership operations as small entre-

[70] The distribution of alms by Orsanmichele and San Paolo is described in Charles de La Roncière, "Pauvres et pauvreté à Florence au XIVe siècle," in *Etudes sur l'histoire de la pauvreté (Moyen Age–XVIe siècle)*, ed. Michel Mollat (Paris, 1974), II, 661–745; and the subsequent history of these institutions can be found in Saverio La Sorsa, *La compagnia d'Or San Michele* (Trani, 1902); and Richard A. Goldthwaite and W. R. Rearick, "Michelozzo and the Ospedale di San Paolo in Florence," *Flor. Mitt.*, 21 (1977), pp. 223–24. The only survey of charitable institutions in Florence is still Luigi Passerini, *Storia degli stabilimenti di beneficenza e d'istruzione elementare gratuita della città di Firenze* (Florence, 1853). An interpretation of the spirit of Renaissance charity is presented by Marvin B. Becker, "Aspects of Lay Piety in Early Renaissance Florence," in *The Pursuit of Holiness in Late Medieval and Renaissance Religion: Papers from the University of Michigan Conference*, ed. Charles Trinkaus (Leiden, 1974), pp. 177–99; R. Trexler, "Charity and the Defense of Urban Elites in the Italian Communes," in *The Rich, the Well Born and the Powerful: Elites and Upper Classes in History*, ed. F. C. Jaher (Urbana, 1974), pp. 64–109; cf. Alberti's rejection of the claims of charity on wealth as discussed by Giovanni Ponte, "Etica ed economia nel terzo libro 'Della famiglia' di Leon Battista Alberti," in *Renaissance Studies in Honor of Hans Baron*, ed. A. Molho and J. A. Tedeschi (Florence, 1971), pp. 306–7.

preneurs and end up with a respectable showing on the lists of the city's taxpayers and share-holders in the public debt. These men, in fact, were the men who spearheaded the revolt of the Ciompi in 1378—not the desperate poor, but men who had improved their economic position in the generation following the Black Death and were seeking a correspondingly higher status in guild society.[71]

The relative prosperity, the economic restlessness, and the mobility of a more fluid society changed men's perception of the economic and social status of the poor. Earlier, poverty was associated with indigence, not with the working poor, and its harsh realities were mediated by religious, not social, notions about charity and the blessedness of Christ's poor. Poverty figured in the plan for redemption: from the poor what was called for was humility and resignation; from the rich, charity. This was the official message from the clergy, delivered in sermons directed to soothe economic realities with spiritual solace. After 1348, however, workers, now better off, had a different perspective on poverty; hopes for a better way of life made some more aware of their impotence in the economic world of guild and governmental controls imposed by the privileged. In addressing the problem of poverty from this point of view the appeal was made more to justice than to charity, and poverty thus became increasingly a social and political problem rather than merely a religious one. The Ciompi revolt in 1378, in fact, has been seen as an expression of a collective consciousness that was beginning to give shape to the working poor as a group distinct from the rich yet subject to the power of the rich and charged with a sense of its importance and resentment. The Ciompi revolt, in other words, was more the mark of how much the lower classes had been affected by the changed economic situation brought on by demographic disasters than an index to the conditions of poverty at the time.[72]

The revolt did not succeed; and if it was, as some have said, the manifesta-

[71] Brucker, "Ciompi," pp. 319–25.

[72] The most determined efforts to penetrate the mentality of the lower classes during this period are being made by Charles de La Roncière: "Pauvres"; "L'Eglise et la pauvreté à Florence au XIVe siècle," in *La Pauvreté des sociétés de pénurie à la société d'abondance* (Paris, 1964), pp. 47–66; "Indirect Taxes or 'Gabelles' at Florence in the Fourteenth Century: The Evolution of Tariffs and Problems of Collection," in *Florentine Studies: Politics and Society in Renaissance Florence*, ed. Nicolai Rubinstein (London, 1968), pp. 140–92; and *Florence*, pp. 1289–1307. The older, Marxian view of the *popolo minuto* of Niccolò Rodolico and its somewhat modified version by the Soviet historian Victor Rutenburg are reviewed and criticized by Brucker, "Ciompi"; see also his "The Florentine *popolo minuto* and its Political Role, 1340–1450," in *Violence and Civil Disorder in Italian Cities, 1200–1500*, ed. Lauro Martines (Berkeley-Los Angeles, 1972), pp. 155–83. Brucker, however, limits himself to political and judicial records. De La Roncière, on the other hand, has been using economic and religious materials, and his occasional use of such phrases as "class," "consciousness," and "veritable proletariat" is perhaps indicative of the direction in which he is moving. Cf. Geremek, 'Salariés," pp. 571–73.

Benedetto Squilli (from a cartoon by Stradano),
Cosimo il Vecchio has a hospital built in Jerusalem (detail),
tapestry, second half of the sixteenth century.

tion of an emerging class consciousness of a proto-proletariat, that development was nipped in the bud by a triumphant elite that proceeded to consolidate its power even more securely. Economic conditions of the lower classes, however, did not worsen. With the population of the city continuing to suffer losses in its periodic bouts with the plague, and with the cloth industry holding on to its foreign markets, the working force maintained its position of strength in the local labor market. After the turn of the century, when wheat prices fell markedly, real wages rose even more, and they remained high throughout two-thirds of the century. It was the period of greatest prosperity for the working classes, when, at least in a statistical view of things, they appear better off than at any other time in our survey. It was also a period of political tranquility for the vast majority of the population that remained outside the orbit of upper-class factions. Momentary problems, especially resulting from tight grain supplies, occasioned some restlessness now and then, but on the whole the city never experienced any breakdown of authority comparable to what happened during the Ciompi revolt. When violence did erupt in any form other than clashes between individuals, it was usually fired by factional strife among the upper classes. In part this stability resulted from a tighter political organization of the ruling elite after 1378 and more zealous enforcement of public order; political order was also the fruit of a more fertile economy.

Putting the working man in a perspective drawn with the statistics of wages and prices hardly brings his overall situation into view. Other kinds of information collected from guild and court records for the purpose of learning about the lower classes have suggested views of the matter that are distinctly grimmer than the purely economic one presented here.[73] The cloth worker, seen as the object of the numerous regulations that sought to subject him to the authority of the guild elite, for the most part cloth merchants, appears the exploited victim of a nascent capitalism, boxed in by controls, policed by the authorities, and enslaved by his dependence on the capitalist. Before the bar of justice, as seen in court records, the working man appears uprooted, debt-ridden, and prone to violence. And yet, we can wonder how realistic guild regulations were, and whether the contents of court records are not typical only in the sense that they reflect some of the most permanent features of deviant behavior, as true now as then. Wages and prices bear more directly on the basic conditions of working-class life than these other sources, however much the statistical skeleton needs to be fleshed out with considerations of other kinds.

Standard of Living

How well off, then, was the worker during the relative prosperity of the fifteenth century? To descend from the generality of graphs and statistics to the reality of the worker's life is not easy. Only by extension can the graph be interpreted as an index to real wages and to the cost of living generally, and in any case wage rates are not earnings. However convincingly the statistics show a relative improvement in the buying power of wages, they do not reveal anything about a standard of living or the quality of life a worker could expect to enjoy on his income. One thing is clear, however: if the wages of unskilled day laborers were determined by subsistence standards, the rise

[73] Brucker, "*Popolo minuto*"; Rutenburg, *Movimenti*, pp. 50–76.

of real wages in the middle of the fourteenth century meant a rise in the standard of subsistence. At the least the worker saw a considerable widening of the margin between earning capacity and mere survival.

It has been estimated that the pre-1348 income level of an unskilled laborer was not sufficient to feed a family of four, even if they lived on wheat alone, the food with the highest caloric return for the money.[74] After the mid-fourteenth century, however, he could afford to substitute wheat for the cheaper and lower quality cereals that he probably relied on earlier and to improve his diet with other items. Wheat, in fact, virtually replaced other cereals in the local grain market after 1348, and in this respect alone the city was eating better as a result. Meat consumption rose (as it did all over Europe after the demographic crisis of the mid-fourteenth century), and even the better kinds—veal, lamb, and sausage—were relatively inexpensive; meat was probably the major addition to the diet of the lower classes whenever budgets permitted it. Wheat, meat, and wine were the staples in the food basket of the time.

Rents were extraordinarily low, whatever housing standards might have been, because the city had lost so much of its population. There is no thorough study of rents in Florence for this period, but data collected by Armando Sapori for the second and third quarters of the fourteenth century show that rents, unlike wages and food prices, were not appreciably affected by the Black Death—which is to say that the relative cost of housing fell. In the fifteenth century a man could put at least a roof over his head for a rent of only 10 to 20 lire a year.[75]

In an attempt to assess the Florentine worker's standard of living on the eve of the Ciompi revolt, Charles de La Roncière created a model budget for a family of four consisting of items whose changing costs he compares with the history of wages during the same period.[76] Besides various food

[74] The difference in living standards before and after 1348 as measured by the value of wages with respect to the caloric content of the wheat they could buy is illustrated by de La Roncière, "Pauvres." The method is not altogether satisfactory, but the results are at least suggestive.

[75] In a sample of returns of the 1427 Catasto, about one-third of rented housing cost under 5 florins, or lb. 20 (Gonfaloni Leon Rosso, Ruote, Carro, Bue, Drago, and Liocorno). Where accounts of property-owners indicate that housing was rented to laborers, the rent generally falls in the range of lb.10 to lb.20: the hospital of San Gallo, Pinto, "Personale" (lb.10 in ca. 1400); S. Miniato 56 (accounts of S. Bartolomeo), fols. 148r (lb.12, then lb.10 for a year, 1465–66) and 179v (lb.11 a year, 1465–66); S. Miniato 58 (accounts of S. Bartolomeo), fol. 81v (lb.8 for six months, 1487–88); S. Spirito 127, fol. 165 (lb.12 plus a goose for six months, 1477). Armando Sapori's study of mid-fourteenth-century rents, "Case e botteghe a Firenze nel Trecento," is in his *Studi di storia economica*, I (Florence, 1955), 314–27.

[76] De La Roncière, *Florence*, pp. 423–54. De La Roncière sees a substantial worsening of the worker's condition in the 1370s preceding the Ciompi revolt, but his analysis is based on a fall in wages that is not confirmed by the data collected for this study.

TABLE 7
Estimated Daily Food Ration for One Adult, 1395–1405

Item	Amount	Calories	Cost	
			Denari	Percentage of Total
Bread	650 gr.	about 1,500	10	42
Wine	0.7 liters	400–500	7	29
Meat	100–200 gr.	about 400	7	29
TOTAL		2,300–2,400	24	100

SOURCE: Giuliano Pinto, "Personale, balie e salariati dell'Ospedale di San Gallo," *Ricerche storiche*, 4 (1974), 158.

items, including meat and wine, adding up to about 3,000 calories daily for the working head of the household and from 8,000 to 8,500 calories for the entire family, this budget accounts for rent, clothing, and even the worker's tools. All kinds of difficulties stand in the way of anyone who attempts to study this kind of detail in a period when documentation is relatively slight and the variables—short-term fluctuations in prices, irregularity of employment, substitution possibilities within the budget, the size of the family and the number of working members therein—so numerous; but de La Roncière's conclusions at the highest level of generalization point clearly and irrefutably to the considerable improvement in the standard of living of the working man in the course of the fourteenth century. Before the Black Death the skilled mason working at optimum wages could scarcely meet the requirement of this budget, and the unskilled laborer could never have earned enough to pay half the expenses. After the Black Death, however, the mason was earning 50 to 100 percent more than what he would have needed to keep a family of four, while the ordinary laborer was able to earn almost enough—from 80 to 100 percent—to meet basic expenses. The continuing improvement in the worker's ability to buy wheat suggests that in the fifteenth century an ordinary worker able to find full-time employment could support a family on his own, while a skilled worker could realistically hope to improve his standard of living much beyond normal (not to mention minimum) requirements.

To proceed to a more precise analysis of what wages could buy in the fifteenth century we can start with the study by Giuliano Pinto of the cost of consumables of all kinds based on an average of prices paid by the hospital of San Gallo from 1395 to 1405 (table 7).[77] Pinto considered a daily ration of food for a single adult as consisting of ⅔ kilo of bread, about ¾ liter of wine, and 1 or 2 hectograms of meat (depending on quality). The

[77] Pinto, "Personale."

2,300 to 2,400 calories provided by these quantities of bread, wine, and meat, though low by modern standards, were probably close to a normal daily calorie intake by standards of that time. On the basis of his study of prices during the decade 1395 to 1405 Pinto estimated the average price of this daily ration at 2 soldi.

This estimate is confirmed by data collected by a contemporary Florentine, Lodovico Ghetti, writing within half a century of the San Gallo accounts, around 1445.[78] The occasion for Ghetti's calculations was his proposal for a one-tenth tax (*decima*) on all earned income in Florentine territory. To support his contention that such a tax would yield sufficient revenue for the needs of the state, Ghetti had to come up with some precise figures for total private income. An important part of his calculations was an estimate of all income from sales, including food; to arrive at a figure he tried to estimate total private expenditures, making assumptions about per capita and food costs for a population of 400,000 (80,000 working men multiplied by five, the number of people who had to be fed between the women, children, and old people who depended on each worker). Even allowing for a certain lack of methodological rigor in Ghetti's calculations, we (like Burckhardt more than a century ago) must respect the strong statistical bent of the Florentine mind, manifested as far back as Villani, whenever it operated in such matters. Ghetti, after all, was presenting a proposal for tax reform, and he had better get his figures right if he wanted to convince anyone that he knew what he was talking about.

Ghetti's data are presented in table 8, along with extrapolations made from them to bring his assumptions (or their implications) into comparison with Pinto's for half a century earlier. Ghetti assumed almost exactly the same per capita consumption of both the basic foods—wheat and wine—that constituted the major part of the diet. His estimate for the per diem expenditure for wine works out to be the same as Pinto's; his estimate for grain is less, but we know from our graph that in fact grain cost less when he was writing. He has a much lower expenditure for meat, but the explanation may lie less in the assumption about how much meat men ate than in the different objectives of the two estimates. Ghetti was not interested in presenting a complete daily ration. He estimated consumption for purposes of determining taxes

[78] "Inventiva d'una impositione di nuova gravezza," in William Roscoe, *The Life of Lorenzo de' Medici Called the Magnificent* (London, 1851), app. XI. To judge from internal evidence of Ghetti's undated proposal, especially the ratio of the florin to the soldo *di piccioli* (1:88), he must have written it toward 1445; the price of s.17 d.6 he uses for a staio of wheat corresponds to the market price of those years. An economic analysis of the data Ghetti provides in his proposal was made by V. Rutenburg at the ninth annual conference of the Istituto internazionale di storia economica "Francesco Datini" di Prato (1977), and presumably it will be published in the proceedings.

TABLE 8

Food Consumption Estimated by Lodovico Ghetti, ca. 1445

Item	Annual Consumption of Population of 400,000 (in florins)	Daily Per Capita Consumption		
			Cost	
		Quantity	denari *a fiorino*	denari *di piccioli*[1]
Wheat (at 14 staia annually per capita)	1,118,150	690 grams	1.84	7.4– 9.2
Wine (at f.3½ a *cogno*)	1,000,000	0.79 liters	1.64	6.6– 8.2
Meat	325,000		0.53	2.1– 2.7
Oil (at f.1½ an *orcio*)	150,000		0.25	1.0– 1.3
TOTAL	2,593,150		4.26	17.1–21.4

SOURCE: Lodovico Ghetti, "Inventiva d'una impositione di nuova gravezza," in William Roscoe, *The Life of Lorenzo de' Medici Called the Magnificent* (London, 1851), app. XI.

NOTE: The data in the first two columns come from the source; the rest are extrapolations. Equivalents used are: 1 *staio* = 18 kg., 1 *cogno* = 406 liters.

[1] F.1. = s.80–100 *di piccioli*. The document is undated, but internal evidence suggests that it was written in the 1440s, when the exchange rate fell into this range.

that could come from sales, and to arrive at his figure for meat he considered only those animals—sheep, pigs, cows, oxen, and horses—that could hardly enter the market unobserved by tax officials. He says nothing about fish and fowl, for although they may have been consumed in large quantities, he may have thought that commerce in them could not be assessed for his purpose. In conclusion, the total cost of a daily ration extrapolated from Ghetti's figures falls into a range of 17 to 21 denari, and with the extras that lay beyond his purpose, the actual amount a person spent for food must have come close to the 2 soldi estimated by Pinto.

The prices of basic foods probably remained at the same level through most of the fifteenth century. Of the three staples in the diet, wheat (which accounts for over 40 percent of the total cost and 60 percent of the caloric content) was subject to the most erratic price fluctuations, and down to the fourth quarter of the century its price was normally lower by 10 percent (and even more) than the s.22 d.5 per staio used in the 1395–1405 estimate. The price of meat as it appears in a price series running from 1491 to 1501 was still at a level it was a century earlier (table 9). By that time, however, the price of wheat had begun its slow rise. When Parenti's series starts in the second quarter of the sixteenth century, the price of meat had gone up about 50 percent, and thereafter it roughly paralleled the inflation of other prices.

The fifteenth century, in short, was a period of price stability when the price of a daily ration, roughly estimated, was about 2 soldi. This was, in fact, the value of the normal food allowance used whenever such an item had to be taken into consideration for accounting purposes—the amount, for instance, paid to an employee of the hospital of San Gallo for meal expenses while he was away from Florence on business for the hospital, the amount a monk at Santo Spirito had to reimburse his convent if a worker employed privately by him for work on his own quarters took his meal in the convent, and the amount normally deducted from a construction worker's daily wage whenever he got a meal (and it would have been his main meal of the day) from his employer.[79] One could easily spend much more, of course, and many did. At one point in the exposition of his tax program Ghetti observes that, besides the working population of 80,000 considered as the basis for his estimation of total consumption, there were 20,000 additional "mouths" that "want many more things than the ordinary mouth"; these, he thought, might spend up to 12 florins a year for food, or from s.2 d.8 to s.3 d.8 *di piccioli* a day (depending on an exchange rate running from 80 to 100 soldi per florin), a not unreasonable increase over what has here been taken as an ordinary ration.

Food was by far the most expensive item in a household budget of the working man; rent and clothing cost much less. At the rate of 2 soldi a day, the cost of food for a year amounts to about 36 lire; with the addition of 10

[79] Pinto, "Personale," p. 159; S. Spirito 67, fol. 101v; and for just one example of a 2-soldi meal deduction taken out of workers' wages, see the accounts of the quarry operations at San Bartolomeo: S. Miniato 174.

TABLE 9

Price of Meat, 1395–1599

(Per pound; in soldi and denari *di piccioli*)

Item	1395–1405	1491–1501	1520–1529	1530–1539	1540–1549	1550–1559	1560–1569	1570–1579	1580–1589	1590–1599
Fish	4/3	3/10								
Sausage	3/0	2/8								
Lamb	2/0		2/10	3/4	3/0	4/0		4/7	4/8	5/5
Veal	2/0[1]	2/3	2/7	3/2	3/0	3/11		4/11	4/8	5/7
Pork loin	2/0[1]	1/7								
Beef	1/2	1/3	1/10	2/6	1/8	2/4	2/4		3/0	3/4
Pork	1/0	1/1								

SOURCES: 1395–1405: Giuliano Pinto, "Personale, balie e salariati dell'Ospedale di S. Gallo," *Ricerche storiche*, 4 (1974). 1491–1501: ASF, Carte strozz., ser. V, no. 69 (accounts of heirs of Lorenzo di Francesco Strozzi), fols. 6–24 and 131–66 (see Appendix 4 herein). After 1520: Parenti, *Prime ricerche sulla rivoluzione dei prezzi a Firenze* (Florence, 1939), table 1, p. 39.
[1] The price of both veal and pork had remained fairly stable at this level ever since the Black Death according to the data presented by de La Roncière, *Florence, centre économique*, pp. 172 and 179.

to 20 lire for rent and as much again for clothing, the expenses to maintain one adult with essentials adds up to 55 to 75 lire a year. This estimate is not out of line with the 14 florins (or 56 lire) that the Catasto officials considered the cost for the maintenance of a single adult in allowing the standard capital deduction of 200 florins (14 florins capitalized at the normal rate of return of 7 percent) for each "mouth" in a household. A manual laborer could afford this level of existence by working about half of a 260-day work-year.[80] With the optimum income of 130 lire, however, which he received only if he managed to work full time, he would have found it difficult to maintain a family, even if a child's food consumption up to the time he could be put to work is estimated to be only one-half of adult capacity. Food alone, of the standard represented by our hypothetical budget, cost 110 lire for such a family of four. This level of expenditure could be met if more than one member worked. Expenses for food could be cut by substituting cheaper meats and cereals, and although any reduction in quantity would obviously lower the caloric and nutritive content of the diet, the family still enjoyed a considerable margin in comparison with the much lower level of real wages before the Black Death. By the fifteenth century, when wheat prices were at their lowest, the worker could eat better, or work less, and perhaps begin to think about supporting a family. He had to make an investment in his tools, and it was not unheard of for a manual laborer to give his daughter a dowry.[81] However low his standard of living was, there was some margin between his earning capacity and survival. Nevertheless, the high percentage of his earnings that had to go for food, his most basic need, indicates how close to subsistence he still was. The margin reveals less the prosperity of the fifteenth century than the misery of the earlier period.

Well over one-half of the labor force in construction was skilled,[82] and with earnings at rates 50 to 100 percent higher than those paid to unskilled laborers, these men could remove themselves from the poverty level if they could work full time. An ordinary mason or smith on a construction site had an optimum income of 175 to 200 lire, and the income range extended up-

[80] The few examples of salaried laborers indicate a slightly lower income. One laborer at Santa Maria Nuova worked for lb.10 a month in 1367 (ASF, S. M. Nuova 4417, fol. 108r); another worked for seventeen months in 1467–68 at the rate of lb.105 a year plus a pair of shoes (ibid., 4509, fol. 73r); and at the beginning of work at the Badia of Fiesole in 1456 a number of laborers were employed at monthly salaries of lb.9 and lb.10 "a tutte sue spese," although within several months all workers were on daily wages (Badia di Fiesole 1, fols. 1–8).

[81] In 1477 one of the laborers at Santo Spirito had his wage account debited for lb.11 s.10, which he had the purveyor pay to his son-in-law as part of a dowry; S. Spirito 127, fol. 165.

[82] This was true throughout Europe; Geremek, "Salariés," p. 569.

wards to a bracket of 250 to 300 lire for better-paid foremen. Nofri di Biagio's salary at the Innocenti went as high as 350 lire (72 florins) in the period from 1445 to 1447. The exceptional builder-architect earned even more. Cronaca had a salary of about 240 lire in his part-time position as head stonecutter and architect at the Strozzi palace; the full-time foreman there, Mariotto di Papi da Balatro, earned about 400 lire, which was also Brunelleschi's salary in the most important post that a mason could hope to have.

With this schedule of incomes the skilled laborer who worked full time could put a comfortable distance between himself and the poverty line, and given the choices of consumer goods available to him in an economy that was not yet organized to entice the consumer to ever higher levels of spending, the psychological distance from poverty must have been even greater. More money could not have improved by much the basic food ration used here, and once the essential needs of food, clothing, and housing were satisfied, the consumer's options were fairly limited. Men in the uppermost range of the income scale of skilled construction workers, in fact, were on the threshold of social respectability. The bracket of the ordinary craftsman approximated that of a cashier in one of the city's business establishments, although a cashier was often a man on the move, coming from a family of some substance and serving a kind of apprenticeship on his way upward in the business hierarchy. The better-paid foreman was in the income bracket of the lower to middle echelon of the professional administrative staff of the government treasury. There was still a gap between the income of the more prosperous artisan and the 100 to 150 florins paid to higher government officials, like the secretary of the Dieci and a second chancellor, and the 100 to 200 florins paid a manager in a merchant-banking house, not to mention the even higher levels that the best lawyers and university professors could expect to reach.[83] Nevertheless, according to Piovano Arlotto, writing about

[83] It is difficult to draw up a table of annual incomes in Florence because annual salaries of businessmen, government officials, and professional men were stated in florins and were therefore continually appreciating in value with respect to the lira, in which workers' and artisans' wages were usually quoted. For some idea of representative incomes see the following references: for the staff at the Strozzi palace project, Goldthwaite, "Strozzi Palace," p. 181; for workers in the cloth industry, de Roover, "Labour Conditions," p. 303; for the staff of the Medici bank in the early fifteenth century, de Roover, *Medici Bank*, pp. 43–45; for treasury officials in the early fifteenth century, Lauro Martines, *The Social World of the Florentine Humanists, 1390–1460* (Princeton, 1963), p. 143 n. 220; for the bureaucracy of Cosimo I in the mid-sixteenth century, Arnaldo D'Addario, "Burocrazia, economia e finanze dello Stato fiorentino alla metà del Cinquecento," *ASI*, 121 (1963), pp. 394–428; for university professors, Gene A. Brucker, "Florence and Its University, 1348–1434," in *Action and Conviction in Early Modern Europe*, ed. T. K. Rabb and J. F. Seigel (Princeton, 1969), pp. 231–32 (in the early sixteenth century a university stipend could go as high as 1,000 florins; ASF, Ufficiali dello Studio 8, fols. 135v–36v).

1480, a man with a wife and three or four children could hope to live quite respectably in Florence on an income of no more than 70 florins (about 400 lire).[84] It was this widespread prosperity among a middling class of Florentines, including artisans, that opened new markets for the decorative arts sector of the economy.

[84] "Sono in Firenze grande numero di uomini dabbene i quali non ascendano alla somma di tanta entrata l'anno [70 florins], e nondimeno vivono civilemente con la donna e tre e quattro figliuoli"; *Motti*, no. 113. At the time Piovano Arlotto was writing (he died in 1484) the florin was worth between 5 and 6 lire.

CHAPTER SEVEN

The Architect

Antecedents

DURING the Middle Ages architecture did not exist as a profession in the modern sense that presupposes a highly technical and formal educational program as the necessary preparation to practice, and no word existed that could be defined as referring exclusively to the practice of architecture. For the most part responsibility for the design of a building lay in the hands of the master mason who headed the works staff. Architecture was an extension of his activity as a builder, a talent he was able to develop only through experience in the normal course of his work.

The medieval architect was trained as a mason and, being an artisan, he had no formal learning or theoretical preparation. After serving as apprentice for four to five years and as journeyman for at least one more, he gained his status as a master of his craft for his work in stone or in wood. Any talent he had for design was nurtured by instruction from the men he trained with and by the inspiration aroused in him on his travels as journeyman or in the course of his employment; his development as an artist depended on the opportunities opened to him by the kind of work he was able to find. Furthermore, a mason could operate as an architect only if he became head of a works staff. To arrive at that position he had to prove himself also as an administrator and supervisor who could be responsible for procuring materials and equipment, hiring and supervising workers, and, in general, directing all the technical operations of the construction enterprise. Getting a medieval cathedral built demanded considerable management skill as well as technical knowledge and design talent. A patron looked for all these attributes in selecting the foreman of any project.[1]

The master mason of a major project was therefore a man who had achieved some stature because of personal qualities that clearly set him apart from the ordinary mason. If he ended up working for the government of a major city, for a great ecclesiastical figure, or for a prince, he in effect entered the bureaucracy of his employer and was in charge of the various works projects undertaken under that auspice. Already in the twelfth century employment by a king could thus lead to a position in the royal household as master of the king's works. With such a career in government service open to him the master mason was one of the few craftsmen in the Middle Ages who could rise above the level of his class. The mason Pierre d'Angicourt (who died in 1284), master of the works of Charles d'Anjou, king of Naples, was knighted and supplied with horses and servants. Henry Yevele, who was in charge of royal works in London and Westminster in the second half of the fourteenth century, enjoyed association with the court, status in the City of London, and enough wealth to be ranked with the lower gentry.[2] It is no wonder that medieval representations of construction work sometimes show the mason-architect wearing robes and gloves to pointedly distinguish him from the ordinary craftsmen working under his supervision.

Medieval culture, however, made little allowance for the conferment of special distinction on painters, sculptors, and architects for their artistic talent alone. In the medieval scheme of social values the artist, because he worked with his hands, was a mere craftsman. Architecture, in any case, was not regarded as the product of what would be called today a creative imagination, and if a building was associated with anyone, he was the patron who paid for it, not its designer. The term *architect* was itself rarely used, at least in any sense that set one mason off from others. The master mason, in other words, had little identity in his own time as an architect; not surprisingly, history has preserved the names of few of the designers of major medieval monuments. Indeed, in view of the extensive use in early medieval churches of painting, lighting effects, and sculptural decoration, there is some question whether the designers themselves had a notion of the building as a completed work with its own integrity as architecture. Only toward the end

[1] Paul Booz, *Der Baumeister der Gotik* (Munich, 1956); L. R. Shelby, "The Role of the Master Mason in Medieval English Building," *Speculum*, 39 (1964), 387–403; idem, "The Education of Medieval English Master Masons," *Medieval Studies*, 32 (1970), 1–26; John Harvey, "The Mason's Skill: The Development of Architecture," in *The Flowering of the Middle Ages*, ed. Joan Evans (London, 1966), pp. 82–132; Pierre du Colombier, *Les Chantiers des cathédrales* (Paris, 1973), ch. 4 (expanded from earlier edition).

[2] John H. Harvey, *Henry Yevele* (London, 1946), especially chs. 2–4.

of the Middle Ages, after masons had solved the major engineering problems of Gothic construction, do great cathedrals reveal attention to architectural detail in a way that suggests that their designers were, at last, asserting greater control over the finished product as a predominately architectural monument.[3]

The mason's opportunities for artistic expression were limited by the conditions of his employment. As works supervisor he was tied down to a single project at a time, and because the construction of a great medieval cathedral lasted for several generations, his position could be a full-time job—and a lifelong one as well. The foreman at a major building site was likely to be called in as a consultant on other buildings in the area, but the extent of his control over what was done at a site when he himself was not in steady attendance remains obscure.[4] The opportunity for designing enlarged if he worked for a public or quasi-governmental authority and the workshop took on other construction. Inasmuch as the cathedral workshop in Florence, for example, was an agency of the commune, the foremen there found themselves responsible for many public works projects away from the cathedral, including civic buildings, fortifications, and any number of more modest projects. Likewise, the master of works for a prince assumed responsibility for whatever kind of building the prince was likely to sponsor—castles, churches, engineering projects—throughout his realm. A mason high up in government service worked primarily as a works supervisor, however, rather than as an architect, for the increase of the number of projects under his purview, given the kind of buildings they were, did not enlarge his opportunities as a designer. His exalted status meant only that his supervisory responsibilities were much greater. While master of royal works in Westminster and London, Henry Yevele, for example, had many official projects widely scattered over southern England, and in addition he took on some work on his own; but the major monuments that established his fame as an architect were those where he was employed virtually full time.

Further development of the mason's talent as architect was stunted by the limited demand for buildings of the kind that qualify as architecture. It was above all in the great cathedral or monastic church, the cultural symbol of the age, where the mason found the greatest artistic and technical challenge. Little secular building was elevated to the realm of architecture. Furthermore, neither the functions of most buildings nor the construction techniques used in putting them up were so innovative and complex that a highly specialized

[3] Andrew Martindale, *The Rise of the Artist in the Middle Ages and Early Renaissance* (New York, 1972), pp. 80–82.

[4] Instances are cited by Booz, *Baumeister*, p. 27, and du Colombier, *Chantiers*, pp. 100–101.

Andrea Pisano, The architect
(or Geometry), ca. 1340.

design talent was necessary. The building techniques and designs passed down for generations and learned in on-the-job training gave the mason what he needed in order to build for a relatively conservative society. The strong traditions of medieval architecture circumscribed the area in which the architect could give himself free rein for working out his own ideas. Indeed, for some critics the glory of medieval architecture is to be explained by the greater independence of craft traditions not yet subservient to the dominant individuality of the architect. As John Harvey put it, "Certainly the system of Gothic architecture left less to individual freaks of fancy than did the highly artificial pack of cards with which the Renaissance masters conjured."[5]

If the architect in the Renaissance began to play with many more of his own peculiar ideas, it was because the market for his services had changed, challenging him to be more inventive and original. This market first opened

[5] "The Education of the Medieval Architect," *Journal of the Royal Institute of British Architects*, 52 (1945), 230.

up in Italy during the Renaissance. Much of Italy's considerable wealth was concentrated in cities, in the hands of merchants who did business there and of princes who took up residence there; as urban dwellers with Roman ruins all around as the obvious models to follow, these men were particularly responsive to what the humanists had to say about the magnificence of buildings. Moreover, the political division of Italy into numerous city-states meant a highly diffused demand and therefore more opportunities for architects—for local masons to make good at home and for the better ones to look for more attractive work abroad. Competition among these states further stimulated building by inducing a rivalry in patronage once buildings came to be recognized as the physical symbols of status. In a more practical realm, political competition also intensified the need for up-to-date fortifications; this, too, contributed to the demand for mason-architects. In short, the surge in demand for building enlarged the opportunities for Italian masons with design talents above all by giving them more work. Architecture flourished in Renaissance Italy, as it was to flourish later in eighteenth-century England, because patrons were numerous and job opportunities for the architect good. Architectural centers were those places not necessarily with the grandest projects but with the greatest concentrations of patrons: Florence in the fifteenth century, Rome and Venice in the sixteenth century. The history of architecture in Italy cannot be reduced to a mere sequence of court architects, as it can for so many places north of the Alps in the early modern period.

There was much more to this new situation for architects, however, than a rise in demand for their services. The revival of interest in antiquity opened a whole new world of architecture, full of models to be followed and accessible to men from outside the building crafts who were excited with the prospect of learning a new vocabulary and stimulated to come up with new ideas of their own. Virtually anyone, from painters to patricians, could aspire to design a building, and with an enlarged range of stylistic options opened to them, architects became self-conscious in asserting their taste and therefore anxious about establishing their credentials to do so. Moreover, the contemporaneous revolution in military architecture brought about by the introduction of firearms and artillery challenged them to add an area of specialization in their preparation so that they could solve increasingly technical problems of design. In a society where industry was still associated with mere craftsmen, these mounting artistic and intellectual pretentions eventually won for the architect an appropriate status distinct from that of a mere mason-builder.

Developments in Renaissance Italy, therefore, generated both a rise in the level of demand for architecture and a refinement of the particular requirements, both aesthetic and technical, of that demand. Ideas about architecture arose independently of the building process. These were the conditions that permitted the architect finally to come into his own as an artist and as a professional. The story begins in Florence.[6]

Training

Building design in Florence before the beginning of the fifteenth century was mostly in the hands of masons who from time immemorial worked in highly traditional ways. Any good mason probably knew enough about foundations and vaulting to solve the structural problems he was likely to encounter putting up the kind of building he usually worked on. Opportunities for inventive design were few, and imitation was widespread. Relatively few buildings can be said to have what could properly be called architectural style. In the normal course of their work, in other words, masons did not have much of an opportunity for working out architectural ideas.

When a patron desired something special by way of architectural design, he looked outside the narrow circle of masons to men who had proved their talent in other artistic areas. The list of foremen at the cathedral workshop is thus studded with names of men not otherwise known as architects. The sculptors Arnolfo di Cambio and Andrea Pisano served there at critical stages of new construction; Giotto, with no previous architectural experience except for interior decoration, was called in at the end of his life to take charge of the new Campanile; Orcagna, identified only as a sculptor and painter in contemporary documents, was for a time foreman when Orsanmichele was going up; the sculptor Giovanni Fetti was in charge during the building of most of the Loggia dei Priori; and the goldsmith-sculptor Ghiberti shared for a few years the direction of the workshop with Brunel-

[6] The Renaissance architect has not been nearly so well studied as the medieval master mason. There are only the highly generalized portraits of W. Braunfels, *Mittelalterliche Stadtbaukunst in der Toscana* (Berlin, 1959), ch. VI (on fourteenth-century city architects in Tuscany); Leopold D. Ettlinger, "The Emergence of the Italian Architect During the Fifteenth Century," in *The Architect: Chapters in the History of the Profession*, ed. Spiro Kostof (New York, 1977), pp. 96–123; James Ackerman, "Architectural Practice in the Italian Renaissance," *JSArH*, 13, No. 3 (1954) (on early sixteenth-century Roman practice); and Catherine Wilkinson, "The New Professionalism in the Renaissance," in *Architect*, ed. Kostof, pp. 124–60. There are also some perceptive remarks about architectural practice of the later Renaissance architect by John P. Coolidge, "La personalità del Barozzi," in *La vita e le opere di Jacopo Barozzi da Vignola, 1507–1573, nel quarto centenario della morte* (Vignola, 1974), pp. 3–9; and by Patricia Waddy, "The Design and Designers of Palazzo Barberini," in *JSArH*, 35 (1976), 183–85. Giorgio Simoncini, *Architetti e architettura nella cultura del Rinascimento* (Bologna, 1969), and Luigi Vagnetti, *L'architetto nella storia di Occidente* (Florence, 1973), are too general to be very useful.

leschi, himself a goldsmith, not a mason, by training. Other foremen, like Francesco Talenti and Neri di Fioravante, are not known for anything but their building activity, although some were stonecutters to whom sculptural work has been attributed. What sets many of these men apart from the stereotype of the medieval master-mason is their independent reputation as artists in other media, and this, in fact, was to be the distinctive trait of the Florentine architecture of the early Renaissance.[7]

It is not difficult to understand why the city fathers regularly had recourse to sculptors, painters, and goldsmiths to manage what was in effect the city's public works office, an office in charge not only of the cathedral but of all the other buildings on which the city staked its claim to monumentality. These men already had established reputations in their own craft. Orcagna and Ghiberti had demonstrated their talents in works that were nothing less than spectacular in the impact they made on the local scene, while Giotto and Andrea Pisano, in addition, enjoyed the prestige of having worked on major commissions abroad. They were also tried and proved as responsible managers, since they worked at their craft in relatively large workshops—as large as the average industrial enterprise of the time. This experience was important in the selection of the foreman of the cathedral works, which was the most demanding, most prestigious, and (for an artisan) by far the best-paying job in industrial management in town. Moreover, until the moment of decision about covering the crossing of the enlarged cathedral project, the cathedral-builders encountered few technical problems that could not be solved in traditional ways. However gigantic, the monumental civic buildings of the fourteenth century posed fewer problems of structure and engineering than of decoration; it was therefore appropriate to turn them over to sculptors and goldsmiths. Critical comment has made much of how their architecture reveals the stylistic marks of these other crafts.

Sculptors, goldsmiths, and furniture-makers were the craftsmen most likely to be called in when someone was needed to design buildings in the early Renaissance, and most of the men we think of as architects came from one of these crafts. These were all craftsmen who (unlike mere wallers) were trained draftsmen with a well-developed design talent and whose sense of design was closely tied to architecture.

Architecture had always been a calling open to stonecutters, given their expertise in basic building materials and their design talent. Challenged by the public commissions for the cathedral in the 1390s to work out new ideas

[7] Some speculation about the medieval sculptor's activity as architect is found in Geza de Francovich, *Benedetto Antelami, architetto e scultore e l'arte del suo tempo* (Milan-Florence, 1952), pp. 305–6. On the Florentine sense of architecture as *disegno*, see Braunfels, *Stadtbaukunst*, pp. 224–30; and Wilkinson, "Professionalism," pp. 134–36.

on a larger scale, a generation of sculptors came into existence in Florence who were highly visible in the vanguard of the renascence of the arts. Much of their work was conceived as part of an architectural context, and in fact the first attempt to evoke a classicizing feeling in architecture is usually thought to be the niche at Orsanmichele for the statue belonging to the Parte Guelfa (about 1422). Although no one of this first generation of Renaissance sculptors has much of a reputation as an architect, the men who made up the group were effective in diffusing a taste for a new style in architectural decoration and in training any number of artisans who could accommodate the demand once the market was opened up by the surge in private building.

Goldsmiths were prominent craftsmen in Tuscany, with its long tradition of working gold, earlier in Siena and later in Florence. Building patrons also turned to goldsmiths for architectural ideas because their design talent and technical expertise gave them a natural affinity for both sculpture and architecture. Many of the objects they made, like shrines and reliquaries, were given architectural forms, and their practical working principles of proportion and their vocabulary of decorative details were derived from, and were therefore applicable to, the design of buildings. They knew how to make drawings and models, and they possessed that working knowledge of geometry known as (to use the term of the traditional historiography on the medieval architect) the "secret of the mason." Lando di Pietro, who among other things made the gold crown for the coronation of Henry VII, and who cast church bells, also worked on fortifications for the commune of Siena and ended up as foreman at the cathedral there in 1339. In Florence Brunelleschi, Ghiberti, and Michelozzo all came out of the goldsmith's shop.[8]

Cabinetmakers also had the kind of knowledge that could lead to architectural practice. Choral stalls, sacristy cabinets, and other church furniture were conceived as part of an architectural setting, and designs for these kinds of objects can be found in medieval architectural drawings. The domestic furniture in growing demand from owners of new palaces also reflected a taste for strong architectonic forms and classical details. To plan the programs for their complex intarsia decorations, cabinetmakers, like goldsmiths, worked from drawings and models in which they had to lay everything out to scale just as the architect did. Carpenters were also involved in building through the equipment they made for construction and, increasingly in the fifteenth century, through the models they made of the buildings themselves. It was altogether natural, therefore, to turn to such an artisan for the design of a building. Giuliano da Maiano, Antonio di Manetto Ciaccheri (Manetti), Giovanni di Domenico da Gaiuole, Francione, Bartolomeo di Fino Pontelli, Giovannino de' Dolci, Nanni Unghero, and Baccio d'Agnolo

[8] For further comments on goldsmiths see herein, pp. 414–15.

and his son Giuliano were all prominent furniture-makers and intarsia artists, who in the annals of art history, however, are better known as architects.[9]

With the exception of Giotto and Orcagna, painters do not show up as architects until the end of the fifteenth century, although they were often called in as consultants by the building committee of the cathedral. Given their preoccupation with perspective, early Renaissance painters were naturally interested in architecture, and like their colleagues in the other arts they were fascinated by nothing more in the classical world, where they sought models for imitation, than architecture. Paintings, in fact, reveal some of the most extravagant architectural ideas of the period, although the fantasy of some of their architectural settings have little to do with anything then being built except in the common reference to the basic classical corpus of motifs and design.[10] Still, half a dozen or so painters, who probably had no practical experience whatsoever in any of the building trades, submitted entries in the 1491 competition for completion of the cathedral facade. By the sixteenth century artists throughout Italy trained as painters, like Leonardo, Raphael, Peruzzi, Vignola, and Giulio Romano, also had active careers as architects, and the list of Florentine painter-architects extends well into the century to include Buontalenti, Vasari, Cigoli, and Santi di Tito.

Leaving aside Alberti and the patrician dilettantes from Lorenzo de' Medici on down the social scale who allegedly designed buildings, it is difficult to find a Florentine architect before Giuliano da Sangallo and Cronaca at the end of the fifteenth century who does not have some reputation as a goldsmith, woodworker, or sculptor. This was not a situation altogether unique to Florence. Most Venetian architects were stonecutters who have some reputation as sculptors, and most of the architects who came from the environs of Como are also known to have carved stone. Many masons in the tradition of brick architecture in the Po River valley, however, seem to have had no talent for other kinds of artistic activity—Alesso Tramello at Piacenza, Biagio Rossetti at Ferrara, Aristotele Fioravanti at Bologna, and the Zaccagni at Parma were known only as wallers. Florentines never used this term when referring to their architects, and apparently no Florentine architect came from that craft. Because of their background in the other arts, Florentine architects were all men who had undergone extensive training to develop design talent. This is why, on the one hand, it was difficult for Cellini to think

[9] Woodworkers in Siena were also active as architects; V. Lusini, "Dell'arte del legname innanzi al suo Statuto del 1426," *Arte antica senese* (*Bullettino senese di storia patria*, 11 [1904]), 183–246. The relation of the craft to architecture is noted by Isabelle Hyman, "Towards Rescuing the Lost Reputation of Antonio di Minetto Ciaccheri," in *Essays Presented to Myron P. Gilmore*, ed. Sergio Bertelli and Gloria Ramakus (Florence, 1978), II, 267–68.

[10] P. Francastel, "Imagination et réalité dans l'architecture civile de '400" in *Homage à Lucien Febvre—Evential de l'histoire vivante*, II (Paris, 1953), 195–99.

that much could be expected of someone like Antonio da Sangallo, who was trained as a mere carpenter, and why, on the other hand, Vasari could so completely overlook the justified criticisms of Bramante for his lack of knowledge of construction techniques.[11]

The recourse to independent artistic talent for the planning of buildings is certainly one of the reasons that architecture flourished in Florence. The notable marks of a Quattrocento building are, after all, the decorative detail of its stonework and the proportional system applied to its design, not (for the most part) any innovation in spatial forms that might have presented a challenge to traditional construction methods. The artisan turning to the planning of a building was not likely to come up against complex technical problems of construction that went beyond his competence to handle with the help of masons working with traditional methods. Moreover, given the particular character of a guild conglomerate embracing all the building and related crafts and the liberal policy of Florentine guilds on membership, little by way of institutional barriers stood in the way of anyone who wanted to design a building and supervise its construction, whether he was a mason or not.

In short, the fifteenth-century artisan came to architecture because he had, in the practice of his own craft, established himself as a man with an eye sensitive to design and alert to contemporary taste. As architectural activity picked up, the aspiring architect made informal efforts to train that eye and thus put his credentials on a more secure basis. In accord with the taste of the times this meant looking at classical architecture, especially traveling to see the ruins of Rome itself. On his trip there Brunelleschi presumably spent much time inspecting sites, measuring details, and examining structural features; and all these things he discussed with no less a humanist scholar than Alberti. Cronaca got his nickname because after his return from Rome he was considered a veritable chronicle of classical architecture. Architects made drawings of plans and details; these sketchbooks, many of which survive, were an important source for their ideas. Their fascination with the architectural monuments of antiquity, however, did not stop with archaelogical recording of what they saw. Their antiquarianism included the fanciful reconstructions of ruins with an imagination that never found a comparable release in their own work as architects. By observing, traveling, and sketching the architect worked up his classical vocabulary and perfected his design technique. These men also had considerable interest in the building techniques of the ancients—in materials, such as cement and bricks, and in struc-

[11] The comment by Cellini is cited by Wilkinson, "Professionalism," p. 138; for Vasari on Bramante see James Ackerman, "Notes on Bramante's Bad Reputation," in *Studi Bramanteschi: Atti del Congresso internazionale (1970)* (Rome, 1974), p. 346.

tural problems, such as vaulting. Finally, some made significant attempts to go beyond mere observation to refine their training by getting down to the very principles of architecture. Brunelleschi studied the proportional system that lay behind classical architecture, and the precise measurements on many architectural drawings show that this was a continuing concern of architects. Rereading Vitruvius they learned that the architect must have theoretical as well as practical knowledge—an intellectual pretension confirmed by the treatise of Alberti, who was, of course, an intellectual, not an artisan.

Design training, consciousness of stylistic models, awareness of theory, intellectual claims—here were all the elements for the eventual definition of professional status, however inchoate that profession still was in the fifteenth century with respect to practice. In addition, the architect as builder became more of a technical expert not so much in construction methods as in the highly specialized functions of two kinds of projects he increasingly found himself in charge of—fortifications and engineering works.

The fifteenth century saw a marked increase in the demand for military architecture. The first half of the century was a period of territorial consolidation by the leading states of Italy on the way to establishing the precarious balance of power at Lodi in 1454, and everywhere military frontiers demarcating the confines of power had to be reinforced with fortifications. Moreover, with artillery becoming a major component of military force, fortifications had to be renewed, and often renewed again, under the changing conditions of the rapidly improving technology of offensive warfare. The use of cannons in Europe goes back to the invention of gunpowder in the fourteenth century, but for a long time cannons had a limited use as seige equipment because their heavy weight precluded easy mobility and the stone balls they fired were not very effective. Only technical improvements in the later fifteenth century made cannons more dangerous. Calibers were reduced, thereby increasing the range of the projectile; the weapon was lightened, making it more mobile; and the use of iron balls increased the weapon's destructive power. Given the precarious political situation among the Italian states, every government was under pressure to take advantage of the new military technology and at the same time update its defensive network of fortifications; those pressures mounted when Italy became the battlefield of Europe—and the proving ground for new battlefield tactics—after the French invasion of 1494. The early history of modern fortifications is written almost entirely on the Italian evidence from the late fifteenth and early sixteenth centuries.[12]

12 Developments in fortifications in the second half of the fifteenth century are surveyed in J. R. Hale, "The Development of the Bastion, 1440–1534," in *Europe in*

Built in the spirit of the new power politics in Renaissance Italy, and in accord with the taste of the times, these military installations had to be monumental statements of the presence of power; they also had practical functions of an increasingly technical nature. On both counts their builders had to be something more than an ordinary mason.

Virtually every architect in Florence had an appointment at one time or another to tend to fortifications somewhere in the city's defensive network. Brunelleschi oversaw fortification works at Castellina, Rencine, and Staggia, toward the southern frontier with Siena; he served in the field during the campaign against Lucca; and he made a model for the fortress of Vicopisano. The commune sent Michelozzo to oversee fortification works at Lucca and Montepulciano and sought his advice on other sites. Giuliano da Maiano directed work at Montepoggiolo. Manetti went to Milan to present the duke his plans for the fortification of Pisa. Francione was responsible for the great fortress put up in Volterra after the suppression of its revolt in 1472, and in the late 1480s he was kept busy by fortification works at Pietrasanta and Sarzana, in the newly acquired territory along the Tyrrhenian coast above Pisa. Giuliano da Sangallo worked at Colle di Val d'Elsa (1479) and Poggio Imperiale at Poggibonsi (1488) on Florence's southwestern flank, at Borgo San Sepolcro (1499) and Arezzo (1503) on the southeastern flank, at Pisa after its reconquest (1509), and at Livorno (1517 to 1518). Antonio da Sangallo worked with him on some of these projects and independently on a few others. The Sangallo, who were on the scene in the period after the French invasions into Tuscany, spent much of their careers on military jobs.[13]

Other governments under greater military pressures had more sustained need for military architects to build up their defense works, and they lured away many a Florentine with the prospect of a better-paying job. When Michelozzo went to the republic of Ragusa at the end of his career he became virtually a full-time military architect. The papal states offered the best employment possibilities, since the pope's vigorous expansionist policy in the second half of the century created a pressing and continuing need for experienced builders as military architects who were capable of dealing with the technical problems inherent in that work. Bernardo Rossellino worked in Rome in this capacity from 1451 to 1455; Baccio Pontelli, Giovannino

---

the Late Middle Ages, ed. J. R. Hale, R. Highfield, and B. Smalley (London, 1965), pp. 466–94. An overview of the problem is provided by Michael Mallett, *Mercenaries and Their Masters* (Totowa, N. J., 1974), pp. 164–72. The importance of military architecture can be measured by the enormous financial burden it imposed on government; see, for example, Judith Hook, "Fortifications and the End of the Sienese State, *History*, 62 (1977), 372–87.

[13] Giancarlo Severini, *Architettura militare di Giuliano da Sangallo* (Pisa, 1970).

de' Dolci, and the Sangallo all spent much of their careers in papal service as military architects.[14] In the High Renaissance architects continued to fall into the pattern. Bramante worked as a military engineer for Lodovico il Moro. Peruzzi and Michelangelo were called on for help with fortifications in their native cities, and Michelangelo was the first choice of the Medici to build the Fortezza da Basso, which was to seal their power over the city. Michele Sanmichele and Antonio da Sangallo the Younger are the most noted among a host of Italian architects of the next generation who spent the better part of their lives supervising the erection of fortifications.

The importance of this work in military architecture for the training, and professionalization, of the architect has never been assessed, although the development of certain artistic ideas by both Michelangelo and Leonardo da Vinci has been attributed to their work on fortifications.[15] Nevertheless, the keen interest of architects in keeping up with the innovations in the technology of warfare that were calling into question the traditional way of preparing defense works is illustrated by a chronological survey of fortifications put up in the second half of the fifteenth century. At times during these years new ideas came so fast that some fortresses seem to have been outdated as soon as they were built.

The challenge of all this military construction was a matter of design and science, not construction techniques; and so what was needed was a veritable architect, not a mason. The problems quite naturally contributed to the growing theoretical literature on architecture. Alberti and Filarete lived perhaps too soon to see fortifications in anything but a traditional way, but by the next generation Francesco di Giorgio had to deal with these new problems. Because his discussion of the subject in fact became the foundation of a new science that had to be mastered by the architect, Francesco di Giorgio has been called the father of military architecture. Thereafter most Italian treatises on architecture include sections on fortifications. Palladio's is the most notable exception, but he was one of the few architects who never worked on military projects. By the sixteenth century military architecture had become so technical in its demands that it was increasingly regarded as a distinct field of specialization, and men came to it from both military and architectural backgrounds. In his treatise on the subject Giovan Battista

[14] Besides the literature cited in the preceding notes see Gaspare De Fiore, *Baccio Pontelli, architetto fiorentino* (Rome, 1963), especially chs. V and VI; and Harriet McNeal Caplow, "Michelozzo at Ragusa: New Documents and Revaluations," *JSArH*, 31 (1972), 108–19.

[15] J. R. Hale, *Renaissance Fortification: Art or Engineering?* (London, 1977), p. 56. The relation between architecture and fortification is remarked by Stanislaus von Moos, *Turm und Bollwerk: Beiträge zu einer politischen Ikonographie der italienische Renaissancearchitektur* (Zurich and Freiburg i/B, 1974), pp. 207–15.

Bellucci (who lived from 1506 to 1554) considered it a profession apart from civil architecture, and although other writers did not exclude the civil architect from working on fortifications, they insisted on the necessity of also having military experts on the job to advise him whenever he undertook such a task.[16]

Architects in the employ of the state were also frequently called upon to supervise civil engineering projects, most notably hydraulic works for land reclamation, river control, and water supply, and many developed a lively interest in technology and machinery. Mariano Taccola, whose treatise on engineering was well known in his own time (although it seems he never was active in the field as an engineer) reports a conversation with Brunelleschi in which the architect refers to some of his ideas on river projects.[17] Francesco di Giorgio's earliest known work for the city of Siena was on fountains and aqueducts, and later, as city architect, he was continually busy on projects related to water supply. A major activity of builders in the Po River valley were the irrigation works undertaken by most governments once the political situation there began to stabilize in the fourteenth century. Luca Fancelli, the stonemason from Settignano who made his career in Mantua, gained much experience there in hydraulic works; in 1487 he wrote to Lorenzo de' Medici about various projects for building a canal in the valley of the Bisenzio toward Signa for purposes of land reclamation.[18] In the sixteenth century Buontalenti worked regularly on river projects in his capacity as the official architect of the grand duke.[19]

Much of Leonardo da Vinci's curiosity and fanciful experimentation reflected all of these current concerns of the architect with weapons, fortifications, and hydraulic engineering. These are the things he advertised about himself when he sought employment at the court of Lodovico il Moro, duke of Milan; and only at the end of his long list of credentials for this kind of work did he add, almost incidentally, that he was also accomplished in civil architecture and could paint pictures. There was hardly an architect around

[16] Horst de la Croix, "Military Architecture and the Radial City Plan in Sixteenth-Century Italy," *Art Bulletin*, 42 (1960), especially 270–75. The study of L. R. Shelby, *John Rogers, Tudor Military Engineer* (Oxford, 1967), shows how the military engineer in England emerged with professional status before the architect. For some evidence of the importance of military engineering in the practice of architecture, see Hale, *Fortification*.

[17] Frank D. Prager and Giustina Scaglia, *Brunelleschi: Studies of His Technology and Inventions* (Cambridge, Mass., 1970), pp. 129–31.

[18] Willelmo Braghirolli, "Luca Fancelli: scultore, architetto e idraulico del secolo XV," *Archivio storico lombardo*, 3 (1876), 630–32.

[19] Anna Cerchiai and Coletta Quiriconi, "Relazioni e rapporti all'Ufficio dei Capitani di Parte Guelfa," in *Architettura e politica da Cosimo I a Ferdinando*, ed. Giorgio Spini (Florence, 1976) pp. 208–9.

who at one time or another did not have to deal with problems of this kind while in government service, and for many these were major preoccupations. Our notion of the architect as artist should not deceive us into thinking that these technical activities were not central to his understanding of the intellectual nature of his profession. That Alberti did not deal with hydraulic engineering in his treatise and only touched on fortifications is the mark of his detachment from the practice of architecture in his own day. For Vasari, on the other hand, machinery characterized the ultimate stage, after necessity and ornament, in the evolution of the craft. In the eyes of contemporaries the architect's expertise in these technical matters helped improve his status as a professional man distinct from ordinary masons.

The labels that came to be attached to the architect in the Renaissance were the distinguishing marks of his emerging professional status. The word *engineer* first appears in the Milanese documents at the end of the thirteenth century with reference to experts in the use of military machines, and in the middle of the fourteenth century engineers commonly supervised irrigation projects. It became the standard term in northern Italy to distinguish architects and foremen of public works from ordinary masons. In the statutes of the masons' guild at Padua, for instance, the head mason of the municipal works authority is alone referred to as an engineer. Florentine architects working in northern Italy were commonly called engineers, although the term seldom shows up in the documents of their native city. The term *architect* also appears during the fifteenth century in its classical sense of a creator and designer of buildings, although, again, the term is not as commonly used in Florence as it is elsewhere in Italy until the end of the century. Perhaps one reason this distinguishing terminology seems to come into more general use sooner in northern Italy is the greater need there for status by one, invariably trained as a waller, who had no independent artisan talent that would qualify him as a designer. Rossetti, Fioravanti, the Zaccagni, and a host of lesser-known architects are often called engineer, architect, and waller in the same breath.[20]

In 1505 four ducal engineers in Milan drew up regulations for land surveying and construction of irrigation works, since there were at the time (as they stated in the preamble) no standard procedures in these matters. The document has been seen as the first step toward the corporate organization of engineers into the College of Engineers, founded in 1563. According to the original statutes the function of the college was to oversee the preparation of aspiring engineers and then to license them. By calling

[20] The usage of the term *architect* is surveyed by Nikolaus Pevsner, "The Term 'Architect' in the Middle Ages," *Speculum*, 17 (1942), 549–62.

themselves a college rather than a guild they emphasized the difference in status between them and mere craftsmen.[21]

The rise in social status is an important theme in the history of the architect during the Renaissance. In the Middle Ages he could achieve some status above his artisan origins simply by virtue of his position as supervisor of a large works project and his often close association with his employer; if he worked for a prince, he could end up in the service nobility of his lord's household. Although he had no intellectual pretensions, he might be able, on his own, to push his education beyond what he got as an apprentice; and if he supervised the construction of a great cathedral, he undoubtedly could get some notion of the sophisticated ideas his employers had about such buildings. The medieval architect did not, however, have a rationale for his own peculiar status as a particular kind of artist and professional.

This is what the Renaissance architects began to articulate. They discovered in Vitruvius the claim to theoretical as well as practical knowledge, and they had in Alberti the program for professional education. For Alberti, the architect must have not only a sense of beauty but sound scientific learning, especially in mathematics and geometry, and since the architect served all mankind as the complete designer, working on everything from simple houses to great cities, Alberti had a sense of the higher purpose of architecture as something socially necessary and useful and of the architect as a kind of universal man. Alberti, of course, directed his remarks more to the typical Renaissance patron with an active interest in the buildings he sponsored than to architects themselves, but his ideas are echoed in Filarete's portrait of the architect and continue to resonate in comments about the craft over the next century. Meanwhile architects became more confident of the intellectual foundations of their art as they enlarged their knowledge of technology, of classical models, of design, and of function; their conscious concern with these subjects surfaced in any number of writings by architects themselves. All of this served to put a definable distance between the architect and the mean craftsman with whom he had traditionally been associated. It also gave rise to the opposing claims of theory on the one hand and of practical knowledge on the other that have competed ever since for the attention of the architect.

It is not that these men had much of a theoretical preparation. Although Italians were more likely to regard their knowledge of geometry in a philosophical context than was the mason north of the Alps, who was still in the medieval tradition of considering the subject as merely a practical working device, some of the scholarly literature has exaggerated the metaphysical stance of the Renaissance architect, attributing to him notions derived from

[21] Gino Bozza and Jolanda Bassi, "La formazione e la posizione dell'ingegnere e dell'architetto nelle varie epoche storiche," in *Il centenario del Politecnico di Milano, 1863–1963* (Milan, 1964), pp. 62–64; Caterina Santoro, *Collegi professionali e corporazioni d'arti e mestieri della vecchia Milano* (Milan, 1955), pp. 10 and 29.

Alberti's justification of the profession. Alberti, however, wrote for the patron, not for the mason, and inasmuch as none of these architects had the humanist education he assumed, we can wonder how well they could have understood his theories even if they had known them firsthand. Certainly Filarete's assertions about the status of the architect sound hollow of philosophical content. It has been said that architects of the High Renaissance did not read the early theorists and, in fact, had little interest in the subject. When architects finally took to writing treatises in the later sixteenth century, their discussions of theory were not well thought out and were largely irrelevant to practice. At the most they tend to codify theory into laws in a way that turns their books into practical manuals. Palladio made by far the most successful efforts to combine theory and practice, and it was no accident that he found his most enthusiastic audience in eighteenth-century England, where a much closer alliance was established between theory and practice than ever existed in Italy.[22]

Practice

In his capacity as architect—that is, as designer and planner of a building—a foreman of the cathedral works in Florence had no more of a problem in getting his ideas across to his workers and his patrons that did any medieval master mason. Being employed more or less full time, he could communicate directly and regularly to his staff as needed. By virtue of his position at the cathedral he was likely to be in charge of other projects concurrently, but all these he directed through one workshop. So long as there was little outside demand for his services as a designer, he did not have to think about devices enabling him to control construction by remote control, so to speak. He did not need to work out a complex medium of communication such as models, drawings, or blueprints. The function of an architect was not yet separated from the function of master builder.

In the fourteenth century most buildings did not present a serious problem in the communication of design intentions to the executing masons. Designs were not complex and in many instances the mason himself was the designer. In any case, to the extent that style in such buildings was traditional it was relatively easy to tell masons what was wanted when they were engaged to put up a building.

The contracts let out for the construction of the hospital of San Matteo during the period 1387 to 1389 illustrate how the design intention was com-

22 Rudolf Wittkower, "English Literature on Architecture," in his *Palladio and English Palladianism* (London, 1974). The Italian treatises are assessed by Wilkinson, "Professionalism," p. 149; and interesting observations on theory and practice in military architecture are made by Hale, *Fortification*.

municated to the builders of one complex that on the one hand was traditional, but on the other made some modest architectural pretensions in its plan for a church, a public loggia on the street with columns and capitals, and an arcaded courtyard within surrounded by service buildings of various kinds.[23] The contracts do not specify an architect in that they make no mention of anyone who had control over the design; nor do they mention any plans or drawings the masons were to follow. The patron communicated his intentions to them in three ways. First, the contracts specify materials and set out, in great detail and precision, all the measurements of walls—their thickness, length, and height—presumably on the basis of a floor plan made out by someone. This was all a waller needed to follow the standard procedures of his craft in putting up a traditional kind of building. Secondly, other buildings are cited as models to be followed in erecting those of San Matteo. The foundations, walls, and construction methods of the new hospital, along with the portico with its vaults, columns, and roof, were to be like those of the recently completed hospital of Bonifazio. The roof of the main ward was to take its model (and all the details were spelled out) the city's principal institution of this kind, Santa Maria Nuova. In other words, the builders were simply to imitate existing buildings, or parts of them, and the models were, quite understandably, notable buildings of the same kind—the hospital of Santa Maria Nuova was the oldest and largest in the city, and the recently completed Bonifazio represented the latest standard in hospital design. The third device in the San Matteo contracts to communicate design to the builders was oral instruction from the patron; doors, window frames, and other stone elments purchased by the patron were to be installed according to his instructions.

The San Matteo contracts probably represent typical building procedures in the fourteenth century. There was no architect, properly speaking, at all. The patron had a general idea of what he wanted, he had worked out all the measurements of walls so that he could both estimate building costs beforehand and provide the masons with all the information they needed to work out technical problems (like vaulting), he looked around the city for certain elements he wanted imitated in his project, and he personally selected decorative elements and told the builders where these were to go. All this may well have been done in informal consultation with a mason in order to have the benefit of expert opinion, but to the extent that the mason himself functioned as architect his on-the-site employment precluded a communications problem. This building tradition continued into the fifteenth century, and it is not improbable that many Renaissance buildings were designed, so to speak, precisely in this way.

[23] S. Matteo 1, fols. 11r–12v and 29r–30v (published by Piero Sanpaolesi, "Alcuni documenti sull'ospedale di S. Matteo in Firenze," *Belle Arti*, I [1946], 77–81); 123, fols. 5r–6r. The contracts are discussed herein, pp. 130–32.

Nevertheless, in the fifteenth century, as more patrons had recourse to design artists of one kind or another for the planning of building projects, these men, many of them not masons and yet finding themselves involved in building, worked out a language to communicate design ideas, in effect separating the function of architect from that of builder. On the one hand, with so many new ideas in the air and with a premium on originality, the architect now more than ever before needed to be sure about conveying his intentions to the client; on the other hand, to the extent that he himself did not work full time (if at all) on the projects he designed, he had to devise some way to communicate those same intentions to the workers so that they could proceed in his absence with some degree of confidence on his part that the job was being done properly. Moreover, the new aesthetic of the Renaissance demanded that the architect have a more coherent and personal view of the finished building as an idea independent of what might result from the vicissitudes of construction. In other words, for both practical and aesthetic reasons the architect could not be altogether satisfied with merely carrying around his ideas about a building in his head. Today the architect works with plastic models, perspective renderings, plans, elevations, and blueprints—all useful in actual construction because builders have learned this language developed by the architect for communicating with them. It was such a language that the Renaissance architect, in the changing conditions of his professional life, began formulating; it had to be a language that both patron and craftsman could understand to varying degrees.

In Florence that language consisted of models and drawings. Surviving examples of these are extremely rare, and evidence for their use comes mostly from literary sources and building accounts. The terminology of these documents, however, is imprecise. The problem of interpretation derives in part from the meaning of *disegno* as both a drawing and a general design idea that can be represented in either two or three dimensions, and in part from the meaning of *modello* as something that incorporates a design idea, be it a model or a drawing. In fourteenth-century cathedral documents both terms are used for both drawings and three-dimensional objects. For the building of the Loggia dei Priori in the late 1370s, models (and *exempla*) are described as being drawn on paper. A wood model made of the church of the Santissima Annuziata in 1384 is repeatedly referred to as a *disegno* in the account for its construction, and Filarete talks about making a *disegno* in wood.[24] As a rule, however, *modello* in Florentine documents of the fifteenth century refers to a plastic object, although there certainly are exceptions. The

[24] Carl Frey, *Die Loggia dei Lanzi* (Berlin, 1885), p. 285 ("quibus est modellus seu exemplum, designatum in quodam folio"); Ss. Annunziata 841 (income-outgo, 1364–84), fols. 28r–v. These terms as used in the cathedral documents are collected in Andreas Grote, *Das Dombauamt in Florenz, 1285–1370* (Munich, 1959), pp. 113–19. Filarete's usage is illustrated in note 39 herein.

context helps to clarify the matter when specific reference is made to wood or carpenters and when the cost is correspondingly high. In the following discussion the word *model* will be used to translate *modello* (or *modano*) when it occurs in the sources; when it is used in a general sense a *model* will be understood as a plastic object.

Architectural drawings were not unknown in the Middle Ages.[25] They are referred to in documents, and many survive, especially for the later period. The earliest drawings that appear to be practical construction aids date to the second quarter of the thirteenth century, and they suggest that the architect was developing new shop procedures for working out his own ideas or for conveying them to his patron. The interest in making these project drawings has been related to the emergence of Gothic style in architecture, when the mason found that he could best refine his growing sense of linearity in both design and structure, first, in full-scale engravings on stone and, later, in drawings. By the fourteenth century masons were also making drawings of buildings they saw on their travels, and these have been credited with widening the architectural world of more sedentary and provincial masons. Most of these early drawings, whether project drawings or memory records, could not have been working plans. They seldom presented a complete picture of the building; most were elevations without ground plans; and they had limited utility as practical guides, lacking technical specifications, for instance, about scale and jointings of stone. At the beginning of work on most medieval buildings the architect was probably in a position to give his patron only a general notion of what his building would look like on completion. He worked out details subsequently, in the course of construction; meanwhile he had to be in steady attendance to instruct the workers so they could realize his intentions, which he carried around only in his head.

In the fourteenth and fifteenth centuries drawings began to take on a more practical function.[26] Plans and drawings are occasionally referred to in English building contracts from this period, and many references to such visual aids show up in Italian construction records. One drawing accompanying a contract for the building of the Sansedoni palace in Siena in 1340 survives. It presents a full view of the facade, and although it seems to be a preliminary freehand sketch, the fact that it accompanies a contract indicates its formal nature as a document. It is, in any case, furnished with detailed dimensions, and since the contract makes repeated reference to it, there is every reason

[25] Du Colombier, *Chantiers*, pp. 72–87; Shelby, "Role," pp. 90–91; Robert Branner, "Drawings from a Thirteenth-Century Architect's Shop: The Reims Palimpset," *JSArH*, 17, No. 4 (1958), 19; idem, "Villard de Honnecourt, Reims, and the Origin of Gothic Architectural Drawing," *Gazette des Beaux-Arts*, 61 (1963), 129–46.

[26] L. F. Salzman, *Building in England Down to 1540* (Oxford, 1967), p. 52; Shelby, "Role," p. 390.

to believe that the masons could use it, at least in a general way, as a guide for measurements and for placement of the doors and windows.[27]

Architectural drawings survive in large number from the latter part of the fifteenth century onward. They were made to copy ancient monuments, to give rein to the architect's fantasy, and to work out his ideas. Given the background of many Quattrocento architects as goldsmiths and intarsia artists, it would be surprising if they did not make extensive use of drawings in the process of going from preliminary sketches of a building to some kind of representation of the final plans, but the extant material is not so complete as to permit a satisfactory reconstruction of that creative process.

Drawings also came to have more of a practical function in the construction process. The fourteenth-century accounts of the Florence cathedral contain payments for the purchase of parchment and for the work of painters in connection with the making of designs.[28] At the Innocenti, in July 1427, parchment was purchased and a painter paid to make designs; a few days later the building committee had a luncheon meeting with the consuls of the silk guild, the masons, and many merchants to make certain decisions on the basis of a design then up for discussion.[29] In 1440 the officials of Montepulciano, who had commissioned Michelozzo to design additions to their town hall, wrote him for the design on paper (*disegno in foglio*) so they could proceed to let out contracts.[30] Michelozzo's design for the new buildings at the hospital of San Paolo is described as containing "the measurements, the form, and the way it was to be built," and although one of the payments mentions a model, the small amount he was paid for his efforts—lb.16 s.10 (about 3 florins)—would suggest that what he submitted was a portfolio of plans and drawings, not a plastic model.[31] They may have been of the sort Filarete had in mind when talking about making drawings preparatory to

[27] The contract is published by Gaetano Milanesi, *Documenti per la storia dell'arte senese,* I (Siena, 1854), 232–40, and the accompanying drawing is reproduced and discussed by Annarosa Garzelli, "Un disegno di architettura civile del 1340," *Antichità viva,* 12 (1973), 36–41. A more thorough analysis by Franklin Toker is forthcoming.

[28] Grote, *Dombauamt,* pp. 113–19.

[29] In July 1427 payment was made to a stationer for "certe carte di pecora avemo per fare disegni per la muraglia" and to the painter Gherardo di Giovanni "per uno disegno fece in su una carta di pechora per cagione della muraglia," and the luncheon was held "per pigliare partito in su certo disegno sopra alla muralglia del detto spedale"; Innocenti, ser. XXI (general administration), 1 (ledger A), fol. 146 (partially published by Mendes and Dallai, "Innocenti," doc. 11).

[30] Howard Saalman, "The Palazzo Comunale in Montepulciano: An Unknown Work by Michelozzo," *Zeitschrift für Kunstgeschichte,* 28 (1965), doc. 7.

[31] "sono per parte di sua faticha del disegno della nostra muraglia, cioè delle misure e della forma e del modo chome s'à a fare"; Richard A. Goldthwaite and W. R. Rearick, "Michelozzo and the Ospedale di San Paolo in Florence," *Flor. Mitt.,* 21 (1977), 272.

construction and explaining them to his masons.[32] No evidence suggests, however, that fifteenth-century working drawings presented elevations or used perspective techniques. The method of using the othogonal projection in architectural drawings was not developed until the early sixteenth century in Rome.[33]

At the same time that project, or working, drawings were coming into use for construction, Italians began also to make plastic models for parts of buildings or for the entire structure, a subject that has been little remarked in the history of architecture.[34] Medieval stonecarvers traditionally used the full-scale mold in wood or plaster as a device for determining decorative details before executing them in stone, but the more ambitious architectural models are unknown in northern Europe.[35] It is said that the Italian custom of sponsoring competitions for the architectural design of cathedral projects, which led to the nomination of the foreman of the works, gave rise to the practice of making elaborate models as a device for displaying the architect's ideas. The model served a particularly important public function in the unique Italian context of communal sponsorship of much cathedral-building, since lay building committees, forever hounding the architect for clarification of his intentions, found a model the easiest way to understand what was involved. At various points in the construction of the cathedrals in both Florence and Bologna models were made of brick that were so large as to be buildings in themselves but so generalized as to have been of slight utility for either the solution of structural problems or the determination of details of the design.[36]

Competitions were common practice in Florence, and aspiring architects had to submit their ideas in one form or another so that the panel of judges

[32] Filarete, *Trattato di architettura*, ed. Anna Maria Finoli and Liliana Grassi (Milan, 1972), I, 241.

[33] The refinement of working architectural drawings has been studied by Wolfgang Lotz, "The Rendering of the Interior in Architectural Drawings in the Renaissance," in his *Studies in Italian Renaissance Architecture* (Cambridge, Mass., 1977), pp. 1–65; for the use of drawings in the architect's design process see Ackerman, "Practice," pp. 8–9.

[34] The literature on the subject, especially for this early period, is slight: Jacob Burckhardt, *Die Baukunst der Renaissance in Italien*, vol. II of his *Gesammelte Werke* (Basel, 1955), pp. 80–83; Martin S. Briggs, "Architectural Models," *Burlington Magazine*, 54 (1929), 174–83 and 245–52; Ludwig H. Heydenreich, "Architekturmodell," in *Reallexikon zur deutschen Kunstgeschichte*, I (Stuttgart, 1937), 925. The importance of models in Renaissance architectural practice is questioned by Ackerman, "Practice," p. 8 (which, however, concentrates on Roman practice in the sixteenth century); and by Howard Saalman, "Early Renaissance Architectural Theory and Practice in Filarete's *Trattato di Architettura*," *Art Bulletin*, 41 (1959), 102–6.

[35] Du Colombier, *Chantiers*, pp. 95–96; Shelby, "Role," pp. 391–92.

[36] Saalman, "Theory and Practice," p. 104; idem, "Santa Maria del Fiore: 1294–1418," *Art Bulletin*, 46 (1964), 476.

could come to a decision. The cathedral authorities held competitions for the vaulting of the crossing and for the lantern to crown it; later in the century no fewer than twenty-nine artists of all kinds participated in the competition for the facade. Cosimo de' Medici must have sponsored some kind of competition for the design of his new palace, for we are told that when Brunelleschi's entry was rejected as too ambitious and inappropriate for a private citizen the architect destroyed it. The son of Filippo Strozzi the Elder recounts how Strozzi endlessly mulled over several plans for his palace in a ploy to arouse Lorenzo de' Medici's interest in the project and at the same time defuse his jealousy, and although the well-kept record of Strozzi's financial dealings reveals no payments for such plans, his son's story must have had a certain verismilitude with respect to how one might proceed in the planning of a building in fifteenth-century Florence. In 1485 the building committee for the new church of Santa Maria delle Carceri at Prato asked Lorenzo de' Medici to look over the many models it had on its hands ("avendo per le mani più modelli di più facte") and make a decision (which was in favor of Giuliano da Sangallo's plan).[37] Competitions of sorts were held even for relatively modest projects. The building accounts for the church of Santa Maria degli Alberighi, which was little more than an oratory, open in 1507 with three equal payments to the two carpenters and the stonecarver who had submitted models for new construction.[38]

Once selected as winner of a competition, the model became, in a sense, a guarantee for the finished product, both assuring the patron of his understanding of the architect's intentions and binding the architect in his capacity as foreman responsible for the execution. In a period when construction often continued beyond the lifetime of all the parties originally involved in the planning of a building, a model could serve as an authority against pressures for modifications of all kinds, even though modifications were inevitably made. That a model, or some similar memory record, became important in Italy, in contrast to earlier architectural practice in northern Europe, says something also about the new attitude Italians were beginning to take toward their buildings in the fourteenth century. A model, or some other kind of representation, becomes important once there is a clear idea of the building in its entirety, and perhaps also in its details, from the moment of its conception.

37 G. Marchini, "Della costruzione di Santa Maria delle Carceri in Prato," *Archivio storico pratese*, 14 (1936), 54–56.

38 ASF, Compagnie religiose soppresse 1425, item 22 (building accounts, 1503–13), fol. 32v; ASF, Acquisti e doni 306 (building accounts, 1501–13), fol. 109r. The three men, paid lb.14 each "per fare uno modello della chiesa overo oratori' della nostra nuziata," were Piero di Nozzo, *legnaiuolo*, Bartolomeo (Baccio) d'Agnolo, *legnaiuolo*, and Chimenti di Taddeo (or del Tasso), *scarpellatore*. The church, now destroyed, was located on the site of Santa Maria de' Ricci.

Vasari and assistants, Filippo Brunelleschi presents a model of San Lorenzo to Cosimo il Vecchio, late sixteenth century.

Few wood models for any building have survived. What is probably Brunelleschi's for the lantern of the cupola, the preliminary one by Sangallo for the Strozzi palace, and Baccio d'Agnolo's for a projected new church of San Marco (1512) can still be seen; others no longer extant were observed by earlier writers, including Arnolfo di Cambio's for the cathedral and Giotto's for the Campanile, both seen by Vasari. A model for the Uguccioni palace (around 1550), seen by Giovanni Cinelli a century later, gave him an exact idea of the cornice that was never executed to complete the facade. Antonio Manetti, Antonio Billi, Giorgio Vasari, and other Renaissance writers on architects and their work take it for granted that models were an aspect of architectural practice of the day. Moreover, architects who themselves wrote about their craft, like Alberti and Filarete, are explicit about the importance of models. Something about how architects made use of them can also be known from the abundance of records of payments in building accounts for their work on models.

Presentation of the architect's ideas, whether in a competition or not, was not the only function of models made to scale and completed in their decorative detail. A Florentine architect, having most likely been trained in the sculptural arts, may have felt a particular need to work out ideas in plastic form. Filarete advises the architect to make a wood model to scale, "measured and proportional to the finished building"; Alberti emphasizes the importance of model-building in helping the architect recognize the full implications of his ideas.[39] Alberti goes on to say that models must be complete in all of their decorative detail. Sangallo's model for the Strozzi palace is unfinished from this point of view, but when Cronaca came on the job as head stonecutter and, in effect, architect, he ordered a new model complete with columns not only for the courtyard but also for the windows. Furthermore, from time to time Cronaca had other models made of details of the palace, including the facade, and until recently models survived for two different rows of windows, presumably made to get a better impression of alternative solutions to a design problem.[40] Michelangelo used models in the same way to work out his ideas about major problems in the design of St. Peter's.[41]

Not all models were completed down to the decorative detail. Some could have been little more than rough three-dimensional sketches, a sort of presentation of the general idea of a building. For all of its expense Sangallo's model for the Strozzi palace was such a "sketch," with no indication of decorative details except for a small section of rustication that could hardly have served in the execution. Rough models, like the one made later in the construction of the Strozzi Palace of the plan of the building, could serve to work out some particular problem relating to design.[42] It has already been noted that at Santo Spirito in 1486, when construction reached the point where placement of doors had to be decided, some of the men involved in the decision wanted to see the options worked out in models.[43]

The construction history of Santo Spirito offers many illustrations of the importance of models in the building process. Brunelleschi made a model of the church, but for the half a century after his death during which con-

[39] Filarete, *Trattato*, II, 40 ("uno disegnio picchoIo rilevato di legniame misurato e proportionato come che à a essere fatto"); Leon Battista Alberti, *L'architettura*, ed. Giovanni Orlandi (Milan, 1966), II, ch. 1; IX, chs. 8 and 10.

[40] Richard A. Goldthwaite, "The Building of the Strozzi Palace: The Construction Industry in Renaissance Florence," *Studies in Medieval and Renaissance History*, 10 (1973), 128–29. The models for window designs are illustrated in Guido Pampaloni, *Palazzo Strozzi* (Rome, 1974), p. 10, figs. 11 and 12.

[41] Henry A. Millon and Craig Hugh Smyth, "Michelangelo and St. Peter's: Observations on the Interior of the Apses, a Model of the Apse Vault, and Related Drawings," *Römisches Jahrbuch für Kunstgeschichte*, 16 (1976), 139.

[42] Goldthwaite, "Strozzi Palace," p. 192.

[43] See herein, pp. 93–94.

struction dragged on, his model—in whatever form it may have taken—was found to be something less than satisfactory as an instructional guide. In 1475 the committee paid for the construction of models for a facade with both interior and exterior details and complete with doors and a portico. In 1479 several architects were called in as consultants on the model of the cupola made by Salvi d'Andrea, the head stonecutter on the project. In 1481 Salvi was paid 25 lire for models of an indeterminate nature, although their high price, including payments for the assistance he needed in making them, indicates they were made of wood; two years later he was paid 6 florins for a model of three doors. In 1489 Giuliano da Sangallo made a model for the sacristy, which was the basis of the committee's decision to proceed with its construction, and six years later they had a separate model made of its cupola. In 1493 the committee concluded deliberations about having a model made for the vault of the vestibule by paying the carpenter-architect Francione 3 florins to make it.[44]

The use of models and drawings to serve the additional function of communicating the architect's ideas to his workers marked an advance over the full-scale wood or plaster model traditional to medieval practice.[45] It is difficult to imagine how stonecarvers could have executed much of the detailing of Renaissance architecture—for example, the complex jointing of stones in the facade of the Rucellai palace—without drawings of some kind. A memorandum made in 1468 by the bookkeeper at the monastery of San Bartolomeo about having let out work for a new bell tower refers to a "design on paper," then in the hands of the stonecutter, to be used for the working of the stone.[46] Manetti tells us that Brunelleschi customarily made models of details for his workers, one of which is referred to in an Innocenti contract with a stonecarver for the architrave, cornice, and oculi of the loggia,[47] although (Manetti adds) he was sometimes reluctant to do this lest his ideas be stolen by someone else. Likewise Filarete says that, after explaining his drawings to the masons, he made models of the ornaments

[44] Most of these models are mentioned by Carlo Botto, "L'edificazione della chiesa di Santo Spirito in Firenze," *Rivista d'arte*, 13 (1931), 477–511; 14 (1932), 25–53.

[45] Shelby, "Role," pp. 393–94; du Colombier, *Chantiers*, pp. 95–96.

[46] "Richordo chome ogi questo dì xxv di settembre 1468 noi abiàno dato a fare uno chanpanile pe' lla nostra chiesa di prieta forte e becchategli di macignio alto braccia otto incircha, e noi gli abiàno a dare la prieta e lui l'à a 'ricidere e àllo a lavorare tutto in quel modo e in quella maniera chome è disegniato in su uno foglio e 'l quale foglio è apresso a Domenicho overo a Mechero di Piero di Bertino scharpellatore a Settigniano, al quale Domenicho di Piero noi promettiàno dare di manifattura e riciditura delle priete del sopradetto chanpanile lire ciento ottanta di manifattura di detto chanpanile, d'achordo con lui"; S. Miniato 57, fol. 17v.

[47] "chome sarà il modello e la forma darà loro Filippo di ser Bruneleschо"; Innocenti, ser. VII, 2 (ledger B), fol. 178 left.

he wanted done first.[48] For the rebuilding of the main chapel at San Martino a Gangalandi, financed from the Alberti bequest, a scale model was made in wood by the carpenter Cristofano di Maso, and the stonecarver Francesco d'Antonio di Vanni, called Il Mancia, was instructed to follow it in making the pilasters.[49] At the Strozzi palace both paper and wood were purchased for the making of designs needed in the course of construction, this work being included in the various tasks Cronaca was specifically paid for; in that workshop wood models made of a doorway, window sills, and various metal ornaments obviously served in the execution of these details.[50] At Santo Spirito, where Cronaca also worked only part time, he was paid for making models for use by the stonecarvers.[51] Architectural details of other buildings executed on the basis of documented models or designs include: the columns at the Santissima Annunziata (in 1357);[52] the columns, cornice, and other details at the Loggia dei Priori;[53] the base of the pilasters at Santa Maria delle Carceri in Prato;[54] the frieze and architrave in the courtyard of the Medici palace;[55] and the columns, with their capitals and bases, at the Da Gagliano palace.[56] In all these last-mentioned instances the documents speak of models or designs, and caution must be used in interpreting them as either plastic models or drawings.

In the fifteenth century neither models nor drawings could have had much value as structural, as distinct from design, aids. Because statics was not yet a science, no theoretical concepts entered into the communications

48 Filarete, *Trattato*, I, 241.

49 Marco Spallanzani, "L'abside dell'Alberti a San Martino a Gangalandi: nota di storia economica," *Flor. Mitt.*, 19 (1975), 248.

50 Goldthwaite, "Strozzi Palace," p. 129 and app. 3 therein.

51 Payment of 3 florins to Cronaca "per la faticha dura in fare modinni e ordinare le chose che achagano a lo scharpello e dire e ordinare suo parere" (1493); Cornelius von Fabriczy, "Simone del Pollaiuolo, Il Cronaca," *Jahrbuch der königlich preussischen Kunstsammlungen*, 27 (1906), Beiheft, 53.

52 "che a' Servi si faciesse intonichare e disegniare l'asempro della colonna e de' chapitelli in vera grandeza, il disengniamento di Franciescho e quel di Giovanni Lapi Ghini"; Grote, *Dombauamt*, p. 116.

53 Frey, *Loggia*, pp. 285 and 295–98 passim.

54 By 21 March 1486 Sangallo had made a "modono per la base" of the pilasters; Marchini, "Santa Maria delle Carceri," p. 57.

55 Payment of lb.3 s.2 on 27 April 1452 from Cosimo de' Medici to Maso di Bartolomeo "per manifattura di due disegni che io gli feci, l'uno fu un fregio alto 7/8 che va sotto el davanzale del chortile, e uno archatrave che va sotto detto fregio"; BNF, Baldovinetti 70 (accounts of Maso), fol. 45.

56 A note of the contracts (1522) with the stonecarver Sandro del Gira for "le 3 cholonne belle fornite di chapitello e cimasa con basa da pie', tutto secondo il modano debbe darlli Baccio d'Angnolo," and "li usci intavolati di falda gientile co' 'l chornice secondo il modano datoli Baccio"; Archivio Salviati, Pisa: ser. IV, 14 (building accounts for the Da Gagliano palace), fol. 2v.

TABLE 10
Prices of Some Architectural Models

Model	Price	
	lb./ s./ d.	Florins
Servite loggia opposite the Innocenti, 1516–18	147/—/—	21.0
Santo Spirito:		
facade, 1475–76	118/ 8/—	*20.8*
sacristy, 1489	77/ 8/—	*12.0*
three doors, 1483		6.0
vault of vestibule, 1493		3.0
Santissima Annunziata, 1384	72/10/—	*19.9*
Strozzi palace, 1489	115/10/—	*17.9*
Santa Maria Maddalena di Cestello, 1491	97/10/—	15.0
Santa Maria degli Alberighi, 1507	14/—/—	2.0
Alberti chapel, San Martino a Gangalandi, 1473	6/—/—	*1.1*

NOTE: Florin prices in italics are not in the documents but have been calculated on the basis of current exchange rates for purposes of comparison.

between designer and builder, and in any case, with the exception of domes—most notably, Brunelleschi's cupola—the structural problems presented by most buildings could be solved by traditional methods. If anything, buildings were overbuilt with respect to load-bearing walls. For this reason the owner of the Strozzi palace could make the decision to vault the second story after foundations were far along and vertical construction started, hence raising the height of the building apparently without any problems (this is the major difference between the completed palace and the original Sangallo model). In building walls and vaults masons applied arithmetical and geometrical rules learned in the tradition of their craft to the basic dimensions given them by the ground plan, which might be represented in a plan or a model, or (as at San Matteo) specified in a contract, or actually measured off on the site. Once the dimensions were given, drawings and models were not essential to the vertical construction of most buildings.[57]

The importance of wood models is reflected in the cost of getting one made, most of which went for labor.[58] The larger models in table 10 represent an investment of three to five months' employment of a highly skilled laborer. The three payments to Guiliano da Sangallo for his model

[57] Saalman, "Theory and Practice," pp. 102–6. Cf. Lon R. Shelby, "The 'Secret' of the Medieval Mason," in *On Pre-Modern Technology and Science: Studies in Honor of Lynn White, Jr.*, ed. B. S. Hall and D. C. West (Malibu, 1976), 201–19.

[58] At the Strozzi palace lb.4 s.15 was paid for the linden wood to be used for the "new model," and an additional lb.6 s.7 was paid for linden to make the various other models needed during construction. At the Innocenti some of the models for stonework were made of walnut and poplar (*albero*).

of the Strozzi palace stretched over five months, and the account for the expenses of the model made for the south front of Santo Spirito was open for six months. Clearly, a great deal of skill went into the making of a model, not all of it, to judge from Sangallo's model for the Strozzi palace, going into the carving of decorative detail. Considerable care must also have been taken to make the model exactly to scale so that it could in fact serve as a practical guide to masons.

Sometimes the architect was paid only for his work on a model, this being the extent of his involvement in a project; sometimes he was paid for models apart from his salary as an employee on the project; and sometimes his salary included the making of models. Giuliano da Sangallo made models for the Strozzi palace, the sacristy at Santo Spirito, and (along with Antonio da Sangallo) the church of Cestello[59] without at the time having any other commitment to these projects. Although both Antonio da Sangallo and Baccio d'Agnolo worked for an annual salary as part-time architects (they are so identified on the accounts) at the Servite loggia opposite the Innocenti, Sangallo alone produced the model "a tute sue spese," for which he was paid apart from his fixed stipend. At Santo Spirito the head stonecutter, Salvi d'Andrea, who worked for daily wages, was also paid separately for his work on models.

Although many of these model-builders were wood sculptors, they did not necessarily do all the work on a model themselves. At least one-third of the fee for Antonio da Sangallo's model of the loggia went to a carpenter, named Bernardino, whom Sangallo paid by drafts on his account with his employer (other unspecified payments to Bernardino on the account were probably also for work on the model);[60] and at least one payment to Salvi d'Andrea for the unspecified models he made in 1481 went for outside assistance. Brunelleschi, on the other hand, seems to have made his models at the Innocenti as part of his job, and, as already observed, Cronaca's salary payments at the Strozzi palace explicitly included model-making as part of his job. Since the large Strozzi workshop included a salaried carpenter, Cronaca could get the help he needed in making his models from his own staff; only occasionally did he have recourse to a specialized carpenter on the outside, in particular a turner. At smaller workshops more outside help was likely to be necessary. The models made in 1475 and 1476 for the facade of Santo Spirito were designed by members of the works staff—the foreman and the head stonecutter—but the building committee paid several carpenters to construct them. In 1384 the building committee of the Santissima Annunziata engaged one carpenter to make the model of the new church who was unable

[59] Alison Luchs, "Documents on the Sangallo Family at Santa Maria Maddalena dei Pazzi," *Burlington Magazine*, 117 (1975), 597.

[60] Ss. Annunziata 846, fols. 11 and 40; 847, fols. 22r–v.

Vasari, Leo X and the construction of St. Peter's (detail), late sixteenth century.

to complete it, and so they gave the job to another, Antonio Pucci, who had just completed a contract for building the scaffolding for the Loggia dei Priori. On the books of both Santo Spirito and the Santissima Annunziata accounts were open for the expenses of making these models.[61] Carpenters employed to make models sometimes must have had to work from drawings alone. The executors of Alberti's estate presumably presented their carpenter with a design to be followed in making his model, and the model for the Uguccioni palace was constructed in Florence by Mariotto di Zanobi Folfi on a design that had probably come from Rome.[62]

[61] Ss. Annunziata 841, fols. 28r–v; S. Spirito 127, fols. 112 and 119.

[62] Janet Ross, *Florentine Palaces and Their Stories* (London, 1905), pp. 349–51; Leonardo Ginori Lisci, *I palazzi di Firenze nella storia e nell'arte* (Florence, 1972), no. 87.

In the fifteenth century drawings and models had by no means replaced traditional medieval ways of communicating design ideas to masons and stonecarvers. One of these traditions was imitation. By simply pointing out other buildings a patron could show his architect what he wanted, and in an age when their practice still depended on strong artisan traditions, architects themselves could get ideas in exactly the same way. In 1026 the bishop of Arezzo appropriated money so that his mason could go to Ravenna to study monuments there, and in 1414 the authorities at the cathedral of Valence sent their masons to various cities to find the best clock tower to be used as a model for their own building programs.[63] What was gained from such travel was inspiration, more than anything else, since without a detailed guide, including extensive plans and drawings, a mason could not replicate a structure other than in its broad outline.

Uncomplicated buildings close at hand could, of course, be more easily copied, a prospect that gave rise to the urban ideal of uniformity found in Italian towns in the fourteenth century, of the kind represented in Florence by the 1363 plan to make the new buildings around the apse of the cathedral all conform in height and placement of openings, and the plan to impose the same standards on the remodeling of facades along Via Calzaiuoli after its widening in 1390. Such criteria, assuring conservatism in architectural practice, reinforced highly traditional working methods. The urban ideal of uniformity may, in fact, derive from the tradition, typical of all crafts, of using standard procedures for working out problems. The medieval mason realized many of his architectural forms, entire buildings as well as details, by starting with certain simple geometric figures and applying rule-of-thumb techniques learned in his on-the-job training as an apprentice. The results of the set ways in which craftsmen were accustomed to work on their own can be seen, for example, in the standardization of arched openings in fourteenth-century buildings and in the similarity between examples of much rusticated stonework.[64] Whatever the relation of such craft traditions to the emergence of the urban ideal, they account for the actual uniformity that characterizes the typical Trecento street scene. The conservatism in building

[63] Du Colombier, *Chantiers*, p. 69.

[64] Staale Sinding-Larsen, "A Tale of Two Cities: Florentine and Roman Visual Context for Fifteenth-Century Palaces," *Acta ad archaeologiam et Artium historiam pertinentia* (of the Norwegian Academy in Rome), 6 (1975), 163–212. The medieval craftsman's use of geometry has been much discussed by Lon R. Shelby, most recently in his *Gothic Design Techniques: The Fifteenth-Century Design Booklets of Mathes Roriczer and Hanns Schmuttermayer* (Carbondale, Ill., 1977), pp. 61–79; and the Florentine mason's knowledge of geometry has been studied by Diane Finiello Zervas, "The *Trattato dell'Abbaco* and Andrea Pisano's Design for the Florentine Baptistry Door," *Renaissance Quarterly*, 28 (1975), 483–503. See also François Bucher, "Architectural Design Methods, 800–1560," *Gesta*, 11 (1973), 37–51.

practice, in any case, largely precluded problems of design communication between patron and mason and between designer and executing craftsman.

Imitation was a practical device by which a mason could be instructed. Instructions to copy already existing features are found in contracts for ordinary buildings in England, and the practice was probably common throughout Europe.[65] Many examples can be cited from the Florentine materials. A 1318 contract for the building of a shop specified that the upper floor and one door were to be like those of one shop, while a second doorway was to be like that of another.[66] The 1359 contract for work on the new palace of the Mercanzia told the masons where they were to look to find what they were to copy in making the windows.[67]

Prominent buildings were an obvious model for others in the same genre. Santa Croce, for instance, was cited for how the roof was to be painted at the new church of Santa Cecilia (1388) in the enlarged square of the Palazzo dei Priori,[68] and for what the steps were to be like at Santo Spirito (1487).[69] We have already seen how, in drawing up the contracts for the hospital of San Matteo, the officials quite naturally pointed to the hospitals of Santa Maria Nuova, the oldest and largest, and Bonifazio, the newest, as models. A generation later, in 1422, the builders of the Innocenti, for all the stylistic innovation of their new project, also had an eye on the city's most prominent hospital when they instructed their masons to make the roof of the children's ward like that of the new church of Sant'Egidio at Santa Maria Nuova.[70] For a guild the obvious model was another guild: the Linaiuoli thus instructed the carpenters of their new hall, in 1419, to make the main door and the door of the audience hall like that of the recently completed hall of the butchers, and the consuls' desk like that of the Mercanzia (the court of the guilds).[71] No sooner was it completed than the cloister at San Lorenzo (begun about 1457) became another such prototype—in 1461 for the thirty-two columns at the Cistercian monastery at Settimo,[72] and in 1465 for the twenty-two columns (and capitals) at the monastery of San Bartolomeo (the cloister at San Lorenzo, however, has twenty-eight columns).[73]

[65] Salzman, *Building*, p. 52; Susan Connell, "The Employment of Sculptors and Stone-Masons in Venice in the Fifteenth Century," Diss. Warburg Institute of the University of London 1976, p. 205

[66] G. Milanesi, *Nuovi documenti per la storia dell'arte toscana dal XII al XVI secolo* (Rome, 1893), pp. 21–22.

[67] Ibid., pp. 57–58.

[68] Frey, *Loggia*, p. 232.

[69] S. Spirito 128 (building accounts), fol. 91r.

[70] Innocenti, ser. VII, 2 (ledger B), fol. 176r.

[71] ASF, Arte dei Rigattieri, Linaiuoli, e Sarti 19, fols. 96v, 97r, 98r.

[72] Alison Luchs, *Cestello, a Cistercian Church of the Florentine Renaissance* (New York, 1977), doc. 13.

[73] S. Miniato 57 (Memoriale of S. Bartolomeo), fol. 8v: "ventidua cholonne pe' 'l nostro chiostro di falda grossa lunghe della misura che sono quelle del chiostro di Sa'

Imitation of prominent new buildings like the hospital of Bonifazio, the guild hall of the butchers, the church of Sant'Egidio, and the cloister at San Lorenzo indicates the impact a new building might make on the architectural scene. Imitation could never result in exact replication, however, and in his resolution of the practical problems of recreating an existing building or any of its details, the mason had room to exercise his own interpretation. It may have been for this reason that the builders of the Servite loggia, not wanting to leave anything to chance in commissioning a duplication of the Innocenti loggia opposite, had an expensive model made to assure the perfect balance of the square.

Communication between designer and workers could also be facilitated by the kind of close personal acquaintance that engendered in the latter a tacit understanding of what was to be done. To the extent that a designing mason could rely on the workers' familiarity with his ideas and practices he could communicate more easily with them. This is probably why Giuliano da Maiano took his entire labor crew with him to Siena to work on the Spannocchi palace (much to the indignation of the Sienese).[74] The director of the hospital of San Paolo, who turned to Michelozzo for the plans of a new building program, employed the same waller and stonecutters who had been working together for a number of years down to that time under Michelozzo's supervision at the church of the Santissima Annunziata. Although at San Paolo Michelozzo served only as an architect and, in fact, left town when construction there was just underway, the workers knew him well, were familiar with his ideas, and must have been capable of understanding on their own what it was he wanted. Since during the forty years it took to finish the buildings at San Paolo these men were replaced, on their deaths, by their sons, there was a continuity of personnel that assured a reasonably correct fulfillment of Michelozzo's original plan.[75] Another, more complete team of workers was associated with Baccio d'Agnolo on two of his projects, the Da Gagliano and Bartolini palaces, where the architect himself showed up only occasionally as a consultant.[76]

Such teams are not to be thought of as architectural firms or construction companies. These craftsmen had no formal partnership with one another and

---

Lorenzo e di quella grossezza che sono quelle di Sa' Lorenzo e mancho un oncia, e cho' lle base e cho' chapitegli lavorate bene e diligientemente, e chapitegli sieno lavorati in quell modo che sono quegli del chiostro di Sa' Lorenzo."

74 "et il capomaestro si chiamò Giuliano del Maiano da Fiorenza, e tutti li altri maestri e manovali erano fiorentini in modo che molti populari ne bollivano"; "L'architetto del Palazzo Spannocchi," in *Miscellanea storica senese*, 3 (1885), 60.

75 See herein, p. 166.

76 The team consisted of the waller Lapo di Fruosino di Lapo from Impruneta, the painter Andrea di Giovanni, and the stoneworkers Giovanni di Sandro del Gira and Antonio d'Antonio di Gherardo; see herein, p. 169.

no formal association with the architect, and it is not known whether they worked together on other projects as well. So far as can be determined they were employed individually. At San Paolo their work was only occasional and was never full time for more than several weeks out of a year, and they are all known to have worked alone elsewhere in the meantime. Nevertheless, belonging to the same guild, and working closely together for long periods of time, they must have built up an informal rapport among themselves that counted for something in enlarging the effectiveness of the new mechanisms being refined for the architect's communication with his workers.

If he could count on teams of craftsmen whose solidarity was enforced by continual association, by a tradition of standard practice and designs, and by an increasingly refined medium of professional communication, the architect could hope to free himself from the necessity of full-time employment on one project without taking much of an artistic risk, confident that these craftsmen could work with a high degree of independence from supervision and without the need of plans spelled out in every detail.

The artistic development of the architect may also have depended on these craftsmen in the way he might have been able to draw on certain elements of design inherent in their own craft traditions. The artistic genealogy of the stonemasons executing Michelozzo's plans at San Paolo went back to two generations of the Marocchi family that worked at the Innocenti, and although we cannot assess the importance of Brunelleschi in the formation of their particular talents, we can be confident that the tradition of craftsmanship represented by them was independent of Michelozzo. It is conceivable, in other words, that the planning of specific decorative details, including perhaps moldings and capitals, was not included in an architect's designs and models but was, instead, implicit in the selection of masons who were to do the work; in this way the architect incorporated their vocabulary into his own architectural language. It has been said that there is hardly a motif in early Florentine Renaissance architecture that cannot be found in Trecento precedents.[77] Drawing on the implications of such a claim, we might hypothesize that the invigoration of a strong tradition of stonecarving by the extraordinary public patronage of the early fifteenth century brought into existence a school of highly intelligent artisans who put a ready-made vocabulary at the disposal of the architect, further facilitating his rise to a higher level where he could operate strictly as a designer.

In short, the extraordinary range of the vocabulary of Quattrocento architecture may be as much the mark of the flourishing of artisan imagination as it is the result of architects' inventiveness. It is clear from the variations among

[77] Howard Burns, "Quattrocento Architecture and the Antique: Some Problems," in *Classical Influences in European Culture, A.D. 500–1500*, ed. R. R. Bolgar (Cambridge, 1971), pp. 269–87.

the capitals in many Quattrocento courtyards that stonecarvers did not hold themselves to strict conformity in the execution of decorative details. The subtle, individual quality of their capitals is hardly to be found in the Cinquecento, when the architect, having completed his rise above artisan status, and being now more informed by classical learning and more anxious about aesthetic control, demanded conformity—much in the way that the diffusion of published pattern books and Palladian taste affected craftsmanship in Augustan England.[78] The Renaissance architect's cards were not packed with "individual freaks of fancy" in just one deal.

The Renaissance architect was still not fully in control of the end product of his design efforts. In the process of planning a building he had to contend with his patron, who, as we have seen, could have an active and informed interest in the matter of design. Inevitably, too, the long process of construction brought forth unanticipated problems whose resolution necessitated modifications in design over which the architect was not always in control. Especially on large projects where he showed up only occasionally, a supervising architect might intervene. The practice of architecture in Italy throughout the sixteenth century and beyond could still be largely a cooperative affair in one way or another.

Employment

The conditions of employment for the architect in many places in early Renaissance Italy were in some respects no different from what they traditionally had been for centuries throughout Europe. The letter patent appointing Luciano Laurana architect of the ducal palace at Urbino proclaims him head mason (*capomastro*) with full authority over the organization of work, including the hiring and firing of workers and the determination of their wages.[79] Biagio Rossetti's official position in the service of the duke of Ferrara was "engineer" in the Office of Public Works, which occupied itself with streets, bridges, and fortifications as well as the duke's private building; his duties included keeping accounts and records, contracting for supply of materials, and overseeing activities at the various work sites.[80] These architects, in other words, were court officials with administrative responsibilities,

[78] See the comment of Clarence Kennedy in Frederick Hartt, Gino Corti, and Clarence Kennedy, *The Chapel of the Cardinal of Portugal, 1434–1459, at San Miniato in Florence* (Philadelphia, 1964), p. 67: "Something of the freedom of invention of medieval capital carvers still lingers on in the Quattrocento, not to be erased until by the dictatorial attitude of the great architects of the High Renaissance."

[79] Pasquale Rotondi, *Il palazzo ducale di Urbino* (Urbino, 1950), I, 109–10.

[80] Bruno Zevi, *Biagio Rossetti, architetto ferrarese, il primo urbanista moderno europeo* (Turin, 1960), pp. 23–25 and 559–60.

and, like any medieval mason, they were inevitably responsible for building operations. Nevertheless, however onerous such duties were, working for a prince interested in building was the best way for enlarging the mason's activity as a designer.

Court service was also the traditional way the mason had been able to improve his social and financial status. Bartolino da Novara (who died around 1410), a mason in the service of the d'Este who also served other governments (including Florence, for military works at Pisa), was given a house and other properties carrying feudal rights he was able to pass on to his sons, who moved up into the ranks of courtly society as lawyers and military men, one, knighted by Niccolò III d'Este, doing a turn as Capitano del Popolo at Florence.[81] Such rewards for service to a prince were not to be taken for granted, however. At the end of his life, in 1494, Luca Fancelli, a Florentine who made his career at the Gonzaga court, among other things executing Alberti's projects, lamented his financial situation in letters to his employer pleading, on the basis of forty-two years of loyal service, for payment of debts still owed him on several accounts.[82]

The only position in Florence comparable to the court architect abroad was that of foreman at the cathedral works.[83] The cathedral works was a large, permanent workshop that functioned as a municipal construction company, and its foreman functioned as something like city architect, responsible for—to cite what Giotto was charged with in the official announcement of his appointment—city walls, fortifications, and any other work undertaken by the commune. Much of this other work did not enlarge his design opportunities, and his job can be best described as low-level industrial management. Like any medieval master mason he was fully in charge of construction, but (unlike some court appointees) he did not enter into the higher level financial administration of the work, and he was subject to a policy-making board. Nevertheless, he enjoyed a certain prestige, if we can believe the rhetoric of official proclamations of appointments, like that which hailed Giotto as the best man to be found in the entire world for the job. The commune's desire to honor the "famous master" Arnolfo di Cambio brought him the more concrete advantage of a tax exemption. The stipend of 100 florins earned by some of these foremen (for example, Giotto and Brunelleschi) made the job one of the best in town for an artisan—but not good enough to launch him on a social ascent out of the artisan class. Once the

[81] Giuseppe Campori, *Gli architetti e gl'ingegneri civili e militari degli Estensi dal secolo XIII al XVI* (Modena, 1882), pp. 11–12.

[82] Braghirolli, "Fancelli," pp. 637–38.

[83] The position of foreman of cathedral works in the Tuscan towns of the fourteenth century is described by Braunfels, *Stadtbaukunst*, ch. VI.

cathedral was finished, after Brunelleschi's death, the job involved little more than maintenance and was often held by two or more masons who, in effect, served only part time. By this time, the later fifteenth century, the city had little other work for them to do. An independent commission with its own staff took care of general urban maintenance—squares, streets, bridges, and so on, and for the considerable task of fortifying—and refortifying—the countryside during these years the city made appointments for each project as it came up rather than assign it to the cathedral foremen.

In contrast to Florence other city-republics had a major bureaucratic post in charge of public works. Francesco di Giorgio held the position at Siena, which was separate from that of foreman at the cathedral and included responsibility for fortifications and hydraulic works throughout Sienese territory. With a salary of 800 lire (at 4 lire per florin) this job paid him much better than the cathedral post in Florence had ever paid, and besides complete job security it gave him the freedom to work at his various other artistic ventures on his own, including making frequent trips abroad as a consultant. In Venice an architect and building superintendent attached to the Salt Office oversaw all government projects, and in 1542 a separate office of superintendent of fortifications was set up. A third works office, corresponding to the post of cathedral foreman elsewhere, was in the division of the Procuratia responsible for the church and property of San Marco. It, too, was a much better job than anything in Florence. Sansovino went to Venice to fill this post in 1529, for which he was given a residence in the Piazza San Marco and a salary (by the second year) of 180 ducats, and he held it until his death over forty years later, always having plenty of time to pick up work on the side as both sculptor and architect.

In Florence there was no one job, like these public works posts, so central to the architect's ambition for success; in fact, there was no one patron from whom he could expect continual employment. He had to pick up work where he could find it, and it was his good fortune to be in a place where the number of commissions increased so considerably in the course of the century. The Florentine architect was not, however, dependent on construction for employment. He was not a waller by training, but invariably an artist in his own right, unlike so many architects elsewhere in Italy, finding his main livelihood as a sculptor, a carpenter, or a goldsmith. Hence, he came much closer to being a full-time designer than the master mason-architect in other places who was heavily burdened by construction responsibilities.

One implication of the increasing involvement in architecture by men who were not builders was the separation of the design function from execution. Whereas in the fourteenth century most of the cathedral architects, in the tradition of the medieval mason, were preoccupied with supervisory duties (although too few details are known about their activities to put together full professional biographies), Ghiberti (for whose career there is a better chronology) was, on the contrary, so busy in his own workshop when first appointed coforeman at the cathedral in 1420 that he could hardly have dedicated himself entirely to the construction project, which was then in full swing; in fact, after Brunelleschi was given major responsibility in 1426, Ghiberti's presence at the site was required for only one hour a day. The practice of naming several foremen suggests a division of responsibilities in the direction of the cathedral workshop in part between design consultation and execution.

Unlike Ghiberti, his associate and rival at the cathedral, Brunelleschi dedicated himself fully to building during the years when he was on the staff of the cathedral workshop. He took on a number of commissions simultaneously, each under different auspices and therefore with its own workshop, but since he was so involved in directing operations at the cathedral, he could dedicate only part of his time to other projects. At the Innocenti, the best documented of his other activities, he was not on the site much of the time, and this may explain why so much of the work there was let out on contract. Nevertheless, there is no reason to think that he did not make frequent appearances at the orphanage, just down the street from the cathedral. At least twice the documents refer to him as *condottore* (or *conducitore*) of the work, and throughout the first decade of building they record payments to him for services rendered. In 1420 he received 15 florins "for his agreed-upon salary at the works." The next year, from May 1421 to April 1422, he served on the building committee itself, representing his section of the guild membership (goldsmiths). Thereafter he received further payments of 10 florins—in November 1422 "for part of the time he put in the building" and "for part of the effort he has endured and endures for the construction of the hospital," in May 1424 "for compensation for the labor he puts in the project," and again in January 1427 (after another stint as a committee member from September 1425 to April 1426) "for the rest of his salary and compensation for the labor and time he has put into the building of the said hospital." In the 1429 Catasto report of the guild a 60-florin deduction for administrative expenses at the hospital included the purveyor's salary and that of Brunelleschi for "the labor he endures in the said construction." None of these payments were on the order of a full-time salary, even for an unskilled laborer, and they are a far cry from the 100 florins he was earning at the cathedral. Brunelleschi can best be described as something like a consulting architect at the Innocenti. The only duties specified in the documents were approval of such things as the iron tie rods needed for the portico and the construction of models, or wooden forms, for decorative stonework. The accountant made a significant comment on Brunelleschi's status at the project when he transferred the 1422 payment to the architect out of the building accounts and into the general accounts "because these moneys are not for construction properly speaking but compensation for work put in toward that construction."[84]

Not enough is known about the building history of the other projects designed by Brunelleschi to assess his involvement in their construction. Although he remained foreman at the cathedral until his death, work slowed down after the completion of the cupola, and during the last decade of his life he was probably less tied down to that job. It is not likely that he worked full time as foreman on any other project, however often he might have showed up at the site to check on progress.

The lack of documentation also hinders any assessment of the practice of Michelozzo, the most active of the architects in the generation after Brunelleschi. He, like Brunelleschi, was probably not tied down to the job as foreman of the works at any of his projects. Michelozzo had an active career as a bronze caster: from 1424 or 1425 until 1433 he had a shop in partnership with Donatello, from 1437 to at least 1442 he worked under Ghiberti on the second baptistry doors, and throughout the 1440s he undertook numerous commissions in association with others, above all, Maso di Bartolomeo. Despite this demanding activity in the foundry he found time to design a large number of buildings, including virtually all of the important Medici projects—if the traditional attributions are to be accepted. (The fact is, however, that only six buildings can be linked to Michelozzo through documentation, and only three of these are in the city.) He succeeded Brunelleschi as foreman at the cathedral after the latter's death in 1446, remaining in that post until 1452. During this time, from 1444 to 1455, he was also foreman at the Santissima Annunziata. Both of these were relatively large workshops that required some attention. During the one year at the Santissima Annunziata reasonably well documented by building accounts (October 1444 to November 1445), Michelozzo received no more than 25 florins, much of this for his labor as a "disegnatore" and for the "labor and skill dedicated to the supervising of the said work" ("fatica e maestiero messa e che de' mettere a condurre la detta opera"). He judged the quality of stonework on its arrival before authorizing payment; he oversaw the measurement of completed masonry work to settle accounts with masons; and on occasion he sent the paymaster written orders of payments for workers, some of whom were paid directly through him. Besides what he earned on this job for such supervisory work, he was also paid as an "intagliatore" for capitals from his own work-

[84] "perchè questi denari non sono per propria muraglia ma sono per provisione di che dura faticha per la edificazione della muralglia." The references in the building accounts to payments to Brunelleschi are cited most recently in G. Morozzi and A. Piccini, *Il restauro dello spedale di Santa Maria degli Innocenti, 1966–1970* (Florence, 1971). The Catasto declaration is 291, fol. 48r. The organization of the Innocenti workshop is discussed herein, pp. 162–63.

shop. During these years at both the cathedral and the Santissima Annunziata, when he was also busy casting, Michelozzo could have done little more on any of the other projects traditionally attributed to him than submit plans and then stop by occasionally to check on progress. For the public hall in Montepulciano he merely sent a drawing. For the hospital of San Paolo he submitted (sometime after 1455) more elaborate plans and a model, but despite one reference to him as foreman, there is no evidence in the wealth of materials documenting this project that he ever did anything at the site.

Michelozzo's career in Florence came to an end on his departure for Ragusa in 1461, where he became director of public works, which included, above all, fortifications. This must have been a full-time job, in contrast to his employment in the numerous part-time jobs he put together to make a living in Florence. His salary of 250 florins plus use of a house was much more than he could have ever hoped to earn in his native city. It is perhaps worth noting, as a comment on the new conditions of patronage in Florence, that at Ragusa, where he had a more traditional kind of job as master-mason, his design imagination as an architect found little outlet, although at that time he must have been at the peak of his life as an artist.[85]

The careers of Brunelleschi and Michelozzo illustrate the varying degrees of involvement the fifteenth-century architect could have with a building, ranging from being merely its designer to being foreman and fully in charge of the works, in the tradition of the medieval master-mason. The tendency, however, was for the architect to avoid the total commitment required of the foreman, even when, like many stonecutters, he found substantial employment at the site. For example, Salvi d'Andrea, who worked as head stonecutter at Santo Spirito throughout the 1470s and 1480s, was probably the supervising architect, since he would have had an expertise in design and decorative detail the foreman, a waller, would not have had (and in fact he was paid extra for construction of models of various kinds)—but he was not the foreman and his wages were no higher than the foreman's.

A clearer instance of this kind of division of responsibility is Cronaca's position at the Strozzi palace. As supervising architect he was a salaried employee with major responsibilities, but his salary of 36 florins as compared to the foreman's 60 indicates only a part-time involvement in the project. He,

[85] Michelozzo's career as a castor of bronze is summarized by Harriet McNeal Caplow, "Sculptors' Partnerships in Michelozzo's Florence," *Studies in the Renaissance*, 21 (1974). A checklist of the numerous buildings attributed to him has been drawn up by Saalman, "Palazzo Comunale," pp. 44–46 (to which now has been added the hospital of San Paolo [Goldthwaite and Rearick, "San Paolo"] and his work at Ragusa [Caplow, "Michelozzo"]). Most (but not all) of the payments to Michelozzo at the Ss. Annunziata (from Ss. Annunziata 842) are published by Cornelius von Fabriczy, "Michelozzo di Bartolomeo," *Jahrbuch der königlich preuss. Kunstsammlungen*, 25 (1904), Beiheft, 82–90.

like Salvi d'Andrea, was head stonecutter, in charge of the entire process of preparation of the stone—a full-scale technical operation involving management of quarries and supervision of stonecutters—but he also made designs and models, dealt with the sculptors on matters of artistic importance, advised the wallers and the owner on all such questions, and in general provided artistic direction to the entire enterprise. Although the documents never refer to him as an architect, the accounting procedures for recording his salary put his position into clear relief, for he was the only salaried employee on the works staff whose payments were not charged to the cost of a specific operation, as were those of the foreman. As only a part-time employee at the Strozzi palace Cronaca could take on additional work (in 1495) as one of the part-time foremen at the cathedral, and he managed both of these jobs in such a way that for two years, from 1495 to 1497, he was able to accept the more demanding position of foreman in charge of the rush job of building an addition to the Palazzo dei Priori to accommodate the constitutional reforms of the Savonarolan regime. If all the other attributions to him are to be accepted, we can infer that he took on other work, probably with less involvement, while holding down his two principal jobs at the Strozzi palace, where he stayed on the payroll until 1504, and at the cathedral, where he remained until his death in 1508.[86]

On these other projects Cronaca, after having submitted a design and plans, was probably something like a consultant, dropping by occasionally to check up on work—the kind of involvement that is documented for Baccio d'Agnolo in the relatively small payments he received during the course of construction of a number of his projects. At the Servite loggia in Piazza Santissima Annunziata both he and Antonio di Francesco da Sangallo, who had been paid apart for the model in 1516, had their own accounts as architects that recorded payments of 8 florins a year for the next three years of construction. At the Bartolini palace Baccio was paid 2 florins a month for almost three years, from 1520 to 1523; during part of this time he was also retained for a much smaller fee at the Da Gagliano palace (receiving 2 florins in December 1521 and then 6 florins over the next year). At this latter project the accounts specify that he made models (*modani*) for the stonework and approved both stonework and interior woodwork. On the building accounts of the bell tower at San Miniato in 1525 the stonecutters were instructed to do their work "a modo di" Baccio, and he shows up for payment of 1 florin in July without any explanation and another in October in compensation for his several visits to the site ("ci era venuto più volte"). On the ledgers of all these projects except the last Baccio has a separate account on which he is specifically identified as the architect, not the foreman. About this same time his son, Giuliano, was paid 79 lire over a period of six months for drawings

[86] Goldthwaite, "Strozzi Palace," pp. 123–27.

he made in connection with construction on a farm belonging to Luigi di Luigi Martelli.[87] This evidence for what in effect were consultation fees suggests that by the sixteenth century it was becoming normal procedure in Florence to have recourse to an architect for the planning of buildings apart from their execution.

These fees reveal the basic economic fact of the architect's professional status: he was paid more for the amount of work put in on a project than for his ideas about its design, and he could not earn enough from his design ideas alone to make a living. If he collected what might seem a large fee for a model, it was to cover the cost of producing the model itself. Michelozzo got 2 florins for his plans for Santa Maria delle Grazie at Pistoia and perhaps only slightly more than that for the plans of the hospital of San Paolo.[88] Baccio d'Agnolo was paid somewhat more for staying on as an occasional consultant on the projects mentioned above, and Cronaca earned a substantially larger stipend at the Strozzi palace because he took on substantially greater responsibilities as head stonecutter. On no one job, however, could the designer hope to earn more than the foreman, and the more lucrative the job he took on as foreman, the more he was tied down there by supervisory responsibilities. To describe the economic situation in altogether anachronistic terms: the architect could not operate entirely from an architect's office.

Nevertheless, design talent gave an architect flexibility as a consultant that somewhat enlarged his earning capacity over that of an ordinary mason. At least at one point in his career Cronaca was able to put together an income of well over 100 florins a year—36 from Strozzi, 25 from the cathedral, 60 the first year and 86 the second from the commune, and (probably) additional fees for plans and consulting jobs elsewhere. Moreover, Cronaca made his living entirely in the construction industry; he did not have (so far as we know) an independent enterprise as a sculptor or furniture-maker like so many Quattrocento architects, whose work was often something they did as an extension of another activity.

For all the patronage in the private sector during the fifteenth century the Florentine architect could not organize his work in such a way that he could substantially improve his economic status through this activity alone. Patron-

[87] Ss. Annunziata 846 (building accounts of the loggia, 1516–25), fols. 11, 40, 53, 90 (cf. 847 [income-outgo journal], fols. 23v, 26r, 29v, 49r); Archivio Bartolini Salimbeni, Villa di Collina (Vicchio di Mugello), 211 (building accounts, 1519–27), fol. 17; Archivio Salviati, Pisa, ser. IV, 13 (building accounts for Da Gagliano palace, 1522–28), fol. 3; S. Miniato 169 (building accounts for bell tower, 1525–26), fols. 7, 9, 27; Carte strozz., ser. V, 1476 (journal and memoranda of Martelli, 1524–33), fols. 6v–7r (Giuliano received five payments, from October 1523 to May 1524, "per sua faticha d'avermi fatto più disegni per la muraglia" at the farm "delle gore").

[88] Ottavio Morisani, *Michelozzo architetto* (Milan, 1951), p. 95; Goldthwaite and Rearick, "San Paolo," p. 272.

age was too fragmented, and demand not enough concentrated in any one agent. Florence, unlike Siena and some other cities, did not have a city architect or surveyor; the biggest job in town, foreman at the cathedral, was filled by two or more part-time maintenance supervisors once major construction was finished. The Florentine architect found bigger rewards, both economic and social, abroad, in the government service of one of Italy's numerous princes, especially now that military architecture had become a major preoccupation of them all. Michelozzo's offer from the republic of Ragusa may have come at a point in his career when he was under a cloud of suspicion for problems at the Santissima Annunziata, but the stipend of 250 florins, with a house thrown into the bargain, was so much better than what he could have earned in Florence that he could hardly have turned it down. For the same reason many Florentines jumped at the opportunities opening up in the expanding papal state. Who in Florence would have been so generous as Pius II in presenting a bonus of 100 ducats plus a scarlet cloak (probably worth again as much) to Bernardo Rossellino for all the work he did in rebuilding the pope's hometown of Pienza?

The employment situation in Florence improved once the Medici introduced a new style of government after the final destruction of the republic, bringing the city more into line with other Italian political systems of patronage. Antonio da Sangallo the Younger was paid 25 florins a month as architect at the Fortezza da Basso, and his assistant, Nanni Unghero, 160 florins a year, far more than the foreman at the cathedral had ever received during the republican period—and Sangallo was able to work elsewhere concurrently. When Ammannati returned to Florence in the later 1550s he worked almost exclusively for the Medici or their courtiers, accumulating a modest fortune; Buontalenti had what was virtually a bureaucratic post as supervisor of the duke's military and civil projects, including hydraulic works; and when Vasari went to work on the duke's new government office building he was given an annual supplement of 150 florins over the 300 florins he was already earning as what might be called his base salary in the ducal service.

The Italian architect generally fared better in the sixteenth century because there was a higher level of demand for his services; there were more patrons and, on the whole, they were prepared to spend more than the Florentine merchant of the fifteenth century had been. With the stabilization of the political order in Italy, resources were released for more elaborate civil engineering projects and for more building in general, and it is significant for patronage that those resources were diffused throughout a highly fragmented political system, not concentrated exclusively in one capital city. Moreover, by this time the upper classes in Italy had become thoroughly conditioned by the artistic culture that had taken root in their midst, so that everyone, from great princes, both secular and ecclesiastical, to provincial urban elites, now sought to assert his public image in building programs.

The mark of the architect's status was not only the higher stipend he could command but also a release from direct responsibility for managing construction work in all of its details. In general, patrons, no longer expecting the architect to assume the position of head master-mason or supervisor of the works, were more likely to set up a construction project as an autonomous operation, independent of the architect and not needing his direct supervision. These were the circumstances under which Cronaca worked at the Strozzi palace and Michelangelo at San Lorenzo. No better example of the situation can be found than at Saint Peter's, the grandest project of the period, where the vast works staff had an hierarchical structure of well-defined tasks and a neat delineation of authority, the architect fitting in not as the manager but as a kind of technical advisor, albeit one with comprehensive authority to intervene at any point in order to assure the full realization of his intentions. In other words, construction and architectural practice tended to become two distinct functions even though the architect still depended on employment at the construction site.

Freed from direct responsibility for management of the construction enterprise and provided with the means to communicate his ideas at least in a general way through drawings, plans, and models, the architect could hope to take on more projects, thereby expanding his creative output. Although he was employed on a large project, it was no problem for him to design other buildings and check in occasionally at their sites. He thus could have major work going on concurrently in several places, requiring a considerable amount of traveling. At one point in his career, in 1538, Antonio da Sangallo was at work on four papal projects in Loreto, Ancona, and Rome, collecting stipends that added up to 85 florins a month.[89] Galeazzo Alessi had clients in various cities and was not always able to show up at some of the sites often. He planned to direct progress at the church of Carignano (1552) mostly through correspondence, having left drawings and instructions with local builders, but his employer, disturbed by his absence, perhaps in part because it had to deal with local Genoese masons who with their strong corporate sense resented working for an outsider, raised his stipend from 160 to 210 scudi on condition that he remain at the site for at least eight months during the building season.[90] Vignola failed to work out the technique for controlling his projects during an absence, and his plans and designs were often not clear when it came to solving a variety of problems that arose during construction; hence he became embroiled in disagreements and arguments over decisions made when he was not around for consultation.[91]

[89] So one can infer from the evidence presented by Ackerman, "Practice," p. 5.

[90] Wolfgang Lotz, "Introduzione ai lavori del Convegno," in *Galeazzo Alessi e l'architettura del Cinquecento*, Acts of the International Congress in Genoa, 1974 (Genoa, 1975), p. 10.

[91] Coolidge, "Personalità."

After a model by Giambologna, Architecture,
late sixteenth century.

The sixteenth-cenutry architect enjoyed a close personal relation with his patrons, the rich and powerful of Italy. He, of course, depended on their personal patronage, but he did not serve them as a mere functionary, however exalted, like his predecessor, the medieval master-mason. He was accepted on his own ground as a quasi-professional in the real sense of the term, with many of the modern overtones that distinguish his status from that of his former category as mere craftsman. His patrons had a vital interest in architecture, now that it had become so much a part of their public image. Architecture had intellectual respectability by their standards, and it was the least manual of the arts. Moreover, its military application was a pressing concern of many a prince, and they had some expertise in the subject. Some patrons, as we have seen, had their own definite ideas about the subject, which they did not hesitate to impose on their architects. Many buildings in the sixteenth and seventeenth centuries were put up in a complicated process by which design ideas from several quarters were fused into a single plan that evolved during construction. But if this involvement of patrons meant that often the architect had to contend with them over design problems and be prepared to accept their interference, it also meant that the patrons learned to appreciate the architect for what he was. They were disposed to give him his due for his expertise as a designer, for his knowledge of classical architecture, especially ornamentation, and for his talent in handling certain kinds of technical problems, all of which added up to recognition of his quasi-professional status. For Galeazzo Alessi this meant being addressed with the respectful titles of Messer, Signore, or Sua Signoria. For Francesco Paciotto it meant knighthood and gifts of 5,000 scudi and a gold chain worth another 1,000 scudi when he accompanied Philip II through the Netherlands. And, finally, for some it meant, as it did for so many other Renaissance artists, the wealth and status to build their own palaces alongside those of their patrons—the ultimate mark of prestige in their society, one that they had done so much to establish.

CONCLUSION

The Results: Art and Architecture as Investment

THE Renaissance of the arts occurred in an economy where immense wealth was spent in conspicuous consumption. Nothing was more conspicuous, and more expensive, than building. It has been the objective of this study to trace the process by which money was channelled into the economy by way of the construction industry. We have seen where wealth came from, why it was spent for architecture, and how the forces of production were organized to meet the demand. It now remains, by way of winding up the scattered strands this study of the construction industry has unraveled, to assess the consequences of so much building on the economy as a whole. This assessment requires that we step back from this one industry in order to enlarge our view of things to take in the entire phenomenon of conspicuous consumption as the wider context in which architecture, in the final analysis, must be seen. Consumption of luxury goods—all those "extras" with which men felt they could embellish their lives—was a much more striking use of wealth in the fifteenth century than was new investment in the staple of the economy (the textile industry), in agriculture, or in any other kind of productive enterprise. If any sector of the Renaissance economy was booming it was that part that produced luxury goods, and since much of this output falls into the category of what today we call art, an assessment of the performance of this sector is nothing less than an economic explanation for the Renaissance of the arts.

Construction and the Economy

Along with agriculture and clothing, construction was the most important industry in pre-industrial Europe since it supplied a universal need for shelter. The relative importance of prestige building within the industry and within the medieval economy as a whole, however, has never been assessed. Cathedral-building in northern Europe has been regarded as detrimental to economic development because it drained capital from investment into conspicuous consumption, since cathedrals were expensive and since the capital they absorbed did not produce further wealth. A debate broke out several years ago over the significance of the cost of a cathedral (or other such prestige project) with respect to gross investment in the Middle Ages, but that debate cooled off about as rapidly as it had flared up without having generated much useful research in the meantime. Otto von Simson suggested a different approach when he observed that the building of cathedrals stimulated development of related skills and industries. Yet, once a cathedral was built, no demand arose from any other quarter of medieval society to sustain those industries and employment beyond the maintenance operations of the structure itself. In medieval Europe cathedral-building was only an occasional activity, like temple-building in the ancient Greek world. In both places some of the most skilled laborers, especially stoneworkers, were in fact highly itinerant, going from one project to another in different and far-away places. Furthermore, building cathedrals was a long process, sometimes taking centuries, and except for moments of great input, their workshops were staffed with a relatively small number of more or less permanent employees. If cathedrals paid any dividends at all, these came from the tourist trade in the form of fees and donations collected from pious pilgrims attracted to these great architectural reliquaries.[1]

The economic importance of the Florence cathedral is to be assessed in the same terms as the cathedral of any other medieval town. It was perhaps the largest of them all, but the town that paid the bills was one of the richest in Christendom. What was new in Florence was the surge of aggregate demand for more prestige buildings within the private sector and the fragmentation of spending into innumerable projects, both ecclesiastical and private. The extent to which this building added up to growth of the construction industry

[1] The scanty literature on this problem is reviewed in H. Thomas Johnson, "Cathedral Building and the Medieval Economy," *Explorations in Entrepreneurial History*, 4 (1966–67), 191–210. Johnson's analysis was challenged by W. E. Alford and M. Q. Smith in subsequent exchanges in the same journal: ibid., 5 (1967–68), 108–10; 6 (1968–69), 158–69, 170–74, 329–32. For building in Greece see Alison Burford, "The Economics of Greek Temple Building," *Proceedings of the Cambridge Philological Society*, new ser., 11 (1965), 21–34.

cannot be measured in precise figures. Unfortunately, for all the fame Florentines enjoy for their statistical turn of mind, no documents have turned up with figures for the number of workers or the size of craft groups in any industry. Nevertheless, the sparse and uncertain statistics that have been collected for a tabulation of the city's skilled workers from the mid-fourteenth to the mid-sixteenth centuries indicate that the building trades along with the related woodworking trades underwent more growth than any other category. The immense size of the building-crafts guild, with perhaps 25 percent of the total guild population, itself marks the impact of construction on employment. It has been estimated that no more than 10 percent of the total labor force of any pre-industrial city worked in construction, but the figure may have been higher for Florence, considering the amount of major construction undertaken there and also the special demands on the labor market by extensive building in stone.[2]

The construction industry was labor intensive, with even cost of materials representing primarily labor charges, and all the labor was concentrated in an area extending no farther beyond the city walls than the quarries and kilns that supplied materials. The cost of building in values of man-years of labor, therefore, suggests something about the impact of new building on employment. We can produce figures for a few notable structures to give an idea of what they cost (evaluating a man-year of unskilled labor as lb.150, or from 20 to 40 florins, depending on the year). The central complex at the Innocenti was built from 1419 to 1443 at a cost of f.2,965 lb. 39,723 (about 350 man-years). In 1449 the abbot of San Pancrazio claimed to have spent f.3,500 for construction, and the next year he received an appropriation of f.2,000 more for a cloister (a total of 176 man-years). The manager of the hospital of San Paolo showed expenditures on his books of f.9,000 (360 man-years) for the new complex built between 1451 and 1495. Tommaso Spinelli spent f.3,000 (96 man-years) on his cloister at Santa Croce in 1452, and Castello Quaratesi bequeathed f.14,000 (worth 523 man-years) in 1465 for the building of San Salvatore. The accounts of the building committee of Santo Spirito show disbursements for rebuilding the church of lb.83,172 (554 man-years) from 1477 to 1491. The Servite loggia cost lb.35,000 (233 man-years), not including completion of the houses behind it. The cost of palaces varied greatly, but some fell into the range of these institutional

[2] Some figures for the percentage of construction workers in a selection of European towns of this period are presented by Carlo Cipolla, *Storia economica dell'Europa pre-industriale* (Bologna, 1974), p. 119; but his figures are probably much too low inasmuch as many construction workers did not fall into the categories that determined the composition of the documents on which these estimates are based. In fourteenth-century Bruges 10 percent of all artisans were in construction; Jean-Pierre Sosson, *Les Travaux publics de la ville de Bruges, XIVe–XVe siècles* (Brussels, 1977), pp. 219–20.

structures. A major one like the Bartolini cost f.13,100 (611 man-years) from 1520 to 1533, and for one of the very largest, the Strozzi spent lb.200,000 (1,333 man-years) down to 1506. The Bardi-Busini palace had remodeling done to it in 1487 adding up to f.3,700 (155 man-years), and Da Gagliano spent lb.15,400 (103 man-years) in the 1520s for what was essentially just a new facade. We have many more price tags for the sale of palaces, but since the market value of a palace was much lower than construction costs, these figures are not an index to the investment such buildings represented. Construction of chapels—for example, at Santa Trinita and Santo Spirito—could cost from 5 to 15 man-years, and their decoration—for example, at the Strozzi and Tornabuoni chapels—three to five times as much again.

The assessment of this labor force involves much more than an estimate of the numbers of men working in the industry, for the new buildings demanded not only a larger labor force but also a more highly skilled labor force. Many of the features we associate with Renaissance architecture were the products of artisans who took up their trade as a result of the demand for higher quality craftsmanship in a number of trades associated with the construction industry: stonemasons, above all, but also smiths, who made decorative bronze and ironwork, like the torch and standard-holders on facades; carpenters, who carved ceilings and did inlay doors and extensive interior paneling; sgraffiti artists, who worked on palace facades. The finished product of a Renaissance building represents a pool of human resources developed to a high level of skill, and this improvement in the training and skill of artisans and the increase in their numbers were the consequences of not merely more building but the elevation of much of that building to the level of architecture.

The Decorative Arts

If at the point where building becomes architecture the construction sector increases its demand for highly skilled labor from the decorative arts, it also opens a consumption linkage to the decorative arts to the extent that buildings, once built, have to be furnished. In Florence the construction of homes and family chapels on a larger scale and in greater quantity, and the new life-style implicit in this development, generated demand for more objects for the decoration and furnishings of these places—gold, silver, and metal utensils; wood, terracotta, and stone sculpture; bronze statuettes and medalions; and, certainly not least of all, pictures (to which must be added picture-frames, now needed to accommodate painting to a function so new as to revolutionize the art itself[3])—in short, the entire range of the interior decorative arts.

[3] An idea suggested by Creighton Gilbert, "Peintres et menuisiers au début de la Renaissance en Italie," *Revue de l'art*, 37 (1977), 14.

Dress, too, was affected by the new life-style played out in the palaces of the rich, becoming more elaborate and more technically demanding in its tailoring to fit the body more closely (reflecting the fascination of artists with the human form).[4] Perhaps this extravagance was partly a result of the freedom the patrician could now find from the sumptuary laws (and more subtle kinds of social censure) by withdrawing from public places into the vast new spaces of his private world.

Before the fourteenth century the decorative arts in Tuscany hardly penetrated the domestic world;[5] by the fifteenth century a considerable variety of objects was being produced to fill up the vastly enlarged residential spaces. Perhaps it would be more correct to say that the domestic world had come into its own by the fifteenth century as both a physical place and a set of values, and that palaces were simply the most grandiose statement of this new fact of life. This new world, at any rate, needed to be filled up, whether the palace of a patrician or the humbler abode of a prosperous artisan, and the rush into the marketplace created a huge new demand for the decorative arts, thus stimulating what was perhaps the most dynamic sector of the economy of Renaissance Florence. And, needless to say, the secularization of art is tied to this process of its domestication.

In this domestic world of the arts demand arose for two basic household items—furniture and glazed pottery—that is of particular note for the economic activity it generated and for the subsequent history of European taste. The furniture industry was not new on the European scene, but it has its first full chapter as a minor art in fifteenth-century Florence. Earlier household furniture consisted mostly of nondescript stools, tables, and, above all, chests of all sizes. Forms were starkly simple, decoration was minimal, and items like chests were usually portable and multifunctional. In the fifteenth century, however, chairs, tables, beds, cabinets, and chests evolved into new forms, and the variety of their decoration introduced a new taste for furniture that soon spread throughout Italy and all Europe.

The cost of furnishings was no object to some of these rich Florentines, who were prepared to pay the equivalent of what a skilled worker earned in a year for a bed or a chest or even an altar picture-frame. The most prominent manufacturer of wedding chests in the mid-Quattrocento, Apollonio di Giovanni, turned out a product that cost on the average considerably more, and on occasion he was able to sell a painted chest to a merchant of this city with a population of a mere 40,000 that cost much more (valued in man-years of labor) than the $35,000 bed recently made by Max Ernst for one of the

[4] See the comments of Elizabeth Birbari, *Dress in Italian Painting, 1460–1500* (London, 1975).

[5] These arts up to the fourteenth century are surveyed in *Atti del I Convegno sulle arti minori in Toscana, 1971* (Florence, 1973).

world's wealthiest men.[6] Local craftsmen could turn out items that were major works of art, something worthy of the household of a prince. Lorenzo the Magnificent had no qualms about presenting a bed as a gift to the sultan of Egypt; Benedetto da Maiano made one for King Ferrante of Naples, and his brother Giuliano made at least two for other Neapolitan noblemen.[7] During the siege of Florence that unscrupulous proto-art dealer, Giovanbattista della Palla, eyed the famous bedroom in the Borgherini palace while the owner was out of town, in the hope of making a deal to get the city fathers to give the entire ensemble of furnishings as a gift to no one less than Francis I; but he had not counted on the stout resistence of the lady of the household, who, anything but flattered, had strong ideas about her matrimonal bed becoming an object of mere commerce, even if among governments and kings.[8]

The colorful tin-glazed pottery—*maiolica*—that covered the ever-expanding shelf and table spaces inside palaces was another distinctively new art form to appear in the domestic world, and Florence enjoys a certain preeminence in its history because the domestic world was so highly developed there. Maiolica is one of the glories of the Italian Renaissance. Inspired by the importations from the Islamic world (much of it by way of Spain), Italians—above all, Florentines—much enlarged the possibilities of this craft once they undertook their own production. Their imaginative elaboration of shapes and decoration, not to mention their perfection of pottery techniques (which in the later sixteenth century brought the Florentines almost to the point of inventing procelain), went much beyond the relatively restricted range of Islamic production. Florentines filled their homes with these things. With prices low enough to bring it within reach of much of the population, large quantities of maiolica turn up in the inventories even of modest artisans, and it was sold in shops throughout the remote territories of the Florentine state. Some merchants took their own pottery with them when they went to live in

[6] Ellen Callmann, *Apollonio di Giovanni* (Oxford, 1974), p. 26.

[7] Gino Corti, "Relazione di un viaggio al Soldano d'Egitto e in Terra Santa (1488–89)," *ASI*, 116 (1958), 9; Dario A. Covi, "A Documented 'Lettuccio' for the Duke of Calabria by Giuliano da Maiano," in *Essays Presented to Myron P. Gilmore*, ed. Sergio Bertelli and Gloria Ramakus (Florence, 1978), II, 121–30.

[8] *Le opere di Giorgio Vasari*, ed. Gaetano Milanesi (Florence, 1973), VI, 262–63. The best survey of interior domestic furnishings is still Attilio Schiaparelli, *La casa fiorentina e i suoi arredi nei secoli XIV e XV* (Florence, 1908). For more interpretive comment see: Wilhelm von Bode, *Die italienischen Hausmöbel der Renaissance* (Leipzig, 1902); Frida Schottmüller, *Wohnungskultur und Möbel der italienischen Renaissance* (Stuttgart, 1921); Eric Mercer, *Furniture, 700–1700* (London, 1969); Mario Praz, *La filosofia dell'arredamento* (Rome, 1945); Siegfried Giedion, *Mechanization Takes Command* (New York, 1948), pp. 258–304. Representations of interiors in manuscript illustrations have been collected by Franca Falletti, "La dimora fiorentina quattrocentesca: analisi e verifica delle tipologie più diffuse quali ci appaiono nella miniatura coeva," *Antichità viva*, 16, No. 3 (1977), 36–54; but these representations are more fanciful than the author is willing to concede.

backward northern Europe, which was still eating off pewter and wooden dishes. Northern Europeans must have found this pottery strikingly beautiful, to judge from the number of these objects that show up in Flemish painting —many more than can be found in the corpus of Florentine painting. It was not until the late sixteenth century that the North began to catch up with Italian taste and manners in the matter of tableware of this kind.[9]

The success of pottery in the local market points up another feature of this expanding decorative arts sector of the economy: the production of items inexpensive enough to be within the reach of customers well below the level of great palace-dwellers. By resorting to materials of lower cost in order to make cheaper products, artisans set new productive forces to work in a wider market. Is this not the significance, for example, of Luca Della Robbia's move away from marble sculpture and his development of the technique of making glazed terracotta pieces, which could be produced more quickly and certainly more cheaply than marble pieces?[10] The extraordinary quantity of Madonna reliefs made of such inexpensive materials as clay, stucco, and cartapesta, and then gilded, painted, or glazed attests the kind of market that had opened up in Florence; it is significant that production of such items was not to be found elsewhere in Italy. In how many places even in Italy was there an art market catering to men like the modest silk dealer Bartolomeo di Lorenzo Banderaio, who in just a few months in 1520 bought a terracotta St. Jerome (lb.1 s.15), a painted terracotta relief of the Pietà (lb.5 s.10), a gesso tondo of the Madonna (lb.5), and a terracotta Mary Magdelain and a gesso plaque of nudes in battle (lb.3 s.12 for both)?[11] Likewise, the abandonment of expen-

[9] The scope and originality of Florentine production is being established on a more sound scholarly basis by current archaeological work, the preliminary results of which have been published by Guido Vannini, ed., *La maiolica di Montelupo: scavo di uno scarico di fornace* (Montelupo, 1977); idem, "In margine alla mostra archeologica di Palazzo Davanzati a Firenze: alcune osservazioni tra archeologia medievale e 'cultura materiale,'" *ASI*, 137 (1979), 91–110. For archaeological evidence for Tuscan pottery in places in England where there were Italian merchant communities, see J.V.G. Mallet, "L'importazione della maiolica italiana in Inghilterra," in *Atti del V Convegno internazionale della ceramica* (Albisola, 1972), pp. 251–59.

[10] Andrea Della Robbia produced a coat of arms for the Bardi in 1490 for f.5 (Archivio Guicciardini, Florence: filza 53, insert 3, unnumbered document of 11 fols. containing remodeling expenses for the Busini-Bardi palace, 1488–90), and his son Luca produced one for the Bartolini in 1523 for f.6 (Archivio Bartolini Salimbeni, Villa di Collina [Vicchio di Mugello]: No. 211 [building expenses for their palace, 1519–27], fol. 41); whereas a marble coat of arms made by Maso di Bartolomeo in 1451–52 for Andrea and Lorenzo Vettori cost f.25 (BNF, Baldovinetti 70 [Maso's account book], fol. 38).

[11] ASF, S. Paolo 129 (accounts and memoranda, 1514–39), unnumbered folios at beginning of book at the following dates in 1520: 16 April ("1° San Girolamo di tterrachotta ttinto a nero, da botteggha di Vincezio Finiguerra orafo"), 17 July ("ttondo d'una nostra madonna di gesso messa d'oro," from the painter Bernardo),

sive ultramarine and gold leaf in painting, more than just a matter of change in taste, meant that more men could afford a painting. Most, of course, bought Madonnas, which are ubiquitous on the household inventories of the fifteenth century, even of artisans. Neri di Bicci sold one (for lb.15) to a stonecutter, Giuliano Sandrini, and another (lb.13 s.6) to the foreman at Santo Spirito, Giovanni di Mariano—just to mention two customers of this productive shop who worked in the building trades.[12] Vasari mentions sales made by painters like Andrea del Sarto and Pontormo to mercers, joiners, tailors, and others of similar economic status.

The expansion of the decorative arts sector of the economy is self-evident in the totality of all its production that survives today, so much more impressive in its range and its quality for this one small city than for any other place in Europe at the time, be it one of the other great Italian cities or a large northern European territorial kingdom. It is impossible to measure the growth of this sector, since the number and variety of craftsmen's workshops that sprung up to meet the demand cannot be known with any precision, but some evidence points to the proliferation of shops of all kinds. Whereas in 1361 a goblet-maker from San Miniato who wanted to set up shop in Florence could hope to get legislation to confirm a monopoly privilege for his production effective for fifteen miles beyond the walls,[13] by the fifteenth century a number of such manufacturers show up in the tax records of any one year. Both tax documents and private accounts are replete with evidence for the impressive growth of pottery works, and business must have been good indeed to induce Francesco di Antonio Antinori, in 1490, to make a contract with twenty-three potters (*orciolai*) by which they committed their full production to him for three years (for what purpose we do not know).[14] For other crafts

---

6 September ("1 Santa Maria Madalena di ttera e 1° quadro di geso di gnudi in battaglia"), 23 November (1ª piettà di tera di rilievo dipintta" from the painter Battista). The originality of Florentine production is remarked by Ulrich Middeldorf, "Some Florentine Painted Madonna Reliefs," in *Collaboration in Italian Renaissance Art*, ed. W. S. Sheard and J. T. Paoletti (New Haven, 1978), pp. 78–79.

[12] Neri di Bicci, *Le ricordanze*, ed. Bruno Santi (Pisa, 1976), p. 424. The sale of the *tavola di nostra donna* to Giovanni di Mariano occurred in September 1475, beyond the period covered in Neri di Bicci's *Ricordanze;* it is recorded in the book of the opera of S. Spirito, whose cashier (the Mellini bank) made the payment to the painter: S. Spirito 127, fol. 83.

[13] Alessandro Gherardi, "Bichieri e altri vasi di vetro," *Miscellanea fiorentina di erudizione e storia*, 2 (1902), 16.

[14] Galeazzo Cora, *Storia della maiolica di Firenze e del contado, secoli XIV–XV* (Florence, 1973), pp. 108–13. For an impressive instance of the extent of the market in Tuscany for Montelupo pottery already in the early fifteenth century, see Marco Spallanzani, "Una bottega di scodellai a Castiglione della Pescaia all'inizio del Quattrocento," *Faenza*, 64 (1978), 13.

we have the statistics included in the survey made by Benedetto Dei in his description of Florence written about 1470: he counted 84 shops specializing in woodcarving and inlay, 54 for the working of decorative stone and marble, and 44 belonging to gold- and silversmiths (not counting those making threads for the silk industry)—182 in all, as compared to his total of 253 for the cloth industry (both wool and silk). Although Dei's figures are not very reliable, not even in their relation to one another—it is not likely that the ratio of these shops to cloth establishments was as high as three to four—his exaggeration about these crafts suggests how contemporaries judged the importance of the decorative arts sector of the economy.

The success of the decorative arts sector did not mean much expansionist growth in the economy. Increased activity of the artisan industries in no significant way expanded Florence's economic frontiers abroad, however much it boosted the city's prestige as an art center. Although probably no city in all Europe was so well known for the variety and quality of its luxury crafts, we can hardly talk about an export industry, at least in the fifteenth century. Francesco di Marco Datini, the merchant of Prato, occasionally sold inexpensive panel paintings abroad,[15] and in the accounts of other great import-export firms of the fifteenth century, such as Strozzi and Cambini, major works of decorative art turn up—terracotta, furniture, gold and silver objects, jewelry, clothwork, pictures—that were sent off to the papal court, to the king in Naples, to princes in northern Europe, and even to the sultan in Egypt. The value of such objects, however, was utterly insignificant within the total international operations of these firms.

Moreover, no large investors can be turned up who had any interest in developing this sector of the local economy, although more than one Florentine took advantage of the market opportunities abroad to turn a profit in the commerce of products in this category—like Netto di Bartolomeo, who declared in his Catasto report of 1427 investments in manufacturies of drinking glasses in Ferrara and Bologna; and like Baldassare Ubriachi, who spent much of his life traveling across all of Europe supplying the market with carved ivory- and bonework, which (toward the end of his life, around 1406, when he was in exile) he had manufactured in his own house in Venice.[16] Later the grand dukes, anticipating mercantilist policy, attempted to develop some of Florence's luxury crafts for the export market, but failed; beyond its traditionally strong cloth industries Florence was never able to promote a significant second line of luxury products for export, as Venice had, for

15 R. Piattoli, "Un mercante del Trecento e gli artisti del tempo suo," *Rivista d'arte*, 11 (1929), 221–53, 396–437, 536–79; 12 (1930), 97–150.

16 Catasto 76, fol. 364 (for Netto di Bartolomeo); Richard C. Trexler, "The Magi Enter Florence: The Ubriachi of Florence and Venice," *Studies in Medieval and Renaissance History*, new ser. 1 (1978), 129–218.

instance, with glass, jewelry, books, embroidery, lace, and soap.[17] Rather than export works of art Florentine artists themselves went abroad, almost in droves, and found work all over Italy—the point hardly need be driven home by illustrating how the Renaissance of art in most of the regional centers of Italy goes back to the arrival of Florentine artists on the local scene. Florentine artists' travel abroad to work, however, had no significant effect on the city's balance of payments.

Nevertheless, this sector did help the balance of payments to the extent that production successfully met the enormous increase in internal demand that might otherwise have damaged the balance by having recourse to foreign markets. Indeed, growth of local crafts probably cut into imports from abroad. Whereas in the fourteenth century all kinds of luxury products were imported for local consumption, from Flemish cloths to the variety of expensive merchandise for which the Levant was famous throughout the Middle Ages, by the end of the fifteenth century (to judge from merchants' accounts and household inventories of the wealthy) the range of such imports had contracted considerably. Items made of raw materials not readily available to Florentine craftsmen continued to come—furs from Russia, pewterware from England, glass from Venice, an occasional tapestry (no longer other kinds of cloth) from Flanders, small rugs and Damascene metalwork from the East—but for the most part, as remarked at the beginning of this book, Florentine merchants scattered all across Europe from Flanders to Egypt brought their profits home in gold because, quite simply, there was little they wanted to buy in any of those places.

In a market where a locally produced piece of furniture or a good picture might cost from 10 to 50 florins and a fine example of Chinese celadon a mere 2 or 3 florins, the criterion for selection was obviously more a matter of taste than rarity, and, in fact, the shrinking of the market for luxury imports at a time when the demand for luxury goods in general was surging reveals just how much the emergence of taste, or fashion, can have significant repercussions in an economy. For evample, Florence had long imported Near Eastern ceramics and Hispano-moresque pottery, but in the fifteenth century its demand for these items became much more particular and selective, and by the sixteenth century imports were reduced to a trickle—and, indeed, there is evidence that Florence had turned the tables and was exporting its own wares to Egypt. Most interesting in the history of this trade is the articulation of a definite taste as, on the one hand, Florentines became more and more selective and, on the other, the local producers of maiolica used those same criteria as inspiration for their own production in their attempt

[17] An example of the grand duke's policy, with Venice clearly in mind, is documented by Gino Corti, "L'industria del vetro di Murano alla fine del secolo XVI in una relazione al granduca di Toscana," *Studi veneziani*, 13 (1971), 649–54.

to give the customer what he wanted. Likewise, in numerous fifteenth-century inventories metalwork is described as "alla domaschina" and glass as "alla veneziana"—objects made in Florence to compete with the imported product.[18]

Little is known about the minor arts in Florence, despite an extraordinary abundance of documentation and numerous surviving examples of that production too often stacked away in museum storehouses. As an index to the history of taste they deserve more attention than they have as yet received from students of the so-called "finer" arts. For the economic historian the history of taste is an important part of the history of demand, and until it is written we cannot have a full understanding of the development of one of the most vigorous sectors of the economy of Renaissance Italy.

The Quality of Economic Efforts

The acquisitive instinct that lay behind the new demand of the rich has intricate psychological roots. In part, if the enlargement of interior private space created many more possibilities for the acquisition of the new objects now being manufactured in greater variety and number to fill it up, this inflated private world may also have generated pressures on men to sustain their increasing social isolation by surrounding themselves with more objects. In part, too, for men whose spending habits betray that liberated sense of individual private wealth described in an earlier chapter, the possession of objects can assume such a psychological significance that the disposition to spend could be aroused even more by the very existence of more objects. Whatever the psychological state underlying acquisitiveness, the greatest success of this sector of the Florentine economy was the ability of the producer to arouse this acquisitive instinct of the rich, thereby generating even further demand for his production.

The quality of the economic efforts of some of these producers is, therefore, not irrelevant to the success of the sector as a whole. In organizing themselves to operate a business, artisans were not unaware of how their rich clients did things in the wider world of capitalist enterprise. They used the formal partnership contract to gain greater flexibility from the pooling of resources and talents so that they were able to increase the number of commissions and lessen the risks of going it alone. Artisan partnerships could have the formal features typical of Florentine business practice—written, renewable, pacts of specific duration, fixed capital, and carefully kept written records. The painter Jacopo d'Antonio had a shop where a wide range of work was

18 See the comments by Marco Spallanzani, *Ceramiche orientali a Firenze nel Rinascimento* (Florence, 1978), p. 138 and note.

undertaken, from pictures to parade banners and military gear, whereas the wedding-chest manufacturer Apollonio di Giovanni went in for a high degree of specialization, using production procedures that were highly standardized.[19] Others diversified by working through more than one shop: at one point the Da Maiano brothers had four for woodworking and another for working stone. The Da Terrarossa investment in brickworks gives us a good idea of how sophisticated artisans were in organizing their capital for an enterprise, just as the surviving accounts of Maso di Bartolomeo testify to the sophisticated procedures with which they kept track of their various financial dealings. We have also seen how easy it was for artisans to deal in credit. All of this may not have increased productivity much, but it does say something about the spirit with which these men went about doing their work.

Impressive, too, was how they called on their own inner resources to make their way in the marketplace. The new conditions created by a wider and more intensified demand prompted them to elaborate their skills, perfect their technical proficiency, come up with new ideas, and especially to demonstrate new knowledge—knowledge of perspective, of anatomy, of optics, of nature, of classical art, even of theory, and eventually (some thought) of the principle of perfection itself. In these ways craftsmanship and fashion became criteria of selection apart from inherent value of materials. Cellini can perhaps be considered the apotheosis of the Renaissance craftsman not so much because he is a fascinating example of an exaggerated Renaissance ego but because he was the supreme product of an economic system that conditioned the virtuoso craftsman to think he could manipulate even the international market. In this atmosphere taste as well as skill could be exploited to entice the customer into the marketplace. It would be anachronistic to talk about the planned obsolescence of the American variety and too brash to suggest that stylistic change was the artist's way of cornering the market; nevertheless, new knowledge, new inventions, and new fashions created a general artistic atmosphere that in itself aroused demand.[20]

This is the spirit behind Vasari's view of the development of Florentine painting as the history of progress, a process of continuing improvement and refinement to the point that no one in his day was astonished at what a Florentine craftsman could do, however superhuman it seemed. He boasted that his generation of better-trained and more knowledgeable painters could turn out six pictures in one year whereas their teachers had been lucky to turn out one in six years. In Vasari's time Florentine craftsmanship reached the full affirmation of its virtuosity, if not imagination, with the mannerists

[19] Ugo Procacci, "Di Jacopo di Antonio e delle compagnie di pittori del Corso degli Adimari nel XV secolo," *Rivista d'arte*, 35 (1961), 3–70; Callmann, *Apollonio*, ch. 3.
[20] See the conference report "Cities, Courts and Artists," *Past and Present*, 19 (1961), 19.

whose work in extravagant materials like crystal, *pietra dura*, and artificial procelain and whose decorative fantasies lavished on objects from salt-cellars to scientific instruments gave the court of the first grand dukes of this little state of Tuscany a veneer of opulence unequaled in the rest of Europe. With our modern notion of style inherited from the nineteenth century we have not found it easy to understand Vasari's concept of progress in art incorporated in his term *maniera* and involving learned principles and conventions, and yet the broadly cooperative effort by artisans implicit in this concept of the advancement of craftsmanship has in fact been seen as the social origin of the rise of modern science with its faith in progress.[21] Vasari, in any case, was talking about the marketplace occupied by ambitious artisans trying to stimulate demand.

The case for the success of this sector of the economy in generating its own demand does not have to rest only on an appreciation of the originality and virtuosity of artisans or on a tabulation of the multiplicity and variety of the objects they produced. The impact these men made on the market can be observed, from their customers' side of the bargain, in the esteem Florentines had for their artisans.[22] When we think about the emerging status of the artist in the Renaissance we always have in mind his struggle for self-assertion as some kind of genius, the status he presumably won for himself at that time and has enjoyed ever since in Western society. There is, however, the necessary other half of this proposition: society's expanding and enhanced appreciation of the handicraft of man. The primacy of Florence in this story of the rise of the modern artist is a comment on a society that somehow changed its view of men who traditionally had been considered lowly "mechanical" craftsmen. Did this not happen because Florentines began to look at the production of these craftsmen through different eyes, and was not this new way of seeing things being conditioned by craftsmen themselves?

It is a remarkable story, unique in the history of western Europe down to that time. It may not be so remarkable that a man of Petrarch's sensibilities took so much pride in the Giotto he owned, which he particularly enjoyed because, as he tells us with characteristic snobbery (in his last will and testament), it was something that could not be appreciated by the unlettered

21 This notion was formulated by Edgar Zilzel, "The Genesis of the Concept of Scientific Progress," *Journal of the History of Ideas*, 6 (1945), 325–49, but it has yet to be explored. Vasari's concept of art is best elucidated by Craig Hugh Smyth, *Mannerism and Maniera* (Locust Valley, N.Y., 1963).

22 Michael Baxandall, *Giotto and the Orators: Humanist Observers of Painting in Italy and the Discovery of Pictorial Composition 1350–1450* (Oxford, 1971), pp. 66–78; John Larner, "The Artist and the Intellectual in Fourteenth Century Italy," *History*, 54 (1969), 13–30; Creighton Gilbert, "The Earliest Guide to Florentine Architecture, 1423," *Flor. Mitt.*, 14 (1969).

masses; but how remarkable it is that a full two generations after Giotto's death a man of only middling status and one certainly unlettered by Petrarch's standards, Giovanni Morelli, could think of no better way to describe the exquisite beauty of the hands of his deeply lamented sister than to say that Giotto himself could have drawn them. To follow the merchant Goro Dati through the streets of Florence, in a description written in the 1420s that has been called the first real guide to any modern city, is to become aware of how sensitive his eye was to buildings and particularly to the working of stone. Giovanni Rucellai revealed something about his sensitivity in the list he drew up of the artists whose work he possessed and whose fame, he boasted, extended throughout all of Italy, including, along with men in the obvious categories of sculptors and painters, the carpenter and intarsia master Giuliano da Maiano and a stonecutter, Giovanni di Bertino, whose work probably consisted of what today we would consider decorative architectural detail rather than sculpture properly speaking. A different kind of statement about the appreciation of artistic work was made by yet another of these Florentine patrons when he permitted an inscription to be put on a female bust commissioned from Mino da Fiesole that leaves the lady anonymous but announces Mino as the one who brought her features to light.[23] If, as has been said, there was a conventional way for a painter to slip his own portrait into the crowd depicted in a narrative scene, it could only have happened because the patron was happy to have him there, perhaps alongside himself and his family.

This sensitivity to art in its various forms reached explicit consciousness in the minds of those intellectuals—and most were Florentines—who began to reassess the eligibility of the visual arts for admission to the higher system of the liberal arts. It was altogether natural, therefore, that Vespasiano da Bisticci, although he included no artists in his collection of biographies of eminent men of his times, nevertheless considered the appreciation and patronage of painting, sculpture, and architecture as a special quality of a man, one worthy of commemoration. Only in a society where such ideas were gaining ground did it make sense for Francesco Albertini, at the beginning of the sixteenth century, to catalogue some of the sculpture and painting in Florence in what was, in fact, the first systematic guidebook to modern art objects anywhere in Europe.

Meanwhile, more and more artists were being admitted to the list of great Florentines. It was not unknown in medieval Europe for an artist to be honored; recognition could come in a courtly society, or at least within the sphere of public service. The so honoring of Giotto by the commune of Florence was in itself not unusual. That he retained his prestige long after in the memory of his fellow citizens is somewhat more notable, and that

[23] "Et io da Mino ò avvuto el lume" (Bargello [Florence], Inv. no. 72).

names are added to his in a list eventually growing into Vasari's *Lives*, one of the longest books written in Renaissance Florence, is, quite simply, extraordinary. Already in the second half of the fourteenth century Filippo Villani dedicated one brief chapter to artists in his book of famous Florentine citizens, and he had a clear view of their historical progress from Giotto onwards. A century later Antonio di Tuccio Manetti's "fourteen singular men in Florence," written to bring Villani's list up to date, included eight artists, and when in 1481 Cristoforo Landino similarly brought Dante up to date in his commentary by listing the artists who followed Cimabue and Giotto, he added some observations that reveal a clear appreciation of their accomplishments. Even a much simpler man like the shopkeeper Luca Landucci, on looking around at the great men of his time, about 1460, came up with a list of fifteen headed by Cosimo de' Medici but including seven artists. It was obviously not just a private elitist whim that Lorenzo de' Medici had in thinking about turning the cathedral into a kind of Westminster Abbey for the city's artists. Appreciation of art and artists was shared by a broad spectrum of the Florentine public. No wonder that the duke of Ferrara, in a public oration he had read before the city fathers of Florence in 1473, praised the place for its painters, whom he mentioned in the same breath with doctors, lawyers, orators, and poets—unlikely company for artisans in any other city of Europe at the time.[24]

It is an old story how this expanding public esteem for artists nourished a self-consciousness among these men and gave them that strong sense of individuality we associate with the Renaissance idea of the artist. The tradition was well established by the time Vasari wrote; otherwise, for all of his fabrications about their lives, he could never have written so much about so many artists over a period of time extending so far back in the past. How did artists win this esteem? It did not depend altogether on the intellectuals, who, after all, were a long time in finally admitting the arts into that scheme of learning they called the liberal arts. Nor did it happen because something like the struggling Promethean spirit of artistic genius finally broke through the shackles of feudal society. It was in the marketplace where the artisan

[24] G. C. Galletti, ed., *Philippi Villani Liber de civitatis Florentiae famosis civibis . . .* (Florence, 1847); Peter Murray, "Art Historians and Art Critics IV: 'XIV Uomini Singhularii in Firenze,' " *Burlington Magazine,* 99 (1957), 330–36; Ottavio Morisani, "Art Historians and Art Critics III: Cristoforo Landino," *Burlington Magazine,* 95 (1953), 267–72; Landucci, *Diario fiorentino dal 1450 al 1516,* ed. Iodoco Del Badia (Florence, 1883), p. 3. Another list is found in a dedication of Alamanno Rinuccini (1473) : *Lettere ed orazioni,* ed. Vito R. Giustiniani (Florence, 1953), p. 106. On Villani's sense of the history of art, see Baxandall, *Giotto,* pp. 66–78; on the popular nature of art see Zygmunt Wazbinski, "Artisti e pubblico nella Firenze del Cinquecento: a proposito del topos 'cane abbaiante,'" *Paragone,* 327 (1977), 3–24. The 1473 oration of the Duke of Ferrara is published in Richard C. Trexler, ed., *The Libro cerimoniale of the Florentine Republic* (Geneva, 1978), pp. 86–88.

enhanced his status, where in selling his wares to customers and seeking new ways to get them to buy more he conditioned public taste to the point that, eventually, he was able to sell himself and everything he stood for as something special. In the sixteenth century he clinched his case with intellectual claims as well, but until that time, ironically, the sense of progress in craftsmanship that he exploited in the marketplace had worked as a countervailing force against the notion of the exalted genius and dignity of the artist and helped stave off that eventual victory of the higher over the so-called minor arts. In the fifteenth century the drive for virtuosity still precluded much of a distinction between artisan and artist.[25]

In short, the decorative arts sector of the economy had built into it the capability of maintaining and even increasing demand for its production. The number and variety of objects aroused the acquisitive instinct in man and sharpened his taste for quality and fashionableness; with variables like these at play as forces stimulating demand the artisan could become more aggressive in the marketplace. His initiative was an important new element in the growth of this sector, and the effect was especially far-ranging in this economy because of the diffusion of demand throughout a large segment of the population. In societies where wealthy consumers constituted a more coalescent group around a single dominating authority, as in almost all aristocratic societies later in the Renaissance and throughout the early modern period with the rise of princely courts, consumers were less independent and their taste more subject to the dictates of court fashions and to the canons of quasi-official artistic authority. In these places, although the structure and level of demand may otherwise have been comparable to the situation in Florence, the nature of demand kept the producer more constricted in his ability to take the initiative in the marketplace.

Social Quality of the Economy

The motivation that inspired these greater economic efforts from artisans is not to be understood simply as a matter of their volition. If on the one hand the opportunities that opened up to them were determined by the level, structure, and nature of demand, on the other their ability to seize those opportunities very much depended on the freedom to develop their talents. In Florence the opportunities were all the greater because the artisan's movement in the marketplace was not largely restricted by social structures—by guilds, by class hierarchy, by large-scale capitalist industrial organization, or by

[25] Ferdinando Bologna, *Dalle arti minori all'industrial design: storia di una ideologia* (Bari, 1972), chs. 1 and 2.

highly personal patronage systems. Perhaps in no other city in Europe at the time was the artisan less confined by these traditional barriers.

Take the guild, one of the most fundamental institutions that shaped the structure of artisan society in medieval Europe. The late thirteenth-century reorganization of the guilds into great conglomerates for purposes of political consolidation threatened the solidarity and exclusiveness of single crafts and precluded the kind of corporate parochialism found elsewhere. The eventual result was the extinction of the protective and collective spirit of medieval guild corporatism. The city's leading master masons, for example, did not control the Maestri, and they could not direct guild policy to assure their domination of construction activity. The industry was therefore much less exclusive than in most places in northern Europe, where artisan dynasties perpetuated themselves through institutional arrangements. Family craft traditions among Florentine masons, as among all artisan groups in pre-industrial society, were strong, but among the leaders of the craft there is remarkably little family continuity. The long list of foremen at the cathedral from Arnolfo di Cambio onwards does not consist of father-son sequences; in fact, hardly any of these men are known to have had any relatives in the same craft. In northern Europe the foreman of a cathedral or royal works commonly fell into a family tradition of at least two or three generations, like the Roriczers at Regensberg and the Parlers at Prague; and to get ahead in the craft, even to become a master, probably depended on one's family connections, whether they were formalized by guild elitism or not.[26] In Florence, on the other hand, innumerable leaders in all the arts came to their trade without the cachet of a family tradition behind them: Brunelleschi's father was a notary, and so was Leonardo's; Fra Filippo Lippi's, a butcher; Botticelli's, a tanner; Fra Bartolomeo's, a muleteer; Andrea del Sarto's, a tailor; Pollaiuolo's, a poulterer.

Furthermore, talent was not confined to narrow guild categories. On the contrary, the economic system encouraged multiple expression, with the result that the arts and crafts encouraged one another, expanding knowledge in a way that is hardly irrelevant to increased productivity. As Bernard Berenson so wisely observed, comparing Michelangelo, Leonardo, Pollaiuolo, and other Florentine painters with Venetian artists: "Forget that they were painters, they remain great sculptors; forget they were sculptors, and they still remain architects, poets, and even men of science." Berenson goes on

[26] John Harvey, "The Education of the Medieval Architect," *Journal of the Royal Institute of British Architects*, 52 (1945), 230–34. See also Lon R. Shelby's account of the Roriczer family of masons, which in three generations during the fifteenth century provided four foremen at the cathedral in Regensberg: *Gothic Design Techniques: The Fifteenth-Century Design Booklets of Mathes Roriczer and Hanns Schmuttermayer* (Carbondale, Ill., 1977), pp. 7–28.

to say that the range of these Florentines' genius could not be contained by the usual categories, but it is more correct to say that in Florence the usual categories were not sanctioned in economic and social institutions like the guilds. The artisan was free to choose his own forms of expression, and versatility as a craftsman was his notable, if not characteristic, endowment as a Florentine.

This versatility is nowhere more striking than among goldsmiths, who left the mark of their identity on so much Renaissance art. Throughout the Middle Ages the goldsmith was considered the aristocrat of artisans because of the materials he worked with and because of his stature as one who could be entrusted with them. Moreover, the peculiar nature of European demand for his work challenged him to develop his talents in virtuoso performances. In the monastic isolation of the early Middle Ages the goldsmith decorated display manuscripts with gold leaf and probably did some of the painting of miniatures therein. His production of shrines, reliquaries, and liturgical utensils took him also into architectural design. He was a designer, an engraver, a modeler, a caster of metal, a jeweler, an enameler, and by logical extension of these talents he had potential as a sculptor. All these skills flourished among the goldsmiths of Florence with the development of their craft in the fourteenth century, and it is a commonplace in the art history of Florence that many of the city's most talented and versatile artists came out of the goldsmith's shop.[27]

The extraordinary versatility and virtuosity of the goldsmith is epitomized by Ghiberti, whose life illustrates how Florentine goldsmiths realized the full potential of their talent and developed their skills beyond the traditional confines of their craft. As a craftsman with a keen appreciation and knowledge of the drawings of earlier Trecento painters, Ghiberti himself made designs for painters and makers of stained glass. Some of the best painters of the next generation—Uccello, Benozzo Gozzoli, and (possibly) Masolino—came out of his workshop. As a modeler in wax and clay he did work for both painters and sculptors. As a metalworker he made his mark in the history of bronze sculpture as one of the great virtuosos of all time with the Doors of Paradise and the first life-size free-standing statues since antiquity, and the tradition of his foundry was carried on by his son and grandson, especially in the area of munitions. As one who knew something about architectural design he submitted proposals for vaulting the cathedral, and although the final solution was not his (as he asserted) he nevertheless served for a while as foreman of that project—until he was edged out by another goldsmith. Ghiberti, in short, embodied the many-faceted talent of the master goldsmith brought to

[27] General remarks about the versatility of medieval goldsmiths have been made by C. R. Dodwell, "The Gospel-Book of Goslar," *Times Literary Supplement*, 19 November 1976, p. 1464; and Shelby, *Design Techniques*, pp. 55–61.

full fruition with enormous implications for the course of Renaissance art.

Goldsmiths were bound to flourish in a city that made up its favorable balance of payments with gold imports and where gold was put to industrial use. Although their artistic versatility was inherent in their craft and therefore not altogether unique to Florence, their mobility into the other arts was made easier here than elsewhere by the absence of rigid guild barriers. Goldsmiths did not have their own guild but were incorporated instead in the Arte di Por Santa Maria, which was dominated by silk manufacturers. Their corporate ties were no stronger than for any other craft group in the Florentine system of guild conglomerates. The easy entry into the craft has already been remarked, and by the same token other guilds did not block them from developing their talents in any direction they wished. It was not until late in his career (1426) that Ghiberti became a members of the Maestri. Many goldsmiths joined the painters' confraternity of San Luca but not the guild to which they belonged.

The looseness of these institutional arrangements contrasts sharply with the situation in northern Europe, where in many places goldsmiths were tightly woven into a traditional guild unity, limited in their activity by both the restrictions of their own guild and the barriers erected by others. In some places they were allowed to work only with precious and semiprecious materials, not with base metals; in others they could not carve their own patterns. In these and other ways the imagination of the northern goldsmith was hemmed in. Even with the great prosperity they enjoyed in the sixteenth century as producers of ever-more extravagant luxury objects for the courts of Europe, northern goldsmiths relied heavily on pattern books or designs of others. They seem not to have been the independent designers the Italians were.[28] In Florence, too, by the time of Vasari, goldsmiths seem to have lost some of their earlier virtuosity, for he felt compelled to explain, in talking about Bandinelli's training as a goldsmith's son, how in those times goldsmiths knew how to draw and model.

If artisans were not held back by corporate guild ties, neither were they, like cloth workers, subordinated to an industrial process controlled by capitalists with an eye on foreign markets; nor were they caught up in the web of personal relations so characteristic of courtly patronage in more established artistocratic societies. Artisans were independent economic agents operating on their own in a marketplace where demand was widely diffused, and the considerable entrepreneurial skill with which they refined the terms

[28] Goldsmiths' guilds in northern Europe are discussed by J. F. Hayward, *Virtuoso Goldsmiths and the Triumph of Mannerism, 1540–1620* (London, 1976), pp. 38–46. R. W. Lightbown, *Secular Goldsmiths' Work in Medieval France: A History* (London, 1978), p. 108, comments on the separation of the design process from the execution of work by goldsmiths toward the end of the fifteenth century.

of their economic existence has been amply illustrated in the careers of many who have shown up in these pages. Even the modest stonecutters formalized the conditions of their employment by drawing up complex schedules of task rates, submitting bids for jobs (sometimes written and sealed), and entering into contracts. Moreover, artisans were fully protected in their contracts by a legal system that showed no prejudice in favor of the upper classes. When, for example, patrician patrons brought court charges of undue delay in contracted work against Luca Della Robbia for the Federighi tomb (in 1459) and against Filippino Lippi for the Strozzi chapel (in 1497), neither artist had reason to be anything but fully satisfied with the final settlement.[29]

As artisans became more aggressive in the marketplace, the more skilled of them were able to claim an added value for individual talent, and this became an increasingly important variable in the determination of prices, which were usually fixed—often by arbitration—only after the completion of work. The art market was never altogether freed from the commission nexus, and retail trade did not develop to the extent that it could sustain the kind of luxury shops that later grew up in London and Paris. Nevertheless, many of these artisan shops probably had ready-made "art" for sale over the counter. Already in the late fourteenth century the local market was well enough developed that at least one wool merchant made some extra money on the side by buying and selling pictures.[30]

Craftsmen operated in a marketplace where social structures were loose, where relations were fluid, where the cash nexus dominated, and where contracts were protected by impersonal legal authority. Hence they were all the less inhibited in seeking to improve their skills and enlarge their imagination. This initiative, above all their claim to *scientia*, or knowledge, as Erwin Panofsky pointed out, gave expression to the emerging self-consciousness of artistic inventiveness so characteristic of the Renaissance, a self-awareness that sharpened competition among them.[31] Who will ever be able to assess the importance of the competitive instinct on the artistic genius—on Donatello, who fearfully locked his workshop door at the cathedral lest

[29] Hannelore Glasser, "The Litigation Concerning Luca Della Robbia's Federighi Tomb," *Flor. Mitt.*, 14 (1969), 1–32; Eve Borsook, "Documents for Filippo Strozzi's Chapel in Santa Maria Novella and Other Related Papers," *Burlington Magazine*, 112 (1970), 737–45, 800–804.

[30] Gino Corti, "Sul commercio dei quadri a Firenze verso la fine del secolo XIV," *Commentari*, 22 (1971), 84–91. Cf. Harriet McNeal Caplow, "Sculptors' Partnerships in Michelozzo's Florence," *Studies in the Renaissance*, 21 (1974), 146.

[31] Erwin Panofsky, "Artist, Scientist, Genius: Notes on the 'Renaissance-Dämmerung,'" in *The Renaissance: Six Essays*, W. K. Ferguson, et al., eds. (New York, 1962), pp. 123–82. Cf. Ernst H. Gombrich, "From the Revival of Letters to the Reform of the Arts," in *Essays in the History of Architecture Presented to Rudolf Wittkower*, ed. D. Fraser, H. Hibbard, and M. S. Lewine (London, 1967), pp. 71–82.

someone see what he was doing; on Ghiberti, who never could admit that the cupola of the cathedral was Brunelleschi's invention and not his own, and who must have shuddered in rage as he worked on the baptistry doors in the growing shadow of that cupola; on Brunelleschi, who was so hesitant to commit his ideas for decorative detail to paper or to plastic models for his workers lest they be stolen, who was indignant when Donatello was allowed to decorate the sacristy at San Lorenzo, and who in a fit of anger destroyed his model for the Medici palace when it was rejected for someone else's? Competition may be just an aspect of artistic temperament (and these instances of it just the age's myth about its artists), but there can be no denying that the terms of competition were much expanded in Florence with the increase in options, with the specialization of skills, and above all with the greater challenge for the artist to demonstrate his knowledge. Competitions were the normal way in Italy to proceed with commissions for great public projects, and because Florence had somewhat more public art than other places, its artists scrambled all the more to get them. Their competition, however, was not limited to these conditions. It was no wonder to Vasari that talented provincial painters (for example, Lorenzo Costa) did not quite reach the highest standards, since they did not live in places where the competition demanded top performance. The competitive drive was a distinct trait of Florentine artists, and it may have been nothing more than good business sense.

It is important to add to all this that the considerable expansion of the artisan's ambitions and his rising stature as a virtuoso craftsman were not accompanied by a comparable enlargement of his hopes to improve his economic status. After the Black Death Florentine workers of all kinds, both skilled and unskilled, enjoyed a period of prosperity that lasted into the sixteenth century, until the inflation we associate with the price revolution began to cut into their earnings. An artisan could realistically hope to build up a modest estate consisting of a furnished house in town and a piece of land in the countryside, and given the economic structure of pre-industrial society, such opportunities were probably sufficient to fire up motivation throughout a wide segment of the population. More substantial wealth, however, lay beyond the reach of all but the most enterprising—and the luckiest—for although wage rates were high the structure of wages was remarkably rigid; with limited investment possibilities open to the man of modest means he could hardly build up a patrimony qualifying him for entry into the ranks of even the lower patriciate.

Artisans who sold their wares rather than working directly for wages or salary could do somewhat better. The value of their work—for example, a painting or a sculpture—was generally estimated on the basis of costs of materials and labor at the going rates, with added value for originality or artistic quality.[32] That variable, however, was never a major component of the final price. As we have seen, no architect in the fifteenth century was paid so much for his ideas as incorporated in plans or models that he did not have to work as a craftsman or construction supervisor in order to make a living. Evaluations made of contemporary works of art, for example on the Medici inventories, make little allowance for artistic quality. Moreover, the artisan-entrepreneur could do little to increase the margin of profit of his business by organizational or technological improvements in the production process, and economies of scale were possible only to a limited extent. The largesse of a great princely patron could, of course, change the artisan's economic situation dramatically, but for that kind of windfall the Florentine artisan had to go abroad—until the establishment of the Medicean duchy in the sixteenth century. Only from a prince could Cellini have made the 200 percent profit he earned on his enormous investment in making the Perseus—a sum roughly equivalent to what it took Ghiberti twenty years to earn working on the Doors of Paradise (and his earnings accounted for no more than a quarter of the total cost).

Nevertheless, however much an artisan's social ambitions were confined by economic structures, his mobility was not blocked by a rigid hierarchical social structure. Not many artisans could realistically look forward to a social climb into the upper class; it is doubtful that any of them really had such hopes, and those whose families eventually made it probably arrived there by routes that lay outside the artisan shop. Yet mobility was possible in a society as fluid as that of Florence. Two of Taddeo Gaddi's sons continued in their father's and grandfather's craft as painters, but their brother Zanobi (who died in 1400) somehow went into business, ending up as a merchant in Venice and the chief correspondent there of Francesco di Marco Datini.[33] In the 1427 Catasto two of Zanobi's sons show up as wealthy wool producers, and a century later their descendants included one of the biggest Florentine bankers at the papal court. The Rosselli, one of the most numerous fifteenth-century families of second-rate painters and masons, who took their name from a forebearer, a mason called Redhead, in the sixteenth century moved into the upper ranges of society, where they are still firmly implanted today with patents of nobility. We have already followed the progress of the Pucci and the Canacci along the same route in the fifteenth century, and

[32] This variable was explicitly recognized for painters by Saint Antonino (Creighton Gilbert, "The Archbishop on the Painters of Florence, 1450," *Art Bulletin*, 41 [1959], 77–78), but it was also built into the sculptor's practice. Cf. Raymond de Roover, "Labour Conditions in Florence around 1400: Theory, Policy and Reality," in *Florentine Studies: Politics and Society in Renaissance Florence*, ed. Nicolai Rubinstein (London, 1968), p. 286.

[33] The career of Zanobi Gaddi is surveyed in the forthcoming study by Reinhold Mueller and Frederic C. Lane on money and credit in Venice.

other names of craftsmen encountered on these pages who appear in sixteenth-century *prioristi* complete with coats of arms are Baccelli, Angeni, and Succhielli (the Succhielli's name, literally represented by gimlets on their arms, betraying their humble origins).

Mobility worked the other way, as well. The vast majority of workers did not use surnames in the fifteenth century, but men with upper-class names occasionally turn up in their ranks—a stonecutter Giovanni Vespucci at San Bartolomeo, a carpenter Bartolomeo Guadagni at the Strozzi palace, a waller Marco Guadagni at the Pandolfini palace, numerous Del Bene as both skilled and unskilled laborers, not to mention the painters Zanobi Adimari, Alesso Baldovinetti, Zanobi Machiavelli, and Zanobi Strozzi.

The pretentious claims of Michelangelo about his family's social status and the obsessive social-climbing of Baccio Bandinelli are symptomatic of the mobility in Florentine society; such social ambitions would have made no sense, for instance, in Titian's Venice. Although a lot of nonsense has been written about how far up the social ladder artists were able to move in the Renaissance, the dissolution of the confining corporate and hierarchical structure of traditional Europe did leave society more fluid, and so incentive and motivation became more prominent in the economic world of the artisan.

Artists, furthermore, enjoyed a definite status in the eyes of their contemporaries, however it has eluded modern observers with their neat categories of sociological analysis. We have already remarked how they gained this recognition by successfully conditioning Florentines to an appreciation of their work. They are included among famous citizens of their times who brought fame to the city, and possession of the works of specific artists gave a man like Giovanni Rucellai considerable pride. The triple portrait of Taddeo, Zanobi, and Agnolo Gaddi (in the Uffizi) expresses already in the fourteenth century the new dignity painters could feel even though represented as artisans.[34] They were certainly literate—most artisans in Florence were—and a surprising number of them, from Ghiberti to Vasari, could claim considerable literary and even scholarly accomplishment. Hence the way was open for them to enter the world of the intellectual if not the patrician. Ghiberti, Brunelleschi, Donatello, and Luca Della Robbia were friends of that first great patrician bibliophile and collector of antiquities, Niccolò Niccoli, and of the humanist Alberti. Michelozzo's sons studied with Ficino; Bernardo Rossellino's son took a degree in law and taught for awhile at the University of Pisa; Bernardo Rosselli's son studied medicine and set up practice in Florence. This intellectual status, however, did not bring the artist the usual advantages the modern historian associates with social climbing—"strategic" marriage, political office, access to good investments and wealth.

[34] This is the sense of the remarks about this portrait made by Miklòs Boskovits, in his review of Bruce Cole's study of the Gaddi, *Art Bulletin*, 60 (1978), 711.

Their own uneasiness about this ineffable but indisputable status lay behind their efforts in the sixteenth century to clarify a distinction between artist and mere artisan and to consolidate their social position in the formal organization of an academy of the arts designed to detach them from the guilds and bring them into the courtly circle.

If social mobility was not such a realistic prospect, geographic mobility was. Many opportunities opened up abroad for Florentine craftsmen, especially with the rise of the courts of the Renaissance princes elsewhere in Italy, who could not draw on local traditions to satisfy all their luxury demands. Florentine painters show up everywhere, whether a great capital with its own artistic traditions like Venice, where they found work even as mosaicists (a bit like taking coals to Newcastle), or a provincial town like Verona, where they outnumbered even the local painters.[35] It was above all stonemasons, sculptors, and architects who saw new horizons abroad—so many that even at the time Tuscany was regarded (in the words of the duke of Urbino) as the "fountain of architects."[36] As many as fifty masons from Settignano worked in Perugia alone in the later fifteenth century, and one, Francesco di Guido di Virio, who arrived in 1484, established a family of masons that dominated building there for the next fifty years.[37] The early diffusion throughout Italy of Renaissance ideas in both the sculptural and building arts is very much the story of the travels of these Florentine artisans abroad. They were the ubiquitous successors to the wandering masters of Como of an earlier era, and, conversely, Florence was about the only place in Italy where the Lombard masters no longer appeared on the local scene.

In a sense emigration meant a loss of the city's investment in skills, but this loss was surely more than compensated for by the stimulus to better performance that came from the ambition of finding employment abroad. These opportunities were often immeasurably greater than anything Florence itself could offer once communal funds for patronage dried up in the late 1420s, since not only might a prince be expected to be more generous in his rewards, but the grandeur of his commissions might arouse artistic ambitions that were no longer realistic at home in patrician Florence. Donatello, Verrocchio, and Leonardo could never have hoped to produce anything as grand as an equestrian monument for a private patron in their native city, not even for the Medici.

[35] David Herlihy, "The Population of Verona in the First Century of Venetian Rule," in *Renaissance Venice*, ed. J. R. Hale (Totowa, N.J., 1973), p. 115.

[36] Giovanni Gaye, *Carteggio inedito d'artisi dei secoli XIV, XV, XVI*, I (Florence, 1839), 214.

[37] Ottorino Gurrieri, "Le opere dei maestri settignanesi nella chiesa e nel monastero di S. Piero," *Bollettino della Deputazione di storia patria per l'Umbria*, 64 (1967), 174–84.

This release of the artisan's imagination was ultimately a matter of motivation. The challenge to his ingenuity, his skill, and his inventiveness occurred in a marketplace intensified by growing demand and evermore crowded with artisans and artists selling their wares to supply that demand, and they developed their skills to the point of gaining considerable leverage also in markets abroad. Yet, the Florentine marketplace was very much an anomaly in Renaissance Europe. Demand elsewhere was more concentrated in the hands of bigger but fewer spenders, of princes and prelates, and many Florentine artists eventually went abroad to reap those higher rewards. But that there were so many artisans in the first place is the point: they were so numerous because the Florentine marketplace was so different from anything abroad. It was a more fluid marketplace, where the level of individual demand was relatively low, however high aggregate demand may have been in its totality, a marketplace relatively crowded with consumers whose taste was conditioned by the competition of artists among themselves.

Vasari clearly understood the economic situation, albeit with some resentment. In the preface to his life of Perugino he explained Florentine preeminence of the arts as a result of three conditions: the superior critical faculty of the city's artists, the intellectual competition among them, and finally, and above all, the necessity of struggling for a livelihood. Ironically, this insight came to Vasari as he fixed an anxious eye on the newly installed Medici duke in the hope that he might be persuaded to change the terms of the artist's economic existence. Vasari regarded Cosimo as a prospective Maecenas, of the kind that Florence had never seen, who could improve the artist's life by taking him out of the grubby marketplace and bringing him into the security of the court. The thrust of much of Vasari's mission in life, in fact, was to exalt the status of the artist over that of the mere artisan. He enthusiastically accepted the princely court, and he saw his highest hopes fulfilled with the establishment of Europe's first art academy, which he regarded as more important for the intellectual and social dignity it conferred on artists than for any academic program it offered them. This sensibility to status was all the keener among Florentine artists because of the competitive market conditions of their professional activity.[38]

The growth in the number of skilled craftsmen, the widening range of their skills, their expanding and sharpened incentives—these all add up to an improvement in the quality of those human resources that contribute to input and constitute the basis of productivity in any economy. These devel-

[38] Vasari's views are discussed in André Chastel, "Vasari économiste," in *Mélanges en l'honneur de Fernand Braudel*, I (Toulouse, 1973), 145–50. See also Carl Goldstein, "Vasari and the Florentine Accademia del Disegno," *Zeitschrift für Kunstgeschichte*, 38 (1975), 145–72.

opments within that sector of the economy embracing the decorative and fine arts probably would not have been so vigorous in a marketplace with a less fragmented demand, nor would incentives have been so pronounced in a society with a tighter corporate and hierarchical structure.

Development of a More Mature Economy

The success of the decorative arts sector of the economy was impressive. Its growth of boom proportions was a response to the rise of a new demand and to a significant shift in the way wealthy men spent their money. Local crafts succeeded in meeting that demand, forestalling potential foreign competion and actually cutting into the import market; and by introducing new criteria of luxury, they generated additional demand that rebounded to the further advantage of that sector of the economy. Growth, however, never reached the point where these crafts entered the export market in a major way, and for all its vitality this sector did not contribute significantly to the expansion of the Florentine economy abroad. Under these circumstances it was inevitable that the vitality of the luxury crafts would eventually wear itself out. The initial dynamism of growth resulted from a new demand, which was therefore high; but society had a limited capacity to consume luxury goods, despite all the efforts of producers to play on the acquisitive instincts of the rich. The history of this sector of the economy, in short, reveals dynamic growth throughout the fifteenth century only to be followed by a leveling off and contraction in the course of the later sixteenth century.

Nevertheless, at least for a moment, in that period we call the Renaissance, the Florentine economy was more successful than the traditional export-centered interpretation of an economy's performance allows. If growth is to be the criterion, Florentines no doubt would have done better to invest their capital in the most productive sector of their economy, the cloth industries—and hope for an industrial revolution. Yet much of the capital invested in the cloth industries was lost to the economy in purchase of raw materials—expensive wool and silk from abroad—and in high transaction and distribution costs; less than half remained in the economy by way of wages of local workers employed in the industrial process.[39] Moreover, the relatively heavy concentration of unskilled labor in this sector, especially in the wool industry, meant that growth would have resulted in many more low-paid, exploited workers. In fact, the long-term trend in the silk industry was toward

[39] F. Melis, "La formazione dei costi nell'industria laniera alla fine del Trecento," *Economia e storia*, I (1954), 31–60, 150–90; idem, *Documenti per la storia economica dei secoli XIII–XVI* (Florence, 1972), p. 115.

less luxurious, simpler cloths produced by lower-paid women and children, who by the later sixteenth century constituted the majority of workers in the industry.

The success of the decorative arts sector was above all in the way it transformed the social structure of the economy. The channeling of wealth into luxury consumption resulted in its transformation into human capital—an increase in the number of skilled artisans, a rise in the level of their skills, a seemingly infinite expansion of the range of their skills, and a constant stimulus to the imagination with which they executed those skills. The immediate economic effects were the rise of per capita income among artisans and an increase in consumption brought about by the larger number of them.

Patrician wealth spent for consumption thus remained in the economy to become redistributed among a larger segment of the population, circulating with greater velocity through the marketplace. If this does not add up to impressive economic growth, it nevertheless represents considerable economic development. The proliferation and refinement of skills, the elaboration of occupational status, and the greater horizontal (if not vertical) social movement among skilled workers meant the diversification of the economic structure away from primary activities. The enlargement of the variety of employment and the widening of the scope for different talents and different styles of living are things that are to be desired in any economy for their own sake. The final result of the growth in this sector, along with the contemporary increase in the luxury crafts linked to cloth production, was a much more mature economy than the city had had a century earlier, at the time of Dante.

In the Renaissance an increasingly large sector of the economy was taken over by forces of production set in motion by great architectural monuments. These forces expanded well beyond the building trades and into all realms of the decorative arts, and they embraced an ever-larger and more diversified labor force. At the same time they raised the quality of labor by elaborating skills, arousing motivation, and calling forth inventive genius. Thus was nourished the arts and crafts tradition in Florence, a tradition that boosted the prestige of the city as an art center and eventually aroused the rest of Italy and much of Europe to lure Florentine artisans abroad, setting in motion the diffusion of the Florentine Renaissance throughout the Continent. The fame of this tradition in the fifteenth century was such that Lorenzo de' Medici could exploit it for diplomatic purposes; his descendants in the sixteenth century called on it to establish the Medici principate with a splendor utterly out of proportion to their political and economic stature, which was shrinking away to provincial isolation on the expanding stage of sixteenth-century Europe; and the tradition carries on yet today, having finally extended its production to international markets from Via Tornabuoni to Fifth Avenue and become the mainstay of the city's prosperity—while the economy of the rest of Italy limps along.

It may be that in this final assessment of the economic importance of the Renaissance of the arts certain negative features of the Florentine economic system have been glossed over a little too glibly. The kind of luxury consumption discussed here reveals, after all, extraordinary inequalities of wealth, and the great concentration of wealth in the hands of relatively few capitalist-consumers was undoubtedly a consequence of economic exploitation of one kind or another. Furthermore, despite intensified activity the craft industries did not attract capital investment or inspire entrepreneurial efforts leading to technological or organizational innovation that might have increased productivity. Whatever stimulus this consumption gave to the arts and crafts, the results fall far short of meeting modern criteria for economic growth.

But who can deny that in the long run this consumption spending in fact increased the resources of Florence? Take, for instance, the patrician palace, the most conspicuous and by far the most expensive kind of consumption: the city is still living in these structures built seemingly for eternity, structures with vast internal spaces endlessly adaptable to the continually changing needs of society over a half millennium. They represent a permanent investment, and a much better one they are than the millionaire mansions—and many other kinds of buildings, for that matter—put up in our own times with flimsy materials and poor workmanship, buildings that require expensive maintenance and even with the best of maintenance too often become obsolete for any useful function in a generation or two and hence either come down to make way for another generation of buildings that will be just as ephemeral or survive only as oddities thanks to the nostalgia of zealots determined to preserve the architectural past at any cost.

Moreover, consumption in Florence called forth a much more significant investment in *human* resources, the success of which is marked by the Renaissance itself as well as by the continuing tradition of high-quality labor that is the basis of the Florentine economy even today. Improvement in the basic factor of production is more than just an aspect of increased productivity, for the quality of labor as much as quantitative growth should be the goal of any economic organization. Economic efficiency is not satisfactory, however high the standard of living it produces, if it sacrifices the quality of the original human effort.

If it is objected that this luxury consumption in Florence imposed elitist consumer taste on the economy to the detriment of the production of more useful objects to meet the needs of a larger segment of the population, let us not forget that those habits of spending nevertheless generated a recognition of a standard of taste and a pleasure in beauty that entered the traditions of the city and are deeply rooted in the sensibilities of Florentines today perhaps as in no other society, not even in Italy. If, finally, it is objected that such consumption habits made the flagrant inequalities in society even more conspicuous, as indeed they did, setting off the life-style of the rich and widening the cleavage between them and the rest of society to an unbridgeable cultural gap, we can perhaps find some solace in the reminder that it was in the Renaissance, after all, when the artist for the first time could hope to break from the ranks of craftsmen (even if he did not always succeed), freeing himself from the meshes of class structures and asserting his own status and dignity as a genius who was no longer a mere practitioner of the mechanical arts.

The phenomenon of conspicuous consumption with its consequence for the luxury industry sector of the Florentine economy was a process of redistribution of wealth, a kind of recycling of over-concentrated wealth. The movement of wealth through the art market was intense in the Renaissance, and although this flow did not generate further wealth it transformed wealth into art—and, what is more, it transformed men and therefore the structure of society in the process. That flow, in short, was the vital force that generated the Renaissance. And the final point is that the Renaissance lives on not just in our museums and universities and (however feebly) in books like this one, but in a city that in a real sense, both materially and spiritually, continues to live off the investment in human capital it made at the height of its prosperity half a millennium ago.

Appendices

APPENDIX ONE

Value of the Florin, 1252–1533

(In soldi *di piccioli*)

Year	Soldi	Year	Soldi	Year	Soldi	Year	Soldi
1252	20	1290	36	1320	65	1345	62
1253	20	1291	38	1321	66	1346	62
1254	20	1292	39	1322	66	1347	61
1255	20	1293	39	1323	67	1348	63
		1294	39	1324	67		
1258	20	1295	39	1325	67	1350	62
		1296	41	1326	67	1351	64
1271	30			1327	66	1352	68
		1299	46	1328	66	1353	68
1274	29	1300	47	1329	65	1354	70
		1301	38	1330	65	1355	69
1276	30	1302	51	1331	60	1356	70
1277	33	1303	52	1332	60		
1278	35			1333	59	1358	70
1279	34	1305	59	1334	60	1359	67
1280	34			1335	51	1360	68
1281	33	1308	54	1336	61	1361	68
1282	33			1337	62	1362	67
1283	37	1313	58	1338	62	1363	66
1284	36			1339	62		
1285	37	1315	58			1365	66
1286	36	1316	57	1341	64		
		1317	57	1342	66	1368	66
1288	37	1318	58	1343	66	1369	66
1289	37	1319	64	1344	66	1370	66

Year	Soldi	Year	Soldi	Year	Soldi	Year	Soldi
1371	65	1412	80	1458	108	1497	134
		1413	80	1459	108	1498	135
1374	73	1414	81	1460	108	1499	137
1375	77	1415	81	1461	102	1500	140
		1416	80	1462	108	1501	130
1378	68	1417	81	1463	110	1502	140
1379	70	1418	81	1464	106	1503	140
1380	70	1419	80	1465	112	1504	140
1381	72	1420	80	1466	112	1505	140
1382	73	1421	81	1467	114	1506	140
1383	74	1422	80	1468	114	1507	140
1384	73	1423	81	1469	114	1508	140
1385	72	1424	81	1470	114	1509	140
1386	74	1425	79	1471	110	1510	140
1387	75	1426	82	1472	110	1511	140
		1427	83	1473	110	1512	140
1389	74	1428	83	1474	112	1513	140
1390	75	1429	83	1475	112	1514	140
1391	75	1430	83	1476	114	1515	140
1392	75	1431	83	1477	114	1516	140
1393	76	1432	80	1478	115	1517	140
1394	76			1479	116	1518	140
1395	77	1441	95	1480	117	1519	140
1396	77	1442	81	1481	120	1520	140
1397	78	1443	95	1482	120	1521	140
1398	77	1444	83	1483	120	1522	140
1399	77	1445	97	1484	123	1523	140
1400	77	1446	97	1485	123	1524	140
1401	76	1447	92	1486	125	1525	140
1402	76	1448	94	1487	126	1526	140
1403	77	1449	96	1488	127	1527	140
1404	76	1450	82	1489	129	1528	140
1405	77	1451	96	1490	130	1529	140
1406	77	1452	96	1491	130	1530	140
1407	78	1453	99	1492	130	1531	150
1408	78	1454	102	1493	131	1532	150
1409	78	1455	108	1494	132	1533	150
1410	80	1456	107	1495	133		
1411	80	1457	108	1496	134		

SOURCE: Mario Bernocchi, *Le monete della Repubblica fiorentina,* III (Florence, 1976), 78–88.

APPENDIX TWO

List of Statutes of Building-Craft Guilds in Italian Cities

AN incomplete guide to these documents is G. Gonetta, *Bibliografia statutaria delle corporazioni d'arte e mestieri d'Italia* (Rome, 1891), which for the earlier period replaces Luigi Manzoni, *Bibliografia statutaria e storica italiana*, I, pt. 2 (Bologna, 1879, pp. 1–78 and 445–67 (guild statutes). With the exception of the items in Milan and Vicenza, I have seen all the unpublished materials on this list.

On the list the archival location of the statute is not indicated if it has been published, and unless otherwise stated all items refer to statutes. The bibliographies include significant discussions of the respective statutes.

BOLOGNA

Archivio di Stato, Archivio del Comune, Società d'arti, busta 9 bis: wallers, 1248–1376.

——, Archivio del reggimento, Assunteria d'arti, Notizie sopra le arti: wallers, kilnmen.

Bibl: A. Gaudenzi, "Le società delle arti in Bologna nel secolo XIII: i loro statuti e le loro matricole," *Bullettino dell'Istituto storico italiano*, 21 (1889), 59–60.

BRESCIA

Civica biblioteca queriniana, Archivio storico civico 1056 (Statuti di Paratici), fols. 108–16 and 266–74: "Statuta marengonorum a muro et lignamine," 1491 (with additions).

FERRARA

Biblioteca ariostea, Mss. I, 616 (eighteenth-century transcription of guild statutes), vol. III, pp. 439–507: masons, 1325, with additions to the eighteenth century. The original manuscript, referred to by Sitta in reference below, is now lost; see Angelo Stella, "Testi volgari ferraresi del secondo Trecento," *Studi di filologia italiana. Bollettino dell'Accademia della Crusca*, 26 (1968), 211 n. 13.

Archivio di Stato di Modena, Archivio segreto estense, Cancelliere ducale, Leggi e decreti, ser. B, reg. IV, fols. 123–26: kilnmen, 1422.

Bibl: Pietro Sitta, "Le università delle arti a Ferrara del secolo XII al secolo XVIII," *Deputazione ferrarese di storia patria: Atti*, 8 (1896), 61–63.

FLORENCE

See text herein, chapter 5.

GENOA

Federigo Alizieri, *Notizie dei professori del disegno in Liguria dalle origini al secolo XVI*, IV (Genoa, 1876), 87 n.: "Capitula Magistrorum Dominorum sculptorum marmarorum et lapidium (sic)" (fifteenth century). Also published in Santo Varni, *Appunti artistici sopra levante* (Genoa, 1870), doc. XIX.

Armando di Raimondo, *Maestri muratori lombardi a Genova, 1596–1637* (Genoa, 1976), pp. 7–12 (summary of 1597 statutes).

Bibl: Ennio Poleggi, "La condizione sociale dell'architetto e i grandi committenti dell'epoca alessiana," in *Galeazzo Alessi e l'architettura del Cinquecento*, Acts of the International Congress in Genoa, 1974 (Genoa, 1975), pp. 360–61.

LUCCA

Biblioteca governativa, Ms 322: "Statuta, capitula et ordinamenta" of the Compagnia di San Bartolomeo delle Sette Arti (carpenters, smiths, wallers, stonecutters, roofers, carters, wood dealers), 1361, with subsequent additions 1519–59. Ms 575: reformed statutes of 1568.

Bibl: Marino Berengo, *Nobili e mercanti nella Lucca del Cinquecento* (Turin, 1965), pp. 70–74.

MANTUA

Archivio di Stato, Archivio Gonzaga, busta 3237, insert 20: kilnmen, 1538 and after.

L. Franchi, *Liber statutorum muratorum. Gli statuti dell'arte dei muratori di Mantova (1338–1520)* (Mantua, 1887).

MILAN

Archivio civico storico, Materie, cart. 675/9: maestri da muro e da legname, 1530. Cited and summarized by Domenico Sella, *Salari e lavoro nell'edilizia lombarda durante il secolo XVII* (Pavia, 1968), pp. 29–32.

MODENA

Archivio di Stato, Archivio segreto estense, Archivio per materiale arti e mestieri. Busta 26: kilnmen in Modena, Reggio and Ferrara, fifteenth to eighteenth centuries. Busta 28: wallers.

Archivio storico comunale, Camera segreta. Parte 4, VII, 1: wallers, 1476–1700. Parte 4, XXI, 1 (Statuti delle arti della città di Modena), fols. 308–21: kilnmen, 1581.

Bibl: Pasquino Fiorenzi, *Le arti a Modena (storia delle corporazioni d'arti e mestieri)* (Modena, 1962), pp. 68–80; Federica Pollastri, "L'arte dei marangoni e l'arte dei muratori a Modena (XV–XVI secolo)," *Deputazione di storia patria per le antiche provincie modenesi: Atti e Memorie*, 10th ser., 9 (1974), 119–34.

PADUA

Museo civico, Biblioteca. BP 913: wallers, 1273 (copy of 1437), with additions (partly published by Giulio Lupati, ed., *Statuto della fraglia dei muratori* [Padua, 1891]). BP 827: stonecutters, 1494, with additions (copy of 1694).

Bibl: Camillo Semenzato, "Note sugli statuti della fraglia dei tagliapietra," *Padova*, 3, No. 11–12 (1957), pp. 13–17; Melchiorre Roberti, "Le corporazioni padovane d'arti e mestieri," fasc. 8 (Venice, 1902) of *Memorie del reale istituto veneto di scienze, lettere ed arti*, 26 (1897–1902).

PALERMO

Ferdinando Lionti, *Statuti inediti delle maestranze della città di Palermo (Documenti per servire alla storia di Sicilia*, 2d ser., III, fasc. 2) (Palermo, 1887), pp. 1–5: marmorai e fabbricatori, 1487–88.

PARMA

Archivio di Stato, Archivio del Comune di Parma, busta 1863 (Statuti delle arti), no. 2: kilnmen, 1459.

Corrado Pecorella, "Gli statuti dell'arte dei muratori parmensi [1425]," *Aurea Parma*, 47 (1963), 13–52.

Bibl: G. Micheli, "Le corporazioni parmensi d'arti e mestieri," *Archivio storico per le provincie parmensi*, 5 (1896), 68–70 and 99–101.

PERUGIA

Biblioteca augusta, Ms 977: "Statuta magistrorum lignaminis et lapidum, 1385" (partly published by A. Rossi, "Alcune rubriche dello statuto dell'arte di pietra e legname della città di Perugia rinnovato l'anno 1385," *Giornale d'erudizione artistica*, 5 [1876], 168–74).

PIACENZA

Emilio Nasalli Rocca, ed., *Statuti di corporazioni artigiane piacentine (s. XV–XVIII)* (Milan, 1955), pp. 93–113: carpenters, wallers, stonecutters, 1544.

PISA

Archivio di Stato, Comune di Pisa. Divisione C (Statuti), no. 2: masons (1477) and carpenters (1496). Divisione D, no. 4: additions to the statutes of the wallers, 1513–1702.

ROME

Archvio storico capitolino, Archivio della Camera capitolina, XI. No. 56: wallers, 1397 (eighteenth-century copy of 1545 ed.). No. 74: sculptors and stonecutters, 1406 (eighteenth-century copy). No. 116: kilnmen, 1605.

Bibl: Gonippo Morelli, *Le corporazioni romane di arti e mestieri dal XIII al XIX secolo* (Rome, 1937), pp. 126–27, 187–92, 264–69; E. Rodocanachi, *Les Corporations ouvrières à Rome depuis la chute de l'empire romain*, I

(Paris, 1894), 407–49; and, of less use, Antonio Martini, *Arti, mestieri e fede nella Roma dei Papi* (Bologna, 1965).

SAVONA

Agostino Bruno, "Capitoli dell'arte dei muratori [Savona, 1417]," *Atti e Memorie della Società storica savonese*, 2 (1890), 379–90.

SIENA

Archivio di Stato, Arti 126: wallers and kilnmen, 1489, with additions to 1616 (seventeenth-century copy).

V. Lusini, "Dell'arte del legname innanzi al suo Statuto del 1426," *Arte antica senese* (*Bullettino senese di storia patria*, 11) (Siena, 1904), pp. 183–246 (at the time this guild included the building crafts).

Gaetano Milanesi, *Documenti per la storia dell'arte senese*, I (Siena, 1854), 105–35: "Breve dell'arte de' maestri di pietra senesi dell'anno MCCCCXLI."

UDINE

Gonetta, *Bibliografia*, lists "Statuti et ordini della Fraterna de' Marangoni et Murari della città di Udine del 1496," but I was not able to turn this up at either the Archivio di Stato or the Biblioteca Comunale.

VENICE

Giovanni Monticolo, *I capitolari delle arti veneziane*, 3 vols. (Rome, 1896–1914), I, 55–57, 79–93, 213–33: kilnmen. II, 283–305: wallers. III, 249–64: stonecutters.

Agostino Sagredo, *Sulle consorterie delle arti edificative in Venezia* (Venice, 1856), pp. 281–310: stonecutters, 1363, with additions.

Bibl: Andrzé Wyrobisz, "L'attività edilizia a Venezia nel XIV e XV secolo," *Studi veneziani*, 7 (1965), 307–43.

VERONA

Archivio di Stato, Casa dei Mercanti 2 (Libro degli statuti dei mestieri e delle arti [a fifteenth-century compilation; see Simeoni, cited below, pp. xxxii–xxxv]): stonecutters, roofers.

Luigi Simeoni, ed., *Gli antichi statuti delle arti veronesi secondo la revisione scaligera del 1319 (R. Deputazione veneta di storia patria: Monumenti storici,* 2d ser., 4 [1914]): carpenters, wallers, kilnmen.

VICENZA

Biblioteca civica: wallers, 1407 (summarized by Felice Pozza, "Le corporazioni d'arte e mestieri a Vicenza," *Nuovo archivio veneto*, 2d ser., 10 [1895], 263–64).

VITERBO

Vincenzo Maria Egidi, "Lo statuto dell'arte o compagnia dei maestri di pietra e di architettura della città di Viterbo [1461]," *Biblioteca degli Ardenti della Città di Viterbo: studi e ricerche nel 150° della fondazione* (Viterbo, 1960), pp. 3–49.

APPENDIX THREE

Workers' Wages: Data and Sources

A. The Data

THE sample of wages of construction workers represented in the graph on pages 318 and 319 consists of data taken from a selection of building projects over three centuries. The average wage has been calculated by taking the arithmetical average of each of these sample units and, in turn, averaging these averages. In this way small projects are balanced against large ones. Otherwise, the data from one large project, like the Strozzi palace, would overwhelm data from a selection of small ones that were, in effect, little more than maintenance or repair operations, whereas employment opportunities at the latter kind of project were certainly much more typical than those at the former. Some of the projects in the list of sample units below were major operations—the hospital of San Matteo, the Innocenti, the Badia of Fiesole, the Ss. Annunziata, Santo Spirito, the Strozzi palace—but some of the surviving records represent no more than a few weeks of work on the project.

There are many problems connected with the selection of the data from the accounts. Entries are not everywhere uniform. Sometimes they include, along with the total amount paid out, all the detailed information one would like to have—the wage rates, the identity of workers, the number of days paid for, and dates—but too often the entries include only some of this information. The mass of highly disparate data cannot easily be organized into uniform categories valid for all sample units. Practical considerations, therefore, dictated a policy of taking as the raw data wage rates as found in separate entries regardless of magnitude of workdays, of the work force, or of the total value paid out as represented by the entry. There are obvious problems here inasmuch as some accounts include comprehensive entries for vast amounts of work over a long period while others record weekly payments for individual workers, but these differences in accounting procedures are somewhat cancelled out in the process of taking averages for each project. The knowledge that wages were so stable throughout much of the period under study somewhat obviated the desire to go any further in refining the criteria by which the data were collected. As explained in the text, the seasonal nature of wages and the specific nature of the work paid for were not used as categories in organizing the data.

Average Daily Wage Rates for Unskilled Laborers
(In soldi *di piccioli*)

Year	Soldi	Year	Soldi	Year	Soldi	Year	Soldi
1310	3.1					1460	10.0
		1384	11.9	1424	9.9	1461	9.8
1339	4.0			1425	8.0	1462	9.0
		1386	11.2	1426	8.0	1463	10.5
1345	4.3	1387	9.4	1427	9.8	1464	9.3
1346	3.7			1428	9.0	1465	9.3
		1389	9.9	1429	9.9	1466	9.5
1348	6.9	1390	8.5	1430	9.3	1467	11.0
1349	8.4			1431	8.2	1468	9.3
1350	10.0	1394	9.6	1432	8.6	1469	9.9
1351	9.5	1395	9.4	1433	8.5	1470	8.5
1352	10.0	1396	9.8	1434	10.0		
1353	8.7	1397	9.9	1435	10.3	1473	11.0
1354	9.4	1398	10.0	1436	10.8	1474	8.0
				1437	11.0	1475	8.0
1356	10.5	1400	9.9	1438	10.4	1476	8.5
		1401	10.4	1439	11.6	1477	9.7
1363	10.0	1402	10.5	1440	11.8	1478	10.9
1364	9.5	1403	10.7	1441	9.0	1479	11.0
1365	11.1	1404	10.9	1442	11.7	1480	11.0
1366	9.9	1405	10.5	1443	10.9	1481	10.7
1367	9.1	1406	11.0	1444	10.8	1482	9.9
1368	8.5	1407	13.1	1445	11.4	1483	9.6
1369	9.5	1408	12.6	1446	12.0	1484	9.4
		1409	10.0	1447	11.0	1485	10.8
1371	9.9	1410	9.2	1448	12.0	1486	10.3
1372	8.8	1411	9.3	1449	12.0	1487	10.8
1373	8.3	1412	9.7	1450	9.7	1488	10.5
1374	7.5	1413	9.2	1451	9.6	1489	10.5
1375	8.0	1414	10.1	1452	9.6	1490	10.0
1376	8.0	1415	10.7	1453	11.7	1491	9.1
		1416	11.0	1454	8.0	1492	8.4
1378	9.0	1417	11.0	1455	8.0	1493	8.4
1379	9.4	1418	9.8	1456	9.7	1494	8.4
1380	9.9	1419	10.5			1495	8.0
1381	10.1	1420	11.1	1458	10.0	1496	8.0
1382	10.8	1421	10.0	1459	10.1	1497	9.0

Average Daily Wage Rates for Unskilled Laborers (*continued*)
(In soldi *di piccioli*)

Year	Soldi	Year	Soldi	Year	Soldi	Year	Soldi
1498	8.0	1526	8.3	1554	12.5	1578	19.7
1499	8.8	1527	9.0			1579	19.5
1500	9.3			1556	13.3	1580	18.5
1501	8.7	1529	12.0	1557	12.5	1581	17.2
1502	9.0			1558	17.3	1582	15.0
1503	8.7	1531	16.0	1559	17.0	1583	20.0
1504	8.7					1584	18.0
1505	8.7	1533	13.4	1561	17.2	1585	16.0
1506	8.0	1534	13.0	1562	18.0		
				1563	13.0	1587	20.0
1516	8.0	1539	12.0	1564	16.0	1588	13.3
1517	9.2					1589	15.5
1518	9.5	1541	14.0	1570	19.3	1590	14.2
1519	9.0			1571	21.0		
1520	9.4	1547	13.9			1592	20.0
1521	9.5	1548	13.0	1573	14.3		
1522	9.3			1574	18.0	1596	17.7
1523	9.0	1551	12.0				
		1552	11.9	1576	20.0	1598	18.3
1525	10.5	1553	12.3	1577	17.5	1599	22.0

Average Daily Wage Rates for Skilled Laborers
(In soldi *di piccioli*)

Year	Soldi	Year	Soldi	Year	Soldi	Year	Soldi
1310	6.8	1360	13.3	1381	15.7	1404	17.3
		1361	14.5	1382	15.5	1405	18.4
1337	7.5	1362	13.3	1383	15.0	1406	18.4
1338	6.5	1363	16.0	1384	17.6	1407	18.0
1339	7.7	1364	14.8	1385	17.3	1408	17.9
		1365	17.8	1386	16.0	1409	16.9
1345	7.0	1366	17.0	1387	16.0	1410	17.9
1346	8.0	1367	15.8			1411	18.4
		1368	15.4	1389	16.9	1412	18.5
1348	12.5	1369	16.4	1390	16.8	1413	16.0
1349	13.4	1370	16.1			1414	17.5
1350	16.8	1371	15.7	1394	17.2	1415	17.9
1351	18.3	1372	15.9	1395	16.0	1416	19.1
1352	17.8	1373	17.9	1396	16.9	1417	18.2
1353	17.8	1374	15.8	1397	16.2	1418	19.1
1354	17.0	1375	16.3	1398	16.3	1419	19.1
		1376	17.0	1399	16.1	1420	17.8
1356	16.2	1377	15.0	1400	16.2		
1357	16.9	1378	18.0	1401	18.0	1424	20.0
1358	17.0	1379	13.5	1402	18.4		
1359	13.7	1380	14.1	1403	18.1	1426	17.0

Average Daily Wage Rates for Skilled Laborers (*continued*)
(In soldi *di piccioli*)

Year	Soldi	Year	Soldi	Year	Soldi	Year	Soldi
1427	18.1	1465	16.0	1502	14.2	1558	28.2
1428	18.2	1466	20.0	1503	14.3	1559	26.7
1429	18.5	1467	14.9				
1430	17.6	1468	15.3	1516	17.3	1561	32.3
1431	17.6	1469	17.0	1517	17.8	1562	26.5
1432	16.5	1470	17.5	1518	17.5	1563	30.5
		1471	20.0	1519	18.0	1564	30.8
1434	16.4	1472	20.0	1520	17.1		
1435	18.4	1473	20.0			1570	40.0
1436	21.3	1474	20.0	1522	18.7	1571	40.0
1437	21.6			1523	18.7	1572	43.0
1438	17.0	1476	15.0			1573	34.6
1439	18.1	1477	16.4	1525	17.3	1574	35.0
1440	19.6	1478	15.1	1526	17.3	1575	33.0
1441	21.5	1479	15.2			1576	40.0
1442	20.0	1480	15.6	1531	30.0	1577	35.0
		1481	13.8	1532	18.4	1578	39.7
1444	20.8	1482	14.0	1533	22.5	1579	41.3
1445	19.1	1483	16.3	1534	23.9	1580	35.8
1446	16.3	1484	16.5	1535	23.0	1581	37.2
1447	19.6	1485	15.7			1582	35.0
		1486	16.0	1539	22.0	1583	40.0
1450	17.0	1487	16.0			1584	37.8
1451	18.9	1488	17.7	1541	25.5	1585	30.8
1452	19.5	1489	15.2			1586	40.0
1453	18.0	1490	15.9	1543	20.5	1587	35.0
1454	18.0	1491	16.0			1588	35.0
		1492	14.0	1547	23.8	1589	30.0
1456	15.0	1493	14.0	1548	21.6	1590	37.5
1457	16.0	1494	16.2				
1458	15.1	1495	12.9	1551	19.5	1592	40.0
1459	16.7	1496	11.6	1552	25.9		
1460	17.8	1497	13.4	1553	23.8	1595	40.0
1461	17.7	1498	11.4	1554	23.6	1596	40.0
1462	17.2	1499	14.9	1555	22.2		
1463	21.0	1500	14.5	1556	23.1	1598	36.7
		1501	12.3	1557	22.6	1599	51.0

Daily Wage of Unskilled Laborers
(In staia of wheat)

Year	Staia	Year	Staia	Year	Staia	Year	Staia
1310	.31	1366	.66			1374	.21
				1371	.35	1375	.16
1364	.79	1368	.27	1372	.46	1376	.33
1365	.79	1369	.37	1373	.49		

Daily Wage of Unskilled Laborers (*continued*)
(In staia of wheat)

Year	Staia	Year	Staia	Year	Staia	Year	Staia
1378	.43	1429	1.10	1476	.29		
		1430	.72	1477	.31	1531	.22
1380	.62	1431	.33	1478	.42		
1381	.40	1432	.29	1479	.58	1533	.19
1382	.45	1433	.50	1480	.67	1534	.21
		1434	.63	1481	.57		
1384	.41	1435	.57	1482	.44	1539	.16
		1436	.43	1483	.26		
1386	.35	1437	.65	1484	.23	1541	.35
1387	.47	1438	.61	1485	.47		
		1439	.46	1486	.47	1547	.46
1389	.23	1440	.42	1487	.42	1548	.24
1390	.26			1488	.44		
		1442	.35	1489	.41	1551	.16
1394	.69	1443	.99	1490	.50	1552	.29
		1444	.72	1491	.46	1553	.31
1397	.34	1445	.95	1492	.50	1554	.17
1398	.42	1446	1.00	1493	.53		
		1447	.69	1494	.37	1556	.14
1400	.58	1448	.67	1495	.28	1557	.14
1401	.50			1496	.20	1558	.20
1402	.52	1450	.61	1497	.14	1559	.28
1403	.63			1498	.22		
1404	.64	1452	.51	1499	.34	1561	.33
1405	.50	1453	.59	1500	.35	1562	.23
1406	.55	1454	.44	1501	.24	1563	.18
1407	.73	1455	.38	1502	.25	1564	.27
1408	.50	1456	.29	1503	.21		
1409	.40			1504	.19	1570	.28
1410	.46	1458	.50	1505	.16	1571	.33
1411	.40	1459	.84	1506	.31		
		1460	1.00			1574	.30
1413	.77	1461	.98	1516	.22		
1414	.63	1462	.82	1517	.34	1580	.25
1415	.59	1463	.66	1518	.42	1581	.29
1416	.42	1464	.37	1519	.37		
1417	.48	1465	.32	1520	.34	1584	.26
1418	.58	1466	.47	1521	.34		
1419	.48	1467	.52	1522	.25	1587	.20
1420	.32	1468	.46	1523	.24		
1421	.38	1469	.55			1592	.14
		1470	.58	1525	.41		
1424	.99			1526	.28	1596	.13
1425	.57	1473	.49	1527	.15		
1426	.50	1474	.26			1598	.14
1427	.70	1475	.26	1529	.16	1599	.25
1428	.90						

B. The Sample Units

The list of sample units follows. No attempt has been made to indicate the magnitude of employment rosters on these projects; as mentioned before, some involved major construction and others were little more than repair work. Dates bracket the years in which the data are distributed, but sometimes that distribution is irregular.

1310 ASF, Carte Del Bene 50: work on Villa di Mezzo.

1337–1469 ASF, S. M. Nuova 4389–4510 (income-outgo journals). These wage data are distributed unevenly throughout this period. Most work was for maintenance on the hospital's extensive property holdings, but at times there were larger concentrations of labor for major building. These include:

1348	*infermeria*
1367–68	general construction
1374–75	vaulting
1395	cloisters, dormitory, etc.
1401–2	*spezieria*
1408–9	a new wing
1412–15	*infermeria*
1418–20	Sant'Egidio
1428–29	chapter house

1345–46 ASF, Balìe 3 (building accounts for work on the Bargello).

1350–52 Bibl. Marucelliana (Florence), C.370.II (building accounts for S. Giovanni Evangelista).

1373 Innocenti, ser. CXLIV, 562 (accounts of Niccolò di Bartolomeo Guidalotti): miscellaneous construction.

1377 Carl Frey, *Die Loggia dei Lanzi* (Berlin, 1885), p. 265.

1384 Ss. Annunziata 841: construction at the church.

1387 ASF, Mss 81 (accounts of sons of Messer Lapo di Castiglionchio): miscellaneous construction.

1395–1406 Giuliano Pinto, "Personale, balie e salariati dell'Ospedale di S. Gallo," *Ricerche storiche*, 4 (1974), 113–68.

1401–9 ASF, Carte dello spedale di Lemmo Balducci 51 (building accounts for San Matteo).

1413 Carte strozz., ser. II, 10 (accounts of Cambio Petrucci): miscellaneous construction.

1416 ASF, San Matteo 251 (income-outgo journal): miscellaneous construction.

1416–19 Carte strozz., ser. V, 7 (accounts of Simone di Filippo Strozzi): miscellaneous construction.

1420–47 Innocenti, ser. VII (building accounts): construction for years 1420–21, 1424, 1436–47.

1424–25 S. Spirito 169 (accounts): miscellaneous construction.

1430 ASF, Conv. sopp. 82 (Sant'Apollonia), 10 (miscellaneous building expenses).

1431–35 S. Spirito 169 (accounts): miscellaneous construction.

1442–49 Archivio di San Lorenzo (Florence), ledger of building accounts for church.

1443–44 Badia di Firenze, 77 (ledger): miscellaneous construction.

1452–73 ASF, San Paolo: numerous accounts for construction in 1452–53, 1460–63, 1467–73 (see R. A. Goldthwaite and W. R. Rearick, "Michelozzo and the Ospedale di San Paolo in Florence," *Flor. Mitt.*, 21 [1977]).

1453 ASF, Conv. sopp. 79 (Sant'Ambrogio), 121 (building expenses): miscellaneous construction.

1453–56 Ss. Annunziata 689 (income-outgo journal): work on church.

1459–60 Badia di Fiesole 1–6 (building accounts).

1460–63 Ss. Annunziata 843–45 (building accounts).

1461 ASF, Conv. sopp. 95, 212 (ledger of Bernardo di Stoldo Rinieri): miscellaneous construction at villa.

1464–67 ASF, Conv. sopp. 168 (San Miniato al Monte), 57 (record book of San Bartolomeo): miscellaneous construction.

1464–68 Carte strozz., ser. V, 1750 (ledger of Bartolomeo di Tommaso Sassetti): construction at rural property near Cercina.

1465 Carte strozz., ser. IV, 574 (accounts of Niccolò di Tommaso Businі): miscellaneous construction.

1469 Carte strozz., ser. II, 17 bis (ledger of Marco di Parente Parenti): work on his house in Florence.

1473 Carte strozz., ser. II, 94 (accounts of the operai of Santa Maria Novella): miscellaneous construction.

1474–77 Carte strozz., ser. V, 1751 (ledger of Bartolomeo di Tommaso Sassetti): work on his house in Florence.

1477–90 S. Spirito 128 (accounts and memoranda of the purveyor of the opera of S. Spirito): major construction on church.

1482–84 ASF, Conv. sopp. 168 (San Miniato al Monte), 174 (accounts of quarry operations at Monte Oliveto).

1483 Carte strozz., ser. V, 36 (ledger of Filippo Strozzi): work on first palace.

1488 Archivio Guicciardini (Florence), filza 53, insert 3 (extract of accounts for remodeling palace of Agnolo di Bernardo de' Bardi).

1489–1506 Richard A. Goldthwaite, "The Building of the Strozzi Palace: The Construction Industry in Renaissance Florence," *Studies in Medieval and Renaissance History*, 10 (1973), 97–194.

1490–97 ASF, Ospedale degli Incurabili 12 (accounts for building a house belonging to the hospital).

1499–1500 Archivio Salviati (Pisa), ser. II, 32 (building accounts for palace of Alamanno d'Averardo Salviati).

1502 ASF, Conv. sopp. 83 (Santa Felicita), 115 (memoranda): work on house.

1516–20 Ss. Annunziata 846 (building accounts): loggia in Piazza Ss. Annunziata.

1517 C. Milanesi, "Due ricevute autografe di Michelangiolo Buonarroti ed un conto di spese concernenti alla facciata di San Lorenzo," *Giornale storico degli archivi toscani*, 1 (1857), 50–54.

1520–99 Giuseppe Parenti, *Prime ricerche sulla rivoluzione dei prezzi a Firenze* (Florence, 1939): maintenance at convent of S. M. Regina Coeli.

1522 Archivio Salviati (Pisa), ser. IV, 14 (building accounts for Da Gagliano palace).

1525 ASF, Conv. sopp. 168 (San Miniato), 169 (building accounts for bell tower).

1532 ASF, Conv. sopp. 168 (San Miniato), 170 (accounts of S. Bartolomeo): quarry operations at Monte Oliveto.

1533–34 Carte strozz., ser. V, 104 (building accounts of Strozzi palace).

1534–41 ASF, S. Paolo 13 (building accounts for work in cloister).

1547–48 Carte strozz., ser. V, 104 (building accounts of Strozzi palace).

1551–61 Ss. Annunziata 848 (accounts).

1577–80 Ss. Annunziata 849 bis (building accounts for houses under loggia in the square).

1578–80 Univ. of Pennsylvania, Van Pelt Library, Mss Lea 559 (ledger of Giovanbattista di Bartolomeo Concini): work on palace.

1581 ASF, Galli Tassi 1480/34 (building accounts for palace of Francesco di Piero Baccelli).

APPENDIX FOUR

Price of Meat, 1491–1501

(Per *libra*; in denari *di piccioli*)

Item	Annual Averages											Eleven-Year Average
	1491	1492	1493	1494	1495	1496	1497	1498	1499	1500	1501	
Vitello	28	23	24	24	24	24	24	28	33	36	28	26.9
Bue	13	13	13	12	14	12	—	15	18	22	—	14.7
Arista	16	17	15	18	18	19	—	20	28	—	—	18.9
"Porco"	15	14	12	15	11	—	—	—	—	—	—	13.4
Salsicce	—	29	28	31	30	34	—	38	38	32	32	32.4
"Pesci d'Arno"	—	—	—	34	43	45	—	—	—	60	—	45.5

SOURCE: ASF, Carte strozz, ser. V, no. 69 (expenses and memoranda of heirs of Lorenzo di Francesco Strozzi, 1491–1501), fols. 6–24 and 131–66.

APPENDIX FIVE

Toward a Checklist of Early Illustrations of Workers in the Construction Industry

THE medieval mason in northern Europe is well represented in art, and the recording of that documentation has been well served by reproductions in numerous publications. It is otherwise with Italian construction workers: I know of no single publication that brings together a significant amount of the visual documentation of their work. The material collected in this book is mostly limited to Florentine or Tuscan artists, and it is presented as a first step toward the collection of the materials of this kind that must exist for other places throughout the vast realm of Italian art. To help complete the Florentine record, here is a list of other items not included among these illustrations:

Anonymous fifteenth-century (Sienese?) miniaturist, wallers at work, illustration in a legendary account of the founding of the convent of Saints Abundantius and Abundius near Siena. Oxford, Bodleian Library (Lyell 75, fol. 4v). Reproduced in O. Pächt and J. J. G. Alexander, *Illuminated Manuscripts in the Bodleian Library, Italian School* (Oxford, 1970), ill. 255.

Apollonio di Giovanni, scenes from the history of Dido and Aeneas (detail showing wallers), mid-fifteenth century cassone panel. New Haven, Yale University Art Gallery (James Jackson Jarves Collection).

Fifteenth-century Florentine workshop, Reconstruction of the temple of Jerusalem (wallers at work), illustration in the Bible of Federigo da Montefeltro, 1476–

78. Rome, Vatican Library (Ms Urbinate latino 1, fol. 196v). Reproduced in Annarosa Garzelli, *La bibbia di Federigo da Montefeltro: un'officina libraria fiorentina, 1476–78* (Rome, 1977), ill. 98 and color plate XVI.

Fifteenth-century wood engraver, illustration of a smith and a mason, from Jacob di Cessoli, *Il giuoccho delle scacchi* (Florence, 1493). Reproduced in Edgcumbe Staley, *The Guilds of Florence* (London, 1906), p. 328.

Fifteenth-century Florentine engraver, Mercury (showing a sculptor). London, British Museum. Reproduced in various places, including most recently the Einaudi *Storia dell'arte italiana* (Turin, 1979), pt. I, vol. II, ill. 76.

Fungai, St. Clement condemned to work in a quarry. Formerly London, Langton Douglas Collection. Reproduced in George Kaftal, *Saints in Italian Art: Iconography of the Saints in Tuscan Painting* (Florence, 1952), p. 282.

Vasari, Paul III follows the construction of St. Peter's. Rome, Palazzo della Cancelleria.

Vasari, Cosimo I among architects and engineers. Florence, Palazzo Vecchio.

Domenico Cresti (Il Passignano), St. Jerome directs the construction of a monastery. Rome, San Giovanni dei Fiorentini.

Machinery, lifting devices, and other equipment used in construction in Italy have been well studied and amply illustrated. For stonecutters' tools see the references in note 95 to Chapter 4 herein. Brickmaking, so far as I know, has not been illustrated in Italian art (kilns for pottery, however, are another matter). I know only the illustration of the making of clay into bricks (no kiln is shown) included in Gio. Antonio Rusconi, *Della architettura* (Venice, 1590), p. 32 (and on p. 101 is an illustration of the mixing of mortar). Some engravings of aerial views of Rome show the large number of kilns located behind St. Peter's. Ten illustrations of brickmaking in Dutch art from the fifteenth to seventeenth centuries have been collected, and extensively commented on, by Hollestelle; see note 13 to Chapter 4 above (where one additional item is noted). An illustration of "Laterarius. Der Ziegler" in H. Schopperus, *Panoplia, omnium illiberalium mechanicarum aut sedentariarium artium genera continens* (Frankfurt am M., 1568), shows a brickmolder and a kiln.

Notable collections of northern European materials from the Middle Ages include Andreas Grote, *Der vollkommen Architectus: Baumeister und Baubetrieb bis zum Anfang der Neuzeit* (Munich, 1959); Kurt Gerstenberg, *Die deutschen Baumeisterbildnisse des Mittelalters* (Berlin, 1966); L. F. Salzman, *Building in England Down to 1540* (Oxford, 1967); Günther Binding, ed., *Romanischer Baubetrieb in zeitgenössischen Darstellungen* (an exhibition catalogue; Cologne, 1972); Pierre du Colombier, *Les Chantiers des cathédrales* (Paris, 1973); Günther Binding and Norbert Nussbaum, *Der mittelalterliche Baubetrieb nördlich der Alpen in zeitgenössischen Darstellungen* (Darmstadt, 1978).

Index

Where possible, workers are identified by the following abbreviations: *f* = founder; *k* = kilnman; *m* = mason; *p* = painter; *s* = stonecutter; *w* = waller